Reconciling Work and Poverty Reduction

International Policy Exchange Series

Published in collaboration with the
Center for International Policy Exchanges
University of Maryland

Series Editors

Douglas J. Besharov
Neil Gilbert

United in Diversity?
Comparing Social Models in Europe and America
Edited by Jens Alber and Neil Gilbert

The Korean State and Social Policy:
How South Korea Lifted Itself from Poverty and Dictatorship to Affluence and Democracy
Stein Ringen, Huck-ju Kwon, Ilcheong Yi, Taekyoon Kim, and Jooha Lee

Child Protection Systems:
International Trends and Orientations
Edited by Neil Gilbert, Nigel Parton, and Marit Skivenes

The Age of Dualization:
The Changing Face of Inequality in Deindustrializing Societies
Edited by Patrick Emmenegger, Silja Häusermann, Bruno Palier, and Martin Seeleib-Kaiser

Counting the Poor:
New Thinking About European Poverty Measures and Lessons for the United States
Edited by Douglas J. Besharov and Kenneth A. Couch

Social Policy and Citizenship:
The Changing Landscape
Edited by Adalbert Evers and Anne-Marie Guillemard

Chinese Policy in a Time of Transition
Edited by Douglas J. Besharov and Karen Baehler

Reconciling Work and Poverty Reduction:
How Successful Are European Welfare States?
Edited by Bea Cantillon and Frank Vandenbroucke

SCHOOL of
PUBLIC POLICY

RECONCILING WORK AND POVERTY REDUCTION

How Successful are European Welfare States?

Edited by

BEA CANTILLON AND

FRANK VANDENBROUCKE

OXFORD
UNIVERSITY PRESS

OXFORD
UNIVERSITY PRESS

Oxford University Press is a department of the University of Oxford.
It furthers the University's objective of excellence in research, scholarship,
and education by publishing worldwide.

Oxford New York
Auckland Cape Town Dar es Salaam Hong Kong Karachi
Kuala Lumpur Madrid Melbourne Mexico City Nairobi
New Delhi Shanghai Taipei Toronto

With offices in
Argentina Austria Brazil Chile Czech Republic France Greece
Guatemala Hungary Italy Japan Poland Portugal Singapore
South Korea Switzerland Thailand Turkey Ukraine Vietnam

Published in the United States of America by
Oxford University Press
198 Madison Avenue, New York, NY 10016

Library of Congress Cataloging-in-Publication Data
Reconciling work and poverty reduction: how successful are European welfare states? / edited by
Bea Cantillon and Frank Vandenbroucke.
pages cm.—(International policy exchange series)
Includes bibliographical references and index.
ISBN 978-0-19-992658-9 (alk. paper)
1. Labor market—Europe. 2. Manpower policy—Europe. 3. Poverty—Europe.
4. Welfare state—Europe. 5. Investments—Social aspects—Europe.
I. Cantillon, Bea. II. Vandenbrouck, Frank.
HD5764.A6R37 2014
339.4′6094—dc23 2013022720

9 8 7 6 5 4 3 2 1
Printed in the United States of America
on acid-free paper

CONTENTS

ACKNOWLEDGMENTS

We are very grateful to Tony Atkinson, Willem Adema, Maurizio Ferrera, Bjørn Hvinden, Paul de Beer, and the participants of seminars and workshops at the University of Antwerp and the KU Leuven for precious comments and suggestions. We have received extremely helpful support from Sarah Marchal, Tim Van Rie, Dieter Vandelannoote, Nathalie Schuerman and Ingrid Van Zele. Finally we wish to express our deep appreciation of the support received from Stephen Windross for language editing.

CONTRIBUTORS

BEA CANTILLON
University of Antwerp
Antwerp, Belgium

VINCENT CORLUY
University of Antwerp
Antwerp, Belgium

JOHAN DE DEKEN
University of Amsterdam
Amsterdam, The Netherlands

KOEN DECANCQ
University of Antwerp
Antwerp, Belgium

RON DIRIS
KU Leuven
Leuven, Belgium

JORIS GHYSELS
Maastricht University
Maastricht, The Netherlands

TIM GOEDEMÉ
University of Antwerp
Antwerp, Belgium

ANTON HEMERIJCK
VU University Amsterdam
Amsterdam, The Netherlands

IVE MARX
University of Antwerp
Antwerp, Belgium

MANOS MATSAGANIS
Athens University of Economics and Business
Athens, Greece

LEEN MEEUSEN
University of Antwerp
Antwerp, Belgium

BRIAN NOLAN
UCD School of Applied Social Science
Dublin, Ireland

Annemie Nys
University of Antwerp
Antwerp, Belgium

Olivier Pintelon
University of Antwerp
Antwerp, Belgium

Karel Van den Bosch
University of Antwerp
Antwerp, Belgium

Frank Vandenbroucke
KU Leuven, University of Antwerp, University of Amsterdam (UvA)
Leuven, Antwerp, Belgium, Amsterdam, The Netherlands

Aaron Van den Heede
University of Antwerp
Antwerp, Belgium

Josefine Vanhille
University of Antwerp
Antwerp, Belgium

Wim Van Lancker
University of Antwerp
Antwerp, Belgium

Natascha Van Mechelen
University of Antwerp
Antwerp, Belgium

Gerlinde Verbist
University of Antwerp
Antwerp, Belgium

INTRODUCTION

Bea Cantillon and Frank Vandenbroucke

This book originated in a soul-searching experience driven by a common concern for social cohesion in Europe. At the time, the co-editors were both actively committed, albeit in different capacities, to the renewed ambition to add a social dimension to the policies of the European Union (EU). But were the concepts, the statistical systems, and the monitoring arrangements that underpinned this ambition creating added value? Were the policies that had been advocated delivering tangible results?

The new social ambition took shape in a context of significant change, both at EU level and within individual European welfare states. The decades around the turn of the millennium had seen the implementation of the Economic and Monetary Union project and the accession of post-Communist countries following the fall of the Berlin Wall in 1989. Increasingly, the EU had been presenting itself as an important player, first in the fields of budgetary discipline and employment, and subsequently in the promotion of social inclusion as an over-arching policy objective. In 2000, the first social agenda in the history of the EU was launched. The Lisbon Council had concluded that "the number of people living below the poverty line and in social exclusion in the Union [was] unacceptable," and boldly asserted that "steps [had to] be taken to make a decisive impact on the eradication of poverty."[1] In what may be regarded as the first move toward "Social Europe," the Lisbon Strategy proposed a loose and flexible policy approach. Known as the Open Method of Coordination, its purpose was to allow the Member States to learn from one another's experiences in outlining national policies toward a common goal. Crucially, a set of social indicators was agreed upon that would enable policymakers "to define in a more precise way the substance of the European Social Model" (Vandenbroucke, 2002a; Atkinson et al., 2002). Subsequently, a stronger emphasis on social rights and solidarity was incorporated into the Lisbon Treaty. Concurrently, combating poverty came to the fore quite prominently and consistently as a specific area for EU policy coordination and cooperation.

This evolution unfolded at the very moment that European welfare states were committing to a process of major reorientation in finding ways to successfully combine budgetary restraint, employment growth, and equality. With hindsight, that reorientation has been interpreted as a turn toward a new policy focus: uneven, disparate, not always consistent, but sufficiently clear across a large group of welfare states to label it a "social investment turn." In Chapter 8 of this book, Hemerijck explains that a key idea in the new concept was to "prepare" individuals and families to adapt to changing career patterns and working conditions, to new social risks and population aging, instead of simply "repairing" damage caused by unemployment, social exclusion, and poverty. The social investment perspective underlines the importance, for the long-term development of human capital, of early childhood development, training, education, lifelong learning, and family reconciliation policies. Looking back, one may say that the Lisbon Strategy was instrumental in promoting "social investment" as a policy recipe for success in the fields of both employment and social inclusion. For sure, at the time, social investment was less of a reference concept in scholarly literature than it is today. Moreover, it has always been a somewhat ambiguous concept, open to many interpretations. One can even debate the actual importance of the Lisbon Council in promoting policy change. To the extent that a "social investment turn" is discernible in European social policy, in many countries this process began well before 2000. Nevertheless, we may look back on the first decade of this century as a period when social investment was put firmly on the agenda of the EU, in a drive to modernize social policy. As the Lisbon Council put it: "Investing in people and developing an active and dynamic welfare state [is] crucial both to Europe's place in the knowledge economy and for ensuring that the emergence of this new economy does not compound the existing social problems of unemployment, social exclusion, and poverty." Aspirations were high, given that the Council conclusions spoke of "the eradication of poverty" as a strategic social policy goal within the Union. Obviously, such a bold statement reflects political rhetoric, but the hope was nonetheless that higher employment would reduce social spending levels and reorient expenditure toward more "productive," activating and inclusive policies, and toward combating poverty, either directly through work or, indirectly, through more adequate, inclusive social provisions.

Prior to the financial crisis, the Lisbon Strategy could be regarded as a qualified success in the field of employment, at least if one assumes there to have been causal relationships between the Lisbon Agenda and growing employment rates across Europe. On the other hand, though, the Lisbon Strategy largely failed to deliver on its ambitious promise concerning poverty, certainly if one uses national at-risk-of-poverty rates (the number of individuals living in a household with less than 60% of the national median household income) as the benchmark. In this book, we focus on poverty rates among the non-elderly population only. By 2007, the overall picture was not one of success in both employment and social inclusion, but rather seemed to combine three features: stability in at-risk-of-poverty rates for the non-elderly population in the majority of countries, increasing poverty rates in some countries, and decreasing poverty rates in yet another subset of countries.[2] In a technical sense, between 2004 and 2007 there was "convergence" of national at-risk-of poverty rates: Poverty rates increased in some Member States, where they had been traditionally low, while they decreased in other Member States, where they had been traditionally high. So conceived, the verdict on the antipoverty ambition of the Lisbon Strategy was unequivocal: Poverty had not decreased in most of the Member States of the Union (Social Protection Committee, 2009). In Chapters 1 and 2 of this book, we assess that verdict on the basis of facts and figures. But Chapter 2 also qualifies it with a pan-European perspective on cohesion among Member States, by proposing a truly pan-European definition of poverty. The reader of this book will soon become aware that the expression "social cohesion in Europe," used without further specification in the opening sentence of this introduction, conveys two meanings: social cohesion in each of the Member States of the European Union, and cohesion among the Member States of the Union.

CENTRAL QUESTIONS, TIME FRAME, AND SCOPE OF THE BOOK

If the poverty record of most European welfare states prior to 2008 is disappointing, from 2008 onwards the overall picture became truly negative. By 2010 the at-risk-of-poverty rate had decreased in only two Member States (Poland and the United Kingdom [UK], but with a concomitant decline in median incomes in the UK), compared to the situation in 2004. In a large group of Member States poverty had increased, sometimes quite substantially. Therefore, against the background of ongoing population aging and the lasting impact of the financial crisis—as a result of which the future is looking much bleaker than the past—it is important to gain insight into what happened before the present downturn. Why did most of the rich welfare states fail to cut poverty levels prior to the financial crisis, and which factors contributed to the success of many of the new Member States? Our purpose is not to assess the effectiveness of European governance as such. Nor do we intend to analyze the details of social policy in individual Member States. Our aim is rather to "map" changes in poverty, employment, and social spending on the basis of data that have become available for those same years via the European Statistical System. Such a "mapping exercise" is a necessary first step in gaining an understanding of the reasons behind what has ultimately been a failure to achieve stated objectives. We thereby confine the analysis to the non-elderly population, given the importance of the employment-poverty nexus in our analysis of welfare state change.

Chapter 1 introduces this "mapping" by focusing on two key parameters, social spending and "household employment," and by exploring their explanatory power with regard to poverty outcomes across European welfare states. We describe different patterns of "household employment" across the EU by distinguishing individuals living in "work-rich households" from individuals living in "work-poor" households. This distinction is based on the "work-intensity" of households: The work-intensity of a household measures the degree of labor market participation by the working-age adults in that household. Work-poor households are characterized by relatively low levels of work-intensity; they typically face much higher poverty risks than work-rich households. Chapter 1 starts from the following observation: at-risk-of-poverty rates correlate negatively both with social spending (though the correlation is far from perfect) and with the share of individuals living in work-rich households (though, again, the correlation is not very strong). This observation is explained by two basic facts: First, in all European welfare states, individuals in work-rich households are confronted with relatively lower levels of poverty than individuals in work-poor households; second, across European welfare states, high levels of social spending are associated with less poverty within both work-poor and work-rich households. This account of cross-country differences in poverty rates sets the scene for the central themes developed in the book, which may be summarized in four sets of *analytical* questions. They all start from observations with regard to at-risk-of-poverty rates among the non-elderly population and should shed light on the fundamental *policy* challenge underlying this book. That policy challenge refers to the notion of *employment-centered welfare reform* and can be summarized as follows: is it possible to structurally replace spending on cash benefits for working-age adults and their families with employment creation, and to simultaneously reduce poverty among working-age adults and their children? We thereby focus on an analysis of the social performance of European welfare states during the good economic years that is substantive rather than related to weaknesses in the Lisbon governance architecture: the transition from the old distributive welfare state to a new social investment state may be more difficult than expected.

A first set of analytical questions derives from a decomposition of changes in poverty rates over time, which is basically an accounting device. Changes in national at-risk-of-poverty rates can be decomposed on the basis of three contributory factors: (i) changes in the share of individuals living in work-poor households; (ii) changes in poverty risks in the population subgroup living in work-poor households; and (iii) changes in poverty risks in the work-rich segment of the population. Such a decomposition allows us to assess the following question: Are disappointing evolutions in poverty rates a consequence of relatively limited reductions in the share of individuals living in work-poor households (despite years of economic growth between 2004 and 2007)? Or, has the reduction in the share of individuals in work-poor households been "neutralized" by increasing poverty within the work-poor and/or the work-rich segments of the population? *In other words, was the distributive upside of creating jobs (fewer people confronted with high poverty risks in work-poor households) offset by a distributive downside (more poverty among the work-poor and/or the work-rich households) that may have been intrinsic to the way in which jobs were created?* Conversely, are we able to discern countries where "poverty success" was clearly the result of "employment success"? This first set of questions refers to a crude observation already made by the Social Protection Committee (2009) in its assessment of the Lisbon Strategy: In the EU15, the proportion of children and working-age adults living in jobless households had hardly decreased during the good economic years before the crisis. Household joblessness constitutes a crucial policy parameter in the Social Protection Committee's analysis, because the risk of poverty is much higher in jobless households than in households where at least one person is in work. This book builds upon that crude observation in two ways. Using relatively recent developments in Statistics on Income and Living Conditions (SILC) and the European Statistical System, we broaden the scope from jobless households to work-poor households, a concept that encompasses households that participate to a limited extent in the labor market[3] and allows a more fine-grained analysis of household employment rates. Simultaneously, we try to understand why household joblessness follows a different trajectory than individual joblessness, which is also the focus of the next set of questions.

The second set of questions refers to patterns of individual and household employment in European welfare states. If the share of individuals living in work-poor households diminished less than one might have expected, is this simply a consequence of the fact that the number of individual jobs increased less than one might have hoped during the boom years? Or, was there a limited "conversion" of increases in individual employment rates into increases in household employment rates? Such a limited conversion of individual employment success into household employment success may be explained by changing household structures and/or by sociological factors leading to a skewed distribution of individual jobs over households (Kalleberg, 2011). The latter phenomenon is coined "polarization" in Chapter 3, which explores this second set of questions.

The third set of questions relates to changes in social spending, notably spending on cash benefits for working-age adults and their households. (Throughout this book we will use "working-age cash benefits" as a short cut for this category of expenditures, and "working-age benefits" when we aggregate in-kind and cash benefits.) It starts from the observation that, in a number of EU Member States, poverty risks increased in the work-poor and/or the work-rich segment of the population. We therefore examine trends in poverty reduction through social transfers, as measured by the difference between pre-transfer and post-transfer poverty headcounts. Can we discern a structural trend toward less poverty reduction by transfers in work-poor households (for whom social transfers are very important) and/or in work-rich households? If so, is this attributable to the fact that the level of spending on working-age cash benefits was reduced, in a *structural* way, to make room for spending on pensions and health care, and/or to make room for spending on "social investment programs," such as child care, active labor market policies, education...? To assess these questions, we will document changes in the structure of social spending. But, apart from aging, increasing healthcare needs, and the shift to service provision related to social investment, there may also have been a paradigmatic shift. The emphasis on "making work pay," which has been part and parcel of the activation strategies pursued in the past, may have justified—and thus contributed to—the retrenchment of traditional unemployment benefit programs and, consequently, may have occasioned a structural decline in the capacity of governments to reduce poverty among working-age people.

This third set of questions prompts a *fourth set*. In the welfare states under review, the structure of social spending gradually shifted toward relatively more spending on services and relatively less spending on cash benefits. Hence, it may be the case that our assessment of poverty increasingly underestimates the redistributive impact of welfare states, since it does not take into account the value and distribution of growing public services when measuring the standard of living enjoyed by households. On the other hand, it can be argued that a shift from cash benefits to benefits in kind implies less redistribution, if the counterfactual benchmark we apply is more spending on cash benefits rather than on public services. In short, more spending on public services may imply more redistribution, if the counterfactual benchmark is less social spending *tout court*; but more spending on public services may be seen to imply less redistribution, if the counterfactual benchmark is substitution of cash benefits for public services, with unchanged levels of social spending. In Chapter 6, Verbist and Matsaganis examine this issue by broadening the income notion, with regard to both inequality and poverty. In Chapter 7, Van Lancker and Ghysels further explore the shift from cash to service spending, with specific focus on family policy (i.e., child benefits, childcare services, and parental leave benefits).

In short, starting from the idea that we can define "household employment rates," by counting the share of individuals in jobless (or, more generally, work-poor) households, our first set of questions decomposes changes in at-risk-of-poverty rates in changes explained by changes in household employment rates on the one hand and changes attributable to poverty evolutions within work-poor and work-rich households on the other. Our second set of questions examines the relationship between household employment rates and individual employment rates. The third examines the impact on poverty of spending on working-age cash benefits in work-poor and work-rich households. Our fourth set of questions, finally, broadens the notions of income poverty and income inequality in order to allow an assessment of the impact of spending on cash transfers and on public services respectively.

The ambition of this book is to formulate answers to these questions by means of survey data from the European Labour Force Survey (LFS), the European Community Household Panel (ECHP), the European Statistics on Income and Living Conditions (SILC), the German Socio-Economic Panel (SOEP), and spending data provided by Eurostat on the basis of the European System of integrated Social Protection Statistics (ESSPROS) system and by the Organisation for Economic Co-operation and Development (OECD) Social Expenditure Database (OECD SOCX). Hence, apart from OECD SOCX, we deliberately rely on the European Statistical System (ESS) and propose analytical tools that use this statistical apparatus creatively. The ESS was developed by the Commission and by Eurostat with a view to informing policymakers about changes in the distribution of work and well-being within and between Member States. In this sense, our book also constitutes a test of the European Statistical System's relevance in that policy perspective.

However, in addition to analyzing data made available in the European Statistical System, we also aspire to enrich the analytical questions listed above, in four ways. *First*, the at-risk-of-poverty headcount based on a threshold of 60% of the national median standardized household income, on which we focus, will be put in perspective. It is only one of the indicators agreed upon by the EU Member States in 2001. Various other indicators build on this notion, including indicators on the depth and duration of poverty. For the sake of simplicity, we mainly report results based on the at-risk-of-poverty headcount. We must of course be aware of the fact that this relative income measure has inherent conceptual and methodological shortcomings that may result in some failures and/or successes being overlooked. These issues are discussed at length in Chapter 2 of this book.

Second, the account of trends in at-risk-of poverty rates, trends in household and individual employment rates, and trends in social spending should highlight the different developments among the European welfare states. Over the past decade, remarkable differences in outcomes have been associated with the strong momentum of growth in the new Member States, instantiating the "convergence machine" that Europe has often been in good times (World Bank, 2012). But even within the EU15, the analysis has to disentangle a mixture of common societal trends and disparity in policies (Chapters 3 and 5).

Third, we consider it necessary to integrate the issue of in-work poverty in our analysis of the Lisbon-era results, and to link in-work poverty with the "household employment" approach that structures much of this book. The expressions "in-work poverty" and "working poor" refer to a situation where an individual is employed but lives in a poor household. Hence, belonging to the "working poor" is conceptually different from being a member of a "work-poor household": A member of a work-poor household may very well not be working at all, so that he or she is not among the working poor. Conversely, an individual in work may, in theory at least, be a member of a work-rich but financially poor household, and thus belong to the "working poor." Nonetheless, it appears that in-work poverty is explained to a large extent by the work-intensity of the household to which the working individual belongs (Chapter 4).

Fourth, one should avoid too narrow a conceptualization, and thus an inevitably poor account, of welfare state change. Both survey data and administrative spending data allow one to test certain hypotheses with regard to the development of welfare states, but caution is urged in both instances. The limitations of survey data, for example with regard to statistical significance, are well-known and quite apparent in our research, too. Administrative data, for their part, may also offer less robust support for welfare state analysis than one may *prima facie* think. Therefore, we also rely on indicators of the generosity of social benefits. In Chapter 5 both average benefit levels measured in the ECHP and SILC surveys and calculated theoretical disposable incomes of standard family types are used to identify the impact of policies. We also make use of microsimulation models in order to assess the trade-offs between benefit generosity and employment traps.

A full understanding of the dynamics of change in welfare states requires a broader analysis that takes due account of changes in discourse, changes in macroeconomic policy, institutional changes, and—last but not least—demographic changes (Chapters 8 and 10, and the Appendix). So, together with the four sets of analytical questions listed above, these four preoccupations guided the organization of this book.

Ours is not the first book to have been prompted by disappointing poverty trends. The OECD publication "Divided We Stand" (OECD, 2011) examines in detail how globalization, regulatory reforms in labor and product markets, altered household structures, and changing tax and benefit regulations impacted rising inequalities. The present book adopts a somewhat different perspective, though, focusing on how pre-transfer poverty evolved, who benefited from expanding labor markets, and how the poverty reducing capacity of cash social spending evolved. Because the main goal is to gain a better understanding of the mechanisms at play during the "good" years (the future is, after all, pregnant with the past), the analysis focuses on the period covered by the SILC surveys 2005–2008; given the fact that the SILC data of year *T* generally refer to year *T-1*, the period considered is actually 2004 to 2007. While this is admittedly a rather limited time frame, the analyses are complemented where possible and useful with pre-2000 data drawn from ECHP and LFS and, in the case of Germany, with SOEP. Moreover, we add a perspective on the crisis years, by integrating results from SILC 2009–2010–2011 in Chapter 1, and from SILC 2009 in Chapter 2. Thus, the reader is able to assess the relevance of our analysis of the "good years" for the present predicament of the Union.

In all chapters, the analysis covers all EU27 Member States insofar as data availability permits. In some chapters, Norway and Iceland are added to the analysis, as their inclusion is deemed to make the analytical framework more robust and richer.

THE BOOK AT A GLANCE

Chapter 1 presents stylized facts concerning at-risk-of-poverty rates for the non-elderly population, household employment, and social spending for 27 EU Member States, Norway, and Iceland.[4] In order to set the scene for the following chapters, Vandenbroucke and Diris focus on the correlation between poverty risks on the one hand and household employment and social spending on the other, as explained earlier.

Chapter 2 considers the measurement of poverty in the European Union and presents a number of key methodological choices in relation to the metric of well-being, the determination of cut-off values, and the question of aggregation. Based on data from SILC 2005–2009, Decancq, Goedemé, Van den Bosch and Vanhille demonstrate that, far from being trivial, the choices for a specific metric of well-being and for a country-specific (as opposed to EU-wide) poverty line strongly impact on observed outcomes.

In Chapter 3, Corluy and Vandenbroucke explore the link between poverty risks and (increasing) employment rates. Because the former are conventionally measured through household income and the latter through individual employment rates, a first step in the analysis considers the distribution of employment at the household level. Focusing on household joblessness (as opposed to the more general notion of household work poverty), actual changes in household joblessness are decomposed in (i) changes due to changing individual employment rates and changing household structures; and (ii) changes in the distribution of jobs over households. This analysis is integrated into the decomposition of changes in the at-risk-of-poverty rates. This technique yields interesting insights into the trajectories that individual EU welfare states have followed over the past 10 years. It reveals the disparity of policy pathways in the EU during the Lisbon era. The results also show that evolutions in "polarization" of jobs over households reflect long-term trends that provide, for most countries, little explanatory power for short-term evolutions in poverty.

In Chapter 4, Marx and Nolan consider the nature of and evolutions in in-work poverty. Contrary to widely held beliefs, they do not observe a secular rise in in-work poverty linked to a general increase in wage inequality. Rather, they find in-work poverty to be strongly linked to work-intensity at the household level, which is associated in turn with institutional settings and the broader welfare state. In view of their findings, the authors consider relevant policy strategies, including the maximization of work-intensity, minimum wage setting, direct income supplements, and tax credits.

Chapter 5 considers changes in the distributional impact of cash transfers and tries to identify the impact of policies. Starting from the hypothesis that against the background of employment-centered welfare reforms the tensions between the objectives of social protection may have become more tense, the chapter considers changes in poverty reduction by social transfers according to household work-intensity. In order to identify the role of policies, it considers trends in spending levels and benefit generosity. It then reflects on the potentials and constraints to achieve more adequate minimum income protection. The most important conclusion to be drawn is the striking—and in many countries rising—inadequacy of social protection for individuals living in households with a low work-intensity. Cantillon, Van Mechelen, Pintelon and Van den Heede conclude that this may point to the tension between the adequacy of income protection and activation, lending credence to the notion that, in some countries, policies have sought to boost employment at least partially by reducing reservation wages.

In Chapter 6, Verbist and Matsaganis analyze the redistributive capacity of services, more specifically health care, education, and child care. First, the authors explore the methodological issues associated with the quantification of social service delivery (which implies an "extended" income concept) and the construction of a counterfactual (that includes needs, but not delivery of publicly provided services). The results show that services reduce inequality more than cash benefits do. To correctly interpret that result, it is, however, important to disentangle the effect of "size" and the effect of "design." Services for non-elderly individuals are, in all countries, much more important in size than cash transfers for the non-elderly, *a fortiori* if education is included. Using concentration coefficients, Verbist and Matsaganis show that, in most countries, cash transfers are more "pro-poor" than in-kind benefits. Yet, compulsory education and health care are weakly pro-poor, given that their distribution is less unequal than the distribution of extended income. Obviously, the larger the share of either spending on cash benefits or spending on services, the larger the equalizing impact on the (extended) income distribution.

In Chapter 7, Van Lancker and Ghysels further explore the shift from cash to service spending, with a specific focus on family policy (i.e., child benefits, childcare services and parental leave benefits). Based on expenditure trends in the realm of family policy, the authors find little support for the hypothesis of a generalized crowding-out process of cash benefits by service spending. Rather, there is evidence of overwhelming diversity across countries, in terms of policy effort, the balance between cash and in-kind spending, and the redistributive impact of family policy. A more possible detailed comparison of family policy in Flanders and Sweden provides indications of the importance of policy design in mediating the adverse distributive impact of policy.

Chapter 8 returns to the "new politics" of the welfare state. Hemerijck argues that, alongside serious retrenchments, there have been deliberate attempts to rebuild social programs and institutions to accommodate the new economic and social realities of the 21st century, roughly in line with social investment priorities, in the fields of family services, gender equality, employment policy, labor market regulation, and human capital formation.

In Chapter 9, De Deken offers a critical review of the concept of social investment and explores the possibilities and limits of operationalizing it on the basis of social expenditure data. He shows that the use of expenditure data to map the skeleton of the social investment state is fraught with conceptual and methodological problems. The chapter comments on the spending data related to old and new social risks that are reported in the Appendix to this book.

Chapter 10 summarizes the main findings and puts them into the perspective of long-term economic, social, and demographic changes that strongly affected the post-war balance between growth, employment, and social inclusion. On the basis of the analyses presented in the book, Cantillon concludes that the experience in the EU before the crisis is indicative of tough trade-offs that should not be taken lightly. She argues that the shift from passive social protection to activation and investment was definitely much more difficult than some might have expected. Disappointing poverty trends in Europe not only point at the structural inabilities of developed welfare states today to reduce income poverty, but also at limitations of the concept of social investment itself to overcome these deficiencies. Cantillon concludes that investment policies are important stepping stones toward social progress, on the condition, that is, that a better distribution of jobs, adequate social protection, and effective social redistribution supported by innovative place-based social action are part and parcel of any effective investment strategy, and vice versa.

The Appendix uses the OECD's Social Expenditure Statistics Detailed Database (SOCX) and the OECD's Education Database to provide country files on the evolution of social spending in 21 EU Member States covering the period 1985–2009. For each country, a distinction is made between "old" expenditures and "new" expenditures. "Old" expenditures represent the traditional core tasks of the welfare state; "new" expenditures represent new programs aimed at social risks inherent in postindustrial societies, which play a central role in the concept of social investment. Meeusen and Nys show the dynamics within "old" spending by distinguishing spending on old-age and survivor programs, spending on health care, and spending on working-age benefits. Until 2007, spending on working-age cash benefits decreased; this seems to reflect both the impact of the economic boom and a long-term trend. The data provided in the Appendix allow one to assess whether there has been (i) a long-term shift in budgetary resources from "old" to "new" programs; and/or (ii) a long-term shift in resources from "working-age benefits" to "old age and survivors programs" and "health care" within the category of "old spending." As a matter of fact, although "new" expenditures have experienced sweeping growth rates from 1990 onwards, the shift within the category of "old" spending seems to have been more substantial in absolute terms.

The book refers to the better years of growth in the second half of the 1990s and the early 2000s, which constitute the main focus of our investigations, followed by the downturn and ongoing crisis, pointing to a worse future. Other recent studies have devoted considerable attention to the incomes of the rich (e.g., Atkinson & Piketty, 2006) and to growing income inequalities (e.g., OECD 2008; 2011). Our focus is primarily on the poor at the lower end of the income distribution and on the considerable differences between rich and poor EU Member States. We believe that the difficulty of sustaining the European marriage of rich and poor nations and the implied need for solidarity and responsibility, not only in times of economic distress but also in eras of prosperity, merit the soul-searching exercise that led to this book project. We hope that this book also strengthens the reader's belief in both the relevance of the ethical program and the value of self-critical scrutiny of facts and figures.

NOTES

1 Lisbon European Council 23 and 24 March 2000. Presidency Conclusions http://www.europarl.europa.eu/summits/lis1_en.htm
2 This assessment is based on a comparison of SILC 2008 and SILC 2005. Except for the UK and Ireland, SILC 2008 covers the income situation in 2007.
3 As will be explained in Chapter 3, "jobless households," under the conventional definition, do not necessarily constitute a subset of "work-poor" households, given the different concepts and time frames applied in the underlying employment notion.
4 In this chapter we will use "the European welfare states" as a shortcut for the EU27, Norway and Iceland. However, references to data on "the European welfare states" provided in other chapters of this book may refer to a smaller set of welfare states.

1

MAPPING AT-RISK-OF-POVERTY RATES, HOUSEHOLD EMPLOYMENT, AND SOCIAL SPENDING

Frank Vandenbroucke and Ron Diris

In this chapter we present stylized facts concerning at-risk-of-poverty rates for the non-elderly population, household employment, and social spending for the 27 EU Member States, Norway, and Iceland.[1] In order to set the scene for the following chapters of this book, we focus on the correlation between poverty risks on the one hand and household employment and social spending on the other. The central question that is thus introduced refers to the notion of *employment-centered welfare reform*, and it may be summarized as follows: Is it possible to structurally replace spending on cash benefits for working-age adults and their families with employment creation and to simultaneously reduce poverty among working-age adults and their children? Because this book explores the poverty-employment nexus, we focus on the non-elderly population. In the present chapter, individuals below the age of 60 constitute the "non-elderly" group. Throughout, we use "population" as a short-cut for "non-elderly population"; at-risk-of-poverty rates should be understood to refer to the non-elderly population.

The at-risk-of-poverty rate applied here is a rather crude headcount: It simply measures the share of individuals in the non-elderly population considered to be at risk of financial poverty, and takes no account of the depth or severity of the poverty faced. Being at risk of poverty means living in a household with an equivalized net disposable income below 60% of the national median equivalized net disposable household income. (See Box on p. 70 for a detailed explanation.) Thus conceived, the poverty headcount defines poverty in relation to the level of income at a given moment in the nation state where an individual happens to be living. In other words, the poverty threshold is a national measure that changes over time. In Chapter 2, Decancq et al. explain that the particular indicator on which we focus here is part of a larger class of poverty indicators, thereby highlighting limitations and possible pitfalls of our approach. They also illustrate the difference between observations that are statistically significant and observations *as such*. In Chapter 10, Cantillon argues that a relative at-risk-of-poverty indicator nonetheless constitutes an important benchmark for assessing the performance of welfare states. Below we present data that we consider essential for the inquiry underlying this book, without entering into any of the substantive or methodological discussions that follow. Our purpose is, first, to show that the income and employment data gathered in the European Statistics on Income and Living Conditions (SILC) suggest both stability and change in the second half of the previous decade, and, second, to introduce and justify the research agenda that is developed in this book.

Underscoring "stability and change" is not redundant in this context. A priori, one might expect that this at-risk-of-poverty headcount is, by its nature, rather inert; because it is a relative measure, it might fail to register a general increase (or decrease) in incomes, including in those of the poor. Moreover, important developments in the income distribution above or below the poverty threshold may also go unnoticed. However, the facts contradict that expectation to some extent. Even over a relative short time span of six years, the poverty headcount turns out not to be inert, as will be illustrated below: In a subset of countries, important evolutions are observed. Against this backdrop, the overall stability of the poverty headcount in another set of countries becomes a relevant observation per se. In a survey that registers change *and* stasis, stasis is as interesting as change. Moreover, even in countries where the overall evolution is suggestive of stasis, important changes occur within subgroups of the population.

Most at-risk-of-poverty and employment data presented in this chapter are based on SILC, the main data source for measuring income and living conditions in Europe. For the 1990s, we rely on the European Community Household Panel (ECHP), while some calculations for Germany are based on data from the German Socio-Economic Panel (SOEP); more detailed information on these data sources is provided in Chapter 2. Data with regard to social spending are taken from Eurostat. The income data in SILC refer to the year prior to the survey, except in Ireland and the United Kingdom. Our definition of "work-poor" and "work-rich" households refers to the same 12-month period as the income data. Below, we introduce a definition of individual employment that refers to realities observed immediately before the survey. To summarize this complex construal accurately, one ought to label the time frame covered by, say, SILC 2005 as "2004/5." We generally avoid this complexity by referring to the SILC survey years (such as "SILC 2005") rather than the actual time frame covered by the survey. For the same reason, we associate observations in SILC *T* with spending data for the year *T-1*. Hence, the reader should be aware that a comparison of, for example,

SILC 2008 and SILC 2005 informs us about changes in *income* and *household employment realities* between 2004 and 2007, except in the case of the UK and Ireland.

Chapters 3 and 5 in this book analyze the change (or lack of change) in poverty rates in European welfare states. They focus on the favorable economic years covered by SILC 2005–2008; Chapter 5 also examines the years covered by ECHP 1995–2001, which was, generally speaking, a period of economic recovery and declining unemployment. In the first section of this introductory chapter, we provide basic facts with regard to at-risk-of-poverty rates in Europe, from SILC 2005 to SILC 2011, that is, up into mid-crisis years. In the second section, we further broaden the time frame and provide some context by the addition of summary data on employment, economic dependency, and social spending for the period 1995–2010. In the third section, we examine the correlation between poverty outcomes, employment (with a focus on household employment, a concept developed in that section), and social spending. We do not pretend to provide causal explanations for cross-country differences in levels of poverty; we rather propose a mapping of levels of poverty based on their association with social spending on the one hand and levels of household employment on the other. Section 1.4 elaborates upon the observation that spending does not seem as "efficient" in some welfare states as in others, and formulates a number of caveats with regard to this important but tricky notion. Section 1.5 introduces the concept of "poverty reduction by transfers," which is an important parameter for describing the dynamics of change in welfare states. Having discussed the concept of "poverty reduction," our attention shifts in Section 1.6 from mapping *levels* of poverty, spending, and employment (in essence, on the basis of regression techniques) to mapping how these variables *change over time* in each of the European welfare states (in essence, on the basis of decomposition techniques). One should be aware that analyzing changes in poverty risks in single countries, from an intertemporal perspective, and making a cross-country analysis of poverty levels are two quite different exercises. Much confusion, both in the academic and in the policy debate, is caused by the unwarranted conflation of these two perspectives. By way of example, perhaps we ought to explain how contemporary Sweden can continue to rank quite well in terms of poverty in a cross-country perspective and yet, as a country, has clearly followed an inegalitarian course in the second half of the past decade. Factors accounting for the Scandinavian "superiority" in terms of social inclusion and employment (relative to performance levels across Europe) are not preventing some Scandinavian welfare states from shifting to less outstanding outcomes (more so than is the case in other European welfare states).

Although we are able to discern some common features, there are no general "laws" that uniformly explain the dynamics of poverty in European welfare states in the previous decade. Therefore, in the seventh section, we provide an overview of eight different trajectories of welfare states, comparing changes in the United Kingdom, Sweden, Spain, Belgium, Ireland, Poland, Norway, and Germany.

1.1 THE EVOLUTION OF POVERTY RISKS FOR THE NON-ELDERLY POPULATION

Several chapters in this book focus on comparisons of SILC 2005 and SILC 2008 because both examine income and employment evolutions in the good economic years 2004/5–2007/8. In order to put the developments during these years in a broader time frame, Figure 1.1 and Table 1.1 summarize the evolution of the national at-risk-of-poverty rates from SILC 2005 to SILC 2011 and simultaneously focus on significant evolutions between SILC 2005 and SILC 2008.

Figure 1.1 ranks European welfare states according to the change in the at-risk-of-poverty rates between SILC 2005 and SILC 2011: Poland is on the extreme left, with a decline of 4.6 percentage points (ppt). Next to Poland, the only country with a substantially lower poverty in SILC 2011 than in SILC 2005 was the United Kingdom (−2.8 ppt). As will be shown in Section 1.6, our interpretation of the poverty decrease in the United Kingdom should be qualified, as it is to a large extent the upshot of decreasing median incomes during the crisis. This leaves only Poland as an unambiguous case of diminishing poverty during the Lisbon era (unambiguous, that is, with regard to the non-elderly; poverty among the elderly increased considerably in Poland in the period under consideration). In contrast, poverty was substantially higher in SILC 2011 than in SILC 2005 in a considerable number of Member States. Starting from the extreme right side of Figure 1.1, these countries are Spain (+4.5 ppt), Germany (+4 ppt),

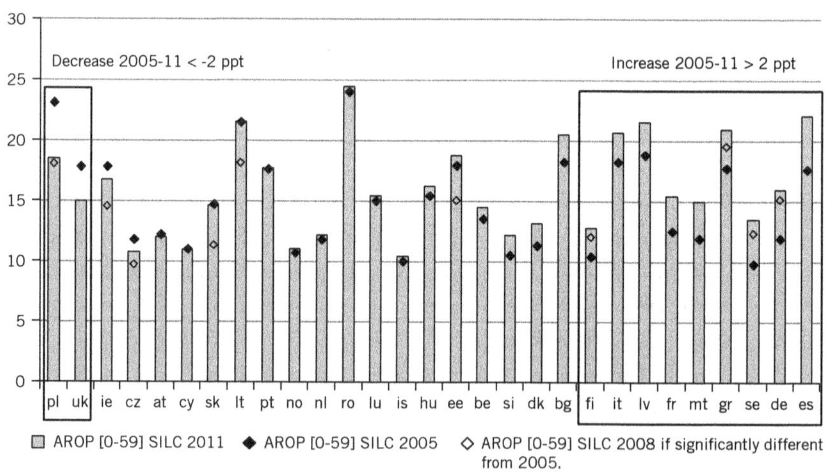

Figure 1.1. At-risk-of-poverty rates, population [0–59]. *Source*: EU-SILC 2005, 2008, 2011. *Note 1:* Bulgaria: EU-SILC 2006 instead of EU-SILC 2005. Romania: EU-SILC 2007 instead of EU-SILC 2005.Ireland: EU-SILC 2010 instead of EU-SILC 2011. *Note 2:* Data for SILC 2008 are shown only when the difference between SILC 2008 and SILC 2005 is statistically significant. *Note 3:* Ranked according to change from SILC 2005 to SILC 2011.

Table 1.1. At-risk-of-poverty rates, population [0–59].

	2008–2005 ppt Δ	Sig. Δ 2008–2005	2011–2005 ppt Δ (*)	2011% (*)
	(1)	(2)	(3)	(4)
Austria	–0.1		–0.2	12.0
Belgium	–0.3		0.9	14.4
Bulgaria	n.a.		2.3	20.5
Cyprus	0.2		–0.1	10.9
Czech Republic	–2.1	**	–1.0	10.8
Germany	3.4	***	4.0	15.9
Denmark	–0.2		1.8	13.1
Estonia	–2.9	***	0.8	18.7
Spain	0.4		4.5	22.1
Finland	1.2	*	2.4	12.8
France	1.0		2.9	15.4
Greece	1.9	*	3.2	20.9
Hungary	–0.9		0.8	16.2
Ireland	–3.1	**	–1.1	16.7
Iceland	–0.4		0.4	10.4
Italy	0.3		2.5	20.7
Lithuania	–3.3	**	0.0	21.5
Luxembourg	0.1		0.4	15.4
Latvia	1.4		2.7	21.5
Malta	n.a.		3.1	15.0
Netherlands	–0.9		0.4	12.2
Norway	0.6		0.3	11.0
Poland	–5.1	***	–4.6	18.5
Portugal	–0.1		0.1	17.7
Romania	n.a.		0.4	24.4
Sweden	2.6	***	3.7	13.5
Slovenia	0.1		1.7	12.2
Slovakia	–3.4	***	–0.1	14.6
United Kingdom	–0.9		–2.8	15.0

Source: (1) & (2) Calculations by Tim Goedemé, on EU-SILC User Database, building on Goedemé (2013). (3) & (4) Eurostat
Note 1: (*) Ireland: SILC 2010 instead of SILC 2011
Bulgaria: SILC 2006 instead of SILC 2005
Romania: SILC 2007 instead of SILC 2005
Note 2: Standard errors take as much as possible account of the EU-SILC sample design
Note 3: *** = sign. at 1%; ** = sign. at 5%; * = sign. at 10%

Sweden (+3.7 ppt), Greece (+3.2 ppt), Malta (+3.1 ppt), France (+2.9 ppt), Latvia (+2.7 ppt), Italy (+2.5 ppt), and Finland (+2.4 ppt).

Figure 1.1 provides the at-risk-of-poverty rates from SILC 2008 for a selection of eight countries, for which there was a statistically significant change between SILC 2005 and SILC 2008. The underlying data are presented in Columns 1 and 2 of Table 1.1, which indicate that we observe a significantly declining at-risk-of-poverty rate between SILC 2005 and SILC 2008 for six countries (Poland, Lithuania, Slovakia, Ireland, Estonia, and the Czech Republic) and a significantly increasing at-risk-of-poverty rate for four countries (Germany, Finland, Greece, and Sweden). In all the other countries there was no significant change in the at-risk-of-poverty rates between SILC 2005 and SILC 2008. For most of the countries under review, these were years of economic boom. During the subsequent years of crisis, some of the latter group deviated from the stability observed between SILC 2005 and SILC 2008: In the United Kingdom, the initially moderate decline in the at-risk-of-poverty rate accelerated between SILC 2008 and SILC 2011, resulting in a significantly lower level of poverty in SILC 2011 than in SILC 2005. In other countries, such as Spain and Italy, the financial crisis led to significantly rising at-risk-of-poverty rates after the standstill during the good economic years.

In some countries the pattern of SILC outcomes is quite irregular for the first years under review, reflecting possible instability in the survey. For Sweden, the poverty headcount calculated on the basis of SILC 2005 is difficult to square with the results in SILC 2004 and SILC 2006, because it suggests a sudden but temporary drop in poverty. For this reason, we cannot exclude that comparisons between SILC 2005 and SILC 2008, which we develop below and in subsequent chapters of this book, overstate the poverty increase in Sweden. Nonetheless, the underlying trend between SILC 2004 and SILC 2011 is suggestive of a rather consistent pattern of increasing poverty rates, as illustrated in Section 1.7. For Germany, the reliability of SILC 2006–2007 has been called into question: Instead of the rather spectacular increase in poverty between 2005 and 2007 registered in SILC, the German SOEP is indicative of stability in the poverty headcount from 2004 onward, which comes after a considerable increase between 1999 and 2004 (Grabka & Schupp, 2012; Frick & Krell, 2010; Hauser, 2008). Therefore, in Section 1.7, we present a separate analysis on the basis of the German SOEP.

When comparing SILC 2011 with SILC 2005, one should note that the picture with regard to poverty risks for the elderly population (60 years or older) is very different. While the weighted average of national at-risk-of-poverty rates of the non-elderly increased with 1.3 ppt for the EU27, poverty rates for the elderly decreased with 2.1 ppt. Consequently, the overall weighted average of poverty rates for the total population did not increase (the Eurostat estimate for the EU27 is an increase by 0.5 ppt). In many European welfare states, the at-risk-of-poverty rate for the elderly declined significantly. For instance, in Spain the decrease was −6.8 ppt; in Portugal −6.4 ppt; in Norway −5.6 ppt; in France −5.1 ppt; in

Greece −3.1 ppt. In some countries, the decline started before 2008; in other countries it was enhanced by the impact of the crisis, because the incomes of the elderly were better protected than the shrinking incomes of many of the non-elderly. There are three important exceptions to this pattern: In Sweden the at-risk-of-poverty rate for the elderly increased by 7 ppt (from a low point of 8.4% in SILC 2005); in Poland the increase was 6.4 ppt, and in Germany 2.6 ppt.

Given the ambition of the Lisbon Strategy, launched in 2000, to eradicate poverty by 2010, this result is plainly disappointing. By 2007/8, when the financial crisis struck, only six of the 27 Member States were on a clearly discernible course of decreasing poverty among the non-elderly population. Using 2004/5 as a benchmark, by the end of the decade, poverty had declined only in Poland and the UK (with the aforementioned qualification); in at least half of the Member States it was higher. In one third of EU Member States, highlighted with the box on the right side of Figure 1.1, the increase in poverty risks was larger than 2 ppt. Should we interpret this outcome as a, possibly diverse, set of domestic policy failures? Or, does it reveal a common trend, associated with the dominant policy discourse in the Lisbon Strategy, with the crowding out of distributive programs for working-age families by old-age programs and health care, with the forces unleashed by European integration and intra-European migration? Or, has the complexity of "employment-centered welfare reform"—the idea that employment creation can structurally replace social transfers—been underestimated? Or is it perhaps symptomatic of a combination of some or all of these factors? Are we witnessing an irresistible convergence in welfare state performance toward a more modest level, characterized by a lower degree of social inclusion than that attained in the 1990s in the best-performing European welfare states?

Scrutiny of Figure 1.1 and Table 1.1 shows that the first part of the period under review, covered by SILC 2005–2008, was indeed one of convergence in national at-risk-of-poverty rates. The group of countries displaying declining poverty rates, consisted mostly (but not entirely) of countries where poverty rates were initially high, such as Poland, Lithuania, Estonia, and Ireland. Poverty rates are growing predominantly (but not exclusively) in countries where they initially were comparatively low, such as Sweden, Finland, and Germany (at least on the basis of SILC). Overall, the data shown in Figure 1.1 are characterized by a process of "catching-up" (beta-convergence) for the period SILC 2005–2008. Simultaneously, there are some notable exceptions, such as the Netherlands, the Czech Republic, and Slovakia (low poverty rates, no increase), as well as Greece and Latvia (high and increasing poverty rates). In other words, there was no "iron law" at play whereby relatively egalitarian welfare states were *all* destined to become less egalitarian, while inegalitarian countries were all set to become more egalitarian. Notwithstanding these exceptions, SILC 2005–2008 suggests growing cohesion on a pan-European level. In Chapter 2, Decancq et al. further develop this insight by considering a pan-European definition of poverty, based on a single European poverty threshold instead of national thresholds. However, between SILC 2008 and SILC 2011, there was no further convergence to be observed: The financial crisis brought a sudden halt to the trend toward greater pan-European cohesion so conceived. Overall, throughout the entire period of SILC 2005–2011, beta-convergence still persists, but less emphatically so than in the early part of this period.

We can summarize the same overall result in yet another way, by contrasting the weighted average[2] of the national at-risk-of-poverty rates for the "old" Member States (EU15) and the "new" Member States (EU12). In the EU15, the at-risk-of-poverty rate for the population under the age of 60 increased from 14.9% in SILC 2005 to 16.9% in SILC 2011; in the EU12, the at-risk-of-poverty rate decreased from 20.1% to 18.6%. The overall result was an increase in the weighted average of estimated poverty rates in the EU27 from 16% (SILC 2005) to 17.3% (SILC 2011).[3] In other words, national poverty rates converged, but there was no evidence of the "upward" convergence previously experienced in the course of European integration, as documented by Lefebvre & Pestieau (2012) with regard to the performance of European welfare states, or by the World Bank with respect to GDP per capita (Gill & Raiser, 2012).

1.2 CHANGING WELFARE STATES: EMPLOYMENT-CENTERED SOCIAL POLICY

A central consideration in this book is the relationship between policy achievements with regard to employment and policy achievements with regard to financial poverty. There is ample historic evidence that "employment success" and "antipoverty success" are not mutually exclusive. On the contrary, a robust employment basis constitutes a precondition for the sustainability of a socially inclusive welfare state. Welfare states that historically have been successful in terms of both employment and poverty, notably the Scandinavian welfare states, typically have also been "big spenders" on social protection. The question we will address goes beyond the familiar observation that employment and social inclusion are friends, not enemies. In a nutshell, it may be formulated as follows: Is it possible to structurally *replace spending* on cash benefits for working-age adults and their families with *employment creation*, and to simultaneously *reduce poverty* among working-age adults and their children? This question pertains to the essence of welfare reform as it has been conceived over the last 20 years: Already in the 1990s, employment-centered welfare reform was the key objective of the changing welfare states Hemerijck describes in Chapter 8 of this book. The Lisbon Council of March 2000 officially endorsed the view that activating an employment-centered social policy, based on investment in people, was the way forward toward reconciling social inclusion and the successful emergence of a new, knowledge-based economy.

With hindsight, the turn toward employment-centered welfare reform may be seen as a logical response to the steady increase in *economic dependency* (i.e., the number of individuals, of all ages, who are not employed divided by the number who are), a process that had been unfolding in the mature welfare states of the EU15 since the late 1970s. Therefore, the focus in this section is mainly on the EU15. In 1994, the economic dependency ratio for the EU15 stood at 1.46; that is, for every 10 persons in work, nearly 15 were not, because they were either too young or too old, or were unemployed, disabled, or inactive for another reason. From 1994 onward, economic dependency steadily decreased, reaching a low of 1.20 in 2008; that is, the number of persons not in work declined to 12 for every 10 persons in work.[4] These figures signal a considerable (positive) change, up until 2008, in the fundamental parameters determining how generous welfare states can be.

Prima facie, one might interpret the 1995–2008 period as one in which employment increasingly replaced social benefits as a means of sustaining individual and household incomes, making it possible to consolidate public budgets with a view to monetary unification *and*, if fiscal consolidation left room for maneuver, in order to enhance the quality of welfare states. However, for various reasons, a decreasing economic dependency ratio does not imply a proportionate decrease in the social policy caseload—which is essential for turning this optimistic prima facie expectation into reality. First, demographic aging leads to more pensioners. Between 1994 and 2008, total demographic dependency (the number of individuals in the 0–14 years and the over-65 years age brackets, divided by the number of individuals in the 15–64 years age bracket), was basically flat (0.49 in 1994; 0.50 in 2008). This overall stability was the outcome of an increase in the old-age dependency ratio (from 0.23 to 0.27) and a decline in the child dependency ratio. Average old age pensions are obviously higher than average child benefits. Second, in a number of countries, a steadily growing number of women were entitled to pensions. Third, the feminization of the labor market, changing family structures, and changes in social policy implied that more and more working-age individuals were entitled to social benefits. In the 1960s and 1970s, economic dependency among non-elderly adults was to a large extent an expression of the male breadwinner model: Women depended financially on their husbands, without intermediation of social benefits. In the 1980s and 1990s, economic dependency increasingly implied benefit dependency. Fourth, decreasing economic dependency at individual level does not result in a proportionate reduction in economic dependency of households. Eurostat provides a rough-and-ready estimate of the share of non-elderly adults living in jobless households (i.e., households where none of the working-age adults were in work, not even for one hour, in the weeks prior to the survey) in the EU15: In 1995 it amounted to 11.5%; by 2008 this share had declined to 9%, while the individual nonemployment rate had decreased from 39.9% to 32.9%.[5] The observation that the percentage point decline in household joblessness is much lower than the percentage point decline in individual joblessness partly reflects a "mathematical truism," as explained in Chapter 3. However, the analysis in Chapter 3 shows that declining family size, increasing female participation rates, and other factors explaining increasing polarization of jobs over households also contributed to the gap between "household employment success" and "individual employment success" over these years. Notably in Southern Europe, the "household employment success" was less than one might have expected on the basis of the "individual employment success." In other words, southern welfare *states* were increasingly replacing *extended families* to cater for economically dependent working-age adults. A final reason why the social policy caseload did not diminish proportionately with economic dependency relates to the development of in-work benefits, which were seen as an important tool for enhancing labor market participation. All these factors, together with deliberate changes in social protection policy, explain why decreasing economic dependency did not convert into a decrease in the social policy caseload. As a matter of fact, the evolution of the social policy caseload was quite disparate in the EU15, with minor decreases or quasi-stability in some countries versus decreases in others. In the UK in 1994, 10.6% of working-age people were on unemployment, social assistance, early retirement, or work incapacity benefits; by 2008, that share had declined to 8.7%. In Germany there was a more marked decrease, from 15.3% to 10.6%. By contrast, the 2008 social policy caseload was comparable to the 1994 caseload in Belgium, Spain, and Sweden. (It should be added, however, that by 2008 in Sweden the caseload was declining from the very high level reached in the early 2000s. All figures are calculated on the basis of De Deken & Clasen, 2011).

Nevertheless, applying a midterm perspective and a highly aggregate level of analysis, one might say that the *decreasing economic dependency* ratios associated with growing employment up until 2008 enabled—or at least helped enable—governments to *replace spending on cash benefits for working-age adults and their families with spending on pensions and health care.* Figure 1.2 displays the evolution of social spending as a percentage of GDP, distinguishing spending on (i) cash benefits excluding old-age and survivor programs (below, we will refer to this category of spending as "working-age cash benefits"); (ii) old-age and survivor programs in cash and in kind; (iii) health care in kind; and (iv) other categories of in-kind expenditures. The data are weighted averages for the EU15.

In 2008, total spending on social protection benefits in the EU15, expressed as a percentage of GDP, was at the same level as it had been in 1995. Spending on working-age cash benefits was 1.33 ppt lower; spending on old-age and survivor programs was marginally higher (+0.34 ppt), while spending on healthcare benefits in kind was 1 ppt higher. So conceived, pension and healthcare spending substituted for working-age cash benefits. The crisis implied a considerable increase in all three categories of spending relative to GDP by 2010 (working-age cash: + 0.67 ppt; old age: + 0.93 ppt; health + 0.70 ppt, all compared to 2008), leading to an unprecedented level of social spending in 2010.

Obviously, not all EU15 welfare states followed this trajectory of substitution between 1995 and 2008. For some welfare states, this was a period of general

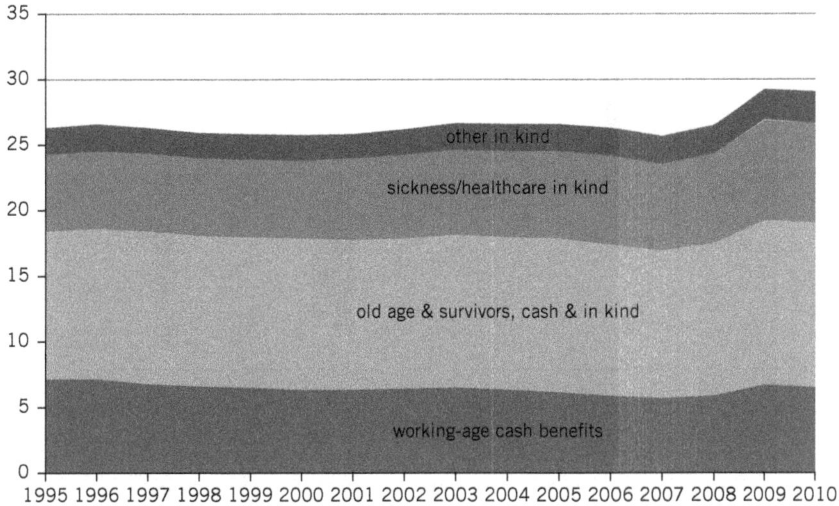

Figure 1.2. Social spending as a percentage of GDP, EU15, weighted average, 1995–2010.
Source: Eurostat.

retrenchment or general expansion; in some welfare states selective expansion also occurred in programs other than old age and health care. Figure 1.3 provides some examples for a subset of EU15 countries and Norway and Poland. Substitution of working-age cash benefits by old-age and healthcare programs can be discerned in Germany (which represents a heavy weight in the EU15 weighted average), Belgium, Spain and the United Kingdom. However, such substitution did not occur in Ireland (where old-age and healthcare spending was much higher 2008 than in 1995, but not at the expense of working-age cash benefits), or either in Sweden (where there was a considerable reduction in working-age cash benefits, but no increase in old-age and healthcare spending) or Norway (where both working-age cash benefits and old-age and healthcare spending declined).

The structure of social spending gradually shifted toward relatively more spending on services and relatively less spending on cash benefits. Hence, it may be the case that our assessment of poverty increasingly underestimates the redistributive impact of welfare states, given that it does not take into account the value and distribution of growing public services when measuring the standard of living of households. On the other hand, it can be argued that a shift from cash benefits to benefits in kind implies less redistribution, *if* the counterfactual benchmark applied is more spending on cash benefits rather than on public services. In short, more spending on public services may imply more redistribution, if the counterfactual benchmark is less social spending *as such*; but more spending on public services may be seen to imply less redistribution, if the counterfactual benchmark is substitution of cash benefits for public services,

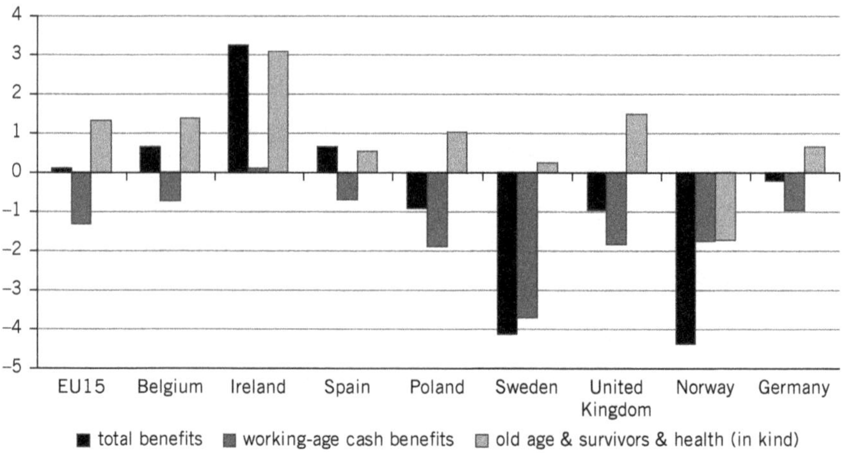

Figure 1.3. Changes in spending on social protection benefits, in percentage of GDP, 1995–2008 (Poland: 2000–2008). *Source*: Eurostat.

with unchanged levels of social spending. In Chapter 6, Verbist and Matsaganis examine this issue at greater length. In Chapter 7, Van Lancker and Ghysels further explore the shift from cash to service spending, with specific focus on family policy (i.e., child benefits, childcare services, and parental leave benefits). Based on expenditure trends, the authors find little support for a generalized crowding-out process of cash benefits by service spending. Rather, there is evidence of overwhelming diversity across countries, in terms of policy effort, the balance between cash and in-kind spending, and the redistributive impact of family policy. A more detailed comparison of family policy in Flanders and Sweden provides indications of the importance of policy design in mediating the distributive impact of policy.

The data referred to in this section permit only a superficial description of spending trends. Would a more finely grained analysis of expenditures allow us to assess whether or not there was a budgetary reorientation toward true "social investment programs" (such as active labor market programs or childcare), rather than just a shift from working-age cash benefits to old-age and healthcare programs? In Chapter 9 and the Appendix to this book, the evolution of social spending is examined in further detail on the basis of the Social Expenditure Database of the Organisation for Economic Co-operation and Development (OECD). In Chapter 9, De Deken offers a critical review of the concept of social investment and explores the possibilities and limits of operationalizing it on the basis of social expenditure data. He argues that the use of expenditure data to map the skeleton of the social investment state is fraught with conceptual and methodological problems. The Appendix should be read with these caveats in mind, but it nonetheless offers some interesting additional insights into the dynamics of social spending.

Common trends with regard to social spending do not imply uniformity. In the same vein, one should be aware that the evolution of employment rates between 1995 and 2008 was far from uniform. Between 1995 and 2001 there was a spectacular increase in employment in Spain and Ireland, while the German employment rate was basically flat. Between 1995 and 2008, nearly one third of the extra employment in the EU15 was created in Spain and Ireland. In Germany employment only started to increase in 2005. In other words, employment-centered welfare reform in Germany only "paid off" in jobs after 2005. In the early 2000s, the Swedish and Norwegian employment rates declined, and did not return to their 2000 level until 2008. Thus, the overall pattern in the EU15 in the years 1995–2008 was one of upward convergence.

The turn toward employment-centered welfare reform and the argument for activating social investment originated in the EU15, as policymakers tried to formulate answers to the dilemmas they perceived in those mature, market-based welfare states (see Chapter 10 and 8 in this book). It is less straightforward to associate this policy paradigm with the transition problems experienced by the former Communist countries. Moreover, identifying any common trends on the basis of spending patterns is difficult for the new European Member States (EU12), because the period for which comparable spending data are available is relatively short. For 2000–2008, no clear trend is observable; the pattern is rather one of stability of spending relative to GDP. An important exception to this pattern is Poland, where spending on working-age cash benefits decreased from an already low level to be partially replaced by spending on old-age and survivors programs. The Polish trajectory should be considered in its proper context, however. Poland went through a deep economic crisis in the second half of the 1990s: The unemployment rate doubled between 1997 and 2002 to 20%, after which it only declined again to its 1997 level by 2007. Poland's employment rate, which is added in Figure 1.4, illustrates the depth of the Polish crisis and the pace of recovery after 2003.

Notwithstanding the country-specific contexts, the common challenge confronting these changing welfare states can be summarized in this one question: Is it possible to *replace spending* on cash benefits for working-age adults and their families by *employment creation*, in a structural way, and, simultaneously, to *reduce poverty* among working-age adults and their children? Or, to formulate it less ambitiously: Is it possible to structurally replace spending on cash benefits for working-age households by employment creation *without increasing poverty*? We add "structurally," because one should distinguish correlations between short-term changes in spending and employment during the business cycle from structural trends. The purpose of this book is not to arrive at a definitive verdict on that matter. In order to enhance our understanding of the issues at hand, we decompose changes in poverty outcomes in the European welfare states during the periods characterized, in general, by rather favorable economic conditions and, for many countries, diminishing spending on working-age cash benefits.

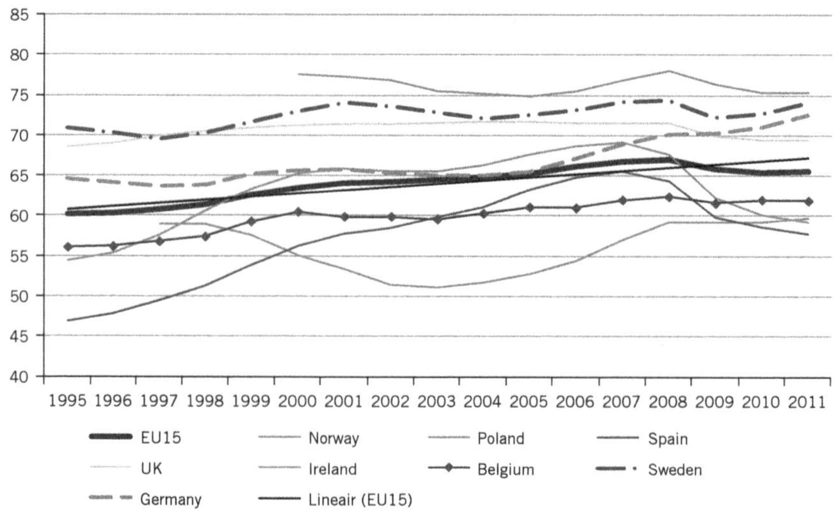

Figure 1.4. Employment rate, population [15–64], 1995–2011. *Source*: Labour Force Survey, Eurostat.

These decompositions are based on a distinction between "work-poor" and "work-rich" households, introduced in the next section of this chapter. Chapter 3 focuses on the period covered by SILC 2005–2008; Chapter 5 examines both the period covered by SILC 2005–2008 and that covered by ECHP 1995–2001. Figure 1.5 shows the evolution of spending on working-age cash benefits for a selection of countries during the periods examined in these chapters. This selection contains countries conforming to the dominant pattern of diminishing spending on working-age cash benefits as well as some notable exceptions (such as Germany in the first period under review, and Belgium, Ireland, and Spain in the second).

It is no exaggeration to say that the years under scrutiny in Chapters 3 and 5 (highlighted with the boxes in Figure 1.5) were economically quite favorable years. At the level of the EU15, overall unemployment diminished steadily between 1994 and 2001, then increased again to reach a new peak in 2004/5, after which it dropped to a low point in 2007/8. The fact that many welfare states cut their spending on working-age cash benefits, relative to GDP, during those years does not necessarily instantiate a long-term trend. It may be attributed at least in part to their role as "automatic stabilizers" in relation to the business cycle; we return to this point in Sections 1.6 and 1.7 below.

The focus in this book is on *changes* in spending, employment, and poverty outcomes in individual, path-dependent welfare states. However, in the following section we first look at *levels* of spending, employment rates, and poverty rates, and how these parameters correlate with one another.

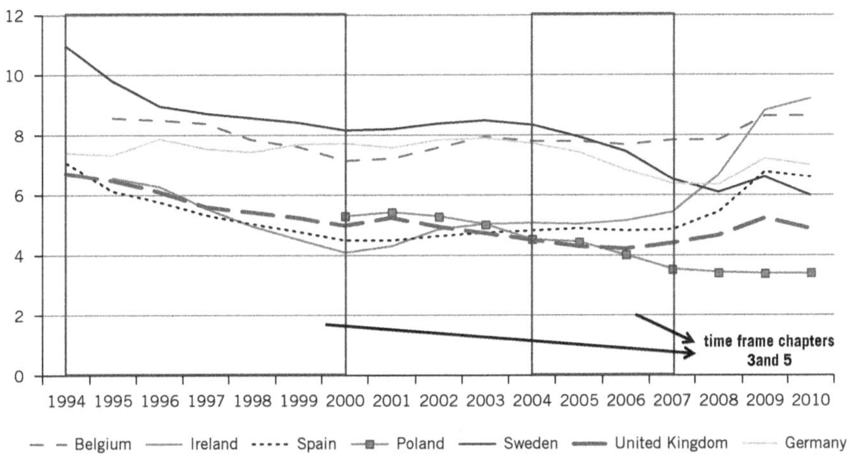

Figure 1.5. Spending on working-age cash benefits, percentage of GDP, 1994–2010.
Source: Eurostat.

1.3 MAPPING POVERTY LEVELS ON LEVELS OF SOCIAL SPENDING AND EMPLOYMENT RATES

In contemporary Europe, it appears that poverty levels correlate negatively with levels of social spending (as a percentage of GDP) and individual employment rates. The first observation is not new and comes as no surprise. The second—the statistical association of high employment rates with low levels of poverty—is less self-evident. After all, we measure poverty at the household level, while employment rates are based on individuals. Therefore, associating employment rates with levels of poverty in a cross-country perspective may represent a *category mismatch*. Distinguishing individuals living in "work-rich households" from individuals living in "work-poor households" (which typically face much higher poverty risks) and measuring the share of individuals living in work-poor households may be more informative than counting the proportion of jobless individuals. This observation, too, has been made previously, and evidence has been tabled to suggest that the correlation between poverty and individual employment rates is quite weak, while the explanatory power of the share of individuals living in work-poor households may be stronger.[6]

What is a work-poor household anyway? Chapter 3 discusses different measures of *household employment* (as opposed to individual employment), implying different definitions of a "work-poor household." In this introductory chapter, we base our presentation on the notion of "household work-intensity," as defined by Eurostat. Work-intensity is conceptualized as the ratio between the total number of months worked by working-age household members (excluding students) and the total number of months that they could, in theory, have worked. For persons who reported having worked part-time, an estimate of the number of months in terms of full-time equivalents was computed on the basis of the number of hours habitually worked at the time of the interview.

In all European welfare states, at-risk-of-poverty rates of individuals correlate negatively with the work-intensity of the household to which they belong. Figure 1.6 shows the weighted average for the EU27 of the national at-risk-of-poverty rates for five different subsets of households, as registered in SILC 2008: We distinguish among households with very high work-intensity (work-intensity ranges between 85% and 100%), households with high work-intensity (between 55% and 85%), households with medium work-intensity (between 45% and 55%), households with low work-intensity (between 20% and 45%), and households with very low work-intensity (20% or less). The at-risk-of-poverty rate in households with very high work-intensity was 5%; the at-risk-of-poverty rate in households with very low work-intensity was more than eleven times higher (56%). *Hence, for individuals in Europe, the work-intensity of the household to which they belong is a crucial determinant of their (individual) poverty risk.*

We now shift our attention from an analysis at the individual level to an analysis at the level of welfare states. To what extent is a welfare state's poverty record determined by spending on working-age cash benefits and the work-intensity of its households? We distinguish two indicators of the "household employment" record of welfare states, based on the data on the work-intensity of households in SILC. The first indicator is the share of individuals living in households with very low work-intensity (between 0% and 20%); we label these households as "very

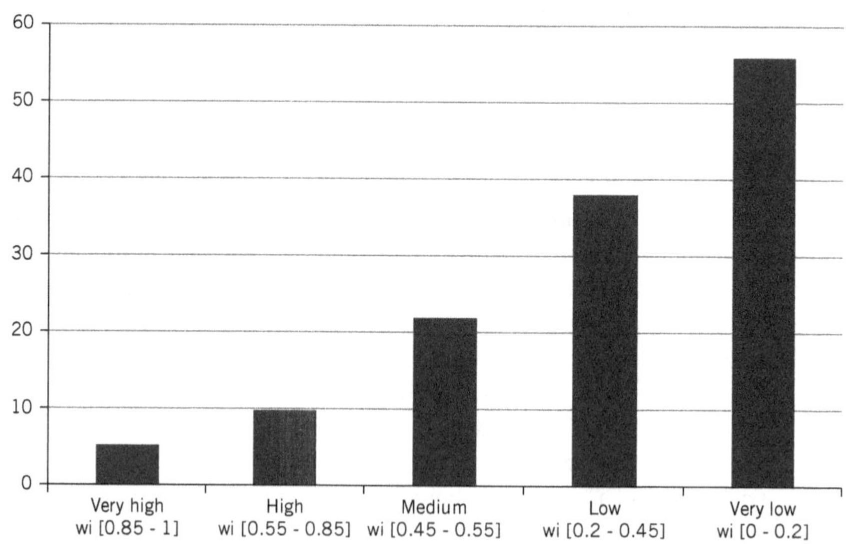

Figure 1.6. At-risk-of-poverty rate, population [0–59], by work intensity (wi) of the household, EU27, EU-SILC 2008. *Note*: AROP defined as at-risk-of-poverty rate (cut-off point: 60% of median equivalized income after social transfers).

work-poor." The second indicator is the share of individuals living in households with medium work-intensity or less (i.e., 55% or less); we label these households as "work-poor." We will use "work poverty" as a shortcut for the share of individuals living in work-poor households, and "severe work poverty" as a shortcut for the share of individuals living in very work-poor households. The reader should note that the expressions "work poverty" and "severe work poverty," as we use them here, refer to features of welfare states, not to characteristics of individuals or households.

Simple correlations on the basis of the SILC surveys from 2005 to 2011, which we do not show here, reveal the following pattern for most of the years under consideration: National at-risk-of-poverty rates correlate negatively with the level of spending on working-age cash benefits; they correlate positively with the individual employment rates and with work poverty, that is, with the share of individuals living in work-poor households. However, these positive correlations with individual nonemployment rates and work poverty are not very strong. If we focus on *very* work-poor households the correlation with financial poverty disappears. Prima facie, the latter observation may seem surprising, given the fact that, at the level of individuals, people living in households with such very low work-intensity are confronted with very high financial poverty risks (Figure 1.6). To assess the impact of 'severe work poverty' on the overall poverty record of welfare states one has to apply a more elaborate model, rather than a simple correlation, as will be shown below.

The values of correlation coefficients of poverty with work poverty and with the individual nonemployment rate are quite comparable for many of the years under review. That should not come as a surprise either, given that individual nonemployment rates and work poverty, as defined by us, correlate strongly on a cross-country basis. Figure 1.7 shows the relationship among individual nonemployment, work poverty, and severe work poverty (i.e., the share of individuals living in very work-poor households). In some countries, notably Luxembourg, Germany, and the Netherlands, work poverty is higher than what one might expect on the basis of a linear relationship between individual nonemployment rates and work poverty. The prevalence of part-time work may be an explanatory factor in those countries. However, as visual scrutiny of Figure 1.7 reveals, the percentage deviation between the actual share of individuals in work-poor households and what one "might expect" given the individual nonemployment rates in those countries is not so substantial. The correlation between individual nonemployment rates and severe work poverty is less. Figure 1.7 shows that Ireland, Belgium, Germany, the United Kingdom, and Denmark have a higher degree of severe work-poverty than one "might expect" on the basis of a linear relationship with individual nonemployment rates. Hence, with regard to very work-poor households, more countries "deviate" from a simple linear relationship with individual employment rates. Moreover, the percentage deviation between the actual share of individuals in very work-poor households and what

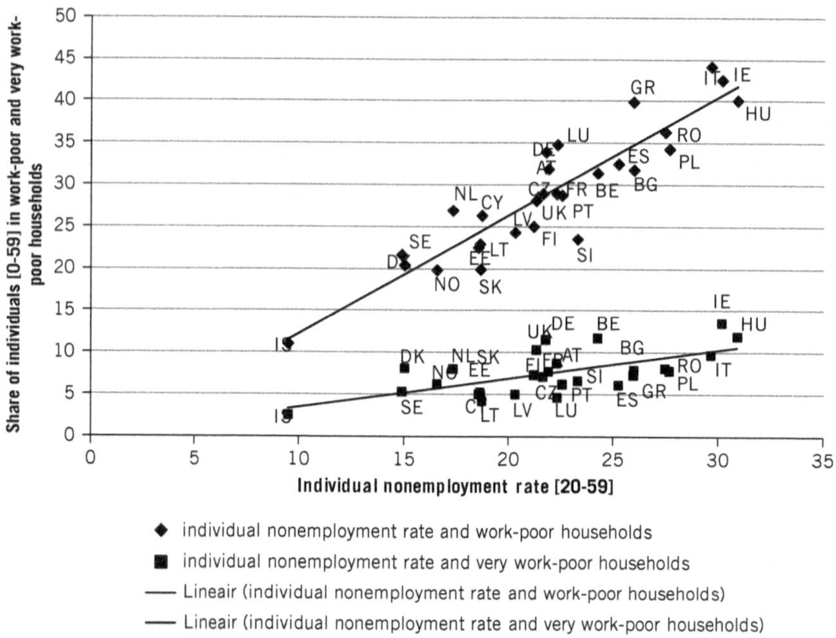

Figure 1.7. Individual nonemployment rates (population, [0–59]) and the share of individuals in (very) work-poor households (population [20–59]). *Source*: EU-SILC 2008.

one "might expect" given the individual nonemployment rates in those countries is important. Chapter 3 explains that household employment rates "one might expect" are not really what one should expect on the basis of individual employment rates. Chapter 3 further examines these deviations, which may be explained by the size structure of households or by the sociological phenomenon of "polarization" in the distribution of jobs over households (in order to decompose polarization, Chapter 3 will focus on jobless households rather than on very work-poor households as defined here).

Table 1.2 introduces a subsequent step in the analysis. It displays the best results of a pooled time-series cross section analysis of national at-risk-of-poverty rates with spending on working-age cash benefits and individual and household employment indicators as independent variables. The analysis covers 29 European welfare states and uses the SILC surveys from SILC 2005 to SILC 2011.[7] All models in Table 1.2 use a logarithmic transformation of spending as a percentage of GDP, because that yields a better fit: This specification implies that the marginal impact of additional spending on poverty diminishes when the level of spending increases. We focus on the two indicators of the "household employment" record of welfare states, already mentioned: work poverty and severe work poverty. The *individual* nonemployment rate is based on the EU Labour Force Survey (LFS) and the so-called ILO (International Labour Organization) concept of employment often used in the context of the LFS: an individual is considered to be "not employed" if he or she was not employed for at least one hour in the week before the survey.

This analysis does not pretend to "explain" poverty rates, but should contribute to a better understanding of the structure of the data reported in SILC. The first set of regressions has as dependent variable the at-risk-of-poverty rate of the whole (non-elderly) population. The second set of regressions focuses on the work-poor segment of the population, with the at-risk-of-poverty rate for individuals in work-poor households as a dependent variable. The third set of regressions uses the at-risk-of-poverty rate of the work-rich population as dependent variable. All models include time dummies, and for each model we present results with "country fixed effects" and without "country fixed effects," that is, with country dummies or without country dummies. The choice between these alternative specifications ("country fixed effects," or not) is not straightforward. An approach without country fixed effects has the drawback that countries that spend more also tend to have a better "underlying fabric of society" and/or a better architecture of spending, which is relevant for the poverty outcomes. Such country-level characteristics will be picked up by the coefficient on spending, leading to an overestimation of the impact of the level of working-age cash benefits on at-risk-of-poverty rates. So conceived, an analysis without country fixed effects provides a clear upper bound on the estimated impact of spending. Including country fixed effects implies that the analysis predominantly reflects the impact of changes of spending levels, rather than cross-country differences. This has the advantage that it focuses on what really is at stake (changes in levels of spending per se, rather than differences in the architecture of spending or the related social fabric). However, for the period under consideration, the coefficient for spending can, for example, be underestimated when social expenditures automatically increase as a response to increased poverty levels in the time of economic crisis. For several reasons, we prefer the model with country fixed effects (see Vandenbroucke et al., 2013). Simultaneously, however, the difficulty of the specification choices implies that one should not infer from such quantitative analysis simple and straightforward conclusions with regard to the impact of social spending and labor market conditions on poverty.

Model 1.1 in Table 1.2 shows that the spending coefficient is insignificant, when we simply regress poverty on spending with country fixed effects. This is explained by the fact that the years under consideration encompass years of boom and crisis. Structural differences in spending are reflected in the country fixed effects. Changes in spending levels partially compensate for changes in the economic situation and dampen the impact of the business cycle on poverty, but are unrelated to the observed poverty rates. *Without* country fixed effects the spending coefficient is important and significant. However, in the model with country fixed effects the spending coefficient becomes significant when we add measures for individual and household employment, because they (partially) pick up the economic situation. Models 1.2 and 1.3 show that there is a sizable

Table 1.2. Effect of spending and work intensity on at-risk-of-poverty rates (AROP)

	COUNTRY FIXED EFFECTS				NO COUNTRY FIXED EFFECTS			
	WACB (logs)	Individual employment rates	Work poverty	Relative severity of work poverty	WACB (logs)	Individual employment rates	Work poverty	Relative severity of work poverty
AROP								
1.1	−0.053				−6.61***			
	(0.505)				(0.308)			
1.2	−1.94***	−1.60***			−4.82***	−1.61***		
	(0.612)	(0.316)			(0.299)	(0.088)		
1.3	−1.70***		0.684***	0.909***	−5.95***		1.46***	0.705
	(0.609)		(0.230)	(0.162)	(0.319)		(0.080)	(0.099)
AROP work-poor households								
2.1	−9.16***				−11.19***			
	(1.22)				(0.598)			
2.2	−8.14***	−0.859			−9.25***	−1.04***		
	(1.49)	(0.778)			(0.865)	(0.299)		
2.3	−8.19***		−2.03***	2.62***	−15.30***		−0.338	2.66***
	(1.40)		(0.533)	(0.409)	(0.801)		(0.252)	(0.214)

AROP work-rich households								
3.1	−0.393				−2.68***			
	(0.408)				(0.259)			
3.2	0.172	0.580**			−2.79***	0.135		
	(0.506)	(0.282)			(0.277)	(0.089)		
3.3	1.23***		−1.08***	−0.074	−2.46***		−0.431***	−0.360***
	(0.464)		(0.160)	(0.116)	(0.285)		(0.068)	(0.096)

Source: EU-SILC.

Note: WACB= Working-Age Cash Benefits.

Note: table shows the effect of spending in working-age cash benefits (WACB) on post-transfer poverty rates (AROP) in the non-elderly population [0–59], for both a model with and without country fixed effects. Both models are GLS estimations with heteroskedastic error structure and include time dummies. Controls are added for either individual employment rates or work poverty (the share of individuals living in work-poor households; i.e., with work intensity 0–55) and the "relative severity of work poverty" (i.e., share of individuals living in very work-poor households within the subgroup of work-poor households; very work-poor households have work intensity of 0–20). Dependent variables are the poverty rate (AROP), the poverty rate for individuals in work-poor households for individuals in work-rich households. Individual employment is based on LFS, and refers to the age bracket [15–64]. Spending data is retrieved from the European system of integrated social protection statistics (ESSPROS), comprising the period 2004–2010. All other data are based on SILC. For SILC 2004–2010, measures of poverty and work intensity are re-estimated by Tim Goedemé on the basis of the SILC User Database. SILC 2011 data are retrieved from the Eurostat-site (1.2.2013). We include 29 European welfare states over these seven time periods. The poverty data from the years 2007 until 2011 are complete for every nation. For 2006, poverty data is missing for Romania. For 2005, both poverty data for Romania and spending data for Bulgaria are missing. This gives a total of 232 observations.

effect of spending on poverty levels, when we control for the level of individual employment or household work-intensity in addition to time and country fixed effects. In other words, time and, especially, structural background features of individual welfare states lead to an initial overestimation of the effect of spending on poverty, but the relation still remains strongly significant when this is controlled for by including country fixed effects in the model, provided we also control for some measure of employment.

When we add individual employment to the analysis (Model 1.2), the coefficient for the log of spending on working-age cash benefits is −1.94, which means the model suggests that, at the mean, a 10% increase in spending reduces the poverty rate by 0.194 (defined from 0 to 100). Individual employment is standardized with a mean of 0 and a standard deviation of 1. Hence, the coefficient shows the effect on poverty of increasing individual employment by one standard deviation. This would reduce the poverty rate by −1.60 in this case. If we would convert employment back to percentage points, it appears that a 10% increase in spending has a similar impact as an increase in the individual employment rate by 1 percentage point. Alternatively, in Model 1.3 we use measures of household work-intensity as regressors. In order to make these different measures comparable, we also standardize them to all have a mean of 0 and a standard deviation of 1. In order to explain at-risk-of-poverty rates, we employ two indicators of household work-intensity: work-poverty (the share of individuals living in work-poor households), and the share of individuals in very work-poor households *within* the subgroup of individuals in work-poor households; we will call this indicator "the relative severity of work poverty." In general, using measures of household work-intensity rather than individual employment levels does not change the model with fixed country effects much. The model that provides the best fit is Model 1.3, which includes *both* the share of the work-poor and the share of the very work-poor in the work-poor. The latter result is particularly interesting: It suggests that one should really study the country-specific distribution of household work-intensity over the population, and that the concentration of individuals in very work-poor households does play an independent role.[8] This finding obviously matches the observation that the poverty rate for people in very work-poor households is typically higher than the corresponding poverty rate in households that are work-poor but not very work-poor. This regression result supports the attention paid in this book to both the share of individuals in work-poor households and the share of individuals in very work-poor or jobless households, and also to the concept of polarization, discussed in Chapter 3. There is a strong correlation between the "relative severity of work poverty," as we define it here, and the absolute polarization index introduced in Chapter 3.

Models 2.1, 2.2, and 2.3 focus on poverty in the work-poor subgroup, that is, individuals living in households with low work-intensity (0–55). The impact of spending on poverty for this group is much larger; in the specification with country fixed effects, it is already strong and significant without controls for employment or work-intensity. This is not surprising, because this is naturally a group that is more vulnerable and more dependent on benefits. Although restricting ourselves to this subgroup already partially controls for differences in work-intensity and changes in the business cycle, adding work poverty and the "relative severity of work poverty" leads to significant coefficients on these indicators. Poverty in the work-poor segment is strongly driven by the "relative severity of work poverty." On the other hand, the extent of work poverty (i.e., the share of individuals in work-poor households) has a negative impact on poverty rates within that group. This result may reflect the fact that the average person in a work-poor household is in a relatively better position when there are many work-poor households. Formulating it slightly bluntly, if work poverty is high, the average "work-poor" is not at the very bottom of the distribution, because the composition of the group changes.

In contrast, the effect of working-age cash benefits on poverty levels in the work-rich segment is insignificant, and even positive in some specifications, as shown in Models 3.1, 3.2, and 3.3. In other words, whereas the level of spending and the pattern of participation in the labor market are clearly important factors in accounting for poverty in the work-poor segment of the population, differences in poverty within the work-rich segment are not readily explained. The analysis in Chapter 3 does indicate that evolutions in poverty in the work-rich segment did play a significant role in the overall evolution in poverty in some European welfare states during the good economic years; explaining these evolutions in the work-rich segment, however, would appear to require explanations that go beyond basic parameters such as welfare state spending or crude employment patterns.

These observations justify the specific focus in the subsequent analysis in this book on levels of spending and work-intensity of households. Simultaneously, they indicate that one should dig deeper into the underlying fabric of welfare states and that a purely quantitative analysis will not suffice. Moreover, neither a correlation nor a decomposition provides an explanation, let alone a causal one, but they do at least apply structure to our understanding of the data.

1.4 THE "EFFICIENCY" OF SOCIAL SPENDING

Some welfare states display poverty outcomes that seem rather feeble given their level of social spending and their employment record. Other welfare states obtain poverty results that are better than one would expect on the basis of their social spending level and employment record. Figure 1.8 illustrates this observation on the basis of some of the regression models listed in Table 1.2.

For each country, Figure 1.8 shows:

- The average residuals in Model 1.1 without country fixed effects (indicator A). Positive values indicate that the observed levels of poverty

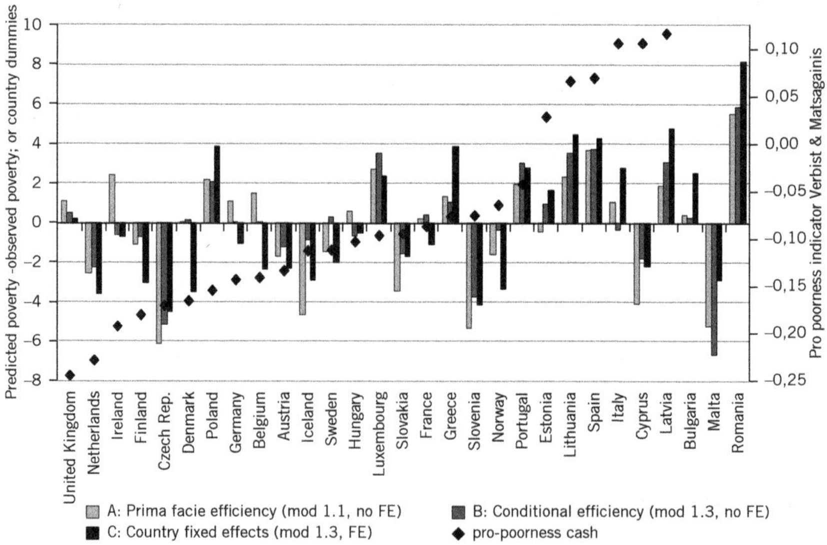

Figure 1.8. Indicators of comparative (in)efficiency of welfare states. *Source:* Results of regression analyses on SILC in Eurostat spending data. Pro-poorness (concentration coefficients) calculated by Gerlinde Verbist on the basis of SILC 2007. *Note 1:* Positive indicators measured on left axis signal comparative (conditional) inefficiency. Pro-poorness indicators below the horizontal axis signal a higher degree of pro-poorness than the average. *Note 2:* No pro-poorness indicator was available for Bulgaria, Malta, and Romania on the basis of SILC 2007.

are higher than what one would predict when using Model 1.1 without country fixed effects, that is, when only controlling for the level of spending on working-age cash benefits;

- the average residuals in Model 1.3 without country fixed effects (indicator B). Positive values indicate that the observed levels of poverty are higher than what one would predict on the basis of levels of spending, work poverty, and the relative severity of work poverty;
- the value of the country dummies in Model 1.3 with country fixed effects (indicator C).

It is tempting to interpret the residuals in Figure 1.8 as alternative indications of the comparative "efficiency" of different welfare regimes. The indicator A might be seen as a prima facie measure of the comparative efficiency of spending on working-age cash benefits: Countries such as the Netherlands, the Czech Republic, Slovenia, Slovakia, Cyprus, Ireland, and Malta perform better than one would expect solely on the basis of their level of social spending; in contrast, countries such as Ireland, Belgium,[9] Poland, Luxembourg, Portugal, and Spain perform less well than one might expect. Next, the indicator B might be seen as an expression of "conditional efficiency," that is, the efficiency of spending, given the employment record of the country. So conceived, it appears that the prima facie efficiency of the Netherlands or the Czech Republic does not diminish when we control for employment: It must be explained by other factors. In the same vein, it appears that the prima facie inefficiency of Poland, Portugal, Spain, and other comparatively inefficient countries is not reduced when we control for their employment record. In contrast, the prima facie inefficiency of Ireland and Belgium is explained by their employment record.

The indicator C (the value of the country dummies) captures fixed institutional and sociological features of countries in a model that explicitly allows for that and thus yields a much lower coefficient for spending. Because the level of spending has a lower impact on predicted poverty in this model, welfare states that are comparatively "big spenders," such as Denmark, Finland, and Belgium, now emerge as having comparatively efficient underlying features (with a view to preventing poverty) when we use indicator C. In general, because the influence of spending is more modest when estimated using country fixed effects, the residuals across nations become wider; high-spending Northern states become more efficient, while low-spending Southern and Eastern states become more inefficient. If we indeed perceive the model including the dummies as a more appropriate one when estimating the true impact of spending, this difference is made up of the fact that the effect of spending when measured across nations picks up on many other relevant country-level characteristics. If these effects are factored out, we would obtain the (in)efficiencies that are truly part of the underlying fabric of the nation (net of the variables included in the model) and (in) efficiencies will become more disperse again.

Both indicators B and C take into account the employment record of welfare states. In that sense, the use of the word "efficiency" might be misleading. A welfare state with a high level of work-poverty and a high level of social spending may appear "efficient" according to indicator B, that is, poverty may be lower than predicted on the basis of that combination of work-poverty and spending. If inadequately organized, however, social protection creates inactivity traps and increases work-poverty. In such a situation this assessment may be misleading: Given its level of social spending, this welfare state may, in fact, be rather inefficient.

It is interesting to combine the results of our regression models (indicators A, B, and C in Figure 1.8) with the indicator of "pro-poorness" of cash benefits developed by Verbist and Matsaganis in Chapter 6. For that reason, in Figure 1.8 we also show a concentration coefficient that is similar to the one on which Verbist and Matsaganis' "pro-poorness" indicator is based. Calculating concentration coefficients indicates how income components are distributed, irrespective of their size. To calculate these concentration coefficients, individuals are ranked according to their income. When the concentration coefficient has a value that is lower than the Gini coefficient of income, lower incomes benefit relatively more: Individuals receive a higher share of the income component than their share of income. Thus, these concentration coefficients provide insight into the pro-poorness of the various income components, irrespective of their size. (Verbist and Matsaganis' indicator is based on an extended income concept and a needs-adjusted equivalence scale. Here we use a concentration coefficient based on cash incomes only and with standard equivalence scales; it is also confined to the distribution of transfers in the non-elderly population. See Vandenbroucke et al. [2013], for the calculation of age-specific concentration coefficients.) There is a positive correlation between the average value of this "pro-poorness" indicator in SILC 2005–2010 and the indicator C. These observations justify not only the focus on "pro-poorness" in Chapter 6, but also the examination of the distribution of benefits over subgroups of the population, defined on the basis of work-intensity, in Chapter 5. However, one must not conclude from this positive correlation that the degree of pro-poorness of working-age cash benefits has *as such* a significant *direct* impact on poverty rates. A more finely grained analysis shows that the unexplained disparity in the residual C reflects differences in the underlying societal fabric of welfare states, which correlate with differences in the level and architecture of social spending, GDP per capita, and past investment in education, training, child care, and active labor market policies. These differences in the underlying societal fabric are not readily explained, however, by any of these factors separately, because they correlate strongly with each other, and possibly with relevant unobserved factors as well. (Vandenbroucke et al. [2013] show this for the analysis of child poverty, but this conclusion also holds for non-elderly poverty.)

To conclude, there are several factors that shed some light on the poverty performance of European welfare states. Spending is a big factor explaining the dispersion of poverty rates, but its exact impact differs strongly across methods and samples. Work-intensity further equalizes the field, but the poor performance of those with the very highest poverty rates remains largely unexplained. Additional indicators that we believe are closely related to the "underlying fabric of the nation" can provide additional insights. Past investments in education and the labor market might help explain why Scandinavian welfare states have such good employment records, and, linked to that, good poverty records. The degree of pro-poorness of benefits may help explain why the Netherlands is a strong performer, and why Spain is a weak one. But also on the side of the winners, there is a big puzzle in the excellent performance of especially the Czech Republic and Slovenia that is left unsolved. Many weak performers have low spending levels, which can also call into question the right fit of the relation between spending and poverty. This can be much steeper for lower levels of spending. However, the success of the new central-European welfare states partly debunks this argument, because they achieve their low poverty levels with very modest levels of spending. In short, there is still an important research agenda with regard to these issues.

Despite these cautionary notes, the issue of "efficiency" is important. Efficiency is not the *prime virtue* of welfare states: We may prefer a welfare state that spends a lot with average efficiency to a welfare state that spends very little with a high degree of efficiency. However, during our inquiry we were struck by the persistence of vast disparities in efficiency, so conceived, of cash benefits for working-age households across the EU. Given that this indicates room for improvement, it should be high on the EU agenda (Vandenbroucke, 2012; Vandenbroucke et al., 2013). However, in addition to some of the cautionary notes already indicated, a number of basic caveats apply with regard to this conceptualization of "efficiency."

First, "efficiency" must be defined in relation to an objective. In our analysis, the efficiency of spending refers to the objective of reducing poverty, not to any other, possibly equally legitimate, objective (e.g., reducing income insecurity, or specific family policy objectives, and/or promoting gender equality). More specifically, efficiency of spending is assessed here in terms of a poverty headcount, using 60% of median income as the poverty threshold. Obviously, the choice of threshold matters. Theoretically, policy changes may reduce the efficiency of spending measured by the 60% threshold and yet enhance efficiency measured by a threshold of 40% of median income; increased targeting of the very poor might yield such an outcome. In such an event, efficiency decreases with regard to the poor but increases with regard to the very poor. For this reason, the efficiency analyses proposed here and elsewhere in this book ideally ought to be repeated with different poverty thresholds (or with the FGT1 and FGT2 indicators, introduced in Chapter 2).

A second caveat concerns the fact that we measure efficiency only in a comparative sense: We construct a benchmark on the basis of the average performance of EU welfare states (i.e., what the regression does). This presupposes that it makes sense to benchmark welfare states vis-à-vis a hypothetical, uniform "European welfare state technology," encompassing welfare states with very different histories and dimensions. The benchmark may, however, be quite sensitive to the inclusion or exclusion of outliers. This approach moreover raises a host of statistical problems: Because this virtual EU average is calculated on the basis of point estimates with wide confidence intervals, we should be extremely cautious when drawing conclusions. Furthermore, Eurostat spending data, which are collected on an administrative basis, and the data on social transfers actually registered in the SILC surveys, may be quite different.

The third caveat relates to the fact that all our measurements neglect the longer-term societal and individual return of welfare programs. As Hemerijck explains in Chapter 8, the core argument advanced by proponents of the social investment turn is that spending on social investment programs creates a return. The assertion that social spending may serve a productive purpose may be extended to some "traditional" social programs, as De Deken argues in Chapter 9. The indicators with regard to welfare state efforts presented in this book measure only the cost of programs, not their return. In the case of education, for example, they measure how much it would cost for a household to provide education for its children without public subsidy, not the longer-term impact on individuals and society of providing education, neither in terms of macroeconomic consequences nor in terms of income distribution. Likewise, they do not measure the impact of childcare on female participation rates and labor market earnings associated with participation. Hence, what we provide here are static indicators of the short-term distributive impact (or rather merely the immediate impact) on household budgets of transferring cash benefits or subsidizing consumption of education, care, etc. We display no dynamic indicators of efficiency in this exercise, so that it does not settle disputes on the strengths and weaknesses of the social investment turn, so conceived.

The final caveat is that the efficiency notion examined here is static in yet another sense: It may be the case that a program that is less efficient than the academic observer may wish nonetheless enjoys broad popular support because of the benefits it creates for middle-class households. The well-known argument by Goodin and Le Grand (1987) that universal programs may be more politically robust, and hence more beneficial to the poor in the longer term, refers to a dynamic notion of efficiency that is not captured by our figures either. Cantillon et al. examine the viewpoint of Goodin and Le Grand in Chapter 5. The same observation might be made in relation to the development of social services when considering the findings of Verbist and Matsaganis in Chapter 6.

1.5 POVERTY REDUCTION BY TRANSFERS AND THE "POVERTY STABILIZING" ROLE OF WELFARE STATES

In order to better contextualize the poverty records of welfare states, we use two additional notions of a counterfactual nature: the at-risk-of-poverty rate "before social transfers" and "poverty reduction by transfers." Pensions are not included in transfers. In the remainder of this chapter, we will use "pre-transfer poverty" and "poverty reduction" as shortcuts. Both counterfactuals should be interpreted with circumspection. Poverty reduction is defined as the difference between post-transfer poverty (i.e., the poverty rates actually observed) and pre-transfer poverty. Following the Eurostat methodology, we exclude social transfers except pensions transfers—but not taxes—from household incomes in the SILC survey results and then calculate "pre-transfer poverty rates" using the same poverty thresholds as in the "post-transfer" calculation. "Poverty reduction by transfers" should not be read as "the level of poverty that would be obtained in the absence of social transfers," for a combination of reasons. First, the poverty threshold is not adapted to what it would be without transfers. Second, the taxes funding social transfers are not added to incomes in the counterfactual. And third, this manipulation of the data does not take into account possible behavioral changes induced by the abandoning of transfer policies and concomitant reductions in taxation. Figures on "poverty reduction by transfers" instead indicate the quantitative significance of social transfers in terms of a counterfactual poverty rate, in a particular equilibrium that is created by, among other factors, those same transfers and the taxes financing them, and with reference to the median income shaped by transfer and tax policies.

Table 1.3 presents the results of regression models, using pre-transfer poverty and poverty reduction as dependent variables and spending and household employment indicators as independent variables, and time dummies; results are presented with and without country fixed effects. The analysis covers SILC 2005 to SILC 2011.

There is a significantly positive relationship between pre-transfer poverty rates and levels of spending. Estimates without fixed effects yield weaker coefficients on spending; this presumably occurs through the fact that high spending is more prominent in egalitarian societies (such as in Scandinavia), which imposes a negative bias. The result either suggests that high spending is a reaction to high pre-transfer poverty or that cash benefits provide strong disincentives to work and stay out of (pre-transfer) poverty, which is not fully picked up by our controls for work poverty. The coefficients on the measures of work-intensity are significant and have the expected positive sign.

The second model in Table 1.3 shows that the relationship between spending and poverty reduction is highly significant. Again, differences in poverty reduction are driven by work poverty and the relative severity of work poverty.

It is worth emphasizing that, in virtually all specifications of this kind, the relative severity of work poverty explains a substantial part of the variation in poverty rates, even when we control for country and time fixed effects, and

Table 1.3. Effect of spending and work intensity on pre-transfer poverty and poverty reduction

	COUNTRY FIXED EFFECTS			NO COUNTRY FIXED EFFECTS		
Outcome	**Spending**	**Work poverty**	**Relative severity of work poverty**	**Spending**	**Work poverty**	**Relative severity of work poverty**
Pre-transfer poverty	7.17***	1.30***	1.67***	2.36***	1.88***	2.04***
	(0.746)	(0.287)	(0.224)	(0.464)	(0.142)	(0.160)
Poverty reduction	7.96***	0.746***	0.449**	7.87***	0.123	1.32***
	(0.508)	(0.265)	(0.177)	(0.411)	(0.119)	(0.148)

Source: Analysis on the basis of EU-SILC and Eurostat spending data.
Note: table shows the effect of spending in working-age cash benefits (WACB) on pre-transfer poverty rates and poverty reduction through transfers, for both a model with and without country fixed effects. Both models are GLS estimations with heteroskedastic error structure and include time dummies. Controls are added for either individual employment rates or work poverty and the "relative severity of work poverty." Dependent variables are the overall pre-transfer poverty rate and poverty reduction.

even when we already include a measure of the share of the work-poor in the model. Hence, this specific measure of the distribution of work-intensity at the very bottom is highly relevant. That observation again supports the focus on jobless households and very work-poor households as a recurring theme in this book.

A high degree of poverty reduction is not necessarily a measure of quality of performance of a welfare state. In the same vein, one should not interpret the relationship between poverty reduction and the level of spending as an indicator of the efficiency of welfare states. It may appear that a welfare state performs "efficiently" in terms of the relation between its level of spending and the extent of "poverty reduction" attained, if the ratio "poverty reduction/spending" is relatively high, compared with other welfare states. But if social benefits create inactivity traps to the effect that pre-transfer poverty is very high in that particular welfare state, describing this as comparative "efficiency" may be misleading. This particular welfare state may merely be "efficient" in remedying a problem of inactivity traps it has actually created itself.

In the next section, we proceed with the analysis of *changes* in the poverty record of individual welfare states on the basis of decomposition techniques. Decomposition analysis does not reveal causality: it is basically an accounting device. However, it yields interesting descriptions of country-specific trajectories of welfare state change. Obviously, in order to be relevant in a comparative perspective, the factors on which these decompositions focus—notably the work-intensity of households—must also have some general explanatory power in a cross-country analysis. As already indicated, the regression results reported in this chapter do support that. Space forbids us to elaborate here upon regression analyses on *changes* in poverty rates, but the results can be summarized as follows. There is an obvious and relatively strong positive correlation between changes in spending and changes in poverty reduction, which can be revealed by applying first difference regression models to the data we explored in the previous section, covered by SILC 2005-2011. This correlation is obvious for the reason that if poverty reduction by transfers increases, one may assume (absent important structural changes in the transfer system) spending on transfers also to increase. In a well-organized welfare state, one may also expect a correlation between changes in household employment and poverty reduction: Increasing employment reduces the need for poverty reduction by transfers, while decreasing employment fuels the need for poverty reduction. Yet, this relationship is less mechanistic, and may depend on the architecture of welfare states and, possibly, on the impact of ongoing policy changes. However, the positive relationship between changes in poverty reduction and changes in the share of individuals living in work-poor households also emerges in first difference regression models.

Welfare states absorb social risks, at the level of both the individual and society in general. Poverty "before transfers" is linked to social risks that are, in part, of a cyclical nature or that may be the result of economic shocks, such as the risk of unemployment. When pre-transfer poverty increases, as in periods of rising unemployment, we expect increasing poverty reduction, as an endogenous mechanism. Welfare states function, to some extent, as automatic "poverty stabilizers," just as, from a macroeconomic point of view welfare states act as Keynesian "automatic stabilizers."[10] Hence, one should distinguish between a welfare state's *structural capacity* to reduce poverty through transfers, as a potential shock absorber, and the *actual* reduction of poverty by transfers at any one point in time, given a specific pre-transfer poverty rate and unemployment situation at that particular juncture. A precise assessment of a welfare state's capacity to reduce poverty requires an examination of the actual poverty reduction at different points in time. If institutions change over time, a counterfactual microsimulation of poverty reduction on the basis of unchanged institutions is required in order to evaluate the impact of those changes on their poverty reduction capacity. Without such an analysis, it may be premature to infer from a decrease in actual poverty reduction in a given welfare state that that welfare state's capacity to reduce poverty through transfers has diminished, or, more generally, that its redistributive capacity has decreased. This being said, the data used in this book, with their focus on household work-intensity, allow some prima facie judgments, as will be illustrated in the next section.

1.6 ANALYZING CHANGES IN POVERTY REDUCTION AND AT-RISK-OF-POVERTY RATES BY MEANS OF DECOMPOSITION

How might we discern *structural changes* in the capacity of individual welfare states to fight poverty? In principle, there are two ways of approaching this challenge, based on prima facie evidence that the structural capacity of a welfare state to fight poverty is declining. Both rely on decomposition of changes.

First, we may look for contradictory changes in pre- and post-transfer poverty that offer such prima facie evidence. If post-transfer poverty increases while pre-transfer poverty decreases, the expectation we hold with regard to the normal functioning of a welfare state on the basis of "unchanged policy" is clearly contradicted. For the years covered by SILC 2005–2008, Finland provides such a clear-cut case, as shown in Figure 1.9a below. Our expectation with regard to the normal functioning of a welfare state with "unchanged policy" is also contradicted when poverty reduction decreases while pre-transfer poverty increases. Germany provides such a case (on the basis of SILC), also shown in Figure 1.9a below.

A *second* approach to looking for such prima facie evidence starts from the notion that, with unchanged policies, poverty reduction will automatically change

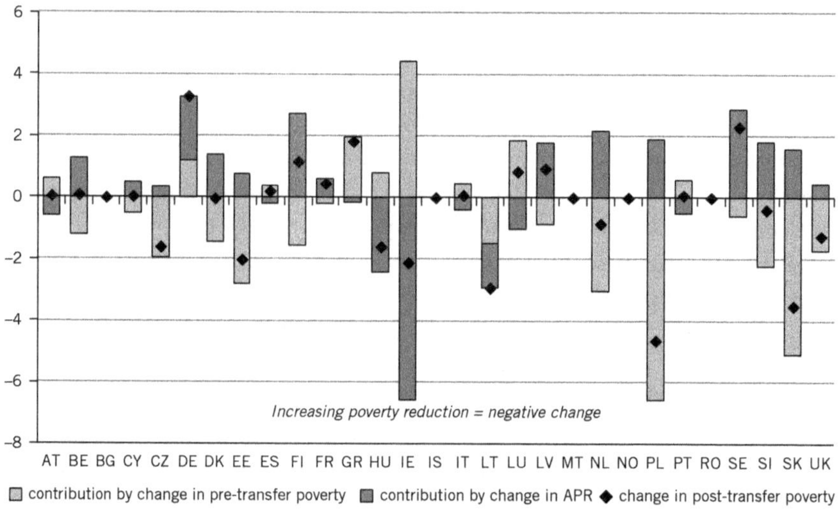

Figure 1.9a. Contribution of changes in pre-transfer poverty and poverty reduction to changes in post-transfer poverty (SILC 2005–2008, AROP , population [20–59]). *Source:* Calculations on data provided by Aaron Van den Heede, based on EU-SILC User Database. *Note* : APR = Absolute Poverty Reduction.

over the course of the economic cycle because the share of the work-poor will change. Typically poverty reduction by transfers is larger in the work-poor subset of the population than in the work-rich subset; an increasing share of individuals living in work-poor households implies an increasing level of poverty reduction for the total population. In yet other words, this approach sees poverty reduction for the total population as the weighted average of poverty reduction in the work-poor and the work-rich segment. A simple decomposition then allows one to calculate the extent to which changes in poverty reduction for the total population are (i) the result of changes in the share of the work-poor (which is the automatic, endogenous change one would expect); and/or (ii) the result of changes in poverty reduction within the work-poor and/or the work-rich segments. The latter may signal, prima facie, a change in policy, or, more generally, a change in a welfare state's structural capacity to fight poverty. However, we should emphasize "*may* signal," because changes in poverty reduction within the work-poor and/or the work-rich segments can also be the result of changes in the work-intensity of households within these subgroups; that is, they can also reflect endogenous countercyclical impacts within these subgroups. However, notwithstanding this caveat, such a mechanical composition yields interesting insights.

Figures 1.9a–b and 1.10a–b illustrate these approaches (here we focus on the population in the age bracket [20–59], as in Chapter 5, which further explores some of these issues). Figure 1.9a represents the changes in pre-transfer poverty, poverty reduction, and post-transfer poverty between SILC 2005 and SILC 2008; the contradictory changes in Finland and Germany are easily recognized.

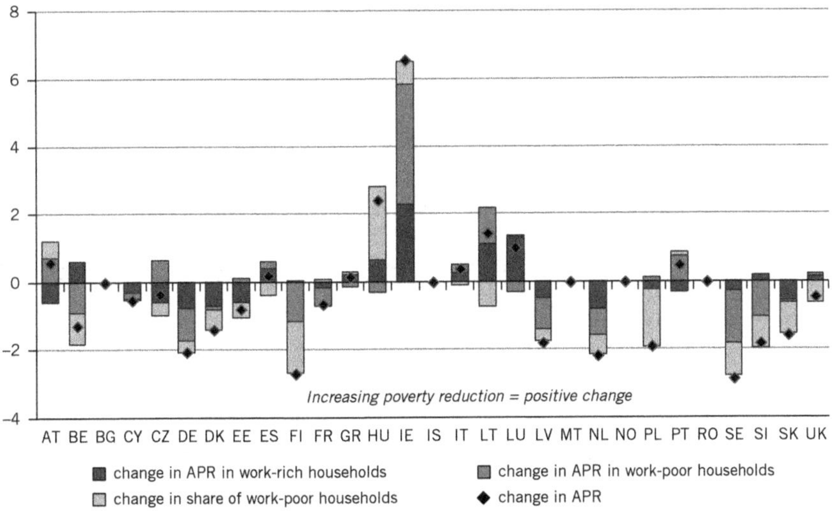

Figure 1.9b. Decomposition of changes in poverty reduction, AROP, population [20–59], SILC 2005–2008. *Source*: Calculations on data provided by Aaron Van den Heede, based on EU-SILC User Database. *Note:* APR = Absolute Poverty Reduction.

Figure 1.9a thus illustrates the first prima facie approach. Figure 1.9b adds to this the decomposition of the changes in poverty reduction. It illustrates the second prima facie approach.

Figure 1.9b shows that poverty reduction by transfers diminished by 2 ppt in Germany and Poland between SILC 2005 and SILC 2008. In Poland this is entirely accounted for by the decreasing proportion of individuals in work-poor households (i.e., the endogenous mechanism prevails); in Germany the decrease in poverty reduction is the result of the decreasing poverty reduction *within* both the work-poor and the work-rich segments, which suggests policy change. In Finland poverty reduction decreased both because of the decreasing proportion of work-poor households (the endogenous mechanism) and the decreasing degree of poverty reduction in the work-poor segment of the population. In Sweden the balance in our account of decreasing poverty reduction tilts even further toward the side of "policy change": The decrease in poverty reduction within both the work-poor and the work-rich segments of the population overshadowed the endogenous impact of improving household employment. Ireland displays exactly the opposite scenario to that observed in Germany: Poverty reduction increased in Ireland because it increased within both the work-poor and the work-rich segments and because the share of the work-poor segment grew during those years (despite rising individual employment rates, according to LFS; see Figure 1.4).

Figures 1.10a–b repeat the same exercise for changes between SILC 2008 and SILC 2010.

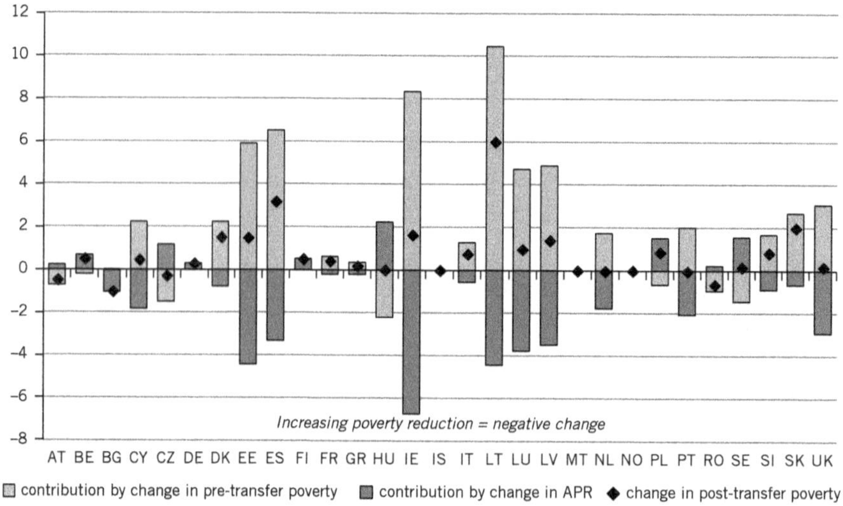

Figure 1.10a. Contribution of changes in pre-transfer poverty and poverty reduction to changes in post-transfer poverty (SILC 2008–2010, AROP, population [20–59]). *Source:* Calculations on data provided by Aaron Van den Heede, based on EU-SILC User Database.

Figure 1.10a clearly reveals the impact of the economic crisis: pre-transfer poverty increases in many welfare states, but this increase is partially offset by increasing poverty reduction. Figure 1.10b shows that increasing poverty reduction is partly attributable to the rising share of work-poor households, which

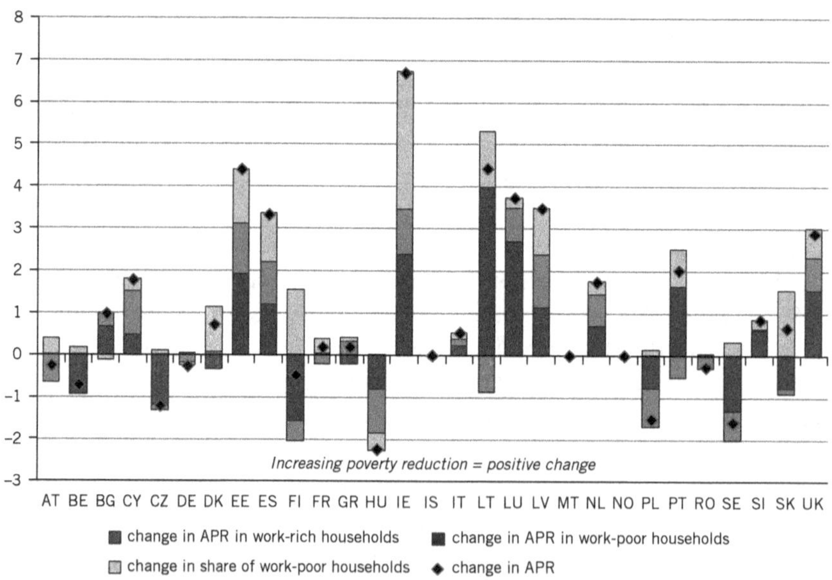

Figure 1.10b. Decomposition of changes in poverty reduction, AROP [20–59], SILC 2008–2010. *Source*: Calculations on data provided by Aaron Van den Heede, based on EU-SILC User Database. *Note*: APR = Absolute Poverty Reduction.

illustrates what we called the "endogenous" mechanism. But in many welfare states poverty reduction also increased within the subgroups of the work-rich and the work-poor. This corroborates our earlier caveat that an endogenous countercyclical mechanism may also be at play *within* the work-intensity subgroups we distinguish here. Because SILC 2010 refers to incomes in 2009, our analysis only covers incomes in the first "full crisis" year, that is, in 2009. Analysis of SILC 2011 suggests that the cushioning effect of increasing poverty reduction by transfers weakened in 2010. Budgetary constraints and austerity measures probably explain the weaker impact of poverty reduction after 2009.

Although they cannot be conclusive, these decomposition analyses show that the countercyclical "poverty stabilizing" character of welfare states in general still prevails, but simultaneously suggest that in some European welfare states the structural capacity to reduce poverty declined in the second half of the 2000s. There is yet another way to approach this question on the basis of decomposition, which is presented in Figures 1.11 and 1.12. Here, our attention returns to changes in post-transfer poverty rates.

Figures 1.11 and 1.12 show the result of a decomposition of changes in at-risk-of-poverty rates, on the basis of five work-intensity subgroups, using the following work-intensity cut-offs: 20%, 45%, 55%,and 85%. The population segment we label "work-poor" encompasses the first three subgroups; the two other subgroups together constitute the "work-rich." Changes in poverty are decomposed in "changes within" and "changes between" the five subgroups. "Changes within" are attributable to changes in the at-risk-of-poverty rates within each

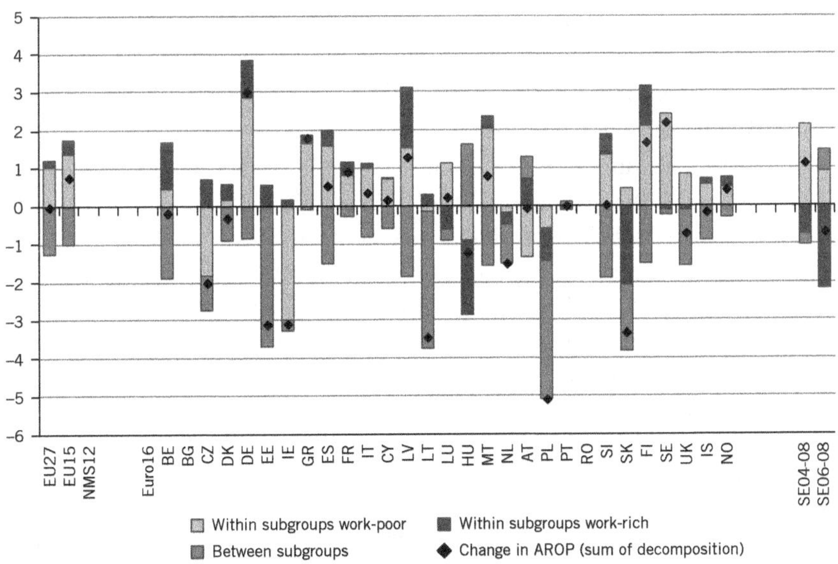

Figure 1.11. Decomposition of change in AROP [0–59], SILC 2005–2008. *Source*: EU-SILC; data retrieved from Eurostat-site.

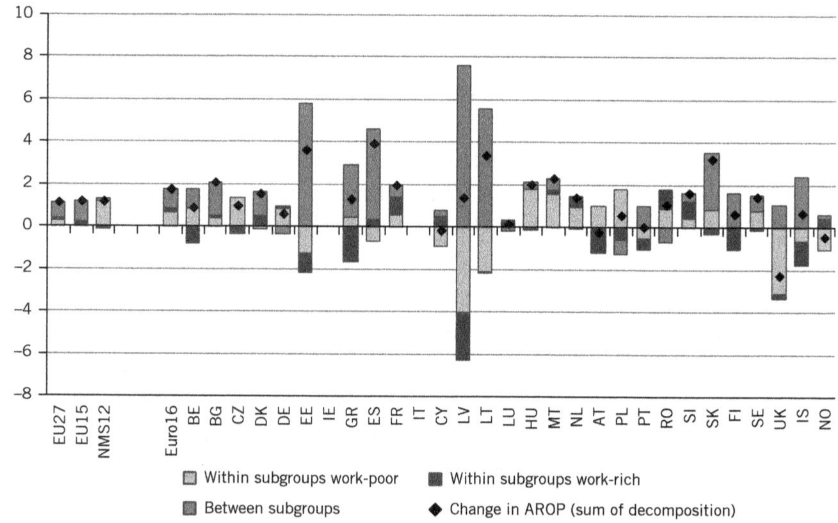

Figure 1.12. Decomposition of change in AROP [0–59], SILC 2008–2011. *Source*: EU-SILC; data retrieved from Eurostat-site.

of the subgroups (keeping their shares constant). "Changes between" are attributable to changes in the relative shares of each of the subgroups (keeping the at-risk-of-poverty rates in each of the subgroups constant). To simplify the visual representation, "changes within" are subdivided into "changes within" in the segment of the "work-poor" and "changes within" in the segment of the work-rich. Thus, Figures 1.11 and 1.12 visualize three factors contributing to changing at-risk-of-poverty rates: (i) changing poverty risks within each of the subgroups constituting the "work-poor" segment; (ii) changing poverty risks within each of the subgroups constituting the "work-rich" segment; (iii) changing shares of the five work-intensity subgroups.

Figure 1.11 includes overall estimates for the EU27 and the EU15, based on Eurostat data. At the level of the EU27, the overall "gain" in poverty rates due to improving household work-intensities between SILC 2005 and SILC 2008 was neutralized by the increase of poverty risks within the subgroups of the work-poor. For the EU15, the increase in poverty risks within the work-poor subgroups was more important than the positive contribution to poverty rates attributable to improving work-intensities.[11] Between SILC 2008 and SILC 2011 the dynamics change, as shown in Figure 1.12. Poverty rates increased in the EU27 and the EU15, and in many individual countries, mainly as a consequence of "changes between," that is, deteriorating household work-intensities. Figures 1.11 and 1.12 together illustrate that the overall increase in poverty rates by the end of the decade can be seen as the combined result of a boom without declining poverty in many Member States—as the gain in household employment was offset in many countries by increasing poverty risks within vulnerable subgroups of the population—followed by a crisis with increasing poverty in many Member States.

1.7 MAPPING CHANGES IN AT-RISK-OF-POVERTY RATES: EIGHT TRAJECTORIES

In this section we provide a "preview" on individual trajectories of European welfare states during those years of boom and bust, which further illuminates the rationale of the inquiry presented in this book. This preview is based on a selection of eight welfare states. Two of those countries, Poland and Ireland, belong to the group of welfare states where poverty decreased between SILC 2005 and SILC 2008. Four welfare states, Spain, Norway, Belgium, and the UK, belong to the group presenting a standstill in poverty between SILC 2005 and SILC 2008. Sweden and Germany belong to the third group, marked by increasing poverty (according to SILC) during the boom years. We will, however, analyze Germany on the basis of the German SOEP data. We have selected these eight welfare states not only because they illustrate divergent trajectories during the Lisbon era, but also because the observed relationships between poverty, poverty reduction by transfers, and social spending are quite different. Figure 1.13 displays the profile of the welfare states under review (excluding Germany), at the end of the boom period, on the basis of SILC 2008. We show levels of poverty, before transfers and after transfers (excluding pensions); levels of spending on cash benefits (excluding old-age and survivors programs) as a percentage of GDP;

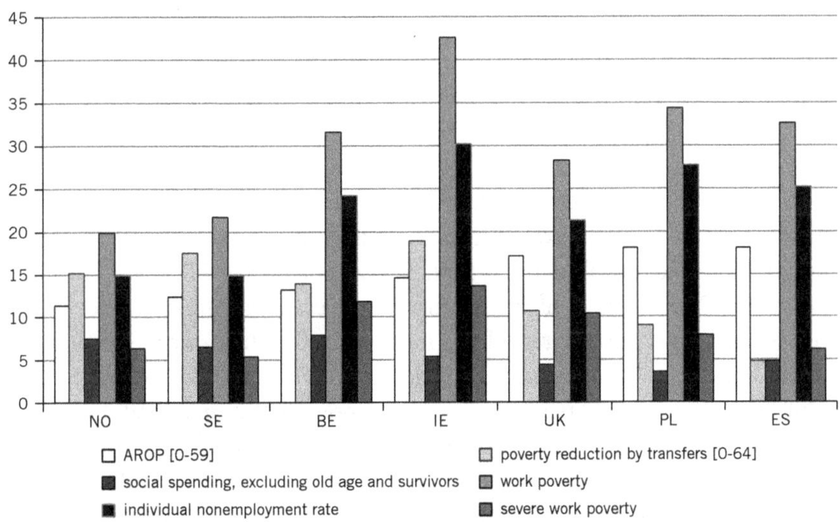

Figure 1.13. Profile of seven selected welfare states. *Source:* EU-SILC 2008 & Eurostat for spending data; spending refers to 2007.

the proportion of individuals living in work-poor households ("work poverty") and in very work-poor households ("severe work poverty"); and individual nonemployment rates.

Figure 1.13 corroborates earlier observations about the "map" of poverty, spending, and employment in Europe. The negative correlation between levels of spending and post-transfer poverty appears to be very strong, given that we gather countries with quite extreme scores on both counts. We also note a strong positive correlation between the proportion of individuals in work-poor households and individual nonemployment rates, and the weaker correlation between the proportion of individuals in very work-poor households and individual nonemployment rates (Belgium and the UK have a high proportion of individuals in very work-poor households, given their individual nonemployment rates; this is illustrative of this weaker correlation). We also see a moderately positive correlation between the proportion of individuals in work-poor households and the level of poverty. Inspection of Figure 1.13, finally, reveals a positive correlation between social spending and poverty reduction by transfers, although it is less strong in this subset of welfare states than it is for the whole set of European welfare states. We deliberately included countries with very divergent profiles in this respect: poverty reduction by transfers appears to be very limited in Spain, given the country's level of social spending, and, by contrast, it appears to be high in Poland and Ireland, given their level of social spending. In short, our sample includes quite divergent welfare state architectures and labor markets.

This section will illustrate the disparity of changes over time in these welfare states and in Germany. However, before elaborating upon the specific trajectories of these welfare states, we should consider one further caveat, in addition to the caveat with regard to efficiency and "poverty reduction by transfers" mentioned earlier. We refer to the fact that changes in poverty rates conceal the movement of the poverty thresholds on which they are based. Figure 1.14 represents the evolution in the poverty thresholds for the seven welfare states under review. Thresholds are compared in Purchasing Power Parities (i.e., thresholds in Euros are corrected for price differentials between countries).

The figure immediately reveals the huge differences in material prosperity across the EU27, but also a considerable dynamic of convergence: Norway's poverty threshold was four times higher than Poland's in SILC 2005; in SILC 2011, it was three times as high. Concurrently, we see striking differences in the evolution of the poverty thresholds. The poverty threshold increased dramatically in Poland (+ 70%), but also considerably in Norway (+ 29%) and Sweden (+ 28%). By contrast, in Spain, the SILC 2011 poverty threshold had dropped to just 10% above the SILC 2005 level and 8% below the SILC 2008 level, reflecting the deep economic crisis and concomitant decline in median incomes. In the United Kingdom and Ireland, the crisis also reversed the upward trend in the poverty threshold; in the United Kingdom the SILC 2011 poverty threshold was identical to that in SILC 2005. Hence, the pattern of changes in relative

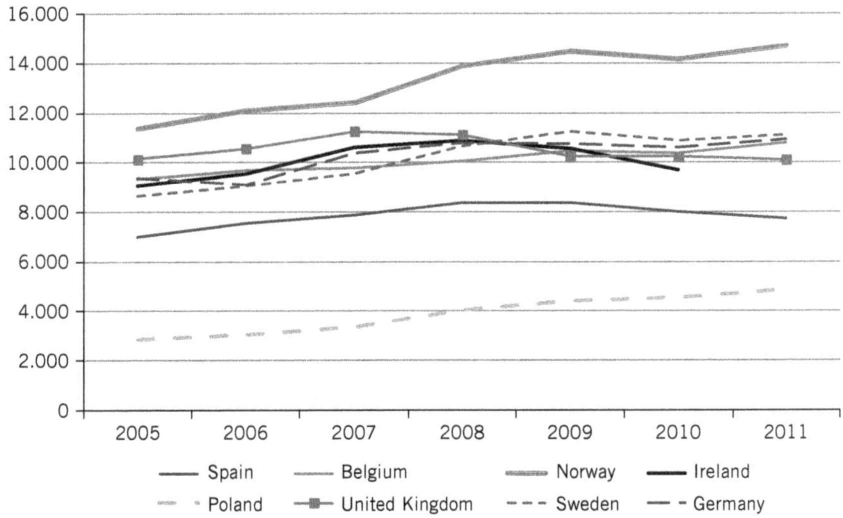

Figure 1.14. Poverty thresholds in Purchasing Power Standard (PPP), 2005–2011.
Source: EU-SILC, data retrieved from Eurostat-site. *Note:* Years are equal to EU-SILC survey years.

financial poverty, calculated on the basis of these floating poverty thresholds, and changes in absolute material prosperity of the worst-off, is extremely disparate. The material deprivation indicator developed by Eurostat also illustrates this. Material deprivation is measured by an index of nine items relating to financial stress and the enforced lack of a list of durables. All persons living in a household that, at the moment of the interview, is deprived on at least three out of nine items are considered to be materially deprived. The contrast between Sweden and the United Kingdom provides a striking example of this disparate pattern: In Sweden, material deprivation diminished to an even lower level in the second half of the previous decade, while the at-risk-of-poverty rate increased; in the United Kingdom, material deprivation increased (starting from an already high level), while the at-risk-of-poverty rate decreased. For Ireland, SILC 2010 shows a dramatic increase in material deprivation while poverty was still marginally lower compared to SILC 2005. In Poland, a boom in material prosperity went hand in hand with decreasing relative poverty.

These contrasting figures provide a warning against one-dimensional interpretations of the changes in poverty risks we consider in the remainder of this section. Below, we will underscore the argument that the increase in poverty reduction by transfers in the United Kingdom during the crisis years reflects the "automatically stabilizing" pattern one might expect to observe in a welfare state, while the decreasing poverty reduction by transfers in Sweden casts doubt on the recent performance of the Swedish welfare state. The reader should bear in mind that the automatic stabilizers at work in the United Kingdom (and Spain) redistributed the impact of a deep economic crisis. Although this is in line with what one might expect from a welfare state, it can hardly be regarded as a satisfactory state of affairs.

In this section we apply the conceptual apparatus developed in the previous sections to the trajectories of eight European welfare states during the Lisbon era. For seven countries, we sketch this trajectory on the basis of SILC, using data from SILC 2004 (or 2005) to SILC 2011. In the case of Germany, we rely instead on the German SOEP.

Figures 1.15 to 1.21 display nine key indicators concerning the non-elderly population during the years of boom and bust, based on SILC and Eurostat spending data, for the UK, Sweden, Spain, Belgium, Poland, Ireland, and Norway:

i. the at-risk-of-poverty rate;
ii. the at-risk-of-poverty rate for individuals in work-poor households;
iii. the at-risk-of-poverty rate for individuals in work-rich households;
iv. work poverty, that is, the share of individuals living in work-poor households;
v. the at-risk-of-poverty rate for individuals in very work-poor households;
vi. severe work poverty, that is, the share of individuals living in very work-poor households;
vii. the pre-transfer at-risk-of-poverty rate (pensions not included in "transfers");
viii. poverty reduction by transfers (pensions excluded);
ix. spending on cash benefits (except old-age and survivor programs), in percent of GDP.

Because of the limited availability of data on SILC 2011 at the moment of writing, the indicators (vii) and (viii) do not refer to the age bracket [0–59], but to the age bracket [18–64].

Figure 1.23 provides a similar analytical grid for Germany but using SOEP and starting from SOEP 1995. We discuss this below.

Each of the graphs consists of three panels. Panel (a) shows the interaction of labor market developments, social spending, and poverty reduction by transfers. Poverty reduction is defined here as post-transfer poverty minus pre-transfer poverty, that is, the more negative the figure, the larger the reduction (when we refer to a "decrease in poverty reduction by transfers," the corresponding figure becomes less negative). Panel (a) clearly illustrates the impact of the crisis, and the countercyclical trajectory of spending and poverty reduction by transfers (except in Sweden and Ireland). Panel (b) shows the evolution of poverty risks in the total non-elderly population, and in its two constituent parts as defined here: people living in work-poor households and people living in work-rich households. In addition, panel (b) represents the poverty risk among very work-poor households, and, again, poverty reduction for the total population. The steady decline in poverty risks among the work-poor and the very work-poor in Ireland is mirrored in the steady increase in poverty reduction. By contrast, the steady increase in poverty risks among work-poor and very work-poor households in Sweden is reflected in the decrease in poverty reduction.

Panel (c) allows us to compare the evolution of post-transfer poverty risks and pre-transfer poverty risks, and the reduction in poverty through transfers. Norway provides a case where changes in pre-transfer poverty are completely neutralized by changes in poverty reduction. In the United Kingdom, the decrease in poverty reduction was less substantial than the decrease in pre-transfer poverty in the first half of the period under review (SILC 2005–2008), while the increase in poverty reduction was more substantial than the increase in pre-transfer poverty in the second half of the period under review (SILC 2008–2011). The net result is a steady decrease in post-transfer poverty. The Swedish figures display some irregularities that are hard to explain (and probably linked to sample problems), but, overall, the opposite pattern is observed: In the first half of the period under review, poverty reduction decreased more than pre-transfer poverty; in the second half of the period under review, again, poverty reduction decreased more than pre-transfer poverty (comparing SILC 2005 and SILC 2011). Hence post-transfer poverty steadily increased.

These graphs thus provide two ways to account for changes in the at-risk-of-poverty rate. First, the at-risk-of-poverty rate (indicator i, listed supra in our description of the graphs) is equal to the weighted average of the at-risk-of-poverty rate for individuals in work-poor households (indicator ii) and individuals in work-rich households (indicator iii), weighted by their respective shares in the population (indicator iv). Second, the at-risk-of-poverty rate is equal to pre-transfer poverty (indicator vii) minus poverty reduction by transfers (indicator viii). The evolution of poverty reduction correlates with the evolution of spending (indicator ix), as one might expect. Also, poverty reduction and pre-transfer poverty tend to correlate, though in different ways in different countries. The graphs also allow us to verify the extent to which the evolution of pre-transfer poverty and poverty reduction correlate with the evolution of the share of individuals living in work-poor households and very work-poor households, that is, the extent to which welfare states interact with changing conditions in labor markets. As already explained in Sections 1.5 and 1.6, a priori, and on a ceteris paribus basis, one might expect to see positive correlations here; however, this is not the case in all the countries under review. Figures 1.8b and 1.9b in Section 1.6 explain why.

The at-risk-of-poverty rate of individuals in very work-poor households is added in the graphs, because this is where the most notable changes occur.

In the United Kingdom, the minor decrease in the at-risk-of-poverty rate before the crisis was mainly due to a decreasing proportion of individuals living

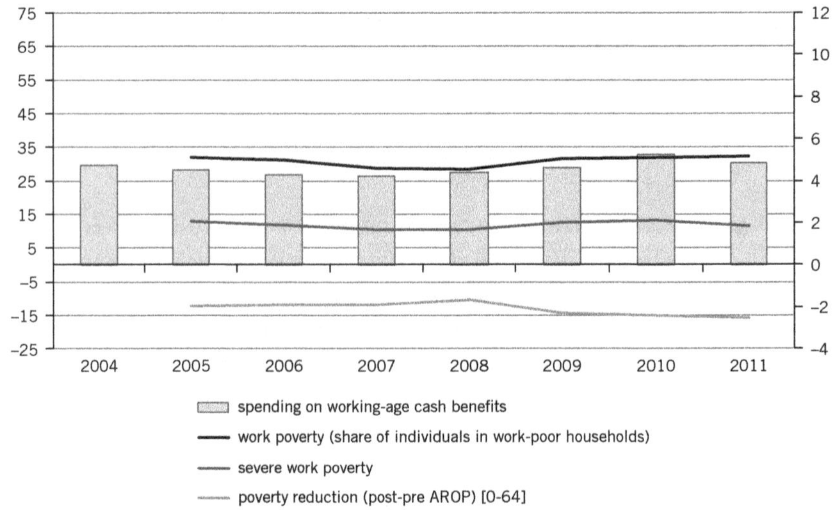

Figure 1.15a. United Kingdom, distribution of population by household work intensity (population [0–59]), poverty reduction by social transfers (excluding pensions) (population [0–64]), 2004–2011. *Source:* EU-SILC & Eurostat for spending data. *Note:* Years are equal to EU-SILC survey years.

in work-poor households (with unchanged poverty risks in both the work-poor and the work-rich segments of the population). From SILC 2008 onward, the at-risk-of-poverty rate declined markedly in the UK, notwithstanding a growing proportion of individuals living in work-poor households; the considerable decrease in poverty risks in both the work-poor and the work-rich segments

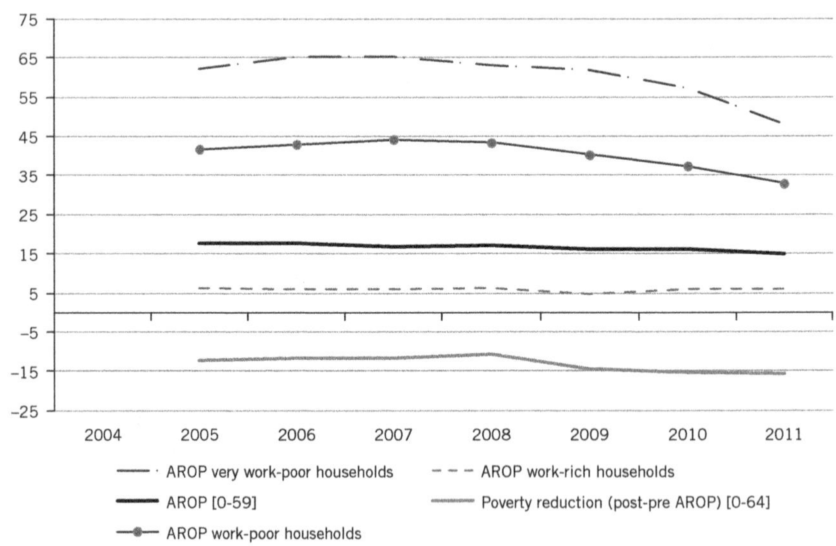

Figure 1.15b. United Kingdom, distribution of population by household work intensity (population [0–59]), poverty reduction by social transfers (excluding. pensions) (population [0–64]), 2004–2011. *Source*: EU-SILC. *Note:* Years are equal to EU-SILC survey years.

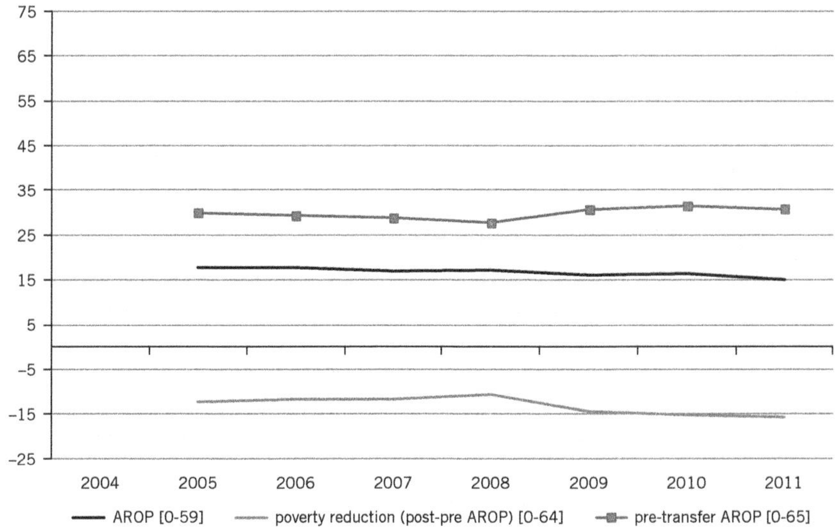

Figure 1.15c. United Kingdom, distribution of population by household work intensity (population [0–59]), poverty reduction by social transfers (excluding pensions) (population [0–64]), pre-transfer AROP (population, [0–64], 2004–2011. *Source*: EU-SILC. *Note:* Years are equal to EU-SILC survey years.

of the population account for this (Figures 1.15a-b-c). In Sweden, the opposite pattern occurred: poverty increased, driven by significant increases in poverty in the work-poor segment of the population (Figures 1.16a-b-c). Notably in the very work-poor segment, poverty increased from a comparatively low level (compared to the other countries under review) to the highest level in the countries under review in this section. The diverging patterns of poverty reduction in the UK and Sweden corroborate this striking difference in trajectory.

Earlier, we mentioned the fact that a comparison between the UK and Sweden should not overlook the fact that the poverty threshold in Sweden stopped increasing during the crisis years but remained considerably higher than it had been at the beginning of the period under review, while in the United Kingdom it declined considerably after which it returned to its initial level. However, one should not conclude from this that there was an inevitable trade-off between the evolution of the poverty threshold and the poverty headcounts during the crisis years: In Norway the poverty threshold kept rising, while the poverty headcount remained stable. This is not happenstance: Spending on working-age cash benefits increased much more in 2009 in Norway than it did in Sweden.

Figure 1.22 shows, for the United Kingdom, Sweden, Spain, and Poland, (A) the share of the population that is at-risk-of-poverty *and* living in a work-poor household (in short: "poor work-poor"); and (B) the share of the population that is at-risk-of-poverty *and* living in a work-rich household ("poor work-rich"). (We compare SILC 2011 and SILC 2005.) Both A and B are expressed as a

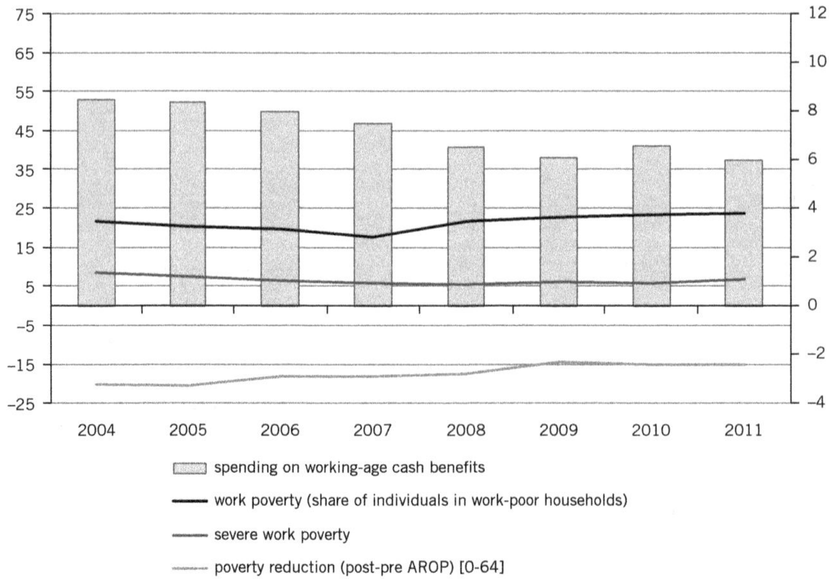

Figure 1.16a. Sweden, distribution of population by household work intensity (population [0–59]), poverty reduction by social transfers (excluding pensions) (population [0–64]), 2004–2011. *Source*: EU-SILC & Eurostat for spending data. *Note:* Years are equal to EU-SILC survey years.

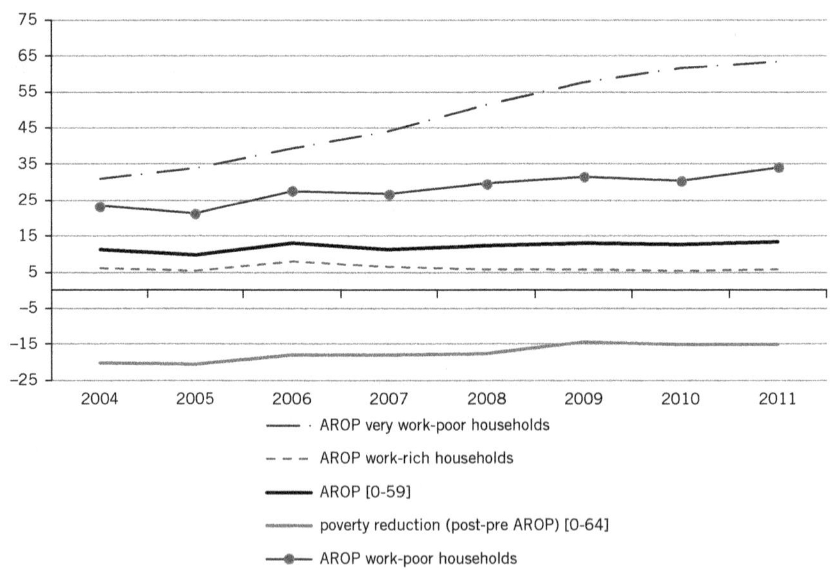

Figure 1.16b. Sweden, distribution of population by household work intensity (population [0–59]), poverty reduction by social transfers (excluding pensions) (population [0–64]), 2004–2011. *Source*: EU-SILC. *Note:* Years are equal to EU-SILC survey years.

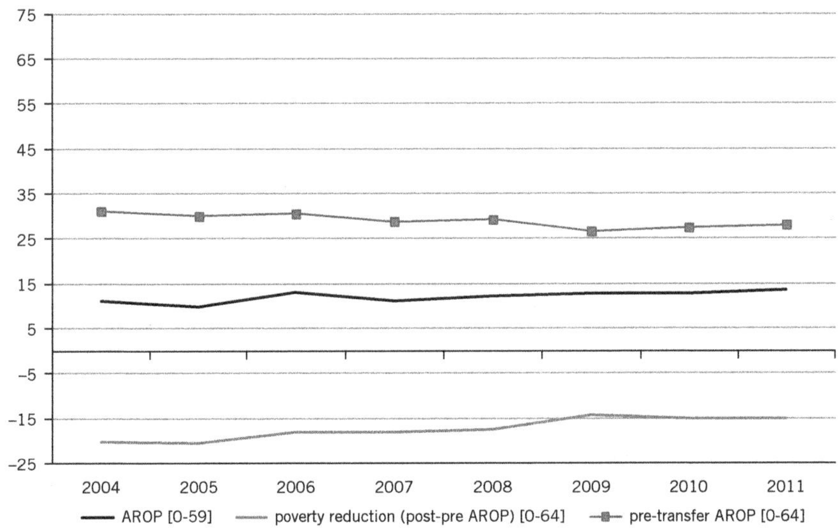

Figure 1.16c. Sweden, distribution of population by household work intensity (population [0–59]), poverty reduction by social transfers (excluding pensions) (population [0–64]), pre-transfer AROP (population [0–64], 2004–2011. *Source*: EU-SILC. *Note:* Years are equal to EU-SILC survey years.

percentage of the total population, hence the sum of A and B is equal to the poverty headcount for the total population. In those four countries, a considerable change in the poverty headcount was driven mainly by the change in the share of "poor work-poor"; the share of "poor work-rich" remained remarkably constant.

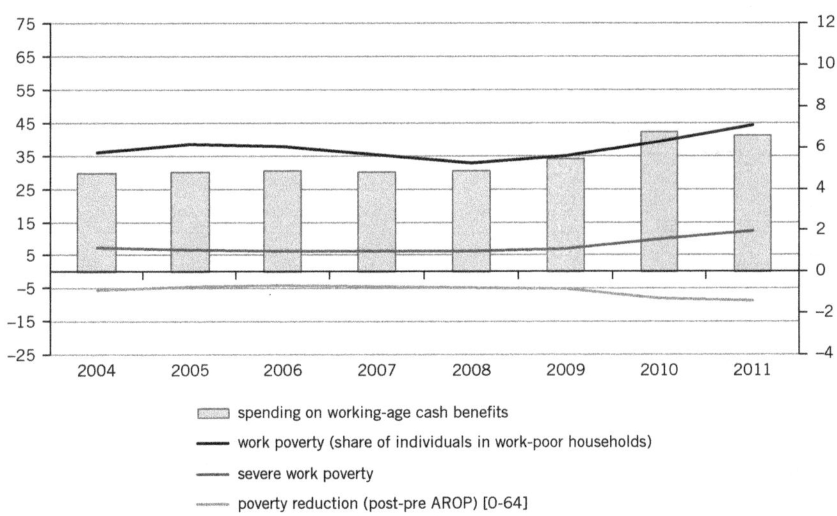

Figure 1.17a. Spain, distribution of population by household work intensity (population [0–59]), poverty reduction by social transfers (excluding pensions) (population [0–64]), 2004–2011. *Source*: EU-SILC & Eurostat for spending data. *Note:* Years are equal to EU-SILC survey years.

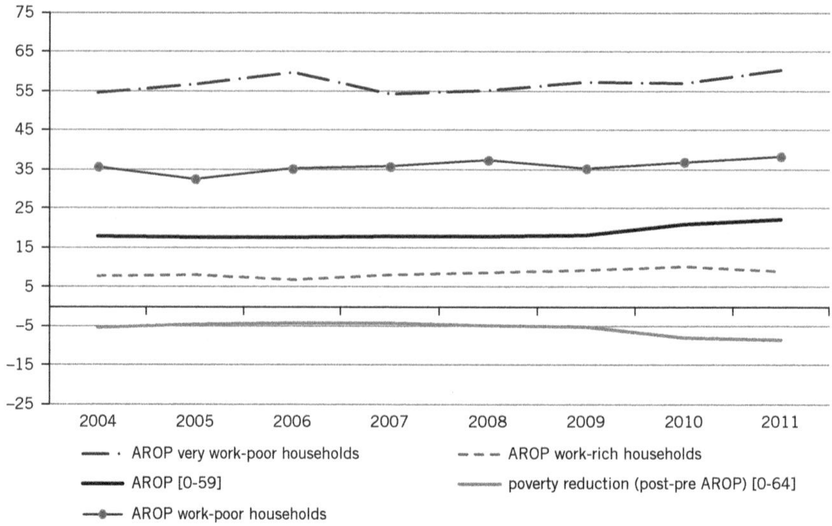

Figure 1.17b. Spain, distribution of population by household work intensity (population [0–59]), poverty reduction by social transfers (excluding pensions) (population [0–64]), 2004–2011. *Source*: EU-SILC. *Note:* Years are equal to EU-SILC survey years.

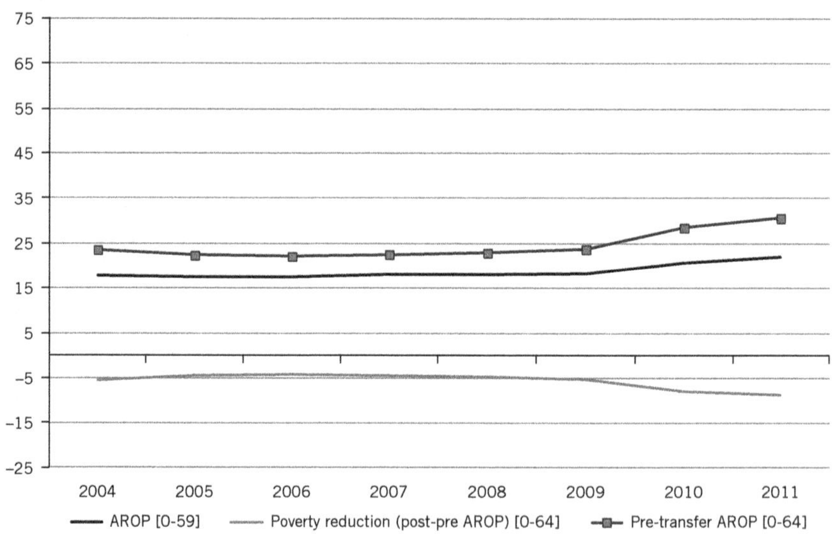

Figure 1.17c. Spain, distribution of population by household work intensity (population [0–59]), poverty reduction by social transfers (excluding pensions) (population [0–64]), pre-transfer AROP (population, [0–64], 2004–2011. *Source*: EU-SILC. *Note:* Years are equal to EU-SILC survey years.

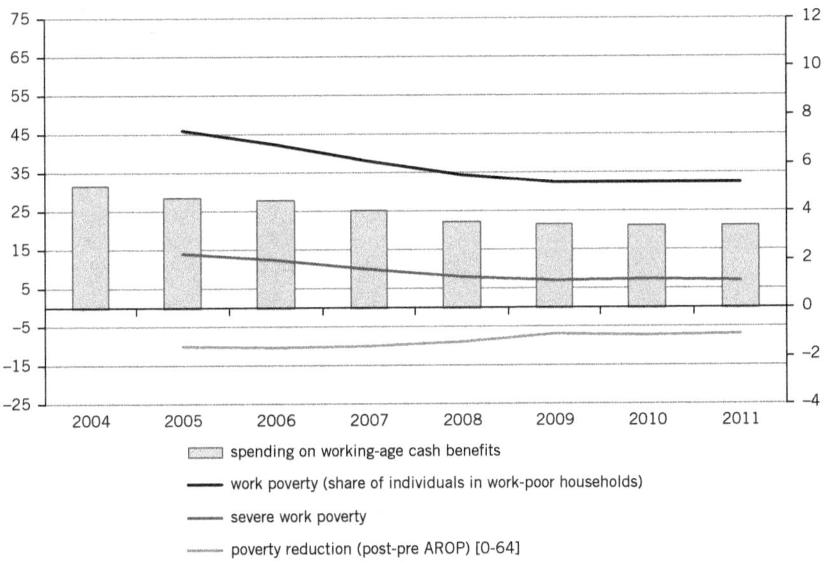

Figure 1.18a. Poland, distribution of population by household work intensity (population [0–59]), poverty reduction by social transfers (excluding pensions) (population [0–64]), 2004–2011. *Source*: EU-SILC & Eurostat for spending data. *Note:* Years are equal to EU-SILC survey years.

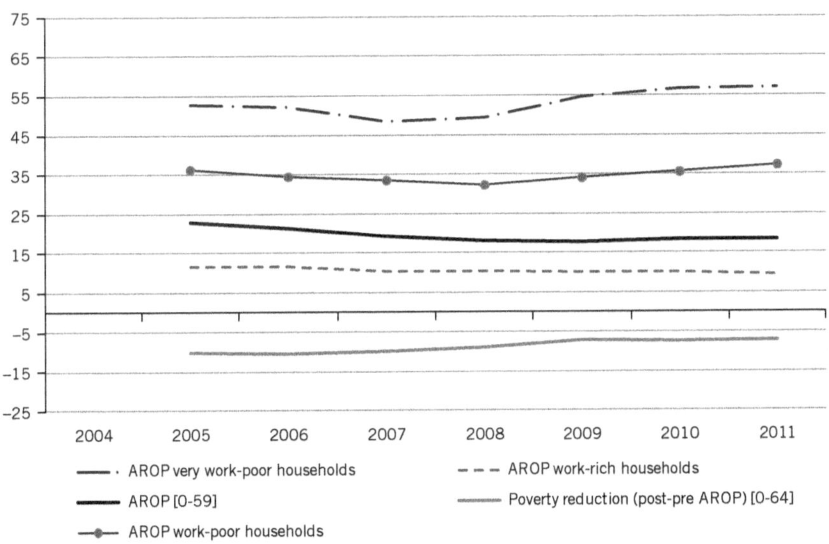

Figure 1.18b. Poland, distribution of population by household work intensity (population [0–59]), poverty reduction by social transfers (excluding pensions) (population [0–64]), 2004–2011. *Source*: EU-SILC. *Note:* Years are equal to EU-SILC survey years.

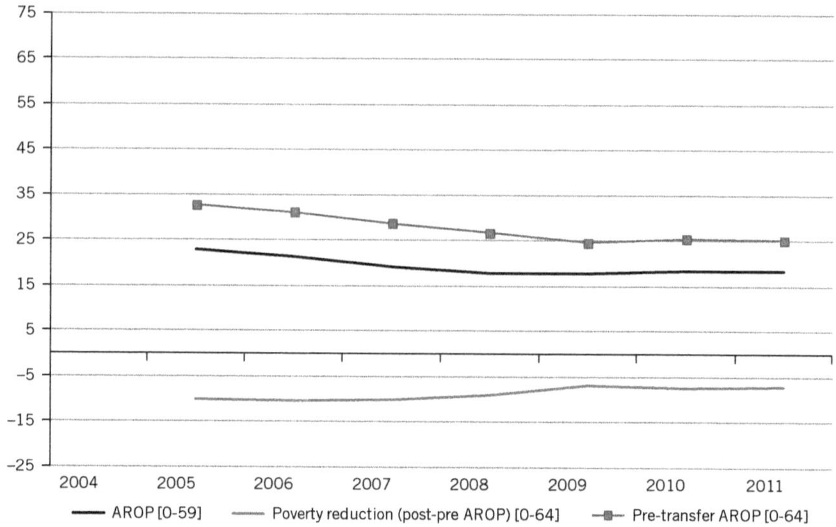

Figure 1.18c. Poland, distribution of population by household work intensity (population [0–59]), poverty reduction by social transfers (excluding pensions) (population [0–64]), pre-transfer AROP (population, [0–64], 2004–2011. *Source*: EU-SILC. *Note:* Years are equal to EU-SILC survey years.

(This observation should not lead us to conclude that the at-risk-of-poverty rate in the work-rich segment was not an important driver of poverty evolutions in a number of countries; see Chapter 3 on this matter.) However, the underlying dynamics were quite different: In the United Kingdom, the share of "poor work-poor" decreased because the poverty risk in the work-poor household

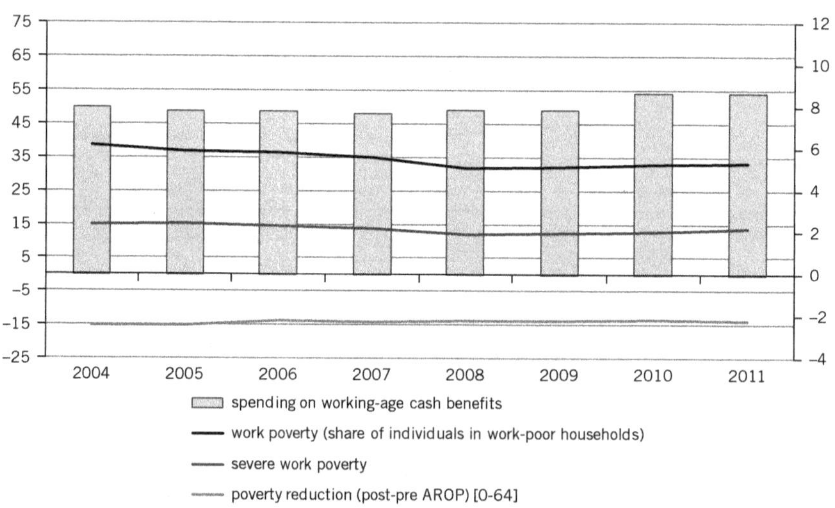

Figure 1.19a. Belgium, distribution of population by household work intensity (population [0–59]), poverty reduction by social transfers (excluding pensions) (population [0–64]), 2004–2011. *Source*: EU-SILC & Eurostat for spending data. *Note:* Years are equal to EU-SILC survey years.

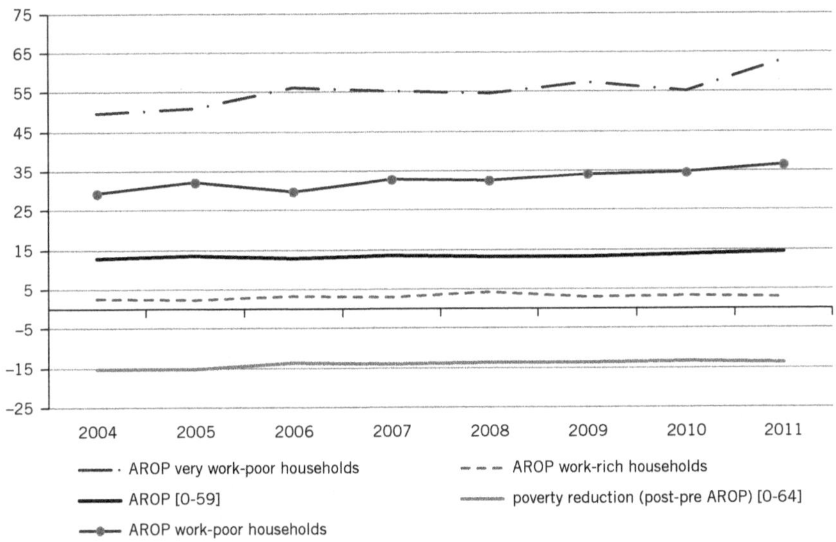

Figure 1.19b. Belgium, distribution of population by household work intensity (population [0–59]), poverty reduction by social transfers (excluding pensions) (population [0–64]), 2004–2011. *Source*: EU-SILC. *Note:* Years are equal to EU-SILC survey years.

segment had declined, while in Poland the share of "poor work-poor" decreased because the share of individuals in work-poor households had dropped. In Sweden, the share of "poor work-poor" increased mainly because the poverty risk of the work-poor rose; in Spain the share of "poor work-poor" increased

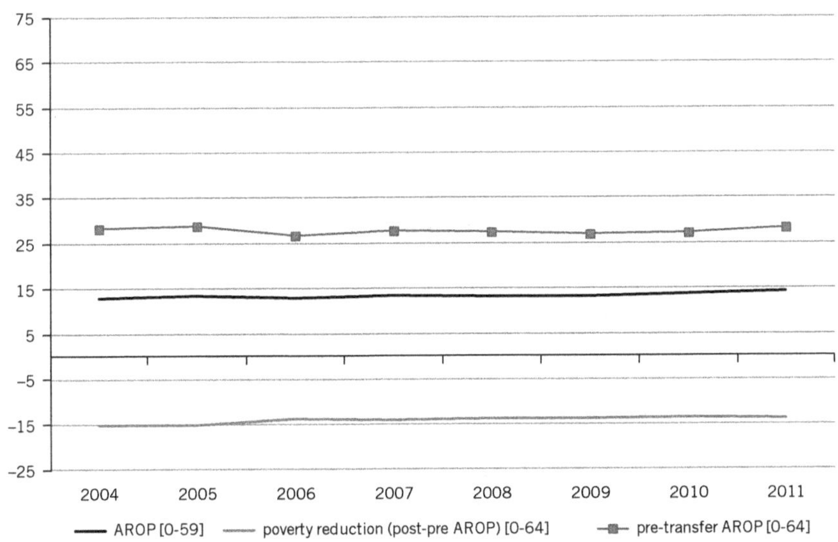

Figure 1.19c. Belgium, distribution of population by household work intensity (population [0–59]), poverty reduction by social transfers (excluding pensions) (population [0–64]), pre-transfer AROP (population, [0–64], 2004–2011. *Source*: EU-SILC. *Note:* Years are equal to EU-SILC survey years.

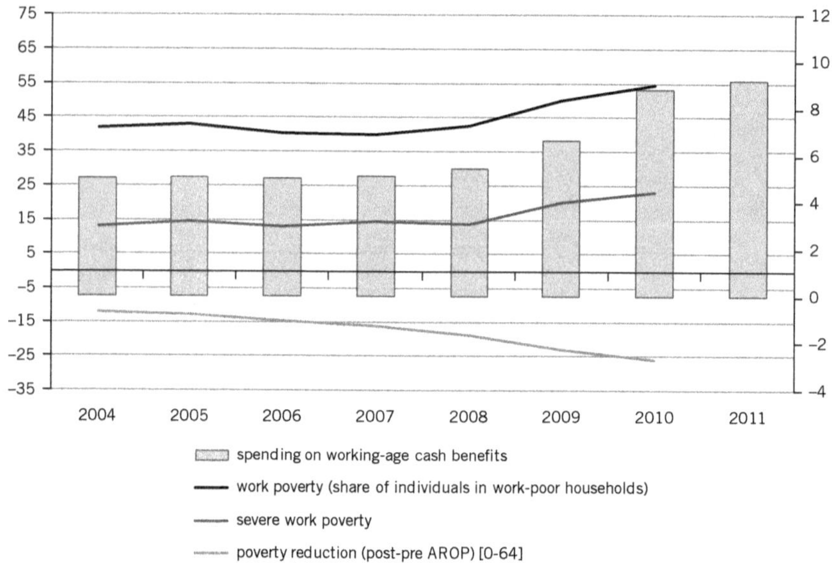

Figure 1.20a. Ireland, distribution of population by household work intensity (population [0–59]), poverty reduction by social transfers (excluding pensions) (population [0–64]), 2004–2011. *Source*: EU-SILC & Eurostat for spending data. *Note:* Years are equal to EU-SILC survey years.

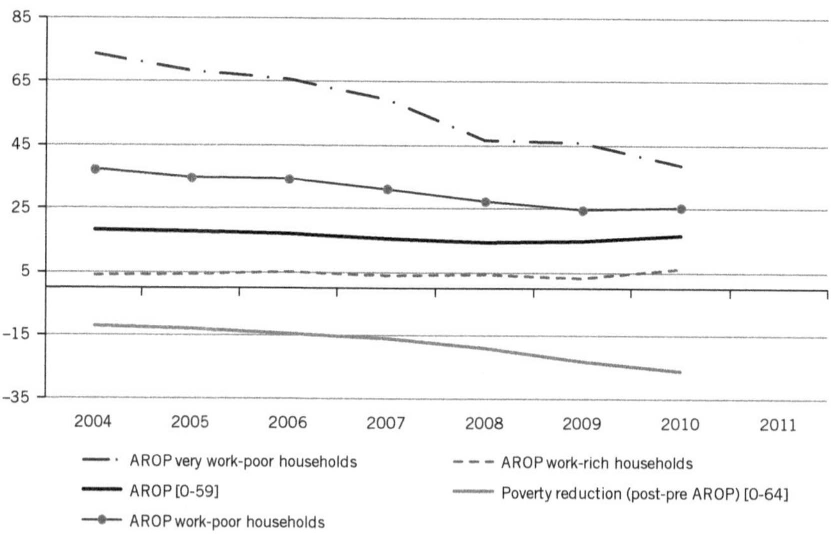

Figure 1.20b. Ireland, distribution of population by household work intensity (population [0–59]), poverty reduction by social transfers (excluding pensions) (population [0–64]), 2004–2011. *Source*: EU-SILC. *Note:* Years are equal to EU-SILC survey years.

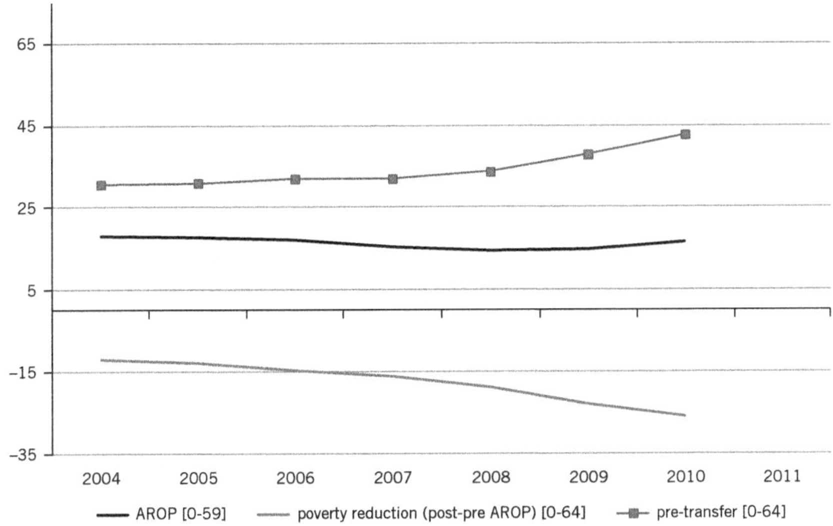

Figure 1.20c. Ireland, distribution of population by household work intensity (population [0–59]), poverty reduction by social transfers (excluding pensions) (population [0–64]), pre-transfer AROP (population, [0–64], 2004–2011. *Source*: EU-SILC. *Note:* Years are equal to EU-SILC survey years.

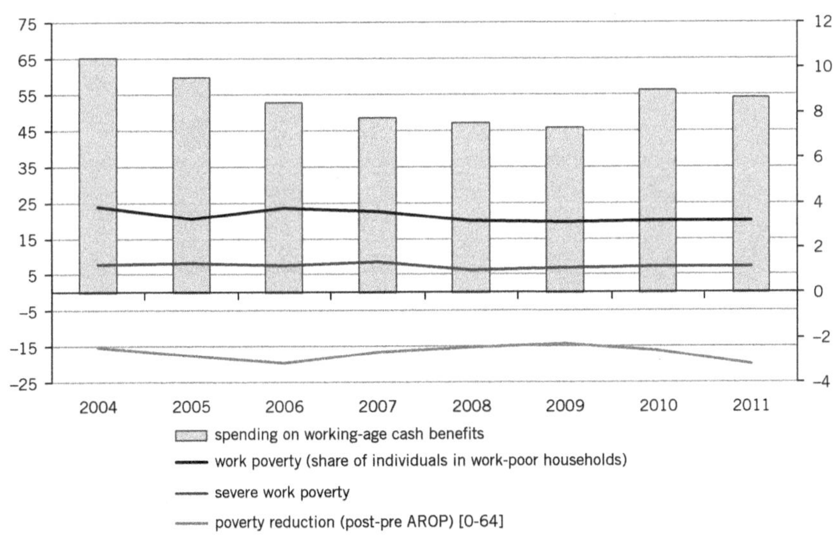

Figure 1.21a. Norway, distribution of population by household work intensity (population [0–59]), poverty reduction by social transfers (excluding pensions) (population [0–64]), 2004–2011. *Source*: EU-SILC & Eurostat for spending data. *Note:* Years are equal to EU-SILC survey years.

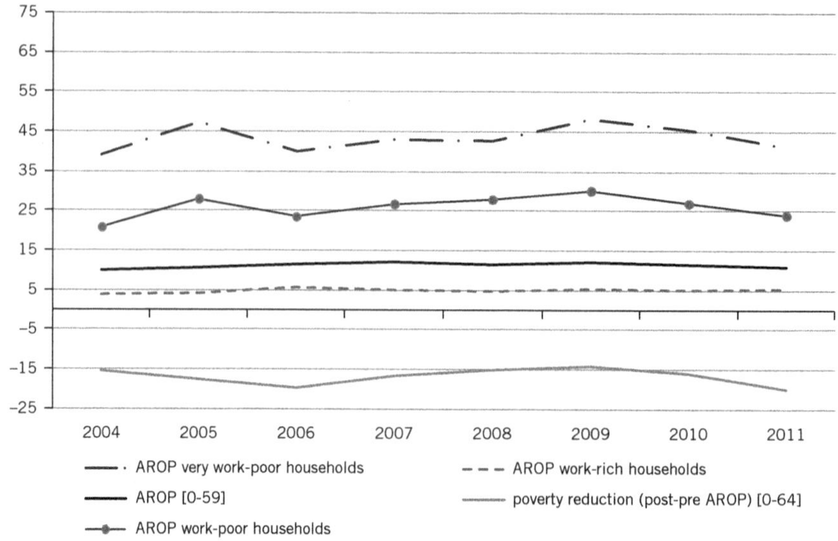

Figure 1.21b. Norway, distribution of population by household work intensity (population [0–59]), poverty reduction by social transfers (excluding pensions) (population [0–64]), 2004–2011. *Source*: EU-SILC. *Note:* Years are equal to EU-SILC survey years.

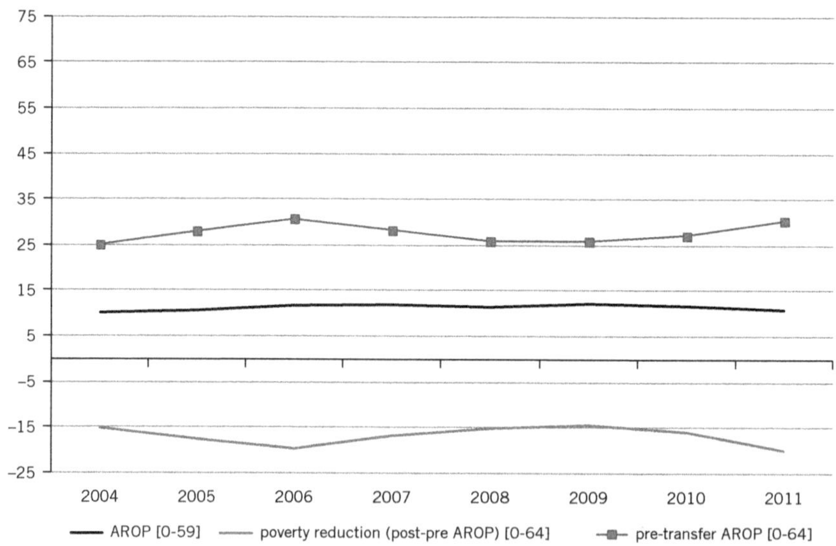

Figure 1.21c. Norway, distribution of population by household work intensity (population [0–59]), poverty reduction by social transfers (excluding pensions) (population [0–64]), pre-transfer AROP (population, [0–64], 2004–2011. *Source*: EU-SILC. *Note:* Years are equal to EU-SILC survey years.

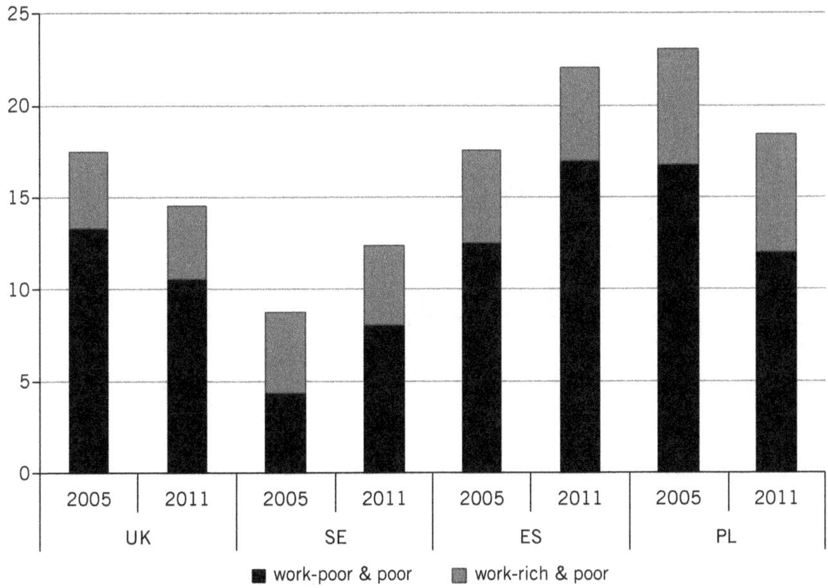

Figure 1.22. Composition of the population [0–59] at-risk-of-poverty, in percentage of total population [0–59], 2005 & 2011. *Source*: EU-SILC. *Note:* Years are equal to EU-SILC survey years.

mainly because the share of individuals in work-poor households grew. Hence, four different trajectories were followed.

The German SOEP allows an analysis over the whole period starting in 1995, provided in Figures 1.23a-b-c.

As previously mentioned, German poverty rates obtained on the basis of SOEP follow an evolution that is very different from the evolution observed on the basis of SILC. According to SOEP, poverty increased considerably between 1997 and 2006, remained basically flat between 2006 and 2010 (with signs even of a decrease). Although the timing is different, we see a development over the past 17 years that shares some features, in terms of poverty outcomes and poverty reduction, with developments sketched on the basis of SILC for some other European welfare states in the second half of the 2000s. Poverty reduction follows a pattern that is, according to our calculations on SOEP, very mildly countercyclical vis-à-vis household employment (poverty reduction increases when work-poverty increases) and vis-à-vis pre-transfer poverty; but the increase in poverty reduction is largely insufficient to counteract rising pre-transfer poverty. Steadily increasing poverty within the work-poor segment of the population corroborates this observation, and signals worrying changes in the German welfare edifice. These trends may in part be attributable to the evolution of social spending, which was basically flat during years in which the population shares in work-poor and very work-poor households increased (2001–2006), as can be

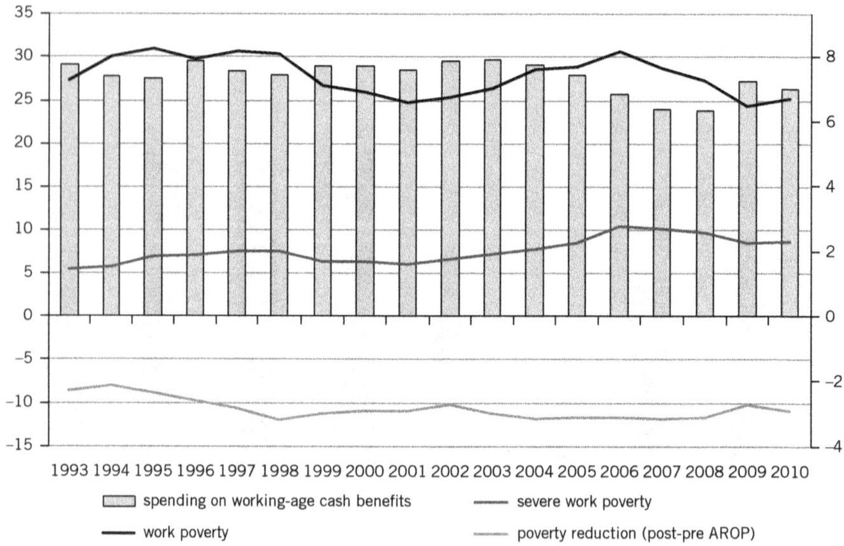

Figure 1.23a. Distribution of German population [0–59] by work intensity of household, 1993–2010. *Source:* SOEP & Eurostat for spending data. *Note:* Spending on working-age cash benefits as % of GDP.

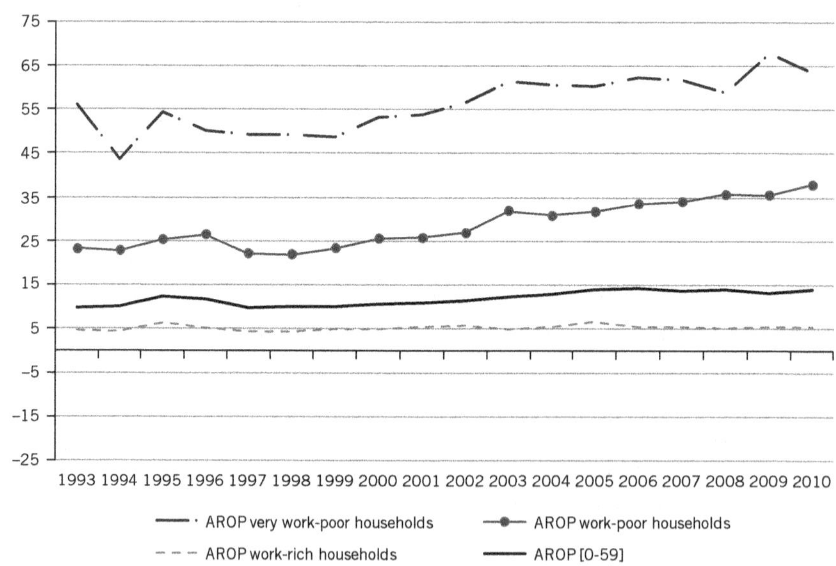

Figure 1.23b. German poverty rates [0–59], by work intensity of households, 1993–2010. *Source:* SOEP & EU-SILC.

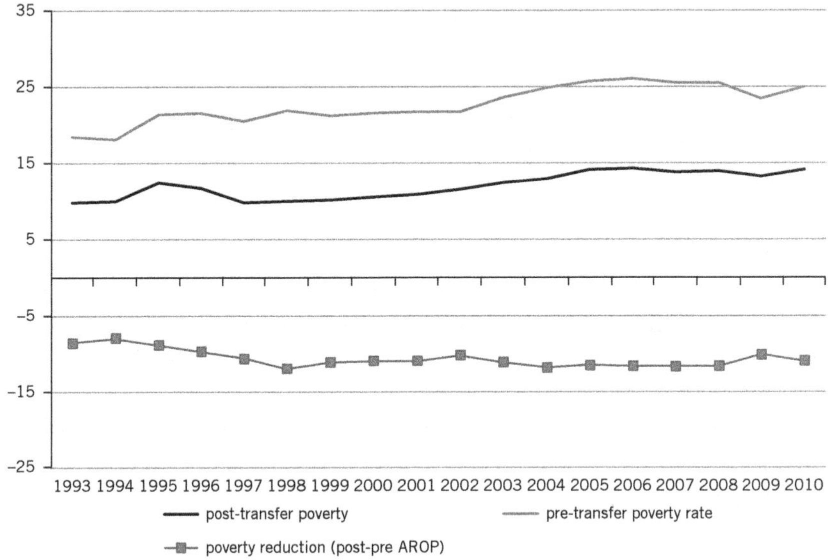

Figure 1.23c. German post- and pre-transfer poverty, poverty reduction, population [0–59], 1993–2010. *Source*: SOEP.

inferred from Figure 1.23a; but aside from less generous spending, evolutions within the labor market, for instance with regard to minimum wages, may have played a role here.

1.8 CONCLUSION

Our main purpose in this introductory chapter was to introduce and justify the research agenda that is developed in this book. This research agenda is motivated by a policy question, which we summarized as follows: Is it possible to structurally replace spending on cash benefits for working-age adults and their families with employment creation, and to simultaneously reduce poverty among working-age adults and their children? Or, to formulate it less ambitiously: Is it possible to structurally replace spending on cash benefits for working-age households by employment creation without increasing poverty? This question pertains to the essence of welfare reform as it has been conceived over the last 20 years. Already in the 1990s, employment-centered welfare reform was the key policy objective in mature welfare states confronted with aging populations and increasing expenditures for health care. We emphasized the word "structurally," because one should distinguish correlations between short-term changes in spending and employment during the business cycle from structural trends.

The purpose of this book is not to arrive at a definitive verdict on this question. In order to enhance our understanding of the issues at hand, we rely to a large extent on decomposition techniques. These decompositions are based on a partition of individuals on the basis of the work-intensity of the households in which they live. Decomposition analysis does not reveal causality: it is basically an accounting device. However, it yields interesting descriptions of country-specific trajectories of welfare state change. Obviously, in order to be relevant in a comparative perspective, the factors on which these decompositions focus—notably the share of individuals in work-poor households and the share of individuals in very work-poor or jobless households—must also have some general explanatory power in a cross-country analysis. The regression results reported in this chapter do support the attention paid in this book to both the share of individuals in work-poor households and the share of individuals in very work-poor or jobless households.

An upshot of these regression analyses is that they shed some light on the poverty performance of European welfare states. Social spending is a factor explaining the dispersion of poverty rates, but its exact impact differs strongly across methods and samples. Work-intensity further equalizes the field, but the poor performance of those with the very highest poverty rates remains largely unexplained. Additional indicators that we believe are closely related to the "underlying fabric of the nation" can provide additional insights. There is suggestive evidence that that past investments in education and the labor market might help explain why Scandinavian welfare states have such good poverty records. In this chapter, we provide data suggesting that the degree of pro-poorness of benefits might help explain why the Netherlands is a strong performer, and why Spain is a weak one. However, the findings on social investment and pro-poorness are purely based on cross-sectional differences and are therefore less robust than those for social spending and work poverty. The performance of especially the welfare states in Central and Eastern Europe presents a number of puzzles that remain unresolved when applying our type of analysis. In other words, there is still an important research agenda with regard to welfare state performance. Despite these cautionary notes and a number of important conceptual caveats listed in this chapter—"efficiency" so conceived is a tricky notion and is certainly not a virtue per se for welfare states—we consider the issue of "efficiency" as crucially important with a view to developing a social policy concept at the EU level.

One should be aware that analyzing *changes* in poverty risks in single countries, from an intertemporal perspective, and making a cross-country analysis of poverty *levels* are two quite different exercises. Much confusion, both in the academic and in the policy debate, is caused by the unwarranted conflation of these two perspectives. By way of example, we ought to explain how contemporary Sweden can continue to rank quite well in terms of poverty in a cross-country perspective and yet, as a country, has clearly followed an inegalitarian course in the second half of the past decade. Factors accounting for the Scandinavian "superiority" in terms of social inclusion and employment (relative to performance levels across Europe) are not preventing some Scandinavian welfare states from shifting to less outstanding outcomes (more so than is the case in other European welfare states). *A fortiori*, with a view to practical policy advice, understanding welfare state change cannot be confined to understanding observable cross-country differences in performance levels.[12]

Although we are able to discern some common features, there are no general laws that uniformly explain the dynamics of poverty in European welfare states over the previous decade. The overall increase in poverty rates by the end of the decade can be seen as the combined result of an economic boom without declining poverty in many Member States—as the gain in household employment was relatively limited and/or offset in many countries by increasing poverty risks within vulnerable subgroups of the population—followed by a crisis with decreasing household employment rates and increasing poverty in many Member States. Although they cannot be conclusive, the decomposition analyses presented in this chapter show that the countercyclical "poverty stabilizing" character of welfare states in general still prevails, but simultaneously suggest that in some European welfare states the structural capacity to reduce poverty declined in the second half of the 2000s.

Because we emphasize the employment-poverty nexus in this book, our analysis focuses on the non-elderly. The picture with regard to poverty risks for the elderly population (60 years or older) is very different than the picture with regard to the non-elderly. Although the weighted average of national at-risk-of-poverty rates of the non-elderly increased by 1.3 ppt for the EU27 in the second half of the previous decade, poverty rates for the elderly decreased by 2.1 ppt. Old-age poverty decreased in many European welfare states, but not in all of them. Where old-age poverty decreased, this is in part the result of trends that started before the financial crisis; in part, it is an upshot of declining incomes of the non-elderly in a number of welfare states that were hit hard by the financial crisis. This observation on poverty rates for the elderly should be related to the observation that in many welfare states, though not in all, pension and healthcare spending substituted for working-age cash benefits. That, in turn, underscores the relevance of the central question motivating this book: Is it possible to structurally replace spending on cash benefits for working-age households by employment creation and to simultaneously reduce poverty?

ACKNOWLEDGMENTS

We thank Tim Goedemé and Aaron Van den Heede for preparation of data on the basis of SILC, Nathalie Schuerman, and Gerlinde Verbist.

NOTES

1 In this chapter, we use "the European welfare states" as a shortcut for the EU27, Norway, and Iceland. However, references to data on "the European welfare states" provided in other chapters in this book may refer to a smaller set of welfare states.

2 In this chapter, the term "average" invariably refers to the unweighted average.

3 We did signal some doubts with regard to the Germany SILC figures for 2005 and 2006, and with regard to the Swedish figure for 2005. Given that approximately one fourth of the non-elderly population of the EU15 lives in Germany and Sweden, excluding Germany and Sweden reduces the increase of the weighted average at-risk-of-poverty rates in the EU15 from 2 ppt to 1 ppt. Excluding Germany and Sweden from the calculation for EU27 reduces the increase for the EU27 from 1.3 ppt to 0.5 ppt. Hence, the German and Swedish figures have a considerable impact, but excluding them does not alter the conclusion with regard to convergence.

4 Confining the scope of our analysis to the working-age population (in the 15–64 age bracket), we observe a decrease in the economic dependency ratio of working-age adults from 0.67 in 1994 to 0.49 in 2008.

5 The figure for adults in jobless households refers to individuals in the 18–59 age bracket; the individual nonemployment rate refers to the 15–64 age bracket.

6 Paul de Beer (2007) analyzes the failure of the Lisbon Strategy with regard to its poverty goal on the basis of the relation between poverty and household joblessness, contrasting long-term changes in individual joblessness and household joblessness. The OECD *Employment Outlook 2001* (2001, 59–61) pointed to the absence of significant correlations between aggregate employment and unemployment rates on the one hand and poverty measures on the other hand. This OECD finding is cited in Gregg and Wadsworth (2008) and may have inspired different authors, such as Dickens and Ellwood (2002) and Nickell (2004), to focus on household joblessness. Our results contradict the findings by the OECD; however, the latter relate to a different sample of countries (ECHP countries and Canada and the United States), a different database (ECHP) and a different time than the correlations we obtain on the basis of SILC for European welfare states in the 2000s.

7 See Vandenbroucke et al. (2013) for a more finely grained analysis of cross-country differences in poverty, which also includes the impact of *pension* spending, which plays a significant role, next to spending on working-age cash benefits. The latter analysis focuses on child poverty, but its conclusions by and large also hold for non-elderly poverty.

8 Note that the difference between this specification and the one with simply the share of work-poor and the share of very work-poor is twofold. For one, it provides a different scale, where more weight is given to increases in the

share of very work-poor when the share of total work-poor is low. Secondly, it provides a different interpretation for the coefficient for the share of the work-poor, given that it holds the relative share of very work-poor constant, rather than the absolute share. This implies that increases in the share of very work-poor occur around the mean of the share of work-poor in our specification, while they occur at the margin in the alternative specification.

9 The result for Belgium is highly dependent on the data we use. The spending data employed here are based on the European system of integrated social protection statistics (ESSPROS) and are very high for Belgium. The analysis in Vandenbroucke et al. (2013) based on EU SILC data gives much lower spending numbers for Belgium, leading to a *prima facie* efficiency for Belgium.

10 Keynesian macroeconomic stabilization and "poverty stabilization" are closely associated, since given that increasing unemployment benefits when the economy goes into recession play a role in both mechanisms, but they are not the same. Keynesian automatic stabilization depends on the support of effective demand; it presupposes that the government deficit increases. The fact that poverty is reduced is not essential for the macroeconomic mechanism to function (although supporting incomes below or close to the poverty threshold may be most efficient with a view to boosting effective demand). For the "poverty stabilization function" to operate, it is not necessary that government spending increases more rapidly than government revenue (although Keynesian stabilization may, through its positive effect on employment, make it easier to prevent poverty from rising).

11 Figure 1.11 also shows the sensitivity of the analysis for Sweden to the choice of the first reference year, by presenting alternative decompositions starting with SILC 2004 and SILC 2006.

12 See Marx et al. (2012b) for an interesting analysis related to this problematic.

2

THE EVOLUTION OF POVERTY IN THE EUROPEAN UNION: CONCEPTS, MEASUREMENT, AND DATA

Koen Decancq, Tim Goedemé, Karel Van den Bosch, and Josefine Vanhille

2.1 INTRODUCTION

Eradicating poverty is arguably one of the greatest challenges facing mankind. In 2010, the European Commission identified as its fifth Europe 2020 target a 20-million decrease in the number of persons in or at risk of poverty and social exclusion within the next 10 years. In order for such a quantitative target to make sense, a clear measure of poverty and social exclusion is required. Indeed, even if it is true that we tend to recognize extreme poverty when confronted with it, the abundance of definitions and measures of poverty in the specialized literature suggests that it is not so easy to pour such intuitions into an operational poverty measure. Yet, as the old motto goes: "to measure is to know." So before proceeding with the rest of this book, it is important to consider in greater detail not just the concept of poverty applied in the European Union (EU), but also how it is measured and on the basis of which data.

In fact, there is a long list of ongoing conceptual discussions on the definition and measurement of poverty. What exactly do we mean by poverty? Is it a one-dimensional or a multidimensional phenomenon? Should the focus be on the severity of poverty or on the extent to which it manifests itself in different life domains? Where should the poverty line be drawn? Should it follow changes in the prevailing living standard? Should a single poverty line be applied across the EU or are country-specific lines preferable? Should one merely count the number of poor or also consider how the depth of poverty varies across the poor population?

The answers to such (complex) questions reflect our value judgments on the notion of poverty. Different people may disagree on how poverty is most appropriately defined and measured. Poverty has many faces, and hence different perspectives on poverty may lead to different empirical conclusions. In this chapter, we identify some of the (implicit) value judgments underlying the various poverty measures applied in this book and the EU's social strategy. Further, we show how different initial choices ultimately lead to different empirical findings.

The measurement of poverty hinges heavily on the availability and quality of appropriate data. For this reason, this chapter briefly reviews some of the methodological features of the main data source for measuring poverty in Europe, namely the EU Statistics on Income and Living Conditions (EU-SILC), and what they imply for the measurement of poverty.

This chapter begins with a discussion of a poverty definition that is widely used in European policy circles. In the third section, this notion is translated into a suitable measurement framework based on the familiar Foster, Greer, and Thorbecke (FGT) class of poverty measures. Three key issues pertaining to the measurement of poverty are discussed: the metric of well-being, the choice of the poverty line, and the sensitivity to the distribution among the poor. The section concludes with a reflection on whether there is room for agnosticism on these issues, taking into account partial poverty orderings and robustness. Section 2.4 shows how the key poverty measures used in this book and in the EU's social strategy reflect specific answers to the conceptual questions posed. Subsequently, in Section 2.5, EU-SILC is introduced as a data set for the measurement of poverty. Section 2.6 considers the empirical relevance of the three central questions identified in Section 2.3 using EU-SILC data from 2005 and 2009. An overview of conclusions is presented in Section 2.7.

2.2 DEFINING POVERTY

Given the focus in this chapter on poverty in the European Union, let us first consider the poverty definition proposed by the Council of the European Communities (1975):

> "Persons beset by poverty: individuals or families whose resources are so small as to exclude them from the minimum acceptable way of life of the member state in which they live."

Many approaches to the measurement of poverty tie in with the above definition and similar definitions have been proposed by other authors, including Townsend (1979). The proposed definition of poverty has three notable features. First, it refers to a lack of resources, suggesting that poverty is a situation that is forced upon people, rather than being a matter of free choice. The list of relevant resources can be defined restrictively or more broadly, so as to include not only cash and other incomes, wealth, and services, but also human resources, such as health and education, and social capital. Second, the notion of a minimum acceptable way of life can likewise be understood in a narrow sense or more broadly, in terms of, for example, Sen's notion of basic "functionings" or "capabilities." Functionings are the doings and beings of individuals, such as being healthy, having a good job, being safe, having a decent standard of living, being able to appear in public without shame and so on. The capabilities are the set of potential functionings that a person can obtain (Sen, 1983, 1985a). Further, the definition implies that what is regarded as the minimum acceptable way of life can vary from one country to another, and that the level of resources needed to achieve that way of life can change as societies become wealthier or poorer. (See Goedemé & Rottiers [2011] for a recent discussion.)[1] Finally, it should be noted that the above definition aims at identifying the poor at the individual level. In order to determine poverty at the societal level, which ultimately is the aim of this chapter, individual poverty needs to be aggregated to an overall poverty figure.

In the Europe 2020 target, as well as the current European discourse, poverty is often linked to the notion of "social exclusion." Social exclusion is a broader, more encompassing and arguably vaguer concept than poverty. The European Commission (2004: 10) defines social exclusion as "A process whereby certain individuals are pushed to the edge of society and are prevented from participating fully by virtue of their poverty, or lack of basic competencies and lifelong learning opportunities, or as a result of discrimination. This distances them from job, income and education opportunities as well as social and community networks and activities. They have little access to power and decision-making bodies and thus often feeling powerless and unable to take control over the decisions that affect their day to day lives." The wide scope and vagueness of the notion social exclusion means that it can encompass many different concerns and fit into divergent, even conflicting, political agendas. At the same time, though, these characteristics undermine its analytical usefulness (Atkinson et al., 2002: 3; Daly, 2010). Hence, the focus in the present chapter is on the notion of poverty.

Furthermore, in the European discourse since the 2001 Laeken summit, the notion of poverty has received the epitheton "at risk of." This prefix may seem to suggest an underlying probabilistic analysis of a person's likelihood of becoming poor (as is customary in the literature on vulnerability; see Ligon & Schechter [2003]). This is not the case, however. The prefix is in fact motivated by the current (political) disagreement on how the complex and multidimensional concept of poverty should be translated into a single indicator. (See also Daly [2010] who argues that the term "at risk of poverty" actually destabilizes the very meaning of poverty.) Some of the relevant points of disagreement are discussed in the next section. Suffice it to say at the moment that the phrase "at risk of poverty" will be reserved for the official headline poverty indicator. (See Box 2.1 for a precise definition.) The next section concludes with an explicit treatment of the room for agnosticism and disagreement in relation to poverty as a concept.

2.3 MEASURING POVERTY

Once an appropriate definition of poverty has been formulated, the next step is to translate this definition into a computable poverty measure. In practice, a wide variety of such poverty measures are used. Some are remarkably simple, others are quite complex. In this chapter, we use a framework for the measurement of poverty that incorporates most of the commonly used approaches in the literature.[2]

2.3.1 A Framework for the Measurement of Poverty

Let $X = (x_1, \ldots, x_i, \ldots, x_n)$ be a vector containing an indicator of well-being x_i for each of the n individuals in a society. A poverty measure attributes to each vector X a number reflecting the magnitude of poverty in that society. In this paper, we make use of the popular class of poverty measures introduced by Foster et al. (1984). These measures have the following mathematical structure:

$$P_\alpha(X) = \frac{1}{n}\sum_{i=1}^{n} \max\left\{\left(\frac{z - x_i}{z}\right), 0\right\}^\alpha,$$

where z is the poverty line and α is a parameter capturing the "sensitivity to the distribution among the poor." The expression $\left(\frac{z - x_i}{z}\right)$ measures the individual normalized poverty gap, which is the distance between the well-being of person i and the poverty line z, normalized by the poverty line itself. To obtain a measure of overall poverty in the society, these normalized poverty gaps of all poor individuals are taken to the power α and then averaged. This class of poverty measures has some attractive properties, such as *additive decomposability* (Foster et al., 1984; 2010).[3]

In the remainder of this section, the focus is on the three main building blocks of the above formula, in other words, x_i, z, and α. Each of these building blocks captures a fundamental question about the measurement of poverty. Although these questions may be distinct, their answers are related. First, x_i is an indicator of individual well-being. In order to be able to say anything sensible about the measurement of poverty in a society, one first needs to ask the question: "Poverty of what?" In other words, poverty needs to be measured in an appropriate *metric* of well-being. Such a metric of well-being may be one-dimensional or multidimensional. Second, a poverty line z needs to be fixed so that a group of individuals is identified as poor. This is the *identification* step. Various methods exist to distinguish the poor from the non-poor. As will become apparent, the selection of an appropriate poverty line in the context of the EU poses some additional challenges. Third, the magnitude of poverty among the individuals of a society should be *aggregated* to an overall poverty figure for that society. The parameter

α plays an important role in this final aggregation step and gives expression to the sensitivity of the measure to the distribution among the poor. Moreover, it allows one to focus straightforwardly on various aspects of poverty, such as its incidence, depth, and severity.

An aspect that is not covered by the proposed class of poverty measure is poverty's persistence over time. In this chapter, however, the focus is on the measurement of poverty based on cross-sectional data, hence intertemporal aspects are beyond its scope.

2.3.2 Selecting a Metric of Well-Being

First, an appropriate metric of well-being for measuring poverty needs to be selected. In this respect, one can distinguish between one-dimensional approaches (where the relevant information on individual well-being consists of a single indicator) and approaches that are multidimensional (where individual well-being is expressed by means of a vector rather than a single indicator). Let us first consider the one-dimensional approaches.

2.3.2.1 One-Dimensional Approaches

Most empirical poverty estimations use either income or expenditure to assess an individual's poverty status. The question of what is the most appropriate one-dimensional metric has been the subject of extensive discussion in the literature. Given the emphasis in the definition of poverty on the lack of *resources*, income seems a natural choice. Yet, as income-based measures often neglect assets and savings, many consider it counter-intuitive to identify as poor an individual who is temporarily income-poor but able to maintain a high level of consumption. Indeed, through saving and borrowing, an individual may be able to smooth consumption over time, so that current total expenditure may be a better proxy than current income for their real (life cycle) economic resources and, therefore, also a more suitable way of assessing an individual's poverty status (Slesnick, 1993; Chaudhuri & Ravallion, 1994; Deaton, 1997). The extent to which individuals actually smooth their consumption is an empirical matter. After a review of research on the topic, Deaton (1992: 218) concludes: "there is much less evidence for low-frequency smoothing, with consumers using assets or loans to smooth their consumption in the face of long-term or life-cycle fluctuations in income." This suggests that, in practice, results obtained through income-based poverty measures may not be misleading, provided that the reference period for income is not unduly short.

Pragmatically, there are some additional considerations to take into account when choosing between income and consumption as a one-dimensional metric of well-being. Consumption or expenditures are more commonly used to assess an individual's poverty status in developing countries, because income is often harder to measure in such contexts (Ravallion, 2010: 2). However, in large-scale surveys in developed countries, income data are easier to collect than expenditure data. Also EU-SILC, the standard data set for poverty analysis in the EU (see Section 2.5), provides only income data, so that almost all recent comparative poverty analyses for the EU are based on such information.

When opting for income as the metric of well-being, a number of additional specifications need to be made in relation to the relevant time span, the exact income concept, the intra-household distribution, and any correction for differences in household needs. In what follows, these aspects are discussed consecutively.

The Expert Group on Household Income Statistics, also known as The Canberra group (2001), has made some recommendations for internationally and inter-temporally harmonized and comparable statistics on household income. First, it recommends a reference period for household income of one year. A sufficiently long reference period reduces the impact of short-term fluctuations, but it also poses higher demands on survey respondents.[4] Moreover, the longer the reference period, the less effective is retrospective questioning (Debels & Vandecasteele, 2008).

Second, the Canberra group recommends a definition of the concept of disposable income as summarized in Table 2.1 (see also Section 2.6). One may want to go a step further by including in-kind income components, especially social transfers through health care and education. The question of how disposable income can be extended beyond its cash components is discussed at length in Chapter 6 of this book.

Although the measurement framework is formulated at individual level, data limitations often force poverty researchers to measure poverty at household level. Typically, only the overall income or expenditure level for the household is observed, without further information on the intrahousehold distribution of resources. Therefore, one often proceeds on the basis of the assumption of equal sharing or full income pooling within the household. This approximation is obviously problematic in contexts where household resources are not shared equally and may lead to considerable underestimations of poverty among certain vulnerable groups, such as children. (See for instance Burton et al. [2007]; Dunbar et al. [2013].)

Finally, one may want to correct for differences in household needs when measuring poverty. To obtain a comparable measure of income across divergent households, equivalence scales are applied to disposable income, aligning the income concept and the needs associated with its use. Equivalence scales are most widely used to adjust for household composition: the needs of a household grow with the number of household members, but arguably not proportionally.[5] Needs for space, electricity, and other shared goods have substantial economies of scale. To correct for such economies, household income and expenditure are divided by an equivalence scale, leading to so-called equivalized incomes. Much

Table 2.1. Recommended definition of disposable household income.

	Employee cash and near-cash income (wages, salaries, bonuses...) including the cash value of "fringe benefits" (goods and services provided to the employee as part of employment)
+	Income from self-employment (profits/losses from unincorporated business, royalties)
+	Net value of home production (for barter or consumption)
+	Imputed rent for owner-occupied dwellings
+	Net income from rentals
+	Property income (interest and dividends received less costs paid)
+	Current transfers received: Social insurance benefits from employers or government schemes Universal or means-tested social assistance benefits Pensions received from individual private plans Regular interhousehold cash transfers received or support received from nonprofit institutions
=	TOTAL INCOME
–	Current transfers paid: Employers' social insurance contributions Employees' social insurance contributions Taxes on incomeRegular taxes on wealth Regular interhousehold cash transfers paid (e.g., to other households or charities)
=	DISPOSABLE INCOME

Source: adapted from Table 2.1 in The Canberra Group (2001: 18).

has been written on what are the most appropriate equivalence scales. (See, for instance, Buhmann et al. [1988]; Coulter et al. [1992a; 1992b]; de Vos & Zaidi [1997]). Moreover, economies of scale are likely to vary across the income distribution, time, and place. However, it is standard practice in empirical poverty research to use the so-called modified OECD scale, which assigns a value of 1 to the household head, 0.5 to each additional adult member, and 0.3 to each child.

2.3.2.2 Multidimensional Approaches

One may want to go even further and also correct for other factors differentiating among households beyond their monetary resources and size. Furthermore, resources in other domains of life (such as health) are not freely exchangeable for monetary resources, or the resulting prices might not be appropriate for poverty analysis. If one wishes to take such additional information into account, individual well-being can no longer be described by a one-dimensional indicator. Inevitably, the measurement of poverty becomes multidimensional. In their report for the Commission on the Measurement of Economic Performance and Social Progress, Stiglitz, Sen, & Fitoussi (2009: 14) assert that, "to define what well-being means, a multidimensional definition has to be used," while Narayan (2000) shows on the basis of a large-scale survey that the global poor likewise perceive well-being and poverty as multidimensional notions.

In a multidimensional approach, individual well-being x_i is described by a vector of outcomes rather than by a single indicator. Let us assume that there are m dimensions of well-being, so that $x_i = \left[x_i^1, \ldots, x_i^j, \ldots, x_i^m\right]$ where x_i^j gives the outcome of person i in dimension j. The formula of the FGT, however, needs to be modified in order for it to capture this multidimensionality. Broadly speaking, two options present themselves.

First, one can apply the one-dimensional FGT to each of the m dimensions separately. This is a dimension-by-dimension approach leading to a dashboard or portfolio of m poverty indicators (one for each dimension). An example of such a portfolio of indicators is the set of common indicators for social inclusion agreed upon at the 2001 Laeken summit. (See Section 2.4 of this chapter and Atkinson et al. [2002]; Marlier et al. [2007]; and Daly [2010] for more details.) A portfolio has the advantage of covering a complex and multidimensional reality while offering the possibility to focus on each of the indicators in detail. Under the assumption that the outcomes in the different dimensions of well-being cannot be compared or if the aim of the analysis is to evaluate the impact of specific policies, a dashboard approach would seem appropriate (see Ravallion [2011] for a defense). However, such a dimension-by-dimension approach by definition excludes information on the correlation structure among the different indicators. The concern of whether or not the same persons fall below the poverty line in the various dimensions is a key motivation for adopting a multidimensional approach in the first place. Pogge (2002: 11) writes: "Consider institutional schemes under which half the population are poor and half have no access to higher education. We may plausibly judge such an order to be more unjust when the two groups coincide than when they are disjoint (so that no one bears both hardships)." (See Decancq [2009] and Ferreira & Lugo [2012] for similar arguments.)

In order to be able to take due account of the correlation between the indicators, an alternative approach is required that begins with the construction of a well-being index for each individual.[6] These individual well-being indices can subsequently be used as x_i variable in a FGT formula (see, for instance, Alkire & Foster [2011]). The question then becomes how to select an appropriate index of individual well-being that aggregates the various outcomes. Designing such an index echoes the eternal philosophical debate on the Aristotelian question regarding the nature of the "good life" (see also Rawls [1971: 80]). In practice, one has to make three interdependent choices in the construction of a well-being index (Decancq et al., 2009; Decancq & Lugo, 2013). The first choice concerns the *transformation* of the outcomes in the various dimensions. Especially if the outcomes involve different measurement units, they need to be transformed or standardized, to allow reasonable comparison and aggregation. The second question relates to the relative *weight* given to the different outcomes. These weights play a crucial role in determining the trade-offs implied by the well-being index. If one dimension is assigned a greater weight, for example, then a higher outcome is required in the other dimensions to compensate for a loss in the former. For reasons of agnosticism or simplicity, the weights are often set equally in empirical analyses.[7] The complex question of which dimensions to select in a multidimensional analysis is a particular case of the weighting problem. Indeed, not selecting a certain dimension is equivalent to attributing to it a weight of zero. Finally, an *aggregation* procedure needs to be agreed upon for aggregating the different standardized and weighted outcomes into a single index. Typically, the method chosen is an additive averaging procedure, which presupposes perfect substitutability among the dimensions, but alternatives with more restricted substitutability are conceivable, for example, through multiplicative averaging (as in the new version of the HDI, UNDP 2010).[8]

A rather crude but empirically attractive example of a multidimensional poverty approach is the so-called *counting approach.* (See, for instance, Atkinson [2003]; Alkire & Foster [2011]). In a counting approach, the outcomes in each dimension are collapsed to a binary scale (taking either the value 0 or 1). These binary values are then (equally) weighted and added, so that a well-being index is obtained that boils down to counting the number of dimensions in which the binary scale takes the value 1. Recent theoretical work on the counting approach has rediscovered and given substance to the old practice in the sociological literature of counting the number of deprived dimensions as a measure of the *width* of poverty (Mack & Lansley, 1985; Vranken, 2002). An example of this approach is the European indicator of material deprivation (e.g., Guio, 2009) described in detail in Box 2.2.

2.3.3 Fixing the Poverty Line

Given a particular metric of well-being, the poverty line identifies those who are to be considered as poor. Where to draw the poverty line is a matter of value judgments and, taking into account the poverty definition applied, should reflect society's views on what are acceptable and unacceptable levels of well-being.

2.3.3.1 Different Methods for Fixing the Poverty Line

There are a number of methods to determine the poverty line.[9] This subsection outlines those methods and considers their merits with respect to constructing an EU poverty measure. (See Deleeck et al. [1992: 3–5] and Atkinson et al. [2002: 83–98] for more extensive discussions.)

Administrative or statutory lines. These poverty lines are equal to the minimum income support offered under the prevailing social security or social assistance system. In some countries, the resulting thresholds might have a prima-facie legitimacy, based upon the assumption that they reflect a political consensus (or at least a majority view) on the minimum level of income acceptable in a particular society. However, the question of whether a guaranteed minimum income suffices to keep persons out of poverty cannot be answered if a statutory poverty line is applied. It is moreover difficult to argue that such country-specific thresholds can be used for cross-country comparisons, particularly in view of the practical complication that some countries do not even have a minimum guaranteed income (e.g., Van Mechelen et al., 2011). Although this approach has been used extensively in the United Kingdom (cf. Morris & Preston, 1986 and references therein) and occasionally in cross-national studies (e.g., Gustafsson & Lindblom, 1993), it has fallen into disuse for the reasons mentioned above.

Statistical lines. Under the statistical method, the poverty line is defined as a function of the underlying distribution, often a certain percentage of median or mean household equivalized income. This is the method most commonly applied in cross-national research on income poverty in the developed world, most likely because it requires no information other than microdata on household income. Statistical lines can differ in their reliance on the mean or the median, and in the setting of the particular percentage. As far as the EU poverty indicators are concerned, the median is preferred to the mean, because it is less sensitive to outliers and extreme observations, unaffected by top-bottom coding, and less sensitive to sampling error (Atkinson et al., 2002: 94). The percentage is largely arbitrarily chosen, but 40%, 50%, and 60% seem the most commonly applied thresholds. The EU headline at-risk-of-poverty indicator uses 60% of the median equivalized disposable income as a poverty line (see Box 2.1 for more details).

Subjective lines. Subjective poverty lines are based on the responses of survey participants to questions such as: "What is the minimum income with which your household could make ends meet?" While the answers to this question correlate quite strongly with income, methods have been designed to derive an estimate of the poverty line that is unbiased by this correlation (Goedhart et al., 1977; Hagenaars, 1985; Deleeck et al., 1992). Unfortunately, the resulting poverty lines vary from country to country, according to patterns that are not only difficult to explain but also unstable over time. One problem is that results are sensitive to small changes in the wording or placement of the survey questions. (Van den Bosch [2001] provides a review.) This is presumably why subjective poverty lines have fallen into disuse in the course of the past decade (Vrooman, 2009).

Budget standards. Budget standards have been used in pioneering poverty studies by Rowntree (2000 [1901]) and others. A budget standard is a specific basket of goods and services, which when priced can represent a particular standard of living for a reference household in particular circumstances and with particular characteristics (Bradshaw, 1993). In principle, the method is simple: First one draws up a list of goods and services that are deemed indispensable; then one estimates the life spans of the goods and corresponding prices; and finally one adds up the resulting amounts. In practice, however, this is of course "a ghastly chore" (Bradshaw, 1993: 236). A variety of sources of information are used in the selection of items, including other budgets, expert opinion, actual spending patterns, public opinion, and value judgments.

Box 2.1. The at-risk-of-poverty indicator

Being at-risk-of-poverty means living in a household with an equivalized net disposable household income below 60% of the national median equivalized net disposable household income. The net disposable household income is equal to the sum of the income of all household members net of taxes. More precisely, it includes cash or near-cash employee income, company cars, cash profits or losses from self-employment (including royalties), social benefits, income from rental of a property or land, regular interhousehold cash transfers received, interests, dividends, profit from capital investments in unincorporated business; minus regular taxes on wealth, regular interhousehold cash transfer paid, and tax on income and social insurance contributions.

Total net disposable household income is equivalized using the modified OECD equivalence scale. This scale attaches a weight of 1 to the first adult, a weight of 0.5 to all other household members aged 14 years and over, and a weight of 0.3 to household members under the age of 14 years. The equivalized household income is obtained by dividing total household income by the sum of the individual equivalence weights. All household members are attributed the same equivalized household income. In other words, it is assumed that the living standard of all household members is the same.

Subsequently, the median equivalent net disposable household income is estimated at the individual level for each Member State. Persons with an equivalent net disposable household income below 60% of the median are considered to be at risk of poverty.

In all countries except Ireland and the United Kingdom, the income reference period is equal to the calendar year preceding the survey year, which means that information on the composition of the household (and the equivalence scale) does not always correspond to the income information. In Ireland, the income reference period consists of the 12 months preceding the interview, whereas in the United Kingdom current income is multiplied by 52 or 12 (depending on whether it is provided as a weekly or a monthly amount). More information on this and other EU-SILC-based indicators can be found in Atkinson et al. (2002), Marlier et al. (2007), and on the Eurostat website.[32]

Budget standards have been put forward recently in various European countries. (See Storms et al. [2011] for a review.) To date, no attempt has, however, been made to define budget standards that allow comparison among countries (although Storms et al. [2011] and Storms et al. [2013] do formulate a proposal in this respect). Given that budget standards are specific to the characteristics and circumstances of the reference households, it is not self-evident to use budget standards as a poverty line for sample survey data. However, budget standards are useful for validating poverty lines derived from other methods, in particular the statistical method. For Belgium, a budget standard for 2008 turned out to be surprisingly close to 60% of median household equivalized income (Storms & Van den Bosch, 2009). It would be interesting to repeat such an exercise for other countries, in particular for the newly acceded EU Member States with lower average incomes (Goedemé & Rottiers, 2011).

Finally, the use of a multidimensional metric of well-being requires one either to set a dimension-specific poverty line (for a dimension-by-dimension approach) or to select a cut-off value of the obtained well-being indices that distinguishes poor from non-poor persons. In the counting approach, one typically selects a number of deprived dimensions as a poverty line. For the severe material deprivation index, this cut-off is four dimensions. (See Box 2.2 for more details, and Nolan & Whelan [2011a] for a critical appraisal of this choice.)

2.3.3.2 Fixing a Poverty Line for the European Union

Unlike in the case of the official U.S. measure of poverty (Orshansky, 1965, 1969; Blank, 2008), most poverty analyses for the EU define the poverty line in relative and in national terms, taking 50% or 60% of the country-specific median income as a poverty line (i.e., a statistical approach).[10] Over time, such poverty lines fluctuate as the median changes. As explained above, though, this choice is just one

Box 2.2. Severe material deprivation

Severe material deprivation is measured by an index of nine items relating to financial stress and the enforced lack of a list of durables (see Table 2.2). All persons living in a household that, at the moment of the interview, is deprived on at least four out of nine items are considered to be severely materially deprived. The list of items and the threshold are the same across all EU Member States. This indicator is currently under revision and will contain an updated list of items by 2015. Guio (2009) provides extensive background information on the current indicator and Guio et al. (2012) present an in-depth study in preparation for the new indicator of material deprivation.

Table 2.2. Items of the material deprivation indicator.

Item	The household...
1	has been in arrears on mortgage, rent payments, utility bills, hire purchase installments, or other loan payments over the last 12 months
2	does not have the capacity to afford paying for one week annual holiday away from home
3	does not have the capacity to afford a meal with meat, chicken, fish, or vegetarian equivalent every second day
4	does not have the capacity to face unexpected financial expenses equal to the at-risk-of-poverty threshold (monthly average) estimated on the basis of EU-SILC of two years ago
5	cannot afford to keep the home adequately warm
6	does not have a telephone because it cannot afford it
7	does not have a colour TV because it cannot afford it
8	does not have a washing machine because it cannot afford it
9	does not have a car because it cannot afford it

of several alternatives, and it should, therefore, be open to public scrutiny and debate (Atkinson et al., 2002; Kangas & Ritakallio, 2007). In what follows, three particularities are discussed of the standard practice in the EU of choosing a *floating, relative,* and *country-specific* poverty line, as opposed to the American approach of setting a *fixed, absolute,* and *pan-U.S.* poverty line (see also Besharov & Couch, 2012).

Floating. A poverty line that is allowed to fluctuate in real terms is called a floating poverty line. A poverty line that, on the contrary, is kept constant in real terms is a fixed poverty line anchored at a point in time, or an anchored poverty line, for short. An anchored poverty line is only adjusted over time for changes in the price level. Some circumspection is appropriate when interpreting poverty figures obtained with a floating poverty line. After all, with a floating poverty line, it is conceivable that a decrease in the well-being of all poor persons is cancelled out by a simultaneous lowering of the poverty line, which may in itself lead to a declining poverty figure.[11] On the other hand, anchored poverty lines may fail to capture possible changes in the perception of the minimum acceptable living standard in a given society, given that they are fixed at construction.

Relative. A poverty line expressed as a percentage of the median varies when the income distribution changes (hence it is not anchored and is floating by definition). Such poverty lines are commonly referred to as relative poverty lines, for obvious reasons. Alternatively, a poverty line may also be conceived as a physiological minimum for human survival, which typically does not vary with a changing income distribution. Such absolute poverty lines may fluctuate, though, with price evolutions of the items necessary to attain the physiological minimum. Ravallion (2010) characterizes poverty lines that are defined as a percentage of the median as "strongly relative," which at once implies an important drawback: a strongly relative poverty line would ultimately approximate to zero in a situation where an entire population becomes extremely poor. Zheng (1997) hints at a potentially counter-intuitive anti-poverty policy that aims at simply deleting some of the non-poor incomes around the median. Atkinson & Bourguignon (2001), therefore, propose a "weakly relative" poverty line somewhere in between the two extremes of an absolute and strongly relative poverty line. In this approach, an absolute poverty line is applied up to a certain threshold and a strongly relative one is used above that threshold. This notion has been further generalized by Ravallion & Chen (2011).[12]

Country-specific. Three different arguments have been put forward in favor of an EU-wide rather than a country-specific poverty line (see Goedemé & Rottiers [2011: 78–79]; Nolan & Whelan [2011b: 207–210]), as discussed below.

First, poverty figures on the basis of country-specific poverty lines may be adequate for distinguishing poor groups within single Member States, but they sketch only a partial picture of the variation in living conditions and poverty across the EU: The purchasing power of the poor in the less affluent Member States is generally lower than the purchasing power of the poor in the richer

EU Member States (see, for example, Lelkes et al., 2009: 23). On this basis, some authors have argued that these poverty figures are not fully comparable cross-nationally and lead to an underestimation of poverty in the less wealthy Member States (see, for example, Guio, 2005a, 2005b; Beblavy & Mizsei, 2006; Juhász, 2006: 100–101).

Second, it has been contended that the group of persons with whom living standards are compared, that is, the reference group, is of crucial importance for the measurement of poverty (or social stratification in general) and that reference groups have to a large extent Europeanized (Förster et al., 2004; Delhey & Kohler, 2006; Fahey, 2007; Whelan & Maître, 2009).[13]

A third argument for a Europeanized poverty line comes from Brandolini (2007) and Fahey (2007), who contend that, even if reference groups were not strongly Europeanized, the national at-risk-of-poverty rate would still miss an important aspect of the heterogeneity and social cohesion in the EU as well as the social dimension of European unification. Therefore, poverty should also be calculated using an EU-wide poverty line (see also Marlier et al., 2007: 153–155).[14]

2.3.4 Aggregation Beyond the Headcount

When an appropriate metric of well-being and a poverty line separating the poor from the non-poor have been selected, aggregation is required to arrive at a single measure of the extent of poverty in a society as a whole.

The headcount poverty measure H is an obvious candidate for this aggregation. It is simply the percentage of poor persons in a given society.[15] The *headcount* can be obtained by setting $\alpha = 0$ in the definition of P_α (so that $P_0 = H$). As an indicator, it is easy to interpret and communicate, and by far the most popular measure of overall poverty, but it is obviously a crude index (Watts, 1969; Sen, A., 1976). It also has some unattractive properties, especially when used as a policy target. Consider the example of a policymaker who aims at maximally reducing poverty with a limited anti-poverty budget. How should he or she best spend the available funds? Well, if the extent of poverty is expressed in terms of a headcount, then it makes sense for him to focus on the better-off poor, as this offers the best chance of lifting a maximum number of individuals out of poverty (Bourguignon & Fields, 1990). Furthermore, an unchanged headcount of people below the poverty line may conceal a sharp rise in the extent of shortfall from the poverty line.

A natural alternative is to use the income gap ratio I, which is the average normalized amount by which poor incomes fall below the poverty line.[16] One easily checks that setting $\alpha = 1$ in the definition of P_α, leads to the overall (normalized) income shortfall divided by the total population (hence $P_1 = HI$). Let us return to the example of the policymaker intending to reduce poverty with a limited antipoverty budget. Using P_1 as a poverty target, clearly it does not matter which poor the policy measures are aimed at, because overall poverty will decrease with the same amount. Conversely, a policymaker may wish to spend the available antipoverty budget on the poorest of the poor. Bourguignon & Fields (1990) show that such a policy is optimal whenever a poverty measure P_α with $\alpha > 1$ is used as a target. This is the case, for example, when α equals 2 such that the poverty gaps are weighted by the poverty gaps themselves (Foster et al., 1984, 2010). When α goes to infinity, only the poorest person matters for the measurement of poverty (reflecting a Rawlsian perspective).

In general, the parameter α may be interpreted as the extent of "poverty aversion." The larger the α, the greater the impact of the condition of the poorest of the poor on the overall measurement of poverty. Alternatively, α may be interpreted as "the elasticity of individual poverty with respect to the normalized poverty gap," so that a 1% increase in the individual poverty gap results in an α-percent increase poverty level of the individual (Foster et al., 2010: 495). One of the practical advantages of the Foster-Greer-Thorbecke class of poverty measures P_α is that the same class of measures allows the researcher to switch easily to the most appropriate perspective given the problem at hand. One can focus on the *incidence* or *prevalence* of poverty by setting $\alpha = 0$, on its *depth* by setting $\alpha = 1$, or on its *severity* by $\alpha = 2$. By now, this terminology has become the standard in the studies of international institutions such as the World Bank, so that P_α has assumed a prominent role as a class of poverty measures (Ravallion, 1994).[17]

2.3.5 Robustness and Partial Poverty Orderings

As demonstrated above, in order to be able to select the most appropriate poverty measure from the extensive toolbox available, at least three (difficult) questions need to be answered. What is the appropriate metric of well-being? Where to draw the poverty line? And how to aggregate poverty figures to society level? The answers to these questions depend to a large extent on value judgments regarding the notion of poverty itself. Hence, it is unlikely that unanimity could ever be reached on these issues. Furthermore, even when value judgments are shared, additional problems can arise due to a lack of accurate data. As mentioned before, the fact that the epithet "at-risk-of" has been added to the headline poverty measures in the EU may be seen to reflect these difficulties.

Rather than look for unequivocal answers to the three aforementioned questions, one can look for ranges of reasonable answers and empirical indications of the evolution of poverty that are robust for all choices within the selected range (as we do in Section 2.6 of this chapter). The following (hypothetical) example clarifies this approach. Four co-authors may disagree on where exactly to set the poverty line, yet agree that it should be set somewhere between 40% and 70% of median disposable income. To resolve their dispute, they might decide to adopt an agnostic perspective and compute poverty for any poverty line within this range. However, agnosticism comes at a price. Consider the unfortunate case where poverty has increased for all poverty lines up to 64% of median disposable income, but decreased for all higher poverty lines.[18] Without narrowing the range of relevant poverty lines (say, to between 57% and 63%), the four co-authors will not be able to unambiguously ascertain whether poverty has increased or decreased.

To allow for such disagreements, partial poverty orderings may be applied. Partial poverty orderings require unanimous poverty rankings for a class of poverty measures or a range of poverty lines (see Zheng, 2000, for a survey). As illustrated above, they cannot order any pair of societies, but where they can, they provide strong results (see also Sen, 2009) on the usefulness of partial orderings in welfare economics in general).[19]

Furthermore, one may want to remain agnostic on the metric of well-being. In several EU Member States, a consistent poverty approach has been introduced whereby individuals are said to be consistently poor only if they are both income-poor *and* poor according to the material deprivation index (Förster, 2005; Nolan & Whelan, 2011b).[20] The four co-authors, who furthermore disagree on the most appropriate metric of well-being, will agree that consistently poor persons should be considered to be poor. They will also agree that a person who is non-poor according to both criteria is not poor. They may well disagree, however, on the status of individuals who are poor according to one criteria but not the other.

The consistent poverty approach requires that both conditions are fulfilled (hence it is a so-called "intersection" approach to multidimensional poverty; see Duclos et al. [2006]). In contrast, the Europe 2020 procedure reflects a "union" approach, where a person is considered poor or socially excluded if he is poor or socially excluded according to at least one of the three criteria (i.e., being income poor, materially deprived, and/or belonging to a jobless household). The Europe 2020 poverty indicators and their relation to other poverty measures used in this book are the topic of the next section.

2.4 POVERTY MEASUREMENT IN THE EUROPEAN UNION: AN OVERVIEW

The object of this section is to show how the set of indicators of poverty and social exclusion used in the EU's social strategy fit into the poverty measurement framework discussed in the previous section. For an in-depth discussion of the EU's involvement in the struggle against poverty, see Marlier et al. (2007) and Frazer et al. (2010).

2.4.1 The European Social Strategy and Poverty Measurement

Though the EU has shown an interest in the living standards of its citizens from its inception, work on poverty indicators was given a boost at the Lisbon European Council of March 2000, where the Member States established the

Social Inclusion Process with the aim of making decisive inroads into eradicating poverty by 2010. A novel method of governance, known as the Open Method of Coordination (OMC), which involves common objectives to be achieved by national policies was introduced. In assessing Member States' progress towards the common objectives, comparable and robust indicators were deemed to be of key importance. A first set of eighteen such indicators on poverty and social exclusion was adopted at the Laeken European Council in December 2001 (hence the often-used term "Laeken indicators"). It is effectively a portfolio of indicators designed in accordance with a number of methodological principles, as formulated by Atkinson et al. (2002). Important considerations were the comparability among Member States and the balance and transparency of the total portfolio. In subsequent years, the portfolio was further extended to include a broad range of indicators covering various aspects of social protection and social inclusion. The EU-SILC data were created specifically as an information source for compiling comparable indicators on social cohesion.[21] In June 2010, the European Council went one step further and defined a specific target in its Europe 2020 strategy: "20 million less [sic] people should be at risk of poverty and exclusion according to three indicators (at-risk-of poverty; material deprivation; jobless household), leaving Member States free to set their national targets on the basis of the most appropriate indicators, taking into account their national circumstances and priorities" (European Council, 2010: 12).

Let us take a closer look at some key measures of poverty and social exclusion as they stood in 2009 (European Commission, 2009). In line with the framework defined above, for each measure a metric of well-being[22], a poverty line, and a method of aggregation are specified. As Table 2.3 shows, the metric of well-being varies substantially. Many measures are defined in terms of disadvantage and, in some cases (e.g., duration of unemployment), it is not straightforward to define a corresponding metric of well-being. Although the choice of indicators is constrained by data availability, it is possible to identify the domains that are regarded as important in respect to poverty and social exclusion: income, material living standard, education, employment, and medical care. No attempt is made to create a composite or multidimensional index of poverty or social exclusion summarizing all indicators. Marlier et al. (2007: 182–185) state that this is to encourage countries to pursue balanced policies aimed at improving their performances in all domains, rather than to concentrate on an opaque overall score (see also Atkinson, 2010, for a discussion). Interestingly, the aggregation method used is nearly always a headcount (FGT with α set at 0), despite the drawbacks of this measure. Presumably the easy interpretability of a headcount overrides other concerns. As an indicator of the poverty gap, the median normalized poverty gap is used. This measure does not belong to the class of FGT poverty measures and is not additively decomposable, but it has the advantage of being more robust to outliers.

Table 2.3. Key measures of poverty: metric of well-being, poverty line, and aggregation.

Measure	Metric of well-being (x_i)	Poverty line (z)	Aggregation
At-risk-of poverty rate (AROP)	Equivalized disposable household income	60% of median household income	FGT ($\alpha = 0$)
Relative median at-risk-of-poverty risk gap	Equivalized disposable household income	60% of median household income	Median poverty gap
Early school-leavers	Educational level	Having only lower secondary education or less	FGT ($\alpha = 0$)
Long-term unemployment rate	Duration of unemployment (reverse)	≥ 12 months	FGT ($\alpha = 0$)
People living in jobless households	Share of eligible persons with paid job in households	= 0	FGT ($\alpha = 0$)
Self-reported unmet need for medical care	Receiving medical care when needed (binary)	n.a.	FGT ($\alpha = 0$)
At-risk-of-poverty rate anchored at a fixed moment in time	Equivalized disposable household income	60% of median household income in 2005	FGT ($\alpha = 0$)
In-work at-risk-of-poverty rate	Equivalized disposable household income	60% of median household income	FGT ($\alpha = 0$)
Persistent at-risk-of-poverty rate	Equivalized disposable household income	60% of median income in 2005 in current year and two of the three preceding years	FGT ($\alpha = 0$)
Employment gap of immigrants	Employment (binary)	n.a.	FGT ($\alpha = 0$), difference between immigrants and nonimmigrants
Material deprivation rate	Number of items lacking (i.e., not able to afford if not possessed) out of nine	≥ 3	FGT ($\alpha = 0$)

2.5 DATA FOR POVERTY MEASUREMENT IN THE EUROPEAN UNION

There are various cross-national comparative surveys providing data for studying poverty and social exclusion in the EU, such as the Survey of Health, Ageing and Retirement in Europe (SHARE); the European Quality of Life Surveys

(EQLS); and the European Social Survey (ESS).[23] However, these surveys either cover only part of the population (SHARE), or they have a small sample size (EQLS), or they contain only limited information on income and living conditions (ESS). Consequently, after its launch in 2004, EU-SILC quickly became the EU reference source for microdata on income and living conditions. Many indicators designed to monitor poverty and social exclusion in the EU are based on EU-SILC (e.g., European Commission, 2006; Marlier et al., 2007).

This section assesses EU-SILC as a data set for measuring poverty in the European Union and, for reasons explained below, the German SOEP data set as complementary data source for Germany.

2.5.1 EU Statistics on Income and Living Conditions (EU-SILC)

The reference population of EU-SILC consists of private households residing in the participating countries at the moment of selection.[24] Currently 32 countries are included in the EU-SILC data set, namely all 28 EU Member States plus the four non-EU members Iceland, Norway, Switzerland, and Turkey. However, some countries are not represented for all years in the User Database (UDB).

In 2004, EU-SILC replaced the European Community Household Panel (ECHP) as the common European source for data on income and social inclusion. ECHP ran as a long-term panel structure in 14 European Member States over the eight-year period from 1994 to 2001. The persistence of quality problems, such as low response rates, steady attrition rates, incomplete geographical coverage, and poor timeliness, led to its termination in 2001. To accommodate these quality problems, EU-SILC pays additional attention to the sample design, internationally harmonized income definitions, and EU-wide coverage (Clemenceau & Museux, 2007).

Common guidelines for EU-SILC ensure output harmonization of the survey results (see, for example, Eurostat, 2010b). Within these guidelines, national statistics offices have a certain degree of discretion to implement the guidelines according to the national conditions. Although basic rules on definitions, time reference, minimum effective sample sizes, etc. are legally binding, considerable differences remain among participating countries in terms of sample design, data collection, and postcollection processing (e.g., Eurostat, 2011), with varying impact on the comparability of the results. These aspects are discussed consecutively.

Sample design. With respect to sample design, the common guidelines prescribe a nationally representative probability sample of the population residing in private households within the country. The guidelines on sample design have been implemented differently in the various countries. In some, the sample consists of a simple random selection of households, individuals, or dwellings/addresses. In others, a more complicated procedure is followed, which in the first stage involves the random selection of clusters (e.g., communities or census areas) from which households are subsequently drawn in the second or third stage. (See the annex in Goedemé [2010] for more details.)[25]

Data collection. Generally, data are collected by means of face-to-face personal interviews. At the same time, the survey design is sufficiently flexible to allow the use of (previously existing) national sources. In a number of countries, the national statistics office opted for reasons of reliability to base many income variables on administrative data rather than on survey data, because this approach avoids the issue of respondents' accuracy in reporting detailed retrospective information. Recently, Lohmann's (2011) research on the relationships among employment, earnings, and poverty has shown that this difference in data collection method may substantially affect estimates based on EU-SILC.

Postcollection processing. Unit nonresponse rates for EU-SILC vary substantially among countries, ranging from 5% in Romania to 45% in Denmark (Eurostat, 2010a). The high nonresponse rates in several countries may compromise data representativeness and thus comparability among countries. Correcting for the resulting potential biases then becomes especially important. Countries have, however, employed different models to deal with the problem of unit and item nonresponse, involving respectively reweighting and imputation (Verma & Betti, 2010; Wolff et al., 2010), which adds to the complexity of intercountry comparison. Furthermore, countries also vary substantially in terms of the manner in which negative and extreme values are treated (Verma & Betti, 2010). In view of this problem, top-bottom coding may be used to mitigate its impact on comparability (see also Section 2.6). Unfortunately, the variables concerning response status of households and individuals are not available to researchers. This rules out the possibility of testing for patterns of nonresponse across the population.

2.5.2 German Socio-Economic Panel (G-SOEP)

For Germany, notable problems arose from the fact that until 2007, at least part of the sample was selected by quota sampling instead of representative probability sampling, preventing the computation of probability sample weights and compromising representativeness, particularly of certain (smaller) population groups (Hauser, 2008; Frick & Krell, 2011). In the context of the present book, whenever applicable and possible, use is made of the German Socio-Economic Panel (G-SOEP) as a second data set to test the sensitivity of the empirical results.

The G-SOEP is an ongoing household panel survey, conducted annually since 1984 and representing the resident population of Germany with, as of 2006, a total of eight subsamples (Wagner et al., 2007). The G-SOEP data used in this book are constructed in such a way that they correspond as closely as possible to Eurostat's recommendations for the EU-SILC data, in order to ensure international comparability in terms of structure (a representative cross-sectional data set for each survey year), the population covered (private households), weighting factors (post-stratified household inverse probability weights), accounting period (previous calendar year), and content of the common variables analyzed (in particular, total disposable income). Having said this, it was impossible to account for all differences between the two surveys with a potential impact on comparability, for example, with regard to postcollection processing (different methods are employed to deal with extreme values, negative incomes, partial unit nonresponse, item nonresponse, etc.) and variable coverage (the G-SOEP data set contains no comparable indicators on material deprivation, for instance).

2.6 AN ILLUSTRATION: POVERTY TRENDS IN THE EUROPEAN UNION BETWEEN 2005 AND 2009

The aim of the analysis presented in this final section is to illustrate the empirical impact of alternative choices with regard to the measurement of poverty (in terms of metric of well-being, poverty line, and sensitivity to the distribution among the poor) on the observed evolution of poverty in the EU between 2005 and 2009. We deviate from other chapters in this book in two important ways. First of all, our focus is on the entire population, including elderly persons. Second, we evaluate the evolution between EU-SILC 2005 and EU-SILC 2009, instead of EU-SILC 2008. We do so, because for most countries this results in a comparison of two independent samples. Because EU-SILC has a four-year rotational panel design in most countries, it is important to take the covariance between samples into account when comparing EU-SILC samples that differ less than five years. Because we have no access to the necessary sample design variables for calculating the covariance (Goedemé, 2012), we opted for comparing EU-SILC 2009 and EU-SILC 2005 to be sure that we are able to distinguish between statistically significant and nonsignificant changes. A first estimation of standard error of year-to-year changes for several central EU-SILC indicators can be found in Berger et al. (2012).

The initial focus is on poverty in the EU as a whole (excluding Bulgaria, Malta, and Romania from the set); subsequently, attention is paid to individual EU Member States. For more elaborate discussions of European poverty trends and what drives them, the reader is referred to the other chapters in this book, as well as to Ward et al. (2009), Atkinson & Marlier (2010), and Notten and de Neubourg (2011).

2.6.1 Poverty in the European Union

Use is made of the two most commonly applied *metrics of well-being*, namely equivalized household disposable income (using the modified OECD equivalence scales) and a counting measure based on an index of nine deprivation items (listed in Box 2.2).[26] The disposable income concept used in the analyses corresponds to the income concept employed in official Eurostat statistics. This diverges slightly from that proposed in the Canberra Group recommendations outlined in Section 3.2.1. First, it does not take account of imputed rent for owner-occupied dwellings and the value of home production.[27] Finally, the extent to which fringe benefits are recorded in the EU-SILC data varies among countries. Additionally, disposable incomes are—in contrast to standard Eurostat practice—top-bottom coded.[28] This procedure reduces the effect of the various treatments of negative incomes across the EU. (See Verma & Betti [2010], for further details.) In order to take due account of relative price differences among countries and differences in exchange rates, income in national currencies is divided by Eurostat's purchasing power parities for final household consumption (see Van Mechelen et al., 2011: 36–37;OECD, 2006).

For the poverty measures based on disposable income, an exploration is made of a range of country-specific *poverty lines* around the standard choice of 60% of the country-specific median disposable income (40%–70% of the country-specific median) and a range of EU-wide poverty lines (40%–70% of the European median). A sensitivity analysis is performed for the threshold for material deprivation on a scale from 7 to 1 (i.e., a person is considered to be deprived if deprived on at least seven items, on at least six items, and so on).

For each case, the three most commonly used *FGT indices* are considered, namely, $\alpha = 0; 1$ and 2. This yields nine alternative comparisons, as shown in Table 2.4, together with the main finding on poverty trends between 2005 and 2009. Because EU-SILC is based on a sample, 95% confidence intervals are estimated and reported in the figures. Maximum account is taken of the sample design and weighting schemes. (See Goedemé [2013] for a full discussion and illustration.)[29]

Proceeding row-by-row, first a comparison is made of the results for the three FGT measures for the metrics of well-being based on disposable income combined with a country-specific poverty line. Each figure consists of three panels showing the 95% confidence intervals for the FGT(0), FGT(1), and FGT(2) for both years. These figures are so-called "poverty incidence curves" as introduced by Ravallion & Bidani (1994). The horizontal axis represents alternative choices for the poverty line, whereas the FGT value can be read from the vertical axis.

In the first row of Table 2.4 we adhere to the official at-risk-of-poverty indicator, which measures country-specific poverty by a headcount using a poverty line defined as a percentage of the country-specific median income and measures European poverty by the population weighted average. As can be seen from the top panel of Figure 2.1, no substantial changes are found between 2005 and 2009.[30] About 16% of the individuals are poor, which amounts to nearly 80 million people, roughly equivalent to the population of Germany. About 5% of the EU population is to be considered poor with a poverty line at 40% of the median. For reasons explained above, we did the same exercise replacing the

Table 2.4. The evolution of poverty in the EU, an overview (EU-SILC 2005–2009).

Metric of well-being	Poverty line	FGT(0)	FGT(1)	FGT(2)
Equivalized household disposable Income	40%–70% of country-specific median income	Figure 6a =	Figure 6b =	Figure 6c =
	40%–70% of EU median income	Figure 7a ↓	Figure 7b ↓	Figure 7c ↓
Deprivation index	1–7	Figure 8a ↓	Figure 8b ↓	Figure 8c ↓

Note: In the case of the last two rows, for all examined poverty lines, changes between 2005 and 2009 are significantly different from zero with more than 99.99% confidence. In the case of the first row, no single change is found to be statistically significant with at least 85% confidence (two-sided test).
Source: EU-SILC User Database 2005, 2009; authors' calculations.

German EU-SILC data with G-SOEP data. To some extent, the poverty standstill observed between 2005 and 2008 is driven by German data. If G-SOEP data are included in the analysis, a slight but significant decrease of about half a percentage point is observed for all levels of the poverty line in the case of FGT(0), and even smaller decreases are observed for higher levels of the poverty line in the cases of FGT(1) and FGT(2).

The picture is very different if one analyzes income poverty with an EU-wide poverty line, corresponding to the second row of Table 2.4, as shown in Figure 2.2. Poverty is then found to have substantially declined between 2005 and 2009, and this is especially so at lower levels of the poverty line for the headcount FGT(0), whereas this evolution is more obvious at higher levels of the poverty threshold in the case of the squared poverty gap ratio FGT(2). For the poverty line set at 60% of the EU-wide median income, the headcount dropped from 23% of European citizens in 2005 to around 21% in 2009 (a decrease of about 10 million persons in poverty, roughly the population of Belgium).

Similarly, if one takes a perspective based on material deprivation (the third row of Table 2.4), the poverty headcount dropped from over 17% to around 15% of EU citizens using at least three items as a threshold. (See Figure 2.3.) Also in the case of FGT(1) and FGT(2) substantial decreases in material deprivation can be observed. As can be seen from the figure, only a very small proportion of the EU population is estimated to be deprived on seven or more items.

2.6.2 Poverty in the Individual Member States

Even though the observed changes for the EU as a whole are remarkable, they mask even larger fluctuations within individual Member States. For this reason, a detailed look is taken at the EU Member States for the FGT(0) measure, which corresponds to the measurement choices summarized in the first column of

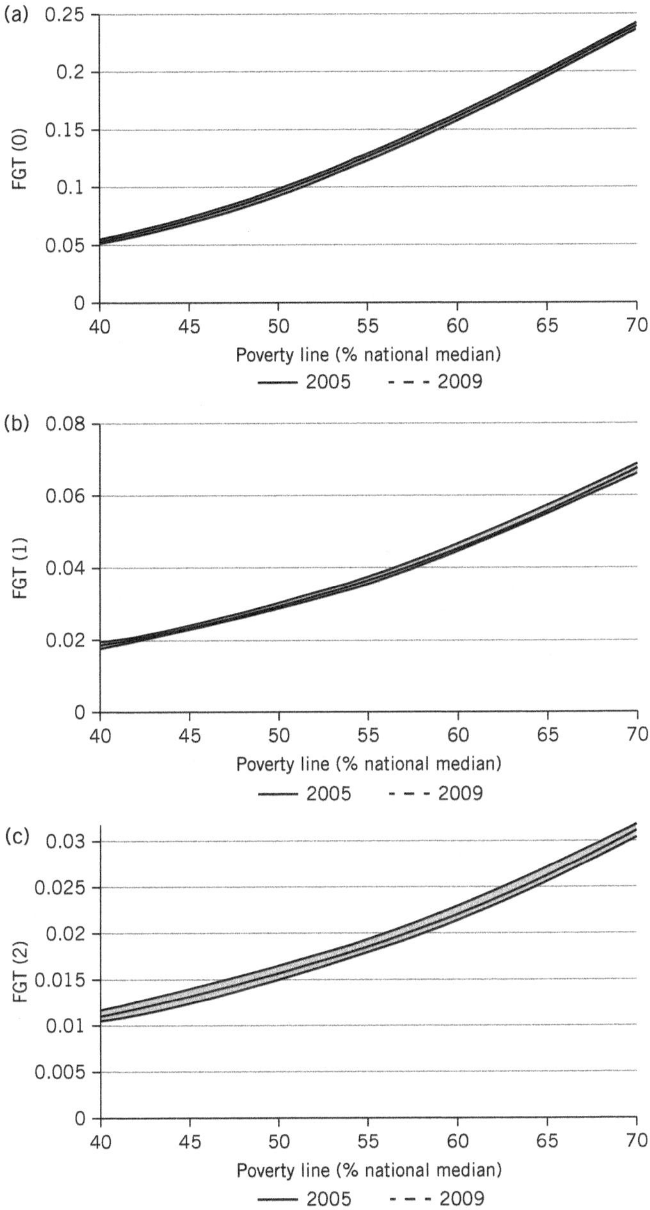

Figure 2.1. Poverty trends in the European Union, EU-SILC 2005–2009 with the poverty threshold expressed as a percentage of the national median income. *Source*: EU-SILC 2005 and 2009 User Database, Eurostat (PPPs), authors' calculations. *Notes*: EU27 minus Bulgaria, Malta, and Romania. Area shaded in grey represents 95% confidence intervals. Standard errors take as much as possible account of the sample design (cf. Goedemé, 2013) and the fact that poverty line has been estimated on the basis of the data (Araar & Duclos, 2007).

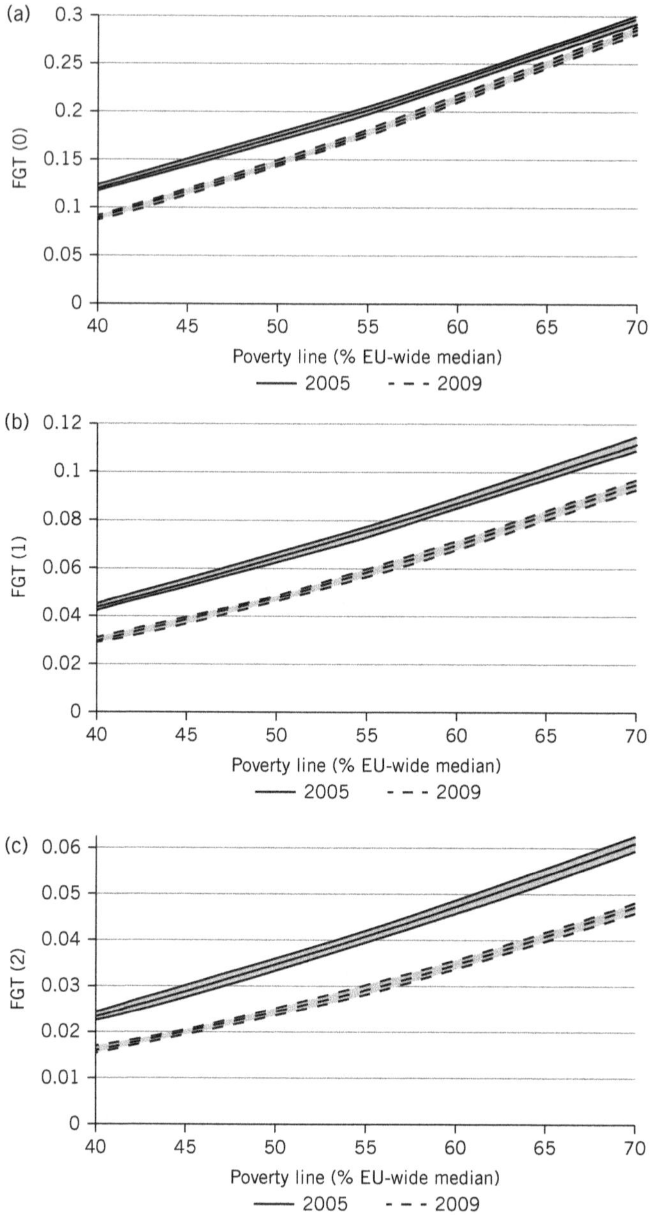

Figure 2.2. Poverty trends in the European Union, EU-SILC 2005–2009 with the poverty threshold expressed as a percentage of the EU-wide median income. *Source*: EU-SILC 2005 and 2009 User Database, Eurostat (PPPs), authors' calculations. *Notes*: EU27 minus Bulgaria, Malta, and Romania. Area shaded in grey represents 95% confidence intervals. Standard errors take as much as possible account of the sample design (cf. Goedemé, 2013) and the fact that poverty line has been estimated on the basis of the data (Araar & Duclos, 2007).

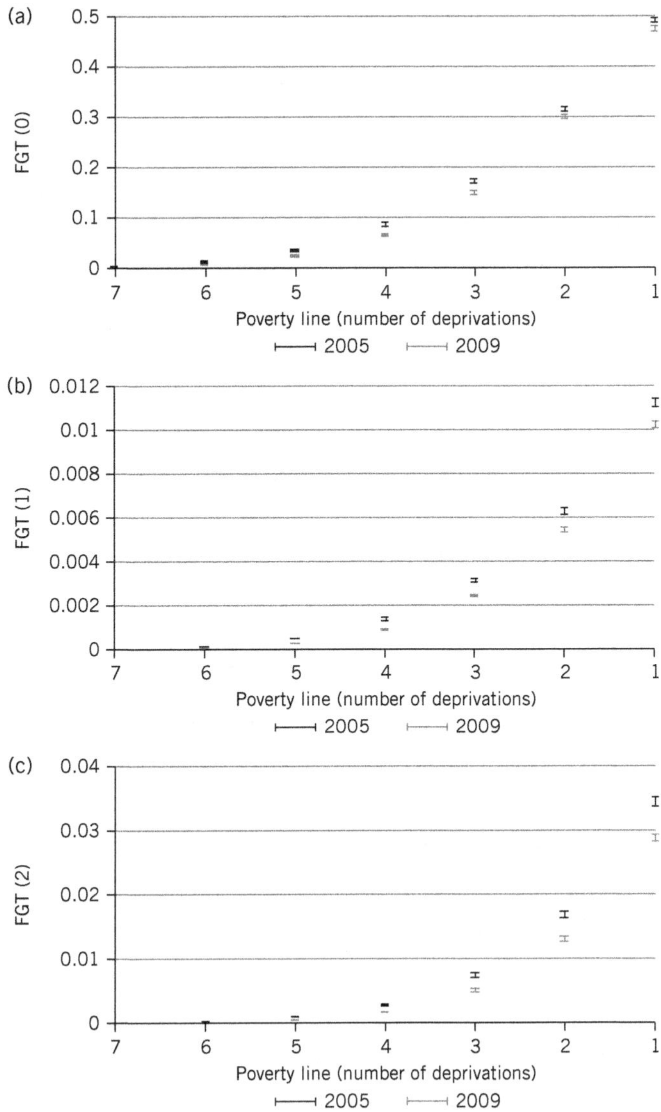

Figure 2.3. The evolution of material deprivation in the European Union, EU-SILC 2005–2009. *Source*: EU-SILC 2005 and 2009 User Database, authors' calculations. *Notes*: FGT(1) and FGT(2) not normalized. EU27 minus Bulgaria, Malta, and Romania. 95% confidence intervals, estimated taking account of sample design (cf. Goedemé, 2013).

Table 2.4). Figure 2.4 represents the country-specific evolution of the poverty headcount between 2005 and 2009 for respectively the official at-risk-of-poverty indicator, the income poverty indicator with an EU-wide poverty line, and the indicator of material deprivation. The poverty line corresponds to respectively 60% of country-specific median income, 60% of the EU-wide median income

(German EU-SILC data) and at least three out of nine items. As it turns out, the type of indicator (income poverty vs. deprivation) and the kind of poverty line applied (country-specific or EU-wide) makes an even bigger difference than was the case in Figures 2.1, 2.2, and 2.3.

Let us again begin with the official poverty measure with poverty lines defined as a percentage of country-specific median income (Figure 2.4a). The difference between the country with the lowest headcount (9% in the Czech Republic) and that with the highest (26% in Latvia) is relatively small. Changes seem to follow no specific pattern. Percentage-point changes in the at-risk-of-poverty rate are substantial in Latvia (+6), Sweden (+4), Poland (−4) and Ireland (−4). Smaller

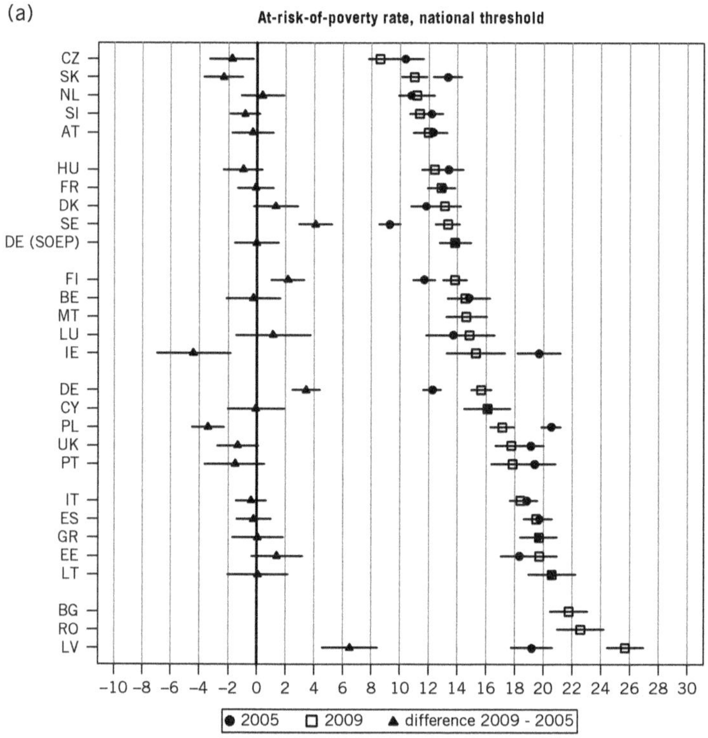

Figure 2.4. FGT(0) of the at-risk-of-poverty indicator with the poverty line set at 60% of the national median equivalized net disposable household income (a); of a similar indicator with the poverty line set at 60% the EU-wide median equivalized net disposable household income (b); and of the EU indicator of material deprivation with the poverty line set at three out of nine deprivation items (c); EU-SILC 2005 and 2009 compared. *Source*: EU-SILC 2005 and 2009 User Database, G-SOEP, Eurostat (PPPs), authors' calculations. *Notes:* Countries sorted by EU-SILC 2009 estimates. 95% confidence take as much as possible account of the sample design (cf. Goedemé, 2013) and the fact that the poverty line has been estimated on the basis of the sample (see Araar & Duclos, 2007). Estimates for Bulgaria, Malta, and Romania in panel (c) are based on an EU-wide poverty threshold including all EU27 countries. In order to maximize cross-temporary consistency, for the other countries the threshold is estimated excluding the latter three countries. In the case of DE(SOEP), the EU-wide threshold has been estimated including G-SOEP instead of EU-SILC data for Germany.

(b)

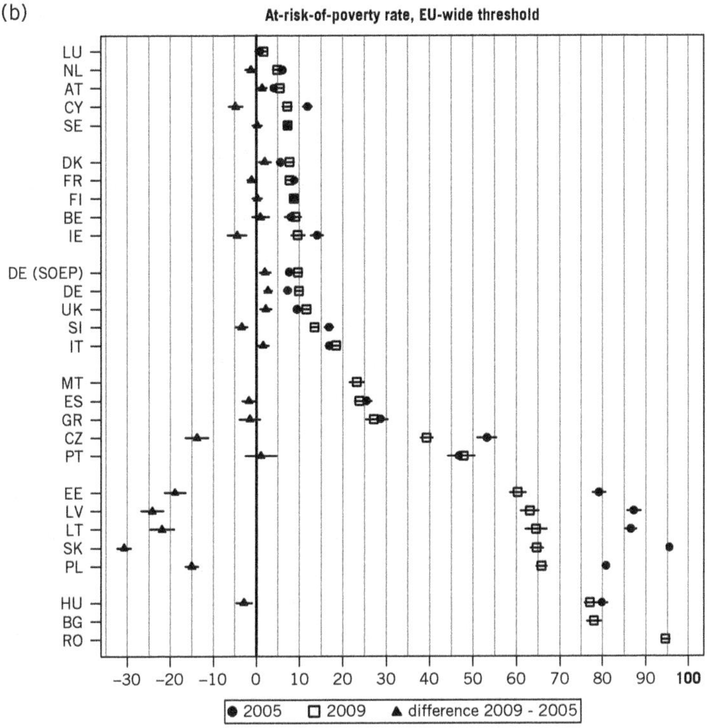

(c)

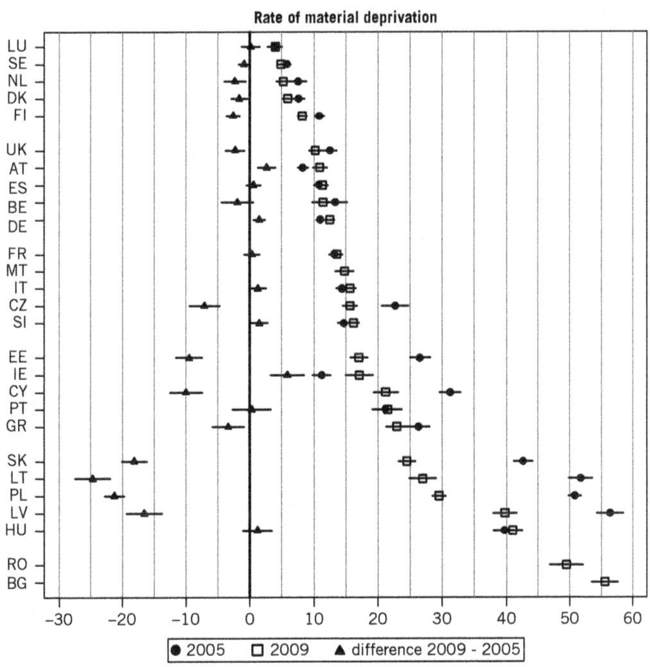

Figure 2.4 (Continued)

changes are observed in Finland (+2), the Czech Republic (−2) and Slovakia (−2). In the other countries, changes are not statistically significant at the 95% confidence level. The increase observed with German EU-SILC data is not corroborated when using the G-SOEP data.

Again, the picture changes if one applies an EU-wide poverty line (Figure 2.4b), which results in a larger cross-national variation in the poverty headcount. In the poorest EU Member States, it exceeds levels of 50%, which is much higher than the headcount in the richest Member States (under 10%). In just four years, the poverty headcount decreased by between 10 and 30 percentage points in the poorest Eastern European EU Member States, who joined the EU in 2004, with Hungary being an important exception. By contrast, in the richest Member States, the poverty headcount did not decline by much; in some cases, it actually increased slightly. As can be seen from Figure 2.4c, results obtained with an EU-wide poverty line are similar to those relating to the indicator of material deprivation, which also uses a single poverty line for all EU Member States, though the observed differences among countries are somewhat smaller.

Finally, the question arises whether the three indicators point in the same direction for all the individual countries. In a quarter of the Member States under consideration, this is indeed found to be the case. For instance, in the Czech Republic, Slovakia, and Poland, all three indicators consistently point to a significant decrease in the poverty headcount. In seven countries, there is agreement only for the two indicators with an EU-wide poverty threshold. Remarkably, only in Latvia are substantial decreases in financial poverty with an EU-wide threshold and decreases in deprivation combined with considerable increases of the at-risk-of-poverty indicator. Finally, it is noteworthy to mention that in Ireland, substantial increases in material deprivation are accompanied by substantial decreases in the income-based indicators.

These contradictory trends may be attributable to the fact that the deprivation indicator more readily captures the impact of the economic crisis than income does, given that the latter concerns the income for the year preceding the time of the interview.

In sum, for our analysis of the evolution of EU poverty it is clear that the choice of the metric of well-being, the placement of the poverty line, and the degree of sensitivity to the distribution among the poorest are not merely theoretical concerns, but that they also matter empirically.[31] In particular, the findings show that the chosen metric of well-being and the setting of the poverty line (country-specific or EU-wide) lead to substantially different conclusions.

2.7 CONCLUSION

The focus in this chapter is on the measurement of poverty in the European Union. The starting-point is a widely accepted definition of poverty in the EU context. The class of FGT poverty measures offers a powerful and flexible toolbox for measuring poverty. Three decisions need to be made in order to be able to measure poverty. These relate to the determination of the most appropriate metric of well-being x_i, the setting of the poverty line z, and the sensitivity to the distribution among the poor α. All three decisions involve value judgments with regard to the notion of poverty, implying that some disagreement among individuals is inevitable.

The famous at-risk-of-poverty measure reflects a particular answer to the three aforementioned questions. Although the official at-risk-of-poverty measure is easy to interpret and communicate, it should be used with care. As a policy target, the at-risk-of-poverty measure provides incentives to focus on the richest among the poor. Moreover, poverty measured by at-risk-of-poverty can decrease in a situation where a deterioration in living standards specifically affects the median of the distribution. Rather than relying on a single poverty indicator, one should apply a broad portfolio of poverty measures including robustness and sensitivity checks (Atkinson et al., 2002).

Some progress has been made recently in the literature on poverty measurement by the introduction of a more encompassing definition of well-being through the application of multidimensional techniques. More sophisticated approaches have been developed for fixing a poverty line, such as the budget standard method; and increased computational power has resulted in more reliable assessment of the statistical precision of results obtained. However, the quality of a poverty analysis obviously depends crucially on the quality of the underlying data. Further improvements of EU-SILC, such as broadening the portfolio of indicators of human well-being (expenditures, objective health characteristics, subjective well-being, and life satisfaction), larger sample sizes, and more precise information on the sampling procedure can only improve the measurement and our understanding of the nature of European poverty.

ACKNOWLEDGEMENTS

We thank Bea Cantillon, Vincent Corluy, Alessio Fusco, Sarah Marchal, Tim Van Rie, Frank Vandenbroucke, Stephen Windross, and participants of the GINI workshop in Antwerp (November 14–15, 2011) for valuable and detailed comments on an early version of this chapter. Of course, we are solely responsible for any remaining errors or shortcomings.

NOTES

1 Traditionally, this issue is referred to as the "relativity" of poverty. There have been heated discussions in the literature whether poverty is indeed relative. See, for instance the exchange between Amartya Sen and Peter Townsend in *Oxford Economic Papers* in 1985 (Sen, 1983, 1985b; Townsend, 1985).

2 See Foster (1984), Seidl (1988), and Zheng (1997) for more comprehensive surveys on the measurement of poverty.

3 An additive decomposable poverty measure increases when ceteris paribus the poverty in a subgroup of the population increases (the larger the population share, the larger the impact). This is a desirable property for a measure of European poverty. Indeed, it is preferable that a European poverty measure should increase with an increase in poverty in any Member State. However, additive decomposability comes at a price: additive decomposable measures are blind for some of the social aspects of poverty, such as considerations about the rank of an individual in the society. (See Bosmans [2011] for an overview on an alternative class of rank-dependent poverty measures.)

4 A number of studies assess the effects of opting for monthly or annual income reference periods, with mixed evidence. Böheim and Jenkins (2006) find little effect of the income reference period on accuracy, while the monthly measure outperforms the yearly income concept according to Cantillon et al. (2003).

5 When in-kind incomes are included in the income concept, the principle of equivalence scales should also be applied to this dimension, in order to correct for differing needs in, for example, health care and education. (See Chapter 6 in this book.)

6 Such an approach is implicit in the multidimensional analyses by Tsui (2002), Bourguignon and Chakravarty (2003), Maasoumi and Lugo (2008), Alkire and Foster (2011), and the references therein. Thorbecke (2008) provides a survey.

7 Decancq and Lugo (2013) survey various approaches to selecting an appropriate weighting scheme, classifying them as either data-driven, normative, or hybrid. Decancq et al. (2013) present an empirical application based on Flemish data where equal weighting receives little support in a simulated voting procedure on alternative weighting schemes among affected individuals.

8 The outcomes in a multidimensional poverty analysis are typically measures of functionings such as indices of living standards, health, and level of education. However, one can apply the same multidimensional toolbox to measure chronic poverty if the outcomes are well-being levels at various points in time (Foster, 2009).

9 For more detailed information, see the surveys by Callan and Nolan (1991), Ravallion (1994), Van den Bosch (2001), and Vrooman (2009).

10 See, among others, Zaidi and de Vos (2001); Atkinson et al. (2002); European Commission (2002, 2007, 2009); Marlier et al. (2007); OECD (2008); Bäckman (2009); European Commission, 2009. Notten and de Neubourg (2011) provide a comparison of the two approaches for the U.S. and 15 EU Member States.

11 This was the case, for example, in Finland during the early 1990s: The economic crisis led to a decrease in the floating poverty line and hence poverty supposedly decreased notwithstanding the decline in living standard at the bottom end of the income distribution (cf. Halleröd & Heikkilä, 1999;

Ministry of Social Affairs and Health, 1999). In a number of countries, most notably Estonia and Latvia, a similar mechanism seems to have been at play during the current economic crisis (Eurostat, on line database, last accessed December 20, 2011).

12 Recent questionnaire surveys eliciting perception of poverty have shown relativist concerns to be widespread among respondents, particularly in coexistence with absolutist concerns (Corazzini et al., 2011).

13 Goedemé and Rottiers (2011), stress however that a distinction should be made between reference groups used for evaluating one's own living standard (i.e., privately oriented reference groups), and reference groups used for defining what should be the minimum acceptable living standard for society at large (i.e., publicly oriented reference groups). Even if the latter seem more relevant, the existing literature focuses on the former privately oriented references groups. The Europeanization of the publicly oriented reference groups is still an open question for further research.

14 A poverty index based on an EU-wide poverty line satisfies the property of *subgroup anonymity*. This means that moving a person between subgroups (i.e., countries) with no change of well-being does not affect overall poverty (Ravallion, 2008). Again, whether or not this is an attractive property for a poverty measure is a matter of debate.

15 The headcount (and all other measures belonging to P_α) is a so-called *replication invariant* poverty measure. Cloning all persons in a society (poor and non-poor) would not affect the extent of poverty in that society. This property allows a meaningful comparison of poverty across societies with different population sizes. Yet, alternatives have been proposed, focusing on the number of poor persons in the society rather than the percentage (Subramanian, 2002).

16 I is defined here in terms of *incomes*. It is obvious that the definition can be applied irrespective the chosen metric of well-being.

17 An alternative graphical representation of the incidence, intensity, and inequality dimensions of aggregate poverty is provided by the so-called *Three* Is of Poverty (TIP) curve (Jenkins & Lambert, 1997).

18 This situation is quite inconvenient for the co-authors, in particular if a policymaker expects them to come up with an unequivocal answer regarding the evolution of poverty.

19 In a series of papers, Foster and Shorrocks (1991, 1988) uncover a powerful link between a unanimous agreement between the class of P_α's for a given α and any poverty line and stochastic dominance of the $\alpha+1$'th order. Furthermore, Atkinson (1987) shows that reaching unanimous agreement for all additive separable poverty measures (which is a much wider class than the FGTs) for all poverty lines is equivalent to second-order stochastic dominance. See Duclos et al. (2006) for a generalization to the multidimensional case.

20 Berthoud and Bryan (2011) study the relationship between households' incomes and deprivation scores over time using longitudinal data for the UK.

21 For a more detailed treatment of the EU-SILC data set, see Section 2.5.

22 Most indicators are in fact defined in terms of disadvantage. Where possible, the corresponding metric of well-being is specified; where not, this is indicated by the word "reverse" in brackets.

23 For more information, see respectively http://share-project.org; http://www.eurofound.europa.eu/surveys/eqls/ and http://www.europeansocialsurvey.org/.

24 It should be noted that people residing in institutions are excluded. This may cause some bias, especially when studying poverty among the elderly (Peeters et al., 2011).

25 Additionally, EU-SILC has an important panel component, in the form of a four-year rotational panel design. This means that, every year, a quarter of the sample is replaced with a new representative sample of households. In other words, every household can participate for a maximum of four consecutive years. Exceptions to this Eurostat recommendation are France and Norway, where the panel duration is nine, respectively eight, years, and Luxembourg, where a pure panel is supplemented annually with a new, additional sample (Wolff et al., 2010: 41).

26 For the income-based indicators, income generally refers to the previous calendar year, whereas most of the deprivation items refer to the situation in the survey year. In some countries, the impact of the financial crisis was already noticeable in 2009: There were increases in the number of deprived households in Ireland, Lithuania, Estonia, Latvia, and—albeit less strongly—Spain, Greece, and Hungary (Eurostat, on line database, last accessed November 25, 2011).

27 The impact of imputed rent on poverty and inequality estimates has been studied by, among others, Frick and Grabka (2003), and Sauli and Törmälehto (2010). The measurement and impact of including production for own consumption is discussed in Paats and Tiit (2010). Brandolini et al. (2010) employ an even wider income concept: They focus on the total net worth, which takes account of as many assets and debts as possible.

28 We use Luxembourg Income Study (LIS) top-bottom coding, that is, top-coding income at 10 times the median of nonequivalized income and bottom-coding income at 1% of equivalized mean income. Our sensitivity analysis has shown that top-bottom coding (and the exact procedure applied) does not strongly affect the qualitative results presented in this chapter. However, especially for FGT(2) the effect on point estimates and estimated standard errors is non-negligible (figures available from the authors; see also Van Kerm [2007]).

29 For the estimation of the 95% confidence intervals of the difference between the two years, it is assumed that the 2005 and 2009 samples are independent, which is true for most countries. This assumption simplifies the estimation

of standard errors of the difference. It should be kept in mind that partially overlapping confidence intervals of two estimates do not necessarily imply that the difference is not statistically significant at the given confidence level (e.g., Schenker & Gentleman, 2001; Wolfe & Hanley, 2002; Afshartous & Preston, 2010; Cumming, 2009). Standard errors and confidence intervals have been estimated with the DASP module for Stata (Araar & Duclos, 2007) as well as standard Stata estimation commands.

30 Given the existing doubts about the quality of the German EU-SILC data, especially during the first years of EU-SILC (Frick, J. & Krell, 2011; Goedemé, 2013), the analyses were run with and without Germany. To some extent, the poverty standstill is driven by German data. Excluding Germany from the analysis, poverty declines significantly: At 60% of national median income, the total percentage of EU citizens at risk of poverty drops by just under a percentage point (from almost 17% to just over 16%). Even though, in percentage points, this change may seem rather small, it amounts to approximately 3.2 million fewer Europeans in poverty. Similar qualifications hold for the (squared) normalized poverty gap ratio.

31 Similar findings have been reached for developing countries, Laderchi et al. (2003) for instance, study the empirical impact of the definition and measurement of poverty in India and Peru.

32 http://epp.eurostat.ec.europa.eu/portal/page/portal/income_social_inclusion_ living_conditions/introduction

3

INDIVIDUAL EMPLOYMENT, HOUSEHOLD EMPLOYMENT, AND RISK OF POVERTY IN THE EUROPEAN UNION. A DECOMPOSITION ANALYSIS

Vincent Corluy and Frank Vandenbroucke

3.1 INTRODUCTION

Is employment the best recipe against poverty of people in working-age? At the level of individual citizens and the households in which they live, participation in the labor market significantly diminishes the risk of financial poverty. However, what seems evident at the level of individuals and households is less evident at the country level.

Prior to the financial crisis, the Lisbon Strategy could be regarded as a qualified success in the field of employment, at least if one assumes there to have been causal relationships between the Lisbon Agenda and growing employment rates across Europe. On the other hand, though, the Lisbon Strategy largely failed to deliver on its ambitious promise concerning poverty. Notwithstanding generally higher employment rates many Member States encountered a standstill in the poverty record. We do not observe a general conversion of employment policy success in antipoverty success. Hence, it is important to understand the *missing links* between employment policy success (or failure) and inclusion policy success (or failure). We explore those missing links, relying on the statistical apparatus of the European Union (EU) Labour Force Survey (EU LFS) and the EU Survey on Income and Living Conditions (EU SILC).

At the poverty side of the equation, our focus is on the share of individuals at risk of poverty in the 20-to-59-year-old age cohort. Because the poverty risk of an individual is determined on the basis of the income of the household to which that individual belongs, the relation between at-risk-of-poverty rates and employment rates must, first of all, be analyzed at the household level. Hence, we will establish measures of *household employment*. Our time frame for the analysis of poverty risks is determined by the use of EU SILC 2005 and EU SILC 2008.[1] This short time frame is linked to data limitations, but is also interesting per se, as we want to study the trajectory of EU welfare states[2] during the "good economic years."

Our inquiry in this chapter is to verify empirically one of the explanations for these disappointing poverty trends during the "good economic years" of the Lisbon era, put forward in Vandenbroucke & Vleminckx (2011) and Cantillon (2011), to wit, that this outcome is partly attributable to a failure to reduce the number of individuals living in jobless or work-poor households, despite increasing individual employment rates.

The analysis of the poverty trends proceeds in two steps.

The first step considers the distribution of individual jobs over households, thus establishing a link between individual employment rates and the configuration of household employment. Following the work by Gregg, Scutella, & Wadsworth (2008, 2010), a "polarization index" is defined in terms of the difference between, on the one hand, the actual share of individuals living in jobless households and, on the other, the hypothetical share of individuals living in jobless households assuming that individual employment is distributed *randomly* across households. This benchmark of "random distribution of jobs" does not carry a normative meaning. The message should be read as follows, in our understanding: to the extent that positive polarization is avoidable, it signals an avoidable suboptimal situation for a welfare state. Not only the (skewness of the) relation between individual and household employment is of interest for our inquiry, but even more important are the changes in its relation. Actual changes in household joblessness are determined by changing individual employment rates, changing household composition structures, and a (potentially) changing distribution of individual employment rates. We pay additional attention to the overall evolution in the distribution of jobs over households in EU Member States over a longer time frame.

The second step in the analysis integrates the two missing links we explore (the link between individual employment rates and the configuration of household employment; the link between the configuration of household employment and poverty) into one single analysis. Therefore, we decompose changes in the at-risk-of-poverty rates on the basis of (i) changes in the poverty risks of jobless households; (ii) changes in the poverty risks of other (non-jobless) households; (iii) changes in household joblessness due to changes in individual employment rates and changing household structures; and (iv) changes in polarization. In principle, this method would allow us to assess the impact on at-risk-of-poverty rates of changes in individual employment rates, ceteris paribus, and the impact on at-risk-of poverty rates of changes in polarization, ceteris paribus. In practice, data limitations make such an integrated analysis hard, and the conclusions we will draw can only be tentative.

The proposed technique does yield interesting insights into the trajectories that EU welfare states have followed over the past 10 years. The analysis uncovers a puzzling combination of convergence and disparity within the EU. Polarization levels and household sizes constitute important structural background features for EU welfare states; together with differences in social spending, they help explain differences in their performance with regard to poverty risks and poverty risk reduction.

This chapter is organized as follows. In Section 3.2 we describe the (mathematical) relation between individual and household employment and explore the distribution of jobs over households over the time span 1995–2008. This empirical analysis is based on EU-LFS using an International Labor Organisation (ILO) concept of employment. In Section 3.3 we will introduce a complementary conception of household employment; we compare those different dividing lines and assess the social stratification of those individuals living in jobless or work-poor households, introducing EU-SILC estimates. Section 3.4 integrates the missing links between labor market trends and at-risk-of-poverty changes. First, we explore whether the upward convergence toward more unequal distribution of jobs is a determining factor in the analysis of poverty evolutions. Second, we decompose at-risk-of-poverty rates, looking more in depth at the impact of changes in the retrospective work-intensity of the household and associated poverty risks.

3.2 THE DISTRIBUTION OF JOBS OVER HOUSEHOLDS

In this section of the chapter we will use an ILO concept of employment. According to this ILO concept of employment, an individual is in work if employed for at least one hour in the week before the survey. The household is jobless if no member in the age bracket 20–59 years is in employment, so defined. As a short cut, we will use "jobless household rate" or "household joblessness" to refer to the share of individuals in the age bracket 20–59 years living in jobless households.[3] In Section 3.3, we will add a different conception of household employment rates, distinguishing "work-poor" from "work-rich" households applying a measurement for work-intensity as defined by Eurostat in the framework of Europe 2020.

3.2.1 Trends in Individual and Household Employment

We first focus on trends in individual and household joblessness in 11 old EU Member States (excluding the Scandinavian countries and Germany) for which LFS data are available from 1995 to 2008 (see Figure 3.1). In all countries, individual joblessness diminished substantially over the sample period, with an

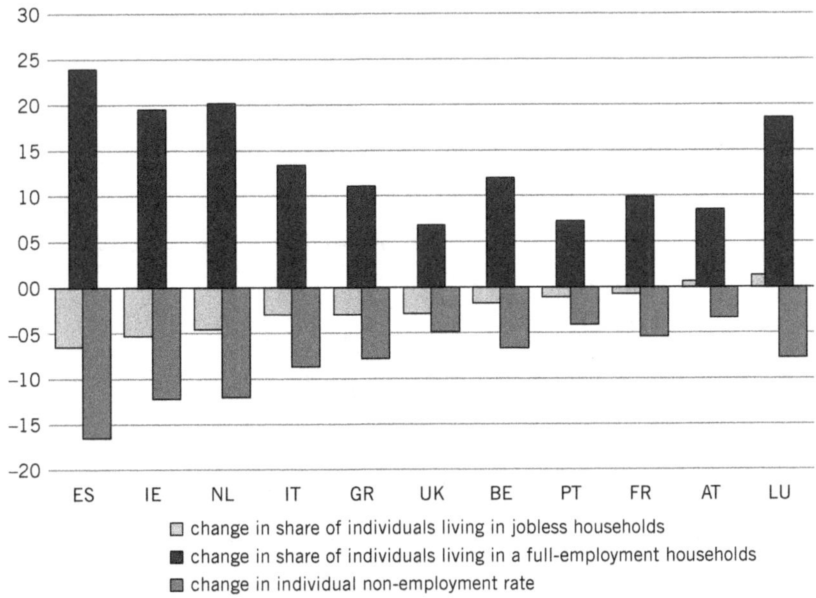

Figure 3.1. Changes in individual and household employment (ILO concept), EU11, 1995–2008, LFS.

average decline of 8.4 percentage points, and improvements of, for example, 16.5 and 12.2 percentage points in Spain and Ireland respectively. However, the share of individuals living in jobless households decreased much less in percentage points.[4] Simultaneously, the percentage point increase of the share of individuals living in "full employment households" (i.e., households where everyone is in work) was larger than the increase in the individual employment rate. As a result, the share of individuals living in "mixed households," where some, though not all, members are in work, declined.

Those trends are in part explainable by a pure "mathematical" effect, reflecting the pooling of individual risks in households. We illustrate this in Figure 3.2 with the Spanish case. Figure 3.2 shows the distribution of Spanish individuals in the age cohort 20–59 years (excluding students) over jobless households, "full employment households," and "mixed households." The actual share of individuals living in jobless households decreased by 6.5 percentage points and the actual share of individuals living in "mixed" households decreased by 17.5 percentage points, while the actual share of individuals living in "full employment households" increased by 24 percentage points. The dotted lines in Figure 3.2 show how the household distribution would have looked if all Spanish households had consisted of two working-age adults and jobs would have been distributed randomly over households: given the rise in individual employment rates, the decrease in household joblessness would have been 11.2 percentage points, the decrease in the "mixed household" share would have been 10.6 percentage

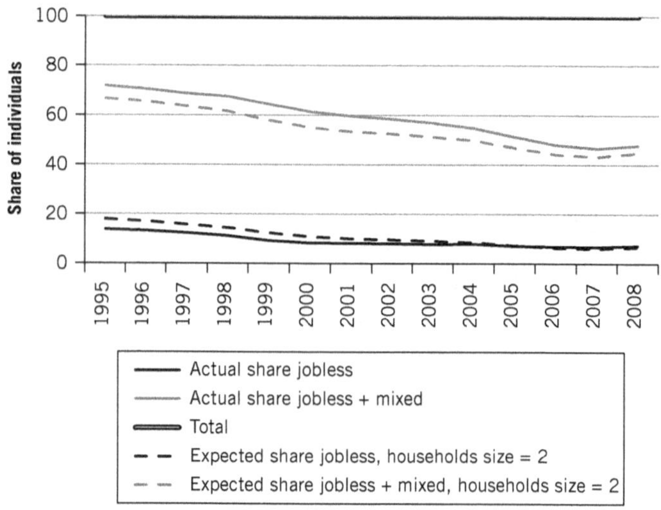

Figure 3.2. Distribution of the population over jobless, mixed, and full employment households in Spain, 1995–2008, LFS.

points, and the increase in the "full employment households" share would have been 21.8 percentage points. The spectacular increase in the share of individuals in "full employment households," from somewhat more than a quarter of the population to more than half of the population (thus making "household full employment" the *median social situation*) is in essence the mathematical corollary of the substantial rise in individual employment rates in Spain. However, the relatively small decrease in household joblessness (measured in percentage points) is only in part explainable as "expected" given the pooling of unemployment risks in households. The gap between the actual decline of household joblessness (6.5 percentage points) and the decline that would have been expected if jobs were distributed randomly over two-adult households (11.2 percentage points) calls for substantial, additional explanations. Household size structure and "polarization" provide such explanations. The fact that the actual share of Spanish individuals living in jobless households was, for most of the period under examination, lower than what one would expect if jobs would be distributed randomly over (two-working-age) households, is rather exceptional in the EU. Specific individual joblessness rate can be consistent with a range of different household joblessness rates, depending on how employment is distributed. In this respect, diversity prevails.

Although one can observe a rather mathematical relation between individual and household employment, this does not mean that its relation carries no societal meaning. In a modernizing society, with increasing individual employment rates, the mitigating impact of risk pooling in households (risk with regard to nonemployment) becomes progressively less important in terms of the (percentage point) reduction of household joblessness that corresponds (in a "probabilistic," expected sense) to a reduction in individual joblessness.[5]

3.2.2 Concept of Polarization

The rather crude distinction between jobless households and other households, based on the ILO concept, allows the construction and decomposition of a polarization index. Later (in Section 3.4.2), we will integrate this measure into the decomposition of at-risk-of-poverty rates.

Gregg & Wadsworth (2008) propose a counterfactual to evaluate polarization in the distribution of household employment. Like the benchmark used in the Lorenz curve, the counterfactual or predicted household joblessness rate is the one that would occur if jobs were randomly distributed in the population, given the specific household size structure in the country under examination. *Polarization* can be defined as the difference between the actual and the predicted household joblessness rate. So it measures the extent to which there are more (or fewer) jobless households than predicted in the case of a random distribution of employment across individuals, given the national household size structure. Formally,

$$P_{it} = wp_{it} - wp^{e}_{it} \tag{1}$$

with:

P_{it} = the polarization of household joblessnes in country i in year t

wp_{it} = the actual share of individuals living in joblessness households (no member of working age is employed) in country i in year t

wp^{e}_{it} = the expected share of ididviduals living in jobless households in country i in year t, in the counterfactual hypothesis that jobs are distributed at random over households given national household structure

Obviously, if the share of smaller households increases, a given rate of individual joblessness may be expected to lead to higher household joblessness, as, all other things being equal, the probability of having no one in work is higher in a smaller household than in a larger one. Ceteris paribus the risk of household joblessness decreases with household size. In what follows, households are distinguished on the basis of size only. Hence, in this analysis, the "predicted rate" of household joblessness is a function of (i) the rate of individual joblessness and (ii) the structure of households in terms of size.

We should emphasize that the expression "polarization" does not carry a normative meaning for us, that is, we do not consider the benchmark used to define the concept—a random distribution of jobs over households, given the household size structure—as a normative ideal. In a context of limited job opportunities "positive polarization" might be seen as a kind of "Matthew effect": a concentration of additional advantage (say, a second job for the partner of someone who is already employed) for those who already have some advantage (compared with a household where both partners are jobless); "negative polarization" might be appreciated as a form of solidarity, that is, as a fair distribution of scarce employment opportunities. However, we do not suggest that either maximally "negative polarization" or the benchmark of "randomly distributed jobs" serve a normative ideal. The message rather is that "positive polarization" comes with a social cost: Jobless households of working-age people need to be supported by social transfers. If that cost is to some extent avoidable, the welfare state is in a sense in a suboptimal equilibrium.

3.2.3 Trends in the Distribution of Individual Employment over Households

In Figure 3.3, actual (X) and predicted (Y) household joblessness rates are presented. If employment is randomly distributed, then the predicted and actual household joblessness rates are identical, so that the polarization rate is zero and the country estimates appear on the diagonal. Countries above the diagonal encounter negative polarization and those under the diagonal positive polarization. The distance to the diagonal reflects the magnitude of the cardinal measure of polarization.

At the start of the sample period, all Southern European countries (most saliently Spain) as well as Luxembourg had negative polarization rates. Negative polarization of work is consistent with theories of the gender division of nonwork (Danziger & Katz, 1996) and added worker theories (Cullen &Gruber, 2000). All other old Member States exhibited limited positive polarization, with

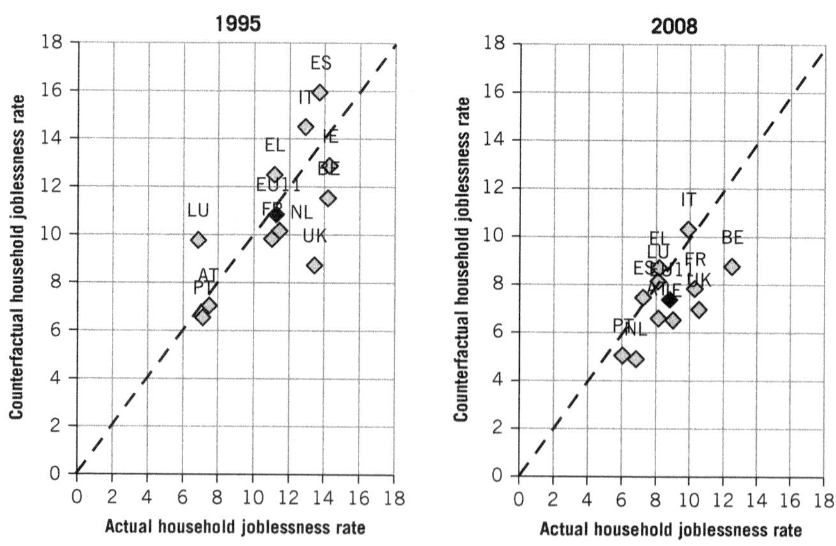

Figure 3.3. Actual and counterfactual household joblessness, 1995–2008, LFS.

only the UK displaying strong positive polarization. Polarization in Spain, Italy, and Greece remained negative throughout the entire period, but approached zero in 2008. In the other countries, polarization became more positive over time, meaning that the distribution of employment grew more unequal. The UK, Ireland, and Belgium display the highest polarization rates, with household joblessness respectively 3.6, 2.5, and 3.7 points higher than would be the case if work were evenly distributed across households.

Why should changes occur in the polarization index? At any point in time, the observed household joblessness rate diverges from the predicted rate if, within certain household subgroups (defined by size), the rate of household joblessness is higher or lower than what one would expect on the basis of a random distribution. Over time, these divergences can decrease or increase in one or more subgroups of the households; this type of change is referred to as "within-household polarization." There may also be a structural shift toward household subgroups where polarization is relatively higher, without change in the subgroup degree of polarization itself; this is referred to as "between-household polarization."

Combining this insight with earlier assertions about the determinants of "predicted household employment rates," the observed changes in the actual household joblessness rate can be decomposed into four terms: (i) changes in the individual nonemployment rate that affect the predicted rate; (ii) changes in the household size structure that affect the predicted rate; (iii) between-household polarization, that is, changes in the household structure that impact upon the degree of polarization, given subgroup degrees of polarization; and (iv) within-household polarization, that is, changes in the degree of polarization in subgroups. Such a shift-share analysis is presented in Table 3.1. Formally, the decomposition has the following form (from Gregg & Wadsworth, 2008):

Observed change in household joblessness

$$\Delta wp = \sum_{k=1}^{k} \Delta n^k \left[0.5\pi_{k,t} + 0.5\pi_{k,t+1}\right] + \qquad (2)$$

(contribution by changes in the individual nonemployment rate n*)*

$$\sum_{k=1}^{k} \Delta n^k \left[0.5\pi_t^k + 0.5\pi_{t+1}^k\right] +$$

(contribution by changes in the household structure)

$$\sum_{k=1}^{k} \Delta\pi_k [0.5(wp_k - n^k)_t + 0.5(wp_k - n^k)_{t+1}] +$$

(contribution by "between household polarization")

$$\sum_{k=1}^{k} \Delta(wp_k - n^k)[0.5\pi_{k,t} + 0.5\pi_{k,t+1}] +$$

(contribution by "within household polarization")

with

n = *individual nonemployment rate in the population*
k = *the size of households (the number of working-age adults)*
K = *the maximal size of households in the population*
π_k = *the share of the population living in households with size k*
wp_k = *the actually observed rate of jobless individuals in households with size k*

The first and the second term in the decomposition add up to the "predicted" rate of household joblessness wp^e in equation (1).

Over the period 1995–2008, household joblessness should have fallen in all countries, given the rising individual employment rates in each country (column 3). Changes toward smaller household structures exert upward pressure on household joblessness rates (column 4). However, the impact of changing household structures on the predicted household joblessness is much smaller than the influence of strongly declining individual joblessness. In most countries, the contribution of polarization to the change in the workless household rate is larger than the household structure component. Most of the divergence between household and individual joblessness stems from an increasingly skewed distribution of employment across households. Moreover, most polarization is within household types. Only in the UK are changes in polarization

Table 3.1. Decomposition of changes in jobless household rates, 1995–2008, 11 EU Member States, LFS.

	Actual change	*Total predicted change*	of which: predicted change (unconditional)		*Total polarization change*	of which: polarization	
			due to Δ nonemployment	*due to Δ household shares*		*between households*	*within households*
ES	-6.48	-8.53	-9.54	1.01	2.05	0.04	2.01
IE	-5.29	-6.37	-6.48	0.12	1.08	0.11	0.97
NL	-4.60	-5.25	-6.03	0.78	0.65	0.32	0.33
IT	-3.02	-4.20	-5.31	1.11	1.18	-0.09	1.26
EL	-2.97	-3.81	-4.43	0.62	0.84	0.21	0.62
UK	-2.85	-1.76	-2.51	0.75	-1.09	0.41	-1.50
BE	-1.72	-2.78	-3.79	1.01	1.06	0.46	0.60
PT	-1.09	-1.49	-1.68	0.20	0.40	0.15	0.25
FR	-0.74	-2.00	-2.95	0.96	1.26	0.11	1.15
AT	0.64	-0.44	-1.53	1.09	1.07	0.12	0.95
LU	1.27	-1.64	-4.13	2.49	2.91	-0.08	2.99

Note:Actual change = total predicted change + total polarization change (column 1 = column 2 + column 5); *Total predicted change* = change due to changes in nonemployment rate + change due to changes in household shares (column 2 = column 3 + column 4); *Total polarization change* = between-household polarization + within-household polarization (column 5 = column 6 + column 7).

negative over time, due to more equally distributed employment within households and notwithstanding the growing share of household types already suffering high polarization. A priori, it seems plausible to assume that policy in the UK, for instance with regard to the activation of lone mothers and the reduction of inactivity traps in tax- and benefit systems, contributed to this result.

Table 3.2 provides an overview of the results of the decomposition for a shorter period. Between 2000 and 2008 individual nonemployment decreased in all countries (except Romania), and substantially in some of the new Member States (Bulgaria, Estonia, Poland, Slovakia) as well as in Italy, Greece, and Spain. However, in all countries except Latvia, Slovenia, and Romania, demographic change reduced the impact of the decreasing nonemployment rates on household jobless rates, as average household size diminished. Polarization of jobs over households had a divergent impact: Negative change in polarization boosted the impact of decreasing individual joblessness on household joblessness in the United Kingdom and most of the new Member States (except Romania and Cyprus); but positive change in polarization reduced it in Italy, Spain, France, Germany, Ireland, and Luxembourg, and, to a lesser extent, in Greece, Cyprus, the Netherlands, Austria, and Belgium. Combinations of the different trends of the components in this decomposition of actual changes in household joblessness offer five emerging clusters of countries for the period 2000–2008, as shown in Table 3.2.

3.2.4 Has Distribution of Jobs Become more Unequal over Time?

In the 11 countries examined (i.e., the Southern, Anglo-Saxon, and Continental members of the EU15, excluding Germany) one observes an *upward convergence* of the levels of polarization. The pattern is one of both beta-convergence, a catch-up process, and sigma-convergence, a reduction in the dispersion of values. In 1995, the average value of the polarization index was 0.39, with a particularly large positive value in the UK and negative values in Luxembourg, Spain, Italy, and Greece (see Figure 3.4). By 2008 the average value of the polarization index increased to 1.42.[6] In the UK, positive polarization diminished, while in Luxembourg, Spain, Italy, and Greece the negative polarization characterizing the beginning of the period was reduced to close to zero. Belgium is an exception in this respect, moving from a rather high level of positive polarization in 1995 to an even higher level (the highest of the group) by 2008.[7]

If one restricts the period under consideration to 2000–2008, the number of countries can be increased to 23 (the EU27 minus Sweden, Finland, Denmark, and Malta). Between 2000 and 2008, one again observes beta and (albeit less robustly) sigma-convergence, both for the group of 23 EU Member States and for the 11 for which data availability stretches back to 1995.[8] There is no real *upward* convergence in the levels of polarization across the 23 EU Members: the average value of the polarization index for the group under review increased from 1.61

Table 3.2. Decomposition of changes in household joblessness rate, 2000–2008, EU27 (except, SE, FI, DK, MT), LFS.

	Actual change	*Total predicted change*	of which: predicted change (unconditional)		*Total polarization change*	of which: polarization	
			due to Δ nonemployment	*due to Δ household shares*		*between households*	*within households*
BG	-6.05	-4.50	-6.48	1.98	-1.55	0.05	-1.60
EE	-4.51	-3.62	-4.70	1.09	-0.89	0.24	-1.14
PL	-3.56	-3.17	-3.51	0.34	-0.39	0.10	-0.49
SK	-2.71	-2.43	-2.80	0.38	-0.29	0.11	-0.39
CZ	-1.67	-0.58	-1.57	0.99	-1.09	0.37	-1.46
UK	-1.01	-0.66	-0.96	0.31	-0.35	0.19	-0.54
LV	-3.82	-2.07	-0.94	-1.12	-1.76	0.01	-1.77
SI	-2.50	-1.80	-1.61	-0.19	-0.70	-0.06	-0.64
HU	-1.09	-0.55	-0.54	0.00	-0.54	0.01	-0.56
IT	-2.07	-2.93	-3.97	1.04	0.86	-0.25	1.11
EL	-2.00	-2.20	-3.06	0.86	0.20	0.04	0.16
CY	-1.50	-2.08	-2.22	0.13	0.58	0.14	0.44
NL	-1.39	-1.79	-2.21	0.42	0.40	0.16	0.24
ES	-1.04	-2.83	-3.60	0.77	1.79	-0.03	1.82
AT	-0.71	-1.06	-1.54	0.48	0.35	0.10	0.25
FR	-0.58	-1.37	-2.01	0.64	0.80	0.08	0.72
LT	-0.43	-1.57	-3.29	1.73	1.14	0.50	0.64
BE	-0.35	-0.71	-1.17	0.45	0.36	0.22	0.14
PT	0.64	0.43	0.19	0.24	0.20	0.11	0.10
RO	1.83	1.46	1.86	-0.40	0.38	0.04	0.34
DE	0.25	-0.46	-1.10	0.63	0.72	0.09	0.63
IE	0.57	-0.80	-0.92	0.12	1.37	0.03	1.34
LU	1.10	-0.55	-1.27	0.72	1.66	-0.13	1.79

in 2000 (with a standard deviation of 1.75) to 1.75 (with a standard deviation of 1.25). In the smaller group of 11 countries for which data are available from 1995 onwards, the *upward* movement is more outspoken: In 2000 the average value of the polarization index for these Member States was 0.73 (standard deviation 1.88) increasing to 1.42 (standard deviation 1.50) by 2008. This trend seems to have been driven mainly by the declining size of households and the rising female participation in labor markets in Spain, Italy, France, and Greece. The 10 new Member States under examination were characterized by high levels of polarization in 2000 (with an average polarization index of 2.72); in this respect

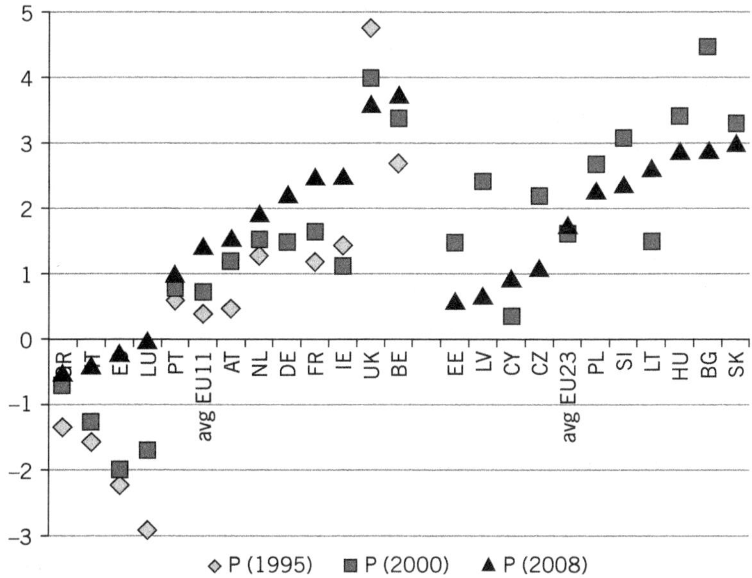

Figure 3.4. Levels of polarization in 1995, 2000, and 2008, old and new EU Member States, LFS. *Note:* average polarization level in EU11 (avg EU11) excludes Germany from calculations, because estimation for 1995 is missing.

their starting position in the beginning of the Lisbon era was very different from that of Spain, Italy, and Greece, which were still characterized by negative polarization in 2000 with extended families still pooling unemployment risks.

The choice of the first year of this shorter period, 2000, is dictated primarily by data availability. However, it appears that 2000 is a useful cut-off in describing the evolution of polarization for some countries. For instance, in Spain and Ireland the increase in polarization accelerated after 2000; in Belgium, and to a lesser extent France, the year 2000 marked the beginning of a deceleration or even a standstill in polarization. Hence, if one takes account of the timing, there appears to be no uniform pattern of evolutions across the EU, apart from the general trend of upward convergence. The difference in pace at which women entered the labor market offers part of the explanation.

A first approach to gaining an understanding of the underlying societal trends that affect polarization consists in the construction of "conditional counterfactuals." We construct a variety of counterfactual household employment rates and allow individual employment rates to vary over gender, age, and educational level of working-age household members. One can then compare the "unconditional polarization" index (the counterfactual being based on household size only) with various "conditional polarization" indices (see Gregg et al., 2010). Subsequently one can calculate the *share* (as a percentage) *of the absolute level* and the *share of the change* (again, as a percentage) *of the unconditional polarization index* that is *explained* by gender, age, education, etc., or by combinations of those factors. Applying this approach shows that the level of polarization is predominantly explained by gender.[9]

A second approach applies regression techniques. A simple regression for the EU11 over 1995–2008 shows that the changes in the ratio of female and male employment rates have a significant and substantial impact on changes in the unconditional polarization index, while changes in the structure of educational attainment of the population seem to have no significant impact.

These findings reflect fundamental societal trends in Europe, some of which follow a clear pattern of convergence, whereas others—surprisingly—show no prima facie convergence at all. The ratio of female and male employment rates displays very strong beta and sigma-convergence in the EU11 over these years. However, there is neither beta-convergence nor sigma-convergence with regard to the proportion of the population with postsecondary education (International Standard Classification of Education (ISCED) levels 5–6) in the EU11 over this period (the correlation between starting values and change is actually positive, and the dispersion increases); with regard to the proportion of the population with lower than secondary education (ISCED levels 0–2), the correlation between starting values and change is mildly negative, but the dispersion is not reduced.

Other results show that "increased homogamy" (increased matching of couples on the basis of education attainment of the partners) is not an explanatory factor for increasing polarization since 1995; that is, there is no increasing gap between the degree of homogamy one sees in reality in couples and the degree of homogamy one would expect if couples are formed at random.

3.3 HOUSEHOLD JOBLESSNESS AND LOW WORK-INTENSITY?

3.3.1 Alternative Definitions of Household Employment

In the previous section of this chapter, we used an ILO concept of employment. In this section, we will introduce a different conception of household employment rates, distinguishing "work-poor" from "work-rich" households. Applying a measurement for work-intensity as defined by Eurostat in the framework of Europe 2020, we consider a household to be "work-poor" if its work-intensity is less than 50%. We will refer to the latter concept with the notation $wp^{0.5}$ and refer to the former concept (joblessness) with the notation wp^{0}. The population reference group is exactly the same for wp^{0} and $wp^{0.5}$: "adults" are defined as those belonging to the 20–59-year-old age bracket excluding full-time students (i.e., household members aged 20–24 years with ILO status inactive). Similarly, the employment status is checked of household members aged 20–59 years, excluding full-time students aged 20–24 years.[10] The underlying employment concept is radically different though. According to the ILO concept of employment, an individual is in work if employed for at least one hour in the week before the survey; the household is jobless if no member belonging to the working-age focus group is in employment, so defined. For the calculation of wp^{0} use can be made of LFS and SILC, differences in the LFS and SILC samples alas leading to divergent results.[11] In contrast, in order to calculate $wp^{0.5}$, work-intensity is defined as the ratio of the total number of months that working-age household members (excluding students) worked to the total number of months that could, in theory, have been worked by them. For persons who reported having worked part-time, an estimate of the number of months in terms of full-time-equivalent was computed on the basis of the number of usually worked hours at the time of the interview. The indicator $wp^{0.5}$ can only be calculated on the basis of SILC.

A comparison of these different dividing lines is not straightforward. The distinction between wp^{0} and $wp^{0.5}$ is a matter not only of degree (no economic activity whatsoever vs. limited economic activity) but also of the time frame applied: wp^{0} is based on the week before the survey, whereas $wp^{0.5}$ is based on the year prior to the survey (income reference period). Thus, the households identified as jobless may be households where the week prior to the survey no one happened to be in employment, even though household members experienced irregular spells in and out of the labor market in the months before; with the work-intensity metric, these households would not be identified as jobless but as work-poor.

Unsurprisingly, the average value of $wp^{0.5}$ across the countries under review is higher than the average value of wp^{0}: 9.5% of the population aged 20–59 years was living in a jobless household and 15.7% of the population was living in a work-poor household, that is, a household with work-intensity of less than 50%. Rather more surprisingly, the poverty risk of the jobless households (pwp^{0}), while typically higher than the poverty risk for the work-poor ($pwp^{0.5}$), is lower in Denmark, Greece, Norway, France, and Estonia (see Figures 3.5 and 3.6). Two factors may explain this. First, the ILO-based measure for wp^{0} is not comparable to the work-intensity measure used by Eurostat, hence one should not a priori expect an ILO-based calculation of pwp^{0} to be higher than a work-intensity based calculation for $pwp^{0.5}$. Second, even when using the work-intensity metric to calculate pwp^{0} (i.e., looking back 12 months, and taking into account both months and hours worked—which we did not do here) the relation between work-intensity and financial poverty risks is nonlinear in most countries. Households with work-intensity equal to zero experience lower poverty risks than households with work-intensity close to zero but non-zero (European Commission, 2011: 157, Chart 21).Prima facie, this may be due to the fact that the group of zero work-intensity households includes a substantial number of households living on

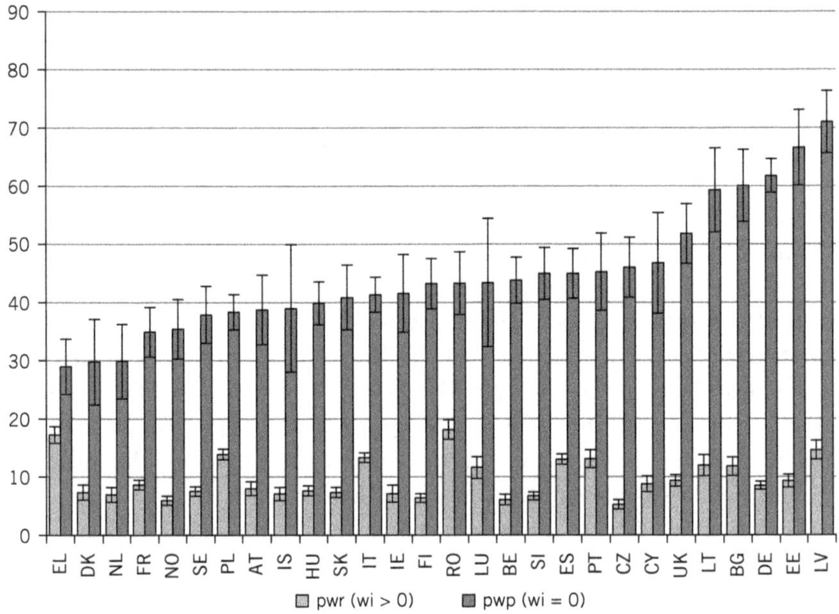

Figure 3.5. At-risk-of-poverty rate for individuals in jobless and non-jobless households, 2007/8 (ILO definition, EU SILC 2008).

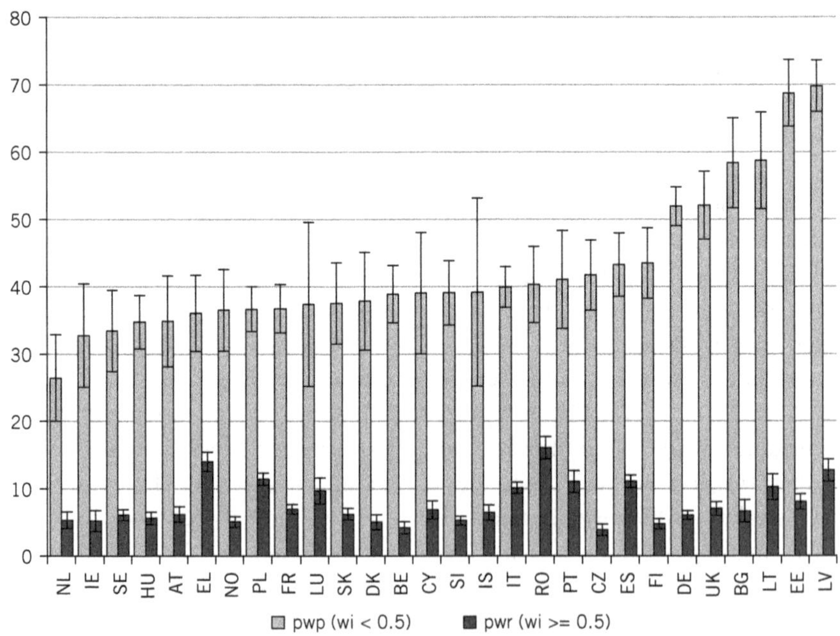

Figure 3.6. At-risk-of-poverty rate for individuals in work-poor and work-rich households, 2007/8 (EU2020 definition of work intensity, EU SILC 2008).

pensions or pre-pensions, even below the age of 59 years; early-exit schemes may yield a better income than the unemployment or social assistance benefits on offer to those who have irregular spells in and out of the labor market.[12]

As a matter of fact, the selection of the population age cohort that is examined influences not only the *levels* of at-risk-of-poverty rates within the work-poor (or jobless) and the work-rich segment of the population, but also the share of individuals living in work-poor or jobless households, and the level of polarization. This corroborates the social stratification analysis in Section 3.3.2 below, which shows that age has an important impact on an individual's risk of living in a jobless household. However, we found that alternative choices for the age cohort, for example, the 20–49-year-old age bracket, did not have much impact on the overall picture of our decomposition results. For that reason, we only present results with regard to the 20–59-year-old age bracket.[13]

The Europe 2020 strategy focuses on households with "very low work-intensity": very low work-intensity means a work-intensity of less than 20%. The European Commission shows that the risk of poverty begins to drop significantly when household work-intensity increases beyond 20%, which explains their choice of this benchmark. Simultaneously, the Commission shows that the poverty risk (for adults) only comes down to the same level as the total at-risk-of poverty rate for adults when work-intensity exceeds 50% (European Commission, 2011: 157, Chart 21). We have chosen to partition the population on the basis of a benchmark of 50% for several reasons. First, the heterogeneity of the subpopulation with work-intensity less than 50% does not differ that much from the heterogeneity of the subpopulation with work-intensity less than 20%. Second, for our purposes the decomposition should focus as much on the work-rich as on the work-poor segment of the population, and within both groups we want sufficient homogeneity. As a matter of fact, the changes in at-risk-of-poverty rates are strongly driven by changes related to the work-rich group. When we expand the work-rich group, by restricting the notion of "work-poor" to "*very* low work-intensity" (less than 20%), (a) the position of the work-rich in the decomposition becomes even more dominant; and (b) their composition becomes more heterogeneous. For these reasons, in Section 3.4.3 we pursue a decomposition on the basis of a 50% work-intensity benchmark.

3.3.2 The Social Stratification of Individuals in Jobless and Work-poor Households

Who are the individuals confronted with a high risk of living in a jobless household (ILO-concept) or a work-poor household with less than 50% work-intensity (EU2020-concept)? A probit analysis on the level of EU15 and EU10 reveals strong social stratification, as can be seen in Figure 3.7 and Figure 3.8. We distinguish the old and new Member States, because a priori one might expect a

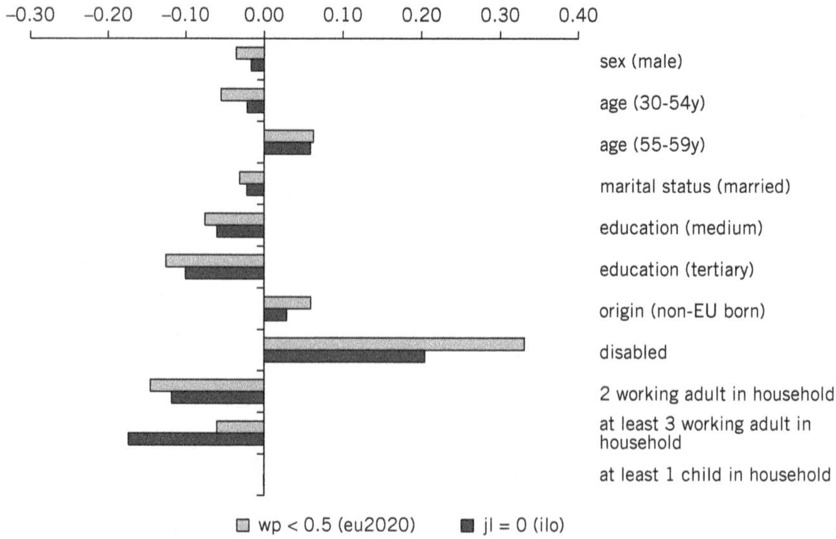

Figure 3.7. Marginal effects on the probability of living in jobless (ILO) or work-poor (wi < 0.5) households, SILC 2008, for EU-15.

sociological difference in the stratification of the post-Communist societies of the EU10. However, the social stratification of jobless and work-poor households in today's "old" and "new" Europe is quite similar; apart from the risk associated with being single, this social stratification to a large extent reflects some deep-rooted social disadvantages with which individuals are born or have come to live with rather early in their lives. This underscores the challenges activation strategies face if they want to reach out successfully to jobless or work-poor households.

First of all and unsurprisingly, individuals with high risks of living in a jobless household or a work-poor household are individuals living in single households. This result is in part attributable to the mere "mathematical" effect of the absence of unemployment risk pooling in single households. Our probit analysis does not reveal whether singles run a higher risk of joblessness or work poverty as a "household" than their peers in larger households (peers in terms of gender, education, and the other factors studied in the probit analysis) *beyond* the higher risk they incur because of the lack of risk pooling.[14] Rather surprisingly, at the level of these pooled EU data, having children does not influence the risk of living in a jobless or work-poor household: This is the result of small positive and negative impacts of having children in different Member States, cancelling each other out at the EU15 and EU10 level.[15] Whatever the household size, we see that disabled individuals[16] and individuals whose educational attainment is lower than secondary education run a higher risk of living in a jobless or work-poor household. With regard to the risk of living in a jobless household, our age-result follows intuition. Compared with individuals aged 20–29 years, individuals between 30 and 54 years of age have a lower risk and individuals between 55 and 59 years of

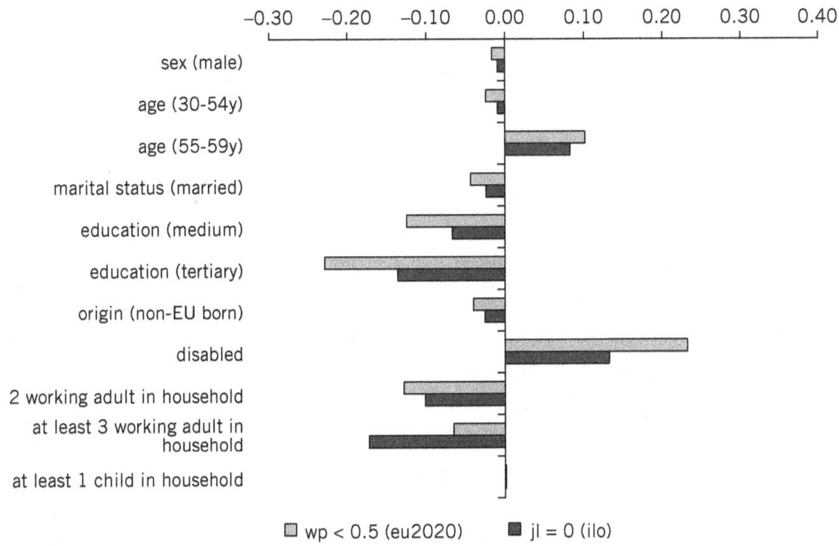

Figure 3.8. Marginal effects on the probability of living in jobless (ILO) or work-poor (wi < 0.5) households, SILC 2008, for EU 10.

age have a significantly higher risk of living in a jobless household. This result for the latter group is in line with what one would expect given early exit from labor markets. The marginal effects are very similar for both the finely grained definition on the basis of work-intensity and the ILO definition.

There are subtle differences between the risk profiles of the two population subgroups (jobless households, work-poor households) we distinguish here. The risks associated with disability and education are similar for joblessness and work poverty, yet the marginal effects of those individual features are more important for work poverty than for joblessness. Also the impact of gender is more outspoken with regard to work poverty than with regard to joblessness. The impact of household size is also different: A larger household size reduces the risk of joblessness and work poverty (compared to the risks of singles), yet the reduction is relatively more important for the two-adult household when looking at work poverty and relatively more important for the three-plus household when looking at joblessness. A low level of education has a larger impact in the EU10 than in the EU15 while disability has a smaller impact in the EU10. The only difference in direction of the effects between the EU15 and the EU10 relates to non-EU-born residents. Their risk of living in a jobless household, compared to the risk of an EU-born resident, is higher in the EU15, yet lower in the EU10.

We conclude from this analysis that both changes in household "joblessness" (wp^0) and in household "work poverty" ($wp^{0.5}$, work-intensity less than 50%) may be of interest in understanding the dynamics of poverty risks over time.

3.4 RELATION BETWEEN CHANGES IN LABOR MARKETS AND POVERTY RISKS

3.4.1 Relationship between Poverty and Employment Rates

On a cross-country level, national rates of household "joblessness" and household "work poverty" calculated on the basis of EU SILC correlate in a different way with national poverty risks for individuals in the age cohort 20 years to 59 years.

Table 3.3 shows that both household joblessness and individual joblessness correlate positively with *pre*-transfer poverty rates, while only individual joblessness correlates positively with *post*-transfer poverty. Contrary to household *joblessness* rates, the share of individuals living in *work-poor* households does correlate positively with post-transfer poverty rates. Household work poverty also correlates with pre-transfer poverty, but less so than household joblessness.

Given our earlier assertion that one should study the link between employment and poverty through *household* employment, it may be rather surprising that, *levels* of *individual* employment rates correlate negatively with post-transfer poverty rates, while *household* joblessness rates show no correlation whatsoever with post-transfer poverty rates, at least for the years covered in EU SILC 2005, 2006, 2007, and 2008.

Different factors explain this prima facie counterintuitive result.[17] First, household joblessness correlates positively with pre-transfer poverty, but the impact of household joblessness on post-transfer poverty is mitigated by social spending. Second, national pre-transfer and post-transfer poverty rates are also influenced by the poverty rates prevailing in "non-jobless" households, which carry a large weight in the overall poverty record of many countries. Third, in a cross-country comparison higher individual employment rates are associated with lower levels of pre-transfer poverty among the "non-jobless" households. Hence, higher individual employment rates reduce pre-transfer poverty rates both because of their impact on household joblessness (individual and household employment correlate with each other) and because of their impact on pre-transfer poverty among the "non-jobless" segment. Finally, higher individual employment rates are associated with higher levels of spending on working-age cash benefits. Higher levels of spending are associated with a larger extent of poverty reduction through social transfers, both within the jobless and the non-jobless segment of the population. Together, all these elements explain why in a cross-country comparison post-transfer poverty correlates with individual joblessness but not with household joblessness.

With regard to *changes* in at-risk of poverty rates between EU SILC 2005 and EU SILC 2008, individual joblessness, household joblessness, and household work poverty all correlate positively but weakly with changes in poverty rates,

Table 3.3. Cross-sectional correlations of post- and pre-transfer poverty and different concepts of employment.

Correlations of *post*-transfer at-risk-of-poverty rates and...			**...employment (*) (ɫ)**		
	2005	2006	2007	2008	Δ 2005–08
...individual employment rates	−0.58	−0.51	−0.48	−0.40	−0.34
...share of individuals in non-jobless households (ILO)	−0.09	0.00	0.04	0.04	−0.35
...share of individuals in work-rich households (wi > = 50%)	−0.42	−0.32	−0.31	−0.16	−0.42
Correlations of pre-transfer at-risk-of-poverty rates and...			**...employment (*) (ɫ)**		
	2005	2006	2007	2008	Δ 2005–08
...individual employment rates	−0.36	−0.27	−0.37	−0.53	−0.78
...share of individuals in non-jobless households (ILO)	−0.73	−0.62	−0.69	−0.76	−0.80
...share of individuals in work-rich households (wi > = 50%)	−0.49	−0.54	−0.42	−0.67	−0.79

Note: These correlations do not imply causality, nor significance; they merely serve to structure our data.
(ɫ) Correlations with joblessness or work-poverty obviously have the opposite sign.
(*) EU SILC, 24 countries.

as can be inferred from Table 3.3 (a correlation coefficient of 0.34 for changes in individual joblessness, 0.35 for changes in household joblessness Δwp^{0}, and 0.42 for changes in household work poverty $\Delta wp^{0.5}$). The decomposition analysis in Sections 3.4.2 and 3.4.3 focuses on these changes over time.

3.4.2 Integrated decomposition of Labor Market Trends and Poverty Changes

In the first section (3.2.4) we described an "upward convergence in polarization" with regard to the distribution of jobs over households. This "upward convergence" had a substantial impact on the evolution of household joblessness, certainly in relative terms. In comparison with the predicted evolution of household joblessness without any change in polarization, over the years 2000–2008 changes in the distribution of individual employment may have been an important factor in the UK (where a negative change in polarization boosted the household employment rate) and in Spain, Italy, France, Belgium, and Luxembourg (where a positive change in polarization reduced the improvement in household employment). The question now is whether polarization is also an important factor in the analysis of poverty trends.

We examine this question by decomposing changes in the at-risk-of-poverty rates on the basis of (i) changes in the poverty risks of jobless households; (ii) changes in the poverty risks of other (non-jobless) households; (iii) changes in household joblessness due to changes in individual employment rates and changing household structures; and (iv) changes in polarization. Thus, we integrate the two missing links we explore in this chapter (the link between individual employment rates and the configuration of household employment; the link between the configuration of household employment and poverty) into one single analysis. In principle, this would allow us to assess the impact of changes in individual employment rates on at-risk-of-poverty rates, ceteris paribus, and the impact on at-risk-of poverty rates of changes in polarization, ceteris paribus. In practice, data limitations make such an integrated analysis hard, and the conclusions we will draw can only be tentative.

Formally, this second step in this integration exercise proceeds as follows. The at-risk-of-poverty rate can be written as a weighted average of the at-risk-of-poverty rate of individuals in jobless households and the at-risk-of-poverty rate of individuals in the other households. Figure 3.5 illustrated that the poverty risk of individuals in jobless households (*pwp*) is much higher than the poverty risk in the other households (*pwr*) in all EU Member States. Labeling these other households as the "work-rich" (the share of individuals in work-rich households $wr = 1-wp$), we can write:

$$pov_{it} = wp_{it}\, pwp_{it} + wr_{it}\, pwr_{it} \tag{3}$$

where:

$pwp_{it} = at\,risk\,of\;poverty\,rate\;for\,individuals\,in\,work\;poor\,(jobless)\,households$

$pwr_{it} = at\,risk\,of\;poverty\,rate\;for\,individuals\,in\,work\,rich\,(non-jobless)\,households$

Changes over time can be decomposed as:

$$\Delta pov_i = \overline{wr_i}.\Delta pwr_i + \overline{wp_i}.\Delta pwp_i + \left(\overline{pwp_i} - \overline{pwr_i}\right).\Delta wp_i \tag{4}$$

where, for a change from t = 0 to t = 1,

$$\Delta pov_i = pov_{i1} - pov_{i0}$$

$$\overline{wr_i} = 0.5wr_{i0} + 0.5wr_{i1}, etcetera$$

In this way, the change in the overall poverty risk is decomposed into three subcomponents or contributory factors:

i. a contribution by the change in the at-risk-of-poverty rate of the work-rich;
ii. a contribution by the change in the at-risk-of-poverty rate of the work-poor;
iii. a contribution by the change in the share of the population living in work-poor households.

De Beer (2007), who applied this technique to long-term evolutions between 1980 and 2000, rightly stresses that a decomposition as such is not a causal analysis. It simply calculates by how much a decomposable variable changes if one of the factors informing the decomposition changes, *all the other factors being equal.* Such a mechanical approach should be interpreted with due caution: It is an accounting device, which does not imply causality. Moreover, changes in one subcomponent may be intrinsically linked to changes in other subcomponents of the decomposition. For instance, reducing the share of people living in work-poor households may be achieved by means of a deliberate policy of increasing the poverty risk of people in work-poor households through stricter conditionality and less generosity in unemployment benefits. Or increasing employment may push up the median income, to the effect that a decreasing share of work-poor households and higher poverty rates go hand in hand. Conversely, work-poor households may become work-rich because their members accept jobs that are at the lower end of the pay scale, thus marginally increasing the average risk of poverty of the work-rich group. Diverging evolutions in household size structure between the work-poor and the work-rich, implying changes in the poverty gap between the two categories, may also be at play. These examples do not invalidate the decomposition as such, but rather illustrate a general caveat concerning its interpretation.

Using equations (1), (2), (3), and (4), it is possible to integrate the decomposition of changes in household employment and changes in poverty on the basis of the following equation:

$$\Delta pov_i = \overline{wr_\iota}.\Delta pwr_i + \overline{wp_\iota}.\Delta pwp_i + \left(\overline{pwp_\iota} - \overline{pwr_\iota}\right).\left(\Delta wp_i^e + \Delta P_i\right) \qquad (5)$$

However, this requires that the data used to decompose changes in individual and household employment and changes in poverty are consistent. Because we must rely on SILC to establish a link between employment and income, it is only possible to pursue this integrated decomposition from 2004 onwards. For some countries, there are considerable differences between individual and household employment data obtained through LFS and SILC, as discussed in de Graaf-Zijl and Nolan (2011). Hence, circumspection is called for when connecting the analysis based on SILC 2005–2008 with the employment analyses for 1995–2008 and 2000–2008 based on LFS, as presented in previous sections. In order to allow some comparison on a conceptual level, the ILO definition of joblessness is applied, even though SILC makes it possible to define joblessness on a retrospective basis for the 12 months prior to the survey.

Figure 3.9 summarizes the integrated decomposition of changes in household joblessness and poverty risks in the 20–59-year-old age bracket on the basis of SILC. The underlying figures are presented in Table 3.4 and Table 3.5 (the statistical significance of the estimated changes in at-risk-of-poverty rates is provided in Table 3.5).

We can draw two sets of tentative conclusions from this exercise.

Table 3.4. Poverty risks and household employment, 2004/5–2007/8: key figures (analysis applied to ILO-based *wp*, SILC 2005–2008).

	Δ *pov*	wp_{2005}	pwp_{2005}	Δwp	Δ *pwp*	Δ *(pwp–pwr)*	Δ *pov(60+)*
AT	0.1	8.4	33.3	0.9	5.5	6.2	0.6
BE	0.1	16.9	36.6	–3.3	7.2	7.1	0.1
CY	0.0	5.3	44.6	–0.5	2.1	2.0	-2.6
CZ	-1.6	10.6	49.2	–3.2	–3.2	–3.3	2.0
DE	3.3	11.6	45.0	–0.3	16.8	15.1	1.8
DK	0.0	10.6	30.1	–2.0	–0.3	–0.8	0.6
EE	–2.9	9.4	65.0	–1.9	1.5	3.7	16.2
EL	1.8	9.0	33.4	–1.5	–4.5	–7.1	–3.8
ES	0.2	7.7	42.4	0.5	2.6	2.7	–1.5
FI	1.2	12.3	39.1	–1.6	4.1	2.7	3.4
FR	0.5	10.6	34.9	0.1	0.0	–0.5	–5.1
HU	–1.6	13.2	40.6	0.8	–0.8	1.3	–2.0
IE	–2.1	12.2	61.7	2.4	–20.2	–19.7	–9.7
IT	0.1	10.6	43.1	–0.5	–1.8	–2.3	–1.6
LT	–2.9	10.3	62.6	–2.3	–3.3	–1.6	11.6
LU	0.9	7.3	33.5	–1.8	9.8	9.1	–1.5
LV	0.9	9.5	66.7	–2.5	4.3	2.1	26.6
NL	–0.8	11.0	25.1	–3.5	4.7	5.4	3.3
PL	–4.6	15.3	40.4	–6.4	–2.1	1.2	3.6
PT	0.1	7.5	39.7	–0.1	5.5	5.9	–4.2
SE	2.3	9.7	27.7	–1.6	10.1	8.1	4.2
SI	–0.4	10.3	41.3	–1.8	3.6	3.7	–0.9
SK	–3.5	8.4	36.5	–2.4	4.3	7.7	2.6
UK	–1.2	12.5	56.9	–2.3	–5.1	–5.5	2.9
Avg	–0.4	10.4	42.9	–1.4	1.7	1.8	1.9
St dev	1.8	2.5	11.6	1.8	6.8	6.6	7.2

First, the poverty record of EU Member States during the economic upswing 2004/5–2007/8 is decomposable in quite different trajectories, which seem in part linked to different *policy* trajectories:

- Belgium: despite a success in the reduction of household joblessness *wp*, there was no significant change in the at-risk-of-poverty rate of the population in the 20–59-year-old age cohort, given a significant increase in the at-risk-of-poverty rate of jobless households.
- Germany (based on SILC, caveat[18]): household joblessness did not decrease, as increasing polarization neutralized the progress in

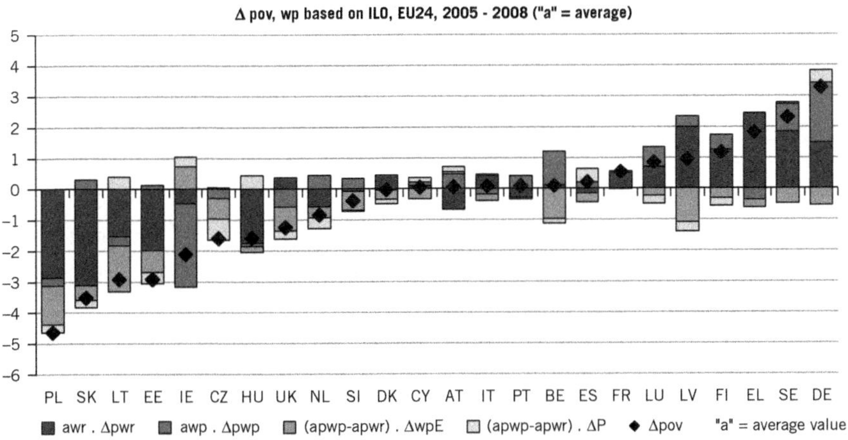

Figure 3.9. Decomposition of changes in poverty risks, 2004/5–2007/8; analysis performed on ILO-based wp, SILC 2005–2008.

employment; but the at-risk-of-poverty rates of both jobless households and other households increased significantly, the overall result being a significant increase in at-risk-of-poverty of the population in the 20–59-year-old age cohort.

- Finland and Sweden follow a trajectory comparable to the German (SILC) trajectory: here, a small decrease in household joblessness was more than offset by increasing poverty risks for both the work-rich and the jobless households; as a result the poverty risk for the population between age 20 and 59 years increased significantly.
- Ireland presents an opposite case: despite an increase in household joblessness, the increasing generosity of social protection diminished the poverty risks of both the jobless households and the other households, to the effect that the overall poverty risk in the 20–59-year-old age cohort decreased significantly.
- UK: both the reduction of household joblessness (helped by the reversal in the British polarization trend in the labor market) and the reduction of poverty in jobless households, contributed to a significant decrease of the overall poverty risk for the population in the 20–59-year-old age cohort.
- In most of the new Member States (notably Poland, Slovakia, Estonia, Lithuania, and the Czech Republic) economic growth led to substantial increases in individual employment rates and decreases in household joblessness (helped by decreasing polarization, except in Lithuania). This contributed to significant improvements in overall poverty risks in the 20–59-year-old age cohort, reinforced by significantly decreasing poverty risks in the work-rich households in Slovakia, Poland, and

Table 3.5. Decomposition of changes in poverty risks, 2004/5–2007/8; analysis on ILO-based *wp*, SILC 2005–2008.

	$\overline{wp}.\Delta\,\overline{pwr}$		$\overline{wp}.\Delta\,\overline{pwp}$		$(\overline{pwp}-\overline{pwr})\Delta\,pwp^{e}$		$(\overline{pwp}-\overline{pwr})\Delta p$	Δpov	
AT	–0.67		0.48		0.07		0.17	0.05	
BE	0.11		1.10	***	–0.98	***	–0.14	0.09	
CY	0.10		0.11		–0.32		0.15	0.04	
CZ	0.05		–0.29		–0.67	***	–0.69	–1.60	**
DE	1.49	***	1.92	***	–0.55		0.41	3.28	***
DK	0.45		–0.03		–0.31	***	–0.15	–0.03	
EE	–1.98	***	0.13		–0.70	***	–0.36	–2.91	***
EL	2.42	***	–0.37		–0.24	***	0.02	1.83	**
ES	–0.15		0.20		–0.29		0.44	0.20	
FI	1.26	***	0.48	*	–0.32	***	–0.25	1.17	***
FR	0.51		0.00		0.05		–0.02	0.54	
HU	–1.75	***	–0.10		–0.18		0.44	–1.59	***
IE	–0.46		–2.70	***	0.74	***	0.31	–2.11	***
IT	0.42		–0.19		–0.20		0.05	0.08	
LT	–1.51		–0.30		–1.49	***	0.39	–2.92	***
LU	0.71		0.63		–0.23	***	–0.26	0.86	
LV	1.99	**	0.35		–1.09	***	–0.30	0.95	
NL	–0.57		0.44		–0.36	***	–0.35	–0.84	
PL	–2.86	***	–0.26		–1.27	***	–0.26	–4.64	***
PT	–0.29		0.41		–0.05		0.01	0.08	
SE	1.84	***	0.90	***	–0.48	***	0.05	2.31	***
SI	–0.08		0.34		–0.61	***	–0.04	–0.39	
SK	–3.11	***	0.31		–0.47	***	–0.24	–3.51	***
UK	0.37		–0.58	**	–0.77	***	–0.26	–1.24	**

Δpov, Δpwp and Δpwr, and (actually observed) Δwp significantly different from 0 at 95% (***), at 90% (**), at 85% (*).

Estonia. Importantly, however, the last column in Table 3.4 shows that poverty risks for the elderly increased in those countries, sometimes very substantially. So, their trajectory is not only employment- and growth-based, but also shows an intergenerational shift.[19]

- In France, Greece and Portugal there was a generational shift in poverty risks in favour of the elderly.

Second, on the basis of this analysis, we can begin to verify one of the hypotheses put forward in Vandenbroucke & Vleminckx (2011) and Cantillon (2011) to explain the disappointing poverty trends in the EU during the Lisbon era. They state that this disappointing outcome is partly attributable to a failure to reduce the number of individuals living in jobless households, despite increasing individual employment rates.

Differences among EU Member States in *levels* of polarization and household size do play a role in explaining the diversity of configurations of individual employment, household employment, and at-risk-of-poverty rates. How important were *changes* in employment polarization in explaining changes in poverty rates? The shaded bars in Figure 3.9 and column 4 of Table 3.5 show the poverty impact of employment polarization across households *as such*. One may conclude that, in the short time span of 2004/5–2007/8, this impact was rather limited and disparate. In some countries it added slightly to the decline in poverty realized over the given period (the Czech Republic, the UK, Estonia, the Netherlands, and Slovakia). In others, most notably Spain, polarization appears to have had the effect of checking any decline in poverty that might have occurred without further polarization. In Germany, on the contrary, polarization apparently added to growing poverty (but, important doubts exist concerning the German SILC figures).

Obviously, polarization is a long-term trend, rather than a short-term event. Given the fact that the gap between the poverty risk of jobless households and the poverty risk of non-jobless households is, on average and across countries, about 33 percentage points, one might say that a one-percentage-point increase in polarization—which is more or less the average increase for the 11 countries studied between 1995 and 2008—structurally adds 0.33 percentage points to the proportion of people experiencing poverty in the 20–59-year-old age cohort. This may seem small, but it is certainly not insignificant. However, polarization does not emerge as "structural," that is, our analysis does not show that it is an unavoidable process in modernizing societies. Policies do play a role. For evidence on the impact of policies regarding patterns of household (non)participation in labor markets, see, for instance, Ellwood (2000), Meyer & Rosenbaum (2001), or Grogger (2003).

3.4.3 Decomposition of Changes in Poverty Rates on the basis of Household Work-intensity

In Section 3.4.1 we pointed out that the correlation between changes in the share of individuals living in work-poor households and changes in poverty rates is positive, but rather weak (Table 3.3). This is also illustrated in Figure 3.10. This figure is constructed with four quadrants, using changes in poverty (Δpov) and the share of individuals living in work-poor households ($\Delta wp^{0.5}$) between 2005 and 2008 (SILC).

In each of the quadrants one can identify specific trajectories. The Finnish trajectory shows a decreasing share of persons in work-poor households, but an increasing overall at-risk-of-poverty rate.[20] In stark contrast, we find the Irish trajectory, with an increasing share of persons in work-poor households but

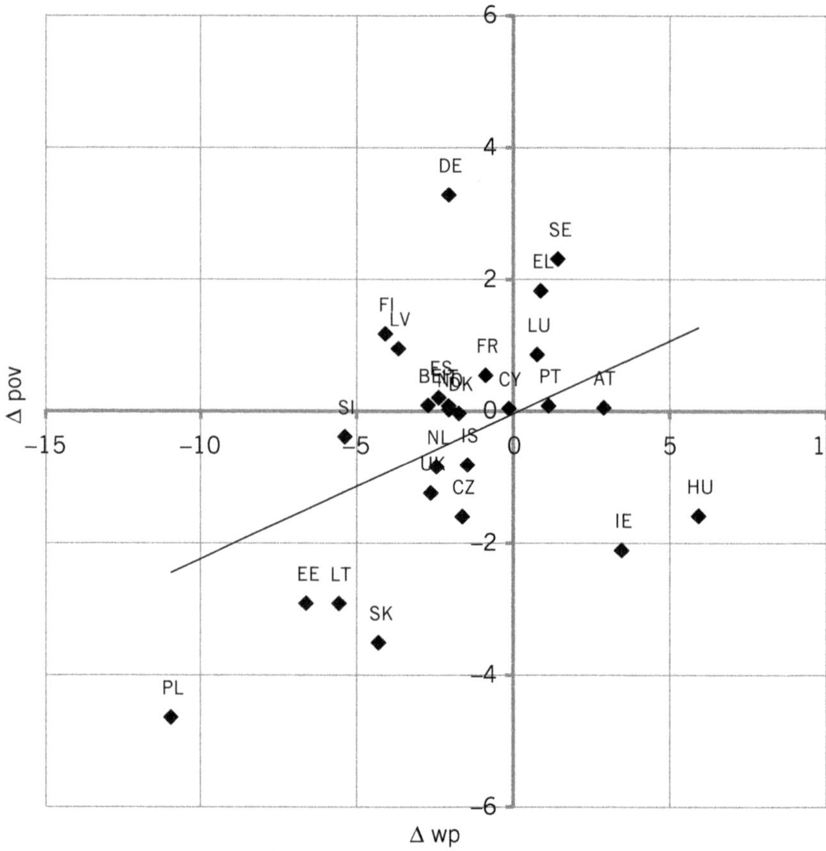

Figure 3.10. Overall poverty risks and the share of individuals in work-poor households: the diversity of EU trajectories (EU 2020 definition of work intensity, EU SILC 2005–2008).

decreasing poverty risks. The Polish trajectory follows a substantial decrease in the share of persons in work-poor households and a strong decrease in poverty risks. Finally, in the right upper quadrant we find the Swedish trajectory, with a slightly increasing share of persons in work-poor households and an increasing overall at-risk-of-poverty rate.

As explained in Section 3.4.2, we can decompose changes in at-risk-of-poverty rates by distinguishing work-poor households and work-rich households. We now apply this technique, formalized in equation (4), using 50% work-intensity as the dividing line between work-poor and work-rich.

The change in the overall poverty risk is decomposed into three contributory factors:

i. a contribution by the change in the at-risk-of-poverty rate of the work-rich;
ii. a contribution by the change in the at-risk-of-poverty rate of the work-poor;
iii. a contribution by the change in the share of the population living in work-poor households.

Table 3.6 provides the basic data with regard to changes in poverty risks and population shares. Table 3.7 displays the components of the decomposition for the period 2004/5–2007/8. Figure 3.11 provides a graphical summary of the decomposition in Table 3.7.

The percentage point differences between the at-risk-of-poverty rates for respectively work-poor and work-rich households varies between 20.2 (for the Netherlands) and 59.2 (for Estonia), with an average of 33.5 percentage points. Correspondingly, the impact of a decrease in the share of individuals living in work-poor households ($wp^{0.5}$) by 1 percentage point on the at-risk-of-poverty rate for the whole population aged 20–59 years ranges from −0.2 to −0.6 percentage points, and is, on average, around −0.3 percentage points.[21] Obviously, given the additional diversity of $\Delta wp^{0.5}$ ($\Delta wp^{0.5}$ ranges from −10.9 in Poland to +5.9 in Hungary), the actual contribution to the poverty rate of the change in the share of people living in work-poor households is very diverse, ranging from −3.9 percentage points in Estonia to +1.7 percentage points in Hungary (see column 3 in Table 3.7).

The observation that the overall cross-sectional correlation between Δpov and $\Delta wp^{0.5}$ is rather weak (Table 3.3) is explained by the highly diversified impact of the *other* factors at work in the decomposition, driven by $\Delta pwp^{0.5}$ and $\Delta pwr^{0.5}$. It would be incorrect to assert that the modest decline in the share of work-poor households was the "main culprit" in explaining disappointing poverty trends across the board in EU Member States. The picture is both more complicated and more diversified. Moreover, to contextualize the decomposition of poverty in the 20–59-year-old age bracket, one must also consider the evolution of poverty in other segments of the population, notably the elderly. For this reason, Table 3.6 also incorporates the evolution of the poverty risk of people aged 60+ years (hereafter "the elderly").

A first set of observations relates to the overall pattern of change between 2004/5 and 2007/8, a period of economic growth, particularly in the new Member States. Not surprisingly, with regard to the poverty risk of both the population aged 20 to 59 years and individuals living in work-poor households, one observes catching-up or beta-convergence (albeit weakened somewhat if one disregards Poland); as regards the poverty risk of the working-age population, there is also evidence of a sigma-convergence (i.e., less dispersion, but this effect is weakened quite substantially if Poland is disregarded). However, simultaneously, the evolution of the gap between the poverty risk of persons in work-poor households and those in work-rich households is quite diverse: It increased by 12.1 percentage points in Germany, 8.6 percentage points in Finland, 6.1 percentage points in Slovenia, and 6 percentage points in Sweden. In that same period of just four years, it decreased by 15.3 percentage points in Ireland and 5.6 percentage points in the Czech Republic. In Germany and Finland, persons in work-poor households lost out in comparison with, not only the work-rich, but also the elderly. In the Czech Republic and Ireland, persons in work-poor households

Table 3.6. Poverty risks and household employment, 2004/5–2007/8: key figures (analysis based on $wp^{0.5}$, Europe 2020 definition of work intensity, SILC 2005–2008).

	Δpov	Wp_{2005}	pwp_{2005}	Δwp	Δ *pwp*	Δ *(pwp–pwr)*	$\Delta pov(60+)$
AT	0.1	13.2	36.1	2.9	-1.3	-0.5	0.6
BE	0.1	23.0	36.0	-2.7	2.9	2.6	0.1
CY	0.0	11.7	39.7	-0.1	-0.6	-0.7	-2.6
CZ	-1.6	13.3	47.5	-1.6	-5.8	-5.6	2.0
DE	3.3	20.6	38.1	-2.1	13.8	12.1	1.8
DK	0.0	14.6	37.6	-1.7	0.3	-0.3	0.6
EE	-2.9	15.6	65.5	-6.6	3.3	3.0	16.2
EL	1.8	18.0	34.1	0.9	2.0	0.5	-3.8
ES	0.2	16.5	40.8	-2.4	2.5	2.3	-1.5
FI	1.2	18.4	33.7	-4.1	9.8	8.6	3.4
FR	0.5	15.9	35.6	-0.9	1.2	0.5	-5.1
HU	-1.6	16.3	37.1	5.9	-2.4	1.1	-2.0
IE	-2.1	21.5	47.8	3.5	-15.0	-15.3	-9.7
IT	0.1	22.2	39.3	-2.1	0.7	0.0	-1.6
LT	-2.9	17.0	60.4	-5.6	-1.7	-1.5	11.6
LU	0.9	12.2	32.7	0.8	4.7	4.7	-1.5
LV	0.9	14.8	63.4	-3.7	6.4	4.0	26.6
NL	-0.8	18.1	25.3	-2.5	1.2	1.8	3.3
PL	-4.6	29.3	40.5	-10.9	-3.8	-2.7	3.6
PT	0.1	14.0	37.8	1.1	3.2	3.9	-4.2
SE	2.3	12.5	26.3	1.4	7.1	6.0	4.2
SI	-0.4	19.2	32.7	-5.4	6.3	6.1	-0.9
SK	-3.5	14.6	35.8	-4.3	1.7	4.4	2.6
UK	-1.2	17.4	53.4	-2.6	-1.3	-1.5	2.9
Avg	-0.4	17.1	40.7	-1.8	1.5	1.4	1.9
St dev	1.8	4.0	10.4	3.5	5.5	5.1	7.2

gained ground on both the work-rich and the elderly, although the reduction in poverty risk among the elderly was quite substantial in Ireland. In yet other countries, such as Poland, Estonia, Lithuania, and Latvia, the gap between the work-rich and the work-poor did not change very much, but the total population aged 20–59 years (i.e., both work-poor and work-rich) gained ground on the elderly, whose poverty risk increased substantially between 2005 and 2008. In other words, Poland, Estonia, Lithuania, and Latvia witnessed an intergenerational shift; the same holds, albeit to a lesser extent, for the United Kingdom. In France and Greece, too, the gap between the poverty risk of the work-poor

Table 3.7. Decomposition of changes in poverty risks, 2004/5–2007/8; analysis on $wp^{0.5}$ (EU 2020 definition of work intensity, EU SILC 2005–2008).

	$\overline{wr}^{0.5}.\Delta pwr^{0.5}$		$\overline{wp}^{0.5}.\Delta pwp^{0.5}$		$\left(\overline{pwp}^{0.5} - \overline{pwr}^{0.5}\right)\Delta wp^{0.5}$		Δpov	
AT	-0.61		-0.18		0.84	***	0.05	
BE	0.20		0.62		-0.91	***	0.09	
CY	0.11		-0.07		-0.04		0.04	
CZ	-0.21		-0.73		-0.67	**	-1.60	**
DE	1.42	***	2.71	***	-0.82	***	3.28	***
DK	0.50		0.04		-0.57	**	-0.03	
EE	0.28		0.41		-3.92	***	-2.91	***
EL	1.24	*	0.37		0.19		1.83	**
ES	0.17		0.38		-0.74	***	0.20	
FI	0.98	***	1.60	***	-1.41	***	1.17	***
FR	0.55		0.18		-0.26		0.54	
HU	-2.83	***	-0.46		1.69	***	-1.59	***
IE	0.17		-3.50	***	1.22	***	-2.11	***
IT	0.55		0.14		-0.62	***	0.08	
LT	-0.20		-0.24		-2.73	***	-2.92	***
LU	0.06		0.60		0.20		0.86	
LV	2.07	***	0.83	*	-2.02	***	0.95	
NL	-0.54		0.20		-0.50	***	-0.84	
PL	-0.82	**	-0.91	***	-2.91	***	-4.64	***
PT	-0.55		0.47		0.32		0.08	
SE	1.01	***	0.94	***	0.35	***	2.31	***
SI	0.22		1.05	***	-1.65	***	-0.39	
SK	-2.36	***	0.22		-1.25	***	-3.51	***
UK	0.17		-0.20		-1.21	***	-1.24	**

Note: Δpov, Δpwp and Δpwr, and (actually observed) $\Delta wp^{0.5}$ significantly different from 0 at 95% (***), at 90% (**), at 85% (*).

and the work-rich changed hardly at all, though here the elderly gained ground significantly, vis-à-vis both the work-poor and the work-rich in the population aged 20–59 years.

We now focus on cases that are in a certain sense exceptional or remarkable. For each of the three subcomponents in the decomposition, values can be identified in Table 3.7 that may be regarded as “outliers” when compared to the average value and standard deviation of those subcomponents for the 26 European countries under review.

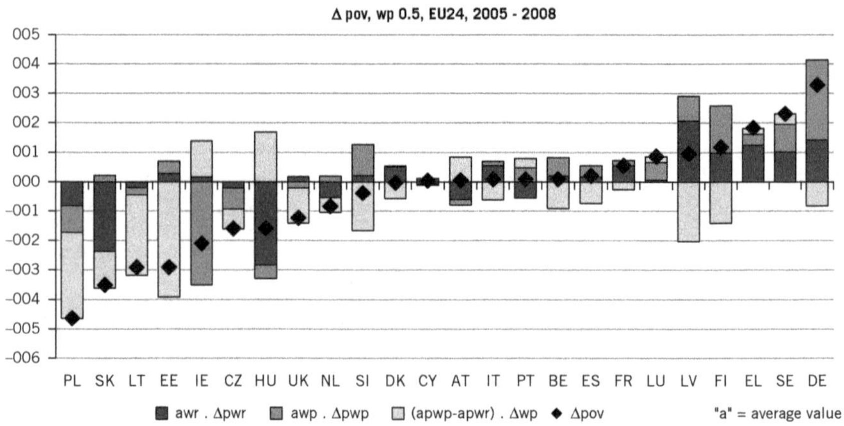

Figure 3.11. Decomposition of changes in poverty, 2004/5–2007/8; analysis based on $wp^{0.5}$ (EU 2020 definition of work intensity, EU SILC 2005–2008).

Finland is an outlier with regard to the contribution of changes in the poverty risk of work-poor households, which adds 1.6 percentage points to the overall poverty risk. The decrease in household work poverty, which was also rather substantial, was not sufficient to offset that impact. Given the fact that the poverty risk of work-rich households also increased, the overall poverty risk in Finland increased.

The data for Ireland paint exactly the opposite picture. The reduction of poverty among work-poor households greatly dwarfed the impact of the increasing share of individuals living in work-poor households over the years 2005–2008. This confirms the intuition on the basis of Figure 3.10 that, in so far as the 1990s and the 2000s were concerned, Ireland represented a striking exception.

Poland is exceptional on two counts: the contribution of the declining share of individuals living in work-poor households (an impact of −2.9 percentage points on the overall poverty rate) and the contribution of the decreasing poverty risk of work-poor households (an impact of −0.9 percentage points). Together with a rather large reduction in the poverty risk of the work-rich, this resulted in a substantial overall reduction in poverty risks. The downside is that the poverty risk of the elderly increased considerably. So one could say that in Poland the decomposition reveals trends (of $pwp^{0.5}$ and $pwr^{0.5}$) that are driven by an intergenerational shift, namely, the relative improvement of the position of the cohort aged 20–59 years vis-à-vis the elderly.

Sweden recorded an exceptional increase in poverty over the years considered. This was the result of the positive impact of all three subcomponents (none were statistical outliers, though all three were rather high up in the distribution of the value of the subcomponents across the EU). In Sweden, the poverty risk of the work-rich, the work-poor, and the elderly increased, and the share of persons in work-poor households also grew.

Although in Greece the overall poverty risk of the population aged 20–59 years increased slightly (though only significantly at 90%), this was mainly due to the increasing poverty risk of persons in work-rich households, which was not offset by any other factor at play within that age cohort; the elderly gained the most ground.

In the United Kingdom, the positive poverty record in the population aged 20–59 years (as opposed to the poverty increase among the elderly) was due mainly to the declining share of people living in work-poor households. This suggests that activation policies were successful in reaching out to work-poor households and moving them to the work-rich group.

Although the underlying employment concept is different, we can now compare both poverty risk decompositions on the basis of $wp^{0.5}$ and wp^{0} (Sections 3.4.2 and 3.4.3). The figures do suggest some interesting stories. A visual comparison of Figure 3.9 and Figure 3.11 shows that the poverty decomposition on the basis of wp^{0} is quite different from the decomposition on the basis of $wp^{0.5}$. The differences are relatively important for Estonia, Finland, Greece, Hungary, Lithuania, Poland, and Slovenia. Some are readily attributable, as in the case of Poland, where the decomposition on the basis of $wp^{0.5}$ gives greater weight to the decline in the share of individuals living in work poverty (as the decrease in $wp^{0.5}$ is much more substantial than the decrease in joblessness wp^{0}) and lower weight to the diminishing poverty risk of the work-rich (because the poverty risk of the work-poor households that hold *any* job decreases more than the poverty risk of work-rich households). Despite those differences, the overall picture that emerges with regard to the diversity of trajectories followed by EU welfare states in the years 2004/5–2007/8 is confirmed by both decompositions.

3.5 CONCLUSIONS

The configuration of individual employment rates and household employment rates on which we focused in this chapter proves relevant for differentiating EU welfare states. We used two concepts to structure data on household employment: "household joblessness," based on an ILO definition of employment, and "household work poverty," based on work-intensity. Although the ILO employment definition is less finely grained than the work-intensity measure, it has the advantage that it can be decomposed on the basis of evolutions in individual joblessness, household size structure, and polarization between and within households.

The shape of this configuration of individual and household employment is driven by forces of modernization that affect all European welfare states in the same direction, such as declining household size, feminization of labor markets,... Nevertheless, the configuration differs from country to country.

At the start of the Lisbon era the individual/household employment configuration was rather different in Spain, Greece, and Italy from most other EU Member States, including new Member States. The level of polarization was negative in Spain, Greece, and Italy—a corollary of the pooling of nonemployment risks in extended families—and became gradually less negative. These southern welfare states were in a trajectory of modernization in which gains in individual employment did not lead to important declines in the shares of jobless households, that is, in welfare state dependency. Their welfare states were still in a process of taking over from familial solidarity.

The pattern in the new Member States after 2000 was very different. Gains in individual employment rates were enhanced by decreasing polarization of jobs over households, that is, by a more even distribution of jobs over households, thus additionally decreasing welfare state dependency. Experience in the UK suggests that the prevalence of jobless households, and thus the extent of "positive" polarization, can be influenced by policy.

However, changes in the share of jobless households cannot explain very much of the diversity in the changes in national at-risk-of-poverty rates during the economic upswing 2004/5–2007/8. Or, to put it another way, it would be incorrect to attribute disappointing poverty trends during the employment boom years solely to the modest conversion of individual employment successes in household employment successes, or more specifically to ongoing polarization of jobs over households. But that does not diminish the importance national and EU policy-makers should attach to the presence of high numbers of jobless households and polarization, as possibly problematic conditions for welfare states. The multidimensional Europe 2020 target on social exclusion and poverty, which includes the reduction of people living in low work-intensity households, may find a justification here.

The disappointing overall "stand still" in national at-risk-of poverty rates during the economic upswing coincides with a convergence of national at-risk-of-poverty rates in the 20–59-year-old age cohort in the EU during those years. We pursued a decomposition of changes in poverty risks both on the basis of "household joblessness" and "household work poverty." Both suggest that the convergence is the combined result of four evolutions:

- first, an overall poverty standstill in a number of countries, with both relatively low and relatively high poverty rates;
- second, a clearly inegalitarian trajectory in some countries with historically low poverty rates, such as Sweden and Finland (and Germany, if we base our assessment on EU SILC);
- third, a successful effort to reduce poverty in the Anglo-Saxon Member States where poverty rates were higher, yet with a different policy

emphasis in the UK (successful activation) and Ireland (much enhanced social protection generosity);
- fourth, the strong economic and employment growth and an intergenerational shift in poverty risks in the new Member States.[22]

Economic and sociodemographic convergence was a dominant background condition in this short time span, but the policy trajectories with regard to public social spending on working-age benefits (including child benefits) were quite different.

These conclusions point simultaneously to the need to refuel economic convergence in the EU, to allow the new Member States to reconnect on a sound basis with the "good years" in terms of growth and employment creation, *and* to the necessary complementarity of employment creation and poverty reduction through social transfers and inclusive labor market policies.

ACKNOWLEDGMENTS

Funding for the research was provided by Net-SILC2, the Second Network for the Analysis of EU-SILC (http://www.essnet-portal.eu/net-silc2). We thank Paul de Beer, Bea Cantillon, and colleagues at the Herman Deleeck Centre for Social Policy, Brian Nolan and the participants at a seminar at the KU Leuven and the UvA for precious comments. The usual disclaimers apply.

NOTES

1 Because the income data in SILC refer to the year prior to the survey, the basis of our poverty data spans the years 2004 and 2007 (except in Ireland and the United Kingdom). The (International Labor Organisation) ILO [author: Please spell out ILO acronym upon first use in Notes]-based definition of jobless households refers to realities in 2005 and 2008 observed immediately before the survey, while the definition of "work-poor" households (see Section 4) refers to the 12-month period as the income data. To summarize this complex construal we label the time frame as "2004/5–2007/8."

2 Currently, 31 countries are involved in the EU-SILC process. Romania, Bulgaria, and Malta were not yet available in the EU-SILC 2005 survey and excluded from the trend analysis. The 2008 EU-SILC user database offers information on 27 countries. These are all EU Member States except France and Malta, but include non-EU members Iceland and Norway. However, as France is again included in the User Database of EU-SILC 2009, information in this wave is used for estimating changes in France.

3 We exclude full-time students both when we count the members of the household who are in employment (to classify the household as "jobless" or "not jobless"), and when we define the population for which we calculate the jobless household rate. In LFS and SILC individuals are considered "full-time students" when they are between 18 and 24 years of age and their status is "inactive."

4 The picture is different when we calculate the growth rates of those shares. Because most of our understanding of the dynamics of welfare states is based on shifts in percentage points of population shares, we stress here the result in percentage points.

5 The argument can best be illustrated in the simple hypothesis that the whole population consists of households with only two working-age adults. For a given individual jobless rate n, a random distribution of jobs implies a household jobless rate $wp = n^2$. Hence, the ratio of "household joblessness" on "individual joblessness" wp/n is equal to n, and thus diminishes with increasing individual employment rates. The marginal impact of changes in n on wp also diminishes with increasing employment rates ($dwp/dn = 2n$). The argument should be interpreted in terms of changes *in percentage points* (i.e., percentage point changes in population shares); the elasticity calculated for marginal changes $\left(\dfrac{dwp/wp}{dn/n}\right)$ is in this case always equal to 2. Our reasoning about poverty rates, employment rates, social spending, etc. is typically in terms of changes in percentage points.

6 Beta-convergence is identified by a negative correlation of −0.81 between the initial values in 1995 and the changes over the period 1995–2008; sigma-convergence is identified by the standard deviation decreasing from 2.16 to 1.50. The sigma-convergence is quite sensitive to outliers, unlike the beta-convergence. Omission of the UK reduces the decline of standard deviation from −0.66 to −0.35; it also reduces the negative correlation from −0.81 to −0.66.

7 Appendix 4 shows that the combined impact of region, origin, and education is an important explanatory factor for the level of polarization in Belgium.

8 The beta-convergence is more robust than the sigma-convergence when eliminating outliers. The negative correlation between starting values for P, signalling beta-convergence, is −0.71 for the EU23 and −0.70 for the EU11. In Appendix 2 we elaborate on the impact of elimination of outliers on the sustainability of convergence.

9 The level of polarization is explained by gender for more than 50% in Spain (for every single year in 1995–2008, with a minimum of 73% explained), in Greece (for every single year in 1995–2008, with a minimum of 109% explained), in Italy (for every single year in 1995–2008, with a minimum of 97%) and in Luxembourg (for most years in 1995–2008). The change in the level of polarization is explained for more than 50% by gender in the following

cases: Austria (2000–2008, change explained for 61%), Belgium (1995–2008, 62%; and 2000–2008, 67%), Cyprus (2000–2008, 146%), Spain (1995–2008, 57%; and 2000–2008, 64%), Greece (1995–2008, 128%; and 2000–2008, 223%), Ireland (1995–2008, 82%), Italy (1995–2008, 70%), Luxembourg (1995–2008, 59%), the Netherlands (2000–2008, 104%; and 1995–2008, 106%), and Portugal (2000–2008, 51%).

10 Hence, whether or not a household, comprised of two 22-year-old students and a non-student adult of the same age, is a jobless household depends on the employment status of the non-student only.

11 This problem is discussed in Nolan and De Graaf (2011).

12 The impact of work-intensity on poverty risks appears to be influenced significantly by the age bracket studied; preliminary results, not shown here, suggest that the at-risk-of-poverty rate for the work-poor groups is considerably higher in a number of countries if the "early-exit generation," that is, the 55–59-year-old age bracket, is excluded from the analysis.

13 A decomposition of changes in poverty rates (2004/5–2007/8, based on the ILO concept of employment) for the age bracket 20–49 years is available on request.

14 In Appendices 4 and 5 of this chapter we refine the decomposition of polarization "within" and "between" households on a conditional basis, which can in principle shed some light on this question.

15 That does not exclude that the impact of having children might be important when analyzing specific subgroups of the population, for instance singles.

16 The variable captures the person's own perception of their main activity at present. The respondent indicates to be permanently disabled or/and unfit to work.

17 This observation contradicts an earlier result by the OECD (2001: 59–61), that no significant correlations are found between aggregate employment and unemployment rates on the one hand and poverty measures on the other hand. This OECD result is quoted in Gregg and Wadsworth (2008) and may have inspired different authors, such as Dickens and Ellwood (2002) and Nickell (2004) to focus on household joblessness. The OECD's result relates to a different sample of countries (ECHP countries and Canada and the United States), a different database (ECHP) and a different time than the correlations displayed in Table 3.3 in this chapter.

18 We entertain serious doubts concerning the validity of the German EU SILC data (Frick & Krell, 2010). They yield a picture that is very different from the German SOEP data, for crucial components of this analysis.

19 Hungary and Latvia present diverging trajectories in the group of new Member States.

20 It is tempting to use Germany as an example of a trajectory where the overall poverty rate increases, despite a decreasing share of work-poor households.

As already indicated in Note 17, doubts exist about EU SILC for Germany. Hence, one should refrain from drawing conclusions on the basis of the former data.

21 A regression of Δpov on $\Delta wp^{0.5}$, $\Delta pwp^{0.5}$, and $\Delta pwr^{0.5}$ yields a coefficient of 0.32 for $\Delta wp^{0.5}$, 0.17 for $\Delta pwp^{0.5}$, and 0.81 for $\Delta pwr^{0.5}$.

22 There was also an intergenerational shift in some of the old Member States.

4

IN-WORK POVERTY

Ive Marx and Brian Nolan

4.1 INTRODUCTION

Although in-work poverty is not a new problem, the degree of attention it is receiving in Europe is more recent, reflecting at least two concurrent sources of concern (Andreβ & Lohmann, 2008; OECD, 2008; European Foundation, 2010; Fraser et al., 2011; Crettaz, 2011; European Commission, 2011). Deindustrialization, intensifying international trade and skill-biased technological change are said to be threatening if not effectively eroding the (potential) earnings and living standards of some workers in advanced economies. Yet at the same time, policy at the European Union (EU) level and in many countries has become focused on increasing the number of people relying on earnings, and particularly on drawing into the labor market those with the weakest education and work history profiles. The Europe 2020 target of boosting employment rates to 75% of the population aged 20 to 64 years shows this drive to be undiminished. Sharply increased unemployment in some countries following on from the onset of the economic crisis has only served to increase the emphasis on getting people into jobs. In light of these trends, there would appear to be legitimate concern that larger sections of the workforce are being expected to rely on jobs that do not generate sufficient income to escape poverty.

This chapter starts with a discussion of current debates about in-work poverty and underlying driving forces. It turns to issues of definition and measurement of in-work poverty, which are central to adequate analysis and policy formulation, and then examines the variation across countries and over time in in-work poverty using data from EU Statistics on Income and Living

Conditions (EU-SILC). With low-paid work often seen as a key driver, we look first at the empirical evidence regarding the extent and nature of low pay, and then at its complex relationship with in-work poverty. This brings out that in-work poverty is strongly associated not so much with low hourly pay per se but rather with single-earnership and low work-intensity at the household level, as well as with working part-time, part-year, or on temporary contract at the individual level. Against this background, the remainder of the chapter is devoted to what policy can do to prevent or address in-work poverty, starting with an examination of what an incremental augmentation/modification of the traditional minimum income protection provisions for workers could potentially achieve. We then ask whether innovative options such as Earned Income Tax Credit/Working Tax Credit (EITC/WTC) type negative income taxes offer a model for emulation. Finally, we discuss the broader implications for effective antipoverty tools and strategies, and how these may differ across institutional settings.

4.2 CURRENT DEBATES ABOUT IN-WORK POVERTY

In-work poverty is widely seen as a "postindustrial" phenomenon, linked first and foremost to the growth of low-paid insecure employment in the service sector. The contrast is often drawn with the golden years of welfare capitalism when manufacturing industry provided stable, well-paid employment even for those with little or no formal education. As Esping-Andersen et al. (2002) put it: "We no longer live in a world in which low-skilled workers can support the entire family. The basic requisite for a good life is increasingly strong cognitive skills and professional qualifications... Employment remains as always the sine qua non for good life chances, but the requirements for access to quality jobs are rising and are likely to continue to do so." By the same token, Bonoli (2007: 496) st ates: "Postindustrial labour markets are characterized by higher wage inequality with the result that for those at the bottom end of the wage distribution, access to employment is not a guarantee of a poverty-free existence."

Research by labor economists shows that this picture of a uniform shift away from low-skilled work needs to be nuanced (Autor et al., 2003). The postindustrial transition and particularly the impact of technological change have not simply entailed a demand shift away from low-skilled labor and toward more highly educated workers. Studies have shown that there is growth in employment in both the highest-skilled (professional and managerial) and lowest-skilled occupations (personal services) with declining employment in the middle of the distribution (manufacturing and routine office jobs). Goos, Manning, & Salomons (2009) document this trend toward "job polarization" throughout Europe, albeit with varying intensity (on which, see also European Commission, 2011). While wage dispersion appears to have increased in a majority of Organisation for Economic Coordination and Development (OECD) countries over the past 25 years, this is more pronounced toward the top than the bottom (OECD, 2011). None the less, the available evidence does provide a basis for legitimate concern regarding a possible rise in low-paid employment, exacerbated by the impact of the economic crisis.

At the same time, an increased policy emphasis on activation has become evident in many European countries, certainly at the level of rhetoric, and gauging by some indicators also in terms of actual policy (Barbier & Ludwig-Mayerhofer, 2004; Kenworthy, 2008; Dingeldey, 2007; Eichhorst & Konle-Seidl, 2008; Aurich, 2009; Weishaupt, 2013). These studies build on mainly qualitative assessments of policy changes, while the 2007 OECD Employment Outlook tentatively concludes, based on country questionnaires, that activation efforts have effectively intensified in a number of countries since the late 1990s. We still lack reliable indicators of actual activation intensity, mainly because implementation aspects are so difficult to measure (e.g., effective sanctioning or effective availability and take-up of training places or subsidized jobs). Within the broad set of activation strategies deployed, an important number specifically target the long-term unemployed, including social assistance recipients. And within this set, an important number of measures are aimed at stimulating these people, who generally have low levels of educational attainment, into relatively low-paid/minimum-wage level jobs. Employment subsidies and employers' social security contribution reductions also generally aim to stimulate the creation and take-up of relatively low-paid, or at least minimum-wage level, jobs.

From a poverty perspective, it is bound to matter who takes up low-paid jobs and under what conditions this is done. If a single person moves from long-term benefit dependency into a minimum wage job this will reduce poverty if (net income at) the minimum wage exceeds the poverty threshold and benefits for the long-term unemployed (social insurance or social assistance) are below that threshold. Similarly, if a potential second earner (e.g., an unemployed or nonemployed partner of someone in work) moves into low-paid work there may also be a positive effect on (in-work) poverty, provided they are living in a household with disposable income below the poverty threshold and the net increase in income (taking any reduction in benefits or entitlements into account) is enough to bring them above that threshold.

However, even taking up a full-time minimum wage job may not suffice to bring the household out of poverty if the minimum wage is not sufficiently high relative to the poverty threshold, or if taxes and social security contributions cause net disposable income to drop below the poverty line. Unemployed sole breadwinners with a dependent spouse and children (and possibly others) to support may not be lifted from poverty if they are forced to take up a low-paid job unless there are supportive measures like child benefits or in-work benefits. Similarly, taking up part-time employment may not suffice to bring the household above the poverty threshold, but that may be all that is available, or all that is feasible where affordable child-care cannot be accessed—a particular problem for lone parents.

It is also important to note that movement from unemployment or inactivity into work may also have an indirect effect on conventional poverty measures, in that relative income poverty thresholds may be pushed up. Depending on whether the increase in employment is for the most part occurring in households above or below the poverty threshold, that indirect effect could dampen down or offset the poverty-reducing effect of successful activation. Countries such as Spain or Ireland saw very rapid increases in labor force participation during the boom, which contributed to the rise in median income and thus poverty thresholds there (see, for example, Whelan et al., 2003).

Hence, the potential impact of such policies in each country will depend on compositional factors (the household composition of the nonactive population) and contextual factors (minimum-wage levels, the presence of childcare benefits and childcare facilities, the presence of in-work benefits, or earnings disregards). We now go on to explore the empirical evidence on patterns and trends over time, first discussing issues of definition and measurement of in-work poverty.

4.3 DEFINING AND MEASURING IN-WORK POVERTY

The literature on the working poor employs a variety of definitions, based on different approaches of what is meant by "poor" and by "working" (for an overview see Crettaz & Bonoli, 2010; Peña-Casas & Latta, 2004). The definition adopted for the indicator of in-work poverty now produced by Eurostat as part of the EU's set of social inclusion indicators is an important focus of attention. For that purpose the working poor are defined and measured as those individuals who have been mainly working during the reference year (either in employment or self-employment) and whose household equivalized disposable income is below 60% of the median in the country in question. Employment status is measured on the basis of monthly calendars completed by survey respondents, with "in work" taken to mean that the status he/she declares to have occupied for at least seven months is employee or self-employed.

It is widely recognized that analysis of in-work poverty needs to distinguish between employees and the self-employed, both because self-employment is quite distinctive in nature and because survey information on self-employment income is normally less reliable than wages and salaries. The EU indicator can be broken down between these two types of employment, and also between full-time and part-time workers, which is another important distinction.

However, in considering this measure a number of other important issues arise:

- Combining two levels of analysis—the individual's labor market status and the household's income (adjusted for household size)—inherently complicates interpretation, because the labor market status of other persons in the household, rather than that of the individual being considered, may be crucial, as may the number of dependent children, if any.

- Using a year as the reference period for labor market status and income position also complicates interpretation: those working for part but not all of the year may be in poverty on an annual basis for that reason even if they were not poor while working—and how much of the year does one have to work to be counted as "working"?
- For these and other reasons, this definition/measure makes it difficult to identify the different factors potentially underlying the phenomenon, as well as the locus(es) of policy failure, which could include:
  - Low (household) work-intensity
  - Inadequate out-of-work benefits
  - Inadequate earnings
  - Inadequate earnings supplements
  - Number of dependent people (children) relative to income.

As we will bring out in reviewing what has been learned from studies of in-work poverty, employing additional measurement approaches can help to clarify the causal processes at work. Some of these are available as breakdowns of the EU's social inclusion indicator—for example, distinguishing employees from the self-employed, and part-time from full-time workers. Others go beyond these, such as measures concentrating on current labor force status and income, or on annual income for those in work all year. We return to these complexities and complementarities, but first look at key patterns and trends using the EU measure, which is now playing a central role in analysis and policy debate.

4.4 IN-WORK POVERTY: PREVALENCE AND TRENDS

Using data produced by Eurostat from the EU-SILC database for the social inclusion indicator described above, we can see how the prevalence of in-work poverty varies across EU countries. Looking first at the right-hand column of Table 4.1, this shows the percentage of persons in work living in households falling below 60% of the median income in their own country for 2010 (or 2009 where that is the latest available). We see that the extent of in-work poverty ranges from a low of 4%–5% in Austria, Belgium, the Czech Republic, Finland, the Netherlands, and Slovenia up to 13%–14% in Greece and Spain and 17% in Romania.

Table 4.1 also shows the corresponding figures for 2006 and 2008, also from EU-SILC, and for 2000 drawn from the European Household Community Panel survey and national sources. It is noteworthy that there was no general tendency for in-work poverty to rise after 2006, despite the onset of the economic crisis: in only six of the 27 countries was a marked increase seen, and in-work

Table 4.1. Percentage of those in work at risk of poverty, EU 2000–2010.

	Percentage with annual equivalized incomes below 60% median			
	2000	**2006**	**2008**	**2010**
Austria	6	6.4	6.3	5.0
Belgium	5	4.1	4.8	4.5
Bulgaria	7*	5.4	7.5	7.7
Cyprus		7.2	6.0	6.8
Czech Republic	3*	3.5	3.6	3.7
Denmark	3*	4.5	5.0	6.5
Germany	4	5.5	7.1	7.2
Estonia	10	7.5	7.3	6.5
Spain	8	9.9	10.6	12.7
Finland	5	4.5	5.1	3.7
France	8	6.0	6.7[b]	6.2
Greece	13	13.8	14.3	13.8
Hungary	6	6.8	5.8	5.3
Ireland	7	6.2	6.5	7.6
Italy	10	9.6	8.9	9.4
Latvia	13	11.2	11.0	9.7
Lithuania	14	10.0	9.3	12.3
Luxembourg	8	10.3	9.4	10.6
Malta	6	4.1	5.0	5.7
The Netherlands	6	4.4	4.8	5.1
Poland	11	12.8	11.5	11.4
Portugal	14	11.2	11.8	9.7
Romania	14	..	17.5	17.2
Slovenia	5	4.8	5.1	5.3
Slovakia	5	6.3	5.8	5.7
Sweden	5*	7.4	6.8	6.5
United Kingdom	6	7.8	8.5	6.8
Iceland		8.8	9.6	8.8
Norway		12.4	11.6	10.9

* 2001
[b]break in time series
Source: EU Social Inclusion Indicators website.

poverty fell in a number of others. It could be that, at least in some countries, those who remained in employment during the economic crises were less likely to be below the income poverty threshold than those who lost their jobs, contributing to a decline in in-work poverty; however, unemployment will also have reduced some multiearner households to a single earner, which would in itself be expected to drive up the number of in-work-poor. Taking the longer span from 2000 to 2010, in-work poverty is seen to have increased over the decade in countries such as Denmark, Germany, Spain, Luxembourg, Romania, and Sweden, but to have decreased in more countries than it rose. Abstracting altogether from the crisis period, comparison of 2000 with 2006 also fails to show a marked rise in in-work poverty in many countries. The common presumption of such a trend is, therefore, not supported, over the period from 2000, by this data and indicator. However, the fact that the sources of data for 2000, unlike the later years, are not EU-SILC means that the trends shown have to be treated with some caution.

The OECD has produced figures relating to trends in in-work poverty covering the decade from the mid-1990s to the mid-2000s, but "working" in this instance is defined as having at least one person in work in the household (see OECD, 2009). Drawing on a variety of sources, but seeking to apply a uniform methodology, the OECD found in-work poverty to have increased substantially in EU countries such as Germany, the Netherlands, and Luxembourg over this decade, while some other countries, such as Italy, saw substantial declines. The study by Airio (2008) of the period 1970–2000 covering six OECD countries (and mostly based on data from the Luxembourg Income Study) concludes that it is difficult to find any common trend in in-work poverty. Great care must be exercised in drawing strong conclusions about levels and trends in in-work poverty across countries, because fundamental differences in approach and definitions, as well as in data and period covered, can all affect the outcome.

This caution must extend to the way "poverty" as well as "working" is defined: Income poverty thresholds held constant in purchasing power terms over time are likely to give very different results than ones moving in line with median household income. The latter will be influenced not only by the trajectory of gross earnings but also by what is happening to other market income sources (notably rent, interest, and dividends) and trends in cash transfers, direct taxes, and social insurance contributions. Where profits are rising more rapidly than wages, where direct taxes or social insurance contributions are being cut so net wages grow more rapidly than gross wages, or where increasing employment is concentrated in households where there is already someone in work, relative income thresholds at the household level may rise considerably more rapidly than average gross earnings for individuals—as seen for example in Ireland, Italy, Poland, and Spain in the period from 2000 up to the onset of the economic crisis. Alternative ways of framing income poverty thresholds can be helpful in disentangling the underlying processes and interpreting headline in-work poverty indicators framed in purely relative terms. They can also usefully be complemented with measures of material deprivation—now included among the EU's social inclusion indicators (see, for example, Nolan & Whelan, 2011). However, most research on in-work poverty has focused on relative income measures, and for current purposes we follow that approach.

4.5 LOW PAY: PREVALENCE AND TRENDS

In view of the strong perceived link between low-paid work and in-work poverty in recent debates, as outlined earlier, we now consider what empirical analysis suggests about trends in low pay and its relationship to in-work poverty.

Is low-paid work becoming more pervasive across Europe?

Service sector employment has become the main source of jobs growth in recent decades, now accounting for more than three quarters of all jobs in several OECD countries. Low-paid employment is more widespread in the services industries, with hotels, restaurants, and retail the sectors where low-paid work is most frequent, even in countries like Denmark where the overall incidence of low-paid work is low (Lucifora &Salverda, 2008).

The OECD's low-pay database, the most widely cited source of comparative data on the extent of low pay, shows the proportion of low-wage workers in rich countries ranging from around one in twenty in Sweden to around one in four in the United States. Although a clear demarcation is often assumed to exist between the Anglo-Saxon countries and the Continental European ones—with substantially more low pay in the former—the evidence does not support this. Nor is it the case that low-paid work has necessarily increased most in the less regulated, more service-intensive economies. Rather, it has remained relatively steady (at a high level in the United States), and though increasing in the UK, this was proportionally by not much more than, for example, in the Netherlands (Lucifora & Salverda, 2008). In fact, the OECD database suggests that the largest increases in low pay (for full-time workers) have taken place in countries like Denmark, Germany, and Poland (OECD, 2011). The overall conclusion advanced by the OECD on the basis of this database, as already noted in Section 4.2, is that wage dispersion has widened in a clear majority of OECD countries in recent years, with this being more pronounced toward the top than the bottom. National studies also show increasing levels of low pay in countries such as Germany, the Netherlands, and the United States.

As of yet, there is also no systematic research available linking low-pay trends with the intensity of activation efforts, in part because actual activation intensity is so difficult to quantify. In the case of the Netherlands, where activation efforts have been significant, there is evidence of an increase in low-paid work, but the link with activation has not been demonstrated (Salverda et al., 2008). In the German case, drastic labor market and social security reform has coincided with a rise in low-paid work (Bosch & Weinkopf, 2008; Kenworthy, 2011).

Most comparative research on low pay has compared the Anglo-Saxon countries with the "Continental" and Scandinavian countries of the "old" EU15, but a more comprehensive picture of low pay in Europe can now be derived from data covering the enlarged EU. These come from the EU Statistics on Income and Living

Conditions (EU-SILC) data-gathering framework designed to produce a range of harmonized indicators for the Union, notably with respect to social inclusion.

In empirical studies of low pay, two broad approaches are used: one focuses on the hourly earnings of those currently working as employees, while the other concentrates on annual earnings for those who worked during the previous year. Each has its own value, with hourly earnings being most strongly related to the pattern of reward for education and skills but annual earnings more directly related to the income measure by which household poverty is usually assessed (including in the EU's Social Inclusion indicators). Because low annual earnings arising from spending much of the year away from work is a very different phenomenon than low weekly or hourly pay, employing an annual perspective is essential to knowing how much of the year was actually spent in work. It is then common (for example, for many countries in the earnings and low-pay database compiled by the OECD) to focus on those who worked all year—"full-year workers." This runs the risk that those who move in and out of work during the year, and who clearly constitute a high-risk group from both a low-pay and poverty perspective, will receive insufficient attention—despite the fact that this may well be a group particularly affected by the enhanced activation efforts of governments in recent years. It is none the less important to home in first on persons with low annual earnings when working all year, given that they pose a particular challenge for income support and broader welfare and labor market policies.

We, therefore, use the microdata from EU-SILC for 2010 to identify those who were in work in all 12 months of the previous year, and whose employee income for that period falls below two thirds of median annual earnings of full-year workers in the country in question (the most widely used threshold in the low-pay research literature). A number of countries had to be excluded because of extensive missing data on the relevant variables. Table 4.2 shows that for all full-year employees the low-pay rate ranges from about 15% to over 30%.

Although most of these employees are working full-time, a significant minority in some countries is only working part-time and may have low annual earnings simply for that reason. Concentrating on full-time full-year employees, the second column in Table 4.2 shows that the extent of low pay then ranges from a low of 10% up to a high of 28%. If one thinks in terms of the conventional categorization into welfare regimes, Denmark and Finland from the Scandinavian regime are among the lowest with 11% or less low paid. Among the corporatist countries the picture is more mixed. Belgium, France, and the Netherlands have relatively low levels of 10%–14%, but Austria and Germany are higher at 17% and 23% respectively. The UK and Ireland, representing the Anglo-Saxon regime, are in the 20%–22% range. Spain is the only one of the Southern "old" Member States covered with 16%, while Cyprus is at 20%. The Czech Republic and Slovenia, among the more affluent post-Socialist countries, are in the 16%–19% range, although Hungary is higher together with Poland and Estonia. Lithuania and Latvia are a good deal higher at 27% or higher. (The change from the ECHP to

EU-SILC as the base for common EU data makes assessment of medium-term trends over time difficult.)

These figures reveal that low pay affects a substantial proportion of those working full-time for the entire year in most EU countries, a proportion in excess of 10% in all but three of the countries covered. There is variation in the extent of low pay across the various welfare regimes conventionally distinguished but none entirely escapes it. This remains the case when we incorporate available estimates for other countries on the basis of the OECD low-pay database. These figures confirm the comparatively high incidence of low pay in countries like Hungary and Poland, where the levels are similar to Canada and the United States.

Research on the varying extent of low-wage employment suggests that labor market institutions, in particular centralized wage-bargaining, union power, and minimum wages, play a key role (Lucifora & Salverda, 2008). Here though our core concern is not chiefly with low pay per se, but with its implications for in-work poverty. In that context, the characteristics of the workers most likely to experience low pay are key. Low pay is generally highly concentrated not just in particular sectors of the economy but among particular kinds of workers—with those having low levels of education, those working part-time, non-nationals, women, and young people having rates well above the average. This has fundamental implications for the relationship between low pay and household poverty, as we shall see.

4.6 LOW-PAID WORK AND IN-WORK POVERTY

Given that in-work poverty is clearly significant across the EU and OECD, then, what is the role of low pay, and the relationship between low pay and household poverty? It is essential to understand that low-paid work and "in-work" poverty are in fact largely separate phenomena. Marx and Verbist (1998), for example, using Luxemburg Income Study (LIS) data for the early 1990s found the overlap between low pay and poverty to be in the order of 5% to 10% in most industrialized economies. Other studies have confirmed this (OECD, 2009). This is because poor households generally do not contain an employee, whether low-paid or not, while most low-paid workers (70%–80% in most countries) live in households with more than one earner. A crucial influence on whether a low-paid employee is in a poor household is thus the extent to which the household relies on his or her earnings. Particularly for low-paid women and young people, their earnings most often constitute a secondary source of income for the household—sometimes a deliberate strategy (Gardiner & Millar, 2006). As a consequence, low-paid workers are often reasonably high up the distribution (in terms of disposable household income relative to need). Studies based on data from the European Community Household Panel (ECHP) showed that in the mid-late-1990s about 80% or more of low-paid workers in EU15 countries were in the 3rd–5th disposable income quintile (Nolan & Marx, 2001). (Some, however, were only just above the poverty line, which points to the role of low-paid work in preventing income poverty.)

We can verify that picture for the enlarged EU by linking the EU-SILC data on earnings and low pay analyzed in Table 4.2 to the incomes of the households

Table 4.2. Low pay for full-year employees, annual income, EU 2010.

	Percentage below two thirds median earnings	
	All full-year employees	**Full-time full-year employees**
Austria	22.1	17.0
Belgium	15.0	9.2
Bulgaria	18.3	17.1
Cyprus	21.1	20.3
Czech Republic	17.9	16.4
Germany	29.1	22.7
Denmark	14.6	11.5
Estonia	21.1	21.2
Spain	21.1	16.0
Finland	11.1	8.2
France	16.2	10.3
Greece	20.8	17.7
Hungary	18.4	17.5
Ireland	29.4	20.9
Iceland	25.3	19.0
Italy	19.2	14.2
Lithuania	29.8	29.0
Luxembourg	27.6	28.0
Latvia	27.8	27.1
Malta	19.0	16.2
The Netherlands	22.6	13.4
Norway	20.9	14.6
Poland	20.6	19.0
Portugal	13.6	13.7
Romania	18.1	18.1
Sweden	18.6	12.3
Slovenia	20.2	20.2
Slovakia	11.3	9.7
United Kingdom	27.3	22.1

Source: Analysis of EU-SILC 2010 microdata.

Table 4.3. Income poverty risk for low-paid earners, by household position, EU-SILC 2010.

	Single person	Single parent	Single earner couple	Dual earner, 1st earner	Dual earner, 2nd earner	Other FTFY worker	Total
Austria	29	59	33	11	3	5	11
Belgium	8	29	37	5	1	9	11
Bulgaria	56	76	43	18	6	15	18
Cyprus	65	22	68	18	2	17	19
Czech Republic	18	63	18	11	1	4	7
Germany	28	55	31	11	1	7	14
Denmark	40		23	1	0	8	17
Estonia	12	56	42	14	3	15	17
Spain	18	71	44	25	6	16	19
Finland	0	0	19	2	0	9	5
France	17	56	37	10	3	8	15
Greece	12	53	71	28	6	9	16
Hungary	29	20	38	14	5	9	14
Ireland	3	9	17	1	0	4	5
Iceland	32	43	25	15	1	6	13
Italy	45	43	65	17	7	17	27
Lithuania	31	93	54	17	5	17	23
Luxembourg	47	75	58	21	3	11	26
Latvia	31	67	51	19	6	15	22
Malta	0	20	81	28	1	8	14
The Netherlands	8	43	23	17	2	8	10
Norway	23	30	21	7	2	5	12
Poland	36	67	56	25	4	12	18
Portugal	11	100	55	25	3	9	15
Romania	23	53	68	23	2	11	16
Sweden	38	29	29	12	2	7	15
Slovenia	17	16	45	8	0	5	8
Slovakia	54	36	40	43	5	10	15
United Kingdom	14	17	28	12	2	7	10

Source: Analysis of EU-SILC 2010 microdata.

involved. Table 4.3 compares the income poverty rates for low-paid workers across different household types. We see that the risk of poverty depends very strongly on the household/income configuration of the low-paid worker. For example, in Ireland 5% of low-paid workers find themselves in financial poverty, which in the context of the overall poverty rate for the working-age population is not a particularly high share. Yet the risk is much greater for a low-paid person who is the sole earner in a couple than it is for a second earner in a couple. More generally, low-paid workers who are the sole or primary earner in their household are at a very substantial risk of poverty, especially when there are dependent children. However, if the low-paid worker is the second earner the poverty risk drops to very low levels. Actually, low-paid workers in this situation have poverty risks far below the average level of working-age persons, pointing to the role low-paid work can have in preventing poverty.

Who are the working poor?

The core of the working poor consists of workers who are sole earners and have a family to support. Poverty rate for persons in work varies markedly depending on the type of household involved. Lone parents or those in households with a couple (and perhaps children), but only one earner, face much higher poverty risks than those in households with two or more earners. Although single parents (lone mothers) are overrepresented, the majority of the working poor are traditional two adult/male breadwinner households with dependent children. Even a moderately well-paid job may not suffice to meet household income needs, depending on the extent of those needs and the other sources of income available to the household.

It is clear, then, that having only one earner in the household has become a poverty risk in an era in which the average living standard, and hence the relative poverty threshold, is increasingly determined by the living standard of double-earner households. As brought out in, for example, European Foundation (2004) and European Commission (2011), the roots of in-work poverty are to be found in the interaction of a variety of factors at individual and household level: These include low educational and/or skill level, gender, and age, but also the size and composition of the household—in particular, single-adult as opposed to couple or multiadult households—and the proportion of working-age adults in work throughout the year.

This helps to explain why in-work poverty is pervasive across Europe and the OECD, and why its extent does not simply reflect the size of the low-wage sector (Lohmann & Andreß, 2008; Lohmann, 2009). Because in-work poverty is strongly associated with single-earnership, it is also associated with a multiplicity of institutional factors that affect household labor market participation patterns, particularly double- and multi-earnership. Lohmann & Marx (2008), comparing the EU15 countries, argue that these institutional factors—relating to decommodification and defamilization—are generally aligned most favorably in the Nordic countries and least favorably in the South, while the institutional constellations in the Anglo-Saxon and Continental European countries have mixed and sometimes contradictory effects. The country differences in in-work poverty risks broadly fit this pattern, albeit with very considerable within cluster variation, particularly within the Continental European countries. A multilevel model by

Lohmann (2009) adds explanatory power, but again highlights the multicausal nature of in-work poverty, in part an inherent consequence of the way in-work poverty is commonly defined. In a similar vein, the expert reports on in-work poverty collected through the EU Network of Independent Experts on Social Inclusion and summarized in Frazer & Marlier (2010) highlight the interaction of a very complex set of factors including individual and household characteristics, institutional factors such as the minimum wage and tax and social protection, and the structure of the labor market and economy. Maitre, Nolan, & Whelan (2011) show that among those employed all year, the likelihood of living in a poor household is much higher for the low-paid than others, but only a minority are in such households; whether the low-paid employee is the only earner in the household is key, bringing one back to the interaction of individual and household characteristics with institutional and labor market structures. The analysis in European Commission (2011) brings out a similar complex set of interactions, highlighting inter alia the high risk faced by those working part-time or part-year, and those in temporary rather than permanent contracts.

Hence, in-work poverty does not lend itself to a simple and uniformly applicable analysis of policy failure. As already emphasized above and explored in Eurostat (2010), this has implications for the way in-work poverty is defined and measured, with alternative approaches having potential for useful insights. From a policy perspective, the implication is that in-work poverty patterns are influenced by a whole range of factors, ranging from labor market institutions (e.g., wage decentralization and coordination, minimum wages), over dual-earner support arrangements (e.g., tax incentives, childcare provisions), to the set-up of social security systems.

4.7 TACKLING IN-WORK POVERTY

We now move on to a discussion of policy options to tackle in-work poverty. Two prior considerations are in place. First, the working poor do not constitute a well-delineated, homogenous group, visible and easily "targetable" for policy. While, for example, social assistance recipients, or more generally people wholly reliant on transfers, are unambiguously at a very high risk of poverty and (seen to be) deserving of policy intervention, the working poor are more heterogeneous. Only a small percentage of workers are at risk, and even the risks for low-paid workers, or for that matter, part-time or atypical workers are not uniformly high. It is only within specific household configurations that workers face a substantial risk. They are also less visible, leading "below the radar" normal lives, going out to work, and raising children.

A second consideration is that which policy action, or set of policy actions, is most appropriate cannot be seen as entirely independent from normative notions that underlie the various ways in-work poverty can be construed. In-work poverty in Europe, as it is conventionally measured, is to a considerable extent concentrated among low work-intensity households, for example, dual adult households with only one working adult. Whether their at risk of financial poverty status is construed as a problem of insufficient breadwinner earnings or as a problem of partner nonparticipation makes a fundamental difference as to what type of policy action is to be examined and possibly favored. This essentially requires a normative judgment. In the case of traditional breadwinner type households with insufficient earnings, the preponderance of opinion in Europe appears to be that this is to be seen as a matter of partner nonparticipation or under-participation. But other cases may be less clear-cut. Even if in-work poverty is construed as largely a problem of low household work-intensity, the question then arises as to what might be a sufficient level of work-intensity. It is not self-evident that this requires all working-age, work-capable adults in the household to be in full-time work the whole year round. Societal norms may differ across countries. In the Netherlands, for example, a four-fifths job per adult appears to be closer to the norm of full-work-intensity. Also, household composition may be deemed to matter. It is not self-evident that a lone parent with young children is expected to work full-year, full-time before additional income support is to be considered legitimate if his or her earnings fall short of the poverty threshold.

A variety of potential tools are available to tackle in-work poverty. One can think of that toolset as consisting of policies distinguishable on two dimensions, as shown in Figure 4.1. One dimension of differentiation is whether the policy in question seeks to have a direct or indirect impact on income. Minimum wages, (child) benefits, and tax measures have a direct impact on personal or household income. Indirect measures can either seek to increase individual earnings potential (e.g., education, training) or to accommodate/stimulate higher work-intensity at the individual or household level (e.g., childcare policies). Another dimension is whether the policy instrument is incremental (i.e.,

	Incremental options	**New options**
Direct income support	– raising the minimum wage/ wage floors through regulation – tax relief – reductions of employee social security contributions – child benefits	– negative income taxes – in work benefits – basic income
Indirect support	– upskilling/training – demand policies (subsidized employment, wage cost subsidies) – active labor market policies – facilitating labor participation (e.g., child care)	– Innovative demand oriented policies (e.g., service cheques) – Innovative supply focused policies (empowerment)

Figure 4.1. The policy toolbox to address in-work poverty.

builds on or augments existing provisions) or whether the policy tool is new and seeks to replace or complement existing policies. Among the set of innovative direct income support measures belong the so-called "negative income taxes" and in-work benefits that are increasingly promoted as solution for in-work poverty. In what follows, the discussion will focus on direct income support measures.

4.7.1 Augmenting Existing Provisions

For decades, gradual increases in legal minimum wages, or de facto minimum wages agreed upon in collective labor agreements, contributed to improving the living standards of low-paid workers and their families. Minimum wages, in combination with child-related benefits, constituted the main pillar of minimum income protection for workers, while in work.

The number of European countries with a minimum wage has increased over the past two decades. The early 1990s saw the introduction of minimum wages in the formerly Communist countries that are now part of the European Union. The United Kingdom introduced a national minimum wage in 1999 and Ireland one year later. Recent developments in Austria point toward an introduction of a national minimum wage, since an agreement between the trade unions and the employers became applicable as of January 2009, establishing a minimum wage covering almost the entire private sector. In 2010, 19 Member States of the European Union had a national minimum wage, set by government, sometimes in cooperation with or on the advice of the social partners, or by the social partners themselves in a national agreement.

What is their effectiveness today in terms of offering protection against poverty? Before we move on to address that question, we should note that, in large part, the historical function of the minimum wage has been to ensure "fair wages" and to prevent "unfair competition." Clearly, here we are mainly concerned with the role of minimum wages in protecting workers against poverty. To gauge this we draw on the Centre for Social Policy (CSB) Minimum Income Protection Indicators (MIPI) Database. This is a national expert sourced database containing data relating to social assistance and minimum wages for the EU25 countries. For the EU15 countries, the database spans the period 1992–2009, for the EU10 countries it spans the period 2001–2009.

Relative to average earnings there is considerable variation in Europe in 2009. As a percentage of gross average earnings, minimum wages range from around 30% to 50%. This would suggest that there may be scope for substantial increases in some countries. However, given that most low-paid workers are not the principal earners in the household where they live, and thus not in poor households, increases in the minimum wage may have a relatively limited impact on poverty, with most of the benefit (even in the absence of possible negative effects on employment) going to non-poor households (Marx, Vanhille, & Verbist, 2012a).

Still, it is relevant to ask how adequate minimum wages are for households that have to rely solely on that income. Table 4.4 shows the net income—taking into account taxes and personal social security contributions—at minimum wage level for a single person household without dependent children. For single persons, net incomes at a full minimum wage exceed the 60% poverty threshold comfortably in most of the EU15 countries, although with some notable exceptions like, for example, Spain. For the EU10 countries, the picture is more mixed.

Turning to a "traditional" single breadwinner household with dependent children the picture becomes entirely different. As also shown in Table 4.4, in not a single EU country, except Ireland, can a two-adult household with

Table 4.4. Net disposable income of a minimum wage earner as a percentage of equivalent median income, by household type, EU, 2009.

	Single	Couple	Couple, two children	Lone parent + 2 children	Lone parent + 1 child
Austria	61	47	45	55	80
Belgium	75	59	49	59	64
Bulgaria	39	26	24	31	29
Czech Republic	52	40	44	51	52
Estonia	50	37	27	39	48
France	68	54	49	58	50
Greece	93	66	44	53	72
Hungary	58	42	43	52	52
Ireland	83	55	63	81	51
Italy	76	56	49	62	76
Latvia	96	67	48	61	57
Lithuania	58	39	50	49	52
Luxembourg	54	54	50	51	54
The Netherlands	73	57	45	61	72
Poland	59	40	38	52	53
Portugal	63	42	47	47	46
Romania	63	43	38	50	48
Slovak Republic	50	33	29	37	45
Slovenia	46	38	39	47	42
Spain	53	35	25	32	47
United Kingdom	62	49	52	67	70

Note: Data for FI, SE, DE, and DK refer to 50% of average wage. Data for Italy are based on the minimum wage in the low-paid leather and fur sector.
Sources: Net disposable income: CSB-MIPI (Van Mechelen et al., 2010); exchange rates and poverty thresholds from Eurostat online data base (extracted in June 2010); own calculations.

two children subside on a net income provided by the minimum wage. Note that the net income calculation in this graph takes account of child benefits and child-related tax allowances. The gap is quite significant in most countries. This is in part a matter of taxation and social security contributions, but even without taxation the gap would remain quite significant in most countries. This is the case despite shifts over the past decade toward tax relief and additional income support provisions for low-paid workers (Marx, Marchal, & Nolan, 2013).

If both partners work and have full-time jobs at minimum wage, they are in few countries at risk of financial poverty unless they have a relatively large number of dependents. Double earnership provides an almost watertight guarantee against financial poverty, even at minimum wage, provided that both partners work full time and that not too many dependents rely on that income.

Clearly, these cases are to be taken as stylized examples. In the real world, these type cases are rare, if only because small proportions of workers actually work for the minimum wage. Minimum wages effectively serve a kind of benchmark purpose in many countries marking the ground floor of the wage building. Also, the stylized examples presented here assume full-time work, even though low-paid work is proportionally more prevalent among part-time workers. Lone parents, in particular, may find it difficult to work full-time.

These stylized cases do, however, help us to think about the potential benefits and limitations of policy alternatives. In that context, it is arguably particularly relevant to consider the policy options as these pertain to full-time workers, simply because they could well be considered those most deserving of direct income support or tax relief.

So what are the prospects for improvement? It is important to consider this question seriously because discussions about reducing in-work poverty tend to focus strongly on the question of raising minimum wages and/or reducing taxes on low-income households.

It is perhaps useful to consider trends over the past decade first. In real terms, minimum wages increased in most EU countries during the period 2001–2009, especially in the EU12 countries. However, these real increases translate into a far more diverse picture relative to average earnings. From Figure 4.2a, in which countries are ranked by their initial level in 2001, it can be seen that by and large the strongest increases occurred in the countries where the initial levels in 2001 were lowest. In the countries where they were highest in 2001, minimum wages generally declined relative to average wages.

Where average living standards, and hence relative poverty thresholds, have been pushed up not by real wage growth but by other factors, the minimum wage has had even more difficulty keeping pace. This is shown in Figure 4.2b, which shows that relative to relative poverty thresholds, minimum wages did not keep

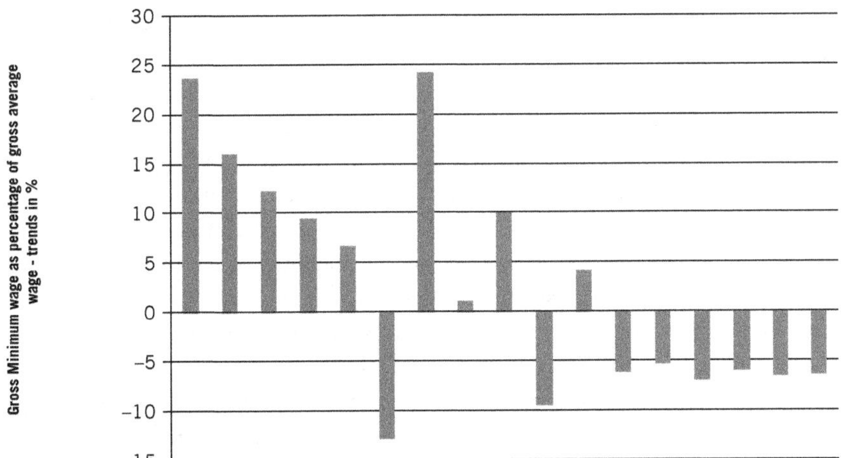

	ES	UK	EE	RO	SK	CZ	LV	LT	PL	HU	SI	IE	PT	FR	BE	IT	EL
trends 2001-2009	24	16	12	9	7	−13	24	1	10	−10	4	-6	-5	-7	-6	-7	-6

trends 2001-2009

Figure 4.2a. Gross minimum trends relative to average wages 2001–2009, countries ranked from left to right by initial level in 2001. *Source:* CSB-MIPI database (Van Mechelen et al., 2010). *Note:* LU is not included as no information is available on gross average wage in 2008.EL is not included as we did not yet receive the Greek data.

pace during the period 2001–2009, except in a minority of countries where these were initially comparatively low. In circumstances where living standards rise faster than average wages, the minimum wage increases needed to improve their potential poverty impact would have to exceed average wage growth, resulting in more compressed wages.

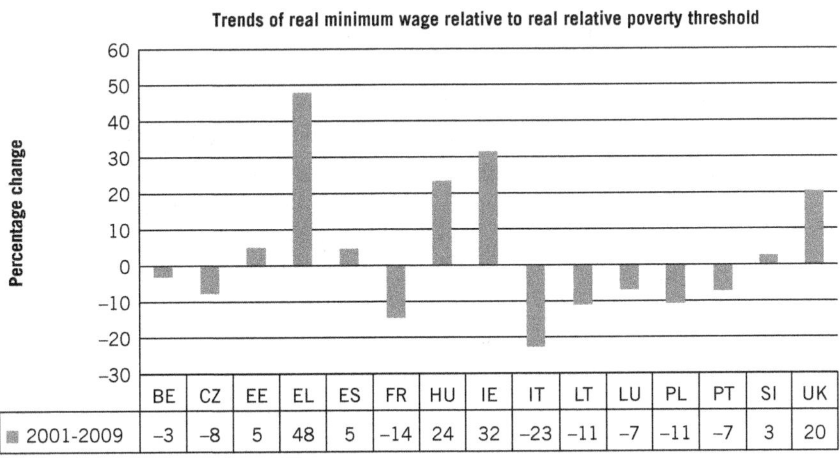

	BE	CZ	EE	EL	ES	FR	HU	IE	IT	LT	LU	PL	PT	SI	UK
2001-2009	-3	-8	5	48	5	−14	24	32	−23	−11	-7	−11	-7	3	20

Figure 4.2b. Real minimum trends relative to real relative poverty thresholds, 2001–2009. *Source*: CSB-MIPI Database (Van Mechelen et al., 2010).

As for the potential of minimum wages at realistic, or at least effectively prevalent, levels in some countries, it is clear that in the case of one adult alone, a sufficiently high minimum wage can clearly provide adequate protection on its own, if tax and social insurance deductions at that earnings level are not prohibitively high. For a single adult with children, a minimum wage at the upper range of the prevailing relative levels can be enough (depending on the number of dependent children), provided that taxes and social insurance contribution are sufficiently low, and child benefits provide sufficient additional income support. In the case of sole breadwinner couples with multiple dependent children, even a minimum wage significantly higher than the currently prevailing relative levels will not nearly suffice, even at hypothetical zero taxation.

In countries where minimum wages are presently low relative to average wages there may be scope for gradual but substantial increases; in countries where these have deteriorated relative to average wages there may be scope for some catch-up growth. However, it is essential to keep firmly in mind that, in most European countries, the vast majority of low-paid workers are not living in households in financial poverty. Studies suggest that even in those cases where the overlap between low pay and household poverty is the greatest, as is the case in the United States, increases in the minimum wage have a relatively limited impact on poverty or income inequality and a substantial spill-over to the non-poor (see, for example, Horrigan & Mincey, 1993; Neumark & Wascher, 1997; Formby et al., 2005; 2010). Similarly, Gosling (1996) and Sutherland (2001) found the potential poverty-reducing effect of the national minimum wage in the UK context to be very small. Marx et al. (2012a) demonstrate that for Belgium, even substantially higher minimum wages would have a limited impact on in-work poverty, and at the cost of significant spill-over to households in the middle and upper regions of the income distribution. Similar results are reported by Müller & Steiner (2008) for Germany, Figari (2009) for Southern European countries, and Formby et al. (2010) for the United States.

It is worth stressing again at this point that we are considering minimum wage only from the perspective of its direct impact on living standards. It may well be the case that low pay forces families to opt for a level of work-intensity that yields a suboptimal level of well-being in comparison with the level of well-being they could legitimately attain by working less—if wages would be higher. Minimum wages may also play a crucial role in countering the possible wage erosion effects of direct subsidies to low-paid individuals and households.

Another potential policy route is not increasing the minimum wage itself but rather reducing taxes and social contributions. Social contributions are by their very logic taken from individual wages while taxes can be either personal or household based. The effective tax rate imposed by personal taxes and social security contributions tends to be substantial in many countries (Immervoll & Pearson. 2009; Marx et al., 2012b). A lot depends on household composition, with households with dependent children generally being treated more favorably. Still, levels are substantial enough to effectively tax households into poverty in some cases.

Thus there is some scope for improving the income position of low-wage households through cuts in employee social contributions and personal income taxes. The most substantial scope for maneuver remains at the level of social security contributions because these tend to be more substantial than taxes. Some countries have already effectively introduced reductions of employees' social contributions on low wages, thus increasing the income progressivity of social contributions and taxes, a route to which there are arguably limits, given that such contributions serve to open rights to social security benefits (Immervoll, 2007; Marx et al., 2012b). The primary motivation here, however, has been to increase work incentives.

When it comes to payroll tax relief, policymakers face the same problem as with minimum wages, but the trade-off is even more severe given that any reduction in social security contributions very directly results in foregone income. Given the very limited overlap between low-paid work and household poverty, this is problematic. A limited number of poor households would see their income improve as a consequence, while most of the benefits would effectively flow to non-poor households.

Income tax alleviation can be better targeted because tax systems tend to take account of household income and circumstances, and the tendency is toward individualization of taxation. Thus tax administrations are generally better equipped to implement measures targeted at low-earning households as opposed to low-earning individuals. The main limitation here is that low-earning households are already taxed very lightly. In addition, an analysis of gross minimum wages relative to poverty thresholds (not shown here, but available from the CSB MIPI data set) makes clear that in many countries even a hypothetical zero taxation of minimum wage workers would not suffice to make that income sufficient to live free from poverty, especially in the case of sole earner households with dependent children (Marx et al., 2012b).

Final incremental options are more generous child benefits and other forms of child contingent income support. It is worth noting here that child benefits have generally lost ground. For a couple with two children, the size of the child benefits package, expressed as a percentage of the gross minimum wage, declined in the majority of countries awarding these benefits. For lone parents with two children the trend was somewhat more favorable in a number of countries. The decline of child cash benefits, both in value, as well as in importance in net disposable income, is discussed more extensively in Van Mechelen & Bradshaw (2013). Child payments may provide the additional income required to escape financial poverty, but this will depend on the set-up of the child support system. If such benefits are universal (i.e., not means tested), the overall increase required to lift a relatively small segment of the population out of poverty would be quite substantial in most countries, at a very substantial spill-over cost to non-poor households. Means-tested (additional) child benefits could be more effective, be it theoretically at the cost of severe wage mobility disincentives and disincentives for potential additional workers. Corak et al. (2005) show that the best performing countries in terms of poverty reduction tend to have systems of universal child benefits and tax concessions that are not particularly strongly targeted at low income children. Indeed, in the best performing countries more tends to be spent on non-poor children than on the poor. Strikingly, countries like the United Kingdom and Ireland, which rank as above average spenders on child contingent benefits, but target most by income, are among the worst performing countries in terms of child poverty outcomes.

4.7.2 In-work Benefits

The option to consider, therefore, are other forms of (targeted) income supplements for households having to make ends meet on low earnings. But governments face a trade-off here. Kenworthy (2011: 44): "Given the importance of employment and working hours for the market incomes of low-end households, policymakers must guard against programmes that provide attractive benefits without encouraging or requiring employment. An ideal transfer would be one that both boosts the incomes of low-earning households and promotes employment by able working-aged adults. As it happens such a programme exists. Referred to variously as 'in-work benefit' [IWB] or 'employment-conditional earnings subsidy,' it is best exemplified by the Working Tax Credit (WTC) in the United Kingdom and the Earned Income Credit (EITC) in the United States."

Clearly, Anglo-Saxon style negative income taxes have been garnering increased interest of late. Immervoll & Pearson (2009): "Even in the mid 1990s, twenty years after such schemes were first introduced in the United Kingdom and the United States, such schemes were seen as interesting but unusual [...] it seems reasonable to conclude that IWB schemes are now mainstream policies in many countries."

Under these schemes households with low earnings do not pay taxes but instead receive additional money through the tax system. In the United States, the 1993 expansion of the Earned Income Tax Credit (EITC) turned it into the country's pre-eminent antipoverty program for families of working-age. The United Kingdom has also implemented and extended several schemes (and, in fact, did so earlier than the United States), culminating in the Working Tax Credit (WTC) of 2003 (Brewer et al., 2006). Several European countries have contemplated introducing Anglo-Saxon-style tax credits, or have done so in some form. Examples here include the "Prime Pour l'Emploi" (PPE) and the "Revenue de Solidarité Active" (rSa) in France, the "Combination Credit" in the Netherlands, and a "Low Wage Tax Credit" in Belgium (Marx &Verbist, 2008a). Yet the reality is that most of these schemes exhibit only a faint resemblance to the EITC or the WTC. The UK Working Tax Credit, to be replaced by the Universal Credit, remains the most important measure of its kind in Europe, both in terms of scope and budget. Sweden has a scheme that goes by the same name in Swedish as its American counterpart EITC. However, the Swedish scheme differs from the American one in that it is a nonrefundable tax credit. Also, because the tax unit in Sweden is the individual and not the household, the scheme works in effect as tax relief on low individual earnings.

Nevertheless, interest remains strong, in the public debate and in the academic literature (Marx & Verbist, 2009; Kenworthy, 2011; Figari, 2011; Allègre & Jaerhling, 2011; Crettaz, 2011; Marx et al., 2012b). That interest seems entirely legitimate. The empirical evidence shows the American EITC, in combination with other policy reforms and several increases in the minimum wage, to have produced some striking results, including marked increases in labor market participation and declines in poverty among some segments of the population, especially single-parent households (Hotz &Scholz, 2003; Eissa & Hoynes, 2004).

Yet whether EITC-type schemes can work elsewhere, as Kenworthy (2011) and others suggest, is not so self-evident. It is worth remembering that the sociodemographic make-up of the United States differs from that of most European countries. There are more single-adult (and single-parent) households but also more multiearner households. The dispersion in earnings is also much more compressed in most European countries, where, in addition, benefits are generally higher relative to wages (including minimum wages) and less subject to means-testing.

As Marx et al. (2012) demonstrate in a microsimulation for Belgium, in order to be effective as an antipoverty device and at the same time affordable within reasonable limits, such measures need to be strongly targeted. However, strong targeting at households with low earnings is bound to create mobility traps, which can only be avoided if taper-off rates are sufficiently flat. That comes at a very considerable cost given that the lower end of the household earnings distribution is so densely populated in Belgium, as is the case in some other Continental European countries. This cost can only be avoided by making the amount of the tax credit itself smaller, but in that case the antipoverty effect is reduced. In addition, from the perspective of horizontal equity and public support for the system, there are probably also limits to strongly targeted tax measures.

A similar simulation by Figari (2011) for four southern European countries (Italy, Spain, Portugal, and Greece) sheds similar doubt over the universal applicability of EITC- or WTC-type systems. The hypothetical introduction of the UK's WTC is shown to yield a limited reduction in poverty at the cost of possibly weakened work incentives for second earners (with female employment rates already low there). Figari also notes that the presence of extended families in southern Europe does not allow for such policies to be well-targeted at the very poorest.

In one of the earliest studies, Bargain & Orsini (2007) investigated the effects on poverty of the hypothetical introduction of the British scheme (as it was in place in 1998) in Germany, France, and Finland, using EUROMOD (Tax-benefit microsimulation model for the European Union) for 2001. They found that the antipoverty effects of a UK-type tax credit (similar in design and relative overall spending) would be very small in these countries, especially relative to the budgetary cost. They concluded that "interest in such schemes is destined to fade away." Whether that is true remains uncertain and indeed doubtful, but EITC-type negative tax credits are not obviously suitable for wholesale emulation throughout continental Europe. In Germany, for example, the labor market has undergone some profound changes over the past decade. Low-paid employment has become far more prevalent and in-work poverty seems to have increased. It is not unlikely that a simulation like the one performed by Bargain and Orsini on 2001 data would yield different results today.

Clearly, simulations demonstrate that in-work benefit schemes that work well in certain settings do not necessarily perform equally well in another setting. Family composition, individual earnings distributions, and family income structures drive outcomes in a very substantial way. It remains to be explored whether alternative designs that have better outcomes in continental European settings and that are realistically affordable are conceivable.

4.8 CONCLUSION

In-work poverty has become a major preoccupation at the same time that policy has become strongly focused on maximizing levels of labor market participation. This chapter has brought out that this may reflect a degree of misperception, namely, that in-work poverty has been increasing strongly in most countries and is very tightly linked to increasing levels of low pay. Empirical analysis of microdata in a comparative setting reveals a much more nuanced picture. Trends in in-work poverty vary across countries, and in-work poverty is strongly associated not so much with low pay as with single-earnership and low work-intensity at the household level, linking in turn to institutional settings and structures in the labor market, tax and benefit system, and broader welfare state.

However, employment-oriented policies remain at center stage and this is reinforced by the challenges posed by the economic crisis. The problem of in-work poverty, as it is conventionally measured and reported, is to a large extent associated with low work-intensity at the household level. This brings into view a wide variety of potential policies that can help households to optimize, if not maximize their work-intensity. These include policies aimed at boosting the demand for workers, and particularly the demand for people with low levels of education or weak work experience. At the supply side, policy can stimulate (e.g., through fiscal reform) or support (e.g., through child care) people to take up work or to increase working hours. What mix of policies will work best in a given context will depend on the composition of the low work-intensity population and on the underlying causes of low work-intensity. These may vary considerably across countries and across population segments, as the chapter by Corluy and Vandenbroucke brings out in this book.

Yet, and this is crucial, it must be recognized that even if such policies succeeded in getting every single nonemployed person into work, or every household to a level of full work-intensity, for that matter (and all empirical evidence to date suggests this to be highly unlikely), this would not guarantee the elimination of poverty (Marx et al., 2012b). What policy can do to help households in these circumstances is again likely to depend on such factors as the institutional and policy context in place, labor market conditions, and the profile of the population in need of support.

In some EU countries minimum wages remain nonexistent or low relative to average wages. As we have seen, minimum wages in a range of European countries do suffice to keep single persons who are reliant on them out of poverty. Thus it would appear sensible for countries with nonexistent or very low minimum wages to contemplate introducing or increasing these. However, the route of introducing or boosting minimum wages to the upper ranges currently prevailing in Europe (relative to average earnings) would, even in the absence of negative employment effects, not be sufficient to eradicate in-work poverty. Even in countries where minimum wages are comparatively high they do not suffice to keep sole breadwinner households out of poverty, especially when there are dependent others or children. Minimum wages have probably become inherently constrained in providing minimum income protection to sole breadwinner households, especially in countries where relative poverty thresholds have become essentially determined by dual earner living standards.

For low-earnings households, only direct household income supplements may offer a reasonable prospect of a poverty-free existence, especially when there are dependent children. Such "in-work benefits" are now often associated with Anglo-Saxon-type "tax credits" such as the EITC in the United States and the WTC in the United Kingdom. We have emphasized that the sociodemographic, economic, and institutional context remains vastly different in much of the rest of Europe and that such "tax credits," while demonstrably effective in particular settings and for particular groups, do not appear to offer a model for wholesale emulation. Moreover, Anglo-Saxon type tax credits are strongly targeted, which implies a potential cost in terms of mobility "traps" and wage erosion. From the perspective of horizontal equity and public support for the system there may also be limits to such strongly targeted measures. By contrast, less strongly targeted income supplements, like, for example, universal (but possibly categorically or otherwise modulated) child benefits, can have an immediate impact on poverty among those at high risk (i.e., child-rich households) without adversely affecting work incentives between workers and nonworkers, although an income effect may have a dampening effect on labor supply among both categories. But for such benefits to be effective across the board as antipoverty devices they need to be high, even when to some extent categorically differentiated or income modulated. This inevitably comes at a significant budgetary cost.

5

SOCIAL REDISTRIBUTION, POVERTY, AND THE ADEQUACY OF SOCIAL PROTECTION

Bea Cantillon, Natascha Van Mechelen, Olivier Pintelon, and Aaron Van den Heede

5.1 INTRODUCTION

Social protection systems traditionally serve a dual purpose: to maintain acquired living standards in the event of the materialization of social risks (*protection*) and to combat poverty by guaranteeing adequate minimum incomes (*poverty reduction*). More recently, these goals—which are basically instances of damage compensation—have been complemented with a third objective, namely to foster "active inclusion" as a means of preventing or rectifying damage (*prevention*). Although this third aspect is present in any insurance system, it has only come to the fore more prominently and explicitly in the context of social protection since the 1990s.[1] Instruments deployed to this end may range from guidance for unemployed or disabled persons toward economic self-reliance, "making work pay", and benefits designed to facilitate the combination of work and family life ("carrots"), to disincentives for prolonged benefit dependency ("sticks"). There are inherent tensions between these three primary purposes of social security. More specifically, as a consequence of the emergence of new social risks (Bonoli, 2006) on the one hand and of the need to develop employment strategies in order to reduce benefit dependency on the other, it may have become more difficult to pursue the goal of poverty reduction. It is against this backdrop that the present chapter explores trends in poverty reductions and the impact of policies.

The chapter begins with a discussion of the relationship between the three primary objectives of social security as previously defined. Subsequently it briefly summarizes the main trends in poverty reduction by social transfers that were identified in Chapter 1. It also examines the years covered by the European Community Household Panel (ECHP), 1995–2001. Then, in an attempt to identify the impact of *policies* and to tackle the "dependent variable problem" (Clasen, 2007), it focuses subsequently on changes in the adequacy of social protection with respect to work-poor and work-rich households, on changes in policy effort vis-à-vis these population groups, on changes in average benefit levels as measured in the surveys, and on changes in calculated disposable incomes of a set of standard family types. The third section uses microsimulation to examine the conditions under which it is possible for European welfare states to guarantee adequate minimum incomes to non-working groups. The final section summarizes and concludes.

5.2 HAVE TENSIONS BETWEEN THE OBJECTIVES OF SOCIAL PROTECTION INCREASED?

Social protection (i.e., cash transfers through social insurance and social assistance) is undoubtedly the most important tool that welfare states have at their disposal for redistributing income. Much more so than taxation, schemes for transferring income from the healthy to the sick (sickness benefits), from the young to the old (old-age pensions), from those in work to the out-of-work (unemployment benefits), and from childless families to families with children (child benefits) contribute to a reduction of income inequality in society (OECD, 2008; 2011). Their impact on poverty reduction is generally also considered to be very substantial (for a comparison with the impact of in-kind spending, see Chapter 6 of this book). If one assesses the distributional capacity of social transfers in the conventional way—by comparing poverty rates before and after transfers—on average they account for a reduction in poverty rates of between 17% and 25% (European Commission, 2010).

There are, however, inherent tensions between poverty alleviation and other purposes of social protection. Systems that are focused strongly on universal maintenance of acquired living standards (i.e., protection) are inevitably less preoccupied with providing adequate (targeted) minimum incomes: such systems are, after all, reliant on insurance principles whereby proportional benefits are linked to the accumulation of social rights through social contributions. Similarly, activation (i.e., prevention) can conflict with the notion of guaranteeing a minimum income, particularly if minimum incomes are seen to create unemployment traps or if it is considered that nonconditional benefits provide insufficient incentives for actively pursuing alternatives to benefit dependency. *Arguably, the tensions between the objectives of social protection have, over the past decades, became more pronounced, partly because of the emergence of "new" social risks, partly because of the persistence of structural unemployment, high benefit dependency, and the ensuing need for work-centered social security reforms.* This section elaborates upon the link between poverty reduction by social transfers, the changing distribution of social risks, and the legitimacy of social redistribution.

5.2.1 Poverty Reduction and the Social Distribution of New and Old Risks

The redistributive and poverty-reducing capacity of social insurance systems is primarily a side-effect of horizontal solidarity schemes between individuals who find themselves in different conditions of life (healthy vs. sick, employed vs. unemployed, families with children vs. childless families, etc.). Even the Anglo-Saxon or Beveridgean system was not expressly designed for the purpose of combating poverty. Already in 1907, Beveridge asserted that "any scheme [...] must be free from the attempt to make their enjoyment dependent upon poverty. Otherwise it does become no better than a new form of Poor Law relief...." (cited in Beveridge, 1954: 56). This rings even more true for the Continental, Bismarckian systems, and for the so-called "demogrant" insurance systems providing coverage for all, as in some of the Scandinavian countries.

The closer the association between the insured conditions with low income, the greater the extent of vertical redistribution induced by systems of horizontal solidarity. Consider the example of unemployment: Given that the risk of unemployment is the greatest among the low-skilled (who, in consequence of mechanisms of homogamy, are moreover more likely to have a low-skilled partner and, therefore, are at a higher risk of household work poverty), unemployment insurance has a strong vertical redistributive effect (Heady et al., 2001). Child benefits, on the other hand, are far less redistributive. Parenthood is distributed rather evenly across the population. Moreover, because children from more privileged families tend to study longer and in greater numbers, compensation is concentrated to some extent among the better-off strata. Unless corrections have been incorporated into their design, child benefit schemes are, therefore, less redistributive. Similarly, one may expect benefits designed to facilitate the combination of work and family life (such as parental-leave schemes) to have a less pronounced vertical redistributive impact, given that this particular new social risk, by its very nature, affects those in work, and specifically members of work-rich dual-income households. The relationship between horizontal and vertical redistribution is, in other words, determined to a considerable extent by the social distribution of those affected by the risks concerned: The greater the concentration among weaker socioeconomic groups, the stronger the redistributive and poverty reducing effect of the insurance scheme, and vice versa.

The existence of strong father-son social gradients for social risks that are statistically likely to induce poverty has been demonstrated time and again (e.g., O'Neill &Sweetman, 1998; Feinstein, 1993; Pintelon et al., 2013; Cappellari & Jenkins, 2002; Nilsson, 2012). "Bad" social risks such as unemployment, low work-intensity, lone parenting, and illness continue to be significantly socially stratified, including (albeit to a lesser extent) in countries that are considered good examples when it comes to effectuating great(er) social equality. As we demonstrated elsewhere (Pintelon et al., 2013), the strongest intergenerational background effects are found in relation to ill-health and living in a jobless household. From a comparative welfare state perspective, there is moreover compelling evidence to support the view that, particularly with regard to social class of origin, stratification patterns are by and large the same across welfare states. In all settings, these social background effects are largely mediated by individuals' own educational attainment.

By contrast, risks related to the combination of work and family and high work-intensity are inversely socially stratified. This is due largely to educational homogamy and the dual-speed emancipation movement discussed in Chapter 10 of this book. Indeed, although in varying degrees, in virtually all developed welfare states we observe multispeed emancipation: The emancipation of highly educated women is reaching completion while poorly educated women still face major obstacles in this respect, especially when young children are involved (Gornick, 1999; Cantillon et al., 2003). This implies that work-related risks associated with the combination of work and family life are characterized by a clearly different social stratification than unemployment, illness, or work-poverty.

The divergent social stratification of social risks—, that is, the combination of work and family mostly among middle and higher-income groups, and unemployment, ill-health, and joblessness mostly in the lower social classes at the bottom end of the income distribution—may be expected to have an impact on the capacity of social protection systems to alleviate poverty. If—in a work-oriented policy framework—one focuses strongly and generously on the work-life balance and other work-related risks on the one hand and on the fight against unemployment traps on the other, the poverty-reducing function of social security may be compromised.

5.2.2 Poverty Reduction versus Prevention

Against a background of budgetary constraints, the emergence of new social needs, and the cost of aging and health care since the mid-1990s, almost all countries implemented policies designed to reduce benefit dependency through employment-centered welfare reform. However, at the *individual* level there was a remarkable stability in caseloads. Aging, the feminization and the ensuing increase of the labor force, in-work benefits, and other new social benefits (parental leave, career break benefits, etc.) and the sluggish decrease in household joblessness accounted for only minor decreases or quasi-stability in individual social security dependency rates in many countries (see Vandenbroucke and Diris in Chapter 1). Therefore, the pressure to diminish caseloads and the associated spending remained invariably high.

Governments aiming to reduce caseloads can rely on negative incentives (shorter duration of unemployment benefits, targeting, punitive measures...) and/or positive incentives (in-work benefits, tax credits, counseling...). On the one hand, people experiencing difficulties in navigating their way to the labor market may be assisted by a broad range of policy instruments, ranging from in-work benefits, tax reductions, and job subsidies to individual counselling, working-time flexibility, and child care (Barbier, 2005 & Lindsay et al., 2007). On the other hand, "activation" may imply the use of "sticks" and the elimination of dependency traps by lowering benefits and tightening eligibility criteria. Depending on the design of the programs involved and depending on the impact of these measures on the number of work-poor households, these kinds of policy reforms may, to a greater or lesser extent, compromise the poverty alleviating capacity of social protection systems (Clasen & Clegg, 2011; Bonoli, 2011; De la Porte & Jacobson, 2011).[2]

5.2.3 The Legitimacy of Poverty Reduction

Much has been written about legitimacy and the relationship between *universalism* and *selectivism,* and *horizontal* and *vertical redistribution* of social protection schemes. A progressive design of social benefits through targeting of low-income groups is more efficient, on condition that the level of protection offered is adequate. However, the prevailing assumption in the social security literature is that targeting (i.e., more vertical redistribution) exerts downward pressure on the level of protection offered (Rosenberg, 1982; Goodin & Le Grand, 1987; Alber, 1988; Sainsbury, 1991; Esping-Andersen, 1994; Rosanvallon, 1995; Barr, 1992: 755–757). Walter Korpi and Joakim Palme have labeled this premise the "paradox of redistribution": "the more we target benefits to the poor...the less likely we are to reduce poverty and inequality" (Korpi & Palme, 1998: 663). The underlying reasoning is that, compared with universal insurance programs envisaging horizontal redistribution, selective poverty programs tend to generate weak results due to their limited political legitimacy. The conviction that selective systems suffer from a lack of legitimacy is forcefully expressed in the often cited assertions that "services for the poor are poor services" (Titmuss, 1969) and that "programs for the poor become poor programs" (Rainwater, 1982: 42), or that "good targeting leads to program shrinkage" (Grosh, 1992).

However, an important caveat applies with regard to research into the relationship between generosity on the one hand and universalism/targeting on the other. It usually considers the totality of social cash transfers, without distinguishing among, for example, parental leave, child benefits, or unemployment benefits. Aspects that have definitely been neglected in this debate are the *type* of risk against which cash transfers are deployed, the social distribution of the risks concerned and—at the same time—which segments of the income distribution those risks tend to affect. The argument that the broad middle classes are more willing to pay for universal protection systems resonates quite differently depending on whether one is considering unemployment or child benefits, work-poor households, or work-rich households. Long-term unemployment is, after all, a highly selective risk affecting primarily the low-skilled, ethnic minorities, and socioeconomically more vulnerable groups. As higher-skilled groups are far less exposed to this risk, it seems unlikely that targeting within unemployment benefit schemes would be detrimental to their willingness to pay; quite the contrary, in fact. On the other hand, the argument seems much more pertinent in the context of so-called "new" social risks that are distributed more evenly across the population (such as parenthood and the combination of work and family life). In this line of reasoning it may be expected that downward pressures on benefit levels may have been stronger in relation to risks typically affecting vulnerable groups (such as long-term unemployment) whereas the logic of universalism may have been more prevalent in the context of pensions, universal child benefits, or parental leave.[3]

Interesting, therefore, is the more recent work from Whiteford (2008) and Kenworthy (2011) who have, on empirical grounds, called into question the "paradox of redistribution." Using OECD data relating to a larger set of countries, Whiteford concludes that the relationship between universalism and redistribution actually turned negative halfway through the first decade of the new millennium. Kenworthy, relying on data of the Luxembourg Income Study (LIS), found that the positive relationship between universalism and redistribution declines strongly over time. For the set of countries studied, he actually found no evidence for 2005 of any relationship between size and pro poorness. Kenworthy's intertemporal analysis suggests that these observations are due to two underlying explanatory dynamics. Danish cash spending became more selective, but expenditure levels remained high, whereas U.S. spending remained low but became more universal (particularly as a result of the increasing proportion accounted for by pensions and the Estimated Income Tax Credit (EITC), albeit means-tested, but aimed at the employed who are not in the lowest income group). On the basis of his findings, Kenworthy formulates a revised size/targeting hypothesis, suggesting that, as long as there is a universal system of cash transfers, policymakers have the option of incorporating greater selectivity toward the weakest without compromising the overall volume of the redistribution mass. Previously in the literature, this was termed "targeting within universalism" (Skocpol, 1991).

To conclude, we may argue that there are reasons to suspect that the poverty-reducing function of social security may have been compromised by (a) a differential social distribution of old and new social risks (old risks such as unemployment are strongly overrepresented in the lower-skilled social segments of the population, while new, work-related, risks are more prevalent among work-richer(er) families); (b) persistent high benefit dependency and the ensuing need for employment-centered welfare reforms (through combating unemployment traps on the one hand and making work more attractive on the other); and (c) a differential middle-class political legitimacy of social protection against social risks affecting work-poor and work-rich(er) families. We, therefore, hypothesize that the decrease in the poverty-reducing capacity of social transfers observed in many countries has affected work-poor households more than work-rich ones.

5.3 SETTING THE SCENE: WORK-INTENSITY AND CHANGES IN POVERTY REDUCTION BY SOCIAL TRANSFERS

With a view to improving efficiency, containing cost, and adapting the systems to new social risks, most welfare states have implemented various reforms (see Hemerijck in Chapter 8). Social protection systems, which form a strong buffer against the negative consequences of successive economic crises (see Vandenbroucke and Diris in Chapter 1), have allowed themselves to be transformed into sometimes quite potent instruments of activation and of employment support through various in-work benefits (Clasen & Clegg, 2011). Moreover, they have supported the transition to dual earnership through all kinds of new benefits that facilitated the conciliation of work and family life. And, in many cases, additional forms of protection have been introduced for (not easily insurable) "new social risks" (Bonoli, 2005; Taylor-Gooby, 2004), such as divorce and single earnership. Even the supposedly inert Bismarckian systems have adapted—albeit generally more slowly than the other types of systems—to the new social, economic, and demographic circumstances (Palier, 2010). These policy changes may have driven divergent evolutions in terms of the poverty alleviating capacity of social transfers. Size clearly matters when it comes to reducing income poverty. Hence, to the extent that cost containment has led to shrinkage, it is likely to have impacted negatively on the poverty-reducing capacity of social transfers, unless such an effect is offset by greater efficiency. As selective targeting may enhance the (relative) protection of vulnerable work-poor households, it may be seen to strengthen the pro-poorness of social security systems. Conversely, trends toward activation and recommodification may have compromised the pro-poorness of social protection if such measures mainly affect work-poor households at the lower end of the income distribution. The effects of new benefits that facilitate the conciliation of work and family life depend on the changing distribution of work over work-poor and work-rich households, and—concurrently—on the social stratification of these risks (Cantillon, 2011).[4]

Striking the right balance among solidarity and insurance, vertical and horizontal distribution, protection, poverty reduction, and prevention is a challenge for all social protection systems. So how have they fared in this respect over the past decade? What has the outcome been of the shifts that the various systems have undergone in response to a drastically changed social and economic environment? How has the poverty-reducing capacity of social protection evolved? Although the Organisation for Economic Co-operation and Development (OECD) continues to consider these questions in a number of influential reports (OECD, 2008; 2011), and notwithstanding the fact that the EU indicators designed for the Lisbon 2010 strategy and currently underlying the Union's 2020 strategy refer among other things to the impact of benefits on poverty, such distribution issues appear to have somewhat faded into the background of policy discourse.[5] Save for a number of important recent studies (Brandolini & Smeeding, 2009; Kenworthy, 2008; 2011; OECD, 2008; 2011; Jenkins & Brandolini et al., 2013), this would appear also to be the case in research. The literature today is focused overwhelmingly on issues relating to the effectiveness of activation measures, on the distributional impact of services, and on assessing the effects of new benefit schemes on the combination of work and family, and far less so than in the 1970s and 1980s on questions of redistribution and the impact of social protection on poverty.

Chapter 1 considered the evolution of the poverty-reducing impact of social transfers among the working-age population in the time frame 2005–2010 (SILC, 2004–2011). Here we broaden the time frame by comparing trends in the economic boom years of the 2000s *and* in the second half of the 1990s (see Figure 5.1). Two different data sources are used: the *European Community Household Panel* (ECHP) and its successor the *European Union Statistics on Income and Living Conditions* (EU-SILC).[6] As some authors have recently called into question the validity of EU-SILC data for Germany (Frick & Krell 2010; Goedemé, forthcoming; Hauser 2008), use is also made of the German Socio-Economic Panel Study (SOEP). Textbox 1 provides an overview of the central concepts used and how they were operationalized.

Figure 5.1 summarizes trends in (post and pre-transfer) at-risk-of-poverty rates and poverty reduction in EU Member States. As a reminder, the most important poverty trends may be summarized as follows. *First*, it emerges that among the countries of the old Europe, Germany (according to SILC), Finland, Sweden and Greece have experienced significant increases in poverty risks in the 2000s, a trend that in the case of Finland and Denmark was also demonstrably unfolding in the 1990s. *Second*, likewise within the group of the "old" Member States, data for Belgium, France, Denmark, the Netherlands and the Southern European countries indicate a general standstill, a pattern that, in the case of France, also predominated in the 1990s. *Third*, the UK and, even more so, Ireland have recorded a decline in at-risk-of-poverty rates among the population of active age. In the UK, this trend has manifested itself since the 1990s. *Fourth*, in many of the new Member States, poverty figures between 2004 and 2007 evolved favorably. This trend was particularly noticeable in Poland, Lithuania, Estonia and Slovakia, and it unfolded as part of a convergence process in at-risk-of-poverty rates across Europe (see Cantillon et al. 2012).

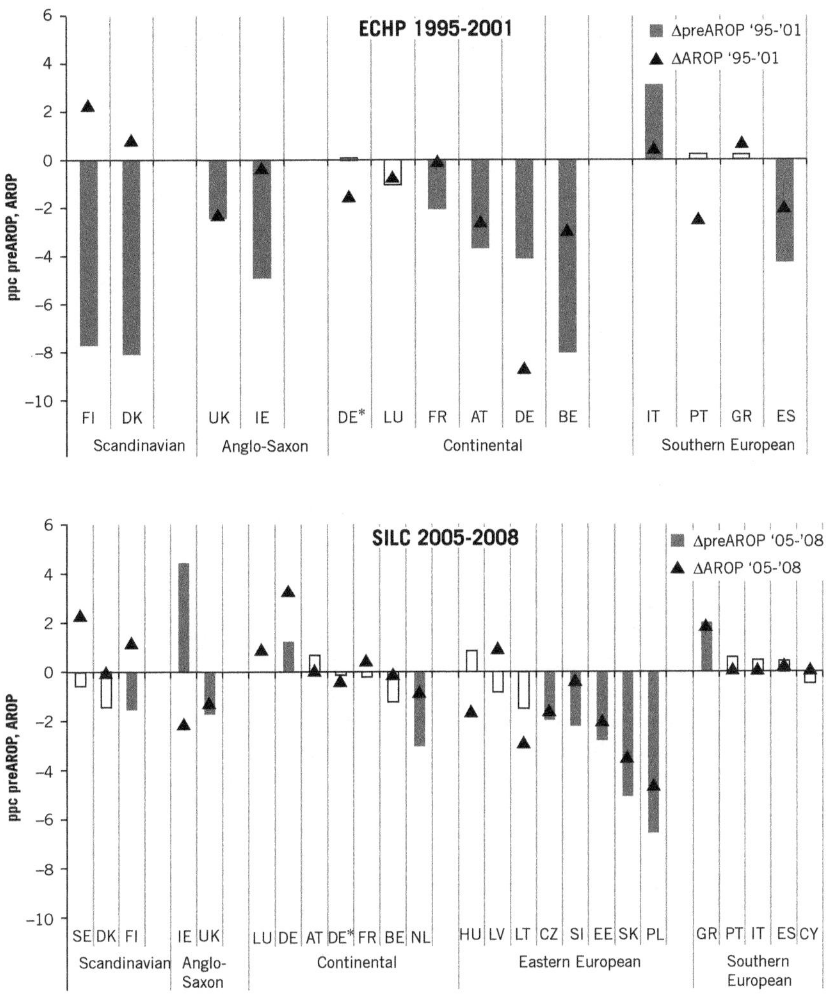

Note: DE* = DE SOEP; the gray bars indicate significant change.

Source: own calculations ECHP (1995-2001), EU-SILC (2005-2008) and SOEP.

Figure 5.1. Percentage point change (ppc) at-risk-of-poverty rate (AROP) (pre- and post-transfers), active age population (20–59 years old), in the 1990s (upper graph) and in the 2000s (lower graph). *Source*: own calculations ECHP (1995–2001), EU-SILC (2005–2008), and SOEP. *Note*: DE* = DE SOEP; the gray bars indicate significant change.

Figure 5.1 analyzes trends in post-transfer at-risk-of-poverty rates as a result of changes in both pre-transfer at-risk-of-poverty rates and the degree of poverty reduction. It shows that the *rise in poverty in Finland and Sweden in the 2000s (and, in the case of Finland and Denmark, also in the 1990s) is largely attributable to a decline in absolute poverty reduction.* As a result of the continuing rise in employment rates and the decline in the proportion of work-poor households (by 2.33% in Sweden and 4.15% in Finland), pre-transfer poverty

Box 5.1. Central Concepts and Their Operationalization

AROP rate = at-risk-of-poverty rate. Headcount of individuals (aged 20–59 years) whose income falls below the at-risk-of-poverty threshold—60% of median equivalent income of total population. (See Chapter 2 for a more detailed explanation.)

Social transfers = all active-age cash benefits accruing to individuals aged 20 to 59 years, that is, unemployment benefits, sickness/invalidity pay, social assistance, family-related allowances, and/or housing allowances (pensions excluded). This broad definition of social transfers corresponds to the notion that benefit schemes often act as communicating vessels.

Pre-transfer AROP rate = at-risk-of-poverty rate calculated by removing all active-age cash benefits (except pensions) from households incomes.[14]

Absolute poverty reduction = the percentage-point difference between the pre-transfer AROP rate (see above) and the AROP rate (see above).

Relative poverty reduction = the absolute poverty reduction relative to the pre-transfer at-risk-of-poverty.

Size = the sum of social transfers (see above) relative to total disposable income as reported in the survey. Size refers to the redistributive effort of social protection schemes.

Households work-intensity (WI) = the average of individual work intensities in a household. The individual work-intensity is the ratio of the number of months worked during the income reference year by a working-age household member to the number of months he or she could theoretically have worked. The ratio ranges from 0 (meaning that no-one at active age worked during the preceding year) to 1 (meaning that everyone at active age was full-time full-year employed). This definition of work-intensity differs from that used in Chapter 3—which controls for the number of hours worked—due to a lack of information on hours worked in the ECHP.

dropped. However, a decrease in poverty reduction by social transfers meant post-transfer poverty actually increased. The *Danish* trends recorded in the 2000s are not statistically significant. However, in the 1990s, the country did record a significant and substantial decrease in pre-transfer poverty, which was cancelled out entirely by a decline in poverty reduction through social transfers. *The Netherlands, Belgium, and France* exhibited no significant changes in poverty rates, even though employment growth resulted in a lower proportion of work-poor households and hence in a drop in pre-transfer needs.

The pattern observed in *Germany deviates from that seen in the above-mentioned countries* in that it *combines an increase in pre-transfer poverty risks with a decrease in income redistribution.* According to the Statistics on Income and Living Conditions (SILC), the strong rise in poverty in Germany was driven by both an increase in pre-transfer poverty and a decline in poverty reduction by the social security system. Although this trend is not confirmed by the SOEP data, according to which recorded changes in the 2000s were not statistically significant, in the 1990s the SOEP data do point to trends similar to SILC in the 2000s.

The strong drop in poverty seen in *Ireland* was driven entirely by an increase of poverty reduction by social security. As a result of weak labor market performance, the extent of pre-transfer poverty increased substantially. This was, however, more than offset by social transfers. In the *United Kingdom*, the decline in poverty in the 1990s and the 2000s was partly the result of lower pre-transfer poverty and higher poverty reduction by social transfers.

The decline in poverty in *Poland, the Czech Republic, Estonia, and Slovakia* was driven entirely by (strongly) expanding labor markets and a drop in the proportion of work-poor households. The corresponding pre-transfer poverty rate declined. Generally speaking, in these countries *poverty-reduction decreased in absolute terms.* Only, in *Lithuania* and *Hungary*, poverty reduction increased.

In sum, most European welfare states saw pre-transfer needs decline during the decades leading up to the crisis. However, whereas in some of the new Member States this trend went hand-in-hand with increasing poverty reduction by social transfers and hence with significant improvements in overall poverty risks, most EU-countries recorded either an increase or a standstill in poverty due to less redistributive social transfers.

So, why did poverty reduction decrease? Given that observed changes in poverty reduction depend in part on shifts in prevailing needs, the simple pre-post observations as such are not very informative about the possible impact of policy choices and the underlying trade-offs among protection, prevention, and poverty reduction. After all, properly functioning systems of social security *automatically* respond to continuously changing needs as a consequence of economic and social changes (e.g., cyclical up- and downturns, changing family structures), demographic changes, etc. More particularly, changes in the number of work-poor and work-rich households may strongly impact the poverty reduction by social security systems. When, as was the case in most countries in the period under review, the number of work-poor households decline, given the much stronger degree of poverty reduction among work-poor households than among work-rich families, this will automatically result in a decline in absolute poverty reduction. To control for changes in the share of work-poor and work-rich households, we, therefore, turn to observed changes in poverty reduction among work-poor and work-rich households. Results are shown in Figures 5.2 and 5.3.

With regard to the *work-poor households* (WI < 0.5), three conclusions emerge. *First*, income poverty among work-poor households is extremely high, reaching levels of 70% in Latvia, 55% in Germany (according to SILC and SOEP), and more than 40% in Finland, Belgium, and Sweden. Although there was no dominant trend in the 1990s, in the 2000s at-risk-of-poverty was rising in most of the countries considered—Ireland being a clear exception. *Second*, cash benefits are clearly very important for these households. Most countries succeeded in reducing poverty among the work-poor by between 20 and 40 percentage points through social transfers. Countries such as Denmark, Sweden, the Netherlands, Ireland, and Hungary, were actually able to reduce pre-transfer poverty among work-poor families by over 50% in this way. *Third*, in all countries

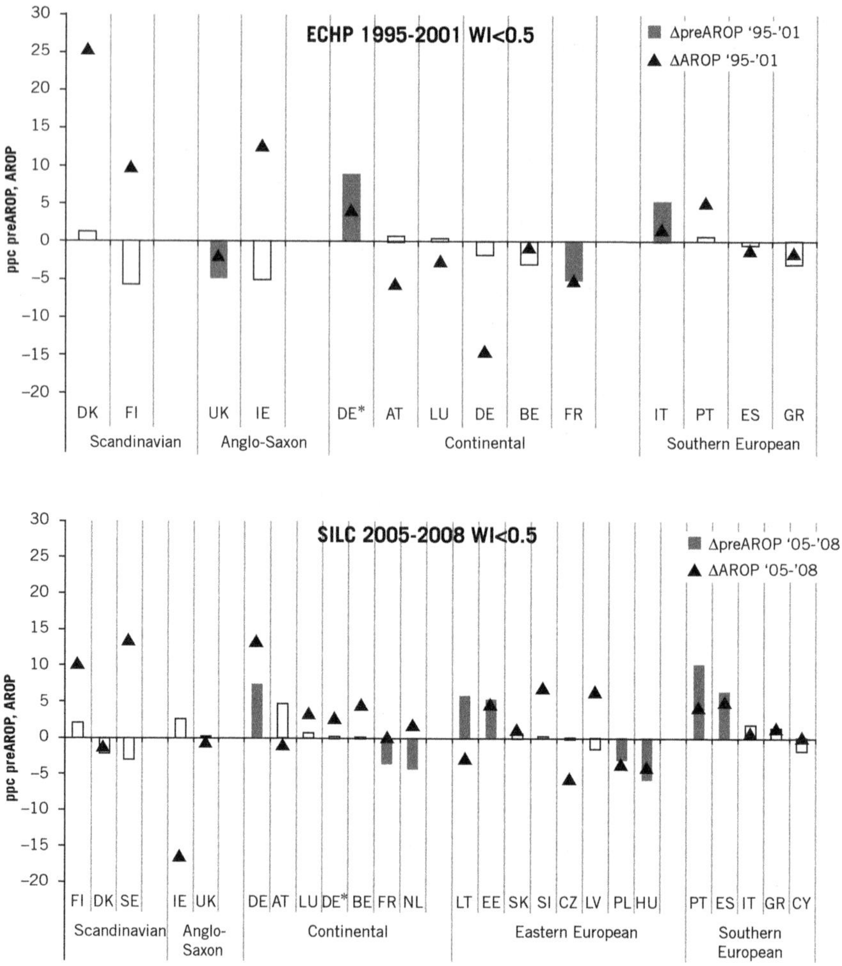

Figure 5.2. Percentage point change (ppc) at-risk-of-poverty rate (AROP) (pre- and post-transfers), active age population (20–59 years old), work intensity < 0.5, in the 1990s (upper graph) and in the 2000s (lower graph). *Source*: own calculations ECHP (1995–2001), EU-SILC (2005–2008) and SOEP. *Note*: DE* = DE SOEP; the gray bars indicate significant change.

experiencing substantial increases of income poverty within the group of work-poor households—most notably in Finland, Sweden, and Germany (SILC)—changes in poverty reduction were the main determinant. Ireland is the only country where poverty reduction among work-poor households increased substantially. In general, in the 2000s within the cluster of work-poor households, relative poverty reduction declined in the Nordic (with the possible exception of Denmark) and in the Continental clusters (with the exception of Austria), while social protection for work-poor households became more adequate only in Ireland, Spain, Portugal, and in some of the new Member States (the Czech Republic and Lithuania) (see Figure 5.2).[7] [8]

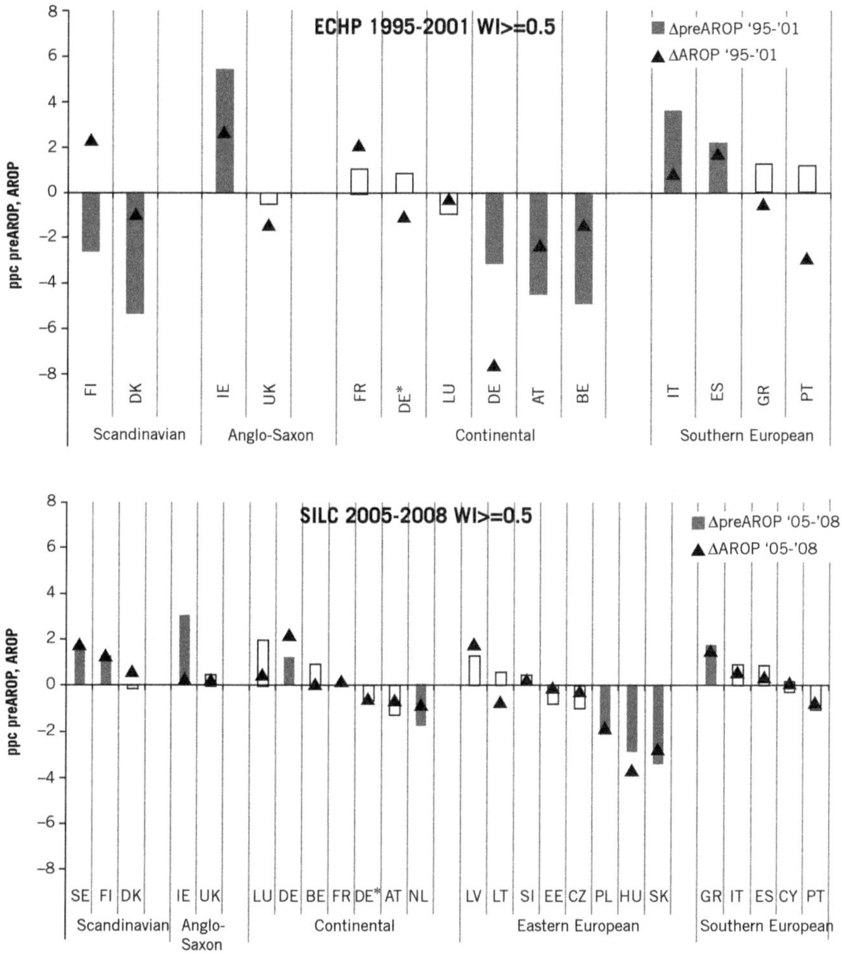

Figure 5.3. Percentage point change (ppc) at-risk-of-poverty rate (AROP) (pre- and post-transfers), active age population (20–59 years old), work intensity ≥ 0.5, in the 1990s (upper graph) and in the 2000s (lower graph). *Source*: own calculations ECHP (1995–2001), and SOEP. *Note*: DE* = DE SOEP; the gray bars indicate significant change.

Among *work-rich households* the poverty risks are lower than those faced by work-poor families in all countries. Still, some countries had relatively many households with a work-intensity above 0.5 who are nonetheless at risk of poverty. In countries such as Latvia, Poland, and Portugal such families faced a poverty risk of over 10%.[9] Changes in poverty reduction by social transfer were much less outspoken than in the case of work-poor households, though by and large they were in the same line. Although the notion of in-work poverty (defined at the individual level, see Chapter 4) and work-intensity (defined at the household level) partly reflect different realities. Figure 5.3 provides some support for the hypothesis formulated in Chapter 4 that in-work poverty is associated not only with low pay but also with low work-intensity at the household level and with shortcomings in tax and benefit systems. Although increasing pre-transfer poverty (pointing to increasing vulnerability in the labor market) accounts largely for the increase in in-work poverty in some countries, *declining poverty reduction by social transfer seems to have been an additional factor*. This was clearly the case in Germany (according to SILC), Finland (in the 1990s), Latvia, and Sweden. Likewise, greater poverty reduction by social transfer accounted at least in part for decreasing in-work poverty in Hungary and in the UK (in the 1990s).

We may, therefore, conclude that (a) in many countries the poverty reducing capacity of social security systems declined in the good years before the great recession; and, (b) work-poor households were more affected than work-rich households, though the direction of the changes was by and large the same.

5.4 THE DEPENDENT VARIABLE: WHAT WAS THE ROLE OF POLICIES?

The observed decline in many EU countries in poverty reduction among work-poor households on the one hand and the far less outspoken trends among work-rich households on the other are suggestive of varied policy foci. Yet behind the changes in poverty reduction lie all kinds of compositional changes that may also have played a part. For example, one may expect that a decline in the number of work-poor households will not have been without consequence for the profile of that group. Conceivably, in countries with a low number of work-poor households what remains is a core of more long-term unemployed with institutionally lower benefits. This idea is supported by the results of the regression analyses (Models 1.1, 1.2, 1.3) presented in Chapter 1 (Vandenbroucke and Diris): there it appeared that "the extent of work-poverty (i.e., the share of individuals in work-poor households) has a *negative* impact on poverty rates within that group." So, in order to gauge policy impact, we must dig deeper. Therefore, in what follows, we present analyses of, consecutively, changes in social protection *effort* (i.e., the size of social spending), changes in *average benefits for the clusters of work-poor and work-rich households*, and *changes in tax benefit packages* for these groups of households.

5.4.1 Effort and the Responses to Declining Needs

Figure 5.4 presents the percentage point change in benefit size (as a percentage of total disposable income in the survey) during the 2000s.[10] The dominant pattern *in the 1990s* was one of decline or stagnation of spending levels for the active-age population, with substantial declines in Denmark, Finland, Sweden, Ireland, the UK, Austria, Belgium, and Spain. The same basic evolutions are observed for the 2000s, except in Ireland, Hungary, the Czech Republic, Lithuania, and Latvia, where the total amount in cash benefits increased relative to total disposable income—as reported in SILC.[11] In general, the size of social spending decreased

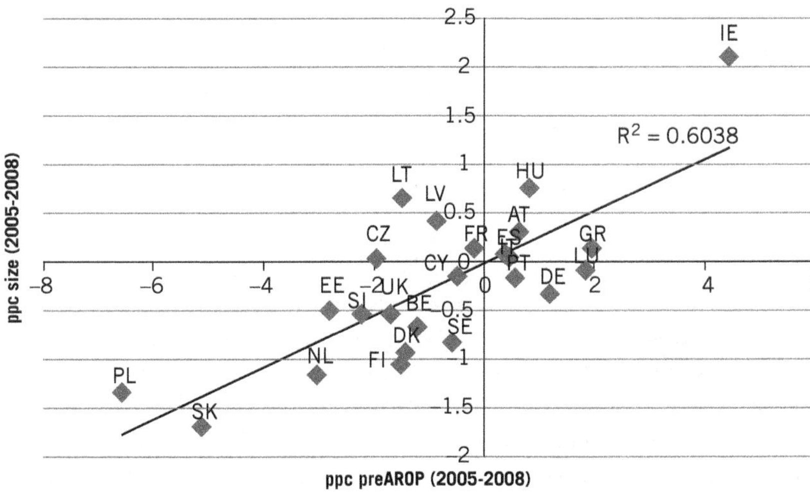

Figure 5.4. Percentage point change (ppc) of benefit size as a function of changes in pre-transfer at-risk-of-poverty rate (pre-AROP), active age population (20–59 years old), 2005–2008. *Source*: own calculations EU-SILC (2005–2008).

most strongly in the "old" welfare states. The decline in spending levels during the 1990s coincided with quite a strong convergence in social expenditure across the then EU Member States (Adelantado & Calderón Cuevas, 2006; Schmitt & Starke, 2011). However, this trend seems to have stagnated somewhat during the years before the crisis, especially across the enlarged EU, but also across the "old" Member States (Caminada et al., 2010; Cantillon et al., 2012).

Figure 5.4 also visualizes the relationship between pre-transfer at-risk-of-poverty and total size of cash benefits. Clearly, there is a substantial positive relationship between the two. Increases or decreases in pre-transfer poverty are associated with rising or falling social spending on cash benefits, which may be assumed to be due to two mechanisms, the relative importance of which is hard to determine. On the one hand, social security systems respond automatically to increases or decreases in social risks. In the boom years under consideration here the decrease of unemployment and of work-poor households resulted in declining spending levels. On the other hand, changing spending levels may also be attributable to *policies*. In Figure 5.4, a linear interpolation has been added of the relationship between size and pre-transfer at-risk-of-poverty. In doing so, we compare changes in national efforts with the "European welfare state technology" (Vandenbroucke and Diris in Chapter 1). Welfare states below the regression line responded less generously than the "European technology" to changes in pre-transfer poverty. More specifically, this was the case in the Nordic countries and in some of the continental and Southern European countries. Germany (according to SILC data) and Greece did not increase the size of social redistribution in line with increasing pre-transfer poverty. On the other side of the regression line, one observes the more generous responses in Ireland and in most of the new Member States. The evidence points at the hypothesis that *in a number of countries (mainly in the old Europe) the response of the social security system to declining pre-transfer needs has been less generous than one would expect under a model of "automatic stabilization."* This is suggestive for policy changes.

5.4.2 Household Work-intensity and Changes in Benefit Generosity

In order to gain better insight into the possible impact of effective policy changes over the past decades, we now consider the percentage-wise evolution of household average standardized benefits for three groups: households with a work-intensity below 0.5, households whose work-intensity equals 1, and an in-between group (Figure 5.5). "Standardized" means here that a correction is made for household composition using the modified OECD equivalence scales. Hence changes in household size do not impact on the evolutions observed. All households (with and without benefits) and all benefits (replacement income, assistance, and child benefits) are considered.

Clearly, work-poor and work-rich households were affected differently by the shrinkage in social expenditures between 2005 and 2008. In many countries, average benefits for the work-richer group evolved considerably more favorably than

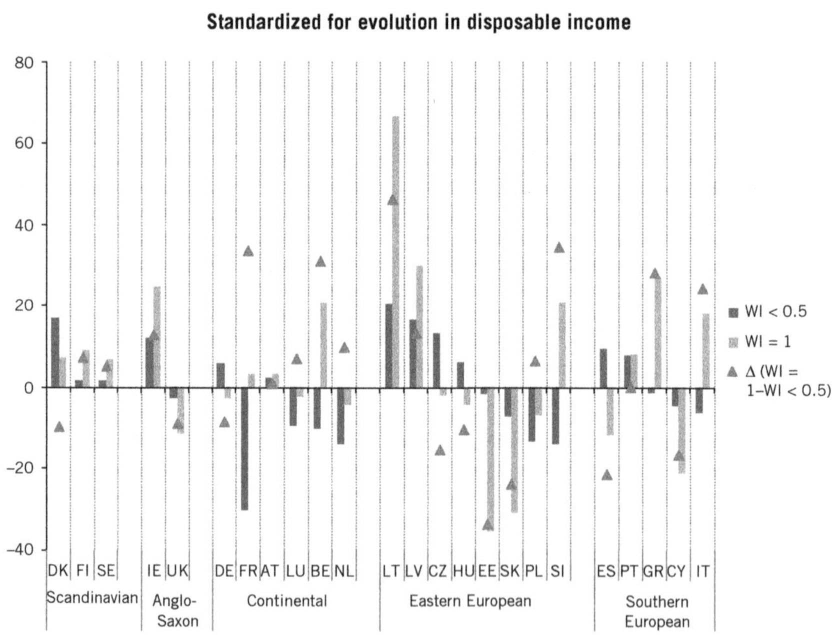

Figure 5.5. Trends in average equivalent social transfers (in %) for three groups: households with a work intensity below 0.5, households whose work intensity equals 1, and an in-between group; active age population (20–59 years old), 2005–2008. *Source*: own calculations EU-SILC (2005–2008).

those for households who failed to fully utilize their work potential. In Belgium, France, the Netherlands, Poland, and Slovenia, the average benefit to work-poor households actually declined, while that to the work-rich group remained stable or even increased. In Finland, Sweden, and Italy the average benefit to work-poor households did not change much while that to work-rich households increased. In a number of countries, we observe the opposite: In the United Kingdom, Slovakia, Estonia, and Cyprus, work-rich families were affected more severely by declining average benefit amounts. Finally, it should be noted that in Denmark, Finland, and Sweden the average benefit did not decline for any of the work-intensity groups observed, while the total size of social transfers did decrease (see Section 5.4.1). The decline of spending levels for the active-age population in these countries, therefore, has fully been driven by compositional changes.

Although the trends are in no way unequivocal, changing average benefit levels may suggest that in a number of countries social protection evolved more favorably for work-richer households than for the work-poor. These trends may support the hypothesis formulated in the introductory section of this chapter, namely, that the poverty alleviation function of social protection may have come under pressure as a consequence of decommodification, on the one hand, and the need to develop work-oriented benefits in order to make work more attractive and to enhance the work-life balance, on the other hand. However, these figures, too, should be interpreted with great circumscription.

Trends in average benefits per work-intensity group are, after all, also sensitive to shifts in the profile of the groups under scrutiny, including any changes that may have occurred in gravity and the type of social risks. The data presented in Figure 5.5 should, therefore, be treated with considerable caution as an indicator of changing welfare state generosity. We, therefore, now turn *to more direct indicators of policy changes*, using a *model family* approach. In Figures 5.6, 5.7, and 5.8 we look directly at the income levels of a specific group of benefit claimants, namely, social assistance benefit recipients who are by definition work-poor. This exercise is based on standard simulations, that is, the net income of a number of hypothetical households is simulated, according to the prevailing tax-benefit legislation in each country. The data draw on the CSB-MIPI data set, that is, a data collection conducted by the Centre for Social Policy (University of Antwerp) through a network of national experts (for a detailed description, see Van Mechelen et al., 2011). This data set contains estimates of net incomes of several model families taking full account of social assistance, child cash benefits, taxes, social security contributions, and housing allowances, on the condition that they are nondiscretionary.

We start by scrutinizing trends in targeted minimum income protection. Ample evidence exists of the inadequacy of minimum social benefits (OECD, 2009; Nelson, 2011; Van Mechelen & Marchal, 2013). In many cases, minimum benefit levels are below 40% of median equivalent income. This is not only so in the relatively new Member States, but also in older, usually richer Member States such as Belgium, Germany, France, Finland, Sweden, and the United Kingdom (see Figure 5.6).

With regard to social assistance, the overall picture for the 1990s in the EU15 was one of almost uniform erosion of benefit levels relative to average wage. Figure 5.7 shows the trend between 1992 and 2009 in the social assistance benefit package of a model family consisting of one adult. (See Van Mechelen & Marchal,2013, for a detailed explanation of methodology.) Especially in Ireland, the Netherlands, Sweden, and the UK, net social assistance benefits were unable to keep up with the rise in net average wages during the 1990s. During the 2001– 2009 period, the pattern was far less unequivocal. In about half of the countries under consideration social assistance benefits rose more quickly than average wages. This was especially the case in Ireland and in post-Communist countries with previously relatively low benefits, such as Hungary, Latvia, Romania, and Slovenia. However, in other East European countries, such as the Czech Republic, Estonia, Poland, and Slovakia, minimum benefits lagged behind average wages. Minimum protection also further declined relative to average wages in the Netherlands, the UK, Sweden, Finland, and Denmark. Relative to median household income, the downward trends in minimum income protection were even more pronounced. In countries such as Italy, Spain, and Lithuania, benefits kept up with wages, but not with median income, and hence not with the poverty line (set at 60% of median income). The adequacy of social assistance benefits thus decreased in many countries. This observation holds not only for single persons, but also for families with children (Van Mechelen & Marchal, 2013).

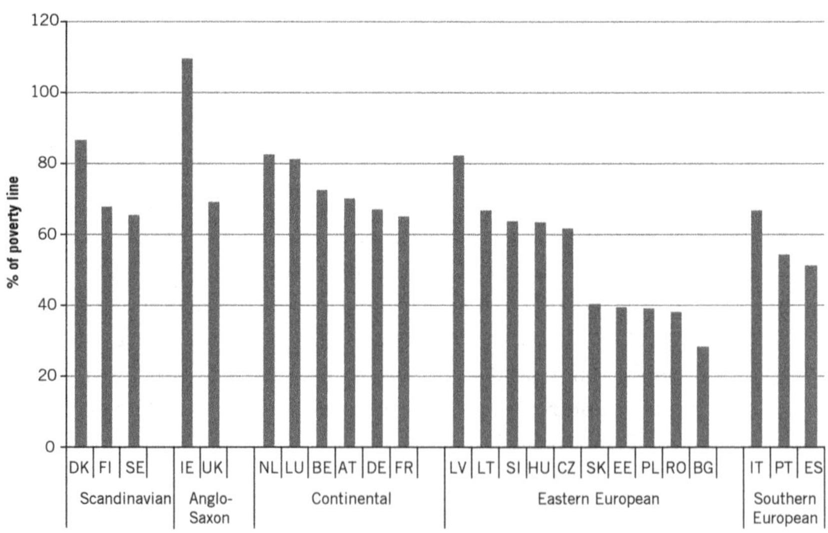

Figure 5.6. The adequacy of social assistance: net social assistance benefit packages as percentage of the poverty line (60% of median equivalent income), three model families, 2009. *Source*: CSB-MIPI (see Van Mechelen et al., 2011).

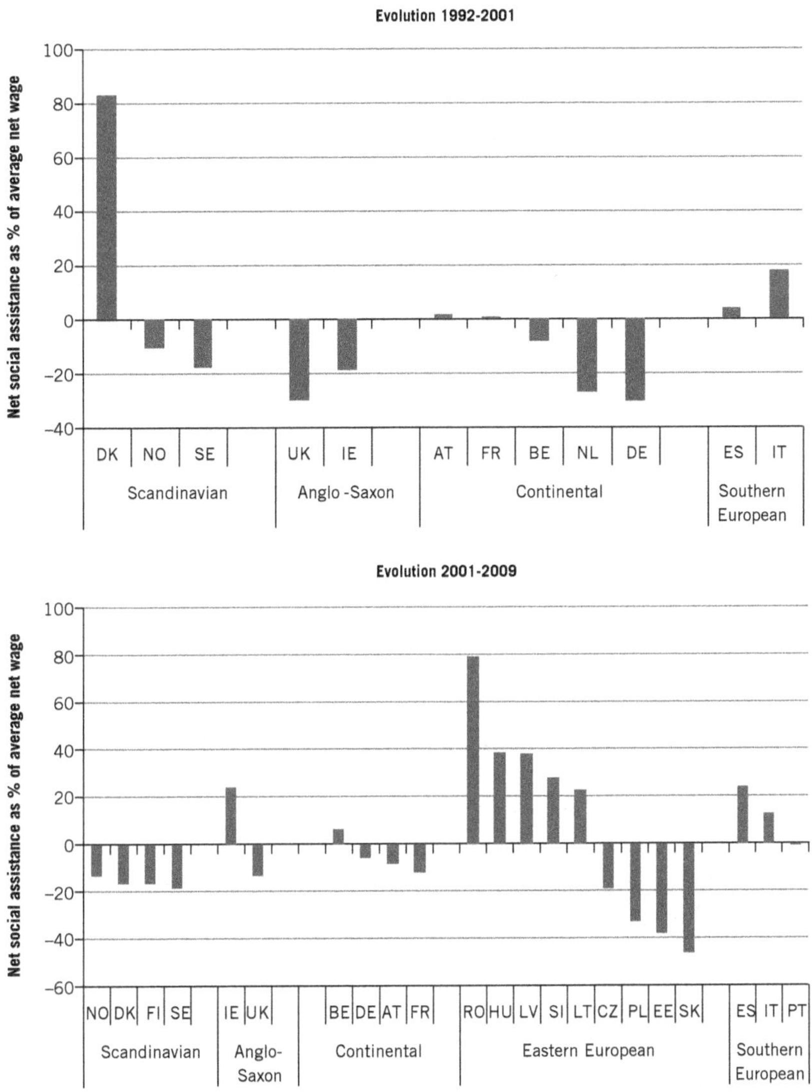

Figure 5.7. Trends in net social assistance benefit packages, single-person households, 1992–2001/2001–2009. *Source*: CSB-MIPI (see Van Mechelen et al., 2011).

Whereas *child benefit packages* were able to escape welfare erosion until the 1990s, over the past decade their adequacy has declined in a majority of countries (Van Mechelen & Bradshaw, 2013; Gauthier, 1990; Kamerman & Kahn, 2001). Figure 5.8 shows the evolution of the child benefit package of a couple with two children on social assistance. The child benefit package here consists not only of child cash benefits and child tax benefits or allowances, which reduce the direct tax liability in respect of children, but also includes housing benefits and social

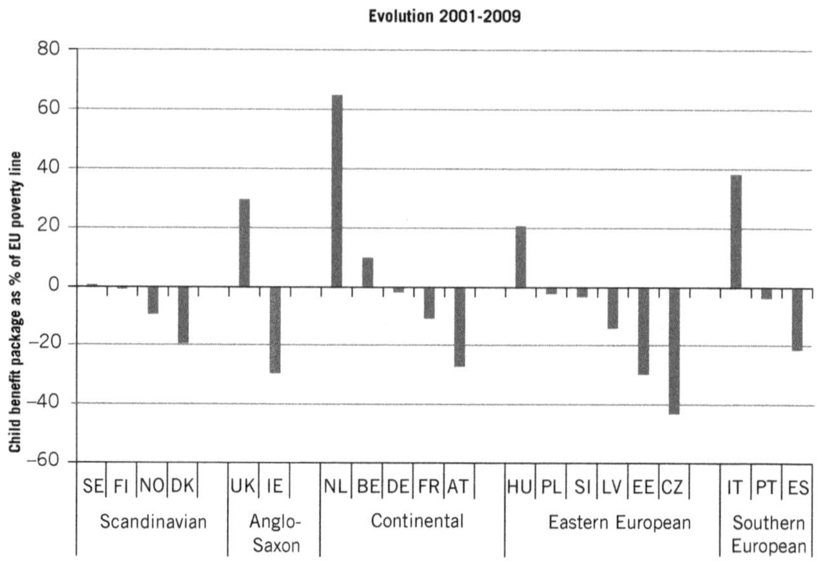

Figure 5.8. Trends in child benefit packages, couple with two children on social assistance, 2001–2009. *Source*: CSB-MIPI (see Van Mechelen et al., 2011).

assistance top-ups that take account of the presence of a child. (See Van Mechelen & Bradshaw, 2013, for a detailed explanation of methodology.) In most countries child benefit packages have decreased relative to the poverty line. This holds true not only for social assistance recipients, but also for other low-income families, such as single-earner households on average or minimum wage, and for double-income families. The gap between the child benefit package of a social assistance recipient and the poverty line has increased by more than 20% in countries such as Austria, Spain, the Czech Republic, Estonia, and Ireland, and by more than 10% in France, Denmark, and Latvia. The main exceptions are Hungary, Italy, Lithuania, the Netherlands, and the United Kingdom where the child benefit package of families on social assistance has grown faster than median equivalent income (Van Mechelen & Bradshaw, 2013).

Table 5.1 shows the evolution of net disposable incomes for a broader range of work-poor and work-rich families in Belgium and the Netherlands. Similar to the figures above, this table draws on model family simulations. Table 5.1 provides evidence that the stark decline in average equivalent benefits for work-poor families between 2008 and 2005 shown in Figure 5.5 is not merely a result of the changing profile of work-poor families but also of shifting policy priorities.

The data for Belgium show that, for households with (relatively) high work-intensity, social protection improved between 1995 and 2007. Further simulation results for work-rich families earning a minimum wage suggest that their real incomes have risen substantially thanks to the reduction in social contributions. The income situation of working *lone parents* observed in Table 5.1 increased

Table 5.1. Trends in net income, 13 model families, 1995–2007 evolution in percentage.

	Belgium	**The Netherlands**
Work Intensity = 1		
Lone parent, full-time employed, minimum wage	11	191
Two earner couple (minimum wage), 35 years	9	15
Two earner couple (minimum wage), 55 years	12	2
Two earner couple (average wage), 55 years	5	-1
Work Intensity = 0.5		
One earner couple (minimum wage), 35years, one partner short-term unemployed	8	–4
One earner couple (minimum wage), 55 years, one partner long-term unemployed	6	–7
One earner couple (average wage), 55 years, one partner long-term unemployed	–1	-5
Lone parent, career reduction 50%, minimum wage	23	10
One earner couple (minimum wage), 55 years, one partner long term disabled	19	–5
Work Intensity = 0		
Social assistance recipient, single person	7	-56
Both partners long-term unemployed (minimum wage), 49 years	13	–7
Both partners long-term unemployed (minimum wage), 55 years	-6	–7
Both partners short-term unemployed (minimum wage), 49 years	0	n.a.

Note: With the exception of young social assistance claimants, all households are assumed to have two children. The age of the children is assumed to be 10 years and 14 years for couples aged 35 years, and 18 years and 25 years for couples aged 49 years or 55 years.
Source: Herman Deleeck Centre for Social Policy.

over the period considered, in consequence of a combination of measures, such as the increase in affordable childcare provisions, the increase in compensatory benefits for parents making part-time use of care leave provisions, and the introduction of a child cash benefit aimed specially at lone parents. Government policy in Belgium during the 1995–2007 period was clearly geared toward, on the one hand, work-rich households with a low earnings potential and, on the other, a number of specific high-risk groups such as lone parents on parental leave, but also the work-incapacitated. The income of households on an average wage, on the one hand and work-poor households dependent on benefits on the other, increased far less strongly. Older work-poor households actually saw their benefits decline in real terms.

The results for the Netherlands are strikingly comparable to those for Belgium. For one thing, in the Netherlands, too, low-income households with high work-intensity saw their income grow quite considerably. This was occasioned by a reduction in social contributions and the introduction of a healthcare allowance to compensate low-income families for the cost of healthcare insurance. Moreover, the incomes of households with a low(er) work-intensity and those working at average wage developed much less favorably. However, the focus of activation policy—at least insofar as financial incentives are concerned—was not so much on the older unemployed as on young social assistance claimants. A further difference with Belgium is apparent from the fact that not a single at-risk group mentioned in Table 5.1 saw a marked improvement in the level of minimum-income protection enjoyed. Likewise, at-risk groups with limited employment prospects (cf. work incapacitation) saw their income grow only relatively modestly. Dutch policy would appear to have been geared entirely toward households with a high work-intensity and low pay. This also holds for lone parents: While the income after deduction of child daycare costs of a lone parent in *full-time* employment at minimum wage increased threefold (thanks to the introduction of a child daycare allowance for low-income families, with a supplement for lone parents), the income of lone parents in *part-time* employment rose by barely 4% (due to the fact that the child daycare allowance was cancelled out almost entirely by cuts in career-break benefits).

5.5 MORE ADEQUATE MINIMUM INCOME PROTECTION: POTENTIAL AND CONSTRAINTS

The most important conclusion to be drawn from the above is the striking—and in many countries rising—inadequacy of social protection for individuals living in households with a low work-intensity. This may point at the tension between the adequacy of income protection, for those who remained outside of the labor market on the one hand, activation and work-centered welfare reform on the other hand, as elaborated in the first section of this chapter, and lend credence to the notion that policies have sought to raise employment at least partially by reducing reservation wages (see, among others, Atkinson, 2010). Arguably, the focus on employment has weakened traditional (passive) social protection as "much of the thrust of labor market reform has been by reducing the level and coverage of social protection and tightening the conditions under which benefits are paid" (Atkinson, 2010: 15; see also Vandenbroucke & Vleminckx, 2011).

The growing inadequacy of social benefits raises the question of whether it is possible (and, if so, under which conditions) to guarantee an adequate minimum income protection given the high number of people who are structurally excluded from the labor market and the necessary activation policies, which inevitably also include the fight against dependency traps. Otherwise stated: Is it possible to reduce poverty among work-poor families and to simultaneously create employment and reduce social spending? Figure 5.9 presents a tentative

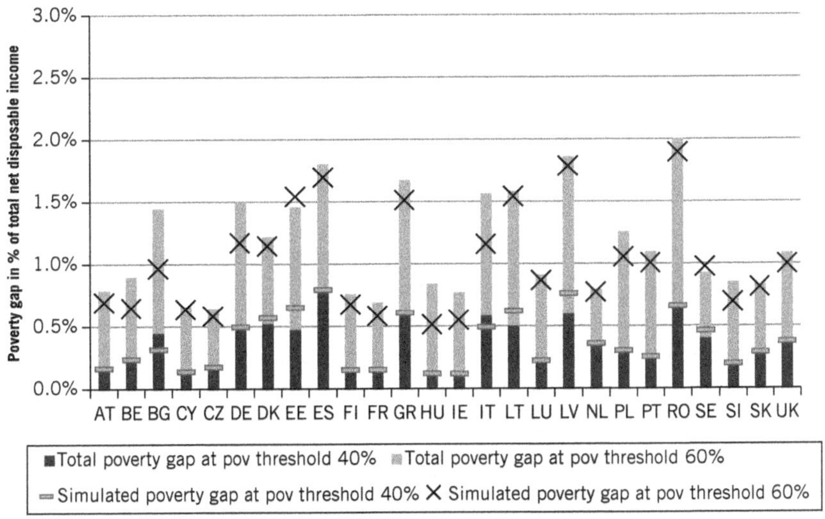

Figure 5.9. The total poverty gap of individuals aged 20–59 years (percentage of total disposable income) at poverty thresholds 40% and 60%, before and after a reduction of the share of households with work intensity lower than 0.5. *Source*: own calculation EU-SILC 2008. *Note*: we assume that poverty risks in both work intensity groups are unaltered.

calculation showing that the total cost of an increase in minimum incomes to the 60% poverty threshold would amount to almost EUR 82 billion, which corresponds to 1.46% of total disposable income in the EU.[12] Clearly the financial effort required for all countries to attain the 60% level is considerable. Moreover, it would be unequally divided between the Member States. In Austria, the Czech Republic, Cyprus, Finland, France, the Netherlands, and Slovenia, the measure would require less than 1.0% of total disposable income; in Bulgaria, Spain, Italy, Latvia, Lithuania, and Romania, it would require over 2.0%. The budgetary impact of increasing minimum benefits across the Union to 40% of median standardized income would represent some EUR 21 billion, ranging from 0.07% of disposable in Cyprus to 0.94% in Romania. Obviously, these differences in simulated costs are correlated with the number of work-poor households, the level of prevailing minimum wage, and with the actual level of means deployed in social security systems.

Moreover, a Europe-wide introduction of social assistance minimums equal to 60% of national median income would create financial "inactivity traps" in no fewer than 10 Member States: in Bulgaria, Estonia, Slovenia, and Lithuania, the net income of a single benefit recipient would be between 25% and 30% higher than the equivalent income of a single person working at minimum wage; in Spain and the Czech Republic, the relative advantage of the benefit claimant would amount to between 14% and 16% (Cantillon & Van Mechelen, 2012; Vandenbroucke et al., 2013).

Not unimportantly, the large differences in the severity of the dependency trap coincide with a great diversity in activation measures and minimum wages (Van Mechelen et al., 2011; Marx et al., 2013). In some Eastern European countries, a genuine activation policy would appear to be lacking thus far. Clearly, here an increase in benefit amounts would appear to be feasible only if minimum wages are increased and a new balance is struck between the rights and duties of benefit claimants.

So what would be the cost of introducing adequate minimum income protection if countries were able to devise successful activation policies and—in so doing—to push down their number of work-poor households? Figure 5.9 illustrates the budgetary impact of an increase in minimum income protection assuming that the proportion of households with low work-intensity (< 0.5) were cut to 7.8% of the population aged 20–59 years in all Member States, that is, the average proportion in the top-five performers (Slovakia, Sweden, Estonia, and Lithuania).[13] Under the admittedly bold assumption of constant poverty gaps in both work-intensity groups, the cost of an increase in minimum social benefits to 60% of median equivalent income would amount to 66 billion, that is, 1.18% of European net disposable income (as compared with 82 billion prior to the reduction in the share of work-poor households). Evidently, the impact of active inclusion policies on the poverty gap would be strongest in countries with a high proportion of work-poor households. In countries such as Bulgaria, Hungary, Italy, and Ireland—where about 20% of working-age households are work-poor—the total poverty gap may be reduced by 30% to 50% by cutting back current levels of low work-intensity to about 8% (under the assumption that the poverty line remains unchanged). In other countries, however, the number of work-poor households scarcely influences the size of the poverty gap. In Spain, Romania, Lithuania, Estonia, and Latvia, the poverty gap would remain large even if the share of families with low work-intensity were to be reduced to 8%. In the latter three countries, the work-intensity of households is already relatively high; hence, one should not expect spectacular employment effects. Here, the poverty gap mainly reflects the inadequacy of current income protection arrangements. In sum, *although active labor market policies can and should play a crucial role in reducing poverty gaps across Europe, income protection schemes remain an important instrument for improving welfare-state poverty alleviation,* even if countries could manage to get their number of work-poor families back to the levels of the best performing countries.

5.6 CONCLUSION

We may summarize the main results as follows. First, as far as the *whole active-age population* is concerned, one may conclude that in the 1990s the redistributive impact of social transfers declined significantly in the traditionally strongest welfare states in the Nordic cluster. In the 2000s figures signal that similiar trends may have prevailed not only in the North but also in many of the old Member States on the Continent, albeit to a much lesser extent. Conversely, the Anglo-Saxon countries (most notably Ireland) and some counties in the clusters of the new Member States in the 2000s, and of the Southern States in the 1990s, displayed *increases* of poverty reduction by social protection. In all, in the period prior to the Great Recession, Europe's social security systems remained important devices in the fight against poverty, but as a consequence of declining poverty reduction, few countries are to be found where the advantages of the favorable pre-crisis employment conditions were translated into declining poverty rates.

Second, considering *work-poor households* in particular, in many (but certainly not all) EU countries significant and substantial decreases in relative poverty reduction through social transfers occurred. Income poverty among work-poor households increased accordingly.

Third, although social transfers are obviously less important for *non-work-poor households* and changes over time were less outspoken than in the case of work-poor households, it is clear that inadequate social protection is not an unimportant factor in explaining *in-work poverty.* The figures shown in this chapter give some mild support to the hypothesis formulated in the previous chapter that in-work poverty is associated not only with low pay but to some extent also with low work-intensity at the household level and with shortcomings in tax and benefit systems.

Fourth, more direct policy indicators such as changing spending levels, observed average benefit levels, and theoretical tax benefit packages for work-poor and work-rich households suggest that—where applicable—the relative decline in social transfers has primarily affected work-poor households. *These trends may support the hypotheses that in many countries the poverty alleviation function of social protection has come under pressure as a consequence of recommodification on the one hand, and the need to develop work-oriented benefits in order to make work more attractive and to enhance the work-life balance, on the other hand.*

Microsimulation and in-depth study of country-specific policy trajectories may provide more insight into the question whether and how it is possible to reduce poverty among work-poor families and to simultaneously create employment and reduce social spending. On the basis of the analyses presented in this chapter, the conclusion can only be that the experience in the EU before the crisis is indicative of tough trade-off inherent to "active inclusion" strategies that should not be taken lightly. Having arrived at this point, the question arises how work, social redistribution, and poverty reduction can be reconciled. How can a maximization of employment and an effective egalitarian agenda be made compatible? Three considerations are in place here.

First, differences in social redistribution observed between individual countries are quite considerable, both in terms of *levels* and *trends*. Although a reduction in the poverty alleviation by social protection has been the dominant (but not unequivocal) pattern, the countries of Scandinavia continue to provide an example of how low poverty, high employment, and economic performance can be combined with a strong social redistribution. Although the adequacy of Nordic social protection decreased, its poverty reducing capacity is still among the highest in Europe (in 2008 only preceded by Hungary and Ireland).

Second, poverty is clearly more prevalent among jobless households, who typically comprise between 10% and 20% of the working-age population. Poverty risks among this population group are generally very high, even though considerable differences between countries are observed. Comparison between countries suggests two things: first, the proportion of work-poor households may certainly be reduced to 10% according to the examples of Slovakia, the Czech Republic, and Denmark; second, guaranteeing adequate minimum incomes to the apparently "noncondensable" groups of work-poor households, while expensive, is not altogether impossible, provided that the policy design is efficient, and that genuine activation measures, as well as adequate minimum wages and an appropriate-level of social redistribution, are put in place. Given the limited economic strength of the poorer countries of Europe and the fact that they usually face a wider poverty gap, they will obviously need to proceed gradually in introducing adequate minimum income protection. The simulations that have been shown in this chapter clearly shown that *although active labor market policies can and should play a crucial role in reducing poverty gaps across Europe, adequate income protection schemes and social redistribution remain an important instrument for improving welfare state performance.*

Third, social budgets are clearly not always deployed efficiently. It has been established that there is generally a negative relationship between spending levels and poverty risks: Successful antipoverty measures clearly require important distributional efforts (see Chapter 1). However, some countries achieve much lower poverty rates despite similar social spending levels. The design and structure of social programs are obviously important, so that certain Member States attain greater "efficiency" in terms of poverty risk reduction than others.

NOTES

1 In a 1992 recommendation to the Council, three primary objectives were formulated at the European level: (1) minimum income protection; (2) earnings-related income protection with a view to safeguarding the acquired standard of living; and (3) social and economic integration.

2 Note that in contrast to individual caseload trends, the share of households receiving cash transfers (pensions excluded)—diminished almost everywhere in the EU, but most notably in Denmark, Finland, and Belgium. In most Western European countries, household caseloads continued to decline between 2004 and 2007. The share of household in receipt of cash transfers

was also cut considerably in Poland and the Slovak Republic. However, most Central and Eastern European countries saw a rise in caseloads. This was most notably the case in Hungary, Latvia, and Lithuania, but also in Ireland. From 2004 to 2007, in many countries household caseloads declined not only among work-poor households but also among the higher work-intensity group. The divergent trends regarding individual and household caseloads can be explained by individualization on the one hand and/or by a concentration of benefit recipients within households on the other hand. This observation is important when considering changes in average benefit levels at household level. We come back to this issue in Section 5.4.2.

3 In addition to the dangers of legitimacy loss and, the consequent downward pressure on the generosity and adequacy of social protection, another major drawback of targeting that is described extensively in the literature is its potential impact on the labor supply through the creation of poverty traps (Atkinson & Micklewright, 1991; Deacon & Bradshaw, 1983; Atkinson & Mogensen, 1993; OECD, 1994).

4 See Chapter 1 for a further elaboration of the issue.

5 Employment and Social Developments in Europe (2011) contains a brief note on the impact of taxes and benefits on income inequality.

6 In the present chapter, we make use of the ECHP waves 1995 to 2001 and the EU-SILC waves 2005 to 2008. Please note that each survey contains information on household incomes from the previous year. There are, however, two exceptions: the United Kingdom (refers to "current income") and Ireland (12 months previous to the interview). Figures from the ECHP and the EU-SILC are not entirely comparable due to differences in the sampling methods used—for more information on both data sources, see chapter 2.

7 See Cantillon et al., 2012 (Table A4) for detailed data on each country.

8 There is, however, one remarkable counterexample, that is, Germany in recent years. Whereas there was an increase in the average volume going to the work-poor, the observed poverty reduction declined, resulting in rising AROP rates. This apparent anomaly is explained by a sharp inefficiency in the allocation of resources going to the work-poor households.

9 Note that this chapter makes use of a household work-intensity indicator, whereas Chapter 4 uses the individual employment status to define in-work poverty.

10 The empirical estimates of spending on cash transfers in both ECHP and SILC are broadly in line with ESSPROS data, although ECHP data tend to report some underestimation of real expenditures whereas SILC data slightly overestimate real size—albeit with exceptions. Notably for Germany and Spain, the 1994 ECHP substantially underestimates the real cash expenditures while the SILC data for Sweden, Ireland, and especially Hungary probably yield an overestimation. As a result, the declining trend in Germany as reported by ESSPROSS is not reflected in the survey estimates.

11 The significant drop in expenditure on cash transfers has in many countries been accompanied by decreasing numbers of households receiving social benefits. (See Figure 2 in Cantillon et al., 2012: 14).

12 The budgetary impact of an increase in minimum social benefits on the national EU poverty thresholds is estimated as the sum of the poverty gaps of all persons aged 20–59 years. The cost obtained is presented as a proportion of the sum of the disposable incomes of the total population. It should be emphasized that many practical and technical aspects are ignored in this exercise, so that the result is an approximation and, therefore, merely illustrative. For example, it is implicitly assumed that introducing such a guaranteed minimum income will affect neither taxes paid nor other benefits claimed by the households. It is also assumed that the poverty threshold is fixed.

13 This idea also underlies the active inclusion strategy of the European Commission. In its recommendation of October 3, 2008 on the active inclusion of people excluded from the labor market, the Commission links adequate income support to other priorities such as inclusive labor markets and access to quality services. The Commission calls on the Member States to adopt measures to ensure that able-bodied persons receive help to re-enter or to remain in the labor market.

14 The same poverty line is applied when calculating the pre- and post-transfer at-risk-of-poverty rate.

6

THE REDISTRIBUTIVE CAPACITY OF SERVICES IN THE EUROPEAN UNION

Gerlinde Verbist and Manos Matsaganis

6.1 INTRODUCTION

Welfare states provide social benefits in cash and in kind. Cash benefits are income transfers, such as retirement pensions, family and unemployment benefits, and social assistance. Benefits in kind are commodities directly transferred to recipients at zero or below-market prices (Barr, 2012).

In Europe, benefits in kind are usually services, such as health, education, child care and care for the elderly. For example, hospital care in most countries is provided either free of charge or at near-zero prices (at the point of use). User fees are even rarer in the case of primary and secondary education: Enrollment is compulsory up to a certain age, while tuition is provided free of charge to all children attending publicly funded schools, irrespective of family income. Moreover, child care is often heavily subsidized; kindergartens are run by the state (most commonly local governments) or government-supervised private organizations, while user fees, where applicable, are usually income-related (in the sense that higher-income families pay higher fees, while lower-income ones pay less or are fully exempted). Elderly care may also be available on similar terms; besides, several countries have developed long-term care insurance schemes, to cater for the future needs of an aging population.

Benefits in kind in the form of goods (rather than services) are rather uncommon in Europe. Housing is a partial exception: In some countries council flats are allocated at subsidized rents (or free of charge) to eligible families.

Nevertheless, in many countries rent subsidies and the direct provision of social housing have been phased out in favor of means-tested housing allowances in cash, except for emergency accommodation, which remains available for selected groups in acute need (i.e., the homeless, refugees, victims of family abuse, and so on). Furthermore, even though food parcels may be handed out by charities and soup kitchens may be organized by municipalities, these are sporadic, or are limited to emergencies, or cater to the needs of marginal groups such as the homeless.[1]

The main sources of internationally comparable data on the size and composition of social expenditure are Eurostat and the Organisation for Economic Co-operation and Development (OECD). In the European Union, although cash benefits constitute the lion's share of expenditure on social protection (which does not include education expenditures), the relative weight of benefits in kind is still significant: In 2007, approximately 38% of all social expenditure involved benefits in kind, corresponding to 8.3% of the combined GDP of the 21 Member States included in this study[2] (Figure 6.1). The significance of services varies considerably between national welfare states. Their relative share was highest (around 50%) in Sweden, United Kingdom, and Denmark, near average (33% to 36%) in Spain, France, and Germany, and lowest (around 30%) in Italy and Poland.

Consistent data going back in time are hard to find, but the data in the Appendix of this book clearly indicate that the relative importance of benefits in kind increased (see also Chapter 1 in this volume). Looking at the European Union of older Member States (the EU15), where a longer statistical series is available, spending on benefits in kind has gone up (from 8.1% of GDP in 1998

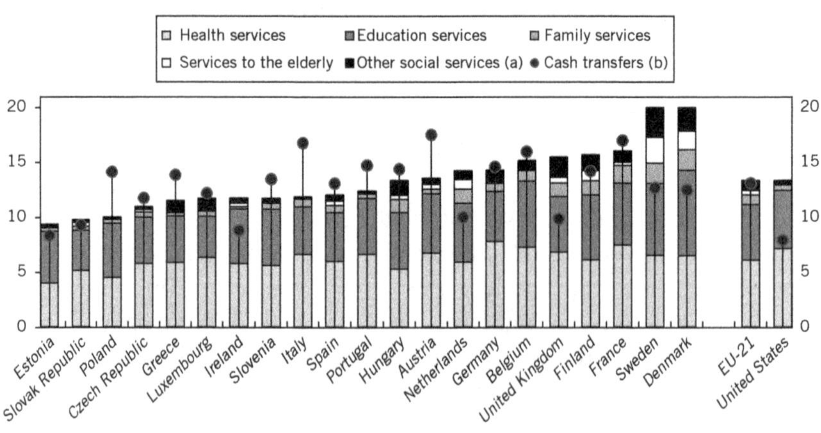

Figure 6.1. Public expenditure for in-kind and cash transfers, in percentage of GDP, 2007.
Source: OECD (2011), data from OECD Social Expenditure database (www.oecd.org/els/social/expenditure) and OECD Education database (www.oecd.org/education/database).
Note: countries are ranked in increasing order of total expenditure on all social services. 2005 data on education services for Greece and Luxembourg.

to 9.2% in 2008), while expenditure on cash benefits has lost ground (from 17.8% to 16.8% of GDP over the same period). As a result, the share of benefits in kind in all social spending clearly has risen, from 31.4% in 1998 to 35.3% in 2008 in the EU15.

Benefits in kind (like most social benefits) tend not to be means-tested, which may have consequences for their distributive impact. In terms of expenditure, a mere 15.2% of benefits in kind were means-tested in 2008 in the EU27 (slightly more as the 8.8% of cash benefits). The relative significance of means-testing for benefits in kind has remained stable since the late 1990s, as data for the EU15 show (15.7% in 2008 compared to 16.2% in 1998), while they slightly increased for cash benefits (9.1% vs. 8.2% over the same period). The share of means-testing in all benefits in kind varies greatly between countries. In the UK, Ireland, and the Netherlands the proportion of benefits in kind that were means-tested was 21%–22%. At the other extreme, this proportion was much lower (around 3% to 4%) in countries like Belgium, Sweden, and Finland, and less than 2% in Romania, the Czech Republic, and Estonia.

Including education expenditures, which are an important in-kind benefit, tips the balance very slightly in favor of benefits in kind: 13.4% of GDP in 2007 in the 21 EU countries included in this study (vs. 13.2% of GDP for cash benefits, Figure 6.1). Spending on in-kind benefits exceeds that on cash benefits in all Nordic countries, as well as in the United Kingdom, Ireland, and the Netherlands. Sweden and Denmark top the league with over 18% of GDP spent on benefits in kind. Education and health (at 5.1% and 6.1% of GDP respectively on average in the EU) make up the bulk of in-kind benefits. Child care, services to the elderly, and other services account between them for another 3.4% of GDP. Compared with this EU average, the United States have similar spending on services, but their cash spending is much lower (Figure 6.1).

Given the increasing importance of services in social spending, it is a natural question to try to gauge their distributional impact. We distinguish three questions. Firstly, do services reduce poverty and inequality, or is it true that they favor the rich more than the poor, as is sometimes asserted in the literature (Le Grand, 1982)? Secondly, how do in-kind benefits from services compare to cash transfers in terms of redistributive impact? And thirdly, has the shift to services eroded the distributive power of the welfare state over time? This chapter attempts to answer these questions by drawing on the latest estimates available and considering the major methodological issues. Its structure is as follows. After this introduction, Section 6.2 reviews the literature on the rationale for in-kind benefits and their possible redistributive impact. Section 6.3 addresses the main methodological questions, presenting an alternative way of taking account of service-related needs in the equivalence scale. Section 6.4 presents the recent findings of analyses on the distributional impact of services, focusing on the first two questions. Section 6.5 concludes, in which we touch upon the third question.

6.2 REDISTRIBUTION *VIA* IN-KIND PROVISION

6.2.1 The Rationale for In-kind Benefits

Services are particularly important in the "social investment state" discourse, emphasizing the role of "social protection as a productive factor." This discourse stresses the contribution of health, education, long-term care, and, crucially, child care to economic efficiency and higher living standards (associated with a healthier, better-educated workforce), as well as to greater equality and lower poverty.[3]

The choice of in-kind versus cash provision hinges on several considerations. In economics, the standard argument in favor of cash benefits is personal autonomy or "consumer sovereignty," while a common justification for benefits in kind is paternalism and interdependent preferences (Curry & Gahvari, 2008).

Under interdependent preferences, if the rich care for the material condition of the poor, a transfer from the former to the latter will leave both better off. However, it could be that the rich are not so much concerned with the welfare of the poor, or with their level of income, but rather with their consumption—and, specifically, with "good" rather than "bad" consumption on the part of the poor, as defined by the rich. Therefore, according to this view, from the point of view of taxpayers, the provision of income transfers may be inferior to the provision of particular goods and services.[4] Paternalism is strongly connected to the idea of merit goods and merit wants. Society may be concerned that certain goods should be available to all, or even that all should be forced to consume certain goods. Therefore, school attendance up to a certain age ought to be compulsory, rather than left to the individual preferences of children or their parents. In-kind provision is also supported by the related notion of "specific egalitarianism." For instance, Tobin (1970) has argued that even those who do not object to income inequality *per se* may still want to see that all individuals receive adequate food, medical services, or housing.

Although paternalism and merit goods can go some way toward explaining why governments provide health and education directly, rather than paying recipients cash benefits to enable them to buy as much health and education as they like, market failures (and, in particular, *information failures* such as moral hazard, adverse selection, and so on) remain a more powerful explanation of in-kind provision (Barr, 2012). In this light, the choice between benefits in cash and benefits in kind to achieve equity objectives is constrained by considerations of efficiency. Specifically, when market allocation is efficient (e.g., in the case of food), equity objectives can be pursued *via* cash benefits that enable recipients to buy what they need at market prices. In contrast, when markets fail (e.g., in the case of health care) cash benefits cannot provide a solution, and equity objectives must be pursued *via* benefits in kind, such as publicly funded health care and school education (see also Le Grand et al. 2008).

The focus on universal provision of a comprehensive range of services (going far beyond health and education to include family services and active labor market policies) has always been a distinct feature of Nordic welfare states (Esping-Andersen, 1990). As a matter of fact, choosing in-kind over cash benefits, even where these may seem interchangeable, has important implications for a number of issues. For instance, it can be argued that paying care allowances in cash (as in much of Continental Europe) favors private provision and reinforces traditional patterns of gender roles within the family, while the direct public provision of child and elderly care (as in Scandinavian countries) limits private sector involvement and promotes gender equality and stimulates labor supply (especially of mothers).

6.2.2 Dimensions of Redistribution

Most of the debate on the distributional impact of services concerns vertical redistribution (e.g., between individuals belonging to different income classes). However, it is worth considering that other dimensions may also be relevant. For instance, we may be simply interested in how resources are distributed between individuals with different needs, quite irrespective of their income. If "the key distributional question is [...] whether what people receive matches their needs" (Hills, 2004: 185), then surely the appropriate dimension is horizontal redistribution. Of course, the difficulty here is that "need" for services is often not observed as such, or cannot easily be disentangled from use of services.

Furthermore, services tend by nature to be mostly used by individuals of particular age groups. For example, health care is more heavily used by the elderly and around birth, education is intended for the young, and child care for the very young (and their parents). In view of that, "a snapshot picture of redistribution may be misleading" (Hills, 2004: 185). The relevant dimension here is life cycle redistribution. This reminds us that the welfare state redistributes resources not just between different individuals, but also between different stages in the life of the same individual.

Again, problems of measurement and data availability abound, making the degree of life cycle redistribution hard to estimate. In spite of such difficulties, it has been estimated that, measured on a lifetime basis, in Britain, "nearly three-quarters of what the welfare state was doing in the late 1980s and early 1990s was more like a 'savings bank,' and only a quarter was 'Robin Hood' redistribution between different people" (Falkingham & Hills, 1995; Hills, 2004; Barr, 2001).

6.2.3 Are Services Redistributive?

Benefits in kind are generally considered to be less redistributive than benefits in cash. In particular, their contribution toward reducing poverty and inequality has been questioned, for instance by Le Grand (1982), who famously suggested that "Public expenditure on health care, education, housing and transport systematically favors the better off and thereby contributes to inequality in final income" (p. 137). OECD (2008; 2011) evidence shows that net cash transfers reduce overall inequality by one third, whereas services reduce inequality only by one fifth.

Part of the difficulty in assessing whether and to what extent this is true lies in the fact that services actually affect the "primary" distribution of incomes (i.e., before taxes and benefits) in a variety of ways, often subtle. For instance, child care and elderly care arguably promote equality through their effect on female employment—both by freeing up women from family responsibilities so as to pursue careers, and by providing women with job opportunities in the social services sector. In this sense, the "equalizing" effect of services goes beyond what a simple "pre-post comparison" would indicate (Esping-Andersen & Myles, 2009). A similar reasoning, however, also applies to cash benefits, especially if they are linked to activation.

Empirical work on the redistributive role of services has proliferated since the pioneering work of Smeeding (1977). In later work, Smeeding et al. (1993) examined the distributional impact of health, education, and housing in seven European countries, while Evandrou et al. (1993) analyzed the role of services in the British welfare state, and their effect on the distribution of incomes. More recently, Harding et al. (2006) compared the redistributive effect of cash and noncash benefits in Australia and the UK. At about the same time Marical et al. (2008) provided estimates of the distributional impact of a range of publicly provided services in OECD countries, an analysis that was updated and extended in terms of country coverage and categories of services in OECD (2011) and Verbist et al. (2012). Furthermore, Matsaganis & Verbist (2009) estimated the distributional effects of subsidies to publicly funded child care in Belgium, Finland, Germany, Greece, and Sweden, while Paulus et al. (2010) estimated the size and incidence of education, health care, and housing subsidies in Belgium, Germany, Greece, Italy, and the UK.

Institutional design may be crucial in determining distributional impact. As the chapter by Van Lancker and Ghysels in this volume demonstrates, the distributional impact of services may be influenced by a number of factors (see also Van Lancker & Ghysels, 2012). The study shows that in terms of equity the Swedish system of child care outperformed the Flemish one. In Flanders, greater use of child care by high-income groups and the generosity of tax deductions offset the pro-poor design of the tariff (parental fees) structure in public child care centers.

The question of redistributive effect is made complex by the fact that services are typically provided in response to greater need associated with the onset of some life event (from child birth to illness and frailty in old age). Ideally, the horizontal and vertical dimensions of redistribution ought to be identified separately. Controlling for need is one way of estimating the distributional impact of services (i.e., the degree of vertical redistribution) net of horizontal effects.

Recently, a comprehensive analysis of Norwegian local public services (Aaberge et al., 2010) concluded that while noncash benefits reduced poverty by almost one third and inequality by about 15%, adjusting for differences in need offset a significant part of that impact. The different methodological challenges reflect the complexity of the topic and are the subject of the next section.

6.3 METHODOLOGICAL ISSUES

Estimating the distributional impact of services (or, indeed, cash benefits) raises the issue of the counterfactual. The European Commission routinely publishes estimates of poverty rates in the EU before social benefits (except pensions) and presents their distance from actual poverty rates (i.e., after social benefits) as a measure of national welfare states' effectiveness in reducing poverty. Although informative, such an exercise explicitly relies on the ceteris paribus hypothesis. But other things are hardly ever equal: If social benefits had not existed, European societies would be completely different. The abolition of maternity, sickness, and disability benefits, for instance, would oblige individuals to work more even when it was better for them that they did not. Simple pre-post comparisons, far from enabling us to draw safe conclusions on the capacity of welfare states to reduce poverty and inequality, thus need to be interpreted with caution.

For a range of reasons, the counterfactual problem is far more serious with respect to services. To start with, incomes in kind (such as free health and education) are not included in standard definitions of income, and their value has to be computed separately in estimations of "extended income." On the other hand, as discussed earlier, services are often provided in response to greater need. For instance, over 90% of all health expenditure for an individual occurs in the last year before death. In view of this, claiming that recipients had high "extended incomes" as a result would miss an important part of the story: controlling for needs becomes necessary. Furthermore, the welfare state not only affects net disposable incomes (i.e., after redistribution through income taxes and social benefits), but also shapes market incomes (e.g., gross earnings before taxes and benefits). For example, service-intensive Nordic welfare states have defamiliarized welfare responsibilities with regard to caring for children and the elderly, as a result of which employment rates are virtually identical for men and women. As a consequence, child poverty in Nordic countries is low *even before social benefits are taken into account.* Ignoring these indirect effects of publicly provided social services on the distribution of market incomes risks seriously underestimating their real distributional impact.

In this section, we discuss the major methodological issues related to including the value of public social services in a distributional analysis (see also, e.g., Aaberge et al., 2010; Garfinkel et al., 2006; Marical et al., 2008; OECD, 2011; Verbist et al., 2012). How should one value the benefits households derive from public social services (valuation)? How should we distribute the aggregate value of these services among individuals (allocation)? How should the equivalence scale be adapted to take account of the needs associated with these services (equivalence scales)? Each of these issues has consequences for the counterfactual against which to measure the distributive effect of these services.

6.3.1 Valuation

The valuation of public services is a particularly difficult issue, given that these services are provided outside market settings, and hence there is no market price valuation. In the literature, the standard practice is to value the benefit deriving from public services at the production cost, which means that its measurement is based on the inputs used to provide these services rather than on the actual outputs produced (see, e.g., Aaberge et al., 2006; Marical et al., 2008; Smeeding et al., 1993). An initial drawback of this approach is that it does not take account of the quality and efficiency in the provision of these services. Both total and public health care spending is, for instance, much higher in the United States than in any EU country. This corresponds to very high-quality care in some areas (e.g., cancer care), but not necessarily in others, such as primary care, in which many other countries (e.g., United Kingdom) perform better (Pearson, 2009). Moreover, U.S. standard health indicators in general are not always better than in many European countries (Anderson et al., 2003; Garfinkel et al., 2006). Within the national accounts framework, attempts have been undertaken to develop output-based measures, which precisely try to capture (changes in) quality. Deveci et al. (2008) find, for instance, that output-based production of health services grew more rapidly than input-based production. Another problem with using the production cost is that it does not necessarily reflect the user's value of the service, given that the public service cannot (easily) be exchanged for other goods. Therefore, economists often assume that in-kind benefits are worth less to recipients than their equivalent in cash (Smeeding, 1977; Nolan & Russell, 2001; Garfinkel et al., 2006; Barr, 2012).

6.3.2 Allocation

The second question relates to the allocation of these benefits across individuals: Who are the beneficiaries to whom the value of public services is attributed? The literature distinguishes two approaches, namely the "actual consumption approach" and the "insurance value approach" (see, e.g., Marical et al., 2008). The actual consumption approach allocates the value of public services to the individuals who are actually using the service; it can, of course, only be applied if actual beneficiaries can be identified. This approach is typically used in the case of education services (Antoninis & Tsakloglou, 2001; Callan et al., 2008), childcare services (Matsaganis & Verbist, 2009; Vaalavuo, 2011; Chapter 7 in this volume) and social housing (OECD, 2011; Verbist et al., 2012).

The actual consumption approach has also been used for public healthcare services, based on detailed data on the effective use of healthcare services by individuals (see, e.g., for the UK Evandrou et al., 1993; Sefton, 2002). Several authors, however, point out that this approach ignores the greater needs that are associated with being ill: It implies that, ceteris paribus, sick people are better off than healthy people because they receive more health care services (see, e.g., Aaberge et al., 2006). Therefore, many studies use an insurance value approach, which means that one imputes the "insurance value" of coverage to each person based on specific characteristics (e.g., age, sex, socioeconomic position). The insurance value is the amount that an insured person would have to pay in each category (e.g., age group) so that the third party provider (*i.c.* the government) would have just enough revenue to cover all claims for such persons (Smeeding, 1982). It is based on the notion that what the government provides is equivalent to funding an insurance policy where the value of the premium is the same for everybody sharing the same characteristics, such as age (Marical et al., 2008). The insurance value approach also incorporates the value of access to this type of service.[5] Both approaches can lead to quite different results. Marical et al. (2008) have applied the insurance value and the actual consumption approach for healthcare services in eight European countries. On average, the reduction in inequality when including healthcare expenditures in the income concept turned out to be considerably lower on the basis of the actual consumption approach than with the insurance-value approach.[6]

6.3.3 Correction for Needs: Equivalence Scales

As the needs of a household grow with each additional member in a nonproportional way, equivalence scales are commonly used in distribution analyses to take account of such economies of scale (OECD, 2005). In this book (as in many recent publications) the equivalence scale used for adjusting household disposable income is the so-called OECD modified equivalence scale.[7] But as some types of noncash income may have needs associated with them that are unmeasured in usual equivalence scales, using a cash income equivalence scale when noncash income components are included in the income concept, may give rise to what Radner (1997) has called the "consistency" problem. Consider two single-person households with each EUR 1,000 cash income. Person A is ill and receives public health care worth EUR 200, whereas person B is healthy and needs no health care. Consequently, person A could be said to have 20% more needs than B because of differences in health care needs, and his equivalence scale should be 1.2 compared with 1 for B.

Despite recognition of this issue in the literature, most empirical studies still apply the same (cash income) equivalence scale for both cash and extended income. Garfinkel et al. (2006) defend this approach because "on the one hand, in-kind benefits do not exhibit economies of scale, which implies they should be divided by household size rather than the square of the household size. On the other hand, in-kind benefits are not shared equally by all family members, which suggests that they should be added to equivalent cash income on an individual basis. (...) Thus our use of the same equivalence scale for both cash and in-kind expenditures is a reasonable middle-of-the-road solution." However, this reasoning neglects the fact that health care or education-related needs do not only depend on economies of scales as captured by a standard cash income equivalence scale. This issue is tackled in Paulus et al. (2010), whose basic point of departure is that the equivalence scale used to measure inequality of disposable income is conditional on the existence of free public services such as education and health care. They propose a *fixed cost approach*, "assuming that the needs of the recipients of these services are equal to a specific sum of money. For example, we could assume that the per capita amounts spent by the state for age-specific population groups on public education and public health care depict accurately the corresponding needs of these groups. Then the recalculation of equivalence scales is straightforward." They propose the following formula, which should be valid for a household to remain at the same welfare level before and after including public services in the income concept:

$$y/e = (y + k)/e' \tag{1}$$

with y being cash disposable income, e the modified OECD equivalence scale, k the value of public services and e' the new equivalence scale that incorporates the extra needs of the household members for public services. Hence, $(y+k)/e'$ can be considered as the income concept that incorporates both the in-kind benefit from services, as well as the corresponding needs for these services.

This formula can be rewritten as:

$$e' = (y + k)\ e/y \tag{2}$$

meaning that for all households (with y different from zero) the new equivalence scale can be derived. Note that this scale is income-dependent, because its value decreases with income level. The value of k differs across countries, and can reflect differences in social priorities. Paulus et al. (2010) calculate this adjusted equivalence scale using EU average values to calculate k (see further), and then calculate how this impacts on inequality measures. They actually do not really calculate the redistributive effect of services, but they basically test the sensitivity of inequality outcomes for differences in relative spending levels on services across countries.

In order to measure the distributive impact of services, an extra step needs to be introduced, which is the track followed in this chapter. We start from formula (1) and decompose it into two steps, thus developing a service-needs-adjusted counterfactual for measuring the redistributive effect of public services. Firstly, it shows the effect of including the needs for the services (e.g., health care) in the equivalence scale by moving from y/e to y/e'[. As e' is an equivalence scale that incorporates a measure for health care needs, y/e' can be considered as an indicator of what the living standard would be if there were no publicly provided healthcare services. Because cash equivalent income is conditional upon the existence of publicly provided services, y/e' is a way of removing this conditionality. Consequently, y/e' can be used as a counterfactual against which to measure the redistributive impact of services, which is represented by the transition from y/e' to $(y+k)/e'$.

The demarcation of needs (of the target groups; see Aaberge et al., 2010) requires careful consideration, and might differ according to type of service. In the case of health care and compulsory education, it can be argued that all individuals have a need for health care, and that all pupils of compulsory school age have a need for education (which is one of the reasons it is compulsory; Callan & Keane, 2009). In the case of other services, this issue is more debatable: Does the use of child care correspond to a need (and thus require an adaption of the equivalence scale), or is it more a reflection of preferences (thus not requiring a modification of the equivalence scale)? We come back to this issue in section 6.3.4.

The level of needs is calculated as the average spending per individual in target group i for the respective services per individual in this target group (*i.c.* age group).[8] The value of k is calculated for each age group using a correction in spending levels (as a share of spending per age group per service in GDP per capita) toward the EU-level based on the formula presented in Paulus et al. (2010):

$$k = \sum_{i=1}^{n} \left(k_{ENi} * \frac{S_{EEUi}}{S_{ENi}} + k_{HNi} * \frac{S_{HEUi}}{S_{HNi}} + k_{ECNi} * \frac{S_{CEUi}}{S_{CNi}} \right) \quad (3)$$

with k_{ENi}, k_{HNi}, k_{ECN} being the country's spending for, respectively, public education, health care, and early childhood education and child care (ECEC) for persons with characteristics i; S_{ENi}, S_{HNi}, S_{CNi}, being the country's spending figures for the different types of services expressed as a share of national GDP per capita and S_{EEUi} S_{HEUi} S_{CEUi} being the corresponding EU averages. The new equivalence scale e' of formula (2) is then recalculated for all households using the new value of k, which reflects EU averages of spending.

6.3.4 Data and Implementation

In our empirical analysis we build on the work presented in OECD (2011) and Verbist et al. (2012), focusing on three major categories of services, namely health care, education (with separate results for compulsory and tertiary education), and ECEC. The underlying database is EU-SILC 2007. We present results for 21 EU countries.[9]

For allocating public education expenditures over the population, we use the actual consumption approach. EU-SILC provides current participation in education for individuals 16 years and older, distinguishing six ISCED (International

Standard Classification of Education) levels (pre-primary, primary, lower secondary, upper secondary, postsecondary, nontertiary, tertiary).[10] As this information is not available for individuals younger than 16 years we have imputed education levels for this group using enrollment rates per education level and age reported in the OECD Education Database. This data source also provides us the average amount of public spending on education per year per pupil/student for the different education levels. These amounts are allocated to pupils/students participating in the corresponding education level.

For health care we have applied the insurance value approach[11] using the health care age profiles as published by the European Commission (2009) to derive public healthcare spending per age group. Note that these age profiles only consider differences in age and gender. This approach might underestimate the equalizing effect of public healthcare services in countries where elements of the system are targeted toward low-income groups (e.g., in the form of reduced out-of-pocket payments). On the other hand, given that research has indicated that poorer people have in general worse health conditions, and consequently greater needs for health care (see, e.g., Hernandez-Quevedo et al., 2006), the results may overestimate the distributive impact if these needs remain unmet.

Beneficiaries of early childhood education and child care are identified in EU-SILC on the basis of their participation (number of hours) in either pre-school education or day-care centers. The amounts for the imputation come on the one hand from the OECD Education Database for pre-primary education and on the other from various national sources for child care facilities (see Verbist et al., 2012, for an overview). The imputations are based on number of hours of reported use, thus incorporating intensity of use. A limitation is that EU-SILC does not differentiate between the use of private and public child care. By treating all child care as "public," our results will overstate the number of recipients of public subsidies and understate the value of such subsidies per user. However, the resulting bias may in practice be rather limited, given that most ECEC is in fact school pre-primary education, which tends to be overwhelmingly publicly funded.[12]

With respect to the choice of equivalence scale, the cash income equivalence scale is the modified OECD scale, which is the starting point for constructing the services needs adjusted equivalence scale. For this adjustment for needs related to services, we first have to specify the target groups for which we assume that there are corresponding needs (see also Aaberge et al., 2010). For health care, all individuals have needs, the extent of which differs with age and gender (in line with the health care age profiles used for the imputation).[13] For education, we assume that all individuals in the age bracket of 6–16 years have education needs (this corresponds for most European countries with compulsory education),[14] which is in line with the approach in Paulus et al. (2010). However, given increased participation in higher education and increased demand for a better educated workforce, it can also be argued that education needs extend to a older age group. Therefore, we use the age group 6–22 years as corresponding to education needs. For ECEC, a similar reasoning can be applied: Given the importance attached to child care (see also Lisbon targets), one can assume that child care use is increasingly recognized as a need. Therefore, we also include in the equivalence scale needs for ECEC. For each target group (based on age), we calculate a value for *k*, which is then averaged over the EU.

6.4 THE DISTRIBUTIVE IMPACT OF SERVICES

In order to show the distributive impact of public services we first present the size and the incidence of these services measured against cash disposable income equivalized with the modified OECD scale. This shows the relationship between the in-kind benefit of services and the indicator of living standards commonly used in distribution analyses. In a next step, we adjust this living standard concept by incorporating the needs for services in the equivalence scale, as well as the value of these services in the income concept. We then use this adjusted measure of living standards to test the inequality and poverty effect of incorporating services both in the income concept and in the equivalence scale. In order to present an indicator of the distributive characteristics of the various policy instruments that is independent of their size, we finally calculate concentration coefficients. Because the social investment strategy is oriented toward the working-age population, we focus here on benefits targeted at non-elderly individuals. This means that healthcare expenditures allocated to individuals age 65+ are not included and that cash transfers do not include pensions.

6.4.1 Size and Incidence of Services

Figure 6.2a presents the value of total in-kind benefits for working-age individuals as a share of disposable income, as well as the distribution over cash income quintiles. With on average 23% of disposable income, these services are important for living standards, and even more important than cash transfers (excluding pensions), which account for 10% of disposable income (see Figure 6.2b). For services, the size ranges from 16% of disposable income in Greece to 30% in Sweden. For cash transfers, Greece reports again the lowest size (3%) and Hungary has the highest score with 15%.

The distributive pattern of services over the cash income quintile distribution is remarkably equal. In most countries, the share of the bottom quintile in total services is around 20%, with slightly more pro-poorness in Poland and Luxembourg (around 25%). The distributive pattern of cash transfers (excluding pensions) is in general somewhat more oriented toward lower incomes than that of services: On average 26% of the total mass of cash transfers goes to the bottom quintile, whereas the top quintile has a share of only 15%. This is most pronounced in the Netherlands (with 35% going to the bottom quintile) and absent in Spain and Italy (15% for Q1).

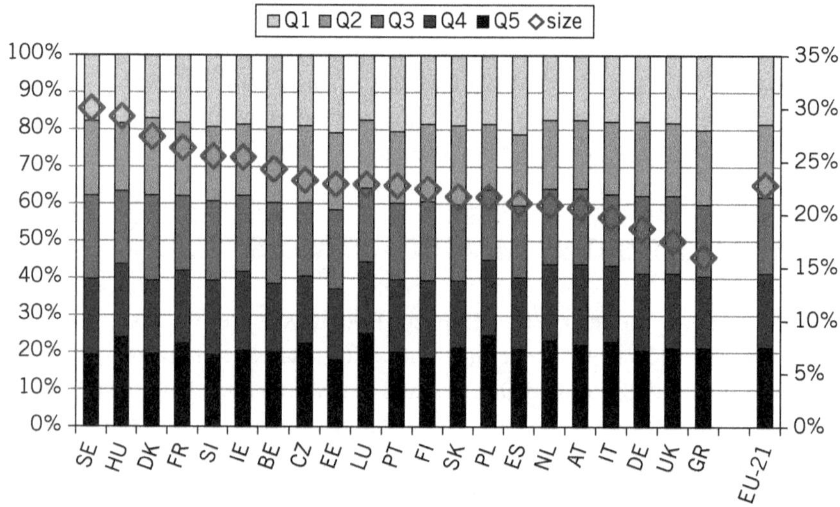

Figure 6.2a. Size (percentage of dpi, rh axis) and distribution of in-kind benefits (non-elderly only) over dpi quintiles. *Notes*: Countries are ranked in decreasing order by share of benefits in disposable income. Dpi = disposable cash income (equivalence scale = modified OECD-scale). *Source*: Calculations based on OECD/EU database on the distributional impact of in-kind services.

Let us now look into the size and distribution of four types of services, namely health care, compulsory education, tertiary education, and ECEC.[15] Health care (excluding expenditures going to the elderly) is the most important type, with on average a share in disposable income of almost 10% (Figure 6.2c). The size is lowest in Greece (7%) and highest in France (12%). On average, the share going to

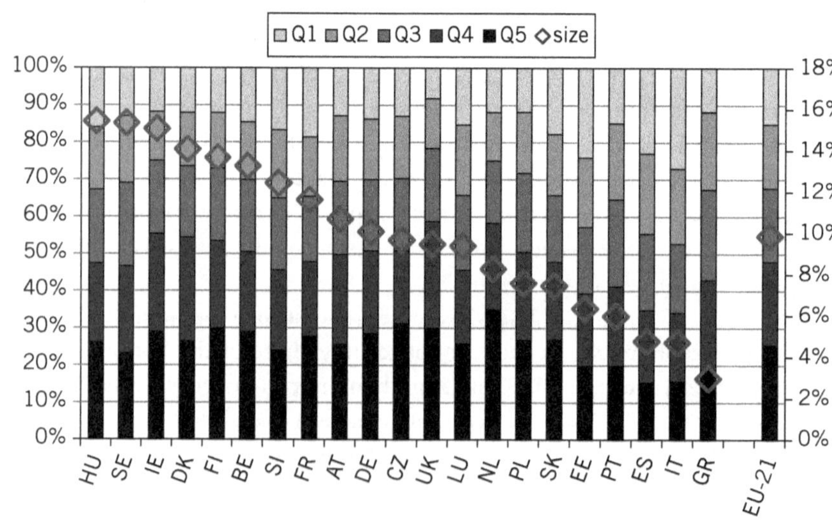

Figure 6.2b. Size (percentage of dpi, rh axis) and distribution of cash benefits (excluding pensions) over dpi quintiles. *Source*: Calculations based on OECD/EU database on the distributional impact of in-kind services. *Notes*: Countries are ranked in decreasing order by share of benefits in disposable income.

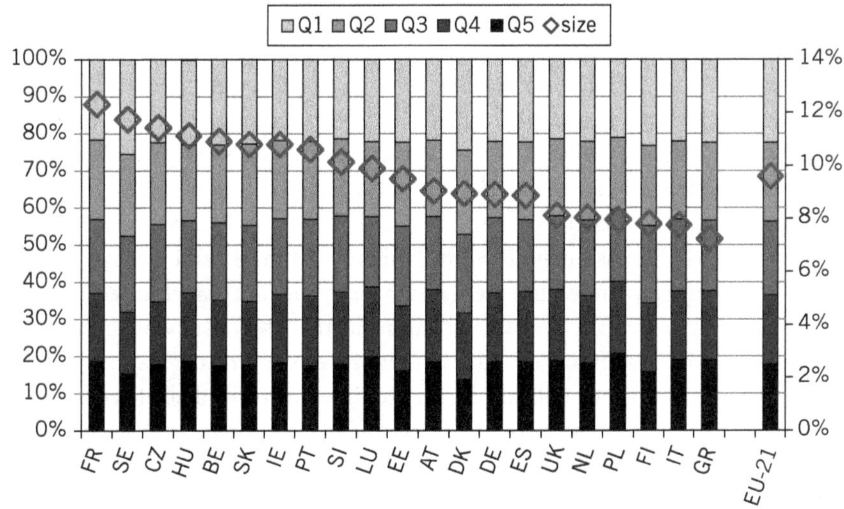

Figure 6.2c. Size (percentage of dpi, rh axis) and distribution of healthcare in-kind benefits (non-elderly only) over dpi quintiles. *Source*: Calculations based on OECD/EU database on the distributional impact of in-kind services. *Notes*: Countries are ranked in decreasing order by share of benefits in disposable income.

the bottom quintile is slightly below 20%, and this is the case in almost all countries (with Poland and Luxembourg as the only exceptions with a share of 20%).

Figure 6.2d gives the distribution over income quintiles of public education expenditures targeted at 6–16-year-old pupils, which corresponds in most countries to compulsory education. After health care this is the second most

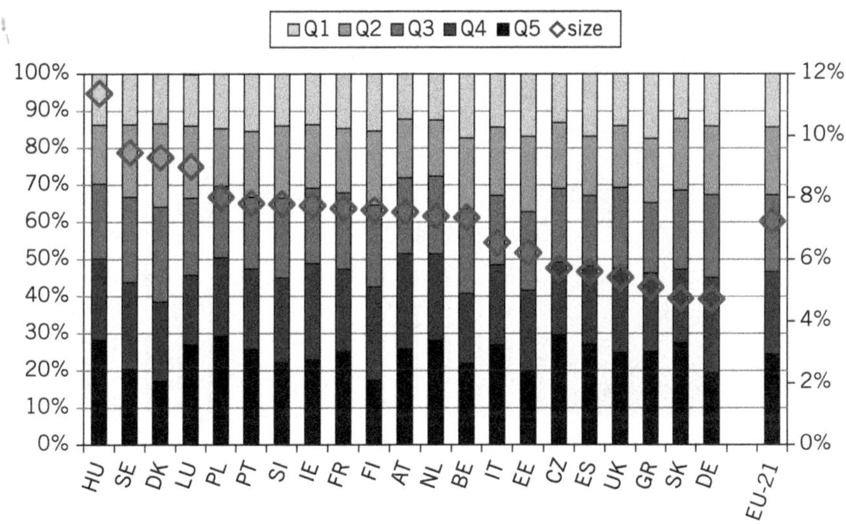

Figure 6.2d. Size (percentage of dpi, rh axis) and distribution of compulsory education in-kind benefits over dpi quintiles. *Source*: Calculations based on OECD/EU database on the distributional impact of in-kind services. *Notes*: Countries are ranked in decreasing order by share of benefits in disposable income.

important component of services (on average 7% of disposable income, with low values in Germany and the Slovak Republic [almost 5%] and a high value of 11% in Hungary). Compulsory education is more oriented toward low incomes: On EU average, the bottom quintile receives 24% of expenditures of this education category, whereas it is only 14% for the top quintile. This pattern is strongest in the Czech Republic and Poland (with a Q1 share of almost 30%), and then decreases gradually over the countries toward 20%. In only three countries the bottom quintile share is below 20% (in Finland, Denmark, and Germany). The general progressive pattern elsewhere is driven by the fact that children in compulsory education tend to be situated more in the lower parts of the income distribution, which is far less the case in these three countries.

The pattern of tertiary education is quite different from that of compulsory education. With on average 2% of disposable income, its size is much lower (ranging from 1% [UK and Italy] to 3% [Slovak Republic and Slovenia], Figure 6.2e). The EU-average appears to indicate a rather even spread of tertiary education expenditures over the entire income distribution. This, however, hides considerable cross-country variation. In Estonia, Portugal, and Slovenia around 10% of tertiary education expenditures are going to the bottom quintile, and, not surprisingly, the share of the top quintile in these countries is, with 30% to 40%, considerable. This is the most common pattern, namely an underrepresentation of the bottom quintile and an overrepresentation of the top quintile. There are, however, some notable exceptions, namely the Nordic countries and Germany. In these countries expenditures to the bottom quintile account for 27% (Iceland) up to

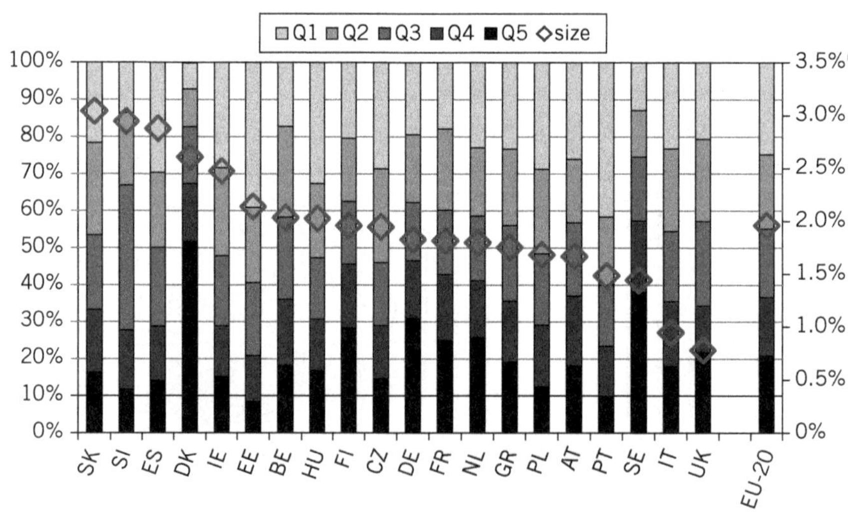

Figure 6.2e. Size (percentage of dpi, rh axis) and distribution of tertiary education in-kind benefits over dpi quintiles. *Source*: Calculations based on OECD/EU database on the distributional impact of in-kind services. *Notes*: Countries are ranked in decreasing order by share of benefits in disposable income.

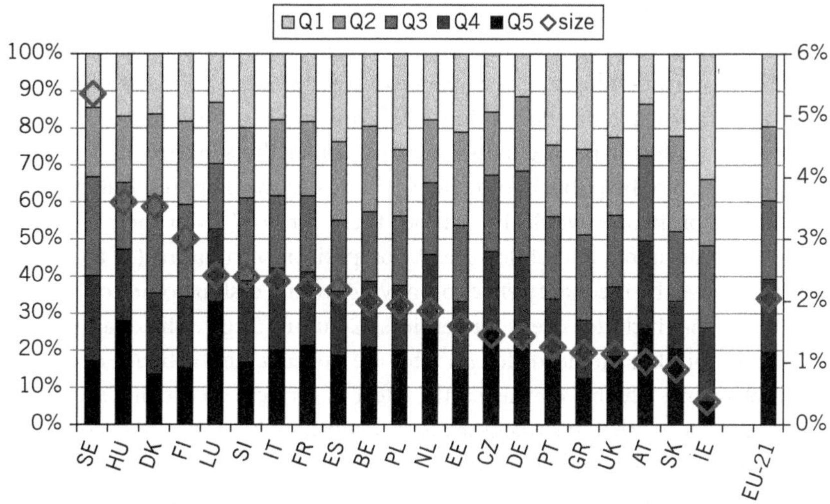

Figure 6.2f. Size (percentage of dpi, rh axis) and distribution of ECEC in-kind benefits over dpi quintiles. *Source*: Calculations based on OECD/EU database on the distributional impact of in-kind services. *Notes*: Countries are ranked in decreasing order by share of benefits in disposable income.

52% (Denmark) of total tertiary education expenditures. This is largely the effect of the compositional factors, as in these countries, large proportions of students live outside the parental home and are thus classified as a separate household. With their low incomes they are often concentrated in the lowest quintile of the distribution. In a study that focuses on the distributive effect of tertiary education spending, Callan et al. 2008 compare for a selection of European countries the distributive effect of excluding students who live independently from the analysis.[16] They find that attributing the public transfers to students living with their parents only, rather than to all students, alters the distribution of higher education expenditures considerably, in the sense that results become less pro-poor.

Figure 6.2f shows the size and distribution of the value of ECEC subsidies over income quintiles. On average it represents around 2% of disposable income, with high levels in Sweden, Hungary, and Denmark and a much lower level in Ireland. In countries like Hungary, Luxembourg, Austria, the Netherlands, the Czech Republic, and Iceland, ECEC expenditures tend to go more to lower incomes than to the top groups: In these countries, the first quintile receives between 23% and 28%. The opposite is the case in the Nordic countries, Greece, and Ireland, where the lowest quintile receives less than 20%.

6.4.2 Incorporating Services in the Income Concept and Equivalence Scale

We now incorporate the needs associated with services in the income concept, in order to construct a counterfactual that can be used to measure the impact of services on inequality and poverty. This counterfactual is cash income corrected with an equivalence scale that accounts for needs of health care (all individuals), education (individuals aged 6 years to 22 years) and ECEC (children aged 0 to 5 years), as explained in Section 3.3.[17] This income concept can be interpreted as an indicator for the living standard under the assumption that these services would not be publicly provided: It indicates in a hypothetical way how much worse off people would be without these services given their needs for health care, education, and child care. A comparison of columns (1) and (3) in Table 6.1 shows the inequality effect of moving from a cash income equivalence scale to one that includes needs for services. Column (3) gives inequality under the assumption that the needs for services are not met, and is hence our counterfactual against which we measure the effect of services on income inequality. This equivalence scale adjustment leads to a considerable increase in measured inequality of disposable income, indicating that these needs are relatively more concentrated at the bottom of the income distribution: On average the Gini increases from 0.2856 to 0.3461. This increase is rather similar across countries.

One may be surprised that the Gini coefficients in columns (1) and (4) are rather similar, suggesting that the redistributive effect of services is rather limited. This outcome follows, of course, from our framework discussed in Section 3.3: The income concept used in column (1) is an indicator of living standards conditional on the existence of free public services, whereas the one in column (4) basically makes this conditionality explicit by incorporating both the needs for and the value of these services—as expressed in formula (1). As we have used an EU-level corrected value of k for each target group to calculate the services-needs adjusted equivalence scale (see formula [3]), the comparison of columns (1) and (4) (as is done in Paulus et al., 2010) is in fact a sensitivity test for differences in relative spending across EU countries.

The difference between columns (3) and (4) in Table 6.1 results in the Reynolds-Smolensky index, which gives the reduction in inequality following from including all services (so also including healthcare expenditures going to the elderly) in the income concept. On average for the 21 EU countries, inequality drops substantially, from 0.3461 to 0.2842, which corresponds to around 18% in the counterfactual scenario. Relative reductions in inequality are strongest in Denmark and Sweden (around 23%) and lowest in Greece (13.4%). In relative terms, these reductions are somewhat smaller than the ones calculated on the basis of the modified OECD scale, which is shown in the first panel of Table 6.1 (RE as percent of (1)). The fact that reductions are stronger in the Nordic countries compared with Southern Europe follows from the fact that the services-needs adjusted equivalence scale is based on the average values of k for the EU. As relative spending levels on services are above average in the Nordics, these countries provide a better coverage of these needs (compared with the EU average) than countries with below average spending levels (such as in Southern Europe).

Table 6.1. Effect of all services on inequality (Gini coefficient; RE = redistributive effect), a comparison of the modified OECD and a services-needs adjusted[1] equivalence scale.

Equival. Scale Income concept	Cash disposable (1)	Modified OECD scale Extended (all services) (2)	RE (1)–(2)	RE as % of (1)	Cash disposable (3)	Adjusted for services needs Extended (all services) (4)	RE (3)–(4)	RE as % of (3)
AT	0.2615	0.2091	0.0524	20.0%	0.3172	0.2591	0.0581	18.3%
BE	0.2622	0.2014	0.0608	23.2%	0.3189	0.2536	0.0653	20.5%
CZ	0.2524	0.1949	0.0575	22.8%	0.3154	0.2535	0.0619	19.6%
DE	0.2995	0.2413	0.0581	19.4%	0.3508	0.2912	0.0596	17.0%
DK	0.2451	0.1894	0.0557	22.7%	0.2973	0.2299	0.0673	22.7%
EE	0.3344	0.2714	0.0630	18.8%	0.4067	0.3457	0.0610	15.0%
ES	0.3125	0.2481	0.0644	20.6%	0.3718	0.3128	0.0589	15.9%
FI	0.2616	0.2137	0.0479	18.3%	0.3174	0.2598	0.0576	18.1%
FR	0.2638	0.2031	0.0607	23.0%	0.3194	0.2529	0.0665	20.8%
GR	0.3427	0.2840	0.0587	17.1%	0.4025	0.3486	0.0539	13.4%
HU	0.2571	0.1961	0.0610	23.7%	0.3273	0.2586	0.0687	21.0%
IE	0.3121	0.2391	0.0731	23.4%	0.3842	0.3138	0.0704	18.3%
IT	0.3216	0.2591	0.0625	19.4%	0.3774	0.3168	0.0607	16.1%
LU	0.2736	0.2147	0.0589	21.5%	0.3460	0.2819	0.0641	18.5%
NL	0.2731	0.2185	0.0546	20.0%	0.3356	0.2751	0.0605	18.0%
PL	0.3217	0.2597	0.0620	19.3%	0.3873	0.3283	0.0590	15.2%
PT	0.3682	0.2888	0.0794	21.6%	0.4319	0.3597	0.0723	16.7%
SE	0.2342	0.1798	0.0544	23.2%	0.2934	0.2255	0.0679	23.1%
SI	0.2278	0.1868	0.0410	18.0%	0.2727	0.2236	0.0491	18.0%
SK	0.2446	0.1921	0.0525	21.5%	0.3093	0.2553	0.0539	17.4%
UK	0.3283	0.2609	0.0674	20.5%	0.3863	0.3222	0.0641	16.6%
EU-21	0.2856	0.2263	0.0593	20.8%	0.3461	0.2842	0.0619	17.9%

[1]Equivalence scale is constructed on the assumption that all individuals have health care needs; 6–22-year-olds have education needs; and 0–5-year-olds have ECEC needs.

Source: Calculations based on OECD/EU database on the distributional impact of in-kind services.

6.4.3 The Impact on Inequality and Poverty

In Table 6.2 we look at the inequality and poverty impact of the various services going to the non-elderly population. Panel A gives the effect on inequality of the different income components. We start from extended income (including all services and using the services-needs adjusted equivalence scale) as the baseline (thus corresponding to Column (4) in Table 6.1). Baseline income inequality is lowest in Sweden, Slovenia, and Denmark (a Gini of around 0.22), and

Table 6.2. Effect of services on inequality (Gini) and poverty, equivalence scale adjusted for needs for services[1,2]

	A: Effect on inequality							B: Effect on poverty rate						
	Gini	Reynolds-Smolensky (change in Gini when excluding income component)						Poverty rate	Change in poverty rate when excluding income component					
	Extended	All services	Health care	Compulsory	Tertiary		Cash (excl pensions)	Extended	All services	Health care	Compulsory	Tertiary		Cash (excl pensions)
	income	non-elderly	non-elderly	education	education	ECEC		income	non-elderly	non-elderly	education	education	ECEC	
AT	0.2591	0.0479	0.0139	0.0221	0.0014	0.0033	0.0399	0.1175	0.1553	0.0501	0.0608	0.0062	0.0097	0.0959
BE	0.2536	0.0465	0.0140	0.0160	0.0027	0.0033	0.0501	0.1410	0.1545	0.0614	0.0415	0.0110	0.0103	0.0942
CZ	0.2535	0.0467	0.0147	0.0163	0.0001	0.0038	0.0363	0.1001	0.1560	0.0550	0.0397	0.0065	0.0090	0.0776
DE	0.2912	0.0460	0.0158	0.0132	0.0036	0.0037	0.0427	0.1451	0.1354	0.0505	0.0347	0.0111	0.0083	0.0778
DK	0.2299	0.0502	0.0062	0.0207	0.0084	0.0046	0.0619	0.1062	0.1730	0.0380	0.0455	0.0203	0.0120	0.1240
EE	0.3457	0.0437	0.0149	0.0130	-0.0006	0.0023	0.0134	0.2106	0.1340	0.0483	0.0392	0.0060	0.0087	0.0395
ES	0.3128	0.0414	0.0146	0.0141	0.0013	0.0029	0.0127	0.2021	0.1223	0.0530	0.0347	0.0097	0.0120	0.0323
FI	0.2598	0.0420	0.0091	0.0170	0.0028	0.0038	0.0590	0.1352	0.1500	0.0372	0.0527	0.0108	0.0148	0.1194
FR	0.2529	0.0563	0.0171	0.0187	0.0028	0.0045	0.0369	0.1198	0.1808	0.0703	0.0500	0.0079	0.0140	0.0944
GR	0.3486	0.0387	0.0145	0.0140	0.0028	0.0018	0.0113	0.2127	0.1005	0.0443	0.0334	0.0091	0.0056	0.0270
HU	0.2586	0.0611	0.0141	0.0305	0.0002	0.0074	0.0458	0.1246	0.1924	0.0602	0.0771	0.0076	0.0201	0.1113
IE	0.3138	0.0576	0.0178	0.0207	0.0013	0.0003	0.0608	0.1608	0.1897	0.0713	0.0573	0.0125	0.0035	0.1403
IT	0.3168	0.0469	0.0136	0.0163	0.0015	0.0031	0.0088	0.1940	0.1232	0.0457	0.0405	0.0060	0.0106	0.0315
LU	0.2819	0.0559	0.0154	0.0230	–	0.0065	0.0301	0.1449	0.1569	0.0646	0.0685	–	0.0144	0.0709
NL	0.2751	0.0509	0.0116	0.0232	0.0024	0.0044	0.0384	0.1108	0.1584	0.0521	0.0648	0.0072	0.0127	0.0822
PL	0.3283	0.0532	0.0157	0.0215	0.0011	0.0032	0.0319	0.1792	0.1400	0.0506	0.0520	0.0077	0.0107	0.0668
PT	0.3597	0.0536	0.0209	0.0212	0.0002	0.0021	0.0205	0.1793	0.1485	0.0559	0.0462	0.0042	0.0058	0.0406
SE	0.2255	0.0517	0.0068	0.0211	0.0037	0.0063	0.0465	0.1028	0.1874	0.0478	0.0505	0.0084	0.0160	0.1164
SI	0.2236	0.0403	0.0119	0.0162	-0.0004	0.0022	0.0383	0.1124	0.1589	0.0439	0.0436	0.0080	0.0075	0.0945
SK	0.2553	0.0407	0.0123	0.0139	0.0023	0.0013	0.0224	0.1201	0.1282	0.0522	0.0348	0.0138	0.0028	0.0571
UK	0.3222	0.0443	0.0161	0.0158	0.0012	0.0013	0.0462	0.1756	0.1155	0.0496	0.0389	0.0044	0.0052	0.0880
EU-21	0.2842	0.0484	0.0138	0.0185	0.0019	0.0034	0.0359	0.1474	0.1505	0.0525	0.0479	0.0089	0.0102	0.0801

[1]Equivalence scale is constructed on the assumption that all individuals have health care needs; 6–22-year-olds have education needs; and 0–5-year-olds have ECEC needs.
[2]Poverty rate is calculated on the basis of 60% of median equivalized extended income.
Source: Calculations based on OECD/EU database on the distributional impact of in-kind services.

highest in Estonia, Greece, and Portugal (more than 0.34). We then calculate the Reynolds-Smolensky index for different income components going to the non-elderly population (total services non-elderly; health care non-elderly; compulsory education; tertiary education; ECEC; cash transfer excluding pensions). This index is calculated as the difference between the baseline Gini coefficient and the counterfactual Gini of income without the income component. On average, the Reynolds-Smolensky index for the total of non-elderly services is with 0.0484 much more important than the one for cash benefits (excluding pensions: 0.0359). Exceptions to this pattern are Belgium, Denmark, Finland, Ireland, and the United Kingdom, where the Reynolds-Smolensky index is higher for cash than for in-kind. In Southern Europe and Estonia, on the contrary, the inequality impact of cash benefits is relatively small (below 0.02), and this is combined with a below average inequality effect of services. Turning to the different categories of services, compulsory education has on average and in most countries the strongest effect on inequality, followed by health care. For tertiary education, the effect is much smaller, and in some countries close to zero or even slightly anti-equalizing (Slovenia and Estonia). The effect of ECEC is relatively small, but positive in all countries.

Panel B of Table 6.2 presents the poverty reducing effect, starting from a similar baseline as for our inequality analysis, namely a hypothetical income concept that incorporates both the needs associated with services as well as the value of these services. The baseline is the at-risk-of-poverty rate calculated on the basis of extended income, with the poverty line set at 60% of median equivalent extended income. The poverty reducing effect is presented as a point change from moving from income without the component to extended income. For example, on average the hypothetical at-risk-of-poverty rate without services (non-elderly) would be 29.8%, implying that incorporating these services in the income concept reduces the poverty rate by 15.1 percentage points to 14.7. It shows that in the absence of these services, and given that individuals have needs for these services, poverty would be much higher than it is currently.

It is striking that the poverty reducing effect of services is much larger than the one of cash transfers (excluding pensions), which is 8 percentage points. This result is found in all countries, even those where inequality reduction due to cash transfers was stronger. The poverty reducing effect of services ranges from 10 percentage points (Greece) to almost 20 percentage points (Hungary), whereas for cash transfers it ranges from around 3 percentage points (Southern Europe) to 14 percentage points (Ireland). The main drivers for services are health care and compulsory education (which have a similar poverty reducing effect of around 5 percentage points), while the effect of both tertiary education and ECEC is rather limited (no more than 2 percentage points on average and in all countries).

6.4.4 The Weak and Strong Pro-poorness of Cash and In-kind Benefits

The stronger poverty and inequality effect of services may come as a surprise, as a comparison of Figure 6.1 showed that cash transfers are on average across EU countries more directed toward lower incomes than services. The distributive impact of polices, however, depends both on size and design (see also, Chapter 5 in this volume). Calculating concentration coefficients indicates how income components are distributed, irrespective of their size.[18] To calculate these concentration coefficients, we rank individuals according to their extended income. When the concentration coefficient has a value that is lower than the Gini coefficient of extended income (which is given in Column [1] of Table 6.1), then lower incomes benefit relatively more: Individuals receive a higher share of the income component than their share of extended income. Thus, these concentration coefficients provide insight into the pro-poorness of the various income components, independent of their size. We can make a distinction here between weak and strong pro-poorness. Strong pro-poorness corresponds to a negative concentration coefficient, whereas weak pro-poorness is captured by a concentration coefficient between zero and the value of the Gini coefficient of extended income.

The concentration coefficients of the various income components (Table 6.3) show that for the EU on average the structure of cash benefits is more pro-poor than that of in-kind benefits (−0.0344 resp. 0.0834). For almost all countries the concentration coefficient for cash transfers is negative, pointing to strong pro-poorness, and much smaller than that of services. Exceptions to this pattern are Spain and Italy, where the concentration coefficients indicate that cash benefits are only weakly pro-poor and less pro-poor than services.

When looking at the different types of services, we found that compulsory education has the strongest inequality reducing effect, even though its size is smaller than that of non-elderly healthcare expenditures. The negative concentration coefficient on average and in most countries indicates that poorer income groups receive a higher share of these services than their share of extended income and points to strong pro-poorness. This result is driven by the distribution of compulsory-aged individuals, which are in most countries slightly more concentrated in the bottom quintile. In almost all countries, the concentration coefficient for tertiary education is the highest of all income components, indicating that this is the least pro-poor of all. Exceptions are Denmark and Sweden, which have a strong presence of students in the bottom quintile, because of students living separately (cf. supra). In some countries the concentration coefficient for tertiary education is even higher than the Gini of extended income, pointing to a pro-rich distribution. This is not only the case in countries where the inclusion of tertiary education expenditures was slightly anti-equalizing (Estonia and Slovenia) but also in, for example, the Czech Republic, Hungary, and Poland.

Health care is rather evenly distributed and is hence only weakly pro-poor. On average the concentration coefficient has a value similar to that of ECEC (both around 0.11), though variation across countries is limited for health care. ECEC services exhibit strong pro-poorness in Austria, the Czech Republic, and Luxembourg, where it is (one of) the most pro-poor policy instruments. In the Nordic countries the pattern is far less pro-poor. A more detailed discussion of this category of services is the subject of Chapter 7 in this volume, which focuses on the distribution of different family care policies across households with children (instead of all households, as is done in this chapter).

Summarizing, these results suggest that the stronger redistributive effect and poverty reduction of in-kind benefits should be attributed mainly to their

Table 6.3. Concentration coefficients of cash benefits and services, equivalence scale adjusted for needs for services.

	All services non-elderly	Health care	Compulsory education	Tertiary education	ECEC	Cash (excl pensions)
AT	0.0402	0.0913	−0.0637	0.2696	−0.1422	−0.0769
BE	0.0811	0.1154	0.0148	0.1702	0.0874	−0.0837
CZ	0.0677	0.1226	−0.0973	0.3525	−0.0546	−0.0961
DE	0.0583	0.0944	−0.0363	0.1554	−0.0005	−0.0900
DK	0.1055	0.1563	0.0273	0.0825	0.1598	−0.1261
EE	0.1597	0.1620	0.0898	0.4331	0.1854	0.1382
ES	0.1235	0.1224	−0.0008	0.3264	0.1936	0.1425
FI	0.1164	0.1311	0.0368	0.2028	0.2021	−0.1255
FR	0.0592	0.0996	−0.0241	0.1463	0.0308	−0.0147
GR	0.0970	0.1182	0.0152	0.2279	0.2018	−0.0077
HU	0.0615	0.1233	−0.0445	0.3207	0.0630	−0.0146
IE	0.0771	0.1193	−0.0361	0.3002	0.2318	−0.1172
IT	0.0910	0.1157	0.0316	0.1460	0.2157	0.1862
LU	0.0293	0.1054	−0.0187	–	−0.0516	−0.0148
NL	0.0460	0.1123	−0.0919	0.2065	0.0143	−0.1579
PL	0.0693	0.0955	0.0006	0.2984	0.1623	−0.0685
PT	0.1162	0.1305	0.0245	0.3877	0.1702	0.0373
SE	0.1088	0.1707	−0.0018	−0.0063	0.2348	−0.0236
SI	0.1044	0.0929	0.0387	0.2883	0.2225	−0.0155
SK	0.0770	0.1390	−0.1237	0.2413	0.1113	−0.0055
UK	0.0614	0.0944	−0.0434	0.1435	0.2278	−0.1891
EU-21	0.0834	0.1196	−0.0144	0.2347	0.1174	−0.0344

Note: Equivalence scale is constructed on the assumption that all individuals have health care needs; 6–22-year-olds have education needs; and 0–5-year-olds have ECEC needs.
Source: Calculations based on OECD/EU database on the distributional impact of in-kind services.

size, rather than to the way they are distributed over the population. The design of cash transfers is apparently more oriented toward lower incomes and is the instrument with the strongest pro-poorness.

6.5 CONCLUSION

Over the last 25 years, expenditure on services, especially health and child care, has increased significantly in many European countries. At the same time, spending on cash transfers other than pensions has declined as a proportion of GDP (Vandenbroucke & Vleminckx, 2011). Given that in-kind benefits are generally considered to be less pro-poor than cash benefits, this trend has been identified as a key reason European welfare states proved unable to reduce relative poverty in spite of favorable conditions in terms of economic and employment growth (Cantillon, 2011).

In this chapter we analyzed empirically the impact of services on inequality and poverty. In view of the conceptual and methodological issues, this task is fraught with difficulties. We have discussed the issues of valuation, allocation, and the use of an equivalence scale adjusted for needs associated with these services. In this chapter we have chosen to build further on a discussion of alternative approaches in Verbist et al. (2012) and the methodology proposed in Paulus et al. (2010) and to construct a hypothetical counterfactual that incorporates service-related needs. We thus compare an estimate of the current distribution of in-kind benefits with a counterfactual that depicts inequality and poverty in a hypothetical situation in which no publicly provided services exist.

In a first instance, we have tried to answer the question whether services targeted at non-elderly individuals (who are the focus of the social investment strategy) are redistributive. When looking at the total of health care, education, and ECEC, the answer is clearly affirmative for the 21 EU countries considered in this chapter. Compulsory education and health care, especially, both reduce inequality and poverty when compared with a hypothetical situation without these publicly provided services. The answer to the question whether these in-kind benefits are less redistributive than cash transfers requires more consideration. When comparing the Reynolds-Smolensky index for cash transfers with that of in-kind benefits, one is inclined to conclude that services reduce inequality more than cash benefits do. However, it is important to disentangle a size and a design effect, as services going to non-elderly individuals are in all countries much more important in size than cash transfers (excluding pensions). Therefore, we have also calculated concentration coefficients of the various instruments, thus allowing us to focus on the distributive structure independent of size. These coefficients tell us that cash transfers turn out to be more pro-poor than in-kind benefits in most countries. In this perspective, cash transfers are on average in the EU the most pro-poor of the policy instruments considered here, closely followed by the in-kind benefit from compulsory education. The in-kind benefits derived from tertiary education expenditures is the least pro-poor (and in some countries even pro-rich). These results are to an important extent driven by the distribution of beneficiaries: In general, compulsory education pupils tend to be situated more in the middle and the bottom of the income distribution, whereas tertiary education students are overrepresented in the higher regions of the income distribution.

For answering the question of evolution, that is, whether the relative shift to services has eroded the redistributive power of the welfare state, there is little evidence on comparisons over time. The only exception is OECD (2011), which compares the inequality reduction through services for 2000 and 2007 for 17 OECD countries (including 14 "old" EU Member States), indicating that, on average across countries, inequality reduction of services has remained remarkably stable over this period. However, countries that improved inequality reduction through services were also those countries that experienced an increase in terms of size (expressed as a share of cash disposable income) (and vice versa). Whether these changes went hand in glove with corresponding (or opposite) changes in the redistributive impact of cash transfers requires further investigation.

ACKNOWLEDGMENTS

This chapter uses data prepared in a joint co-funded project of the OECD and the European Commission (see also, OECD, 2011; Verbist et al., 2012). The authors are grateful to Bea Cantillon, Michael Förster, John Hills, and Frank Vandenbroucke for their constructive remarks and valuable suggestions.

NOTES

1 Outside Europe, the direct provision of food to the poor as a matter of course (i.e., not only in the case of famine relief and other emergencies) is still quite common in the United States and some Latin American countries. Examples are Programa Apoyo Alimentario (PAL) in Mexico or food stamp programs in the United States.

2 The selection of countries is driven by data availability, see section 6.3.4.

3 The "Samaritan's dilemma," proposed by Buchanan (1975), may be thought of as the libertarian case for social investment. The argument goes along the lines of the Chinese proverb that it is better to teach someone how to fish than simply give them a fish. In Buchanan's formulation, recipients have an incentive to remain poor if they are entitled to benefits as long as they are poor. Hence benefits should primarily be designed to discourage benefit dependency and eliminate moral hazard. The latter may arise when the availability

of benefits (when poor) undermines the willingness of individuals to invest in human capital (so they avoid poverty). While the argument can be evoked to support cuts in social provision, it can and has been used to support the public provision of in-kind transfers, whether in the form of job training or social insurance (Coates, 1995).

4 Sen's approach (1993), redefining well-being in terms of capabilities like being able to read, write, remain healthy, etc., can be seen as a more enlightened form of paternalism (cf. Deneulin, 2002), justifying social investment in public services such as education and health.

5 A more pragmatic reason for using the insurance value approach is that most data sets used in distributional analysis (e.g., EU-SILC) do not contain information on effective use of healthcare services.

6 This rather surprising outcome is largely due to the effect of re-ranking. Because part of the expenditures (notably those on in-hospital care) are concentrated among a very small group, this may lead more easily to re-ranking of individual beneficiaries, which dampens the equalizing effects of healthcare services (5% of the population in the survey data accounted for more than 90% of the nights spent in hospital, whereas out-of-hospital care was more widespread over the population; see Marical et al., 2008 for more details).

7 This scale assigns a value of 1 to the household head, of 0.5 to each additional adult member, and of 0.3 to each child. See OECD (2005) (http://www.oecd.org/dataoecd/61/52/35411111.pdf) for further explanations and specifications. This is a pragmatic equivalence scale, which takes into account only differences in household size.

8 This means that higher spending levels (either due to high use of the services or high expenditures per user) result in higher corresponding needs (and vice versa). Thus a higher level of spending corresponds to a higher recognition of needs. Remember that, as already indicated in section 6.3.1, differences in efficiency or quality of services cannot be accounted for in this analysis.

9 Bulgaria, Malta, and Romania are not included in EU-SILC 2007. Cyprus, Lithuania, and Latvia are not included in the analysis because for these three countries we do not have estimates for the value of ECEC. Moreover, their amounts for tertiary education include expenditures on research and development, reducing comparability with other countries.

10 Note that EU-SILC does not allow us to distinguish between participation in publicly or privately funded educational institutions, nor between general and technical secondary education, nor between Type A and Type B tertiary education. For tertiary education, amounts exclude direct expenditures for research and development activities.

11 This approach is defendable for EU-countries, where public healthcare coverage is quasiuniversal in most countries.

12 In some of these countries (Denmark, Germany, and Sweden), the distinction between day care and pre-primary education in EU-SILC is probably erroneous: The number of children in the former is probably overestimated, while the number in the latter is underestimated (when compared with enrollment rates in pre-primary education in the OECD Education Database). In most countries where child care is more frequently used, day-care centers tend to be heavily subsidized.

13 Unfortunately, there is no information available that would allow us to differentiate according to other parameters such as socioeconomic background.

14 The starting age of compulsory education is six years in most countries, whereas some countries start earlier at age five years (Hungary, the Netherlands, and the United Kingdom), and others at age seven years (Denmark, Estonia, Finland, Poland, and Sweden). (See OECD, Education at a Glance 2010.) The ending age of compulsory education varies between 14 years and 18 years in Europe. Ninety percent of the population are enrolled in education for at least 13 years, ranging from 11 (e.g., Greece) to 15 years (Belgium, France, Norway, and Sweden).

15 These four categories do not sum up to the total presented in Figure 6.2a, which includes also non-tertiary education outside the age category 6-16.

16 This was a relevant exercise for five of the seven countries in their study, namely Germany, Greece, Ireland, the Netherlands, and the UK. In Belgium and Italy students in the survey are included together with their household of origin, thus making this kind of correction unnecessary.

17 The calculations have also been done for other specifications of needs (e.g., only children aged 6 years to 16 years have education needs). Overall, the results are similar to those with the broader definition of needs as used here.

18 The concentration coefficient of an income component is calculated in a similar way as the Gini coefficient (see e.g., Kakwani, 1977; Lambert, 2002; OECD, 2008). The difference between the two lies in the variable according to which income units are ranked. With a concentration coefficient of an income component, income units are ranked according to extended income (and not by the income component itself), while for a Gini coefficient the variable of interest and the ranking income variable are the same (namely, extended income). Because extended income is used for all income components as the ranking variable, concentration coefficients can be used to compare the distributive structure across income components. They can be considered as a summary indicator of the information provided by quintile distributions. Note that in Figure 6.2, quintiles are constructed on the basis of cash incomes (with modified OECD scale), whereas here units are ranked on the basis of extended income equivalized with the services-needs adjusted equivalence scale.

7

WHO BENEFITS FROM INVESTMENT POLICIES? THE CASE OF FAMILY ACTIVATION IN EUROPEAN COUNTRIES

Wim Van Lancker and Joris Ghysels

7.1 INTRODUCTION

Family policy is a constituent part of the traditional social policy mix that has been subject to profound changes in terms of both scope and substance following the emergence of the social investment state. Initially in the post-War era, most measures in the field of family policy were entirely income-oriented and served the main purpose of making society share in the monetary cost of child raising and ensuring children's well-being. Working from diverse ideological foundations, European welfare states crafted a combination of cash benefits (e.g., child benefits, maternity benefits) and fiscal measures (e.g., tax allowances, derived rights) (Ferrarini, 2006; Montanari, 2000; Gauthier, 1999). The design of such family support measures was geared entirely toward coping with the "old" social risk of child-rearing and served no activation agenda whatsoever.

In the past three decades, however, the family policy mix has undergone a remarkable transformation. Its traditional pillar of "passive" cash measures has been complemented with "activating" services and measures, such as early childhood education and care (ECEC) services and parental leave schemes, designed to reconcile work and family life, to foster female employment, and to promote child development, all of which are important pillars of the social investment idea (e.g., Bonoli, 2005; Esping-Andersen, 2008). More generally, under the umbrella of European-led initiatives aimed at boosting employment rates and enhancing competitiveness and growth, family policy (and investment in young children) has come to be seen as a "productive factor" and an integral part of employment-centered social policy strategies (European Commission, 2000; Lewis, 2009). It is often assumed that this emphasis on activation and the accompanying change in discourse has led to a shift in government expenditures from "old" to "new" family measures (e.g., Cantillon, 2011).

This chapter considers the outcome of government investment in the present-day family policy mix, defined as policy measures aimed at families with young children (under 6 years old). The focus is on the three mainstays of family policy, representing old as well as new forms of family support: ECEC (briefly: child care) services, parental leave schemes, and child benefits. The key question addressed is *who benefits from changing government expenditures on family policy?* More specifically, we want to unravel (1) whether the assumed shift in government expenditures for family policy has actually occurred; and (2) how expenditures are allocated over different households in European societies. Our research question is fueled by growing concern over the distribution of family-oriented benefits under activating policy measures (Ghysels & Van Lancker, 2011; Van Lancker & Ghysels, 2012; Esping-Andersen, 1999; OECD, 2011). Traditional cash programs of family support (child benefits) redistribute income between households with and without children and generally entail elements of vertical distribution from high to low incomes in order to ensure children's well-being in families with more limited economic resources (Immervol, Sutherland, & de Vos, 2001; Wennemo, 1992). It is, however, much less evident which households are the beneficiaries in the case of parental leave and childcare services. Considering their underlying employment logic, it can be hypothesized that government expenditures for those measures will first and foremost benefit families with two earners. Given the fact that dual earnership is not equally dispersed among income strata, with higher educated women being more often employed and living in a dual earner household (Cantillon et al., 2001; Evertsson et al., 2009), the implication is that social expenditures for activating family support are biased against the lower incomes and that government expenditures will flow first and foremost toward dual earner households, which have more financial resources at their disposal and thus greater opportunities to ensure their children a better future. More generally, if policy measures are grafted on an underlying logic of (previous) employment, then government investment will favor those already better-off. In this respect, it was claimed in a recent European Commission review on employment and social developments in Europe that "the resources devoted to early childhood education and childcare (ECEC) services are seen to benefit the rich more than the poor" (European Commission, 2011: 107; see also Van Lancker, 2013). This phenomenon has been designated a "Matthew effect," after the Gospel of Matthew (Merton, 1968; Deleeck, Huybrechs, & Cantillon, 1983).[1] Our analysis aims to demonstrate whether the above considerations hold true and, if so, whether this Matthew effect may be an unavoidable feature of current family policy.

The next section investigates whether a shift in social expenditures has taken place from old to new measures. Subsequently, we study the variable use of the aforementioned measures by different income groups using European-wide survey data. This is followed by an in-depth distributional analysis of two specific cases: Sweden and the Flanders region of Belgium. We end this chapter with a discussion of the results and their implications for social investment policies related to families with young children.

7.2 PRODUCTIVE FAMILY POLICY IN THE EUROPEAN UNION: SCOPE AND EVOLUTION

Social policy became embedded in an employment-driven logic and accommodating responsibilities at work and at home became an important policy issue at European Union (EU) level since the early 1990s (Mätzke & Ostner, 2010; Lewis, 2006; Council of the European Union, 1992). Although gender equality, equal opportunities for men and women, and the reconciliation of work and family life were added in 1998 as a separate "pillar" to the European Employment Strategy (EES), governed by the soft policymaking approach of the Open Method of Coordination (OMC) (Hardy & Adnett, 2002), these three interrelated principles were paid lip service in official EU communication and were de facto subordinated to an all-encompassing "employment mainstreaming" under the Lisbon Strategy in 2003 (Jenson, 2008; Lewis, 2006; Rubery et al., 2003). In a nutshell: Family measures are expected to contribute to increasing female employment in conjunction with broader EU labor market measures; their potential for enhancing gender equality and equal opportunities, both in the domestic sphere and in the job market, has been watered down and encapsulated within the employment objective.

In the field of family policy, the EU promoted various measures for removing disincentives to female employment and balancing paid work and family duties. A first lever is the provision of childcare services. It is generally considered an efficient labor market instrument that removes barriers to labor market participation by mothers, while at the same time contributing to gender equality and investment in young children (Vandenbroucke & Vleminckx, 2011; Lewis, Campbell, & Huerta, 2008). Women still face the main burden of child care, and, without the possibility of externalizing care duties (be it through informal or formal channels), they are often unable to engage in paid employment (Van Lancker & Ghysels, 2012). In the absence of decent care provisions, women often cut back on their working hours or quit the labor force altogether to take care of their (pre-school-age) children (Uunk, Kalmijn, &Muffels, 2005). Indeed, it has been shown that the availability of formal care services in particular is a strong determinant of female labor supply in industrialized countries (Jaumotte,

2003; van der Lippe & van Dijck, 2002). Child care became an official EU policy issue with the adoption of the 1992 Childcare Recommendation, followed by the adoption of explicit targets to provide child care by 2010 to at least 33% of children under 3 years old and to at least 90% of children between 3 years old and mandatory school age at the Barcelona Summit in 2002 as part of the Lisbon Strategy. A new benchmark for at least 95% of children between 4 years old and mandatory school age to participate in child care was set in 2009. At present, child care is seen as a means to reach the EU2020 targets for employment, early school leaving, and poverty (European Commission, 2011c).

Parental leave is a second important aspect of EU concern for the reconciliation of work and family life. Leave entitlements interact with childcare services, because they enable parents to interrupt employment to care for their children, which reduces the need for external childcare services during that period. Nevertheless, parental leave and childcare service provision are both activation-oriented. Leave schemes ensure parents' bond with the labor market by maintaining the contractual link between employer and employee during the latter's temporary retreat from work (Ghysels & Van Lancker, 2011). However, their employment effect is harder to assess than that of childcare services, because that depends on the length of the leave, the conditions of entitlement, and the generosity of the benefit (Gornick & Hegewisch, 2010). Short periods of particularly well-paid leave have been shown to be beneficial to female employment rates: Young women are encouraged to strengthen their labor market attachment before childbirth through the knowledge that they will incur only minor income loss during their leave and that they will be able to safely return to their jobs subsequently (Del Boca et al., 2007; De Henau, Meulders, & O'Dorchai, 2007). However, longer leave from the labor market (the exact tipping point is rather unclear)[2] provides women with fewer incentives to start a career and fewer postleave career prospects (Morgan & Zippel, 2003; Gornick, Meyers, & Ross, 1997). If remuneration is too low or even nonexistent, there are few incentives for taking leave, especially for low-income families who cannot afford to give up earnings (Fagan & Walthery, 2007). Like childcare services, leave is a potentially powerful instrument to ensure gender equality in both care arrangements and on the labor market (see Ray et al., 2010 for further reading on this issue). Generally, four types of leave entitlements are available in European welfare states: maternity, paternity, parental, and home-care leave (OECD, 2011). In contrast to the soft targeting in the case of childcare services, the EU has influenced national policymaking on leave rules in a legislative way by introducing legally binding Directives. Examples are the 1992 Pregnant Workers Directive (92/85/EEC), which stipulated that workers who have recently given birth or who are breastfeeding should be granted the right to maternity leave of at least 14 continuous weeks with continuous receipt of either their salary or an adequate allowance, and the 1996 Parental Leave Directive (96/34/EC), which stipulated a minimum right to three months of parental leave as an individual entitlement for both men and women. In 2010, the 1996 Directive was revised (2010/18/EU) inter alia extending the period of leave to four months.

A final policy measure we incorporate into our comparative exercise is child benefits, which constitute a more traditional pillar of family policy. All European welfare states have child benefit schemes, but, as with childcare and leave policies, there are considerable differences in design, structure, and generosity. Previous research on the history and evolution of child benefit systems has shown them to be shaped by ideological considerations and gendered views on society and the role of men and women as breadwinners and/or homemakers. Hence, they may serve different purposes (Gauthier, 1999): (1) as a complement to household income so that mothers can stay at home and take care of the children; (2) to encourage parenthood and increase fertility; or (3) as a means of horizontal and/or vertical redistribution in response to a concern for the well-being of children (Montanari, 2000). The particular design of the system of child benefits in the various countries often reflects such historical objectives and ideological motives: They may be income or nonincome related, variable with the age or parity of the children, taxable or nontaxable, have a contributory or noncontributory financial base and operate through the tax system, via cash benefits, or a combination of the two (Immervoll, Sutherland, & de Vos, 2001; Kamerman, 1980).

One of the assumptions underlying this chapter is that the transition from the traditional welfare state to the social investment state has coincided with a shift in expenditures from passive cash benefits to activating family support. Ultimately, this is an empirical issue. How does the hodgepodge of family policy measures of different origins, with divergent ideological foundations and varying modalities translate into government expenditures, our main area of interest? Moreover, given the above-described shift in the dominant EU policy discourse to an emphasis on work/family reconciliation and activation, is there a parallel evolution to be observed from old to new family support measures?

Figure 7.1 shows total gross government spending on child benefits, parental leave, and child care for 21 EU Member States and Norway compiled from the OECD Social Expenditure database (SOCX; see Chapter 9). We also take government spending via the tax system (by means of tax credits or tax allowances) into account, which is an often overlooked fact in comparative spending exercises (Adema, Fron, & Ladaique, 2011).

The amounts of spending are made comparable across countries and over time by converting them into purchasing power parities (PPPs) using the EU27 average as basis. To ensure that differences in spending between countries are not driven by demographics, we control for the number of children between 0 and 6 years of age for child care and parental leave spending, and for the number of children between 0 and 18 years of age for spending on child benefits. In effect, what is shown in Figure 7.1 is the average spending per child on the three mainstays of family policy in 2009, while Table 7.1 shows the evolution of average spending per child for the three measures between 2001 and 2007 and between 2007 and 2009.

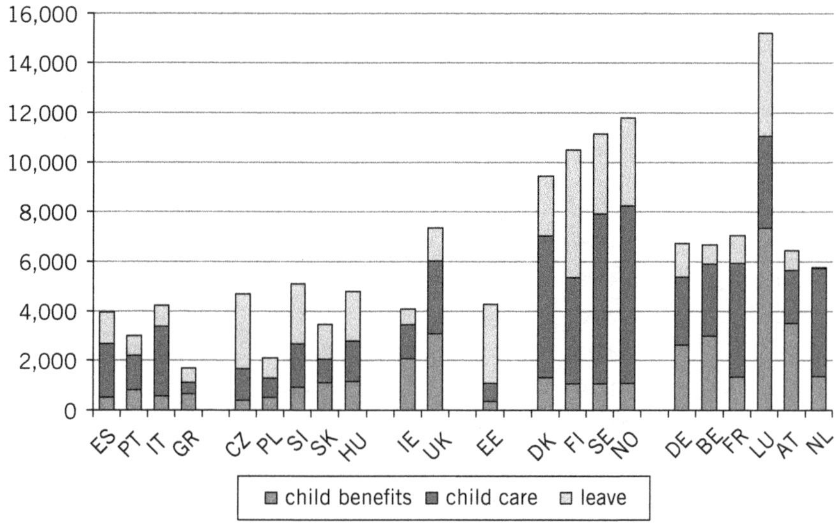

Figure 7.1. Average net government spending on child benefits, parental leave, and child care, per child in €PPP, 2009. *Source*: own calculations on OECD SOCX database and Adema et al. (2011). No information available for Bulgaria, Romania, Latvia, and Lithuania. *Note*: childcare includes spending on day-care services, pre-primary (ISCED0) education and, if applicable, tax credits for childcare. Leave includes maternity as well as paternity and parental leave. Child benefits include benefits in cash and benefits working through the tax system.

Although diversity is without doubt the main feature of a cross-country comparison of spending on family policy, certain patterns emerge. In the Southern welfare states, spending on family policy is comparatively low and heavily concentrated on child care (nurseries for 3–6-year-olds in particular). The highest overall spending is observed in the Continental and Nordic countries. In the former, child benefits are relatively more important (with Luxemburg as emblematic example), while in the latter the focus is on productive family policy (childcare services and parental leave). This mirrors choices made in the past.

The Anglo-Saxon countries differ from each other. While spending in Ireland is comparatively low and focused on child benefits, the UK spends above average, emphasizing childcare services. Although the former Socialist economies share a history of extensive day-care provisions for pre-school-age children combined with generous and extensive leave schemes, today only the latter is clearly reflected in the expenditure data. Czech Republic, Slovenia, Estonia, and Hungary only devote a minor share of family policy expenditures to childcare services, although they have retained their focus on leave entitlements and display a rather high average level of spending per child. Poland finds itself at the bottom of the league table with total spending at Mediterranean level.

Finally, the data shed light on the question of whether government spending on new family policy measures, that is, employment-related policy, increased during the Lisbon period. Table 7.1 shows changes in government spending per

Table 7.1. Change in government spending on three family support measures per child in €PPP, 2001–2007–2009, European countries.

	Child benefits		Leave schemes		Childcare services	
	Δ01-07	Δ07-09	Δ01-07	Δ07-09	Δ01-07	Δ07-09
Spain	+313%	-2%	+105%	+31%	+40%	+8%
Portugal	+35%	+36%	+120%	+25%	+45%	+11%
Italy	+15%	-1%	+52%	+4%	+20%	-1%
Greece	+43%	25%	+52%	+53%	+2%	-5%
Czech R.	-29%	-50%	+196%	-16%	+41%	+10%
Poland	+245%	-10%	+43%	+27%	+139%	+17%
Slovenia	+18%	+6%	+27%	+34%	+15%	-10%
Slovak R.	+113%	+11%	+56%	+9%	+47%	10%
Hungary	+68%	+3%	+81%	+8%	+49%	0
Ireland	+103%	+9%	+176%	+17%	+83%	+6%
UK	+88%	+12%	+507%	-16%	+56%	-9%
Estonia	+50%	+3%	+170%	+54%	+226%	+2%
Denmark	+12%	+3%	+44%	+5%	+21%	+3%
Finland	+11%	-1%	+122%	+8%	+36%	+9%
Sweden	+16%	-6%	+54%	-1%	+71%	+2%
Norway	-3%	-8%	+19%	+3%	+124%	+16%
Germany	+82%	+4%	+46%	+11%	+58%	+20%
Belgium	+21%	+2%	+26%	+3%	+28%	0
France	+13%	+4%	-9%	-1%	+22%	0
Luxemburg	+32%	+33%	+39%	+9%	+48%	+7%
Austria	+36%	+7%	-49%	+7%	+48%	+28%
Netherlands	+28%	+21%	+192%	+17%	+133%	+26%
Mean	+37%	+9%	+61%	+8%	+50%	+7%

Source: Own calculations on OECD SOCX and Adema et al. (2011).
Note: see Figure 7.1.

child in €PPP for the period 2001–2007–2009. It is immediately clear that, generally, *spending on all three measures increased* in the pre-crisis period (2001–2007). Only Czech Republic (–29%) and Norway (–3%) have seen a decline in spending on child benefits, and spending on leave declined in France (–9%), Luxembourg (–5%) and Austria (–49%). All other countries report increasing budgets for child benefits, leave schemes, and childcare services. Eight countries have more than doubled their budget for leave (Spain, Portugal, Czech Republic, Ireland, United Kingdom, Estonia, Finland, and the Netherlands); four countries their budget for child benefits (Spain, Poland, Slovak Republic, and Ireland); and four countries their budget for child care (Poland, Estonia, Norway, and the Netherlands). For the sake of clarity, we do not discuss the evolution of government spending in every particular country. Yet we may conclude from the data that the assumed shift in government expenditures for family policy has not occurred: Although spending on new family measures has increased, the same holds (although to a somewhat lesser extent) for spending on old measures. In other words, spending on leave and child care has not led to a crowding out of spending on child benefits.

Recent OECD data allow some preliminary light to be shed on the evolution of spending in the first years of the crisis. In several countries, spending on child benefits came to a halt or even decreased (Czech Republic, Poland, Sweden, and Norway) while in others spending did increase but at a slower pace than in the pre-crisis period (exceptions: Portugal, Luxemburg, and the Netherlands). A similar picture arises for spending on leave schemes (cuts in Czech Republic, United Kingdom) and childcare services (cuts in Greece, Slovenia, and United Kingdom). Generally speaking, the data show that spending on family policy slowed in the period 2007–2009.

7.3 THE FAMILY POLICY TRIAD: EXPLORING THE DISTRIBUTION OF ITS USE

In the previous section we clarified total spending, its recent evolution, and policy background. Yet this chapter is not just about spending on family policy, but also about its distribution among families with children. This section explores the social distribution of the use of existing family policy schemes as a first step in determining who benefits from public investment in these areas. Later on, we will complete the picture by coupling usage with government spending. It will be argued below that the interaction of use and government funding is complicated by the modus operandi of the various policy measures. Therefore, the detailed analysis of the social distribution of public spending on family policy will be limited to two countries. The Europe-wide comparison of family policy measure usage in this section thus concludes the European part of our analysis.

7.3.1 Child Benefits

In order to gain insight into the social distribution of child cash benefits in Europe, and hence grasp the relative generosity of child benefits toward different income groups, use is made of the "model families matrix method," which allows cross-country comparisons for different "model family" types at different earnings levels. Figure 7.2 compares a low-income family (single earner, working at minimum wage) with an average-income family (dual-earner couple, both working at average wage) and a couple living on social assistance. For the sake of comparability, amounts have been converted into €PPPs, so that the cross-country assessment takes due account of price differences.

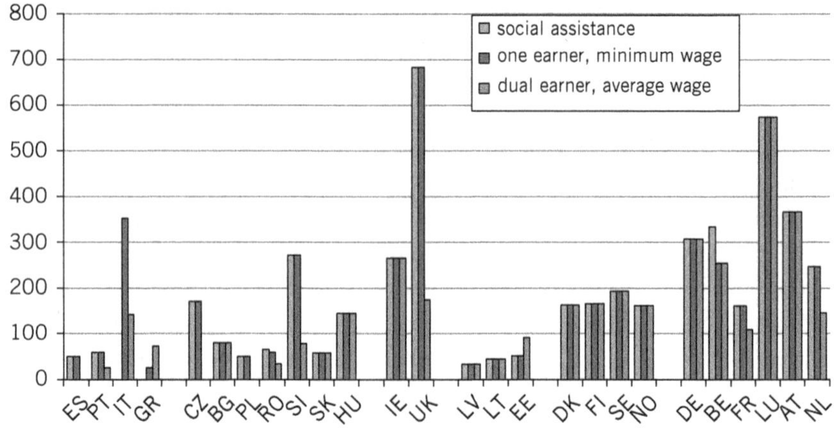

Figure 7.2. Child cash benefit levels for families on social assistance and low-income families compared to average-income families, European countries, €PPP, 2009. *Source*: CSB MIPI (Centre for Social Policy – Minimum Income Protection Indicators) database (Van Mechelen et al., 2011). Couples with two children (7 and 14years old). If the bar is not shown, the family type does not receive any cash benefit (see Spain, Italy, Greece, Czech Republic, and Poland).

In 11 of 26 countries under study, the child benefit package takes account of the higher needs in low-income families, while in others child benefits are provided on a universal basis (at least for the model families under consideration). Only in Greece and Estonia are child cash benefits biased against the lowest incomes, while in Italy the benefit system is biased against the non-employed. The high overall level of generosity in the Continental and Liberal welfare states illustrates once again its importance in these countries, as reflected in Figure 7.1. The Baltic and Southern European countries have the lowest levels (except Italy, with its system of employment-related yet generous benefits for low incomes), while the Central and Eastern European countries display considerable variation. All in all, child benefits are in most countries not linked directly with employment and are awarded on a universal basis. Additionally, several countries have made room for "targeting within universalism" (Skocpol, 1991): degrees of selectivity offering additional resources to low-income families within a universal framework. Hence, government investment in these measures can be expected to be either distributionally neutral or allocated more than proportionally toward low-income families (assuming complete take-up).

7.3.2 Childcare Services

To gauge the social stratification of the use of childcare services in European countries, the households in our sample (households with a youngest child under the age of 6 years) were divided into five income groups (quintiles). The average outcome is compared with results for the highest and lowest income groups in Figure 7.3 and Figure 7.4, respectively, for the youngest children and for pre-school-age children. Overall, the pattern of care use is socially stratified: In almost

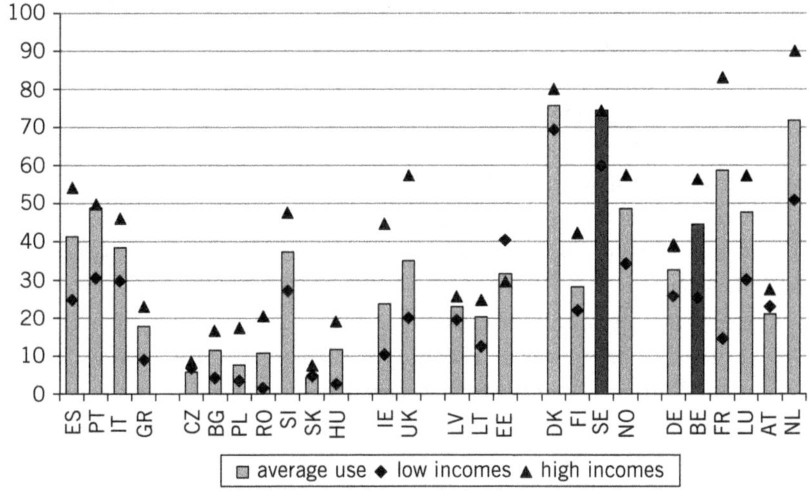

Figure 7.3. The social distribution of childcare use for children aged 0–2 years by income group, SILC 2009, European countries. *Source*: EU-SILC 2009.

all countries, the higher-income households (represented by triangles in the figures) make far more use of formal care services than the lower-income households (diamonds in the figures). Obviously, these findings should be interpreted in conjunction with the labor market participation of mothers in the different social groups. This is certainly the case in Belgium, for example, where mothers

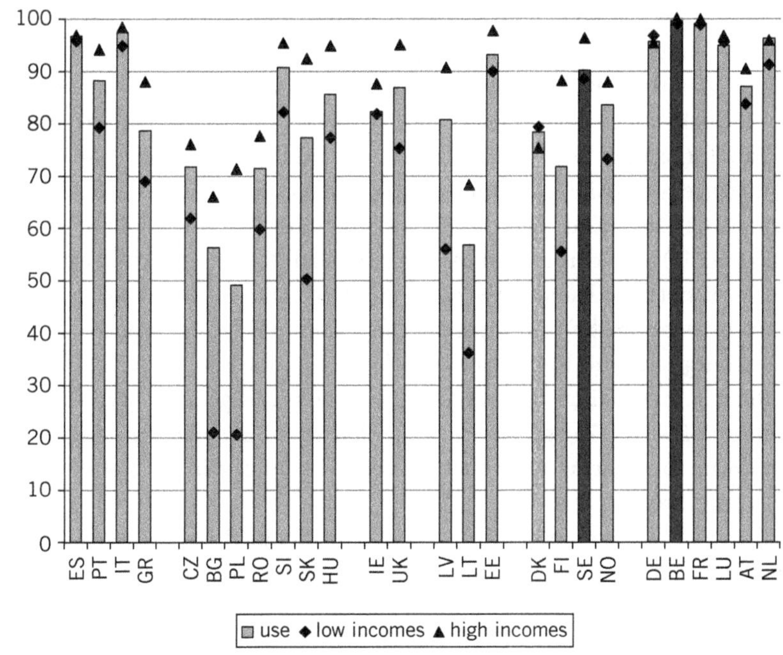

Figure 7.4. The social distribution of childcare use for children aged 3–5 years by income group, SILC 2009, European countries. *Source*: EU-SILC 2009.

living in low-income households are more likely to be inactive than mothers in higher income brackets, and this pattern is reflected in the social distribution of formal care use (Ghysels & Van Lancker, 2011). Nevertheless, the magnitude of the inequality in Belgium is striking: In spite of the high average use of child care for the youngest children in general, around 60% of the households in the highest income quintile make use of formal care services compared to only 25% of the households in the lowest income quintile. Countries with similar unevenly distributed care use patterns are France, United Kingdom, Ireland, the Netherlands, Luxemburg, and Spain.

Furthermore, all countries with low rates of childcare use display a very unequal distribution among households (with Latvia as the only exception). In contrast, Denmark and Sweden succeed in providing extensive care services while almost equalizing the social distribution of opportunities, which to an extent reflects the inclusive childcare policies pursued in these two countries, although it is also related to their high female employment rates. Indeed, the employment gap between high- and low-skilled mothers is much smaller in Sweden (Evertsson et al., 2009) than, say, Belgium (Cantillon et al., 2001). Be that as it may, the Danish and Swedish pattern of childcare use is reminiscent of basic arithmetic: Equal (universal) access for all social groups must be ensured in order to reach high overall levels of formal care use, which is an important lesson in the light of the European ambitions laid down in the Barcelona targets.

In many countries, the pattern for the 3-to-5-year-old age group runs parallel to that for the youngest, though at higher average levels of use. In most countries, children between ages 3 years and 5 years are served by the school system. Often this entails a shift from the policy sphere of social welfare to education, which commonly results in a clear break in the usage pattern. In Spain and Italy, for example, childcare services are used by about 40% of the youngest (an intermediate position within the EU), whereas kindergarten is attended by almost all children aged 3 years to 5 years (making them top-ranking countries within the EU). As a corollary, the uneven social distribution of child care for the youngest is not found among the older group of children. The same gap-closing pattern is found in the Continental welfare states (Belgium, France, Germany, Luxembourg, and the Netherlands) and—albeit to a lesser extent—in Ireland and the UK. Interestingly, however, gap closing is not general, even though an expansion of use is. The graphs illustrate that social inequality among children aged 3 years to 5 years is larger than among the youngest in the Slovak republic, Latvia, and Estonia.

All in all, the above shows that social inequality in childcare use is the norm rather than the exception in European countries. Moreover, we are reminded of a basic lesson: An equal distribution is hard to achieve without high levels of service use.

7.3.3 Parental Leave Entitlements

The empirical data for parental leave entitlements are drawn from the 2005 ad hoc module of the EU Labour Force Survey (EU-LFS). This module offers uniquely comparable information on the use of parental leave, but as a source it also has some drawbacks. First, no income data is available in the publicly available version of the EU-LFS. Therefore, we limit our distribution analysis to educational groups instead of income groups. Second, to ensure that data were available for all countries, the sample had to be widened to working women with a child under the age of 15 years. Still, a table for a sample of families with children under the age of 3 years for a selection of countries (excluding Denmark, Sweden, Norway, Finland, and France) does confirm the results.

The distributional picture shown in Figure 7.5 is quite homogeneous, despite the considerable differences in generosity of parental leave schemes. All significant divergences between educational groups point in the same direction: Households with a low-educated mother use parental leave opportunities to a smaller extent than other households do. As in the analysis of childcare

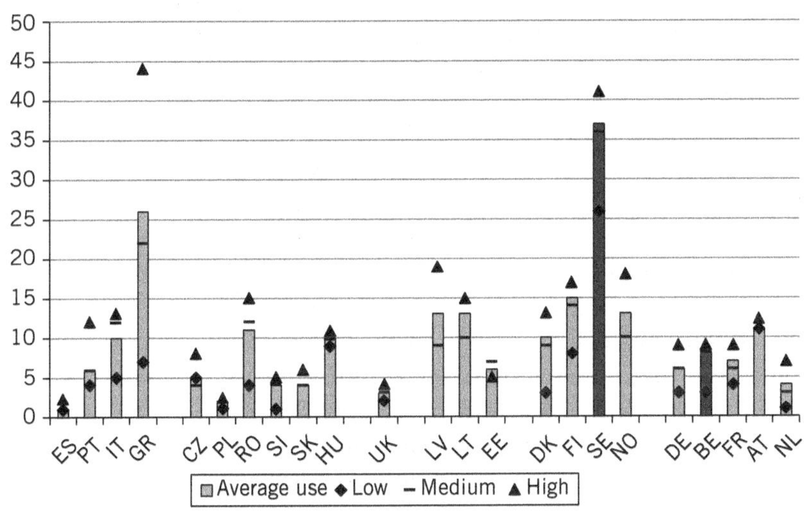

Figure 7.5. The educational distribution of remunerated parental leave among families with a working mother and at least one child under the age of 15 years, European countries, 2005. *Source*: EU-LFS 2005. Cells with fewer than 50 observations are not shown, resulting in the omission from the table of Luxemburg, as well as the group of low-skilled mothers for several countries. Selection: women having a job at the moment of the interview and living together with at least one own or partner's child younger than 15 years. *Note*: Paid parental leave refers to all types of remunerated parental leave schemes, including both full-time and part-time leave and leave taken by either one or both parents during the last 12 months. Bulgaria and Ireland are not included, because there was no paid parental leave scheme in place in these countries in 2005. Other countries lacking a paid parental leave scheme, such as the UK and Spain, are included because a number of respondents reported some kind of remuneration (e.g., specific regulations in the public sector, following a collective agreement or with a particular employer).

services, a second observation applies: Some countries do not exhibit an unequal distribution at all. In Spain, Poland, and UK, the reason for this outcome is quite obvious: The overall use of parental leave is almost zero. In these countries, parental leave is either unpaid (Spain and UK), or an income test applies to what is, moreover, a rather low benefit (Poland).

In Austria and Hungary, a relatively high level of take-up is equally dispersed among the social strata. Characteristics of the leave system do not offer an immediate explanation for the relative attractiveness of leave to low-skilled mothers in these countries. Leave is paid at a flat rate in Austria, but the payment period can exceed the leave period (which is an attractive option for low-income families), while in Hungary, for example, it covers 60% of the previous wage for a period of more than two years (OECD, 2011). Yet, the specific characteristics of the leave entitlements are not the only factor determining take-up. Other factors such as the availability of child care, employment opportunities for women, and cultural aspects, are equally important (Gornick & Hegewisch, 2010).

Moreover, the equalizing logic we observed in the childcare sector is not reproduced in parental leave. None of the countries with high take-up rates display an equal distribution across educational groups. The difference between high- and low-skilled working mothers is statistically significant among the three countries with the highest average take-up rates, for example (Sweden, Finland, and Greece). Yet, it should be stressed that take-up of parental leave is typically much lower than childcare coverage. Hence, the mathematical rule tending toward an equal distribution with rising coverage rates does not come into play yet.

It is worth reiterating that Figure 7.5 is limited to working mothers only. This demonstrates that even among the selected group of employed low-skilled mothers, parental leave is not used to the same extent as among the high-skilled (with the exceptions noted above). Consequently, inequality in the use of parental leave is not only the result of unequal labor force participation but also a consequence of inequalities in the effective access to parental leave within the working population. Compared with the analysis of the use of childcare services, Figure 7.5 also shows that the Nordics do not always achieve equal distributions. Although childcare use is hardly skewed against the low-skilled in Denmark, Norway, and Sweden, the use of parental leave clearly is.

7.4 THE SOCIAL DISTRIBUTION OF FAMILY EXPENDITURES: THE CASE OF SWEDEN AND FLANDERS (BELGIUM)

The above analyses suggest that the more recent work-family reconciliation measures (childcare and leave schemes) may have distributional effects that countervail the redistributive or distributionally neutral design of long-standing income protection measures such as child benefits. Yet, the interaction between the measures and their resulting overall effect (i.e., the presence of a Matthew effect) cannot be ascertained on the basis of the use of those measures only. For instance, if one observes that the use of child care is unequally distributed among households with young children in some countries but not in others, it does not necessarily follow that government expenditures are unequally distributed. The distribution of government expenditures on policy measures depends not only on their use or take-up, but also on the modus operandi. In the case of child care, this includes inter alia the out-of-pocket costs and the subsidizing method of (public or private) childcare services. In the case of parental leave, it depends on the benefit levels, be they income-related or not, the leave period duration, entitlement conditions, etc. For child benefits, due account should be taken of whether the system is universal or means-tested, how it incorporates age, rank, and number of children, and the extent of targeting. Dysfunctions in any of these aspects can induce a Matthew effect, so that detailed data and level of analysis are required to gain genuine insight. For this reason, we concentrate on two case studies.

In the following paragraphs, the focus is on Sweden and the Belgian region of Flanders, which accounts for approximately 60% of the country's population. The purpose is to arrive at a fine-grained analysis of the social distribution of subsidized childcare services, parental leave entitlements, and child benefits.[3] The descriptive overview above indicated that child care and parental leave use is heavily biased against the lowest incomes in Belgium, while this is only the case for parental leave, not child care, in Sweden. Child benefits are expected to be targeted more at the lowest incomes in Belgium, while they are assumed to be distributionally neutral in Sweden. In what follows, we investigate whether these patterns of entitlement, use, or take-up translate into a Matthew effect, in other words, an unequal allocation of government investment in these policies.

7.4.1 Data and Methodology

The proposed analysis of the social distribution combines administrative data on government outlays with detailed data from national surveys containing information on usage and parental contributions (for child care) and on benefit receipt (for child benefits and parental leave). For Flanders, we rely on the 2005 Flemish Families and Care Survey (FFCS), while for Sweden we draw on the Level-of-Living Survey (LNU) Wave 2000 (relating to income for the year 1999), complemented by register data on benefits drawn from the Luxembourg Income Study (LIS) database. All data on government expenditures on relevant policy measures are derived from official and administrative sources and recalculated to reflect government efforts to reach the group of young children (0 to 6 years of age) that the present chapter is concerned with. For the sake of clarity and conciseness, the calculation of the amounts cited is not shown, but details can be obtained from the authors upon simple request.

For readers of the chapter by Verbist and Matsaganis (Chapter 6), it should be clarified that we apply the standard techniques of budget allocation (a production cost logic and equal distribution within the household), yet use data allowing for a higher level of detail. We refer to the above-mentioned chapter for a discussion of the benefits and drawbacks of potential alternatives.

One should also refrain from making simple comparisons between Sweden and Flanders in so far as the total budget for a particular measure is concerned. Differences in volume of the total budget do not necessarily reflect genuine differences in policy choices or total government investment, but might simply be occasioned by compositional differences (population size, number of children). Similar to Figure 7.1 and Table 7.1 above, we control for the number of children in a particular household to make sure that potential differences between income groups do not stem from differences in the number of children across these social groups. In effect, the graphs presented below show the amount of government investment received by an average child in five different income groups. As such, the results reflect the joint outcome of use or take-up of a measure (access, perceived affordability) and its funding (proportion of public support). Hence, if differences are observed between the funding received by an average child in different income groups, these may stem from variation in both usage and mode of operation (government funding rules, legislation, entitlements), as will be discussed for every policy measure separately.

Finally, it should be noted that the amounts relied upon are based on the year 2000 for Sweden and the year 2005 for Flanders, but in order to allow comparison, the Swedish amounts have been uprated to the year 2005 and converted into €PPPs. Still, although great care is taken to maximize comparability, the difference in policy setup does not allow very precise comparisons. The focus is rather on the patterns of social distribution constituting the central question addressed in this contribution: Which income groups benefit from government investment in the three mainstays of contemporary family policy?

7.4.2 Child Benefits

Let us first consider (cash) child benefits. In Belgium, child benefit rights for employees were first introduced in 1930 and the system has expanded ever since (Cantillon & Goedemé, 2006). Today, the system encompasses child benefits (*kinderbijslag*) and childbirth allowances (*kraamgeld*). Hence, Flemish families with children may claim universal child benefits (with supplements according to age and rank of the child), additional child benefits for vulnerable families (e.g., single or unemployed parents) and one-off allowances at childbirth (or at the moment of adoption) from the federal state and municipal authorities. In 2005, the total government budget for this combined scheme for children aged 0 to 5 years in the region of Flanders amounted to EUR 686 million, which works out to EUR 1,821 per child per year.

In Sweden, prior to the 1930s, support measures for families with young children consisted mainly of tax subsidies. A universal system of child benefits for all parents (*barnbidrag*) was only introduced in 1948 as a flat-rate fee that did not vary according to rank or age of the child. This principle has been retained to date. However, the universal benefit was complemented in 1982 with an additional benefit for large families of three or more children (*flerbarnstillägg*), the rationale being that full-time work is hard to maintain for mothers with more than two children. As in Flanders, parents are entitled to cash childbirth allowances, but these are provided under the (insurance) scheme of parental leave, which will be discussed in the next section. In 2000, the total Swedish budget for child benefits for children aged 0 to 5 years amounted to EUR 660 million, or roughly EUR 1,135 per child per year. The difference in average public investment per child between Sweden and Flanders corresponds with the different expenditure structures observed in Figure 7.1: Belgium (and thus Flanders) spends most on cash benefits and least on parental leave, while in Sweden childcare services and parental leave schemes represent a much more substantial item of public expenditure than do child benefits.

All in all, given the design of the Swedish system, government spending on child benefits may be expected to be quite evenly distributed among the different income groups. In Flanders, on the other hand, expenditures are expected to be targeted more at the lowest incomes (given the system of supplementary benefits). Figure 7.6 shows that the public subsidy for an average child in the five income groups indeed follows the expected pattern in Sweden, but surprisingly not so in Flanders. In reality, the supplementary benefits are highly selective and cover only a small proportion of the population. Moreover, families in the lowest income quintile tend to have more children than other households. Combined, these characteristics explain why there is no statistically significant difference between the social groups in terms of average child benefit amounts. The same mechanisms are at play in Sweden: Although lower income families tend to be larger families (and hence should be the main beneficiaries of the supplementary

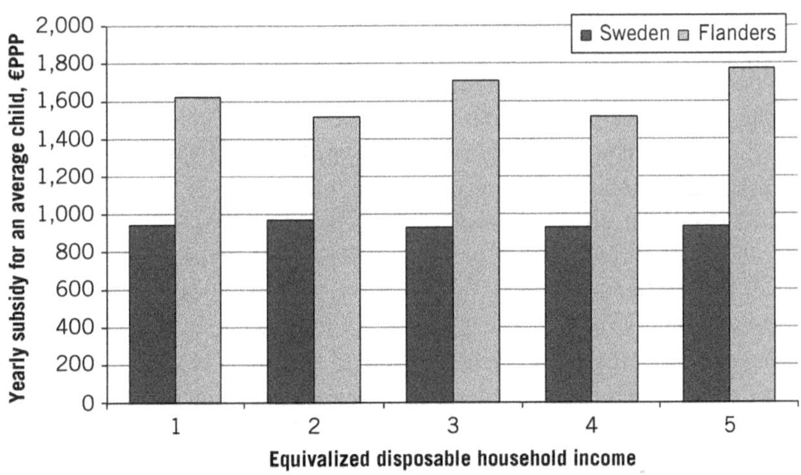

Figure 7.6. Social distribution of government investment in child benefits.

benefit for large families), the weight of the benefit is too insignificant to show up in the results. In sum, in both Sweden and Flanders, children receive on average a more or less equal share of child benefit expenditures, regardless of their parents' financial resources.

7.4.3 Parental Leave

In 1974, Sweden abolished its system of maternity leave and replaced it with a system of remunerated parental leave (*föräldrapenning*). It was the first Western democracy to impose a strictly gender-neutral program of this kind (Ferrarini, 2006). Since 1989, the leave period has been 360 days per child, with an income replacement of 80% of previous wage up to a certain earnings level, followed by a flat fee during 90 days (guaranteed minimum). Eligibility depends on the payment of national insurance contributions through employment for a minimum of 240 consecutive days before childbirth. Those who do not meet this requirement are entitled to the guaranteed minimum for the full period. The benefit may be taken up by the mother from 60 days prior to confinement onward, and by either of the parents up until the child reaches the age of eight. Additionally, fathers are entitled to 10 days of leave ("daddy days," *pappadagar*) under the same income replacement rate as parental leave, to be taken up any time during the first 60 days after childbirth.

In 1994, a so-called "daddy month" was introduced. This is a period of four weeks within the total leave length earmarked for fathers on a use-or-lose basis, with the explicit aim of increasing gender-equality in childrearing (Duvander, Ferrarini, & Thalberg, 2006).[4] Presently, 60 days of the leave are reserved for either parent, and the remaining time may be divided between the parents as they see fit. The system is very flexible: It can be used partially by both parents, allowing both to work and be on leave on the same day, and parents can opt to receive only part of the benefit even if on full-time leave in order to extend the total leave period. In effect, most Swedish children stay at home with a parent for approximately a year, regardless of household income or labor market status of the parents. Finally, parents are entitled to 60 days of "temporary parental leave" per child (below 12 years of age) per year in case the child or child minder is sick. The latter benefit is not included in the analysis. In 2000, total government spending on parental insurance and the additional "daddy days" amounted to EUR 1,272 million, an average of EUR 2,187 per child.

In Belgium, parental leave (*ouderschapsverlof*) is a strict implementation of the European Directive (supra). Introduced in its current form in 1997 by Royal Decree, it entitles each individual parent to 12 weeks of parental leave (recently extended to 16 weeks following the revision of the Directive). The parental leave benefit consists of a flat fee (federal plus Flemish supplement). The strict individualization implies that families stand to lose half of their entitlement if the father does not participate. However, fathers' take-up-rate is low. This may be due in part to the lack of proportional income replacement, though employer reluctance is also believed to be a factor. This system, too, is quite flexible: Leave can be taken on a full-time or part-time basis, including the option of taking leave at a rate of one day a week. This way, the entitlement period of twelve weeks may be proportionally extended to a maximum of 60 weeks. Additionally, in 1999, the Belgian government introduced a generalized system of career breaks (*loopbaanonderbreking*) as an individual right for all workers. Although such leave may be taken for any reason,[5] it is often associated with child-rearing (Clauwaert & Harger, 2000).

The benefits included in the analysis are those for parental leave and the related scheme of career breaks (as well as its more recent "time credit" variant). Because the career break scheme is not confined to parents with young children, only that part of the budget that is assigned to parents with young children is taken into account. It should, however, be noted that due to data limitations, no distinction is made between full-time and part-time leave. In 2005, government spending on the various types of parental leave for young children amounted to EUR 132 million, an average of EUR 351 per child.

Figure 7.7 shows that government subsidizing of parental leave in Flanders and Sweden is not distributed evenly across social strata. An average child in the first income quintile receives considerably less in leave benefits than a child in the upper quintiles. In Flanders, the highest income quintile is the main beneficiary, while in Sweden it is the middle-income group. Hence, despite large differences in their policy frameworks, both Sweden and Flanders fail to reach children in the lowest income group with measures of parental leave. As parental leave is directly linked to active participation in the labor market, a Matthew effect seems inevitable, regardless of the design of the measure. However, as demonstrated in Section 7.3.3 the unequal distribution of use is only partially explained by differences in employment. Other potential factors are the types of

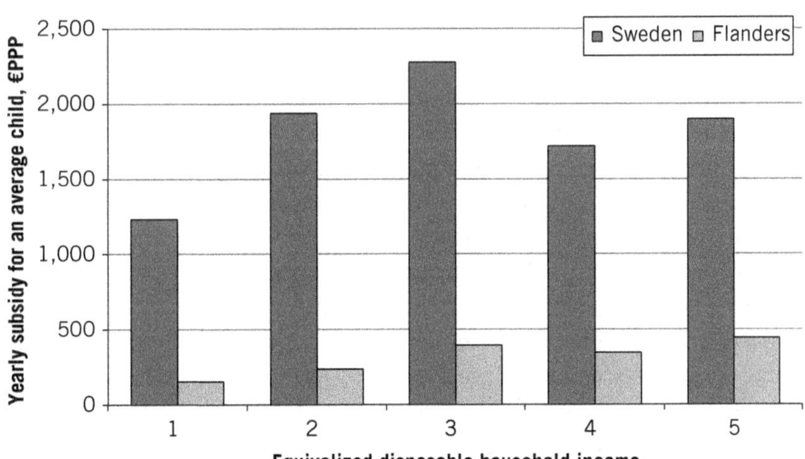

Figure 7.7. Social distribution of government investment in parental leave.

jobs held by parents in the lowest income group, which may not be sufficiently stable for them to qualify for parental leave and/or (under the Belgian scheme) to convince an employer to sanction such leave, and insufficient household resources, which may impede use of the scheme. The rather odd observation that, under the Swedish system, the main beneficiaries are families in the middle quintile rather than the highest quintile may be due to the ceiling imposed upon the wage-related benefit level. After all, this may be assumed to make the system less attractive to high-earning families, in terms of career advancement and wage penalties (Moss, 2011). By contrast, it allows middle-income mothers and fathers to profit fully from the wage-related benefit system. However, the precise causes of the socially stratified allocation of government investment in parental leave systems have yet to be established.

7.4.4 Childcare

From the mid-1970s onwards, childcare services developed quite rapidly in both Belgium and Sweden. Child care in Sweden serves the dual purpose of enabling parents to combine paid work with parenthood and providing support for the development of children (Skolverket, 2000). The latter goal has gained in prominence since the responsibility for child care was transferred in 1996 to the Ministry of Education (*Skolverket*), putting it outside the realm of social welfare. Child care in Sweden is organized at the municipal level, but with a national financial framework and curriculum and centrally determined regulations. Municipalities are obliged to provide child care to the extent necessary for parents to be able to work and study without "unreasonable delay," which usually means within three to four months. The bulk of childcare services is provided publicly, although private facilities are becoming more widespread. In any case, the latter must meet identical standards and they are funded in the same way as the public services.

In the early 2000s, major reforms were implemented, imposing a ceiling on parental fees (*maxtaxa*). By the year 2003, all municipalities had introduced a uniform income-related tariff system as a result of which any remaining regional differences in fees were smoothed out (Skolverket, 2007). Although prior to the reform, municipalities were free to set rates, almost all had already implemented an income-related tariff system (Brink, Nordblom, & Wahlberg, 2007). Another important aspect of the reform was the introduction of the additional obligation for municipalities to provide child care for children whose parents are unemployed or on parental leave. In effect, while children under 1 year old were almost always cared for at home, due to the system of parental leave (supra), about 85% of children yet to start school (aged 1 to 5 years) participated in public child care. Total government outlays for childcare subsidies for the year 2000 amounted to EUR 2,297 million, or an average of EUR 3,951 per child per year.

Unlike in Sweden, child care and education are separate policy areas in Flanders. In general, education starts at age 2.5 years, when almost all children enter kindergarten up to the age of 6 years. Kindergartens are free of charge and entirely state funded, although many are privately organized (Vandenbroeck, 2006). Child care for children under the age of 3 years is a responsibility of the Welfare Department (a competence that was devolved to the Belgian regions under the 1980 state reform). The monitoring of care for those under the age of 3 years is entrusted by decree to the public institution Child and Family (*Kind en Gezin*, K&G hereafter), which sets forward three objectives: reconciling work and family life; supporting the development of children; and promoting the social inclusion of vulnerable groups. It should be noted that K&G does not organize childcare services itself and that, unlike in Sweden, there is no such thing as a statutory childcare entitlement for young children. Even though child care is privately organized, a distinction can be made between facilities accredited and subsidized by K&G on the one hand and facilities registered with and supervised rather than subsidized by K&G on the other (Van Lancker & Ghysels, 2012).

Subsidized services receive funding that covers staffing (salaries) and operating costs. They must apply centrally determined income-related fees. Private facilities, by contrast, may set fees freely. Moreover, unlike in Sweden, parents can claim tax deductions for their childcare expenses, even if their children attend a nonsubsidized service (which makes all childcare services de facto indirectly subsidized).

Flemish parents are each entitled to three months of parental leave (supra), which means that most infants enter childcare services before their first birthday. Around 1990, about 20% of children under 3 years of age (0–2.5) were in child care. This proportion has since increased to 63% (45% for Belgium as a whole) (Moss, 1990; Kind en Gezin, 2009). In 2005, total government subsidies for childcare services and kindergarten amounted to EUR 1,014 million, an average of EUR 2,691 per child per year.

As pointed out above, in Sweden, children from different social strata are represented quite evenly in subsidized childcare services, while in Belgium there is a bias in childcare use against the lowest incomes. (See Van Lancker & Ghysels [2012] for a further elaboration on the use of child care in both cases.) The reason for this inequality lies in factors of supply and demand: It is well-established that Flanders suffers from a general shortage in childcare supply, despite its high coverage rate, resulting in an underrepresentation of the lower income groups. In Sweden, the system of guaranteed places ensures equal access. However, as argued in Section 7.3.2, the different labor market circumstances in the two countries obviously play a crucial role here. Yet, previous analyses of the FFCS data revealed that 70% of non-working mothers in the lowest quintile who are not using child care would prefer to be employed if possible (Ghysels & Van Lancker, 2010). In other words, there is an untapped labor supply among low-income families who are disproportionally hit by the current lack of child care slots in Flanders. Following the employment logic of the European discourse on child care, the provision and use of child care acts as a precondition for labor market attainment of mothers with young children, and the unequal use in Flanders warrants concern.

Figure 7.8 represents public subsidy allocation given the divergent usage patterns and substantial systemic differences between Sweden and Flanders.

When analyzing the various components of government funding of childcare services in Flanders, it is important to keep in mind the underlying compensation mechanisms. The starting point is the net government subsidy to childcare providers. Because the tariff system is beneficial to lower income groups, subsidies net of parental contributions are larger in the lower income groups than in the higher income groups. In other words, the tariff system compensates for the unequal use of childcare services, to the extent that the direct government subsidy is not statistically different between the income groups. However, the equalizing effect of the income-related tariff system is undone by the indirect subsidy of the tax reduction scheme, which allows parents to deduct part of their childcare outlays from income tax. All things considered, then, direct and indirect subsidies for child care are beneficial to the upper income groups. In Sweden, however, one observes the opposite pattern. Because there is no comparable tax deduction scheme, the income-related tariff system combined with a more equal usage among income groups results in higher average investment per child among the lower income groups.

On a side note, it should be mentioned that this outcome differs from what is found in Chapter 6 by Verbist and Matsaganis: They report that the distribution of government subsidies in Sweden is biased against the lowest incomes in Sweden. The reason for the difference is twofold. First, the applied methodology differs: The investigation of specific cases allows us to grasp more in detail the role of the design of the service. Here, the individual allocation of out-of-pocket parental fees is included in the analysis, which is not the case in the aforementioned chapter, and these play a major role in the distributional outcomes of government

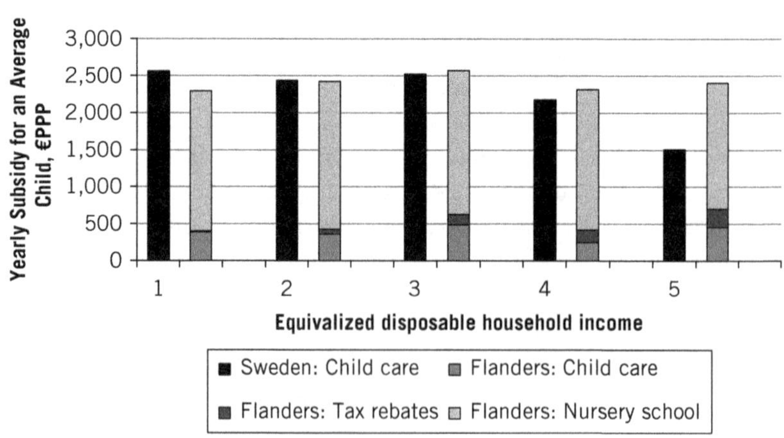

Figure 7.8. Social distribution of government investment for child care.

subsidies for child care because the income-related tariff system gears more subsidies toward the lower incomes relative to high-income families. Second, the population under consideration differs: Here we focus on households with young children while Verbist and Matsaganis take the whole population into account. If households with young children are found higher up the income distribution, government subsidies are by default biased against the lower income groups if one takes the whole population into account.

However, due account must also be taken of nursery school use in Flanders. From age 2.5 years, children are able to enter the school system. By age 3 years, attendance is quasiuniversal and by age 4 years almost all have become full-time users of the system. Thus, in the age group between 3 and 6 years, government funding is divided equally among the social groups. Moreover, funding is high relative to funding for the youngest children, because attendance approximates to 100% and tends to be full-time. Consequently, social inequalities in government funding of childcare services in Flanders are confined to the youngest age group. A strongly income-sensitive tariff system has proven insufficient to counteract this tendency, due to a combination of persistent inequalities in use (in consequence of supply and demand factors) and a "perverse" system of tax compensations that undoes the effects of the tariff system.

7.4.5 The Total Distribution of Old and New Family Measures

As a final step, the three measures of family support for young children are integrated into Figure 7.9, in order to compare the total distribution of government investment in the two cases considered. For Flanders, it suggests a rather uniform distribution. This follows from the relative dominance of two universal measures: child benefits and nursery schools. Indeed, the amounts of child benefits and nursery schools are clearly much higher than the government funding of

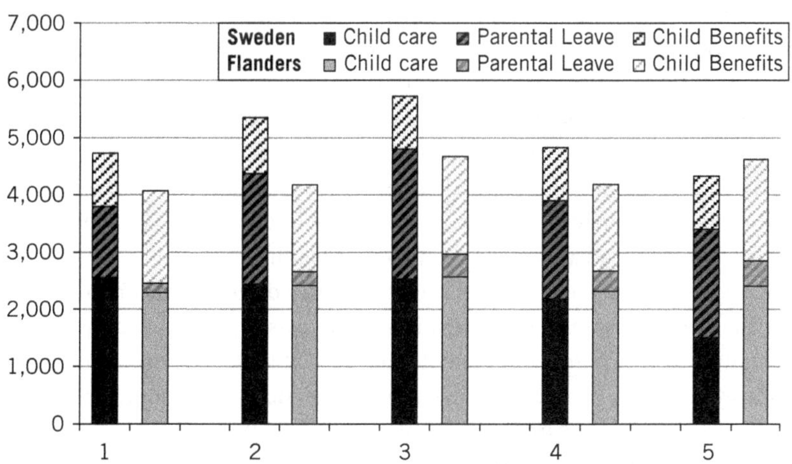

Figure 7.9. The social distribution of total government investment for family policy.

pre-school childcare services or parental leave (see also Figure 7.8). This should not come as a surprise, given that child benefits reach all children and attendance at nursery school is nearly universal, while the latter policy measures are selective by design. As shown above, this selectivity implies a certain bias. In the lowest fifth of the income hierarchy, children benefit significantly less from government funding for pre-school childcare services and parental leave. In Sweden, the allocation of government investment tends to benefit the lower and middle income groups most, while children in the highest income quintile receive the least.

7.5 DISCUSSION: ARE MATTHEW EFFECTS UNAVOIDABLE?

This chapter has considered the question of who benefits most from government investment in family policy. The starting point was the observation that the nature of family policy has changed dramatically from passive cash payments (such as child benefits) to more activating and employment-related services and measures (such as parental leave and child care). Given this, it is often assumed that there has been a shift in government expenditure toward the latter type of schemes, the main beneficiaries of which are assumed to be the higher income categories, which is a so-called "Matthew effect." Using this insight as a conceptual tool, this study looked into the social distribution of three measures, namely child benefits, parental leave, and child care, representing respectively an old and two new forms of family policy, in order to ascertain whether or not the presence of a Matthew effect could be confirmed and, if it could, to establish whether it is an inevitable feature of employment-related forms of family policy.

The analysis began with a European overview, which yielded a rather unexpected picture: Countries spend increasing proportions of their budgets on *both* old and new forms of family policy. There is no clear evidence to be found in the data for the assumption that spending on child care and parental leave schemes is crowding out spending on child benefits. In the first years of the crisis (between 2007 and 2009), however, in many countries the expenditure increase came to a halt. We also found that high relative spending on one type of policy may or may not be accompanied by generosity in other areas of family policy. What is more, spending is not tightly linked either to the social distribution of use. As a matter of fact, relatively high degrees of equality in the use or take-up of family measures are observed at both high and low expenditure levels.

Our results underscore the importance of policy design in the broadest sense; hence the need for careful consideration of the existing policy framework and close monitoring of policy implementation. In reality, a policy measure may be undone by competing adjacent policies or citizens may choose not to respond to a newly introduced measure, undermining its anticipated impact.

To illustrate the complexity of design and outcome interactions, detailed analysis was made of family policies in two different settings, namely Sweden and Flanders (Belgium). In a European comparative perspective, the two countries report high average spending per child on family policy. Moreover, they both have a universal child benefit system and rank among the countries with the highest use of childcare services. When it comes to parental leave, however, Sweden spends proportionally more than Flanders, where leave is comparatively short and not very generous.

At first sight, the overall distributional picture looks favorable for both countries: In Flanders, an average child younger than 6 years is likely to benefit equally from family policy measures across the income distribution and the same is (largely) true for Sweden. However, this overall and average picture is deceptive. It is biased by the age brackets chosen and stems in large part from the child benefit system. Traditionally, child benefits are the mainstay of family policy. In Flanders, this is true up to the present day; child benefits represent 37% of the amount an average child under the age of 6 years receives through the three measures scrutinized here. Consequently, the largely uniform and universal nature of the child benefits dampens potential disruptions of more selective family policy measures such as parental leave and childcare services, which are further discussed below. In Sweden, however, child benefits are less important. Here they represent 19% of the total amount received by an average child under 6 years of age. Conversely, the average amount spent by the Swedish government on parental leave is much more substantial (36% of the average total), and hence its distributional pattern also has a much greater impact on the overall distribution than is the case in Flanders. As has been demonstrated, neither Flanders nor Sweden achieves a socially uniform distribution of either parental leave usage or funding.

A widely applicable lesson to be learned here is that unequal distribution, although a legitimate cause for concern, only becomes crucial in the context of policy measures that have a large relative weight in the total policy mix. Hence, if other European countries should opt to follow the Swedish route, with large increases in the use of parental leave and much greater spending on such measures within the family policy mix, they must give due consideration to the design issues involved. In Sweden, parental leave is proportional to the previous earned income, which is likely to motivate parents to make use of the measure. Yet, this design feature also entails a Matthew effect, which, under the premise that all children should be treated equally, is detrimental to those living in lower-income families.

However, the case of child care in Sweden demonstrates that, even when a large share of government outlays is devoted to a policy measure, Matthew effects are not inevitable. The Swedish childcare system is beneficial for the lower incomes thanks to its design and the universality of its use: Child care slots are guaranteed for every child from age 1 year onward and the tariff system is related to disposable income. A second lesson to learn here is that policymakers should be aware of the internal consistency of their policy initiatives: The Flemish regional government aimed for the inclusion of low-income families in its implementation of childcare services by designing an income-related tariff system, as exists in Sweden. However, the Belgian federal government concurrently introduced a measure whereby parents of young children who remain in work are compensated for their childcare expenses through a tax deduction scheme. The latter undoes the income-sensitivity of the tariff system completely.

A third lesson relates to exogenous factors such as the state of the labor market. Even when carefully designed, employment-related policies can generate Matthew effects because labor market participation is unequally distributed across social strata. Especially parental leave, but in many countries also childcare services, are tightly linked to parental employment. Without employment, parents may not be (or they may perceive themselves not to be) entitled to such newer strands of family policy. A generalization of the latter thus requires universal parental employment and, hence, accompanying labor market policy.

A final lesson concerns the age group taken into account. In earlier work on this issue (Ghysels & Van Lancker, 2011; Van Lancker & Ghysels, 2012), the focus was on families with children younger than 3 years. In the present study, the scope is widened to children under 6 years of age. This makes a considerable difference, because age 3 years is when universal childcare schemes (as part of the general school system) become applicable in many European countries. In other words, the distributional concern is often limited to the youngest age group, as the Flemish example indeed shows. For children aged 3 to 5 years, Flanders succeeds in equalizing its allocation of government investment in child care through its nurseries, which are free of charge and used almost universally. Again, this stresses the importance of expanding service use across income groups in order to avoid Matthew effects and a subsequent bias against the lowest incomes.

ACKNOWLEDGMENTS

We would like to thank Dieter Vandelannoote and Willem Adema for their valued help with the data, and Frank Vandenbroucke, Bea Cantillon, and the participants of the Gini workshop in Antwerp (November 14–15, 2011) and the SOCLIFE Research Seminar in Cologne (December 21, 2011) for their comments and suggestions.

NOTES

1 We refer the interested reader to Rigney (2010) for a general overview of how the Matthew effect manifests itself in several aspects of social life.

2 Jaumotte, for instance, found that the impact of parental leave on employment becomes negative beyond a duration of 20 weeks, while others assert

that the optimal leave period may be more than 40 weeks (see Jaumotte 2003; OECD, 2011).

3 The focus is on the Flemish community rather than on Belgium as a whole, because family policy has been devolved to the communities. When relevant (i.e., in the case of overlapping competences), reference is made to Belgium as a whole.

4 For further details on the system of parental insurance and its effects on gender equality, see Haas and Rostgaard (2011).

5 The Di Rupo I government, however, pledged to reform the system. Here, we report on the system as it was in December 2011.

8

THE REFORM CAPACITIES OF EUROPEAN WELFARE STATES

Anton Hemerijck

8.1 THE "NEW POLITICS" OF THE WELFARE STATE REVISITED

The study of the welfare state over the past quarter century has been strongly advanced by the theoretical perspective of historical institutionalism. Surely the most successful research program has been the so-called "new politics" of the welfare state perspective, which rose to intellectual hegemony over the 1990s. Paul Pierson, the leading advocate of this approach, has in numerous publications advanced the conjecture that welfare states have in recent decades become exceedingly change-resistant, despite *irresistible* social, demographic, economic, and fiscal pressures (1994; 1998; 2002; 2004). At the heart of the so-called "new politics" of the welfare state literature lies a shrewd political analysis of why the welfare status quo ex ante has become increasingly difficult to alter. Pierson's key claim is that once a certain policy is in place, this creates groups of beneficiaries with strong interests in preserving the status quo. In an era of "permanent austerity," fiscal pressures confront policymakers with the more daunting challenge of "blame avoidance" (Pierson, 1994). Because "dismantling the welfare state" is not an attractive ticket for electoral competition, according to Pierson, policymakers are well advised to try to disperse, obfuscate, and hide the costs of unpopular cutbacks as much as possible. Moreover, precommitted resources of past policy choices, such as old age pensions, "lock in" social provisions, which in turn constrain budgetary leeway for present-day social reform. There have surely been curtailments in replacement rates and coverage in social programs, but by and large such retrenchment efforts have been relatively modest in the more affluent democracies in the period leading up to the global financial crisis of 2008.

To say that the modern welfare state is pretty resilient, however, is not to say that it is in good shape. In the wake of the global financial crisis, costly bank bailouts, automatic stabilization, tax cuts, and other initial stimulus measures, drained the public purse. This has resulted in a "double bind" of rising social protection expenditures and declining government revenues. In the spring of 2010, the Greek sovereign debt crisis confronted the European economy with a new and challenging crisis aftershock, and contagion fears spread across the weaker periphery of the eurozone. The European Union (EU) ultimately came to the rescue of Greece and other weak economies with a general bail-out package. Next, Greece, Spain, and Portugal staged impressive fiscal consolidation programs, including significant welfare retrenchment and labor market reforms. Soon after, conservative governments in Germany, France, Italy, the UK, and the Netherlands launched severe austerity measures. Will the aftermath of the crisis usher in a period of more social retrenchment? Pierson is not optimistic: After four decades of institutional tinkering, he believes, the era of austerity has finally begun (Pierson, 2011)! Because the modern welfare state, as a popular and deeply anchored policy system, has been so single-mindedly driven by the politics of fear of electoral retribution, special interest capture, and past policy lock-in, it runs the risk of becoming obsolete. In their obsession with fighting for and defending the welfare status quo, the majority of social policymakers and organized interest constituencies have been unable to adjust, adapt, and update their welfare programs to the new rules of international competition, the new shape of family life, the new flexibility of labor markets, and the new realities of immigration and demographic aging. Pierson is not expecting, however, another full-blown assault on social protection akin to the 1980s high-profile ideological attack on the welfare state of the likes of Margaret Thatcher and Ronald Reagan. Rather, he believes that the heavily fortified welfare state will most likely be outflanked, just as the "Maginot Line," built before World War II on the eastern frontier of France, failed to prevent invasion by the Nazi army. Welfare state opponents, including right-of-center governments and the international business community, are more likely to use political tactics of "policy drift," tailoring tax, financial, social and corporate governance policies to the interests of the economically privileged in an attempt to restore growth and competitiveness. In this respect, Pierson conjectures that the recent experience of the United States may serve as a precursor for Europe. A frontal political attack is neither wise, nor necessary, as incremental program exhaustion will see to the welfare state's gradual demise in the 21st century. In the process, to be sure, the social needs and welfare preferences of the middle and lower classes will take a residual back seat (Hacker & Pierson, 2010).

Although Pierson's highly evocative account of past policy experience, together with his speculative conjecture about the welfare state's non-future in the aftermath of the banking crisis, is highly plausible, in this contribution, I take issue with the "new politics" of the welfare state thesis on both empirical and theoretical counts. My argument below is more nuanced about the extent of social policy change over past decades and more positive about the welfare state's future. To be sure, we are very familiar with cases of stalled social reforms that fit Pierson's social policy inertia story line. The failed pension reforms of Juppé in France and Berlusconi in Italy in the mid-1990s immediately spring to mind. But how widely applicable is the welfare state immobility conjecture really? To what extent is political backlog or "Reformstau" the rule or the exception to contemporary welfare state development? The issue at stake is whether what has been coined a case of institutional inertia is really representative of the more general evolution of contemporary social policy since the last decade of the 20th century?

I agree with Pierson that the seemingly mundane empirical question *how much change is there to explain?* is riddled with ambiguity. It very much depends on where one looks empirically on the basis of what prior expectations. *What kind of policy change do we consider significant?* Most comparative welfare state scholars focus on large-scale programs of social insurance, ranging from unemployment insurance, disability and sickness benefits, survivors and old age pensions, as they define the core of the modern post-War welfare state. As a consequence, these scholars tend to overlook critical social provisions, including macroeconomic management, taxation, labor market policy and regulation, and education and vocational training, which clearly also shape, albeit more indirectly, but no less importantly than social insurance, citizens' material life chances.

It is true that social insurance, together with health care, constitute the largest expenditure items of the modern welfare state, but to view social insurance as the pars pro toto of the modern welfare state hides an important selection bias. Such a selection bias is particularly problematic when the aim is to answer the question whether welfare states are responsive to new economic realities and new social needs. It is true, with respect to government social expenditures; mature European welfare states indeed seem remarkably stable. From the early 1990s to 2003, total public social spending as a proportion of GDP generally absorbed between 25% and 30% of GDP (Begg et al., 2008; Castles, 2004; 2005; see also OECD, 2008; Hemerijck, 2012a). Cumulative research into social insurance has surely deepened our understanding over the past two decades. But by declining to take seriously how social insurance programs are embedded in and interact with broader economic and social policy provisions, we may well have lost sight of welfare-relevant public policy changes over the recent period of rapid social and economic restructuring in other relevant policy areas. The welfare state is more than the "social insurance state." Welfare states are multidimensional. A singular focus on spending and social protection blinds us to important changes in the institutional architecture of social policy and in the political strategies of (non-) reform.

8.2 A SHORT HISTORY OF PROFOUND SOCIAL REFORM

Behind stable government social spending, and only tepid benefit retrenchment, in terms of coverage and replacement rates, the welfare state, it is my contention, has experienced profound institutional transformation. From a public policy perspective, modern welfare regimes can be conceptualized as complementary packages of interdependent social policy provisions (Hemerijck & Schludi, 2000). As an encompassing policy repertoire, the welfare state stabilizes effective demand, and regulates labor markets, far beyond the traditional instruments of employment protection legislation and unemployment insurance. Effective labor market policies are contingent upon social insurance activation, but also upon education and training, and even health care. All these provisions impact on life chances. Furthermore, childcare provision critically influences female labor market participation. Pensions regulate orderly transitions out of employment in old age, enabling employers to effectively manage their labor force. Together, different social provisions shape the life course by creating predictable transitions between work, care, and spells of inactivity and the timing of education, family formation, and retirement.

For an adequate understanding of the dynamic of especially contemporary welfare state development under the new rules of global competition, the new shape of working life, the new realities of family and gender relations, and demographic aging, there is an even greater need to unravel the interaction and spillover effects across a broad range of interdependent areas of social and economic regulation, beyond passive social insurance protection. Welfare states are multidimensional policy systems, made up of interdependent social and economic policy repertoires with different dimensions. As a social risks mitigating device, it is particularly necessary to consider how macroeconomic policy, labor market regulation, social insurance, and taxation work together to reduce the risks of poverty, unemployment, and social and labor market exclusion. Drawing on an expanding literature of comparative welfare reform, I propose to briefly look at some key policy changes across time: (1) macroeconomic policy (including fiscal, exchange rate, and monetary policy); (2) wage bargaining and industrial relations; (3) labor market policy; (4) labor market regulation; (5) social insurance and social assistance; (6) old age pensions; (7) family and social servicing; (8) welfare financing; and (9) governance and social policy administration. I concentrate on the recent social reform momentum in the older EU15 Member States of the European Union.

In *macroeconomic policy*, Keynesian priorities were prevalent until the late 1970s, with full employment as the principal goal of macroeconomic management.

After 1980, macroeconomic policy gave way to a stricter rule-based fiscal and monetary policy framework centered on economic stability, hard currencies, low inflation, sound budgets, and public debt reduction, culminating in the introduction of the European Monetary Union (EMU) (Dyson & Featherstone, 1999; Scharpf, 2000; Eichengreen, 2007; Lindvall, 2010). Especially, the swift liberalization of capital markets precluded the kind of reflationary fiscal and monetary policy strategies that were pursued in the 1970s. Moreover, EMU restrictions on monetary and fiscal policies led many policymakers across Europe to bring social and employment policy to the center of welfare state adjustment over the 1990s.

In the field of *wage policy*, the 1980s saw a reorientation in favor of market-based wage restraint in order to facilitate competitiveness, profitability, and employment growth, prompted by the new rule-based macroeconomic policy prescription. Wage moderation has in many countries been pursued through social pacts among the trade unions, employer organizations, and government, often linked with wider packages of negotiated reform that have made taxation, social protection, and pension and labor market regulation more "employment friendly." Social pacts spearheaded by internationally exposed sectors, under close monitoring by central banks and wage growth among European trading partners, gained policy preference in many countries over the alternative of straightforward labor market deregulation and wage bargaining decentralization. In the 1990s, the EMU entrance exam played a critical role in national social pacts in the so-called hard-currency latecomer countries, such as Italy, Spain, and Portugal (Pochet & Fajertag, 2000; Dølvik, 2004; Baccaro & Simoni, 2008; Avdagic et al., 2011).

In the area of *labor market policy*, in the 1990s the new objective became maximizing employment. Spending on active labor market policies in most OECD countries has increased considerably from the 1990s and the mid-2000s, in the context of falling unemployment rates, mobilizing women, youth, older workers, and less productive workers through early intervention, case management, and conditional benefits gained sway (Clasen & Clegg, 2011; Van Vliet, 2010). Bonoli (2011) convincingly argues that the novelty of the new approach lies in the combination of investment in human capital and stronger work incentives. In all countries (except Italy) we see a general convergence in active labor market policies, although some countries stress human capital investment (the Nordic countries and France), while others emphasize labor market re-entry (the Netherlands, Germany, the United Kingdom). A series of labor market reforms in Denmark over the 1990s gradually implemented a right and a duty to activation. This included the introduction of mandatory, individual action plans to activate the unemployed within three to five months and the abolishment of a system that passively accorded generous benefits (Goul Andersen, 2011).

With respect to *labor market regulation*, several European countries have moved toward greater acceptance of flexible labor markets. The introduction of these "active" elements into the Danish labor market, mentioned above, gave rise to the "flexicurity" model (Campbell & Hall, 2006). Flexicurity entails the view that social policies and labor market regulation should simultaneously augment labor market flexibility to address the needs of firms while expanding social policies to enable workers to find employment (Wilthagen, 1998; Wilthagen et al., 2004). Flexicurity triangulates flexible labour markets, generous unemployment benefits, and active labour market policies, so as to reduce unemployment and improve the quality and supply of workers to the labour market, with the aim of correcting the imbalance between an inflexible labor market for core workers and precarious work for the growing contingency workforce. It builds on the concept of the 'transitional labor market' (Schmid 2006; 2008), which underscores the need to adjust the qualifying criteria for social policies to accommodate more frequent transitions in and out of employment. The Danish arrangement of easy hiring and firing, generous unemployment benefits, and active labor market policy, was hailed by the European Employment Strategy (EES) as an *example par excellence* for simultaneously enhancing flexibility and security in the labor market, reconciling employers' need for a flexible work force with workers' preference for employment security. In the Netherlands, the 2000 Working Hours Act now gives part-timers an explicit right to equal treatment in all areas negotiated by the social partners (Hemerijck, 2003). Meanwhile, governments in many European countries have increased the scope for temporary work and fixed-term contracts.

In terms of *social insurance* and *assistance*, the generosity of benefits has been curtailed. There have been reductions in benefit levels and benefit duration, the eligibility criteria of social provisions have been tightened, and the coverage of benefits has been limited. Through the weakening of earnings-related benefit provision and by harmonizing benefits across different risk categories, social insurance benefits have become less status confirming. As income replacement policies have been curtailed, activation and active labor market policies have expanded significantly (Kenworthy, 2008; 2010; Eichhorst et al., 2008; Bonoli, 2011; 2012). Access to social insurance for inactive able-bodied persons has become progressively conditional on participation in training and counselling programs and behavioral requirements, such as job search obligations (Van Gerven, 2008; Weishaupt, 2011). Clasen & Clegg (2011) observe a trend toward benefit homogenization, suggesting a reduction in variation and conditions of entitlement across different tiers of social protection, such as unemployment insurance and social assistance in countries like the UK, the Netherlands, Germany, Denmark, and Belgium. In the Netherlands, reforms increased the employment requirements of the disabled, single mothers, and older workers (Hoogenboom, 2011). Conditionality and job search requirements have been tightened in Denmark and Sweden (Goul Andersen, 2011; Sjöberg, 2011). In Denmark, the so-called "passive period" without the right and duty to activation was reduced sequentially from four years in 1990 to six months for jobseekers under 30 years of age and to nine months for adult jobseekers in 2007 (Kvist et al., 2008: 227). Similarly, successive British Labour governments have departed from the liberal path since 1997 by developing an "enabling" welfare state that makes most of its provisions contingent upon paid employment (Clasen, 2005). The introduction of the New Deal in 1998 built on the requirement that the unemployed actively seek work in exchange for benefits. Even where insiders remain protected by strong insurance policies, new activation policies have expanded the range of mechanisms to help workers (re-)integrate more quickly into the labor market. In addition, policymakers have strengthened minimum income protection, coupled with more "demanding" activation and "enabling" reintegration measures (Palier, 2011a). In countries like Belgium, France, and the Netherlands, activation programs based on individual guidance and training opportunities, primarily targeting "outsiders" like the young, female, or low-skill workers, have gained momentum over the past two decades. These reforms have also begun shifting privileges away from insiders (male breadwinners and their dependents) by opening insurance benefits to outsiders, introducing paid maternity leave, and improving social rights for part-time workers and minimum income protection (Hemerijck, 2013).

In 2004 and 2005, the influential Hartz reforms expanded the low-wage sector through new tax and contribution exemptions and reductions. Although most measures were related to active labor market policies, the most controversial element included the merging of unemployment assistance and social assistance (Fleckenstein, 2008). These changes involved drastically shortening benefit durations for all unemployed, hiking the early retirement age for elderly unemployed from 60 years to 63 years, tightening requirements to accept suitable jobs, simplifying insurance regulations, and merging unemployment assistance with social assistance. The latter implies that only those unemployed who fulfill certain qualifying conditions are entitled indefinitely (Weishaupt, 2011). The French *Revenu minimum d'insertion* (RMI) is a case in point. The general trend is the shift from "out-of-work benefits" to "in-work benefits," including job-search obligations, in many European countries with greater "targeting" and "selectivity" of resources for those most in need (Eichhorst et al., 2008). Several European countries have experimented with "employment-conditional earnings subsidies," ranging from the Working Tax Credit (WTC), the "Prime Pour l'Emploi" (PPE) and the Revenue de Solidarité Active (rSa) in France, the "Combination Credit" in the Netherlands, and a "Low Wage Tax Credit" in Belgium (Marx, 2007).

Old age pensions are often seen as the most resilient artifacts of the post-War welfare state, "least likely" to confront profound reform. Financing problems due to population aging and lower growth prompted widespread reform. Steps have been taken to reverse the trend toward early retirement policies, together with initiatives to promote longer and healthier working lives. A string of adjustments, however, have fundamentally altered retirement welfare over the past two decades (Ebbinghaus, 2011; Bonoli & Palier, 2008). A key shift has been the growth of (compulsory) occupational and private pensions and the development of multipillar systems, combining pay-as-you-go and fully funded methods, with relatively tight (actuarial) links between the pension benefits and contributions, with strong incentives to delay early exit from the labor market and award those working longer (Clark & Whiteside, 2003; Häuserman, 2010). Countries responded to initial financial difficulties by increasing contributions or transfers from the state budget. A strong trend toward development of funded pensions, the third pillar of pension policy, is apparent throughout Europe. The role of funded pensions is particularly developed in the Netherlands, Switzerland, and Iceland. There also have been efforts to improve the regulatory framework of funded pensions. Many countries have shifted from defined benefits to defined contributions (Ebbinghaus, 2011). Virtually all European countries have introduced fiscal incentives to take up supplementary private pension insurance. While Germany and the United Kingdom are about to raise the official retirement age, Finland is bent on improving occupational health, work ability, and the well-being of aging workers so as to keep them in the workforce (Immergut et al., 2007). In Italy and Spain, pension reform has gone hand-in-hand with attempts to upgrade minimum retirement guarantees. In addition, measures to combine work and retirement, with tax allowances and partial pension benefits, have been introduced in Denmark and Finland. One of the most profound pension reforms was enacted by Sweden in the mid-1990s, introducing a small mandatory funded element and transferring an important part of the risk associated with aging onto (future) retirees, by way of indexing future benefits to the life expectancy and net wages, while at the same time ensuring a universally guaranteed pension for low-income pensioners (Palme, 2005).

Social services have significantly expanded, especially in the 2000s, to boost female participation through active family policy (Lewis, 2006; Mahon, 2002; 2006; Ungerson, 2004; Orloff, 2006; 2009; 2010). Spending on family services, child care, education, health, and care for the elderly, as well as on training and employment services, has increased as a percentage of GDP practically everywhere in the European Union (Jenson, 2006; 2009; OECD, 2007; 2011). Family policy, which covers child care, parental leave, and employment regulation, as well as work and family life reconciliation policies, has been subject to profound change in both scope and substance over the past decade and half (Daly, 2010). Since the 1950s, most measures taken in the field of family policy primarily concerned passive income support measures to help male breadwinner family households in the costs of child rearing (Gauthier, 1996). Since the 1990s, family policies have experienced a remarkable metamorphosis. Traditional "passive" cash measures were complemented with "activating" services, such as childcare and parental leave schemes, to help reconcile work and family life, as well as to foster higher levels of female employment, reflecting a change in orientation toward the norm of dual-earner households (Bradshaw & Finch, 2010; Plantenga et al., 2012). A core feature concerns new provisions to resolve dilemmas associated with women's new career preferences (Gautier, 1996; Hakim, 2000; Orloff, 2006; Esping-Andersen, 2009). The available evidence suggests that many countries have moved toward the expansion of policies to facilitate work-life reconciliation.

Pioneers in such reconciliation policies include the Nordic countries and France, followed by the "path-shifters" of Germany, the Netherlands, and the UK, and finally slow reformers, such as Austria, Italy, and Spain (Morgan, 2008; 2012). For Denmark, the 1990s witnessed the expansion of services for children and the elderly, the expansion of parental leave opportunities, and the introduction of specific activation instruments for mothers returning to work (Pfau-Effinger & Rostgaard, 2011). Leave arrangements have been expanded, in terms of both time and scope of coverage, including the frail elderly. In the United Kingdom, a variety of legislation was initiated to promote the reconciliation of work and family life (more childcare facilities, paid maternity leave, a leave entitlement for fathers, and flexible working time (Clasen, 2005). Child care has expanded since the late 1990s in Germany and the Netherlands (Morgan, 2008). German and Dutch governments increased spending and pushed for more flexible childcare facility opening hours in order to enlarge the number of available and affordable childcare places, although this has not gone so far as to indicate a commitment to a "service state." To help reconcile work and family life, childcare and parental leave arrangements were expanded, including for part-time workers. Germany offers two "daddy months" for working fathers (Korthouwer, 2010). Dutch life course schemes grant an additional payment worth 50% of the minimum wage during periods of parental leave. Finally, social service provision to the frail elderly is rapidly becoming a new modern social policy issue, as younger generations, increasingly adhering to dual-earner family norm, are less able and inclined to provide informal care than previous homemaker/caregiver generations (Knijn, 2012).

With respect to the *financing of the welfare state*, policies have been sought to relieve public finances and to shift some of the responsibility for welfare provision to individual workers or the social partners, and to reduce charges of business and labor. Although a straightforward privatization of social risks has remained a marginal phenomenon across Europe, except for pensions, we do observe an increase in user financing in social services—child care, school education, medical care, old-age care. Especially, private provision of publicly financed services has increased substantially. In parallel, market-oriented administrative practices have also become more widespread. In addition, most countries have reviewed the incentives of their tax/benefit systems in order to make them more "employment-friendly." This development has been motivated by competitiveness concerns, but also by the wish to neutralize the vicious spiral of "welfare without work" generated by "contribution-heavy" Continental social insurance systems (Palier, 2010b). Although many observers feared that tax competition would come to underfinance the welfare state (Sinn, 1990; Steinmo, 1993; Tanzi, 1995; Rodrik, 1997; Swank, 2002; 2006; Swank & Steinmo, 2002), Philipp Genschel & Peter Schwarz (2011) observe that a "race to bottom" through competitive tax cutting does not stand up to empirical scrutiny. Moreover, they found that governments increasingly engage in tax cooperation to reign in tax competition, especially after the financial crisis of 2008, triggered mostly by domestic constraints.

A final overarching reform trend has been *administrative reform*, most important of which is the attempt to bring social insurance and assistance and labor market policies institutionally under one roof in so-called "one-stop centers," thus ending previous separation of social security and public employment administration. Beyond important substantive policy innovation in social security, labor market, and social service provision, many policy changes also implied important reforms in the governance structure, toward more decentralization, marketization, and competition; interagency cooperation; and new public management (Berkel & Borghi, 2008; Berkel et al., 2011). Ideas of New Public Management (NPM) and novel concepts of *purchaser-provider* models within public welfare services have been especially instructive with respect to the restructuring of Public Employment Services (PES), since the 1990s (Weishaupt, 2011). The trend toward greater marketization is perhaps most pronounced. Contracting out integration services and expanding temporary employment agencies in labor market allocation are widely followed strategies in European countries. Marketization has often but not always increased the number of actors involved in the governance of unemployment benefit regimes. Although increased cooperation among different levels of government has expanded in practically all cases, the UK remains the most centralized system, along with Finland. The Netherlands has moved toward the opposite on the other extreme. Germany and Sweden initially decentralized and then later recentralized active labor market policies (Clasen & Clegg, 2011; Dingeldey, 2011). Further variation exists regarding whether the social partners retain a role in the governance of unemployment benefits and active labor market policies. Social partners remain deeply involved in the administration of the system in France (Palier, 2010c), whereas a diminishing role of the social partners is apparent in Germany and the Netherlands (Dingeldey, 2011; Hemerijck, 2003). The general shift from income maintenance programs to services in welfare provision, moreover, has been accompanied by individualization and customization of new public-private mixes in capacitating local social servicing, requiring high-quality institutional competencies for policy administration and discretionary implementation in career guidance, (re-)training and rehabilitation services, and child and elder care provision adjusted to the specific needs and capabilities of individual clients. In short, the division of labor in welfare provision among family responsibilities, commercial market social services, and public provision has been redrafted throughout the EU (Le Grand, 2007; Pollitt, 2003; Pollitt & Bouckaert, 2004).

Although we live in a world of path-dependent solutions, the wide-ranging postformative welfare reform momentum, with significant domestic variation, adds up to a broad, cumulative process of welfare state (self-)transformation across the Member States of the European Union (Hemerijck, 2002). The inventory of social reforms from before the economic crisis reveals, contrary to

Paul Pierson's conjecture of change-resistant welfare states, that the majority of European welfare states have, interactively, made complementary reforms across macroeconomic policy, industrial relations, taxation, social security, labor market policy, employment protection legislation, pensions, social services, welfare financing, and social and employment policy administration. These are big policy changes, many of which also apply to the allegedly most "inert" and "locked-in" German model of the turn of the century (Vail, 2010; Eichhorst & Kaiser, 2006; Stiller, 2010; Palier, 2010a; Weishaupt, 2010)! Even though public social spending has been consolidated, practically all advanced European welfare states have been recasting and reconfiguring the basic policy mixes upon which they were built after 1945. The economists Duval & Elmeskov (2006), in an attempt to quantify reform intensity across the OECD, have reached the conclusion that, over the period between 1994 and 2004, the propensity to enact welfare and labor market reforms has been greater in the EU15 countries as compared to a number of OECD countries outside the EU. Based on alternative indicators from 1995 to 2005, Bertola et al. (2011) and Boeri & Garibaldi (2009), similarly, observe a strong acceleration of social reforms, with eurozone member states significantly intensifying the reform momentum over the period of the establishment of EMU. Especially since the mid-1990s, the welfare state has been in a constant state of flux. Has the "era of austerity" become an epoch "permanent welfare change"?

8.3 TOWARD SOCIAL INVESTMENT?

Because social policy repertoires have almost constantly been evolving, it is imperative to appreciate the dynamic of the recent reform momentum. I agree with Pierson that taking the long view is essential here. However, without proper contextualization, any list of intense social policy changes remains unsatisfactory. Are we not risking exchanging a social protection bias for the selection bias of hunting down each and every adjustment effort without correcting for important dimensions of institutional continuity? To invoke a notion of profound welfare state change suggests that after a certain interval of time welfare regimes substantively differ significantly from before. The emergence and diffusion of the so-called "social investment perspective" in the second half of the 1990s can be employed as a benchmark for gauging substantive social policy redirection over the past two decades (Morel et al., 2012).

The social investment turn, pioneered by leading experts and intellectuals like Gøsta Esping-Andersen (1999; 2002) and Anthony Giddens (1998; 2001), was advocated in terms of a determinate departure from the institutional and ideological foundations of both the post-War male breadwinner, social insurance, welfare state, and its 1980s neoliberal successor of labor market deregulation and welfare retrenchment. The philosophy underpinning the social investment perspective was given more substance by the publication of a book edited by Esping-Andersen et al. in 2002, *Why We Need a New Welfare State* (Esping-Andersen et al., 2002). Commissioned by the Belgian presidency of the EU in 2001, it endorsed the view that "the single greatest challenge we face today is how to rethink social policy so that, once again, labor markets and families are welfare optimizers and a good guarantee that tomorrow's adult workers will be as productive and resourceful as possible" (Esping-Andersen et al., 2002: 25). The key idea, in terms of policy, was to "prepare" individuals, families, and societies to adapt to various transformations, such as changing career patterns and working conditions, the development of new social risks, population aging, and climate change, instead of simply "repairing" damage after passive social policies prove inadequate. Central to *Why We Need a New Welfare State* is the argument that the prevailing inertia in male breadwinner welfare provision fosters increasingly suboptimal life chances in labor market opportunities, income, educational attainment, and intra- and intergenerational fairness, for large shares of the population. The new social risks of social segmentation, skill erosion, and structural poverty dynamics in the knowledge-based service economy—pressed by demographic aging—make traditionally passive, employment-related, social insurance provision extremely expensive and ultimately unsustainable. Instead, they underline the importance of early childhood development, training, education and lifelong learning, and family reconciliation policies, so as to promote the long-term development of human capital. And because the heaviest burden of new social risks falls on the younger cohorts, in terms of policy redirection, Esping-Andersen et al. explicitly advocate a reallocation of social expenditures toward family services, active labor market policy, early childhood education, and vocational training, so as to ensure productivity improvement and high employment for both men and women in the knowledge based-economy. It is also important to add that Esping-Andersen et al. (2002) emphasized—*contra* the Third Way—that social investment is no substitute for social protection. Adequate minimum income protection is a critical precondition for an effective social investment strategy (Vandenbroucke, 2002). In other words "social protection" and "social promotion" should be understood as the indispensible twin pillars of the new social investment welfare edifice. In terms of concrete policy advice, linchpin policies of the social investment edifice included a child-centered investment strategy, human capital formation, employment activation, labor market flexibility with generous social security and adequate minimum support, gender mainstreaming, family servicing, reconciling work and family life, avoiding early retirement, encouraging more flexible patterns of retirement, while raising the statutory pension age.

Given that many of these ideas of social investment were first ventured over a decade ago, it is worthwhile to take note of the more general direction of European social policy transformation: Have European welfare states recalibrated their social policy systems in accordance with the teachings of social investment perspective? Or has social investment been a political cover for stealthy retrenchment and deconstruction or a Machiavellian foil for reconsolidating old social contracts, pressed by the strong and long-established clientelistic networks around the welfare state? To what extent does the reform inventory listed in the previous section suggest that social investment priorities have been incorporated into social reform? I wish to highlight three overarching, long-run changes that indeed lend plausible empirical support to the social investment turn (Hemerijck, 2013; Chapter 5).

8.3.1 From Fighting Unemployment to Raising Labor Market Participation

Different policy provisions have been brought into new institutional relationships with each other based on important redefinitions of salient social policy problems across time. In line with the general shift to supply-side economics, the overarching social policy objective shifted in the 1990s from fighting unemployment to proactively promoting labor market participation. As income protection remained the key function of social insurance policy, it was increasingly complemented with employment activation and reintegration measures, evident in augmented conditionality for unemployment insurance and social assistance benefits and supported by active labor market policy measures. Employment protection legislation, a quintessential old social risk category, serving to protect labor market insiders, has been curtailed in many countries, especially with regard to restrictions on part-time and temporary work. The integration of vulnerable groups into the labor market, improved coverage of the social risks associated with family instability, policy support for accommodating the feminization of the labor market, as a consequence, have generally received preferential treatment.

8.3.2 Toward Capacitating Social Services

Loosely aligned with the shift toward activation, the development of capacitating social services for dual-earner families marks a clear departure from the longstanding male breadwinner/female homemaker legacy, especially in continental Europe. Family support, gender roles, and particularly child care, have indeed moved to the center of recent social reform. One of the fundamental reasons why the "active" welfare state today must provide enabling and capacitating social services is inherently related to the erosion of the effectiveness of the social insurance principle, upon which the post-War transfer-biased male breadwinner welfare state was based. When the risk of industrial unemployment was largely cyclical, it made sense to administer collective social insurance funds for consumption smoothing during spells of demand-deficient unemployment. When the risk of unemployment becomes structural, caused by radical shifts in labor demand and supply, however, unemployment insurance can no longer function as a reserve income buffer between similar jobs. For the effective mitigation of *new social risks*, such as skill depletion and tension between work and family responsibilities, the new welfare state must provide capacitating services tailored to particular social needs. Such services, in fact, better protect citizens against new labor market risks than unemployment benefits. What is important to underscore here, is that 21st century welfare provision addresses a wider range of social risks with a broader array of policy intervention, far beyond social insurance narrowly understood.

8.3.3 From "Freedom from Want" to "Freedom to Act"

We seem have entered a distinctively new phase of welfare state development, characterized by an incipient move toward active *service-oriented* welfare states, away from the traditional passive, *transfer-oriented* systems of the past. Today, the highest levels of employment are found in the Nordic countries, which have been able to hold on to more generous welfare systems in the affluent world, by shifting emphasis from social compensation to citizenship empowerment with state-provided or regulated human capital investments and social service quality improvements throughout the life course.

The welfare state, it should not be forgotten, is a normative concept based on the image of a social contract, with claims on equity and fairness, which goes far beyond issues of economic redistribution and insurance, to include dimensions of gender roles, the work ethic, child rearing and intergenerational equity. In times of transformation, the articulation of competing value perspectives is essential to changing welfare states. The changes listed above have contributed to a slow redefinition in the very idea of social justice: a shift away from understanding fairness in terms of static income equality toward an understanding of solidarity and fairness as an obligation to give due support to the needs of each, individually, so as to enable all to flourish (Jenson, 2009; 2010; 2012). At the heart of the new welfare state gestalt also lies a reorientation in social citizenship, away from the compensating *freedom from want* logic toward the capacitating logic of *freedom to act*, under the proviso of accommodating work and family life through social servicing and a guaranteed *rich social minimum* serving citizens to pursue fuller and more satisfying lives. In order to connect social policy more fully with a more dynamic economy and society, citizens have to be endowed with capabilities (Sen, 1999; 2001) through active policies that intervene early in the life cycle rather than later with more expensive passive and reactive policies.

8.4 THE ECONOMICS OF SOCIAL INVESTMENT

An emphasis on the productive function of social policy stands as the distinguishing feature of the social investment perspective. From this perspective, social investment is essentially an encompassing human capital strategy with an explicit focus on helping both men and women balance earning and caring (Bernard & Boucher, 2007). Welfare states need to be recast to optimize their potential. By raising employment and citizens' productivity the financial sustainability of the welfare state is best guaranteed (Esping-Andersen et al., 2002). If successful, social investments relieve dependence on passive social insurance provision, without having to further retrench benefits.

Social investment protagonists hold the relationship between substantive social policy and economic performance to be critically dependent on identifying institutional conditions, at the micro-, meso-, and macrolevels, under which it is possible to formulate and implement productive social policies. The economic and institutional policy analysis of social investment relies heavily on empirical data and case-by-case comparisons. It is crucial to consider the "fine" structures of the welfare state. Social policy is never a productive factor *per se*. One cannot turn a blind eye to the negative, unintended, and perverse side effects of excessively generous social security benefits of long duration, undermining work incentives, raising the tax burden, and contributing to high gross wage costs. And, by the same token, rigid forms of dismissal protection making hiring and firing unnecessarily costly can result in high levels of inactivity (Hemerijck, 2013; Chapter 7).

Beyond these caveats, in agreement with Keynesian economics, the social investment paradigm makes a virtue of the argument that a strong economy requires a strong welfare state. Social protection expenditures are powerful stabilizers of economic activity at the macrolevel, because they consolidate effective demand during recessions. This kind of Keynesianism through the back door is still operative today, as we have experienced from the early days of the 2007–2010 financial crisis. Alongside this nuanced reappreciation of the Keynesian welfare policy legacy, the economic policy analysis of social investment shares with the neoliberal critique of the welfare state a strong focus on the supply-side. Social investments today generate private and public dividends in the mid- to long-term. There is also a deliberate orientation toward "early identification" and "early action" targeted on the more vulnerable new risks groups.

A fundamental unifying tenet of the economics of the social investment perspective bears on its theory of the state. Distancing themselves from the neoliberal "negative" economic theory of the state, social investment advocates view public policy as a key provider for families and labor markets. They do so on the basis of a far less sanguine understanding of efficient markets. Neoclassical economic policy analysis, based on perfect information and market clearing, theoretically rules out the kind of social risks and market failures that the welfare state seeks to address. Also, because neoclassical economics focuses only on the (public) cost side of the welfare state, it is unable to appreciate its core macro- and microeconomic benefits (Atkinson, 1999). Two economic rationales theoretically support the proficiency of social investment. The first relates to imperfect information (including important information asymmetries) and the capacity of citizens to make adequate choices on the basis of the information that is available. Therefore, the first rationale for public intervention harks back to the original economic rationale for collective social insurance, countering market inefficiencies caused by asymmetric information, and to the economic rationale for social policy interventions related to the problems of imperfect information and the framing of choice in a more general sense (see Barr, 2004). This is what Nicholas Barr has coined as the "piggy-bank" function of the welfare state (Barr, 2001). Because citizens often lack the requisite information and capabilities to make enlightened choices, many postindustrial life-course needs remain unmet because of the market failures of service under provision at too high a cost.

But the economics of social investment and its reaffirmation of the role of the state do not stop with "piggy-bank" rationality. The more fundamental reason why the welfare state today must be "active" and provide enabling social services is inherently bound up with the declining effectiveness of the logic of social insurance ever since the 1980s. When the risk of industrial unemployment was still largely cyclical, it made perfect sense to administer collective social insurance funds for consumption smoothing during spells of Keynesian demand-deficient unemployment. However, when unemployment becomes structural, caused by radical shifts in labor demand and supply, intensified international competition, skill-biased technological change, the feminization of the labor market, family transformation, and social and economic preferences for more flexible employment relations, traditional unemployment insurance no longer functions as an effective reserve income buffer between jobs in the same industry. Basic public income guarantees, therefore, have to be complemented with *capacitating* public services, a term coined by Charles Sabel, tailored to particular social needs caused by life course contingencies (Sabel et al., 2010; see also Gilbert, 2002). Because it is difficult to privately and/or collectively insure new social risks, and because capacitating social services are not self-evidently supplied by private markets, it becomes imperative for public policy to step in for effective protection against new social risks. At the same time, however, capacitating services must be customized to individual needs across the life cycle to be effective.

Social spending organized so as to make people more productive (through public education, support for child care and parental leave, and public health), and universal programs to minimize administrative costs and work incentive problems, require highly professional institutional capabilities in terms not only of policy-making, but also in terms of policy implementation and evaluation. The importance of institutional capacities so as to make social investments work cannot be overstated. What matters at the policymaking level are coordinated and mutually reinforcing complementary policy packages affecting all welfare and labor market institutions, many of which have to be negotiated with various stakeholders, such as the social partners and care professionals. What matters at the level of policy implementation is that, as welfare states become ever more service-oriented, local service provision offers highly qualified professional care workers, able to help clients to make timely choices in areas of childcare placement, job search and training, and elder and family care. Finally, in terms of policy analysis, because the devil of social investment is in the details of policy interdependencies between passive and active social policies over the life cycle, there is constant need for reliable ex post and ex ante evaluation of the strength and weakness of various policy options and interdependencies in light of variegated social and economic contexts, with appropriate and independent monitoring functions.

Extensive comparative empirical research has since the turn of the century revealed that there is no trade-off between macroeconomic performance and the size of the welfare state. The presence of a large public sector does not necessarily damage competitiveness; there is a positive relationship between fertility and high levels of female participation in most Scandinavian countries; and finally, high numeracy and literacy rates can be achieved with educational policies that abide by the principle of equal opportunity. Inequality is reduced by diminishing the human capital gap between high- and low-wage individuals. Universal and high-quality care increases equity, in labor force participation and earnings, while mitigating the risk of poverty, especially for women and children. To the extent that social investment policies are coordinated along a life course perspective, they, in turn, produce the highest payoffs in participation and productivity. In addition, socialized welfare servicing not only enables women to work on a full-time basis, it also allows them and their partners to have the number of children they aspire, which in turn serves to mitigate the social and financial pressures of demographic aging (Hemerijck, 2002; 2012; Eichhorst, & Hemerijck, 2010; Swank, 2002; Fouarge, 2003; Kenworthy, 2004; 2008; 2011). To be sure, social investment does not come cheap. High social spending has to be matched by high taxes or social contributions to which many people contribute. For this, fiscal and transfer policies need to be finely tuned and closely monitored, in a way that maximizes employment and economic growth (Lindert, 2004). High social spending can thus help promote productive capacity, reconciling workers and citizens to the social and economic challenges of the 21st century of aging populations, changing households, and the rise of internationally competitive knowledge economies (Ferrera et al., 2000).

Social investments harbor a reliable positive impact on the economy, although it takes considerable time for them to pay off. Under the rule-based macroeconomic framework of EMU, the explicit reappraisal of the role of the state as a necessary social investor, however, is confronted with a disconcerting public finance limitation, stipulating balanced budgets and price stability as overriding conditions for macroeconomic stability, anchored in the Maastricht criteria and the Stability and Growth Pact. While all the available evidence suggests that investments in child care and education will, in the long-run, pay for themselves, EMU public finance constraints consider any form of social policy spending as pure consumption. This may be true for the modus operandi of the post-War welfare state, which was indeed income-transfer biased. Today, as the welfare state is in the process of becoming more service based, there is a clear need to distinguish social investments from consumption spending. A new regime of public finance that would allow finance ministers to (a) identify real public investments with estimated real return, and (b) examine the joint expenditure trends in markets and governments alike, has become imperative. This would be akin to distinguishing between current and capital accounts in welfare state spending, just as private companies do, as Esping-Andersen argues (2006). A new public accounting regime can comply with fiscal orthodoxy, suggesting tightening of current spending, as long as leeway for social investment spending with the effect of improving health of the economy and its growth potential in the long run is allowed. There is even an argument to be made that public deficits and debt wisely spent on social investment in education and family support, can help stabilize the macroeconomy. This in two ways: first, by depriving financial institutions of excess liquidity for short-term speculation, and, second, by nourishing sustained job and productivity growth with social progress and well-being.

8.5 BEYOND FROZEN WELFARE STATES

The overall scope of social reform across the Member States of the European Union, surveyed in this contribution, is, of course, heterogeneous, disparate, and uneven. On balance, however, I observe trajectories of welfare reform in many countries that are more proactive and reconstructive, rather than purely defensive and deconstructive. Alongside serious retrenchments, there have been deliberate attempts to rebuild social programs and institutions to accommodate policy repertoires to the new economic and social realities of the 21st century, roughly in line with social investment priorities, in many advanced European welfare states, in the fields of family services, gender equality, employment policy and labor market regulation, and human capital formation.

Because of the emergence and proliferation of these novel welfare mixes, preceding the global financial crisis, we are in dire need of an alternative analytical perspective that allows for a better and nuanced understanding of these more positive, multidimensional, and dynamic trajectories of social reform, in comparison with the biased "new" politics conjecture of change-resistant social insurance provision. If policymakers, contrary to received wisdom, do engage in major social reforms, in spite of highly relevant political and institutional obstacles, to the extent of potentially undermining (re)election chances, what distinguishes them and the institutional setting within which they operate from the purported general case of welfare state inertia?

Welfare reform is difficult, but it happens. Institutional inertia is an ordinary part of postformative welfare state development. Paul Pierson's path-breaking studies on the political incentives of blame avoidance and organized interest opposition continue to be extremely valuable contributions to our understanding of the modern social politics in affluent democracies. But when taken too far, Pierson's conjectures become unnecessarily overgeneralized and deterministic, and unlikely to offer much analytical purchase on complex processes of profound postformative welfare state change.

The inputs of the *irresistible forces* welfare states are facing up, together with the outputs of welfare states as *immovable objects* are well defined in the "new" politics literature; their mutual interaction, however, is unduly neglected. Fiscal strain coming from demographic aging, intensified market competition from low-wage manufacturing around the globe, the removal of national economic boundaries through the European integration, are practically all understood in *regressive* terms, ready to undermine the redistributive scope of the welfare state. On the output side, the welfare status quo is preserved through self-serving blame-avoiding politics, reform-opposing collective action, and institutional inertia per se. There is hardly any feedback effect between outside pressures and policy responses through relevant policy actors.

It is my contention that the past two decades have not been merely ones of straightforward regressive institutional liberalization. *On the input side* of external challenges, both demographic aging and greater gender equality should count as important welfare successes. Population aging, to the extent that it reflects increased life expectancy in good health, through the introduction of old age pensions, is one of the great achievements of post-War welfare state innovation. More recently, gender equality, also pressed for by the EU, liberating women to choose a career and decide under which conditions they form families and raise children, also represents real social progress. Moreover, the effects of social and economic change are never uniform. Pressures of economic internationalization, labor market change, and adverse demography, trigger different reform agendas, but they do not determine policy content, and the timing and scope of policy change. The term "permanent austerity," suggesting long-term economic stagnation, moreover, is somewhat misleading. With an average growth rate of above 2.3% of GDP per year over the past three decades of alleged austerity, the EU15 economy has nearly doubled. This has been largely sufficient to sustain comprehensive welfare commitments.

On the output side of institutional responses, in the decade leading up to the crisis, the Nordic welfare states have achieved the highest rates of growth and employment participation, while preserving generous unemployment, disability benefits, old age pensions and expensive active labor market policy, and expanding quality family servicing and long-term care. Other European countries, Germany, the Netherlands, the United Kingdom, Ireland, and Spain followed suit with important social reforms in labor markets, retirement policy, and family servicing, supporting women and lone parents' employment, early childhood education and care, and specific forms of labor market regulation and social protection institutions that promote flexible security, suggest forms of welfare reconstruction, which—in conjunction—are difficult to locate on a straight line between the poles of radical retrenchment and reform resistance.

Beyond the recalibrated Scandinavian welfare states, whose social investment roots can be traced back to the 1930s (Andersson, 2004), very few countries can be said to have implemented social investment policies in a comprehensive fashion, enough to stem the tide of income polarization, rising in-work poverty, precarious work and social segmentation, and economic dualization (Palier & Thelen, 2010). Despite growing evidence that social investment priorities are being broadly pursued in many European welfare states, many empirical studies reveal significant limits. Activating reforms in the UK, for instance, are found to impinge on the autonomy of lone parents by failing to fully address adverse barriers in combining care and earner responsibilities (Daly, 2010; Wright, 2011). Other studies criticize active labor market policies in terms of low-quality employment (Graziano 2007; 2011) or restricting access (Betzelt & Bothfeld, 2011) to education and training. Especially, in the more "segmented" labor markets of Continental Europe and most Mediterranean countries, the position of nonstandard workers hardly has been improved (Palier, 2010a). In Germany, various reforms lowered the benefits for low-wage and atypical workers through revaluation and the elimination of pension credits during periods of education or long-term unemployment (Hinrichs, 2011). The Italian case is criticized as promoting flexibility without security (Jessoula & Alti, 2010). Even in countries broadly recognized as successful cases of pension reform and "homogenous" labor markets, atypical workers face greater risk today as a result of reforms. In the Netherlands, although part-time workers receive access to normal occupational pensions, temporary and on-call workers face gaps in coverage (Anderson, 2011). Finally, there are important questions as to whether all social groups benefit equally from social investment policies, and, if not, whether social investment supports are really only truly available to the middle class (Cantillon, 2011; Vandenbroucke & Vleminckx, 2011).

Notwithstanding these social investment ambiguities, most EU Member States have undertaken profound social reforms since the 1990s, and not by singularly following the neoliberal and deregulation recipes of the 1980s. The recent reform momentum amounts to neither "neoliberal" convergence nor change-resistant "frozen" welfare states. In some cases, welfare state change has been accompanied by deep social conflicts, while in other instances unpopular social reforms received broad consent from opposition parties, trade unions, and employer organizations (Hemerijck, 2002; 2013; Starke. 2006; 2008). The focus has been on social pacts, activation, active aging/avoidance of early retirement, part-time work, lifelong learning, parental leave, gender mainstreaming, and labor market "flexicurity." In the process, additions and innovations in some policy areas have been accompanied by subtractions in others. The novelty of the recent epoch lies in the simultaneous application of both positive incentives of active and investment-oriented labor market policies and negative incentives of retrenched welfare benefits of shorter duration, increased targeting, and sanctioning. Most recently, in the shadow of the looming fiscal crisis of the state and the euro, countries like Greece, Ireland, Portugal, and Spain, but also France and Italy, have pushed through bold, austerity-oriented social reforms. These reforms, to be sure, draw attention to the mechanism of deep crises as rare opportunities for far-reaching social policy reconfiguration. In Spain, the government has approved giving employers more control over how they deploy workers, while making it cheaper to fire—and, therefore, easier to hire—permanent employees. In Greece, the era of retiring at 50 years of age on full pension has come to an end; people will need to work until 65 years of age, with 40 years' full contributions. Also, France and Italy are taking steps to raise the retirement age from 60 years to 62 years. All these reforms have met with industrial conflict. In the post-crisis context, these protests have hardly led to an insider-biased watering down of reform efforts. Many of the problems in Southern Europe, now critically exposed by the crisis, it is true, lie in inefficient clientelist bureaucracies and organized interests. In the broader experience of European welfare state change, many of the reforms now being enacted in Greece, Spain, and Portugal were implemented in the majority of other West European polities before the onslaught of the Great Recession, under less dire economic conditions and in a far more incremental and negotiated fashion, in the 1990s and early 2000s (see Hemerijck, 2013; Chapter 9).

As I have argued in this chapter, the "new politics" of the welfare state perspective amounts to a denial or downplaying of change in the face of seemingly irresistible epochal forces of social and economic change. In its political analysis, as popular programs are successfully defended by the veto-powers of policy insiders, there is no room for social learning or for incremental, corrective policy making. Political decision-makers merely defend ideological turf, and thus lack any capacity to engage in policy evaluation and information feedback. As a consequence, existing institutional orders simply reproduce themselves. Stein Ringen (1987 [2006 edition]: xlvi) reminds us that the "welfare state is reform on a grand scale. It is an attempt to change the circumstances individuals and families live (...). No less; no wonder it is controversial. *If the welfare state works, reform works*" (my emphasis). A careful analysis of key economic and social changes, together with an understanding of how changing social risks are voiced and mobilized, are indispensible for an empirically grounded, dispassionate and open, theoretical conceptualization of contemporary social policy change. Elsewhere I elaborate upon the imperative of *open institutionalism* for the comparative study of changing welfare states (Hemerijck, 2013; Chapter 4). Any attempt to analyze social policy change should follow a differentiated approach that takes account of the complex character of welfare states—their normative and ideological foundations, their distributive portent, the institutional structures of social programs, and the division of labor of welfare provision and administration among state, market, families, and civil society.

The European welfare reform momentum of the past two decades is best captured as a *search for a new welfare state*. This search process remains incomplete, resulting from the institutionally bounded and contingent adaptation to new social realities. Welfare state change is work in progress, leading to patchwork mixes of old and new policies and institutions, on the lookout perhaps for more coherence. This should not surprise us. The post-1945 modern welfare state was also not built from scratch. Key differences among European welfare states find their origins in the remnants and legacies of earlier episodes of social policy experimentation in the late 19th and early 20th centuries. Also the rise of neoliberal retrenchment was largely evolutionary. Neoliberalism emerged gradually from the elections of Margaret Thatcher and Ronald Reagan three decades ago to achieve global influence with the fall of the Berlin Wall 20 years later. More important still is that neoliberalism did not spell the death of Keynesianism either, as evidenced by the important role of unemployment insurance systems as automatic stabilizers for individual incomes and the European economies as a whole, in the aftermath of the global financial crisis.

What remains in the final analysis is the hypothetical possibility that many items in the concrete policy portfolios that make up modern welfare states have been profoundly transformed, without touching constant spending, near universal social insurance coverage, and high replacement rates. From this reading, social insurance consolidation at the macrolevel has been achieved through determinate reform efforts of raising levels of employment, especially of women and older workers, through activation; active labor market policies and improved child care; and parental leave and family servicing; all following the logic so elegantly portrayed in Giuseppe Tomasi di Lampedusa's novel *Il Gattopardo* (2007 [1958]: 28), when Tancredi Falconeri says "if we want things to stay as they are, things will have to change!" However plausible Pierson's final portrayal of the new early 21st century crisis of the welfare state, this surely is no longer a tale of institutional resilience, in its meaning of the ability and agility to bounce back into shape. Crossing the evocative "Maginot Line" metaphor, rather, suggests the opposite; namely, a tale of institutional atrophy until the welfare status quo ultimately succumbs and breaks down under the weight of the aftershocks of global financial crisis.

I hold the view—or at least working hypothesis—that modern welfare states, administered by democratic polities are able to rebound as they rely on the recuperative resources of their past successes. Welfare states are complex systems, whose goals, functions, and institutions change over time, however slowly and incompletely. They defy easy explanation. In the current context, changing welfare states necessarily follow trajectories of postformative path-dependent transformation and innovation. For this reason, it is imperative to study the politics of changing welfare states, not as models, but, more dynamically, as open systems caught up in processes of evolutionary social and economic reconfiguration.

9

IDENTIFYING THE SKELETON OF THE SOCIAL INVESTMENT STATE: DEFINING AND MEASURING PATTERNS OF SOCIAL POLICY CHANGE ON THE BASIS OF EXPENDITURE DATA

Johan De Deken

The budget is the skeleton of the state, stripped of all misleading ideologies... (Joseph Schumpeter 1918)

9.1 INTRODUCTION

The concept of the "social investment state" appeared in the debates on welfare state reform toward the end of the 1990s (see, for example, Esping-Andersen et al., 2002; Jenson & Saint Martin, 2003; Morel et al., 2011). It can be seen as part of various attempts to justify social policy as a "productive factor" rather than a mere "drain on the economy," an idea also found in the Varieties of Capitalism approach (Hall & Soskice, 2001). Advocates of these kinds of reforms want to reorient social policies from merely compensating misfortunes through income insurance toward instead preventing those misfortunes from occurring in the first place by investing in people's capacities. Activation policies are at the center of such preventive strategies (Bonoli, 2011). The return on investment that is hoped for is an increased labor market participation of the population as well as a higher productivity of those participating. This chapter offers a critical review of the concept of social investment and explores the possibilities and limits of operationalizing it on the basis of social expenditure data.

Ever since the Organisation for Economic Co-operation and Development (OECD) and the statistical office of the European Union (Eurostat) started to make available social expenditure data broken down according to branch and program, it has become possible to carry out a disaggregated analysis of the structure of social expenditure. Such an analysis can offer insights into cross-national differences in the policy priorities of different welfare states, as well as into longitudinal changes within the same country. The metaphor of investment makes the analysis of expenditure data an obvious choice for both attempts to identify to what extent governments have adopted the agenda of an "activating" and "enabling" welfare state (i.e., to use it as a dependent variable in comparative welfare state research), as well as to operationalize policies that can potentially account for cross-national differences in poverty trends (i.e., to use it as an independent variable in research on inequality). In this chapter we will discuss the possibilities and limitations of using expenditure data to measure the social investment state. As such we want to qualify the spending trends that are presented in Meeusen & Nys (2012). In this chapter we will begin by critically reviewing the notion of social investment, elaborate its multiple facets, and link it to identifiable social policy areas. We will develop a typology of social investment that seeks to go beyond a conceptualization based on a mere dichotomy between "compensation" and "investment" by differentiating the concept of investment. We will draw distinctions among different forms of investment: (1) maintenance: maintaining or restoring the capacities of the existing stock of labor market participants; (2) expansion: facilitating the entrance of new labor market participants; (3) enhancement: improving the human capital of new labor market participants. These three types of investment are juxtaposed to policies that offer compensation to those exiting the labor market. Next we will seek to operationalize this typology by placing the different policy branches that the OECD distinguishes in its social expenditure database within the proposed typology. The chapter concludes by discussing a series of methodological problems of interpreting cross-national and longitudinal variation in spending patterns to qualify the observed changes.

9.2 THE SOCIAL INVESTMENT PARADIGM

One could argue that the reproduction of society and the labor force has always been a central goal of welfare state intervention, but the social investment state perspective seems to narrow down the expected return to the reproduction, extension, and enhancement of the labor force. This more narrow conception seems to be related to concerns about the economic sustainability, in particular to the necessity to limit the deterioration of the ratio between the productive capacity of the active population and the needs of the inactive population. As such, the discourse on the social investment state is intimately intertwined with the activation turn in welfare state policies, and calls for building a "knowledge economy" that promotes development of human capital. The main aim of such policies is to produce an adaptable, skilled, and educated workforce that can respond to demands of a so-called "knowledge based" labor market. A second related aspect of the social investment state paradigm is that policies must transform needy citizens from passive recipients of benefits into citizens capable of organizing their integration into society, an integration that primarily is to take place via labor market participation. Such policies are expected to endow the population with the capacity to come to terms with new risks, such as the instability of family structures and the de-standardization of the employment relationship (Bonoli, 2007).

The development of a social investment state entails policy changes along three interrelated dimensions: (1) from "old" to "new" social risks; (2) from "cash benefits" to "social services"; (3) from "ex-post" remedies toward "ex-ante" prevention. Before we will examine to what extent one can use expenditure data for that purpose, we first would like to briefly and critically review these three dimensions.

9.2.1 "Old" and "New" Social Risks

It is not always clear what is "new" about the social risks that are targeted by the social investment state. According to Taylor-Gooby (2004), the novelty lies in the fact that those risks are all related to social changes associated with the transition toward a "postindustrial" society. These changes include the increased entrance of women into the labor market and the difficulties that women, in particular low-skilled women, experience in balancing this paid work and family life; the increase of the absolute and relative number of older people and the implications these increases have for social care and health care; the technological developments that have reduced the proportion of low-skilled manual jobs in industry, which, combined with an intensification of international competition from low-wage countries, have tightened the link between education and employment. According to Taylor-Gooby these changes have resulted in new kinds of needs that existing welfare state programs are incapable of adequately addressing: the need to balance paid work and family responsibilities (in particular for women to take care of their children and of their frail elderly relatives); and the need to upgrade the skills and the kind of training that are required for an adequately paid and secure job, or the need to upgrade skills and forms of training that have become obsolete.[1] Other proponents of the social investment state also cite labor market polarization, the incidence of structural unemployment, and the emergence of work-poor households, in the list of "new" risks, and relate these to the erosion of the effectiveness of the social insurance principles of the "old" welfare state (Esping-Andersen et al., 2002). What are often referred to as "Bismarckian" welfare states, are criticized for their "welfare without work traps," "insider-outsider segmentation," and "perverse familialism" (Palier & Martin, 2007: 542). In order to mitigate the spread of these "new forms of labor market segmentation" those critics call for "employment friendly reforms" intended to reinforce "preventive employability" through policies that weaken dismissal protection, but also ought to generate better security for employees in flexible jobs (Hemerijck & Eichhorst 2009: 28).

One can question though to what extent the rise of structural unemployment can be seen as something really new. Moreover, the polarization of the labor market and the growing army of outsiders are as much a consequence of a retrenchment of the social-insurance-based welfare state and reforms that have reinforced the conditionality of social insurance benefits (Clasen & Clegg, 2007), as they are caused by this very organizational principle. Even though many advocates of an "active welfare state" in principle call for both social investment and stronger incentives to get people to work, in reality governments endorsing the "new welfare settlement" appear to have been more focused on deregulating the labor market, reducing employment protection, restricting access to social insurance, and relying more on means-testing benefits, than they have been pursuing policies that seek to enhance human capital and facilitate labor mobility (Taylor-Gooby, 2008).

Furthermore, the disapproval of the insurance principle by the advocates of the social investment paradigm sits uneasy with the benefits that the Varieties of Capitalism approach attributes to unemployment *insurance* (as compared with flat rate or means-tested forms of *assistance* to the unemployed). Insurance kind of arrangements are said to encourage the acquisition and preservation of skills (Estevez-Abe et al., 2001). One could argue that in some cases unemployment insurance might be rewarding skills that are no longer needed, but this appears to be more a temporary problem, typical for the period of the kind of labor shedding that was adjunct to the transition from a predominantly industrial economy to an economy more based on service sector employment—a conversion that in most European countries was already largely completed by the time the social investment paradigm became en vogue.

The new labor market risks might be less related to the ever changing skill requirements than the advocates of a skill offensive may want us to believe, and rather more a consequence of the erosion of the standard employment relationship and changing career patterns. On the one hand, this does entail the kind of problems Taylor-Gooby associated with attempts to combine full-time paid work and caring responsibilities. On the other hand, the new risks are adjunct to the precarious labor market position of the low-skilled workforce. This precariousness is faced by existing labor market participants, whose industrial skills have become obsolete because this kind of employment was outsourced to low wage countries, as well as by new (primarily female) labor market entrants who seek jobs in the expanding low-skill service economy that predominantly offers non-standard employment contracts.

Moreover, the "new" risk of "insufficient social security coverage" (Bonoli, 2005) is not only a consequence of new career profiles that are typical of postindustrial labor markets, but is also brought about by some of the activation reforms. For example, by making eligibility and entitlement subject to stricter conditions (such as the reduction or abolishment of the periods equivalent to contributory periods), or by changes in conditions of conduct that force those who are out of work into precarious forms of employment (such as activating behavioral requirements that require benefit recipients to accept nonstandard employment contracts) (Clasen & Clegg, 2011). If unemployment benefit systems do not require beneficiaries to take on just any type of employment, atypical employment is less likely to proliferate (De Deken, 2011).

9.2.2 Social Services Facilitating Labor Market Participation and Stimulating the Long-term Development of Human Capital

The social investment state seeks to expand public services to increase the rate of (female) labor force participation, and to foster child development through quality care. Quality care services can "make work pay," in particular for low-income parents, while also providing developmentally enriching services to young children. On first sight the distinction between cash benefits and social services appears relatively straightforward, though in practice it might be more difficult to uphold: Some schemes, such as the service voucher scheme in Belgium, might work with cash transfers to promote the provision of private social services. Even though technically such a scheme can be considered a form of cash benefits (and is classified as such by the OECD), its effects on female labor force participation are pretty similar to those of directly providing public services. It can be seen as a hybrid form of "defamilialization" (Esping-Andersen, 1999) that through public subsidies and regulations tempers the inequality effects of market-based service provision. But because such schemes facilitate (full-time) female employment, they should be seen as a form of social investment and not as a compensatory payment. In addition they contribute to the creation of low-skilled service jobs, in particular for women, without expanding precarious employment conditions.

The effects of some cash benefits, in particular of parental leave schemes, on female labor force participation remains contested.

"Extensive periods of parental caring time can be justified by aspects of the social investment logic and have often been politically popular with the female constituency politicians are trying to reach. Yet, long leaves (...) also undermine employment equality, creating a policy conundrum that no country (...) has yet resolved" (Morgan, 2011: 152).

A similar argument could be made to qualify the beneficial effects of unemployment insurance benefits as suggested by the Varieties of Capitalism approach. Typical insurance kind of features of unemployment benefit systems, such as earnings-related benefits or the ability to reject job offers below one's level of qualification, may protect skill investments in the short or medium term. But in the long term, they might encourage the unemployed to hold onto skills that have become obsolete.

9.2.3 "Ex-post" Remedies and "Ex-ante" Prevention

The social investment state seeks to go beyond merely reproducing the existing labor force, in order to come to terms with the problem of worsening dependency ratios that come with an aging population. Hence, in the social investment paradigm there is a strong emphasis on getting people (back) to work who previously did not work or who were a victim of the labor shedding that came in the wake of deindustrialization.

Preventive action to avoid precariousness and vulnerability can also include various "productive constraints" (Streeck, 1992) such as employment protection and health safety regulations at work, or encompassing accessible health care. The social investment paradigm, however, emphasizes *individual* human capital investments that are expected to enable people to care for themselves in a deregulated labor market, and under the conditions of a trimmed social policy regime in which citizens have far more individual responsibility for their welfare. Nevertheless, many proponents of the paradigm seek to distinguish themselves from the Third Way, which sought to make the entitlement to social rights conditional on "satisfying a corresponding productive obligation" (White 1999: 168). They insist that social investment should not be seen as a substitute for social protection (Esping-Andersen, 2002). Nevertheless, there remains a tension between, on the one hand, calls to reorient policies away from merely passively repairing the damage, toward actively preparing individuals to adapt to various transformations, and, on the other hand, the intention to maintain adequate passive social protection, especially in an era of "permanent austerity" (Pierson, 2001). The only exception to this emphasis on individual agency of the social investment approach appears to consist of measures in the area of family policies. Here preventive action also includes measures to reduce child poverty and to promote the development of cognitive skills of children in early life by providing high-quality public childcare services.

9.2.4 Linking the Social Investment Continuum to Identifiable Policy Categories

On the basis of these three dimensions, social policies can be placed along a continuum of the extent to which they can be expected to generate the kinds of returns that the social investment paradigm seeks to generate: raising labor force participation and productivity. At one end of this continuum one can situate those policies that offer compensation to those exiting the labor market. Though this can boost the productivity of the economy by taking out the less productive elements of the labor force, these policies do reduce the overall productive capacity of the economy because they result in low labor force participation rates. These policies include (early) retirement pensions, disability pensions, survivor pensions, and social and unemployment *assistance* benefit schemes. Next along the continuum one can find policies that allow members of the labor force to maintain or regain their capacity to participate in the labor market. These policies include unemployment *insurance* (in the sense of an earnings-related scheme that protects investment in specific skills). (See Estevez-Abe et al., 2001.) They also include part of the active labor market programs, reintegration programs, and to some extent short-term sickness benefits, health care, and housing (in so far as they all can contribute to the health of the workforce).[2] Further down the line one can find policies that facilitate the entrance of new participants who were not part of the labor force (in particular women of working-age who might have been occupied with caring for their own children or for frail relatives). Policies in this area include public care services for children, the elderly, the sick, or the disabled. Finally, there are policies that seek to invest in the capacities of new or of future labor market participants. Here again, we find child care, though this time not in its function of unburdening women so that they can pursue paid work, but rather as an institution that allows us to upgrade the cognitive skills of children, in particular those with a disadvantaged background. Some of the active labor market policies might also be considered as part of this category, in particular when they try to repair failures in the training of adolescents during the regular schooling period. An important function can also be attributed here to primary, secondary, and even tertiary education. Finally, one could even consider family cash benefits as supporting the potential for children to prepare for participation in the labor market.

In Table 9.1 an attempt is made to place concrete policy areas in this conceptual map of the social investment state. A major problem is that some policies can fulfill different functions (like child care) or cannot be exclusively categorized in

Table 9.1. Linking social investment to identifiable social policy categories.

Compensatory policies	**Social investment policies**		
Compensating exit of labor market participants	Maintaining or restoring capacity of labor market participants	Facilitating entrance of new labor market participants	Investing in the capacity of new labor market participants
– *Old age pensions* – *Survivor pensions* – *Incapacity benefits (LT)* – *Early retirement* – *Unemployment assistance* – *Social assistance*	– *Unemployment insurance (ST)* – *Maternity and parental leave (ST)* – *Reintegration of work incapacitated* – *Active labor market policies*	– *Care for elderly and frail* – *Child care* – *Active labor market policies*	– *Active labor market policies* – *Child care* – *Education* * *pre-primary education* * *primary education* * *lower secondary education* * *upper secondary education* * *tertiary education*
– *Maternity leave (LT)* – *Unemployment insurance (LT)* – *Housing benefits* – *Sickness pay* – *Health care*			

LT = Long Term; ST = Short Term.

one of the four categories (like unemployment insurance, and to a lesser extent various leave schemes) partially because their effect on social investment in part depends on whether they allow for temporary or relative long-term exit from the labor force. Finally, some policies, in particular social housing and health care, can in part contribute to maintaining or restoring the capacities of the labor force, but can as much simply support the population that exited the labor force.

9.3 SOCIAL EXPENDITURE DATA AND THE MEASUREMENT OF THE SOCIAL INVESTMENT TURN

During the 1990s, the OECD developed the Social Expenditure Database (SOCX) to monitor trends in social expenditure and analyze changes in its composition. Over the years, the number of countries included in the database was extended. At the time of writing, SOCX covers some 34 countries for which data disaggregated at the level of branches and programs are available from 1980 up to 2007, with shorter time-series for countries that were only added to the database during the mid-1990s. Social expenditure is defined by the OECD as "the provision by public and private institutions of benefits, and financial contributions targeted at, households and individuals in order to provide support during circumstances which adversely affect their welfare." It includes both cash transfers and the direct provision of goods and services "provided that the provision of benefits and financial contributions constitutes neither a direct payment for a particular good or service nor an individual contract or transfer" (Adema et al., 2011: 90). Depending on who controls the relevant financial flows, the OECD distinguishes public, mandated private, and voluntary private forms of expenditure. Even though the SOCX data for the countries of the European Union are based on European System of Integrated Social Protection Statistics (ESSPROS), the OECD uses a more restricted conception of "public" than Eurostat (De Deken & Kittel, 2007). In its expenditure database, the OECD does not always include statutory sickness pay and mandated occupational pensions in its "public" or "mandatory private" category. It even lists expenditure for civil service pensions as a "voluntary private" item in countries (including the Netherlands, Denmark, Sweden, and the UK) where these pensions are paid through autonomous funds for which the government does not on a regular basis make up possible deficits.

The SOCX database has a number of distinct advantages over ESSPROS for researchers interested in identifying a shift toward a social investment state. On the one hand, it includes an increasing number of countries outside the European Union and covers a longer times series. On the other hand, the OECD has been regrouping some ESSPROS items and combining them with data from its database on labor market programs in order to create the expenditure category "Active Labor Market Policies," an item that is central to social investment strategies. The OECD was also able to complement family benefits with spending items from its education database to get a more comprehensive picture of early childhood education and care.

The SOCX and the related labor market and educational databases of the OECD have, in principle, made it possible to disaggregate social expenditure at the level of individual programs and recombine it into new categories. But some theoretically necessary distinctions (such as between expenditure on short-term vs. long-term unemployment insurance and maternity leave, or between health care spending on the labor force and health care spending on the inactive population) cannot be made. That is why rather than matching OECD spending categories to our conceptual map of the social investment state, we will rather use them to qualify the distinction between "old" and "new" programs that has inspired the present volume.

A number of attempts have been made to measure the extent to which the social policies of a country show signs of the characteristics of a "social investment state" by analyzing changes in the spending patterns of welfare states. Such an approach builds upon the idea of resource competition that is inherent in the fiscal sociology of Schumpeter, and has become possible ever since the OECD started to make disaggregated social expenditure data available. In principle, an examination of the structure of the social budget can provide valuable estimates of shifts in the magnitude and political salience of different welfare state programs (Siegel, 2007), and ought to allow us to identify cross-national differences, as well as changes over time of the extent to which countries embarked on the path of a social investment state. Earlier attempts to identify the social investment state on the basis of expenditure data opted for a rather basic dichotomous distinction between "compensatory" and "investment" (Nikolai, 2009) or "old" and "new" social spending (Vandenbroucke &Vleminckx, 2011). Both studies tried to make the best out of amalgamating the spending categories of the OECD to tap cross national differences, and to analyze policy changes over time.

The study by Nikolai juxtaposed two groups of exemplary expenditure items: the "compensatory" category in this analysis only included spending on old-age and survivor pensions and spending on "passive" labor market policies (a category only consisting of unemployment compensation and early retirement, which left out functional equivalent programs such as work incapacity schemes). The "investment" category, on the other hand, included spending on families (which appears to include childcare services as well as various family cash benefits and maternity or parental leave schemes); spending on active labor market policies; and spending on primary, secondary, and tertiary education. Again some spending categories that are potentially important from a social investment perspective, such as elderly care, were left out of the analysis.

The study by Vandenbroucke and Vleminckx seeks to adopt a more encompassing approach, which tries to integrate most of the original spending categories of the OECD into one analytical framework.[3] Their "old" spending category is intended to be related to "old social risks," and includes three subcategories: (1) health care; (2) old-age and survivors pensions; and (3) cash benefits for the working-age population (ranging from work incapacity benefits, to unemployment compensation and income maintenance, to family benefits). Their "new" spending category includes programs that seek to alleviate "new social risks" and that can be linked to the social investment paradigm. Again they distinguish a number of subcategories: (1) parental leave; (2) elderly care; (3) child care and pre-primary education; (4) active labor market policies; and (5) primary and secondary education. By distinguishing subcategories it becomes possible to control for demographic effects and the effect of cross-national and longitudinal differences in unemployment levels.

After all, differences in the skeleton of a welfare state do not need to be a consequence of deliberate choices by governments, but can as much be caused by divergent population structures or by variations in the incidence of unemployment. Spending on retirement and survivor pensions or on care for the elderly is bound to be higher in countries with a relatively older population, or can be expected to rise in countries with an aging population. Healthcare spending might also be affected by the progress of aging, even if a series of studies have come to the conclusion that the proportion of the elderly population "may not be decisive in determining how health care expenditures change" (see, for example, Payne et al., 2007). There is general agreement that most healthcare expenditure takes place at the very extremes of the life course and that the costs for the elderly are concentrated in the final year. An increase in life expectancy might simply delay "the high cost of dying" (Seshamani &Gray, 2004). Hence, to the extent it is related to an increase in the life expectancy of people, the share of the population over 65 years of age does not need to drive up the costs of health care. However, the increase in the number of persons in their final "high cost" year might still drive up the cost of health care: to the extent that ageing is not only a consequence of an increased life expectancy, but also due to years of declining fertility health costs may well be rising. Yet, in that case a correction of expenditure for the share of the population over 65 years of age would be far too crude a factor to take into account the share of elderly in their final years.

Spending on child care and pre-primary education, on the other hand, can be expected to be higher in countries with relatively more children, just as spending on primary and secondary education is in part driven by the size of the population between 5 and 19 years of age. Finally, the level of spending on active labor market policies can to some extent be seen as a function of the incidence of unemployment.[4]

One of the main advantages of the categorization used by Vandenbroucke and Vleminckx is that it was inductively constructed out of the original OECD spending branches and programs. This, however, also raises a number of questions if one attempts to link back their (sub)categories to the three dimensions of social investment and the different theoretically relevant aspects of social investment.

Only one of the three "old" categories can be considered without reservation as solely compensating for an exit from the labor market: the category that amalgamates old-age pensions, early retirement pensions, and survivor pensions. The category that includes health care can have both ex-post compensatory function, but also contribute to an ex-ante prevention.[5] The third subcategory of "old" includes on the one hand spending items (such as incapacity pensions), that are not very different from those in the second category and can unambiguously be considered as being solely compensatory. On the other hand, the third category of Vandenbroucke and Vleminckx also includes items that have a far more ambiguous status: Unemployment benefits are not merely compensating exit; if constituted on an insurance basis they can, as we argued, also contribute to maintaining the capacities of labor market participants. They can do so by giving the unemployed the possibility to look for a job in accordance with their formal qualification, and by rewarding past investment in human capital. Other forms of unemployment compensation, in particular benefits for the long-term unemployed such as unemployment or social assistance, by contrast have a compensatory character. Family allowances, another important spending item in the third category, can be considered investments in the capacities of children as future labor market participants (by preventing child poverty), but can also weaken incentives for lower skilled mothers to participate in the labor market (which could justify allocation as a form of compensatory spending). Residential care for the incapacitated is no different from elderly care in relieving families from caring responsibilities and allowing women to make optimal use of their human capital in the labor market. Finally, rehabilitation services for incapacitated workers are not a compensatory item, but should rather be seen as an investment in restoring the capacities of former labor market participants.

9.4 METHODOLOGICAL PROBLEMS WITH THE USE OF THE ORIGINAL SOCX CATEGORIES

9.4.1 The Problem of Dual Purpose of Certain Policies and Spending Categories

In the above discussion it became evident that it is hard to allocate spending categories exclusively to one of these four categories of our continuum. Public child care ("New 3") can be seen as a policy instrument that enables women to pursue a labor market career (which, from a social investment strategy perspective, increases in importance the more those women are skilled, given that the opportunity costs of their educational investment and training become higher). However, the same spending item can also be considered as an instrument to invest in the capacities of children (in particular those born in families with lower cultural and social capital). In other words, it can serve the investment function of facilitating new entrants to the labor market, or as an investment in the human capital of future labor market participants. Moreover, both investment functions can serve less "productivist" goals: gender equality in the case of enabling female labor market participation, and equal opportunity in the case of enhancing the capacities of children.

Active labor market policies can be oriented toward investing in the capacity of new participants who have so far failed to enter the labor market, as well as an investment to revitalize the capacities of labor market participants whose skills have become obsolete. They can also be used to mask the extent of expenditure on unemployment benefits, as some argue is the case with direct job creation programs.

And as we already pointed out, unemployment benefits can serve the purpose of compensating exit from the labor market, but they can also form an incentive for skill investment.

9.4.2 The Problem of the Differential Composition of Benefit Packages

The social spending data as reported by the OECD are in essence an aggregation of spending on cash benefits, benefits in kind, and social services. A major problem one faces when trying to use such data to deduce cross-national variation in the architecture of welfare states, is related to the different composition of the benefit packages directed at the same target population. Take for instance the case of unemployment compensation: In some countries the unemployed are only entitled to an unemployment insurance benefit and hence most compensatory payments to those out of work appear under the expenditure category "unemployment." In other countries, the unemployed are entitled to various additional benefits from the family allowance system, social housing funds, or the social assistance budget. In Figure 9.1 we give a few illustrative examples based on the gross benefits for two types of unemployed (singles with no children, and single-income couples with two children) in five countries. These benefit packages were simulated using the OECD tax benefit calculator, for someone who before becoming unemployed was earning the average wage (in the case of couples, the partner has no labor market income). Whereas in Belgium, compensatory payments are more than 90% obtained from the unemployment expenditure budget, in the UK this is only the case for about a third of those payments. In the UK, a very sizable part of unemployment compensation originates from the social housing budget, which in earlier studies on measuring the social investment state were ignored (Nikolai, 2009) or deliberately left out (Vandenbroucke & Vleminckx, 2011). For a country like the UK, this may severely distort the relative importance of the kind of expenditures that are associated with social investment, given that it underestimates compensatory spending items.

Although the UK forms the most extreme case of the five countries we looked at, in three other cases housing benefits do play a role in compensatory payments

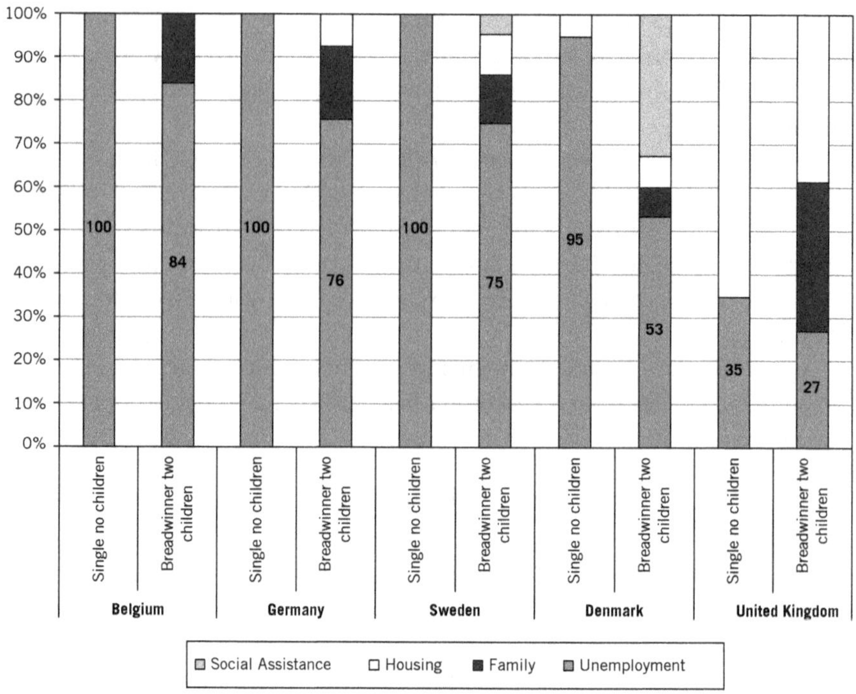

Figure 9.1. Benefit packages for the unemployed in five countries in 2009. *Sources*: own calculations based on simulations by the OECD tax benefit calculator, accessed November 28, 2011.

to the unemployed. In all countries some unemployed are also entitled to family benefits, but whereas, for instance, in Denmark this only makes up a minor part of the benefit package, in the UK it can form up to a third of the total benefit and in Belgium and Germany still about one sixth.

9.4.3 The Problem of Allocating Policies to Expenditure Categories

The SOCX database distinguishes nine main social expenditure groups, but because of differences in the structure and organization of national welfare states, it is not always evident to which category certain expenditures are allocated. This problem poses itself, in particular, for services that facilitate labor market participation of women by freeing them from caring for their children, and for their older or frail relatives. In some countries long-term care for elderly and frail relatives is largely financed via general health insurance (e.g., Belgium) or is part of the national health service (e.g., the United Kingdom) (and hence would appear under the "old" spending item of health care). Other countries have set up dedicated long-term care insurances (e.g., the Netherlands and Germany) and the costs of care for frail and elderly might end up in the "new" investment category of "elderly care." What makes matters worse is that cross-national differences in spending on long-term care vary dramatically depending upon which OECD source one consults. From the SOCX database one can retrieve data for residential care and home-help services in the categories "old age" and "incapacity." The problem is that for some countries, this appears to severely underestimate total expenditure on long-term care. This problem becomes evident when one compares these sums of SOXC categories with figures reported in the OECD's Health Statistics and with data published in a recent report on long-term care *Help Wanted, Providing and Paying for Long-Term Care* (OECD, 2011). Table 9.2 reports some illustrative discrepancies among the three data sources.

In countries such as Belgium and France where long-term care is still largely financed out of the general health care budget, the expenditure reported for long-term care in the Health Statistics portal and in the 2011 report is significantly higher than the sum of residential care and home-help services for old age or incapacity. In other countries, such as Sweden and Denmark, the opposite is the case. Germany scores very low on all indicators, which is surprising given that this country was one of the pioneers of setting up a branch in it social insurance system solely dedicated to long-term care. (Even in the health expenditure series on long-term care this country appears to spend very little.) Finally, the

Table 9.2. Expenditure on care for elderly and frail relatives in six countries 2007–2009.

		Social expenditure (SOCX)			Health Expenditure	
		Elderly care, old-age-residential care, home-help services, and other benefits in kind	**Incapacity related residential care and home-help services**	**Total**	**Services for long-term nursing care**	**Help Wanted? Providing and Paying for Long-Term Care**
Belgium	2007	0.1	0.4	**0.5**	**1,9**	
	2009				**2,1**	**1,7**
The Netherlands	2007	0.8	na	**na**	**1,2**	
	2009				**2,5**	**3,5**
Germany	2007	0.0	0.3	**0.3**	**1,3**	
	2009				**1,3**	**0,9**
France	2007	0.3	0.2	**0.5**	**1,2**	
	2009				**1,4**	**1,7**
Denmark	2007	1.7	0.9	**2.6**	**2,3**	
	2009				**2,7**	**1,8**
Sweden	2007	2.3	1.4	**3.7**	**0,7**	
	2009				**0,7**	**3,6**

Source: SOCX and Health Statistics databases (last consulted November 30, 2011); and OECD, 2011.

Dutch case shows a very inconsistent pattern: with very low expenditure levels in SOCX, medium spending levels in the health statistics series, and very high spending in the 2011 report on long-term care (which in view of the very large long-term care insurance (AWBZ) budget seems to be the more credible figure). In brief, it seems to be very hard to use data on elderly care and care for frail relatives to make sensible cross-national comparisons. This is unfortunate because these play a pivotal role in our theoretical category of investments that facilitate entrance of new labor market participants and in the "New 2" spending item.

A similar problem exists if one tries to relate early childhood education and care services for children aged 0–6 years to the spending categories of the OECD. Except for the Nordic countries, childcare services for toddlers (those aged 0–2 years) are normally organized by the Welfare Department, while provisions for pre-school children (those aged 3 years to 5 years) are the responsibility of the Department of Education. The fundamental problem is how to avoid double counting in countries where the distinction between these two kinds of childcare services is less clear. Eurostat's ESSPROS database only includes spending on child care and leaves out spending on pre-primary education. The OECD has sought to improve this by complementing these data with expenditure on pre-primary education, which they retrieved from their database on educational expenditure. To ensure the comparability of the data, the OECD adjusted these data for cross-national differences in the compulsory age of entry into primary school. But unfortunately, here too, the SOCX data suffer to some extent from a category mismatch: Spending on child care and pre-primary is lumped together with spending on "home-help services" and "accommodation," and both these categories cannot simply be equated with early childhood education and care services. Moreover, when one examines in detail the items grouped under childcare spending, one is faced with a number of discrepancies between the ESSPROS and SOCX data for which it is hard to account.[6] Despite these problems, however, SOCX offers the most sophisticated account of countries' spending on childcare services. One should, however, bear in mind that for some countries the SOCX data might underestimate genuine government efforts for child care.

9.4.4 The Problem of Public and Private Expenditure

Countries vary significantly in the degree to which their social protection systems rely on private forms of provision. Private social spending is less private than it often appears to be. On the one hand, such initiatives are made possible and encouraged by very sizeable tax expenditures. On the other hand, the state regulates and sometimes even mandates private forms of welfare. Such regulation is one of the reasons that those programs are still considered to have a social dimension of some sort. Even though the SOCX database seeks to document both public and private expenditure, the reporting of the latter appears to be far less systematic than the former. As a consequence, social expenditure in countries that strongly rely on private social protection may be underestimated in the database. The (quasi) private nature of some programs inherently leads to such underreporting. Hence it is hard to estimate the full magnitude of some of the items that make up the third category of compensatory expenditures, such as statutory sickness pay, or of forms of early retirement based on collective agreements.

The OECD makes a distinction between "mandated" and "voluntary" forms of the private provision social benefits, yet in practice that distinction is marred by problems. Mandated schemes are "stipulated by legislation but operated by the private sector" (Adema et al., 2011: 93). Other privately operated programs are considered "voluntary" forms of private expenditure, but are categorized as "social" if they involve a redistribution of resources across households and include benefits provided by NGOs, or if the benefits accrue from tax advantaged individual plans.

In practice, benefits that are granted because employers have signed up to a collective labor agreement are categorized as a form of "voluntary" private social spending; whereas in cases where they are granted because employers are required by law to pay the same benefit they are categorized as "mandated" private social spending. This leads the OECD to categorize the Swiss occupational pensions as a form of "mandated private social expenditure"; while Dutch occupational pensions are considered to be "voluntary" because they are formally organized by employers who signed up to a collective agreement. But given that in the Dutch context the central government almost always uses its legislative power to subject such agreements to administrative extension, the effect is pretty much the same as the Swiss direct mandate.

Moreover, there is reason to suspect that not all schemes required by law are registered in the SOCX as mandatory. This, for instance, appears to be the case with statutory sickness pay in the Netherlands. When the government decided in 1996 to phase out the public insurance for sickness benefits and replace it with a system in which employers are required to continue to pay wages to sick employees (initially only for one year, but since 2004, for a period of up to two years), one would have expected the private expenditure for paid sick leave to go up somehow. But in the SOCX database, mandated expenditure remains stable, and one can at best observe a decline of public expenditure in 2005 (without any concomitant shift toward the mandated expenditure category). This is the more surprising because since 1994 the absenteeism rate has been constantly hovering around 5% (Hartman et al., 2010: 174) even though the labor force has expanded significantly during that period (hence the number of beneficiaries of statutory sickness payments rose).

From a social investment perspective, it does not really matter whether the state requires employers to continue to pay wages to sick or child bearing employees, or whether it has legislated a public insurance fund that pays a sickness benefit or maternity or parental leave benefit. This problem can in principle be addressed by including all three types of social expenditure (public, mandated private, and voluntary private), but this still leaves us with the problem that payments by private programs are often inadequately recorded. For example, even though the Netherlands have known a system of mandatory paid maternity leave,[7] since the 1990s, SOCX no longer reports any expenditure: not public, nor mandated, nor voluntary private.[8] In other words, to the extent that countries rely for their "compensatory" expenditures on private programs, the relative importance of social investment items may end up being severely overestimated.

9.4.5 Problem of Gross versus Net Expenditure

There are basically three ways in which the tax system can affect social expenditure: (1) direct taxation of benefit income; (2) indirect taxation of the consumption by benefit recipients; (3) tax breaks for social purposes (Adema et al., 2011). Governments levy income tax and social security contributions on cash transfers. As cash transfers form the bulk of noninvesting compensatory policies, cross-national differences in this direct taxation may lead to an over- or underestimation of the relative importance of social investing.

Countries also differ significantly in the extent to which they rely upon indirect taxes on consumption, and as most of the transfer income is used by beneficiaries to finance their consumption, a substantial part of social transfers ends up being clawed back by the state. Because many of the services that are provided in the context of social investment policies are not taxed or taxed at reduced rates, in countries with high indirect levies the importance of social investing might be underplayed if measured on the basis of gross expenditure data.

In Figure 9.2 we illustrate the potential impact of taxation on reducing the importance of cash benefits. The diagram shows how much from total gross public expenditure is clawed back by direct taxes and social contributions and by indirect taxes. Because of the lack of detailed information from benefit recipients and because income surveys tend to underreport indirect tax payments, the OECD estimates the impact of indirect taxes by calculating an average implicit tax rate based on the OECD *Revenue Statistics* and the OECD *National Accounts*.[9]

There are not only important differences among countries, but also within the same country over time. It would be preferable to know the tax rate for each separate cash benefit program, but unfortunately so far the pioneering work of Willem Adema offers only overall estimates. But many countries apply different tax rules to different kinds of benefits. Thus, whereas in Germany unemployment benefits are not subject to direct taxes, while sickness benefits, disability pensions, and old-age pensions are subject to reduced taxes, in Denmark the same tax rules apply to all these benefits (MISSOC, 2011). In Belgium almost two thirds of the revenue of direct taxes on cash benefits comes from taxing public old-age pensions, whereas taxation on unemployment benefits and sickness benefits only makes up a few percentages of that revenue. In the Netherlands, public pensions are taxed at a far reduced rate, while disability pensions, early

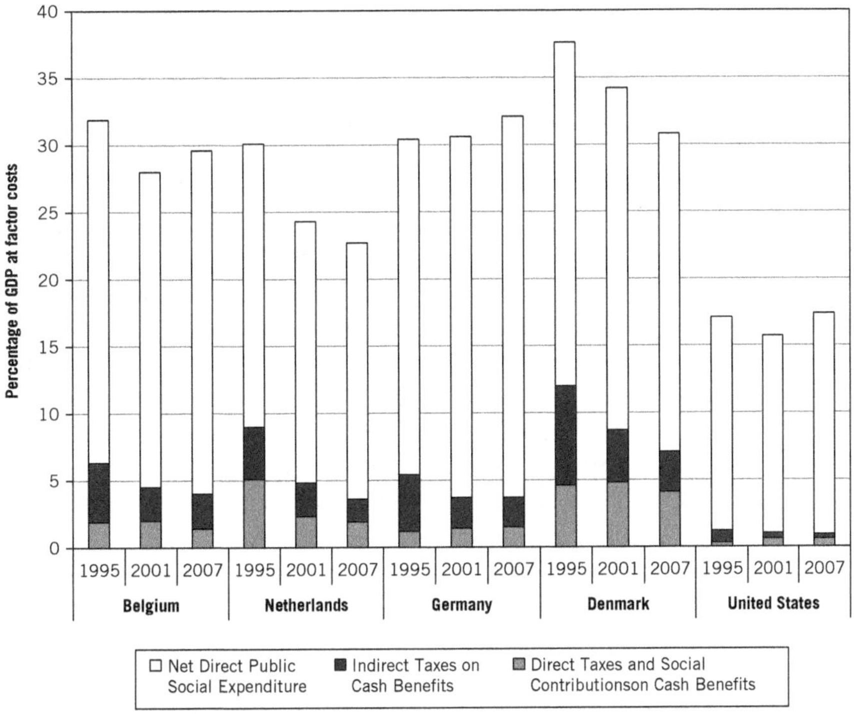

Figure 9.2. Breakdown of gross public social expenditure into net expenditure, direct and indirect taxes 1995–2007. *Sources*: own calculations based on data reported by Adema, 1999; Adema & Ladaique, 2005; and Adema et al., 2011. Gross Public Social Expenditure is the sum of "Net Direct Social Expenditure," "Indirect Taxes on Cash Benefits," and "Direct Taxes and Social Contributions on Cash Benefits."

retirement, and unemployment insurance benefits are subject to normal tax rates (Adema et al., 2011).

If one takes the impact of the tax system into account, the expenditure items linked to social investment are likely to become more important, in particular in countries where taxes on cash benefits are high. If one deduces policy priorities only from gross spending patterns, one is likely to overestimate the magnitude of social transfers that form the bulk of "compensatory" policies.

The fiscal measures the government uses to pursue social policy goals are a third way in which the tax system can affect the level of social expenditure. Some countries offer tax breaks with a social purpose that are similar to cash benefits. For example, child tax allowances can function as a replacement (in, for instance, the United States) or co-exist next to family benefits (like, for instance, in Germany or Belgium). Fiscal measures can also stimulate the provision of private benefits (e.g., tax relief toward the provision of private health plans in countries such as the United States and Germany); or can reduce the costs of private social services (such as child care in the Netherlands) and favorably treat contributions to or income from charities.

The OECD makes a distinction between tax breaks toward current private social benefits, and fiscal welfare aimed at future benefits, in particular old-age pensions. These arguably form the most important form of tax exemptions, but calculations are complex and "there is no comparable data set available on the value of tax breaks for pensions" (Adema et al., 2011: 29). One of the main problems here is related to the intertemporal nature of pension schemes: Tax relief can be granted at various stages of building up the entitlements and paying out the benefits, and some of this foregone revenue will be clawed back when pension benefits are finally being paid out.[10] Because of these difficulties the OECD does not include these measures in its calculations of net social expenditure, but merely lists them as a "memorandum item." In the year 2007 the value of this item ranged close to 0% of GDP in countries such as France or Austria, to as much as 2.1% in the Netherlands or 3.0% in Australia. Given that pensions are forming the most important branch of compensatory social policies, not taking into account these tax effects can make social investment policies more important in countries that have sizeable tax breaks for pensions.

Finally, there are a series of in-work benefits such as the Earned Income Credit in the United States, the Working Tax Credit in the United Kingdom, or the Employment Tax Credit (*Arbeidskorting*) in the Netherlands. These are not included in the OECD database, but could be considered as part of a social investment to facilitate labor market entry of people previously living on benefits. Such measures also include preferential tax treatment of certain problematic groups of workers to make them more attractive for employers.[11]

9.5 CONCLUSION

The use of expenditure data to map the skeleton of the social investment state is fraud with conceptual and methodological problems. Social investment is a multifaceted concept and it is hard to relate the different dimensions it entails to mutually exclusive policy areas. Moreover, some policies can have both a compensatory as well as an investment function. This does not need to imply that one cannot use spending data to depict cross-national differences or basic trends in the kind of welfare settlement prevailing in countries. The purpose of this chapter was to qualify the interpretation of such regional and intertemporal differences. Meeusen & Nys (2012) present an attempt to map both kinds of variations that builds upon the approach of Vandenbroucke and Vleminckx. It uses a refined and extended version of their distinction between "old" "compensatory" expenditures and "new" "investing" type of expenditures. Apart from adding certain programs or shifting some programs between expenditure categories, the main difference is that family benefits are no longer automatically considered to be a form of compensation (but rather, in line with the argument in this chapter, can to some extent also be considered a form of social investment); and that voluntary private

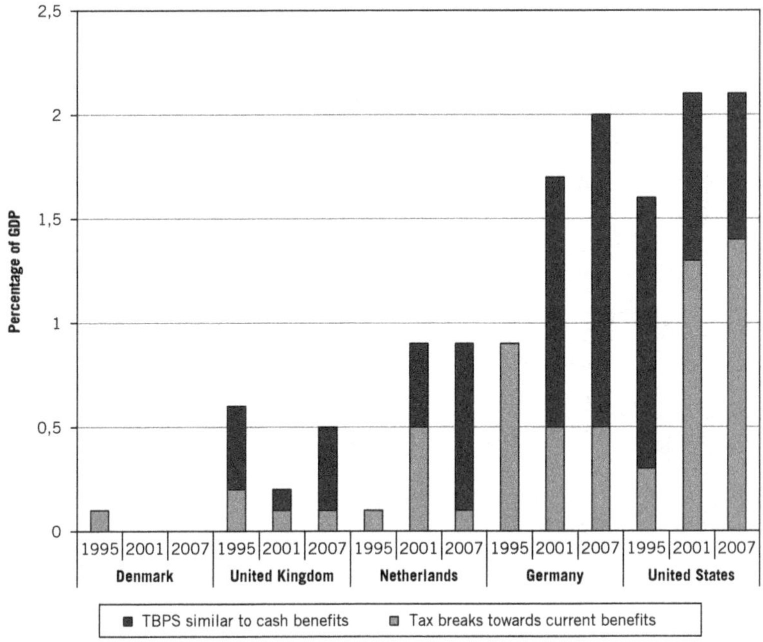

Figure 9.3. Tax breaks with a social purpose as a percentage of GDP 1995–2007. *Sources*: own calculations based on data reported by Adema, 1999; Adema & Ladaique, 2005; and Adema et al., 2011.

expenditure has been taken into account. On the compensatory side, Meeusen & Nys (2012) draw distinctions among "Old 1" (health care); "Old 2" (retirement and survivor pensions); and "Old 3" (working-age benefits with or without family benefits).[12] On the investment side, distinctions are made among "New 1" (parental and maternal leave schemes); "New 2" (elderly care); "New 3" (child care with or without family benefits); "New 4" (active labor market policies); "New 5" (primary and secondary education); "New 6" (tertiary education).[13]

Table 9.3 gives an overview of how the different measurement problems discussed in this chapter, in principle, affect the accuracy of the measurement of the different spending categories[14] in countries where these problems manifest themselves. A zero means that for the particular spending categories there is no significant impact to be expected. A minus means that in some countries the measurement problem is likely to lead to an overestimation of the real magnitude of the spending category (as compared with what is reported in Meeusen & Nys [2012]), in other words, that "real" spending can be expected to be *lower* than what is reported in Meeusen and Nys. A plus means the opposite: that is, if one would be able to adequately take into account the problem, real spending can be expected to be *higher* than is reported in Meeusen and Nys.

Of course the actual impact differs according to the institutional structure of the welfare state of a country.

Table 9.3. Overview of how the five methodological problems can impact the accuracy of the measurement of the different expenditure items.

	OLD "compensatory"			NEW "investing"					
	Old 1 health care	**Old 2 retirement**	**Old 3 working age**	**New 1 parental/ maternity leave**	**New 2 elderly care**	**New 3 child care**	**New 4 ALMP**	**New 5 primary & secondary education**	**New 6 tertiary education**
Dual purpose of the same policy	0	0	++	0	0	0	-	0	0
Composition of benefit package	0	0	+	0	0	–	0	0	0
Allocation policies to spending	–	0	-	0	+	+	+	–	0
Private expenditure:	+	++	++	+	+	+	0	0	0
*mandated	++	++	+	+	+	+	0	0	0
*voluntary									
Net expenditure:	0	–	–	–	0	0	0	0	0
*direct taxes	0	–	–	–	0	0	0	0	0
*indirect taxes	++	++	+	+	+	+	0	0	0
*tax breaks									

ALMP = Active Labor Market Policies.

In Table 9.4 we examine a few exemplary countries to illustrate how moving from gross to net expenditure significantly changes the ratio between "old" "compensatory" policies and "new" "investment" policies. In this table we distributed the effects of direct taxes among the three "Old" items and "New 1," relative to the share these items have in total expenditure. In a similar procedure, the effects of the implicit indirect tax rate were distributed among the three "Old" items, "New 1," and "New 3" (whereas family benefits are not subject to direct taxes, they are affected by the implicit indirect tax rate). Hence the tax system is assumed to change only the magnitude of cash benefits, not of the social services that make out the bulk of the "new" social investment expenditures.

Even though we also report tax benefits with a social purpose (TBSP), we did not allocate these to "old" or to "new" expenditures, because in countries such as Belgium and Germany the bulk of these tax benefits consists of "New" tax credits for children; whereas in the Netherlands they include primarily "Old" deductions for those with medical disabilities or for the chronically ill, while in the case of the United Kingdom they consist of working tax credits and child tax credits. Hence it is hard to uniformly allocate the TBSP to our "old" or "new" categories.

Because the magnitude of taxation of cash benefits is far more important than tax benefits similar to social benefits or tax breaks on current benefits, using net expenditure data increases the relative importance of social investment in all countries. But this effect varies significantly among countries and within the same country over time. In the UK, where the relative share of social investment expenditure is the lowest, the tax effect is even slightly negative in 2007. In Denmark social investment is by far the most important among the five countries, and in addition significantly increases, if we take into account the effects of the tax system. But in this country this kind of expenditure has become less important in 2007 as compared with 1995. In Belgium the importance of social investment has not changed at all during the 12 years under study, and is somewhere in-between Denmark and the United Kingdom. In the Netherlands, social investment has become more important since 1995, but more so in gross than in net terms. Still, by 2007 it became as important as in Belgium. Finally, Germany continues to give a comparatively low priority to social investment policies, and compensatory expenditures even became more important in 2007. For this country the picture hardly changes if one moves from gross to net expenditure.

If one would be able to quantify the other methodological problems we have been discussing, the ratios would be likely to change further. For countries such as Belgium, social investment might become more important, as for this country a significant part of care for elderly or frail relatives is included in the "old" health expenditure category. In countries such as the Netherlands, that know an important underreported private component to social spending, social investment might turn out to be less important than our ratios suggest.

All this means that the data that are reported in Meeusen and Nys have to be interpreted with much caution. Even though they allow a cursory overview of

Table 9.4. Impact of taxation on measuring social investment in five countries.

	UK		The Netherlands		Germany		Belgium		Denmark	
	1995	**2007**	**1995**	**2007**	**1995**	**2007**	**1995**	**2007**	**1995**	**2007**
"Old 1" Health care	*5.85*	*6.92*	*6.83*	*6.50*	*9.19*	*8.81*	*6.47*	*7.81*	*4.66*	*6.67*
"Old 2" Pensions	*10.09*	*9.85*	*8.53*	*8.26*	*11.33*	*11.45*	*10.65*	*11.66*	*8.07*	*7.74*
"Old 3" Working-age benefits	*7.10*	*5.90*	*9.16*	*6.90*	*4.13*	*3.34*	*4.17*	*4.19*	*5.61*	*4.98*
Gross Total "Old" as % GDP	23.04	22.67	24.52	21.67	24.65	23.59	21.29	23.66	18.34	19.40
"New 1" Maternity and parental leave	*0.07*	*0.36*	*0.00*	*0.00*	*0.30*	*0.27*	*0.16*	*0.18*	*0.85*	*0.55*
"New 2" Care for elderly and frail	*0.47*	*0.73*	*0.50*	*0.79*	*0.48*	*0.32*	*0.37*	*0.51*	*2.68*	*2.63*
"New 3b" Child care and family benefits	*1.36*	*1.87*	*1.24*	*1.97*	*1.70*	*1.54*	*2.11*	*2.37*	*2.99*	*2.74*
"New 4" ALMP and rehabilitation	*0.41*	*0.32*	*1.54*	*1.42*	*1.39*	*0.93*	*1.22*	*1.24*	*2.06*	*1.45*
"New 5" Primary and secondary education	*3.34*	*4.01*	*3.39*	*3.71*	*3.27*	*2.84*	*3.57*	*4.10*	*4.23*	*4.26*
Total Gross "New" as % GDP	5.64	7.29	6.67	7.89	7.14	5.90	7.42	8.39	12.80	11.62
Ratio of Gross "New" versus Gross "Old"	**0.24**	**0.32**	**0.27**	**0.36**	**0.29**	**0.25**	**0.35**	**0.35**	**0.70**	**0.60**
Direct taxes as % GDP	*0.40*	*0.30*	*5.10*	*1.90*	*1.20*	*1.50*	*1.90*	*1.40*	*4.60*	*4.10*
Implicit indirect tax rate	*14.30*	*12.80*	*15.20*	*16.80*	*13.30*	*14.20*	*14.10*	*15.10*	*24.40*	*26.00*
Effect of implicit indirect tax rate as % GDP	*1.70*	*1.40*	*2.00*	*1.70*	*2.20*	*2.20*	*2.60*	*2.60*	*3.60*	*3.00*
TBSP similar to benefits	*0.40*	*0.60*	*0.10*	*0.90*	*0.90*	*1.30*	*0.90*	*0.60*	*0.10*	*0.00*
Tax breaks toward current benefits	*0.20*	*1.40*	*0.00*	*0.10*	*0.00*	*0.50*	*0.00*	*0.00*	*0.00*	*0.00*
Net Total "Old" as % GDP	21.45	21.71	17.62	19.11	22.33	21.37	17.96	20.52	11.10	12.86
Net Total "New" as % GDP	*5.53*	*7.15*	*6.57*	*7.74*	*6.96*	*5.72*	*7.16*	*8.13*	*11.95*	*11.06*
Ratio of Net "New" versus Net "Old"	**0.26**	**0.33**	**0.37**	**0.41**	**0.31**	**0.27**	**0.40**	**0.40**	**1.06**	**0.86**

Sources: own calculations based on SOCX (last consulted November 30, 2011) and data reported by Adema, 1999; Adema & Ladaique, 2005; Adema et al., 2011; and revised figures on recalculations of the effects of the implicit direct tax rate directly provided by Willem Adema of the OECD.
ALMF = ?; TBSP = Tax benefits with a social purpose.

cross-national and longitudinal variation of the importance of social investment policies, detailed case studies are necessary to get a full picture of the state of affairs.

ACKNOWLEDGMENTS

We would like to express our gratitude to Willem Adema of the OECD who took a lot of time to clarify a number of questions related to the social expenditure database; and provided us with some unpublished data.

NOTES

1 Taylor-Gooby also adds a third change to his list of trends that resulted in new risks. The expansion of private services, which occurred in the wake of attempts to limit public spending, resulted in a new need whereby people increasingly have to be able to offset the consequences of having made the wrong decision when choosing privatized welfare services and utilities.
2 One could argue that when unemployment assistance or social assistance kind of benefits are made conditional upon participating in activation measures or are topping up employment that is remunerated under the poverty threshold (as often is the case with the German ALG II benefits), these transfers ought to be considered to have an aspect of social investment as well. However, the costs of the investment part are likely to show up in the ALMP[Author: Although this acronym is in a footnote, rather than the text of the chapter, please consider expanding it for the benefit of the reader.] budget, while the coercive aspect of this conditionality (or the employment-forcing nature of schemes such as ALG II) cannot really be considered as positively enhancing human capabilities, something that is supposed to be at the center of social investment.
3 They only excluded the OECD categories "housing," "family in kind," "capacity in kind," and "other benefits in kind" from their analysis.
4 Though such an argument could also be made for unemployment compensation (and functionally equivalent schemes, such as early retirement and work incapacity benefits), Vandenbroucke and Vleminckx decided to only estimate the impact on ALMP.
5 The establishing of public health insurance systems has often been motivated by a concern for the productive capabilities of the labor force. A similar case can be made about social housing: good housing conditions can be essential for a healthy labor force as already paternalistic employers in the 19th century discovered when they were building decent housing for their employees.

6 In the case of Germany, for instance, the total amount of child care in SOCX includes both child care and pre-primary, as shown in the OECD's Family Database (FDB). But when looking at spending for pre-primary education only, the FDB, the OECD Education Database, and ESPROSS report different numbers. In France and Belgium, SOXC and ESSPROS report far lower spending for child care than in FDB. In Sweden, by contrast SOXC and ESPROSS report higher expenditures on child care than the FDB. For the UK, SOCX reports significantly higher spending on both child care and pre-pre-primary [author: do you intend pre-pre-primary?] education. Moreover, in some of the countries that Van Lancker and Ghysels (in this volume) scrutinized more in detail, a series of classification errors appeared. In Belgium, for instance, only childcare expenditures in the Flemish Community are classified under the heading "day-care," while childcare expenditures in the French community are classified in the category "other benefits in kind."

7 With a total of 16 weeks (4–6 weeks are intended to be taken as pregnancy leave (*zwangerschapsverlof*) prior to the confinement and the remainder as childbirth leave (*bevallingsverlof*) after the confinement, it is comparatively short.

8 It might be that this expenditure is recorded under sickness benefit expenditure, which would bring us back to the problem of allocating policies to expenditure categories. In this case, it would really be problematic as a "social investment" item and would be counted as a "compensatory" item.

9 This average implicit tax rate is the ratio of the revenue from general consumption taxes plus excise duties to a broad consumption tax base, that is, private consumption and government consumption minus government wages (Adema et al., 2011: 108).

10 Tax breaks for pensions include exemptions from income tax and social security levies for contributions to private pension plans, tax relief for the investment income of pension funds, or lower rates for benefits paid by pension funds.

11 For example, in the Netherlands the Employment Tax Credit rates are higher for workers close to retirement age. None of these in-work tax benefits are included in what the OECD registers as "employment incentives in its ALMP module," as that only concerns payments to individuals that are conditional upon the take-up of a new job *and* have to be targeted at specific groups (e.g., restricted to the long-term unemployed).

12 As we demonstrated in Figure 9.1, housing allowances can, in the UK in particular and to a lesser extent in Denmark and Germany, be considered to form an important part of compensatory benefits for those out of work. They have been included in the "Old 3" category. In SOCX this item does not include spending related to directly provided social housing (which, as we argued, can have both a compensatory as well as an investment function). Expenditure for this direct provision is hence not included in the data

used in this volume.[Author: please review edits to the preceding sentence for accuracy.]

13 Primary and secondary education on the one hand, and tertiary education on the other hand, are in separate categories because the time series of the latter is much shorter (there is no substantial consideration behind this differentiation).

14 In this table family benefits are part of the "New 3" (child care).

10

BEYOND SOCIAL INVESTMENT. WHICH CONCEPTS AND VALUES FOR SOCIAL POLICY-MAKING IN EUROPE?

Bea Cantillon

10.1 INTRODUCTION

Since the beginning of the Great Recession, poverty has, not unexpectedly, increased in many countries of the European Union (see Figure 1.1 in Chapter 1).[1] More worrying in view of its structural significance is the observation that, in the decade leading up to the present downturn, despite years of growing employment and increasing average incomes, Europe failed to make substantial progress in combating relative income poverty, particularly among the working-age population. Certainly, Europeans became richer and material deprivation declined. Similarly, using a pan-European definition of poverty, the number of Europeans living on an income below the European Union (EU)-wide poverty line decreased. However, if we take the perspective of relative income poverty defined at the national level, the proportion of individuals living on an income lower than 60% of the median income in their country remained invariably at the level of approximately 16% of the European population. Of course, below the surface of an apparent stasis there were divergent national trends to be observed. Consistent increases of at-risk-of-poverty were noticeable in the Nordic countries. There were clear and significant decreases in Ireland, the UK, and in many of the new Member States, while other countries displayed no significant change. *On average, however, on the national escalators of income growth and employment rise, the discrepancy between those at the bottom and those in the middle did not decrease*. Not unimportantly, the available data equally suggests a poverty standstill in the economically favorable years during the second half of the 1990s (see Chapter 5).

These observations constituted the starting-point for the analyses presented in this book. Why should we worry about this?

Taking the perspective of relative income poverty we must of course be aware of the fact that this measure has inherent conceptual and methodological shortcomings, which may lead to overlooking some failures and/or successes. These issues are discussed at length in Chapter 2 of this book. However, the premise in this book is that each household should have at its disposal the minimum income required for participation in its society. The value of these incomes—defined by the EU "at-risk-of-poverty" thresholds—are given on the EUROSTAT website.[2] By way of example, for a single person they amounted in 2011 (in euro per year) to 11,426 in Germany, 7,509 in Spain, and 3,015 in Poland. Clearly, someone with less than 60% of median income has a low income.[3] Therefore, reducing the number of people who must, for the duration of a whole year, make ends meet on an income below these amounts—which, again by way of example, is the case for 16% of the German population on working-age, 21% in Spain, and 18% in Poland—is prominently present as an objective in the European policy discourse. It implies that in the good years before the crisis the poor in each of the countries concerned should have benefited most from expanding labor markets and increasing prosperity. This is, however, *not* what we observe.

The reduction of relative income poverty requires macroeconomic and social policies. Unfortunately, this is not always well understood. The National Strategy Reports on Social Protection and Social Inclusion contain numerous references to innovative social projects that are focused on very specific and often localized problems. Most of these initiatives are extremely important and necessary as complements to macro policies. Much as social security and social welfare states in general were developed from the bottom up, starting from local initiatives and with much benevolence and creativity, so seeds for social progress today lie in innovative place-based initiatives. I will return to the significance of this observation in the conclusion to this chapter. However, despite large and meritorious efforts, one should not expect these projects to have a significant impact on national at-risk-of-poverty rates. In order to achieve a better distribution of the fruits of economic growth and, in so doing, to reduce the number of relative poor, countries must develop sustainable growth strategies, effective employment policies, and adequate social redistribution.

Eradication of poverty also implies that minimum incomes from work and from social protection must be above the poverty thresholds. However, as outlined in Chapter 5, only a tiny minority of EU countries reaches that goal: In many countries, minimum protection levels are well *below 40%* of these thresholds (see Figure 5.6 in this volume). Moreover, there is ample evidence of an erosion of minimum social benefits, primarily in the 1990s but, in many countries, also in the 2000s (Marx & Nelson, 2013). Although social progress can certainly not be measured exclusively in terms of the adequacy of minimum income protection, the verdict may well be damning. To cite Goodin: "A state that did not even try to relieve distress when it was clearly within its power to do so simply could not credibly claim to constitute a welfare state" (Goodin, 1988: 22).

The question, then, is whether European welfare states *had* the power to decrease relative income poverty. Since the second half of the 1970s, welfare states have undeniably sailed into choppy water. As will be explained in this chapter, social, economic, and demographic change has disrupted the post-War virtuous cycle of growth, employment, and social inclusion. However, in the second half of the 1990s and the first years of the 2000s, many social, economic, and demographic circumstances were rather favorable for a successful drive to reduce poverty and social inequalities: Employment and incomes were on the rise; demographic dependency rates were still rather favorable; social spending remained high; deliberate attempts were being made to transform passive welfare states into "investment states," while the fight against poverty was prominent on the political agendas of regional, national, and international bodies. European aspirations in particular were very high: In 2000, the Lisbon European Council spoke of "the eradication of poverty" as a strategic policy goal within the Union. Although it is still a matter of debate as to what extent policies have effectively veered in the direction of "social investment" (see Hemerijck, De Deken, & Vandenbroucke in this volume; Morel, Palier, & Palme, 2011), prior to the crisis, most European welfare states achieved a degree of success in creating jobs. Various other indicators of investment type outcome also make for positive reading: The number of early school leavers has decreased consistently and the number of working women and mothers has gone up.

So the long poverty standstill in the developed European welfare states before the crisis is clearly a point of concern. *Is it indicative of a structural inability of active welfare states today also to combat poverty in a structural way? Does it point at imbalances in the prevailing policy paradigm? Or is it suggestive of ill-considered national policy trajectories in individual countries?*

In the previous chapters these questions were approached through analyses of the volume and the distribution of labor, the evolution of poverty among work-poor and work-rich households, and changes in terms of the pro-poorness and the adequacy of social spending. However, a full understanding of the dynamics of change in welfare states requires a broad perspective that also captures changes in discourse, changes in macroeconomic policy, institutional change, and social and demographic transitions. The origins of the evolutions that unfolded in the more recent past—lay in a more distant history. It is only against the broader backdrop of structural societal and policy change that we can begin to understand why welfare states are today experiencing such great difficulty in making headway in the fight against poverty and social exclusion and why the new policy paradigm of "social investment," too, has failed to deliver in terms of poverty alleviation. Therefore, this chapter starts with a general historical sketch of the strongly changing interface between work, social redistribution, and poverty. Subsequently, it considers how contemporary European welfare states have responded to these changes, and questions how, when, and why the European social agenda and its underlying social investment paradigm came to the fore. The third section provides a macroscopic summary of the main findings reported in this book. Finally, the chapter reflects on new policy paradigms and the values, the concepts, and inclusive visions of and for Social Europe and beyond.

10.2 WELFARE STATES AND CHANGE IN THE 1970S AND 1980S

The moment that Europe's rich welfare states reached a high level of maturity coincided with a period of social and economic upheaval. Growth was slowing down, unemployment was rising, and the post-War institutions of the welfare states seemed unable to cope with the consequences of demographic evolutions and changing family relations, globalization, the tertiarization of employment, the massive entry of women into the labor market, and new migratory flows. Designed to cope with traditional social risks such as sickness, injury, unemployment, old age, and the burden of raising children, the welfare state now had to find adequate responses to a set of unfamiliar challenges and newly emerging social risks such as low skills, single parenthood, and combining care duties with paid work. Although welfare states have proven to be remarkably robust (Pierson, 2011), they adapted—reluctantly at first—within the confines of the prevailing system, restricted by the laws of path dependence; subsequently, supported by European discourse and policy, they developed—as explained by Hemerijck in this volume—a stronger common focus on work, social investment, and cost containment.

10.2.1 The Big Transformations

Since the early 1970s, welfare states have been confronted with immense economic, demographic, sociological, and normative changes that fundamentally threaten the post-War balances among markets, families, and "the social" sphere.

As a consequence of the so-called postindustrial transition (Touraine, 1969), globalization, technological change, and concomitant *shifts in the labor market*, an increasing number of people lacking the necessary skills and abilities have become economically redundant, resulting in changing employment relations (Gallie, 2007; Kalleberg, 2011), greater structural reliance on social benefits, and thus in higher dependency rates (and costs) in social security, an evolution that Pierre Rosanvallon (1995) has termed *la nouvelle question sociale*, the new social question. Concurrently, employment has become more important for individual social status, self-confidence, self-esteem, and social inclusion, a process that has been significantly amplified by individualization and the changing role of women, as discussed below.

The post-War welfare settlement was firmly grounded on gendered assumptions (Orloff, 2006; Lewis, 2001). However, the male breadwinner model began to erode from the second half of the 1960s onwards, as the *emancipation of women* caused a massive influx of female workers into the labor market, a trend that was accompanied by changing patterns of family formation and rising divorce rates (Lewis, 2009; Crompton & Lyonette, 2006; Blossfeld, 1995; Cantillon, 1989). The consequences for the functioning of the welfare state were far-reaching.

First and foremost, the emancipation of women meant that the active population grew strongly, which inevitably translated into great imbalances in a labor market already in full transition (Salverda, 2011). As a result, the socioeconomically weak (be they men or women) saw their position further deteriorate.

Second, the outsourcing of care work, previously performed unpaid by women, came at a cost. Although the commodification or collectivization of care work undeniably created new jobs—as the Scandinavian example already demonstrated very early—there was a price-tag to be met by the public authorities, who were henceforth required to supply and organize care provisions for children and frail elderly persons and/or to provide financial support for working families with children.

Third, marital instability led to growing numbers of lone-parent families, a trend that is often associated with an intensified poverty risk. As dual earnership became more generalized and double incomes increasingly became the norm, one-parent households (and, more generally, single-earner families) increasingly slipped beneath the poverty line (Cantillon, 1989; Esping-Andersen et al., 2002; Fritzell, Bäckman, & Ritakallio, 2012; European Commission, 2010a).

Fourth, the individualization in sociological terms coincided with an individualization of income redistribution through policies: Increasingly, gender neutrality called for less progressive and less redistributive individual taxation and individualized social rights.

The emancipation of women is arguably the greatest social achievement of the past 40 years. However, while it contributed substantially to combating poverty among women and probably had a leveling effect on income distribution (see, among many others, Esping-Andersen, 2009; Harkness, 2010; OECD, 2008), women's liberation was paradoxically, also at odds with the struggle against social and income inequalities. For one thing, the process of emancipation invariably unfolded at two speeds: It reached the higher skilled sooner than the lower social groups, unskilled individuals, and migrant population groups (Cantillon et al., 2001). This fact, combined with household dilution and homogamy, in many countries resulted in a polarization in the labor market, with a simultaneous increase in work-rich and work-poor households (cf. the analyses in Chapter 3).

Second, a policy in support of individualization processes and labor-market participation by women inevitably pressurizes the redistributional capacity of social security and taxation: If individuals rather than households as a whole become the object of redistribution, the progressiveness of fiscal and social systems is eroded. Moreover, policy devices designed to buttress dual earnership (such as child daycare services) also may give rise to so-called *Matthew effects* (as discussed in the present book by Verbist and Matsaganis, and by Van Lancker and Ghysels) due to the fact that they disproportionately benefit work-rich households (Cantillon, 2011).

Importantly, in Europe the processes of individualization and emancipation are unfolding at different speeds. The Scandinavian countries have clearly taken the lead in this respect, to the extent that the process of individualization has been almost completed. Most new Member States also traditionally have high female employment rates. The "conservative" Continental Welfare States (in the wording of Esping-Andersen) made the transition mainly in the 1980s and 1990s, while the countries of Southern Europe and Ireland are still in full transition today. The various speeds at which the emancipation of women is unfolding largely explain the divergences between countries in terms of employment trends and the distribution of work among work-poor and work-rich households.

The past 40 years have seen a *large baby-boom generation* move slowly through the active age span. Its substantial inflow into the labor market from the 1970s onwards aggravated the disequilibria between supply and demand occasioned by the previously mentioned economic and social changes and contributed to the strong increase in benefit dependency and social security case load. Moreover, there has been the *increase in and changing nature of migratory movements*. Unlike with the organized labor migrations of the 1960s, the affluent West has since attracted a rapidly growing flow of Eastern European migrants and of unsolicited economic immigrants and asylum seekers (OECD, 2006a; Hooghe et al., 2008; European Commission, 2010b). These processes have unfolded quickly and concurrently with the problematic integration in education and the jobs market of the migratory flows of the 1960s. This has resulted in a high prevalence of work and income poverty among immigrants, especially in the large urban centers, and in the emergence of a subclass of illegal immigrants in search of a better future (Corluy & Verbist, 2010; Lelkes & Zólyomi, 2011). Although governments felt compelled to attribute them certain social rights (Corluy et al., 2011), the inclusion of groups that in the perception "do not belong" (Mau & Burkhardt, 2009) in the social protection system affects public attitudes on deservingness (Vanderstraeten, 2005, 2006; Roemer et al., 2007; Finseraas, 2012; van Oorschot, 2000; Taylor-Gooby, 2012). Indeed, there is clear evidence that individual approval of welfare state solidarity and redistribution is negatively associated with migratory influx, certainly in situations where employment rates among immigrants are low (Mau & Burkhardt, 2009; Finseraas, 2012).

Arguably, the substantial growth of top incomes (Atkinson & Piketty, 2006) and, more generally, rising inequalities, too, have been detrimental to the willingness to pay for social redistribution (Rosanvallon, 2011; OECD, 2009, 2012).[4] After a consistent decline in inequality in the 1950s and 1960s, it would seem that many welfare states began to evolve in the opposite direction in the second half of the 1980s. This trend first manifested itself in the United States (from the 1970s onwards), followed by the United Kingdom. In the literature, it is generally attributed to a real decline in the lowest wages combined with weak welfare state institutions (relatively weak labor market regulation and ungenerous social benefits). More recently, however, different sources speak of an increase in inequalities, including in the more egalitarian and strong welfare states of Scandinavia and Continental Europe. The OECD's 2008 report *Growing Unequal*? concludes on the basis of empirical data concerning the evolution of income distribution and financial poverty that "there has been an increase in income inequality that has gone on since at least the mid-1980s and probably since the mid-1970s. The widening has affected most (but not all) countries" (OECD, 2008:17). The report identifies the following explanatory factors: growing earnings inequality, growing income from assets, and a reduction in the redistribution achieved through social benefits and taxation.

In sum, social, economic, and demographic transitions occasioned a *strongly changed interface between growth, work, and social redistribution*. Growth slowed down, structural disequilibria emerged in changing labor markets, additional social and demographic transitions—most notably changing women's roles—gave rise to new social risks and to a steady increase in levels of welfare dependency. Meanwhile, changing social norms and values put pressures on traditional social redistribution by family-based progressive taxation, rights-based social protection, and social insurances. "New social risks" such as low educational levels, single earnership, and divorce are, after all, of an entirely different nature than the old risks. The lines dividing "risk," "behavior," and "choice" have become thinner and, in the case of long-term unemployment, they concern a highly asymmetric risk, to which an "insurance paradigm" is unable to formulate an adequate answer (Vandenbroucke, 2011). As a consequence, those lacking the skills and abilities to function in the knowledge economy saw their position deteriorate while the reliance on social protection increased dramatically (trends in economic dependency rates and the social policy caseload are presented by Vandenbroucke and Diris in Chapter 1). The required investment in human capital, with a view to education and activation among other things, has additionally burdened public budgets, as have the costs of aging, the impressive but costly technological improvements in health care, and new family support needs in the era of dual earnership. Moreover, in the knowledge economy, activation policies and the creation of adequately remunerated low-productive jobs has implied either tax reductions or public funding. At the same time, the inclusion of migrants has negatively affected public attitudes on deservingness and on the legitimacy of social redistribution. *Clearly, then, since the 1970s, in the era of "permanent austerity"(Pierson, 2001), there are reasons to believe that it has become much more difficult for modern welfare states to successfully pursue their core objectives of growth, full employment, and social inclusion.*

10.2.2 First Accommodations and the Social Service Trilemma

Welfare states accommodated—within the confines of the prevailing architectures—in different ways. The literature of the 1980s and 1990s points to at least three[5] "path-dependent" accommodations inherent in the worlds of welfare capitalism (Esping-Andersen, 1990: 191–229; Esping-Andersen, 1996; Hemerijck & Bakker, 1994; see also Pierson, 1994: 181; Pierson, 1995: 39; Mishra, 1990; Schmidt, 1983; Lessenich, 1995: 77–84).

The "*market model*" (Ferrarini, 2006), with weakly regulated labor markets and feeble social protection systems, was able to attain substantial overall job growth. Low-paid precarious work in services (including in domestic care work, the hotel and catering industry, and the entertainment sector) expanded strongly, a trend that was enhanced by a further deregulation of the labor market combined with less social protection (Kalleberg, 2011). The Anglo-Saxon countries saw a far-reaching individualization with relatively high proportions of lone-parent households and single persons, combined with a notably high female labor market participation rate. Demand for care work was mainly covered by the market. This way unemployment was kept relatively low, but at the cost of an unresolved redistribution issue, increasing in-work poverty, and deteriorating earnings, income, and social rights for the lower segments of the working population (or, in Esping-Andersen's words, the "service proletariat" [Esping-Andersen, 1993]). Particularly in the 1980s, liberal welfare states experienced rather spectacular increases in income inequality and relative poverty (Förster, 1993; Hanratty & Blank, 1992).

The "*social service model*," for its part, did simultaneously address the employment and the redistributive issues by, on the one hand, controlling wage development in sectors able to achieve strong productivity growth and, on the other, a far-reaching subsidization of social services. A substantial proportion of the job growth achieved consisted in services offered by local authorities geared to substituting social provisions for care and chores performed within households. In Lindbeck's terms, the family was "nationalized" (Freeman et al., 1997: 81). Poverty remained low while employment increased, albeit at the cost of high and increasing social expenditures. Apparently, the Scandinavian countries were best equipped against rising unemployment and they had also prepared most adequately for growing female labor market participation (Esping-Andersen, 1996). As a result, poverty in the Scandinavian welfare states remained unchanged at comparatively low levels (Ritakallio, 1994; Gustafsson & Uusitalo, 1990).

The transition from industrial to postindustrial employment was more difficult in the Continental European welfare states, because the high cost of labor and more regulated labor markets stood in the way of an adequate creation of low-qualified jobs in the services industry. Moreover, these welfare states continued to be geared primarily to providing cash transfers, so that the burden of the unfolding employment transition was borne almost entirely by their social security systems, either through policy-induced reductions in the labor force (early retirement schemes for those over 50 years of age, schemes encouraging women with children to exit the labor market,...; see Von Rhein-Kress, 1993) or through (long-term) benefit systems for the unemployed. In this *labor reduction* model, the process of individualization proceeded more slowly and female employment rates remained comparatively low: Care work continued to be performed primarily within the family (see, among others, Skocpol & Ritter, 1991; Orloff, 1993; Sainsbury, 1994). The employment issue associated with the postindustrial transition remained unresolved, and employment rates remained low, whereas poverty was addressed through social transfers. In the welfare states of Continental Europe, the first line of defense consisted of the traditional social security systems. Here, too, poverty and income inequality remained remarkably stable (Förster, 1993; Coder et al., 1993; Cantillon et al., 1997).

These courses may be summarized as the *Scandinavian route, combining high employment, high public expenditure, and low poverty; the Anglo-Saxon route, with high employment, low public expenditure, and high poverty; and the Continental European route, characterized by a constellation of low employment, high social expenditures, and low poverty* (Figure 10.1).

Based on these observations, *the prevailing view in the 1990s was that, in the new social and economic context, it was no longer possible to combine low poverty with high employment as well as budgetary discipline.* In a seminal article,

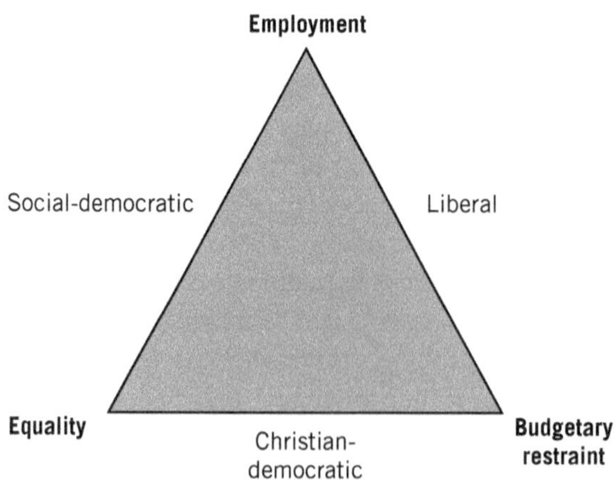

Figure 10.1. The trilemma. *Source*: Iversen & Wren, 1998.

Iversen and Wren considered the relationship between wage inequality, service employment, and changes in public outlays for wages as a proportion of GDP in Germany, the Netherlands, the United States, the UK, Sweden, and Denmark, leading them to identify the three aforementioned policy routes. The authors argued that, as a consequence of the transition from an economy dominated by manufacturing production to one dominated by service production, modern welfare states are no longer able to successfully enhance both employment and equality within a tight budgetary framework: "...governments and nations confront a three-way choice, or 'trilemma,' between budgetary restraint, income inequality and employment growth. While it is possible to pursue two of these goals simultaneously, it has so far proved impossible to achieve all three. Private employment growth can be accomplished only at the cost of wage inequality. Therefore, if wage equality is a priority, employment growth can be generated only through employment in the public sector—at the cost of higher taxes or borrowing" (Iversen & Wren, 1998: 508).

Of course, Iversen and Wren's influential notion of a *social service trilemma* concerned just one aspect of the puzzle discussed in the present chapter: They were referring to wage inequality and public outlay for wages only. Moreover, Iversen and Wren's claim has been challenged by many authors (see, among others, Kenworthy, 2008) while in a recent revision of the trilemma, Wren, Fodor, and Theodoropoulou argue that more recent developments have altered the economic environment in which services are produced: "...in this environment, the constraints on policy making may not be as tight as previously understood" (Wren, Fodor, & Theodoropoulou, 2013: 109). Yet, albeit understood in a more generic manner, as successfully combining employment growth, lower social spending, and more social cohesion, Iversen and Wren's notion is relevant to the context discussed here. In what follows, it will become clear that, the social investment discourse and, more generally, the perceived need for a radical reorientation of social and economic policies may be regarded as voluntaristic alternatives offering a way out of the trilemma in which welfare states found themselves. In the second half of the 1990s, welfare states began to alter their policy approach in order to deal with rising budget deficits, high structural unemployment, and/or rising poverty. In trying to overcome these difficult choices, all hope was placed on employment-centered welfare reform and, more generally on the so-called "social investment strategy."

10.3 FROM TRILEMMAS TO VIRTUOUS CYCLES?

After a period of divergence, there were signs from the second half of the 1990s of a degree of convergence in policy discourse and implementation toward employment, activation and social investment. This new era in the history of European welfare states was further colored by the Economic and Monetary Union project and by the accession in 2004 of the transition countries of Central Europe after the fall of the Berlin Wall in 1989. Increasingly, the EU presented itself as an important player, first in the fields of budgetary discipline and employment and subsequently (yet far more modestly) in the promotion of social inclusion.

10.3.1 Enlargement, Coordination, and the Cascade of EU Initiatives

The EU launched the Economic and Monetary Union project in 1990. In preparation for the introduction of a common currency, an encompassing program of macroeconomic convergence was installed, with a number of criteria for entry into the eurozone. Targets were set with regard to inflation, exchange rates, long-term interest rates, and government finance (budgets deficits and government debt). No target was set for (un)employment rates, yet labor market policy became highly salient in this context.

With the possibility of fiscal transfers between Member States ruled out, and currency devaluations and deficit spending no longer an option, the common currency was expected to generate pressure for structural reform, in product and, importantly, labor markets. Therefore, in 1994, the Heads of State or Government laid the foundations of a process of open coordination of employment policies, calling for a convergence of policies on best practices. In 1997, it was officially launched as the "European Employment Strategy."

Concurrently, the Treaty of Amsterdam (1997) enshrined *a new coordinating role for the EU in the fields of employment and social policy*. With a view to supporting the convergence process, a number of common social objectives were agreed upon at the Lisbon Summit of March 2000. The conclusions of the 2000 Lisbon Council with regard to social inclusion were ambitious: "The number of people living below the poverty line and in social exclusion in the Union is unacceptable. Steps must be taken to make a decisive impact on the eradication of poverty by setting adequate targets to be agreed by the Council by the end of the year."[6] To this end, a loose, open-policy approach was developed that was supposed to enable the Member States to learn from one another's experiences. The *Open Method of Coordination* (OMC) was extended to the domain of social inclusion at the Nice European Council of 2000. The following year, at the Laeken European Council, a set of social indicators was defined for the purpose of measuring the progress made toward the social objectives (Atkinson et al., 2002).[7]

Because the social protection agenda remained "politically and institutionally fragile" (Vandenbroucke, 2002b: 1) adequate income support, inclusive labor markets, and access to quality services were incorporated into the *Lisbon Treaty* (Verschueren, 2011; Dawson & De Witte, 2012). The so-called "horizontal social clause" (Article 9 TFEU) stipulates that the Union must "take into account requirements linked to the promotion of a high level of employment, the guarantee of adequate social protection, the fight against social exclusion, and a high level of education, training, and protection of human health."

The recent European story was further shaped by the experiences of the *transition countries of Central Europe*, a group that joined the EU in 2004. These countries, in addition to catching up with general globalization trends, have undergone major structural adjustment processes, and large volatility of economic cycles, as well as budgetary expansion and austerity cycles. This added to the effects of the technological catching up process and the consequent shifts in demand and supply of skilled labor, as well as in household formation patterns and in changes of welfare state arrangements, all having substantial effect on poverty trends in this very heterogeneous part of Europe.

10.3.2 The Social Investment Strategy and Employment-centered Welfare Reforms

The European focus on growth, work, and social inclusion has been increasingly incorporated into the broader policy narrative on "Social Investment," where investment in social policy plays a critical role as part of a virtuous cycle combining adaptability, flexibility, security, and employability (European Commission, 2004). The expectation was that a *virtuous cycle* could be generated whereby *growth would create employment (and vice versa), and more jobs in turn would lead to less poverty and lower (and/or more efficient) social spending* (Figure 10.2).

Obviously this is, to a large extent, political rhetoric, but the hope was nonetheless that higher employment could indeed reduce or reorient the level of social spending to more "productive," activating, and inclusive policies and lower poverty, directly through work or, indirectly, through more efficient, inclusive social spending. Recent literature refers to an "activating," "enabling," or

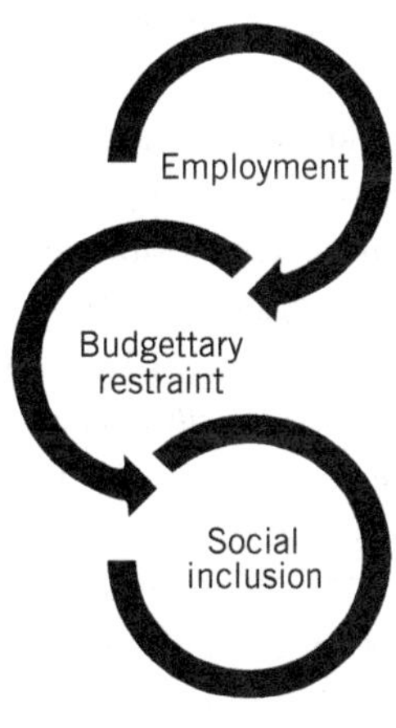

Figure 10.2. The virtuous cycle.

"developmental" welfare state, a "new" social contract and a new social agenda behind which one can discern a policy shift toward what has been termed a "social investment" agenda. In this volume Hemerijck elaborates on this new social policy approach, which focuses on investment rather than on direct provision of economic maintenance, and on equal opportunities rather than on equality of outcomes (see, among others, Esping-Andersen et al., 2002; Gilbert, 2004; Morel et al., 2009, 2012). This approach was evident in the Social Policy Agenda adopted by the European Union in 2000, which identified as its guiding principle the need to strengthen the role of social policy as a productive factor. In 2001, during the Belgian Presidency of the EU, Frank Vandenbroucke—then Minister of Social Affairs—commissioned Esping-Andersen, Hemerijck, and others to draft a report, later published with Oxford University Press under the title *Why We Need a New Welfare State* (2002). The book puts forward the idea of social investment to assist in the management of structural change while minimizing negative social consequences.

Although it is a matter of debate as to what extent policies actually veered in that direction (Morel et al., 2012; Hemerijck and De Deken in this volume), most Member States have experienced to a greater or lesser extent a shift in focus from passive social protection to activation and investment in education, more and better jobs, flexicurity, and family-oriented services with a view to enhancing people's ability to work and to balance work and family life (Taylor-Gooby, 2004; Bonoli, 2005).

In general terms, although the actual implementation differs greatly between welfare states, the policy ingredients have included the following: (1) *An all-encompassing focus on work*, for example, by making work attractive, by acting against unemployment traps, by imposing restrictions on early retirement schemes, by activating benefit recipients, by providing in-work benefits, by subsidizing low-productive labor, and—more generally—by making the labor market more flexible (Serrano Pascual, 2004; Eichhorst et al., 2008; Clegg, 2007; Grover & Stewart, 1999); (2) *Cost containment*, for example, by making social benefits in social security and social assistance schemes less generous, by imposing greater selectivity, by increasing dependence on activation programs, by introducing stricter eligibility requirements such as the obligation to accept "suitable jobs" or community services, and by shifting responsibilities to other actors such as private bodies and local governments (Cantillon, 2011; Weishaupt, 2011; Van Mechelen et al., 2010; Van der Veen, 2009; Kazepov, 2010; Cantillon, Van Mechelen, Pintelon, & Van den Heede in this volume); (3) *Family policy as a productive factor*, for example, by implementing career break schemes, and expanding parental leave schemes and pre-school services such as childcare, as well as long-term elderly care services (Esping-Andersen et al., 2002; Van Lancker & Ghysels in this volume); and (4) *Investment in human capital*, for example, a move toward early childhood services and equal opportunities in education, as well as encouraging lifelong learning and vocational training (Esping-Andersen, 2008; OECD. 2006b).

It is quite clear that the underlying rationale of these reforms is the belief in welfare through work, exemplified by investment in human capital and the enhancement of individual opportunities (Van der Veen, 2009). Otherwise (and briefly) stated, social investment strategies put emphasis on "the ability of everybody to accumulate skills and to find one's way on the labor market" (Gazier, 2009: 153). It is asserted that it is more opportune to affect income-generating attributes than to enhance transfers of income. In other words, it is expected that "poverty alleviation will, in the longer term, be attained more sustainably through the optimization of opportunities in education and training than through a system of progressive taxation and extensive social transfers." This insight is, of course, by no means new. In fact, the above quotation is taken from Herman Deleeck's Ph.D. from 1966.[8] This quotation, especially considering that it dates back to 1966, is important for yet another reason, as I will explain later.

10.3.3 Employment, Social Spending, and Poverty before the Crisis

So, how have employment, social spending and poverty evolved? *How successful has the new policy agenda been in trying to strengthen national welfare states capable of creating more employment and greater social cohesion?* Let us, by way of summary of the insights emerging from the analyses presented in this book take a bird's eye view of the *relationship between the changes in employment and social spending on the one hand and poverty trends on the other.*

Table 10.1 displays trends in at-risk-of-poverty, employment, and social spending for the Nordic, Anglo-Saxon, Continental, Eastern, and Southern-European countries. The positive and the negative signs are derived from the data presented in Chapter 1 and in the Appendix. At-risk-of-poverty data stem from SILC 2004–2008 and relate to the working-age population only. It appears that only the new Member States were successful in closing the virtuous cycle: at-risk-of-poverty declined while employment rose and social spending dropped. The Scandinavian countries displayed an increase in employment and a decrease in spending levels but an increase of relative income poverty. In the Anglo-Saxon countries, at-risk-of-poverty declined, employment rose moderately, but social spending went up, most notably in Ireland. The Continental and Southern EU countries combined an increase in employment and a decrease in social spending with a poverty standstill. Of course, within these geographical clusters of countries, there were divergent national trends to be observed: Within the Southern and Continental clusters Greece and Germany (according to SILC) stand out with significant increases in poverty; in comparison with the other new Member States, Latvia followed a clearly diverging course with a rising poverty rate; and although Denmark displayed significant increases of at-risk-of-poverty in the second half of the 1990s, with its stable poverty rate in the 2000s, this nation

Table 10.1. Trends in at-risk-of-poverty (AROP, SILC 2005–2008), employment, and social spending (2004–2007), working age population.

	AROP	Employment	Social expenditure
Scandinavian	+***	+	–
Anglo-Saxon	-	+	+
Continental incl. DE	+***	+	–
Continental excl. DE	+	+	–
Eastern Europe	–***	+	–
Southern Europe	+	+	–

Note: Scandinavian = DK, FI, and SE; Anglo-Saxon = IE and UK; Continental = BE, LU, FR, NL, AT, and DE; Eastern Europe = PL, CZ, LV, LT, SI, EE, SK, HU; Southern Europe = ES, IT, GR, and PT
Note: AROP defined as 60% of the median equivalized disposable income after social transfers (Eurostat), for people aged 0–59 years.
Note: *** significant change with 95% confidence interval (ci)
Source: EU-SILC (AROP, 2005–2008), EU-Labour Force Survey (employment, 2004–2007) & OECD SOCX (social expenditure, 2004–2007).

diverged from the other Scandinavian countries. The Irish trajectory clearly exhibited an exceptional pattern. (For more detailed overviews I refer the reader to Chapters 1, 3, and 5, and to the Appendix on evolutions in social spending and employment.) In general terms, however, the countries within each of the geographic clusters display sufficient similarities to justify the choice to maintain the classification for the sake of clarity.

This book has delved into the reasons why the EU15 was unable to deliver on the Lisbon Agenda in relation to the "eradication of poverty" and why Ireland, the UK (albeit to a much lesser extent), and many of the new Member States were more successful. As has been demonstrated, *changes in both the levels and the distribution of employment as well as social spending were instrumental.* Figures 10.3 and 10.4 summarize the trends in the contributory factors that are analyzed in detail in Chapters 1, 3, and 5. Figure 10.3 shows that in the Scandinavian countries and—though much less outspoken—in the Continental European states, employment growth and the ensuing decline in pre-transfer poverty were cancelled out by a decline in the poverty reducing impact of cash transfers. Figure 10.4 makes clear that this occurred within the work-poor and, although much less outspoken, also within the work-rich segments of the population. The southern EU countries displayed an increase in pre-transfer poverty as a consequence of job polarization and the ensuing increase of the number of jobless households. This was compensated for by a slight increase in poverty reduction through social transfers both in the work-rich and work-poor segments of the population. In the new Member States, employment strongly benefited the work-poor households. In addition, with a strengthened poverty reduction among work-rich households, this accounted for decreasing poverty trends in these countries. The exceptional favorable poverty trends observed in

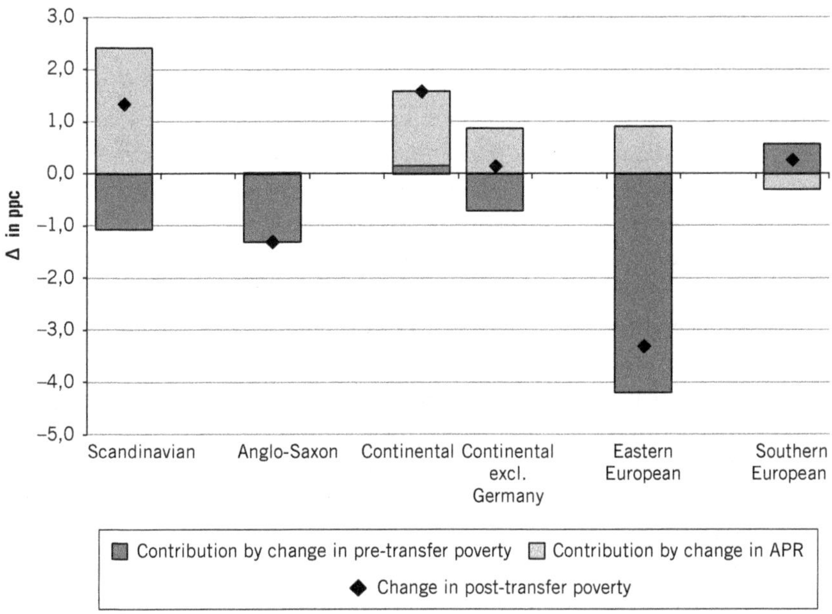

Figure 10.3. Contribution of changes in pre-transfer poverty and poverty reduction through social cash transfers to changes in post-transfer at-risk-of-poverty rates within the working age population, SILC 2005–2008). *Source*: based on Figure 1.9b in Vandenbroucke (this volume). *Note*: weighted averages, Scandinavian = DK, FI and SE; Anglo-Saxon = IE and UK; Continental = BE, LU, FR, NL, AT and DE; Eastern Europe = PL, CZ, LV, LT, SI, EE, SK, HU; Southern Europe = ES, IT, GR and PT.

Ireland were the result of a strong increase in the poverty-reducing impact of social spending for both work-rich and work-poor households, which compensated for a growing number of jobless households. The moderate decrease of at-risk-of-poverty in the UK was accounted for by a decrease of pre-transfer poverty and an increase of poverty reduction by social transfers.

Importantly, as Figures 1.9b and 1.10b in Chapter 1 show, only seven countries—Ireland, Austria, the Czech Republic, Lithuania, Portugal, Spain, and the UK—realized greater poverty reduction through social transfers among work-poor households. In Ireland and (to a lesser extent) in Austria, this did, however, coincide with an *increase* in the share of this group of households in the total population. We thus observe in only five countries, a concurrent increase of poverty reduction in the work-poor segments *and* a decrease of the share of these segments in the population.*In other words, the answer to the central question put forward in this book is that in most countries the distribution upside of creating jobs (fewer people confronted with high poverty risks in work-poor households) has been affected by a distributive downside (more poverty especially among the work-poor households) that may have been intrinsic to the way in which jobs were created.*

These observations point to different *obstacles in the looping "work," "spending," and "at-risk-of-poverty."*

The *first* obstacle relates to the distribution of work between work-poor and work-rich households. In general, in the old Europe, compared with the work-richer households the *work-poor households benefited less from job growth* (see Table 3-1 in Chapter 3). Corluy and Vandenbroucke explain that, to an extent, this is purely a mathematical truism, but they also point to the importance of individualization, increasing female participation rates, and other factors explaining the observed polarization of jobs over households (see also Vandenbroucke and Diris in Chapter 1). Although the authors of Chapter 3 explain that the modest conversion of individual employment successes into household employment successes cannot explain very much of the changes in national at-risk-of-poverty rates during the economic upswing, they also ascertain that "this does not diminish the importance national and EU policy-makers should attach to the presence of high numbers of jobless households and polarization, as possibly problematic conditions for welfare states."

The *second* obstacle relates to the poverty reducing impact of social cash transfers. Considering work-poor households, the authors of Chapters 1 and 5 observed a decline in poverty reduction through social transfers in most of the Continental and Nordic welfare states. In many of these countries *income poverty among work-poor households increased* accordingly. Moreover, the evolution in average and theoretical protection levels for work-poor and for work-rich households shown in Chapter 5 is suggestive of diverging developments: Average benefits, as measured in the SILC samples, as well as the theoretically calculated income levels, indicate that in many countries especially the protection for work-poor households came under pressure while, in some countries, the protection for work-rich(er) households even increased. This trend tallies with the hypothesis that the poverty-reducing function of social security is compromised by (a) a differential social stratification of old and new social risks (unemployment and disability overrepresented in lower social segments of the population while new work-related risks are more prevalent among higher skilled work-rich(er) families); (b) persistently high benefit dependency and the ensuing need for employment-centered welfare reforms; and (c) a differential political legitimacy of social protection against social risks affecting work-poor and work-richer families (see Chapter 5).

The *third* obstacle is discussed in Chapter 4 and relates to in-work-poverty. There it is argued that social protection is not an unimportant factor explaining in-work-poverty. Although in-work-poverty and poverty according work-intensity point at least partially to different realities, Figure 10.4 gives support to the hypothesis developed by Marx and Nolan that in-work-poverty is associated not only with low pay but also with low work-intensity at the household level and with shortcomings in tax and benefit systems. The *decreasing poverty reducing capacity of social protection* vis-à-vis households with higher work-intensity as it

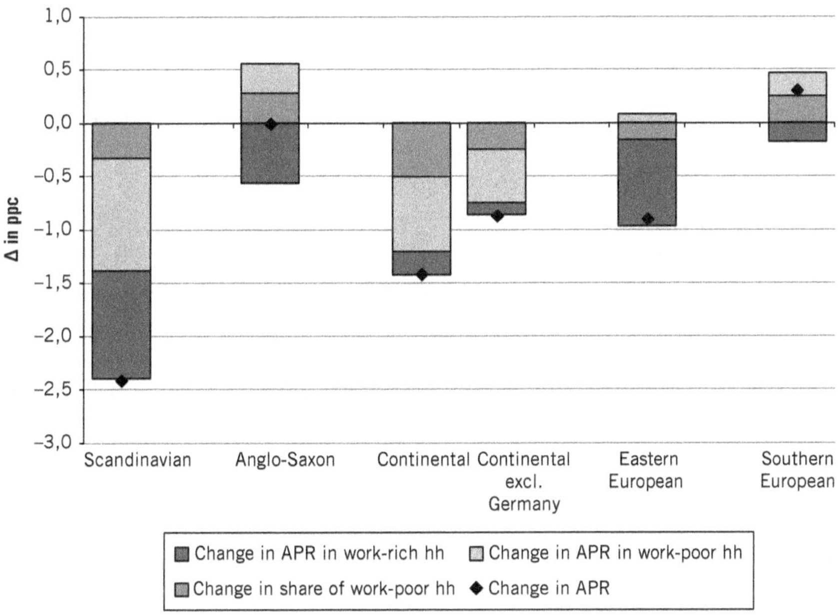

Figure 10.4. Contribution of changes in the share of work-poor households, in absolute poverty reduction in work-poor and work-rich households to changes in post-transfer at-risk-of-poverty rates within the working age population (SILC 2005–2008). *Source*: Based on Figure 1.10b in Vandenbroucke (this volume). *Note*: weighted averages, Scandinavian = DK, FI and SE; Anglo-Saxon = IE and UK; Continental = BE, LU, FR, NL, AT and DE; Eastern Europe = PL, CZ, LV, LT, SI, EE, SK, HU; Southern Europe = ES, IT, GR and PT.

appeared for the Nordic, Continental, and Eastern clusters in Figure 10.4 should thus be regarded as a potential additional hindrance in the virtuous cycle.

A *fourth* obstacle that impacts the relationships among job growth, relative income poverty, and social spending relates to the not unimportant shift that occurred in overall social spending from cash to in-kind spending (see Chapter 9 and Appendix). As the impact of in-kind spending is not visible in the income-poverty measure, assessments of the poverty reduction capacity of welfare states are in danger of overlooking a growing proportion of social expenditures. Chapter 6 by Verbist and Matsaganis, therefore, introduced a methodologically innovative model whereby the distributive impact of in-kind spending is also taken into account. They show that, while total public spending on health care, education, and childcare has the effect of reducing inequality and poverty, when size is taken into account, *cash transfers turn out to be more pro-poor than in-kind benefits.* I will come back to this issue in the next section.

These observations lead us to our initial question: *was* and *is* it possible to reduce benefit dependency (and the associated expenditures) in a structural way while at once achieving progress in the fields of employment as well as poverty reduction, given (a) the expenditures necessitated by job creation (particularly on child daycare, leave schemes, and in-work benefits); (b) the requirement to combat employment traps in order to make work more attractive at the bottom end of the labor market for individuals possessing lower-productive skills; and (c) the more adequate social protection that is necessary in order to reduce poverty among work-poor households? *On the basis of the analyses presented in this book, the conclusion can only be that the experience in the EU before the crisis is indicative of tough trade-offs that should not be taken lightly.* They are indicative of the structural difficulties active welfare states face today to combat poverty in a structural way. Undeniably, trends are not unequivocal and many of the new Member States were successful in relation to all three dimensions. There, the circumstances were, however, quite exceptional: After a period of major socioeconomic crises, the European convergence drive achieved very strong economic and job growth, although much of this convergence has since been reversed in consequence of the crisis. Admittedly, this book has focused on a brief period: the synthesizing figures above relate to the SILC surveys of 2004–2008. Hence, the conclusions drawn are inevitably tentative. Nonetheless, wherever possible, we have presented analyses that relate to the economically favorable 1990s, and these are by and large in the same line as evolutions observed in the 2000s (see Chapters 3 and 5).

10.4 BEYOND SOCIAL INVESTMENT

So, *are Social Investment Policies to blame for the new trade-offs*? (Hemerijck, 2013: 286). Of course not. As I explained in the first part of this chapter, the difficulty in successfully combining job growth, budgetary restraint, and social inclusion results from the big social, economic, and demographic transformations that occurred since the early 1970s. The social investment paradigm should, on the contrary, be considered as a rational and functional response to these changes, offering an alternative to the traditional social policy paradigm.

Are Social Investment Policies to blame for disappointing poverty outcomes? For many reasons this question remains largely unanswered; first of all because the counterfactual remains unknown. The age and family structure of the population, migration movements, global competition, and technological innovation are all potentially strong drivers of poverty growth. Secondly, it may be too early to pass judgment on a policy paradigm that, by definition, incorporates an important temporal dimension—achieving a return on investment in human capital does after all require time. Thirdly, the focus in this book on *changes* may lead to overlooking successes. After all, although the Scandinavian countries have been losing ground, they continue to set the example when it comes to simultaneously achieving high employment, low poverty, and high-performance economic activity, albeit accompanied by high social spending. However, it is equally true that in many developed welfare states the social investment turn and employment centered welfare reform did not deliver in terms of poverty alleviation.

While education, along with the emancipation and empowerment of the *working classes* were obviously already deep-rooted concerns in the design of the post-War welfare state, it is clearly the case that the addition of "positive" measures, aimed at social investment, the emancipation of *women*, and social promotion, on top of the traditionally "negative" forms of protection, has gained momentum since the 1990s. Much as labor law slowly evolved in the early 20th century from a merely "negative" focus on protection against the forces of the free market (e.g., through a prohibition on child labor) to a "positive" focus on improving the social status of individuals (e.g., by introducing compulsory education), so, too, the "old" Welfare State ("Etat Providence" in French, "Verzorgingsstaat" in Dutch, "Estado de Bienestar" in Spanish, "Welsyn Staat" in Afrikaans) with its emphasis on care and welfare (in the sense of health and well-being) should be complemented with "developmental," "enabling," and "investment" strategies whereby a new dimension is added to that of protection from cradle to grave.

Yet, the qualified analyses presented in this book suggest that the shift from passive social protection to activation and investment was definitely much more difficult than some might have expected and that the new policies failed to deliver in terms of poverty alleviation. *This points not only at the structural inabilities of developed welfare states today to reduce income poverty, but also at some limitations of the investment paradigm itself to overcome these deficiencies.* Insofar as investing in human capital, maximizing employment, and facilitating the work-life balance is the only possible response to new needs and circumstances, governments cannot be too ambitious in radically applying the social investment recipe to social policy renewal. However, this must not impede us from locating its possible shortcomings and problems. Influential ideas should withstand a critical assessment, certainly so if they are to become the encompassing concept of social policy in Europe and beyond.

10.4.1 Three Shortcomings of Social Investment

In a general way it would appear that, although there are clearly different intellectual and political influences that have shaped the notion of social investment, and while some authors have forcefully argued that "income security is a precondition for an effective social investment strategy" (Esping-Andersen, 2002: 5), the political translation of "social investment" and "social policy as a productive factor" entails the danger of *instrumentalization* and *undervaluation* of social protection, care and redistribution *per se* and of the underestimation of the difficult trade-offs with which developed welfare states today are confronted.

10.4.1.1 Exaggerated Expectations with Regard to Equal Opportunities Policies

The *first* and most important shortcoming of the social investment notion lies in the *exaggerated expectations* it may create *with regard to the possibilities of combating social inequalities through* equal *opportunities policy*. More than a century of historical, sociological, economic, and psychological research leaves little doubt as to just how determining social, economic, and cultural contextual factors are for one's life chances. In their seminal work *The Constant Flux*, Erikson and Goldthorpe (1992) showed that there is a high degree of constancy and commonality in social stratification (as measured in terms of father-son class mobility). More specifically, with regard to inequalities in education, few have argued against the classic "persistent inequality thesis" of Shavit and Blossveld (1993). It is true that Breen et al. in their important contribution "Nonpersistent inequality in educational attainment" (2009) found, contra Shavit and Blosveld, a widespread decline in educational inequality in the first two thirds of the 20th century in eight European countries. Importantly, however, the decline took place "for the most part during a relatively short period of around 30 years in the middle of the century, between the oldest cohort (born 1908–24) and the second youngest (born 1945–54 and thus *in the educational system during the period 1950–75*)" (Breen et al., 2009: 1514). The general picture subsequently is one of mainly stasis. This observation (which is corroborated in numerous country-based studies) inspired Erikson and Goldthorpe to make the following highly relevant assertion in the context of social investment discourse.

"In sum, intergenerational inequality has important self-maintaining properties. It creates conditions under which individuals in less advantaged positions choose and act in ways that can in themselves be understood as adaptively quite rational (rather than, say, being the expressions of 'dysfunctional' subcultures) yet which, in aggregate, serve to perpetuate the status quo. Educational expansion and reform alone should not therefore be expected to serve as very effective instruments of public policy at creating greater equality of opportunity in the sense of 'a more level playing field.' Complementary efforts to reduce inequalities of condition, and especially class inequalities in economic security, stability and prospects, will also be required" (Erikson & Goldthorpe, 2002: 42).

Some have called into question the structuring impact of social class in modern societies (e.g., Clark & Lipset, 1991; Lee & Turner, 1996; Pakulski & Waters, 1996; Scott, 1996). Beck (1992), for example, argues that we have evolved into a so-called "risk society," characterized by greater as well as more diffuse social risks. However, "bad" social risks such as unemployment, low work-intensity, and illness continue to be significantly socially stratified, including (though to a lesser extent) in countries that are considered good examples when it comes to effectuating great(er) social equality. The existence of strong father-son social gradients for social risks that are statistically likely to induce poverty—particularly unemployment, low work-intensity, ill-health, and low pay—has been demonstrated time and again (e.g., O'Neill & Sweetman, 1998; Feinstein, 1993; Pintelon et al., 2013; Cappellari & Jenkins, 2002; Nilsson, 2012). Social class is also observed to influence the duration of poverty spells (Whelan et al., 2003; Dewilde, 2008; Biewen, 2009), while risky life events clearly do not trigger identical poverty effects for different social classes (Vandecasteele, 2010). Moreover, compelling evidence is found to support the view that stratification patterns are by and large the same across welfare states, be it the Scandinavian, the Anglo-Saxon, or the Continental European ones (Pintelon et al., 2013). Clearly, then, social background is an overwhelmingly important factor. The universal nature—in terms of both space and time—of the gravity of social class calls for moderation of expectations in respect to the impact of social investment. Herman Deleeck, in the previously cited 1966 quote, argued that, from a long-term perspective, social investment is more effective than merely passive protection. While it is undoubtedly the case that some welfare states (notably the Scandinavian ones) are in a higher league thanks to persistent social investment, Deleeck's words sound slightly bitter in the context of the aforementioned studies and insights.

10.4.1.2 Little Guidance in Respect to Care and Protection for the Most Vulnerable

The notion of investment implies a return, and hence one would expect there to be a tendency in social investment policy design first to help forward the relatively strong in the hope that the weaker will be carried along. That is why social investment—however important it may be—must not and cannot be the only, or even the principal, objective of social policy in the new welfare state. After all, there is no denying that the notion loses much of its significance in the context of care for frail elderly, for disabled persons, the long-term ill, or more generally for individuals seriously deprived by circumstances of life. Remarkably, and perhaps symptomatically, the most recent literature on social investment (see, for example, Morel et al., 2012; Bonoli et al., 2012) as well as the work of Esping-Andersen (2002) and Giddens (1998) is mute on the adequacy of social protection of persons who cannot or will not be activated due to disability, illness, or old age—people who are vulnerable and require care. The focus is overwhelmingly on "active aging," "capacitating" policies and "empowerment." Although these actions are obviously extremely important tools of "social inclusion," a one-dimensional perspective of an all too voluntaristic activation and investment discourse may become very threatening for some of the most vulnerable. So, although ambitions should be as great as possible and "the social scientist's circumspection should not unduly overtake the policymakers voluntarism," social protection, redistribution, and care *should and will* always remain important tools for fighting Beveridge's five "Giant Evils" of "Want, Disease, Ignorance, Squalor and Idleness."

10.4.1.3 A One-sided Focus on Economic Activity

The *third* shortcoming relates to the fact that growth and paid work are considered to be aims in themselves. This may lead to a *one-sided focus on economic activity* as a means of attaining social inclusion, as if goals such as societal recognition, social belonging, and the development of social capital—cf. the previously mentioned notions of "bienestar," "welsyn," "well-being"—were achievable only through more paid labor, and as if activities in the informal sphere were, by definition, devoid of economic and social utility.[9] It speaks for itself that more jobs should lead to lower benefit dependency, as previously mentioned in this chapter. Against the backdrop of population aging and Europe's shrinking workforce, this is obviously an important socioeconomic objective. Moreover, in today's welfare state more than ever before, labor participation is a key instrument for attaining social integration: In an individualized society, the absence of "work" often holds a danger of social exclusion and detachment from the prevailing lifestyle and culture in a given society. This should, however, not lead to societies where the cement of giving and receiving care remains undervalued in the general policy framework.

10.4.2 The Case of the Disabled

In *Frontiers of Justice*, Martha Nussbaum (2006) takes the situation of Jamie, Arthur, and Sesha, three seriously disabled children as a starting point for expounding her views on the ethical foundations of a fair society.[10] By analogy let us briefly consider the three aforementioned shortcomings of the social investment paradigm in relation to the *disability sector*.[11] On average, the disabled as much as the parents of children with an impairment have *lower levels of education* (OECD, 2010). Children's behavioral disorders are moreover positively correlated with *relational conflict* leading to high divorce risks in families with disabled children (Al Kremani, 2011; Bennet & Hay, 2007; Kersh et al., 2006; Ghysels & Van Vlasselaer, 2008). Children's disabilities have also a clear *negative impact on mother's employment* (Gorden et al., 2007; Ghysels & Van Vlasselaer, 2008). As a consequence, the disabled are strongly concentrated in work-poor households (see Chapter 4). This raises many (normative) questions: What is the realistic and desirable work-intensity norm for these households? Should domestic care work be rewarded? And if so, in which cases? Clearly, the low-skilled, divorced, non-working mother of a severely disabled child who wants to take care of her own child is in great need of (financial) support, a nurturing environment, and adequate services.

In most countries, those who give or receive care face *very high poverty risks.* Three percent of the population of active age declare themselves to be permanently disabled. However, this group represents 9% of the people at risk of poverty (European Union, 2012). In Europe, 6.5 million of those who are at risk of poverty or exclusion declare some form of disability (European Commission, 2010b: 5). On the caregiving side it appears that persons without employment and fulfilling domestic tasks, such as caring for a disabled child or other dependent persons, are strongly overrepresented in the population at risk of poverty (European Union, 2010). As has previously been argued, this is due to a number of factors. There is the *inadequacy of a single household income* in what is effectively a dual-earnership era;[12] caregivers often face *more substantial costs* and they often have a *weaker socioeconomic and educational profile.*

Clearly, *the disability risk is illustrative of the three aforementioned shortcomings entailed by a unidimensional use of the social investment concept*—the lack of guidance it offers for a social policy that provides care and protection for the weakest, the exaggerated expectations it may create in respect to equality of opportunities, and the one-sided focus on economic growth and activities as a way to social inclusion. The notion of social investment wrongs care, caregiving, and the associated value of compassion—so neatly captured by the American and Canadian social security term of a "*compassion allowance*"—as the cement of society.

That is not to say that—as a general trend—social protection has become less generous toward the disabled. In a number of countries, including Belgium and the Netherlands, the adequacy of benefits has actually been enhanced for these groups (see Table 5.1 in this volume). However, Organisation for Economic Co-operation and Development (OECD) figures make clear that in the last decade the relative income situation of people with disability has deteriorated in more than half of the countries for which trends could be observed (OECD, 2010: 57). Clearly, in many countries compensation policies became less important compared with integration policies (OECD, 2009: 234). In a discussion on activating disability policies, as opposed to redistributive ones, Hvinden quite rightly concluded that "the current criticism against redistributive disability provisions... tend to downplay the significance of income transfers and services for the dignity, autonomy, and participation for a great number of persons with disabilities" (Hvinden, 2009: 26–27).

10.4.3 New Matthew Effects[13]

Social investment aims to move beyond redistributive, consumption-based social welfare centered around benefits and rights to a social welfare whereby investment in human capital enhances people's capacity to participate (see, among others, Jenson & Saint-Martin, 2003). If, however, it is true that—due to the gravity of social stratification and given that more vulnerable segments tend to find it hard to navigate their way to the labor market and/or work-related benefits—"new" spending[14] is beneficial more to the socioeconomically stronger groups, then it is *unintentionally resulting in an adverse redistribution of resources* and in new Matthew effects.[15]

Generally speaking, there would appear to be good reasons to assume that "new policies budgets," less so than the traditional cash transfers, tend to flow to the higher income groups.[16] Depending on the policy design and the social stratification of employment, one may indeed expect more or less adverse redistributive impacts of work-related social expenditures, such as in-work benefits, child care, or parental leave, etc.[17] If one wishes to increase labor force participation, then a policy is required that facilitates the combination of work and family life and, more generally, makes work more attractive. Obviously such a policy will first benefit those already participating in the labor process, but the underlying rationale is that others will follow suit. As poverty is typically high in workless households, effective work-related spending is expected to be pro-poor at least in the long term. However, if job growth does only partially benefit work-poor households, work-related social spending will tend to accrue permanently to middle and higher income groups. This is especially true with regard to policies aiming to achieve a better work-family balance. So long as women's roles remain socially stratified and while there is no adequate support for those for whom the combination of work and family life is (temporarily) not an option (e.g., mothers and fathers of a child with an impairment), the new-risk policy is bound to generate adverse redistributive effects.[18] In Chapter 6, Verbist and Matsaganis show that, while total public spending on health care, education and child care has the effect of reducing inequality and poverty, when size is taken into account, cash transfers turn out to be more pro-poor than in-kind benefits in most countries. Depending on the policy design and the social stratification of employment, one may similarly expect more or less adverse redistributive impacts of other "new" work-related social expenditures, such as in-work benefits, subsidies, tax credits, and parental leave. Using data from the Labour Force Survey, Ghysels & Van Lancker (2010) find that, in most countries, households with a low-educated mother use parental leave opportunities to a lesser extent than do other households. This would appear to be the cumulative outcome of unequal labor force participation and inequalities in the effective access to parental leave within the working population (Van Lancker & Ghysels in this volume). Of course, as shown in Chapter 9, appropriate policy designs may no doubt help reduce or even neutralize such adverse effects. However, this requires that the redistributive issue should be firmly addressed in policy and discourse.

10.4.4 Social Spending is Not Synonymous with Redistribution

So the implication of the foregoing is that policymakers should be aware of possible *Matthew effects* in the distribution of jobs, social benefits, and of social services and, more generally, of the redistributive aspect of social spending as discussed in Julian Le Grand's classic book *The Strategy of Equality* (1982). The growing body of investment literature is very quiet on this matter. However, a simple quintile distribution of social spending reveals a clear but troubling pattern. The diagrams below provide an overview for the geographic clusters in Europe of the distribution by income quintiles of cash benefits and spending on in-kind services for the working-age population as calculated in the chapter by Verbist and Matsaganis. It is striking how broadly dispersed social spending is

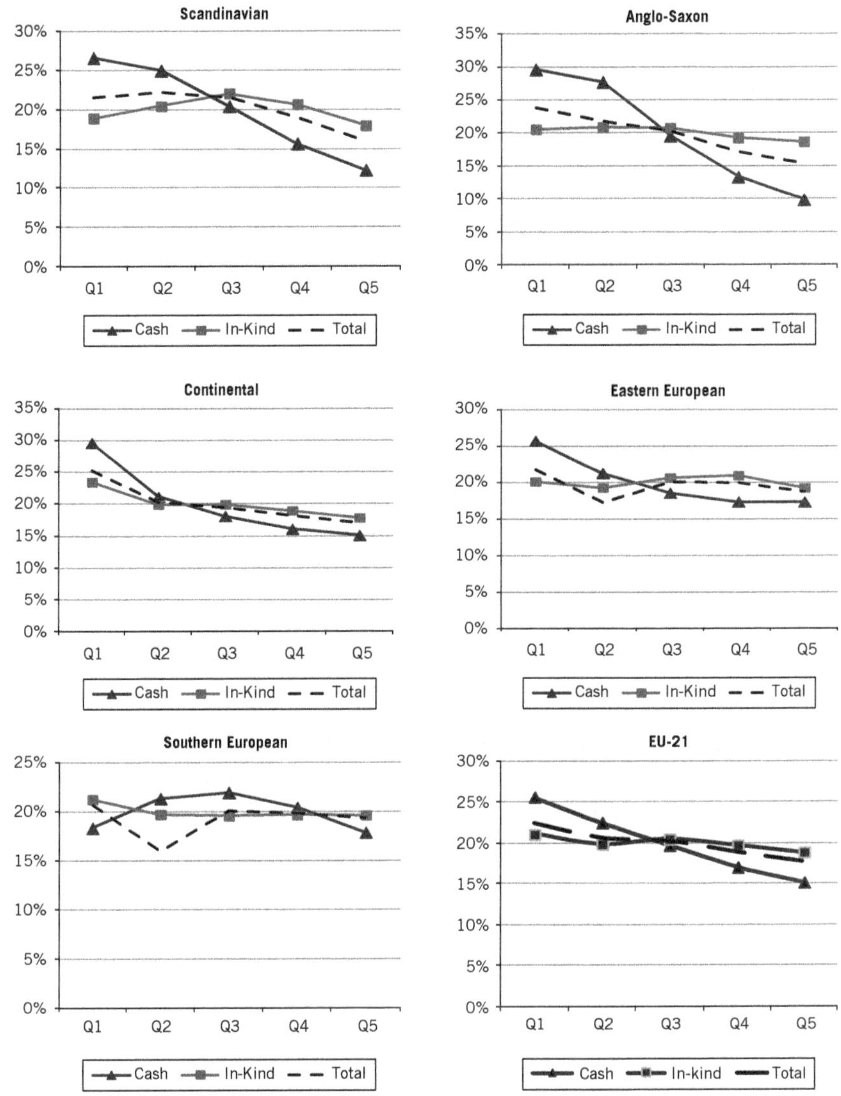

Figure 10.5. Distribution of cash and in-kind benefits (non-elderly only) over Dpi quintiles.
Notes: Dpi = disposable cash income (equivalence scale = modified OECD-scale), calculations based on the data presented in chapter 6 in-kind-benefits include health care, education, ECEC.

across the income distribution. In the 21 countries represented in the first graph, just over 22% of total social spending accrues to the 20% poorest households, while the highest quintiles still take up over 17% of spending. In-kind spending is clearly less pro-poor than cash spending, even though the latter category is also very broadly dispersed across the income distribution: Some 15% of cash benefits go to the 20% best-off households. Social spending is most pro-poor in the Anglo-Saxon and Continental countries. In Eastern and Southern European countries the distribution of social spending across income quintiles is almost completely flat (Figure 10.5).

In other words, social spending is not at all synonymous with social redistribution. Hemerijck, therefore, rightly points out that "we should not overestimate the impact that the welfare state has on inequality" (Hemerijck, 2013: 286). However, *if* we take poverty reduction seriously, this issue needs to be placed firmly on the agenda. Effective antipoverty policy with limited resources requires indeed an *enhancement* of the redistributive capacity and the pro-poorness of social spending. Against the backdrop of population aging, rising health care costs, and budgetary restraint there is simply no other way.

This is clearly a complex debate in which considerations of efficiency need to be balanced with a policy design that is legitimate in the eyes of the broad middle classes and the higher-income segments of society. They must, after all, bear the burden of social redistribution. In Chapter 1 of this book, Vandenbroucke and Diris recall the now familiar and generally acknowledged relationship between the volume of social spending and poverty levels. Effective anti-poverty policy presupposes a substantial commitment of resources. This spending should not be targeted exclusively at the most needy, for at least three reasons. *First and foremost*, social spending should *prevent* poverty, including by offering risk protection to all individuals—including those belonging to the less needy middle classes—and by ensuring that households facing such circumstances should not get caught in a downward spiral toward social exclusion. The saying "prevention is better than cure" holds in this sense, too. This is where the purpose of universal social protection schemes lies. *Second*, it is a known fact that social redistribution that benefits only the weakest tends not to have the degree of legitimacy among the middle classes that is required in order for those middle classes to be prepared to contribute. Here we refer to Korpi and Palme's influential notion of the "paradox of redistribution," which is also briefly discussed in Chapter 5. *Third*, as it is generally assumed in the context of such in-kind benefits as child care and education, a mix of socially strong and socially weak children or pupils is beneficial for social promotion. This also presupposes universal provisions according to quality standards set by the broad middle classes.

However, this does not mean that there are no opportunities for enhancing elements of targeting within a framework of universality. The relationship between social spending and poverty is, after all, not particularly strong. At a given level of resources, some countries succeed better than others in combating poverty, as the diagrams presented in Chapter 1 show. There are, moreover, also indications that the relationships among the volume of social spending, the degree of universality, and poverty are less outspoken today than used to be the case (see Kenworthy, 2011; Whiteford, 2008).

Matthew effects have been widely observed throughout the history of the advanced welfare state (Goodin, 1986; Deleeck et al., 1983; Merton, 1968), but today they seem to manifest themselves differently. The principal new social risk in the contemporary welfare state is undoubtedly joblessness. It is a risk that is complexly composed of different socioeconomic factors, as explained in Chapter 3. If the more vulnerable in society benefit less from expanding labor markets or if they are hit more severely by economic crisis and—under strongly work-oriented policies—are, therefore, less able to benefit from a variety of "work-related" spending schemes, while also seeing their income decline due to decommodification and anti-poverty-trap measures, then the inevitable implication is that money will tend to flow more to the higher and socioeconomically stronger groups in society. Unless, that is, the gamble of the social investment strategy pays off and education, as an important mediating factor, is able to smooth out intergenerational inequalities. However, the gravitational pull of social inequality in education is so strong that any effects in this respect would only become apparent in the (very) long term.

Due to the commitment to equality of opportunities rather than equality of outcomes (e.g., the emphasis on schooling and training, which presupposes commitment and hence responsibility from individuals) and the focus on employment as a fast-track to social inclusion (which—again—presupposes a commitment to look for a job and the responsibility to accept suitable employment), benefit recipients and persons in need are increasingly expected to act upon opportunities that are opened up to them. Several examples are to be found, such as behavioral management contracts[19] or social benefits conditional on school enrollment (Cantillon & Van Lancker, 2012).[20] The CSB-MIPI data set (Van Mechelen et al., 2011) shows that the conditionality of child benefits on school enrollment is now commonplace in several Central and Eastern European countries. Here, again, Matthew effect can come into play. In real life the dividing line between "circumstances" (e.g., social background) for which an individual should be compensated and "ambitions or efforts," for which an individual is held responsible, is indeed very thin.[21] Not only the actual living conditions but also family histories, deprivation, and social hierarchy can influence judgments and behaviors: "Suffering is not typically ennobling; more often it can deform or maim the personality" (Nussbaum, 2001: 411). More generally, "bad" social risks such as unemployment or ill-health remain truly "social" in that they are not coincidentally connected with life courses. The strong social selectivity of these risks significantly qualifies the notion of "individual responsibility." Conditionalities should, therefore, only be deployed if they stand a good chance of achieving success, in accordance with human dignity, with *compassion,*[22] and in the service of agency and social justice.[23] That is why great modesty is called for in policy outlining and implementation. In that matter, social policy should continue to be primarily concerned with the even distribution of capabilities, of equal opportunities for functioning and social rights[24], instead of enforcing desirable functionings by means of conditional policies. Otherwise, new policies risk encouraging new forms of exclusion.

10.4.5 Trade-offs, Political Choices, and Conflicts

For the reasons mentioned before "social investment" cannot take the place of the welfare state. What it can and must do is add a further dimension to the ethical project underlying the welfare state. Given budgetary constraints, aging and health care costs, this process, however, inevitably involves trade-offs, which—if inadequately acknowledged and identified—may lead to less social redistribution, care, and protection for the very weakest in society. This book deals with several such trade-offs. Chapter 5 touches briefly upon the question I already mentioned of whether social policies should be poverty-preventing and/or more middle-class oriented and, if so, then how. A second trade-off worth mentioning here is that between expenses for "services" versus "cash transfers." Healthcare expenses will undoubtedly continue to rise in the future, while the need for education, child care, and elderly care is expected to increase. If we are not alert to this, this may reduce the redistributional capacity of social spending. Central to this book is the trade-off between employment-centered welfare reform and adequate social protection for those who remain outside the labor market. By overemphasizing the productive side of social policy, these (and many other) trade-offs may well be minimized, as a result of which the redistributive aspect is in danger of being overlooked.

10.5 CONCLUSION: PROGRESS FOR THE POOR THROUGH SOCIAL INVESTMENT, PROTECTION, AND INNOVATION

Building on the empirical data presented elsewhere in this book, the analysis in this chapter may be summarized as follows. The Western welfare states have experienced momentous change in recent decades, driven primarily by three concurrent evolutions: the emancipation of women and the rise of the knowledge and service economy against a background of globalization. More recently, migration and population aging (and the ensuing substitution of working-age cash benefits by pensions and health care) have emerged as two further impeding factors to achieving progress in the fight against income poverty and social inequality. There are undoubtedly reasons to believe that it has become and will remain difficult for modern welfare states to successfully pursue their core objectives of growth, full employment, and social inclusion. Against this backdrop, a broad consensus has grown in recent years regarding the need for a thorough rethink of the post-War policy paradigm toward social investment and employment-centered welfare reform and prevention rather than damage compensation. Clearly, governments cannot be too ambitious in deploying investment strategies for the long-term development of human capital, early childhood development, training, education and lifelong learning. However, this must not stop us from locating shortcomings and problems, as employment central welfare reform and the investment turn, too, did not deliver in terms of poverty alleviation.

In this book, we more specifically presented empirical indications of the following elements: (a) in many countries of the EU15 job growth has benefited work-poor households less than it has benefited work-rich households; and (b) welfare states structural redistributive capacity to reduce poverty has declined for the generation under 60 years of age, in consequence of (c) a declining adequacy of protection for vulnerable subgroups of the population, work-poor families in particular and (d) a shift from working-age cash spending to pensions, health care, and working-age in-kind spending.

As argued in this chapter, a one-sided implementation of social investment entails the danger of an underestimation of the workings of labor markets and the strong gravitational pull of social class, and thus an overstatement of the potential of activation, enabling and developmental strategies, and a depreciation of the question of redistribution, of social protection, and of care for the most vulnerable. This should be seen not as a criticism of the investment concept as such, but rather as a warning against too simplistic an interpretation and the exaggerated expectations it may engender. A unilateral focus on activation, investment, and promotion might turn against the weakest in society and it could moreover obscure other promising policy alternatives.

In our understanding, the European social objectives can only be attained if a new balance is struck in the investment concept that now is often referred to within the EU and beyond: Without a renewed focus on social redistribution—a notion whose prominence has faded in discourse and policies alike—and without effective guarantees regarding basic social rights for those in and those out of work, and without a reappraisal of activities that are currently regarded as economically nonproductive, it will become increasingly hard to achieve social progress in a future that promises to be bleaker than the past. The analyses presented in the consecutive chapters of this book point to different policy options for doing so. Some of them are briefly mentioned here by way of concluding remarks. *First*, the proportion of work-poor households may probably be reduced to at least 10% according to the examples of the best performing EU countries. Successful activation and part-time work can arguably be considered as good practices of how a better distribution of work can be attained. *Second*, guaranteeing decent minimum incomes in general and adequate child benefit packages in particular, while expensive in some countries, is not altogether impossible, provided that the policy design is efficient, and that genuine activation measures as well as adequate minimum wages are put in place. *Third*, social spending is clearly much less redistributive than one might expect. The evidence presented in this book shows that a greater "efficiency" in terms of poverty reduction can be achieved by a proper design not only of cash benefits but also of in-kind services. *Fourth*, from the data shown in Chapter 1 it appears that in many European countries old-age poverty declined significantly. When these trends lead to a situation where child poverty is *higher* than poverty in old age (which is actually the case in a sizable group of countries) the issue of intergenerational income distribution should urgently be placed on the agenda.

After *Les Trentes Glorieuses* (Fourastié, 1979), for more than thirty years most of the rich welfare states failed in making substantial headway in the fight against poverty. In these disconcerting circumstances, from the late 1970s onwards, a whole range of place-based social innovative policies and actions emerged in the institutional margins of welfare states. Their importance and value should not be underestimated. Responses to the persistence of poverty, the concentration of disadvantage in multicultural urban areas, and the individualization of social exclusion by locally embedded civil society, all suggest that place-based institutions and social enterprises should be considered as potential powerful seeds for progress. Therefore, to borrow the metaphor from Oosterlynck et al. (2013), the "elephants" (the welfare states) should firmly promote and support "the butterflies" (the socially innovative practices and actions).

With the Lisbon Strategy, the 2020 targets and—more recently—the Social Investment Package the EU put forward ambitious social projects. Although the shortcomings of the chosen instruments and prevailing policy paradigms are evidenced by the poor performance in the favorable years prior to the crisis, they certainly are a stepping stone toward more effective tools, on the explicit condition, that is, that a better distribution of jobs, adequate social protection, effective social redistribution supported by innovative social action are part and parcel of any effective investment strategy, and vice versa.

ACKNOWLEDGMENTS

I thank Frank Vandenbroucke, Maurizio Ferrera, and Bjørn Hvinden for critical comments; Tim Van Rie and Nathalie Schuerman for preparation of data and figures. The usual disclaimers apply.

NOTES

1 While it is certainly too early to make statements about the consequences of the great crisis on poverty levels, there is the hypothesis that welfare states today are less resilient to the consequences of crises than they used to be: In many countries, the strong increase in unemployment during the 1970s and 1980s did *not* cause rising poverty rates (Jenkins, et al., 2013).

2 http://epp.eurostat.ec.europa.eu/portal/page/portal/employment_ social_policy equality/introduction

3 In his foreword to the report written for the conference in which the establishment of common European social indicators was discussed, Frank Vandenbroucke rightly stated that "it is the combination of low income with other factors that leads to poverty. These additional factors may differ from country to country... What a 60% line indicates, therefore, is the number of people 'at-risk-of-poverty.' Whether or not that risk materializes depends on other factors, such as the cost of chronic illness..." (Atkinson et al., 2001: V).

4 See on the relationship between wage inequality and social spending: Cantillon, B., I. Marx, and K. Van den Bosch. 2003. "The puzzle of egalitarianism. The relationship between employment, wage inequality, social expenditure and poverty." European Journal of Social Security 5(2):108–127.

5 Ferrera (1996) rightly pointed to the specificities of the Southern welfare regimes with a high degree of familialism and less developed social redistribution.

6 Lisbon European Council, March 23 and 24, 2000. Presidency Conclusions http://www.europarl.europa.eu/summits/lis1_en.htm

7 Important in the present context is the agreement at the highest policymaking level on the setting of income poverty indicators, one of which is the *at-risk-of-poverty threshold at 60% of median standardized income in any given country*. Various other indicators build on this notion, including those relating to poverty in jobless households, and to the depth and duration of poverty. These income indicators are prominently present within the portfolio of indicators. The indicators were subsequently refined and enhanced, not least thanks to the excellent work by the Indicators Sub-Group (See Decancq et al., in this volume; Atkinson & Marlier, 2010; Zeitlin, 2010).

8 Morel, Palier, and Palme trace the origins of the social investment perspective back to the Great Depression when the Swedes Alva and Gunnar Myrdal developed a new conception of social policy (Morel et al., 2012: 3).

9 See, for an important critical analysis, Stiglitz et al. (2009). Report by the Commission on the measurement of economic performance and social progress. http://www.stiglitz-sen-fitoussi.fr; see also the Beyond GDP initiative http://www.oecdbetterlifeindex.org/2012/05/the-better-life-index/ and the OECD Better Life Index http://www.oecdbetterlifeindex.org/2012/05/the-better-life-index/.

10 See also Sen (2001: 258) who pays attention to the disabled in developing arguments in favor of his capability approach.

11 In the disability sector this is referred to as the "citizenship" model (Brett, 2002; Van Gennep, 2000; Dowling & Dolan, 2001).

12 In many households, a "medium work-intensity" no longer suffices to stay out of poverty (European Union, 2010: 158).

13 The "Matthew effect" refers to the phenomenon, widely observed across advanced welfare states, that the middle classes tend to be the main

beneficiaries of social benefits and services (Deleeck et al. 1983; Merton 1968; Rigney 2010).

14 For a discussion of new and old social risks, see De Deken in this volume.

15 See Rigney (2010) for further reading.

16 The factors contributing to the redistributive capacity of cash transfers are discussed in Chapter 5.

17 See Van Lancker and Ghysels in this volume.

18 Albeit to a much lesser degree, this is also a reason for concern in the Scandinavian countries, the undisputed forerunners of the active welfare state (Fritzell et al., 2012).

19 Job seekers agreements, youth offender contracts, parenting contracts (Vincent-Jones, 2009).

20 The CSB MIPI data set (Van Mechelen et al. 2011) learns f.i. that the conditionality of (some) social benefits on school enrolment is nowadays present in *inter alia* Belgium (Flanders), Netherlands, Germany, Denmark, Finland, Slovakia and United Kingdom. In some of these countries, social benefits are dependent on a status of "material need," a status which can be retracted when a families' children are playing truant. Some countries even go further: in the UK, truancy is considered a criminal offence for parents and they face penalty fines and prosecutions, and recently (September 2011), the government has proposed to cut child benefits of parents whose children regularly play truant. Similar proposals have been made in Belgium.

21 Drawn by responsibility-sensitive egalitarians Dworkin (1981a,b), Sen (1980, 1992), Arneson (1989), Cohen (1989), and Roemer (1993, 1998).

22 Note the difference between "compassion" and "pity": "compassion is based on an awareness of suffering, an intrinsic condition of a person" (Andersen: 306).

23 For a discussion on the relationship between Investment policies and "citizenship," see Hvinden and Johansson (2007) and Rosanvallon (2011).

24 "Some political views deny this: they hold that the right thing for government to do is to make people lead healthy lives, do worth-while activities, exercise religion, and so on. We deny this: we say that capabilities, not functionings, are the appropriate political goals" (Nussbaum 2011, 25).

EPILOGUE: WHAT WE KNOW, DON'T KNOW, AND NEED TO KNOW

Frank Vandenbroucke and Bea Cantillon

We are not the first to observe worrying trends in poverty or inequality (OECD, 2008, 2011; Brandolini & Smeeding, 2009; Banting & Myles, 2013; Jenkins et al., 2013; Kenworthy, 2011). The specific approach taken in this book is the link between poverty in the working-age population on the one hand, labor market participation and the distributive capacity of welfare states on the other hand, with an emphasis on evolutions during the "good economic years" before the financial crisis. To gain a better understanding of the nexus of labor market participation, social redistribution, and poverty, we focused on the distinction between work-poor and work-rich households (Chapters 3 and 4). We augmented a traditional "pre-post approach"—the drawbacks of which were discussed in Chapter 1–with regression analysis and indicators that reflect the impact of policies (Chapters 1 and 5). We refined the common method of measuring the redistributive effect of social expenditure, particularly for in-kind benefits (Chapters 6 and 7) and gave due consideration to concepts (Chapter 2) and data (Chapter 9). Most analyses were based on the European Statistics on Income and Living Conditions (SILC), but when it was relevant and feasible, we included alternative surveys (in the case of Germany, SILC and SOEP data) and additional data, that is, administrative expenditure data and indicators that inform directly on policy (Chapter 9 and the Appendix). Finally, we discussed our observations with reference to paradigmatic evolutions in contemporary welfare states, and linked the analysis with a broader perspective on the socioeconomic, demographic, and policy changes that were prominent in the European countries in the past two decades (Chapter 8 and 10). So, what do we know and what do we need to know?

THE USE OF SURVEY DATA AND THE LIMITATIONS OF OUR KNOWLEDGE

The thrust of our analysis is based deliberately on survey data gathered by the European Union (EU).[1] The development of that statistical capacity is in itself an important outcome of the momentum created by the Lisbon process, to which this book bears testimony. Surveys are, however, also sensitive to methodological flaws, and coverage and measurement errors. The EU cannot develop a credible policy monitoring system if investment in surveys is not a priority in every Member State. Furthermore, our experience indicates that we need sufficiently long series: Breaks in series are the most important obstacle to current research on social Europe. Hence, *continuity* should be the overriding concern: It may sometimes be better to resist the temptation to make marginal improvements to the database if such action will result in breaks in series. The French phrase "*le mieux est l'ennemi du bien*" is appropriate in this respect.

Even if our survey data were impeccable, though, we would still be unable on this basis alone to make a detailed assessment of the quality of social and employment policies pursued in Europe's welfare states. Without recourse to contextual evidence, other data, and in-depth analysis of policy, one cannot assess with great certainty the adequacy of policy trajectories. In general, we feel that one should resist making sweeping generalizations about such complex questions on the basis of statistical analysis of survey data alone. Not only microsimulation, policy indicators, and in-depth studies of national policy, but also a broader perspective capturing discourse, social and demographic transitions, institutional change, and macroeconomic policies are needed for an appropriate understanding of welfare state performance.

WHAT WE DO KNOW

Since the 1990s, social policy has become increasingly employment-centered, both in its aims and in its outcomes. But, was and is it possible to reduce benefit dependency and the associated expenditures in a structural way while at once achieving progress in the fields of employment as well as poverty reduction? At this level of generality, the initial question formulated at the outset of our book, must remain largely unanswered. Trends were not unequivocal, the book focused on a brief period and cross-country differences in social redistribution are considerable, both in terms of levels and trends. In cross-section, the Nordic countries continue to provide an example of how low poverty, high employment, and economic performance can be combined. This suggests that effective social protection and work-oriented policies can be complementary strategies. However, the trends presented in this book illustrate tough trade-offs that should be taken seriously.

The available data allow us to measure the differential impact, the successes, the weaknesses, and the limitations of the employment turn. Our analysis underscored the relevance of increasing individual employment rates and reducing household non-employment. However, it also revealed an inherent limitation in the drive to increase household employment. Increasing individual employment rates yield a "diminishing marginal utility" in terms of household employment: The elasticity of household employment creation with respect to individual employment creation is larger than one, but tends to decrease. This observation first and foremost reflects a mathematical truism, related to the nature of employment risk pooling in households; but in some countries trends in the polarization of jobs over households contributed to this phenomenon (notably in Southern Europe), while in others (such as the UK and most new Member States) an improving distribution of jobs over households reinforced the positive impact of job creation on poverty risks. Policy has a role to play in that respect. Moreover, the link between household employment rates and the poverty record of welfare states is an indirect one, mediated by the quality of jobs and by the level and efficiency of social spending. Hence, our analysis highlighted the importance of social protection policy per se: EU Member States pursued quite different policy pathways during the Lisbon era, which explains the different observed outcomes in terms of social inclusion; moreover, we see persistent differences among Member States in terms of efficiency of social spending.

On the positive side of the overall assessment, one may say that employment-centered social policies have gradually allowed many welfare states to shift resources to health care and pensions, thus responding to social needs in the field of aging and wellbeing. So conceived, increased employment has proven to be a successful substitute for "passive" working-age benefits as an antipoverty strategy in a number of European welfare states, including—primarily even—in some of the new Member States. At the same time, on the negative side of the assessment, this means that, despite the high-minded declarations at the Lisbon Summit, poverty did not decrease in most of the mature welfare states of the EU. Delivering on this promise would have required at least the maintenance of the poverty reduction capacity of social policies, which in many countries did not materialize. On the contrary, there was a worrying increase in at-risk-of-poverty rates in those countries that are considered to be in the vanguard of welfare reform and the social investment turn, such as Sweden and Finland. This should make us pause and think.

In some Member States the poverty risks of work-poor households increased substantially, while poverty reduction through social transfers declined. Additional indicators (such as changing spending levels, observed average benefit levels, and theoretical tax-benefit packages for work-poor and work-rich households) suggest that in a number of countries the relative decline in social transfers primarily affected work-poor households. Hence, in some of the rich and most developed welfare states, the poverty alleviation function of social spending seems to have come under pressure as a consequence of the development of work-oriented (cash and in-kind) benefits in order to discourage benefit dependency, to make work more attractive, and to enhance the work-life balance. Conceptually one can contrast a "high road" to employment creation, based on training, education, and decent jobs, with a "low road" to employment creation, pushing unemployed people into low-paid, low-quality jobs or into inadequate benefit schemes. Increasing poverty for work-poor households may signal that, at least in a number of countries, the "low road" dominated, or, in yet other words, it may signal re-commodification. We do not think that was inevitable. We are strongly in favor of a "high road" to employment creation, based on adequate social protection and social investment in high-quality child care and education. The chapter on family policy illustrates how intelligent and consistent design of policies may make the different objectives on this agenda easier to attain. There is, however, no denying of the tensions and trade-offs involved.

There are fundamental indications that the pressure on budgets for working-age cash benefits will not go away in the foreseeable future: The trend in health care and old-age spending remains upward, and not without reason. Welfare states must increasingly cater to working-age people's legitimate expectations with regard to (health) care and retirement. But this raises the question of whether compensation for traditional social risks and the concomitant vertical redistribution of incomes among working-age people, typically belonging to different social strata, are bound to deteriorate. This disquieting thought is one of the reasons why it is important to examine the efficiency of social spending with regard to poverty outcomes (as it is important to assess the efficiency of health care spending, and the intergenerational balance in social protection efforts and social investment spending). In the end, a strategy that sacrifices redistribution among working-age households may be self-defeating—including with regard to investment in human capital and to fairness in old age and health. That is the reason why it is necessary to study the impact of social spending on the working-age population, as this book set out to do, in order that it would remain firmly on the agenda.

Our analysis at once points at a lingering normative issue: What is the level of work-intensity households should ideally attain? On a more fundamental level, the "win-win" approach to social policy that relies on its "productive role" is unhelpful when considering the indispensable role of social protection for people, such as the disabled, who are unable to work. Welfare states should be underpinned by a strong sense of reciprocity. But reciprocity cannot be the only rationale for welfare state intervention.

WHAT WE NEED TO KNOW

Our analysis was not complete. To give but one example, the impact of migration on levels and trends in poverty was not incorporated (see Corluy, Marx, & Verbist, 2011). Apart from signalling difficult trade-offs in social policy, it also indicates where future social research is needed. *First*, when it comes to poverty alleviation, the Southern European welfare states continue to display low efficiency relative to their levels of spending. It would be wrong to attribute this solely to a social investment deficit in those countries, however real that deficit may be. Sufficiency and efficiency of spending in traditional domains of social protection are potentially equally important, and both should, therefore, be an integral part of the European social agenda. Given the prospect of aging, tight budgets, and the need to rebalance the EU's financial situation on the basis of mutual support and understanding among EU Member States, persistent deficits in the efficiency of some national welfare states are particularly worrying. It is, therefore, important that research should focus on the legitimacy of a notion of "efficiency" (see Lefebvre & Pestieau, 2012, for a critical approach) and on characteristics that make welfare states comparatively less efficient in dealing with poverty (see Vandenbroucke, Diris, & Verbist, 2013, for a further exploration). With regard to policy, this also shows that the Open Method of Coordination on Social Inclusion should be more incisive and intrusive with regard to the overall efficiency of social spending in EU Member States (Vandenbroucke et al., 2013). Another necessary line of research, associated with the question of efficiency, follows from Marx and Nolan's analysis of in-work benefits: it should study normative and empirical issues with regard to the potential role of in-work benefits and child benefits in European welfare states.

Second, in a country such as Poland, decreasing poverty among working-age people has gone hand-in-hand with increasing poverty among the elderly. Moreover, the Polish pensions data gathered by the EU suggest that, without a change in policy, the future might be even bleaker for the country's elderly. Hence, despite the undeniably positive impact of Poland's "employment-centered" social policy in so far as working-age people are concerned, the model as it stands today may not be socially sustainable. This observation, too, is indicative of unfinished business, both in social research and in policymaking.

Third, to the extent that employment-centered social policy contributed to improving social cohesion at the EU level, it critically depended on "convergence-in-growth." The financial crisis now has a dramatic impact on standards of living and poverty risks in a number of European welfare states: these recent developments are not covered in this book. The crisis revealed the fragility of the underlying economic processes, such as the housing bubbles in Spain and Ireland. Our analysis adds another factor to this sobering economic assessment, to wit, the relative weakness or vulnerability of the social policy trajectory in some countries (including, once again, the Southern European welfare states, but also Ireland), which can be traced back already to "the good economic years." In those years, EU governance remained largely blind to both the economic and the social fragility of developments in a number of welfare states. Given the persistent trend of demographic aging, a consistent combination of sustainable economic growth, employment-centered social policy, and effective social protection is key. How to improve economic and social governance at EU level, and how to ensure the necessary link between the "economic" and the "social" is a crucial question on our agenda.

NOTES

1 These data are not all "survey" data in a strict sense; for a number of countries (DK, FI, IS, NL, SE, SI, LV, NO), the majority of (income) data are not collected through surveys, but derived from administrative sources.

APPENDIX: THE EVOLUTION OF PUBLIC SOCIAL SPENDING 1985–2009

Leen Meeusen and Annemie Nys

This Appendix structures data on social expenditures for the 21 European Union (EU) Member States (*Austria, Belgium, Czech Republic, Denmark, Estonia, Finland, France, Germany, Greece, Hungary, Ireland, Italy, Luxembourg, The Netherlands, Poland, Portugal, Slovakia, Slovenia, Spain, Sweden, and the United Kingdom*).

The information is gathered in country files, containing public expenditure variables. The different variables are constructed based on the Social Expenditure Statistics Detailed Data (SOCX) from the Organisation for Economic Co-operation and Development (OECD) and the OECD's Education Database (01/2013). The classification of social expenditures is based on a distinction between "Old" and "New" programs, which is inspired by the distinction between "old" and "new" social risks, as formulated for instance by Bonoli (2006). In this context, "Old" should not be interpreted as "out of date"; rather it is meant to imply that these programs belong to the core tasks of the welfare state of the "golden age" and were well-established before the emergence of programs that specifically address the risks related to changes associated with the transition toward a "postindustrial society" (see Chapter 9).

As previously done by Vandenbroucke & Vleminckx (2011), we distinguish among three "Old" expenditure categories and 6 "New" expenditure categories. Those categories include the following expenditure items of the OECD's SOCX database:

"OLD 1": *healthcare;*

"OLD 2": *old age*; including both *old age* (pension, early retirement pension, and other cash benefits) and *survivor* programs (pension, as well as other cash benefits for the elderly, and compensation of funeral expenses and other benefits in kind);

"OLD 3": *working-age cash benefits;* including *incapacity-related* programs (excluding residential care/home-help services and rehabilitation services), active labor market policy (ALMP) programs (unemployment compensation/severance pay and early retirement for labor market reasons), *other* social benefits and *housing* (housing assistance and other benefits in kind); *family* programs are also included in this category, but because they can also be seen as an investment in the capacity of children, the Appendix also adds them to one of the "New" categories;

"NEW 1": *parental leave*; which includes *family* programs (maternity and parental leave);

"NEW 2": *elderly care*; including *old-age* programs (residential care/home-help services and other benefits in kind);

"NEW 3": *child care services*; including *family* programs (day care/home-help services and other benefits in kind; *incapacity-related* programs (residential care/home-help services) and, as explained under "Old 3," two variants (one including family allowances and one excluding them);

"NEW 4": *active labor market policies*; and *incapacity-related* programs (rehabilitation services);

"NEW 5": *primary and secondary education*

"NEW 6": *tertiary education*

The country tables (Table 12.1 to 12.21) provide the average levels of the above-defined spending categories as a percentage of GDP for the years 1985–1989, 1990–1994, 1995–1999, 2000–2004, and 2005–2009.

One can interpret family allowances both as a social investment, congenial to the other programs captured under "New 3," or, alternatively, as a traditional welfare state program congenial to other cash benefits for working-age people (cf. De Deken, Chapter 9, this book). Hence, in the tables we provide two variants of "Old 3" and of "New 3." In the first case family allowances are included in the working-age cash benefits ("OLD 3"). In the second case they are included in the "new" spending category, *child care* services ("NEW 3"). In the figures, family benefits are included in the "Old 3" category.

The tables also display employment and unemployment rates as those may to some extent explain the level and evolution of the "Old" spending category.

In the tables, the following percentages were calculated:

- Row A–K: public spending as percentage of GDP (average for period)
- Row L–N: the different types of public expenditures (cash, in-kind, and not classified[1]) as a percent of total spending (education excluded; average for period)
- Row O–P: employment and unemployment rate (average for period)

Changes in social spending can also be driven by demographic changes. To control for this impact (as well as for the impact of changes in the level of unemployment), four additional indicators are provided in row Q–T. These indicators take public spending into consideration and are expressed as indices against a baseline period:

- spending on retirement pensions ("OLD 2") divided by the number of people older than 64 years, compared with GDP/capita;
- spending on child care services ("NEW 3" excluding incapacity-related programs) divided by the number of children younger than 5 years, compared with GDP/capita;
- spending on active labor market policy (ALMP) ("NEW 4") per unemployed, compared with GDP/capita;
- spending on primary and secondary education ("NEW 5") divided by the population from 5 years to 19 years old, compared with GDP/capita.

For each indicator, we calculate an annual correction by dividing the total annual spending of year "x" (of the category of interest) by the number of "claimants" of year "x" and then relate this figure to the annual GDP/capita of year "x."

In the table, the averages of the periods 1990–1994, 1995–1999, 2000–2004, and 2005–2009 are shown, expressed as an index of basis period 1985–1989. For some countries, the data for the period 1985–1989 are lacking and other baseline periods (1990–1994, 1995–1999, and 2000–2004) had to be used. These indices can refer to deliberate efforts to invest in resources (or the willingness to disinvest) in specific functions of the welfare state; we call these budgetary efforts.

The last column of each table displays percentage point change in spending (percent GDP):

- Average levels for the years 2005–2009 are compared with the average levels for the years 1985–1989 (in case no data are available for the period 1985–1989, a different period for comparison, which is indicated in the table, has been used)
- The percentage point changes for rows "J" and "K" are only displayed when data is available for all spending categories concerned. In case of missing data, we have omitted these figures to avoid misinterpretation.

The graphs (Figure 12.1 to 12.21) depict for each country the evolution of public spending on "Old" and "New" programs. The four "new" spending categories were aggregated into a single category. In the graphs, family allowances were included in "working-age benefits" (OLD 3) (as is done in the analysis in Chapter 5, based on EU-SILC, though in Chapter 9 they were included in "New 3").

Table 12.1. Austria: total social spending (public), percentage of GDP 1985–2009, OECD SOCX.

AT		1985-1989	1990-1994	1995-1999	2000-2004	2005-2009	ppt change (05-09)–(85-89)
	PUBLIC SPENDING, AS A PERCENTAGE OF GDP						
(a)	"OLD1" HEALTH CARE	5.12	5.72	6.22	6.58	6.88	1.76
(b)	"OLD2" OLD AGE	11.30	11.78	12.32	12.52	12.54	1.24
(c)	"OLD3" OTHER BENEFITS + ALLOWANCES	6.10	6.22	6.30	6.08	5.70	–0.40
	"OLD3" OTHER BENEFITS	4.10	4.38	4.46	4.00	3.60	–0.50
(d)	"NEW1" PARENTAL LEAVE	0.40	0.56	0.50	0.34	0.12	–0.28
(e)	"NEW2" ELDERLY CARE	0.20	0.20	0.24	0.36	0.42	0.22
(f)	"NEW3" CHILD CARE	0.30	0.36	0.48	0.58	0.64	0.34
	"NEW3" CHILD CARE + ALLOWANCES	2.30	2.20	2.32	2.66	2.74	0.44
(g)	"NEW4" ALMP	0.24	0.24	0.34	0.54	0.72	0.48
(h)	"NEW5" PRIMARY & SECONDARY EDUCATION		3.65	4.12	3.66	3.53	
(i)	"NEW6" TERTIARY EDUCATION			1.35	1.13	1.20	
(j)	TOTAL NEW 1-4 (a)	1.14	1.36	1.56	1.82	1.90	0.76
	TOTAL NEW 1-4 (b)	3.14	3.20	3.40	3.90	4.00	0.86
(k)	TOTAL OLD & NEW (education excluded)	23.66	25.08	26.40	27.00	27.02	3.36

	CASH, IN KIND, AND NOT CLASSIFIED SPENDING, AS A PERCENTAGE OF TOTAL SPENDING						
(l)	TOTAL CASH	75.86	72.01	70.69	69.04	66.84	–9.01
(m)	TOTAL IN KIND	23.10	27.03	28.03	28.97	30.50	7.40
(n)	TOTAL NOT CLASSIFIED	1.05	0.96	1.29	2.00	2.66	1.61
	CONTEXTUAL FACTORS						
(o)	EMPLOYMENT RATE		68.44	68.11	68.39	70.78	
(p)	UNEMPLOYMENT RATE		3.90	4.20	4.12	4.58	
	BUDGETARY EFFORTS (INDICES)						
(q)	(“OLD2” / 65+) / (GDP/cap)	100	99	101	101	93	
(r)	(“NEW3a”/<5) / (GDP/CAP)	100	122	148	161	176	
	(“NEW3b”/<5) / (GDP/CAP)	100	97	104	130	138	
(s)	(“NEW4”/UN) / (GDP/cap)	100	91	112	174	202	
(t)	(“NEW5”/5-19) / (GDP/cap)		100	113	101	103	

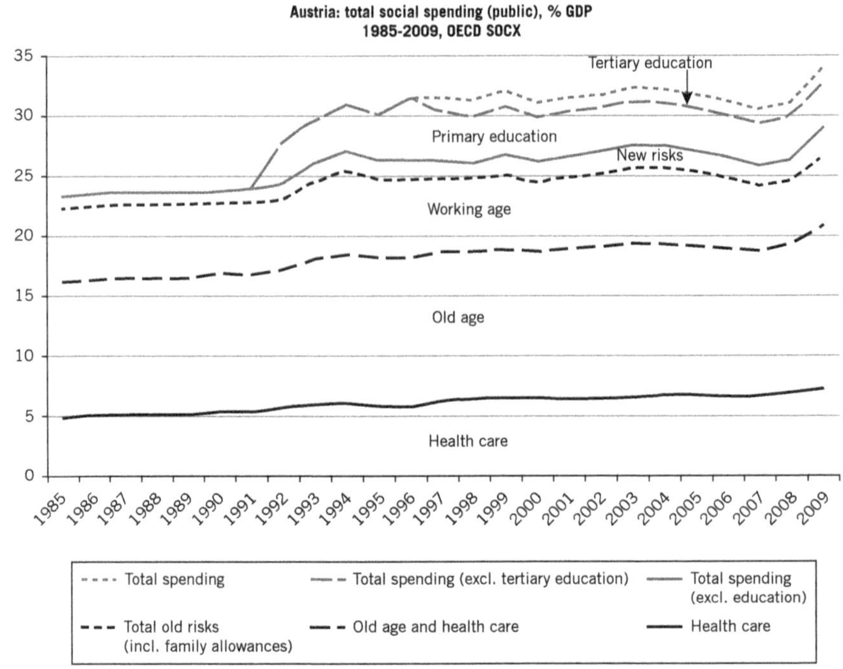

Figure 12.1. Austria: total social spending (public), percentage of GDP, 1985–2009, OECD SOCX.

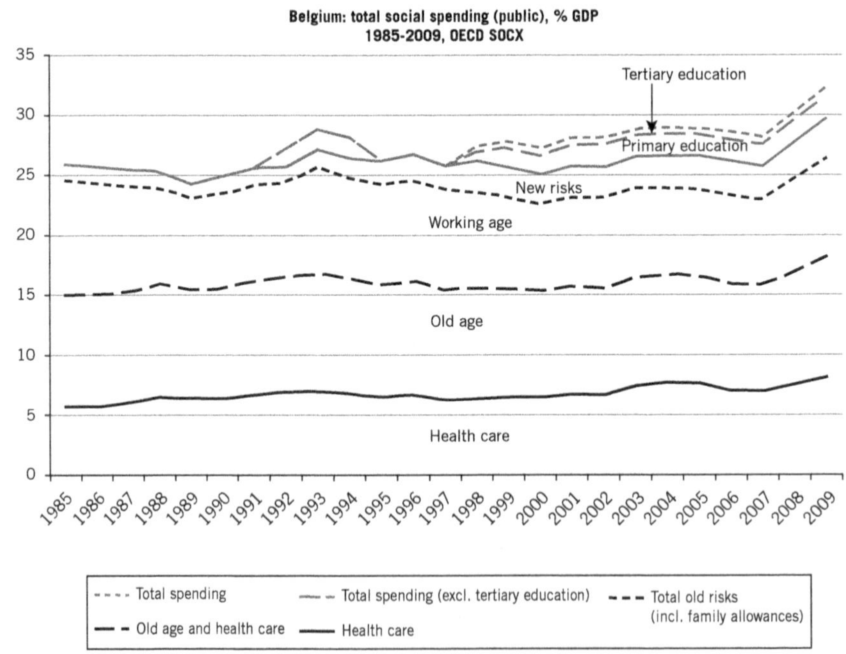

Figure 12.2. Belgium: total social spending (public), percentage of GDP, 1985–2009, OECD SOCX.

Table 12.2. Belgium: total social spending (public), percentage of GDP 1985–2009, OECD SOCX

BE		1985-1989	1990-1994	1995-1999	2000-2004	2005-2009	ppt change (05-09)–(85-89)
	PUBLIC SPENDING, AS A PERCENTAGE OF GDP						
(a)	"OLD1" HEALTH CARE	6.06	6.76	6.48	7.00	7.46	1.40
(b)	"OLD2" OLD AGE	9.26	9.52	9.22	8.94	9.22	–0.04
(c)	"OLD3" OTHER BENEFITS + ALLOWANCES	8.72	8.20	8.14	7.42	7.50	–1.22
	"OLD3" OTHER BENEFITS	6.50	6.26	6.30	5.86	5.98	–0.52
(d)	"NEW1" PARENTAL LEAVE	0.10	0.20	0.20	0.20	0.20	0.10
(e)	"NEW2" ELDERLY CARE			0.10	0.10	0.20	0.20
(f)	"NEW3" CHILD CARE	0.10	0.14	0.74	1.24	1.40	1.30
	"NEW3" CHILD CARE + ALLOWANCES	2.32	2.08	2.58	2.80	2.92	0.60
(g)	"NEW4" ALMP	1.14	1.10	1.26	1.02	1.18	0.04
(h)	"NEW5" PRIMARY & SECONDARY EDUCATION		1.63	1.16	1.79	1.88	
(i)	"NEW6" TERTIARY EDUCATION			0.49	0.54	0.59	
(j)	TOTAL NEW 1-4 (a)	1.34	1.44	2.30	2.56	2.98	
	TOTAL NEW 1-4 (b)	3.56	3.38	4.14	4.12	4.50	
(k)	TOTAL OLD & NEW (education excluded)	25.38	25.92	26.14	25.92	27.16	

(continued)

Table 12.2. (Continued)

BE		1985-1989	1990-1994	1995-1999	2000-2004	2005-2009	ppt change (05-09)–(85-89)
	CASH, IN KIND AND NOT CLASSIFIED SPENDING, AS A PERCENTAGE OF TOTAL SPENDING						
(l)	TOTAL CASH	70.81	68.08	64.70	61.27	61.06	–9.75
(m)	TOTAL IN KIND	24.70	27.68	30.48	34.80	34.61	9.91
(n)	TOTAL NOT CLASSIFIED	4.49	4.25	4.82	3.94	4.33	–0.16
	CONTEXTUAL FACTORS						
(o)	EMPLOYMENT RATE	52.87	55.71	57.15	60.08	61.62	8.75
(p)	UNEMPLOYMENT RATE	9.24	7.70	9.26	7.52	7.82	–1.42
	BUDGETARY EFFORTS (INDICES)						
(q)	("OLD2" / 65+) / (GDP/cap)	100	96	87	81	83	
(r)	("NEW3a" / <5)/(GDP/CAP)	100	135	453	956	1049	
	("NEW3b"/<5)/(GDP/CAP)	100	87	100	113	114	
(s)	("NEW4"/UN) / (GDP/cap)	100	99	103	126	137	
(t)	("NEW5"/5-19) / (GDP/cap)		100	71	112	120	

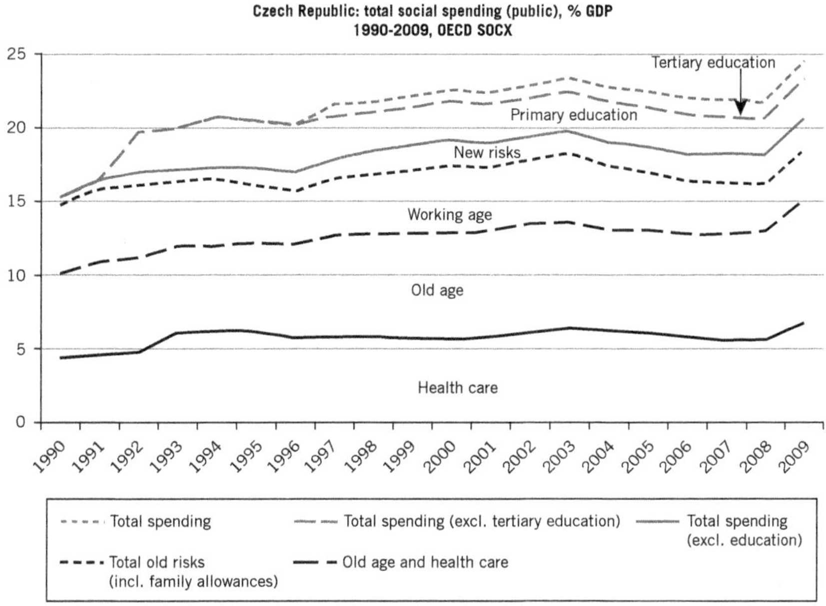

Figure 12.3. Czech Republic: total social spending (public), percentage of GDP, 1990–2009, OECD SOCX.

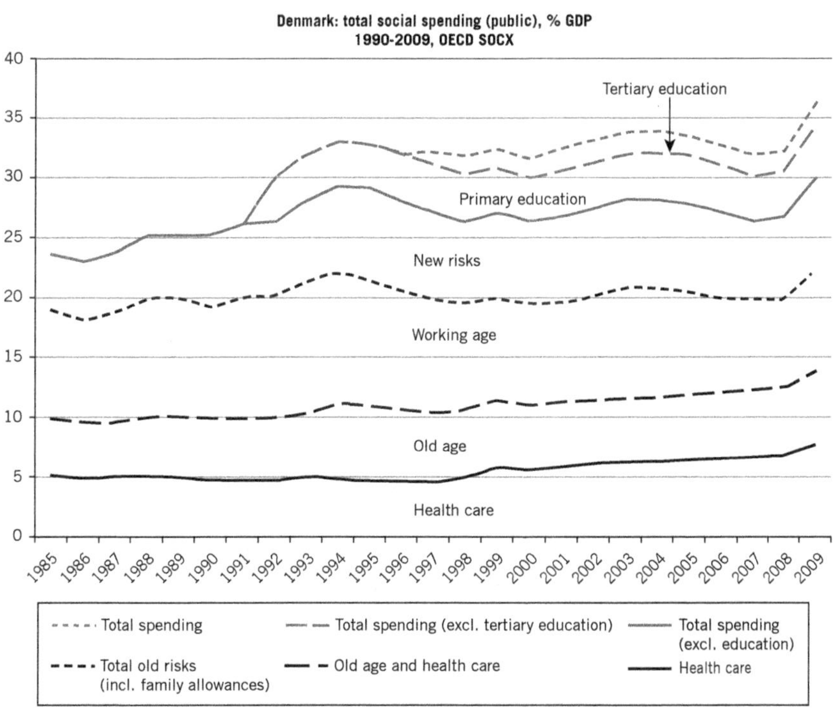

Figure 12.4. Denmark: total social spending (public), percentage of GDP, 1985–2009, OECD SOCX.

Table 12.3. Czech Republic: total social spending (public), percentage of GDP 1985–2009, OECD SOCX

CZ		1985-1989	1990-1994	1995-1999	2000-2004	2005-2009	ppt change (05-09)–(90-94)
	PUBLIC SPENDING, AS A PERCENTAGE OF GDP						
(a)	"OLD1" HEALTH CARE		5.20	5.84	6.04	5.96	0.76
(b)	"OLD2" OLD AGE		6.06	6.68	7.18	7.36	1.30
(c)	"OLD3" OTHER BENEFITS + ALLOWANCES		4.66	3.94	4.42	3.56	–1.10
	"OLD3" OTHER BENEFITS		3.52	3.26	3.92	3.30	–0.22
(d)	"NEW1" PARENTAL LEAVE		0.58	0.50	0.50	0.82	0.24
(e)	"NEW2" ELDERLY CARE			0.34	0.38	0.30	
(f)	"NEW3" CHILD CARE		0.10	0.50	0.62	0.62	0.52
	"NEW3" CHILD CARE + ALLOWANCES		1.20	1.18	1.12	0.88	–0.32
(g)	"NEW4" ALMP		0.13	0.10	0.14	0.18	0.06
(h)	"NEW5" PRIMARY & SECONDARY EDUCATION		2.97	2.90	2.65	2.60	–0.37
(i)	"NEW6" TERTIARY EDUCATION			0.74	0.88	1.13	
(j)	TOTAL NEW 1-4 (a)		0.81	1.44	1.64	1.92	
	TOTAL NEW 1-4 (b)		1.91	2.12	2.14	2.18	
(k)	TOTAL OLD & NEW (education excluded)		16.69	17.90	19.28	18.80	

	CASH, IN KIND, AND NOT CLASSIFIED SPENDING, AS A PERCENTAGE OF TOTAL SPENDING					
(l)	TOTAL CASH	64.60	61.00	60.27	60.96	–3.64
(m)	TOTAL IN KIND	34.81	38.44	39.00	38.08	3.27
(n)	TOTAL NOT CLASSIFIED	0.59	0.56	0.73	0.96	0.37
	CONTEXTUAL FACTORS					
(o)	EMPLOYMENT RATE	69.11	68.16	65.06	65.62	–3.49
(p)	UNEMPLOYMENT RATE	3.34	5.56	8.02	6.30	2.96
	BUDGETARY EFFORTS (INDICES)					
(q)	("OLD2" / 65+) / (GDP/cap)	100	104	109	107	
(r)	("NEW3a"/<5) / (GDP/CAP)	100	398	683	715	
	("NEW3b"/<5) / (GDP/CAP)	100	110	124	95	
(s)	("NEW4"/UN) / (GDP/cap)	100	53	47	83	
(t)	("NEW5"/5-19) / (GDP/cap)	100	107	112	125	

Table 12.4. Denmark: total social spending (public), percentage of GDP 1985–2009, OECD SOCX

DK		1985-1989	1990-1994	1995-1999	2000-2004	2005-2009	ppt change (05-09)–(85-89)
	PUBLIC SPENDING, AS A PERCENTAGE OF GDP						
(a)	"OLD1" HEALTH CARE	5.00	4.78	4.88	6.02	6.84	1.84
(b)	"OLD2" OLD AGE	4.78	5.44	5.90	5.34	5.66	0.88
(c)	"OLD3" OTHER BENEFITS + ALLOWANCES	9.38	10.36	9.52	8.80	8.02	–1.36
	"OLD3" OTHER BENEFITS	8.64	9.38	8.52	7.80	7.06	–1.58
(d)	"NEW1" PARENTAL LEAVE	0.40	0.56	0.64	0.54	0.56	0.16
(e)	"NEW2" ELDERLY CARE	2.14	2.16	2.00	1.78	1.84	–0.30
(f)	"NEW3" CHILD CARE	1.74	2.40	2.72	2.92	3.10	1.36
	"NEW3" CHILD CARE + ALLOWANCES	2.48	3.38	3.72	3.92	4.06	1.58
(g)	"NEW4" ALMP	0.72	1.34	1.90	2.02	1.62	0.90
(h)	"NEW5" PRIMARY & SECONDARY EDUCATION		3.80	3.87	3.84	4.00	
(i)	"NEW6" TERTIARY EDUCATION			1.42	1.76	1.72	
(j)	TOTAL NEW 1-4 (a)	5.00	6.46	7.26	7.26	7.12	2.12
	TOTAL NEW 1-4 (b)	5.74	7.44	8.26	8.26	8.08	2.34
(k)	TOTAL OLD & NEW (education excluded)	24.16	27.04	27.56	27.42	27.64	3.48

	CASH, IN KIND, AND NOT CLASSIFIED SPENDING, AS A PERCENTAGE OF TOTAL SPENDING						
(l)	TOTAL CASH	56.77	56.71	54.23	49.81	47.49	−9.28
(m)	TOTAL IN KIND	40.50	39.19	39.38	43.53	47.24	6.74
(n)	TOTAL NOT CLASSIFIED	2.73	4.09	6.38	6.65	5.28	2.54
	CONTEXTUAL FACTORS						
(o)	EMPLOYMENT RATE	75.65	73.87	75.03	75.79	76.70	1.05
(p)	UNEMPLOYMENT RATE	5.82	8.18	5.66	4.86	4.40	−1.42
	BUDGETARY EFFORTS (INDICES)						
(q)	(“OLD2” / 65+) / (GDP/cap)	100	113	126	115	117	
(r)	(“NEW3a”/<5) / (GDP/CAP)	100	101	95	101	107	
	(“NEW3b”/<5) / (GDP/CAP)	100	106	100	105	110	
(s)	(“NEW4”/UN) / (GDP/cap)	100	131	276	365	334	
(t)	(“NEW5”/5-19) / (GDP/cap)		100	104	99	99	

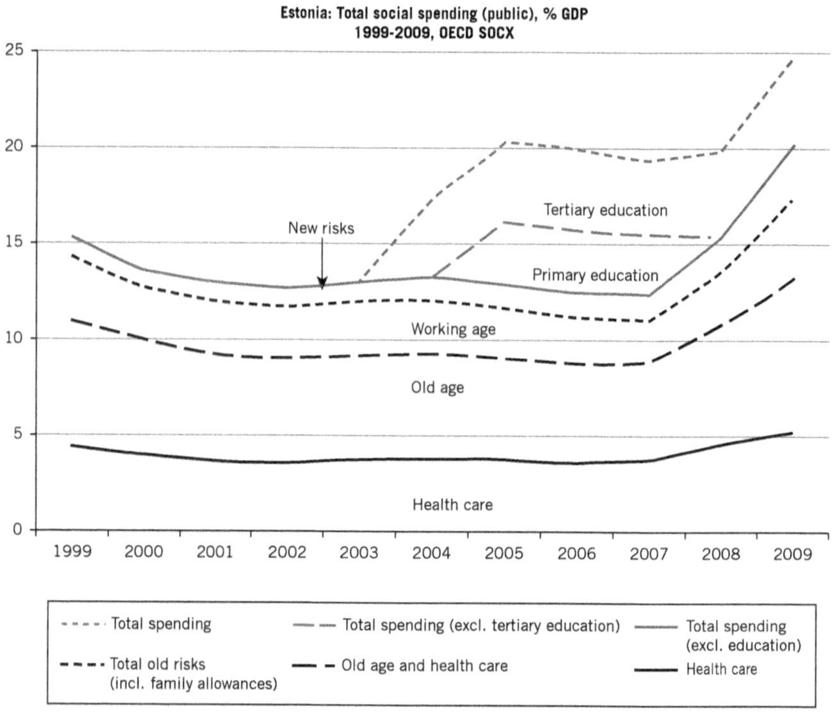

Figure 12.5. Estonia: total social spending (public), percentage of GDP, 1999–2009, OECD SOCX.

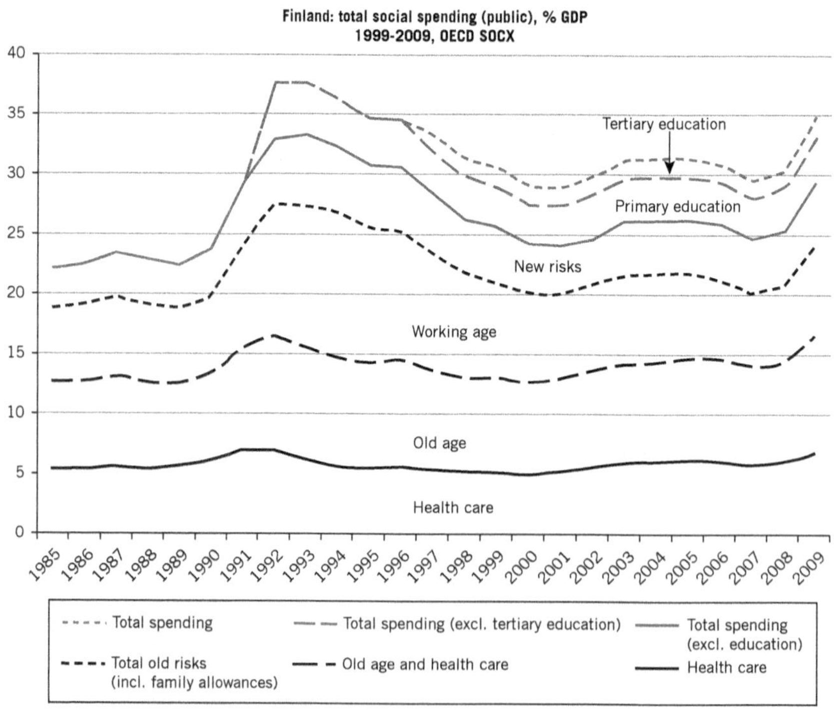

Figure 12.6. Finland: total social spending (public), percentage of GDP, 1985–2009, OECD SOCX.

Table 12.5. Estonia: total social spending (public), percentage of GDP 1985–2009, OECD SOCX

EE		1985-1989	1990-1994	1995-1999	2000-2004	2005-2009	ppt change (05-09)–(95-99)
	PUBLIC SPENDING, AS A PERCENTAGE OF GDP						
(a)	"OLD1" HEALTH CARE			4.40	3.78	4.20	–0.20
(b)	"OLD2" OLD AGE			6.60	5.56	5.96	–0.64
(c)	"OLD3" OTHER BENEFITS + ALLOWANCES			3.30	2.76	2.84	–0.46
	"OLD3" OTHER BENEFITS			2.40	2.14	2.36	–0.04
(d)	"NEW1" PARENTAL LEAVE			0.40	0.54	1.00	0.60
(e)	"NEW2" ELDERLY CARE			0.20	0.10	0.10	–0.10
(f)	"NEW3" CHILD CARE			0.40	0.38	0.50	0.10
	"NEW3" CHILD CARE + ALLOWANCES			1.30	1.00	0.98	–0.32
(g)	"NEW4" ALMP					0.30	
(h)	"NEW5" PRIMARY & SECONDARY EDUCATION					3.17	
(i)	"NEW6" TERTIARY EDUCATION				4.07	4.27	
(j)	TOTAL NEW 1-4 (a)			1.00	1.02	1.90	
	TOTAL NEW 1-4 (b)			1.90	1.64	2.38	
(k)	TOTAL OLD & NEW (education excluded)			15.30	13.12	14.90	

(*continued*)

Table 12.5. (Continued)

EE		1985-1989	1990-1994	1995-1999	2000-2004	2005-2009	ppt change (05-09)–(95-99)
	CASH, IN KIND, AND NOT CLASSIFIED SPENDING, AS A PERCENTAGE OF TOTAL SPENDING						
(l)	TOTAL CASH			66.67	66.92	66.69	0.02
(m)	TOTAL IN KIND			33.33	33.08	33.11	–0.22
(n)	TOTAL NOT CLASSIFIED					0.20	0.20
	CONTEXTUAL FACTORS						
(o)	EMPLOYMENT RATE			64.70	62.01	66.92	2.22
(p)	UNEMPLOYMENT RATE			10.10	11.26	7.60	–2.50
	BUDGETARY EFFORTS (INDICES)						
(q)	("OLD2" / 65+) / (GDP/cap)			100	80	79	
(r)	("NEW3a"/<5) / (GDP/CAP)			100	138	146	
	("NEW3b"/<5) / (GDP/CAP)			100	81	64	
(s)	("NEW4"/UN) / (GDP/cap)						
(t)	("NEW5"/5-19) / (GDP/cap)						

Table 12.6. Finland: total social spending (public), percentage of GDP 1985–2009, OECD SOCX

FI		1985-1989	1990-1994	1995-1999	2000-2004	2005-2009	ppt change (05-09)–(85-89)
	PUBLIC SPENDING, AS A PERCENTAGE OF GDP						
(a)	"OLD1" HEALTH CARE	5.52	6.36	5.38	5.58	6.24	0.72
(b)	"OLD2" OLD AGE	7.28	8.74	8.36	8.02	8.68	1.40
(c)	"OLD3" OTHER BENEFITS + ALLOWANCES	6.40	10.10	9.66	7.32	6.76	0.36
	"OLD3" OTHER BENEFITS	5.70	8.98	8.36	6.36	5.92	0.22
(d)	"NEW1" PARENTAL LEAVE	0.76	1.22	0.82	0.60	0.62	–0.14
(e)	"NEW2" ELDERLY CARE	0.68	0.82	0.84	0.86	1.04	0.36
(f)	"NEW3" CHILD CARE	1.34	1.66	1.72	1.56	1.74	0.40
	"NEW3" CHILD CARE + ALLOWANCES	2.04	2.78	3.02	2.52	2.58	0.54
(g)	"NEW4" ALMP	0.76	1.46	1.64	1.16	1.26	0.50
(h)	"NEW5" PRIMARY & SECONDARY EDUCATION		4.32	3.63	3.50	3.55	
(i)	"NEW6" TERTIARY EDUCATION			1.51	1.57	1.54	
(j)	TOTAL NEW 1-4 (a)	3.54	5.16	5.02	4.18	4.66	1.12
	TOTAL NEW 1-4 (b)	4.24	6.28	6.32	5.14	5.50	1.26
(k)	TOTAL OLD & NEW (education excluded)	22.74	30.36	28.42	25.10	26.34	3.60

(continued)

Table 12.6. (Continued)

FI		1985-1989	1990-1994	1995-1999	2000-2004	2005-2009	ppt change (05-09)–(85-89)
	CASH, IN KIND, AND NOT CLASSIFIED SPENDING, AS A PERCENTAGE OF TOTAL SPENDING						
(l)	TOTAL CASH	61.12	63.06	63.38	60.51	57.39	–3.73
(m)	TOTAL IN KIND	35.54	32.57	31.85	36.06	38.95	3.42
(n)	TOTAL NOT CLASSIFIED	3.34	4.37	4.77	3.42	3.66	0.32
	CONTEXTUAL FACTORS						
(o)	EMPLOYMENT RATE	72.57	66.61	63.93	67.97	69.64	–2.93
(p)	UNEMPLOYMENT RATE	4.98	10.90	12.88	9.16	7.50	2.52
	BUDGETARY EFFORTS (INDICES)						
(q)	("OLD2" / 65+) / (GDP/cap)	100	113	102	93	93	
(r)	("NEW3a"/<5) / (GDP/CAP)	100	124	129	127	144	
	("NEW3b"/<5) / (GDP/CAP)	100	138	153	139	143	
(s)	("NEW4"/UN) / (GDP/cap)	100	100	81	77	103	
(t)	("NEW5"/5-19) / (GDP/cap)		100	84	83	88	

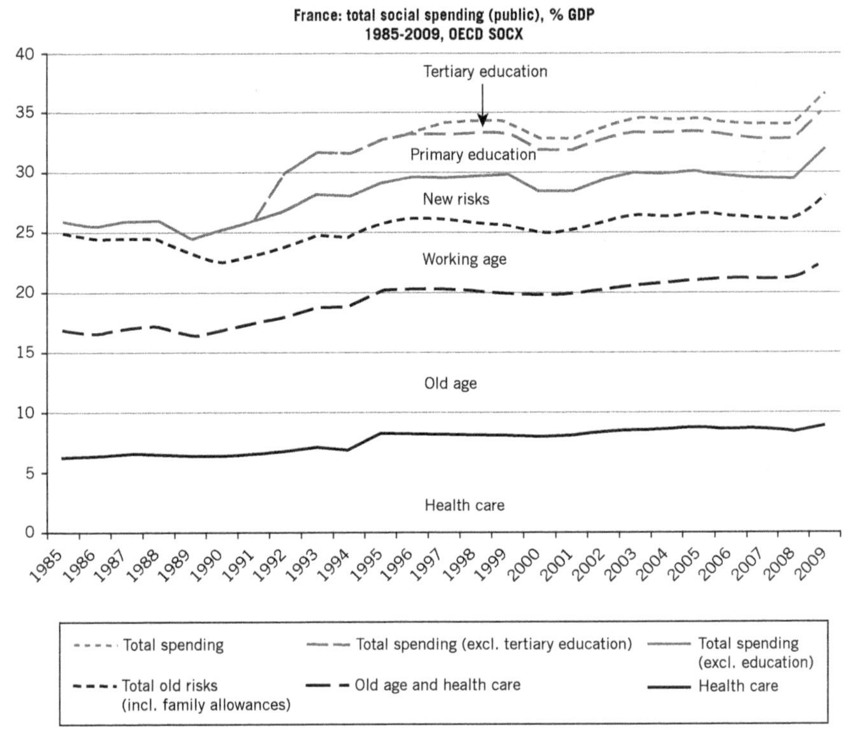

Figure 12.7. France: total social spending (public), percentage of GDP, 1985–2009, OECD SOCX.

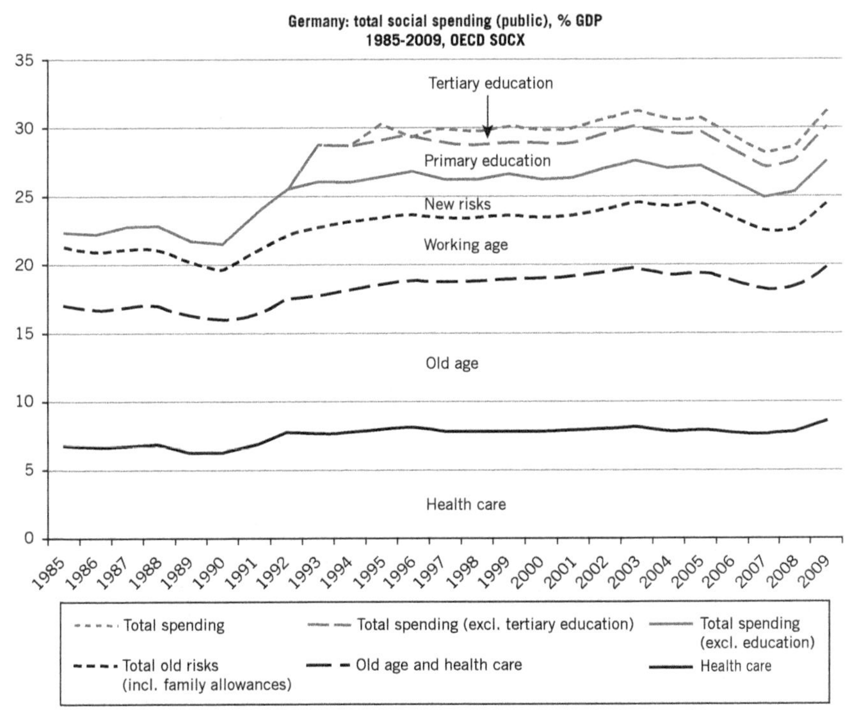

Figure 12.8. Germany: total social spending (public), percentage of GDP, 1985–2009, OECD SOCX.

Table 12.7. France: total social spending (public), percentage of GDP 1985–2009, OECD SOCX

FR		1985-1989	1990-1994	1995-1999	2000-2004	2005-2009	ppt change (05-09)–(85-89)
	PUBLIC SPENDING, AS A PERCENTAGE OF GDP						
(a)	"OLD1" HEALTH CARE	6.48	6.78	8.20	8.36	8.72	2.24
(b)	"OLD2" OLD AGE	10.36	11.26	12.06	11.94	12.78	2.42
(c)	"OLD3" OTHER BENEFITS + ALLOWANCES	7.50	5.76	5.70	5.50	5.26	−2.24
	"OLD3" OTHER BENEFITS	5.70	4.58	4.54	4.42	4.24	−1.46
(d)	"NEW1" PARENTAL LEAVE	0.28	0.30	0.38	0.40	0.32	0.04
(e)	"NEW2" ELDERLY CARE	0.10	0.20	0.20	0.26	0.34	0.24
(f)	"NEW3" CHILD CARE	0.30	1.54	1.84	1.70	1.86	1.56
	"NEW3" CHILD CARE + ALLOWANCES	2.10	2.72	3.00	2.78	2.88	0.78
(g)	"NEW4" ALMP	0.60	1.04	1.24	1.10	0.94	0.34
(h)	"NEW5" PRIMARY & SECONDARY EDUCATION		3.44	3.56	3.43	3.32	
(i)	"NEW6" TERTIARY EDUCATION			1.02	1.05	1.21	
(j)	TOTAL NEW 1-4 (a)	1.28	3.08	3.66	3.46	3.46	2.18
	TOTAL NEW 1-4 (b)	3.08	4.26	4.82	4.54	4.48	1.40
(k)	TOTAL OLD & NEW (education excluded)	25.62	26.88	29.62	29.26	30.22	4.60

	CASH, IN KIND, AND NOT CLASSIFIED SPENDING, AS A PERCENTAGE OF TOTAL SPENDING						
(l)	TOTAL CASH	65.95	61.41	58.21	58.03	58.10	–7.85
(m)	TOTAL IN KIND	31.71	34.75	37.61	38.20	38.79	7.08
(n)	TOTAL NOT CLASSIFIED	2.34	3.84	4.19	3.77	3.11	0.76
	CONTEXTUAL FACTORS						
(o)	EMPLOYMENT RATE	60.66	59.97	59.79	63.01	64.08	3.42
(p)	UNEMPLOYMENT RATE	8.92	9.48	10.76	8.74	8.84	–0.08
	BUDGETARY EFFORTS (INDICES)						
(q)	(“OLD2” / 65+) / (GDP/cap)	100	100	100	95	100	
(r)	(“NEW3a”/<5) / (GDP/CAP)	100	396	502	563	613	
	(“NEW3b”/<5) / (GDP/CAP)	100	115	133	137	141	
(s)	(“NEW4”/UN) / (GDP/cap)	100	169	180	198	165	
(t)	(“NEW5”/5-19) / (GDP/cap)		100	106	106	105	

Table 12.8. Germany: total social spending (public), percentage of GDP 1985–2009, OECD SOCX

DE		1985-1989	1990-1994	1995-1999	2000-2004	2005-2009	ppt change (05-09)–(85-89)
	PUBLIC SPENDING, AS A PERCENTAGE OF GDP						
(a)	"OLD1" HEALTH CARE	6.70	7.32	7.98	8.02	8.00	1.30
(b)	"OLD2" OLD AGE	10.10	9.86	10.86	11.34	10.92	0.82
(c)	"OLD3" OTHER BENEFITS + ALLOWANCES	4.18	4.60	4.72	4.70	4.60	0.42
	"OLD3" OTHER BENEFITS	3.28	3.60	3.80	3.70	3.74	0.46
(d)	"NEW1" PARENTAL LEAVE	0.16	0.26	0.20	0.20	0.24	0.08
(e)	"NEW2" ELDERLY CARE	0.20	0.20				
(f)	"NEW3" CHILD CARE	0.30	1.16	1.40	1.26	1.32	1.02
	"NEW3" CHILD CARE + ALLOWANCES	1.20	2.16	2.32	2.26	2.18	0.98
(g)	"NEW4" ALMP	0.78	1.36	1.34	1.38	1.12	0.34
(h)	"NEW5" PRIMARY & SECONDARY EDUCATION		2.66	2.57	2.52	2.36	
(i)	"NEW6" TERTIARY EDUCATION			1.02	1.04	1.08	
(j)	TOTAL NEW 1-4 (a)	1.44	2.98	2.94	2.84	2.68	
	TOTAL NEW 1-4 (b)	2.34	3.98	3.86	3.84	3.54	
(k)	TOTAL OLD & NEW (education excluded)	22.42	24.76	26.50	26.90	26.20	

	CASH, IN KIND, AND NOT CLASSIFIED SPENDING, AS A PERCENTAGE OF TOTAL SPENDING						
(l)	TOTAL CASH	63.52	58.90	58.04	58.96	57.86	–5.67
(m)	TOTAL IN KIND	33.45	36.33	37.66	36.81	38.64	5.19
(n)	TOTAL NOT CLASSIFIED	3.03	4.78	4.30	4.24	3.51	0.48
	CONTEXTUAL FACTORS						
(o)	EMPLOYMENT RATE	62.67	65.41	64.53	65.27	68.45	5.78
(p)	UNEMPLOYMENT RATE		6.75	8.96	8.98	9.10	
	BUDGETARY EFFORTS (INDICES)						
(q)	(“OLD2” / 65+) / (GDP/cap)	100	117	129	122	103	
(r)	(“NEW3a”/<5) / (GDP/CAP)	100	438	559	559	641	
	(“NEW3b”/<5) / (GDP/CAP)	100	189	218	235	241	
(s)	(“NEW4”/UN) / (GDP/cap)	100	161	118	125	95	
(t)	(“NEW5”/5-19) / (GDP/cap)		100	94	95	94	

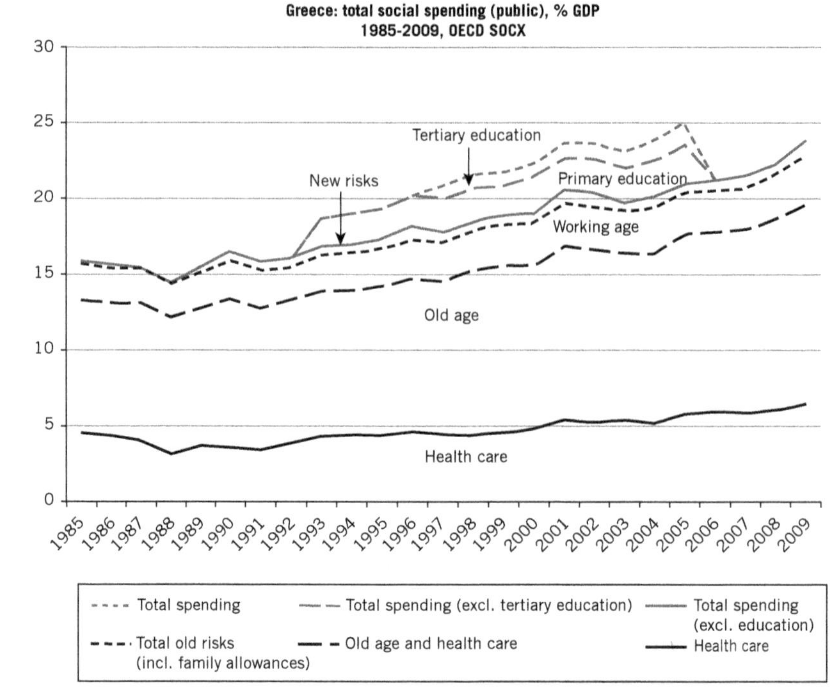

Figure 12.9. Greece: total social spending (public), percentage of GDP, 1985–2009, OECD SOCX.

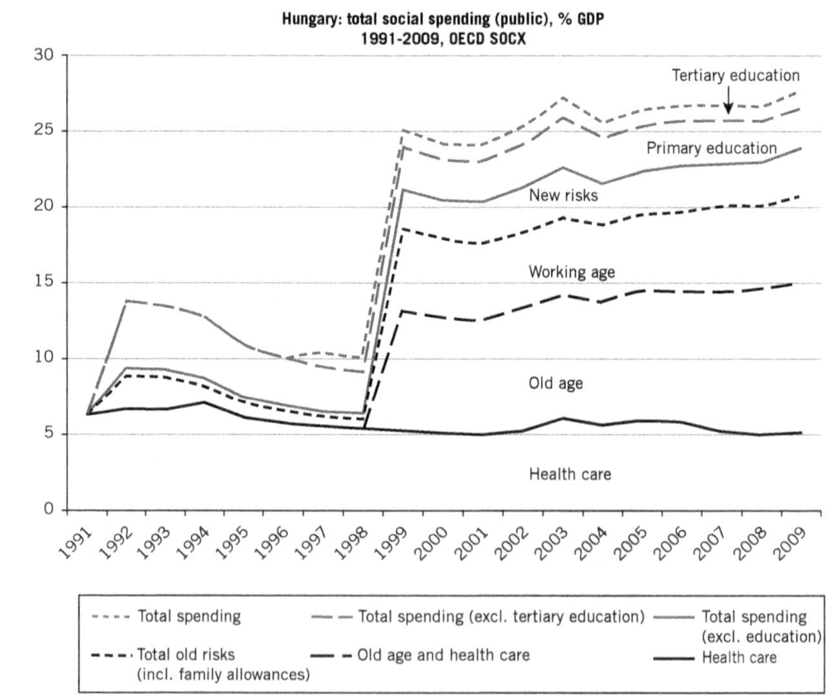

Figure 12.10. Hungary: total social spending (public), percentage of GDP, 1991–2009, OECD SOCX.

Table 12.9. Greece: total social spending (public), percentage of GDP 1985–2009, OECD SOCX

GR		1985-1989	1990-1994	1995-1999	2000-2004	2005-2009	ppt change (05-09)–(85-89)
	PUBLIC SPENDING, AS A PERCENTAGE OF GDP						
(a)	"OLD1" HEALTH CARE	3.98	3.94	4.52	5.22	6.06	2.08
(b)	"OLD2" OLD AGE	8.94	9.52	10.36	11.18	12.26	3.32
(c)	"OLD3" OTHER BENEFITS + ALLOWANCES	2.30	2.42	2.58	2.84	2.90	0.60
	"OLD3" OTHER BENEFITS	2.10	2.00	2.02	2.36	2.46	0.36
(d)	"NEW1" PARENTAL LEAVE	0.10	0.10	0.10	0.10	0.12	0.02
(e)	"NEW2" ELDERLY CARE			0.10	0.10	0.10	
(f)	"NEW3" CHILD CARE		0.30	0.30	0.38	0.40	
	"NEW3" CHILD CARE + ALLOWANCES	0.20	0.72	0.86	0.86	0.84	0.64
(g)	"NEW4" ALMP	0.16	0.20	0.24	0.20	0.18	0.02
(h)	"NEW5" PRIMARY & SECONDARY EDUCATION		1.95	2.09	2.30	2.60	
(i)	"NEW6" TERTIARY EDUCATION			0.92	1.06	1.45	
(j)	TOTAL NEW 1-4 (a)	0.26	0.60	0.74	0.78	0.80	
	TOTAL NEW 1-4 (b)	0.46	1.02	1.30	1.26	1.24	
(k)	TOTAL OLD & NEW (education excluded)	15.48	16.48	18.20	20.02	22.02	

(continued)

Table 12.9. (Continued)

GR		1985-1989	1990-1994	1995-1999	2000-2004	2005-2009	ppt change (05-09)–(85-89)
	CASH, IN KIND, AND NOT CLASSIFIED SPENDING, AS A PERCENTAGE OF TOTAL SPENDING						
(l)	TOTAL CASH	73.20	69.33	67.72	65.98	65.50	–7.70
(m)	TOTAL IN KIND	25.77	29.45	30.95	33.22	33.87	8.10
(n)	TOTAL NOT CLASSIFIED	1.03	1.21	1.33	0.80	0.63	–0.40
	CONTEXTUAL FACTORS						
(o)	EMPLOYMENT RATE	55.03	53.82	55.05	57.41	61.11	6.09
(p)	UNEMPLOYMENT RATE	6.76	7.70	10.26	10.50	8.86	2.10
	BUDGETARY EFFORTS (INDICES)						
(q)	("OLD2" / 65+) / (GDP/cap)	100	99	97	95	97	
(r)	("NEW3a"/<5) / (GDP/CAP)		100	105	140	141	
	("NEW3b"/<5) / (GDP/CAP)		100	125	131	123	
(s)	("NEW4"/UN) / (GDP/cap)	100	112	103	82	87	
(t)	("NEW5"/5-19) / (GDP/cap)		100	115	145	177	

Table 12.10. Hungary: total social spending (public), percentage of GDP 1985–2009, OECD SOCX

HU		1985-1989	1990-1994	1995-1999	2000-2004	2005-2009	ppt change (05-09)–(95-99)
	PUBLIC SPENDING, AS A PERCENTAGE OF GDP						
(a)	"OLD1" HEALTH CARE		6.70	5.66	5.44	5.40	–0.26
(b)	"OLD2" OLD AGE			7.80	7.90	9.20	1.40
(c)	"OLD3" OTHER BENEFITS + ALLOWANCES		1.80	1.68	5.04	5.46	3.78
	"OLD3" OTHER BENEFITS		1.08	1.38	3.78	4.08	2.70
(d)	"NEW1" PARENTAL LEAVE			0.50	0.62	0.72	0.22
(e)	"NEW2" ELDERLY CARE			0.50	0.54	0.54	0.04
(f)	"NEW3" CHILD CARE			1.20	1.30	1.28	0.08
	"NEW3" CHILD CARE + ALLOWANCES			2.70	2.56	2.66	–0.04
(g)	"NEW4" ALMP		0.50	0.40	0.44	0.40	0.00
(h)	"NEW5" PRIMARY & SECONDARY EDUCATION		4.22	2.98	2.86	2.80	–0.18
(i)	"NEW6" TERTIARY EDUCATION			0.98	1.13	1.05	0.07
(j)	TOTAL NEW 1-4 (a)			2.60	2.90	2.94	0.34
	TOTAL NEW 1-4 (b)			4.10	4.16	4.32	0.22
(k)	TOTAL OLD & NEW (education excluded)			18.94	21.28	23.00	4.06

(*continued*)

Table 12.10. (Continued)

HU		1985-1989	1990-1994	1995-1999	2000-2004	2005-2009	ppt change (05-09)–(95-99)
	CASH, IN KIND, AND NOT CLASSIFIED SPENDING, AS A PERCENTAGE OF TOTAL SPENDING						
(l)	TOTAL CASH		14.66	20.64	60.46	63.18	42.54
(m)	TOTAL IN KIND		81.23	74.31	37.46	35.43	–38.88
(n)	TOTAL NOT CLASSIFIED		4.11	5.05	2.08	1.39	–3.66
	CONTEXTUAL FACTORS						
(o)	EMPLOYMENT RATE		55.32	53.47	56.44	56.72	3.25
(p)	UNEMPLOYMENT RATE		11.00	8.86	5.98	7.98	–0.88
	BUDGETARY EFFORTS (INDICES)						
(q)	(“OLD2” / 65+) / (GDP/cap)			100	99	109	
(r)	(“NEW3a”/<5) / (GDP/CAP)			100	113	110	
	(“NEW3b”/<5) / (GDP/CAP)			100	99	102	
(s)	(“NEW4”/UN) / (GDP/cap)			100	153	100	
(t)	(“NEW5”/5-19) / (GDP/cap)			100	106	112	

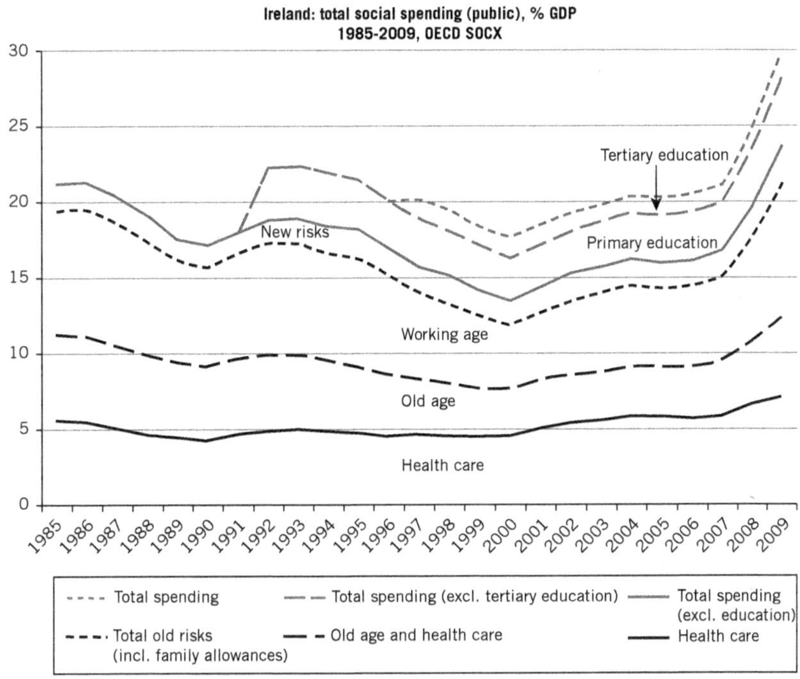

Figure 12.11. Ireland: total social spending (public), percentage of GDP, 1985–2009, OECD SOCX.

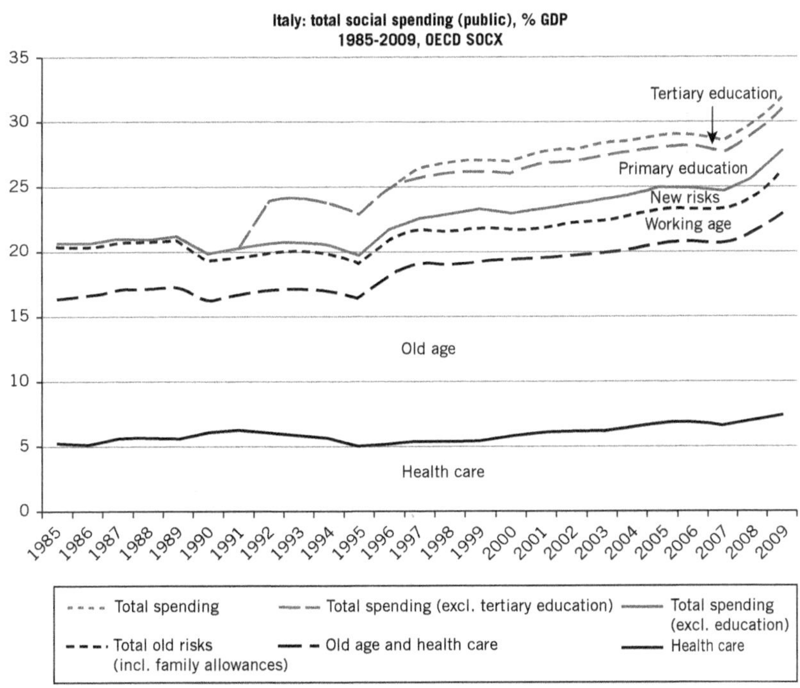

Figure 12.12. Italy: total social spending (public), percentage of GDP, 1985–2009, OECD SOCX.

Table 12.11. Ireland: total social spending (public), percentage of GDP 1985–2009, OECD SOCX

IE		1985-1989	1990-1994	1995-1999	2000-2004	2005-2009	ppt change (05-09)–(85-89)
	PUBLIC SPENDING, AS A PERCENTAGE OF GDP						
(a)	"OLD1" HEALTH CARE	5.08	4.76	4.64	5.30	6.24	1.16
(b)	"OLD2" OLD AGE	5.36	4.92	3.74	3.22	3.94	–1.42
(c)	"OLD3" OTHER BENEFITS + ALLOWANCES	7.78	7.04	5.88	4.80	6.38	–1.40
	"OLD3" OTHER BENEFITS	6.86	6.04	4.98	3.68	4.94	–1.92
(d)	"NEW1" PARENTAL LEAVE	0.10	0.10	0.10	0.10	0.14	0.04
(e)	"NEW2" ELDERLY CARE	0.48	0.40	0.32	0.30	0.36	–0.12
(f)	"NEW3" CHILD CARE	0.10	0.10	0.22	0.46	0.62	0.52
	"NEW3" CHILD CARE + ALLOWANCES	0.96	1.06	1.12	1.58	2.06	1.10
(g)	"NEW4" ALMP	1.06	0.98	1.16	0.84	0.78	–0.28
(h)	"NEW5" PRIMARY & SECONDARY EDUCATION		3.53	3.07	2.90	3.59	
(i)	"NEW6" TERTIARY EDUCATION			1.31	1.22	1.28	
(j)	TOTAL NEW 1-4 (a)	1.74	1.58	1.80	1.70	1.90	0.16
	TOTAL NEW 1-4 (b)	2.60	2.54	2.70	2.82	3.34	0.74
(k)	TOTAL OLD & NEW (education excluded)	19.90	18.26	16.06	15.02	18.46	–1.44

	CASH, IN KIND, AND NOT CLASSIFIED SPENDING, AS A PERCENTAGE OF TOTAL SPENDING						
(l)	TOTAL CASH	62.23	62.77	56.93	51.81	54.55	–7.68
(m)	TOTAL IN KIND	32.43	31.86	35.87	43.24	41.75	9.32
(n)	TOTAL NOT CLASSIFIED	5.34	5.37	7.20	4.95	3.70	–1.64
	CONTEXTUAL FACTORS						
(o)	EMPLOYMENT RATE	49.84	51.33	57.68	65.41	67.17	17.33
(p)	UNEMPLOYMENT RATE	16.22	14.70	9.44	4.34	6.34	–9.88
	BUDGETARY EFFORTS (INDICES)						
(q)	(“OLD2” / 65+) / (GDP/cap)	100	89	68	60	74	
(r)	(“NEW3a”/<5) / (GDP/CAP)	100	121	283	577	749	
	(“NEW3b”/<5) / (GDP/CAP)	100	127	137	188	237	
(s)	(“NEW4”/UN) / (GDP/cap)	100	100	168	237	157	
(t)	(“NEW5”/5-19) / (GDP/cap)		100	94	102	141	

Table 12.12. Italy: total social spending (public), percentage of GDP 1985–2009, OECD SOCX

IT		1985-1989	1990-1994	1995-1999	2000-2004	2005-2009	ppt change (05-09)–(85-89)
	PUBLIC SPENDING, AS A PERCENTAGE OF GDP						
(a)	"OLD1" HEALTH CARE	5.50	6.00	5.32	6.16	6.94	1.44
(b)	"OLD2" OLD AGE	11.40	10.84	13.10	13.58	14.34	2.94
(c)	"OLD3" OTHER BENEFITS + ALLOWANCES	3.72	2.94	2.64	2.46	2.74	–0.98
	"OLD3" OTHER BENEFITS	3.16	2.58	2.30	2.06	2.36	–0.80
(d)	"NEW1" PARENTAL LEAVE	0.10	0.10	0.10	0.14	0.20	0.10
(e)	"NEW2" ELDERLY CARE		0.10	0.10	0.10	0.10	
(f)	"NEW3" CHILD CARE	0.20	0.20	0.36	0.66	0.78	0.58
	"NEW3" CHILD CARE + ALLOWANCES	0.76	0.56	0.70	1.06	1.16	0.40
(g)	"NEW4" ALMP		0.26	0.44	0.58	0.50	
(h)	"NEW5" PRIMARY & SECONDARY EDUCATION		3.28	3.13	3.30	3.15	
(i)	"NEW6" TERTIARY EDUCATION			0.79	0.93	0.90	
(j)	TOTAL NEW 1-4 (a)	0.30	0.66	1.00	1.48	1.58	
	TOTAL NEW 1-4 (b)	0.86	1.02	1.34	1.88	1.96	
(k)	TOTAL OLD & NEW (education excluded)	20.92	20.44	22.06	23.68	25.60	

	CASH, IN KIND, AND NOT CLASSIFIED SPENDING, AS A PERCENTAGE OF TOTAL SPENDING						
(l)	TOTAL CASH	72.19	67.89	71.81	68.34	67.48	–4.70
(m)	TOTAL IN KIND	27.81	30.84	26.22	29.21	30.55	2.74
(n)	TOTAL NOT CLASSIFIED	0.00	1.27	1.97	2.45	1.97	1.97
	CONTEXTUAL FACTORS						
(o)	EMPLOYMENT RATE	51.97	52.32	51.85	55.61	58.15	6.18
(p)	UNEMPLOYMENT RATE	9.22	9.32	11.16	8.86	7.04	–2.18
	BUDGETARY EFFORTS (INDICES)						
(q)	("OLD2" / 65+) / (GDP/cap)	100	84	91	87	87	
(r)	("NEW3a"/<5) / (GDP/CAP)	100	216	397	735	832	
	("NEW3b"/<5) / (GDP/CAP)	100	92	117	179	189	
(s)	("NEW4"/UN) / (GDP/cap)		100	159	262	294	
(t)	("NEW5"/5-19) / (GDP/cap)		100	106	118	116	

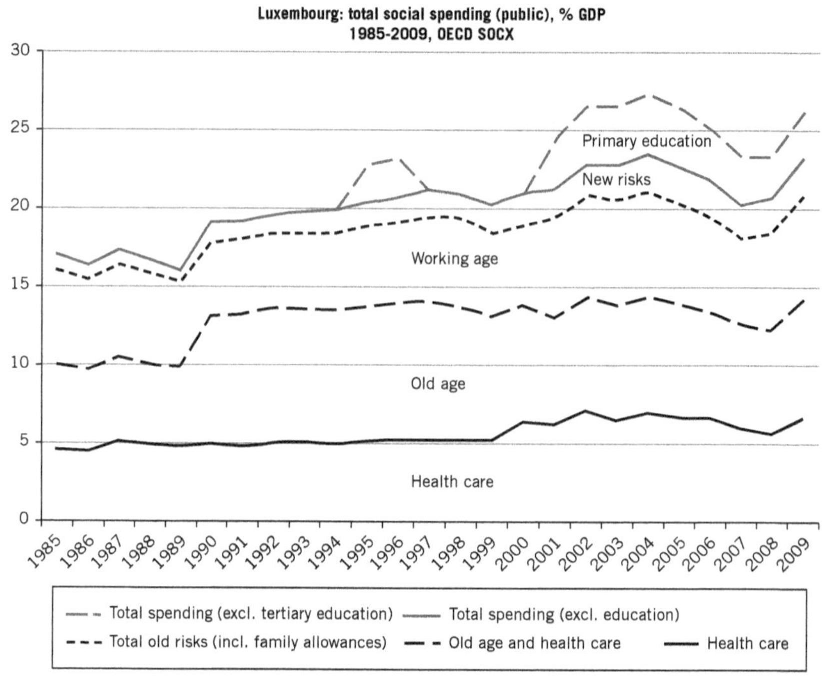

Figure 12.13. Luxembourg: total social spending (public), percentage of GDP, 1985–2009, OECD SOCX.

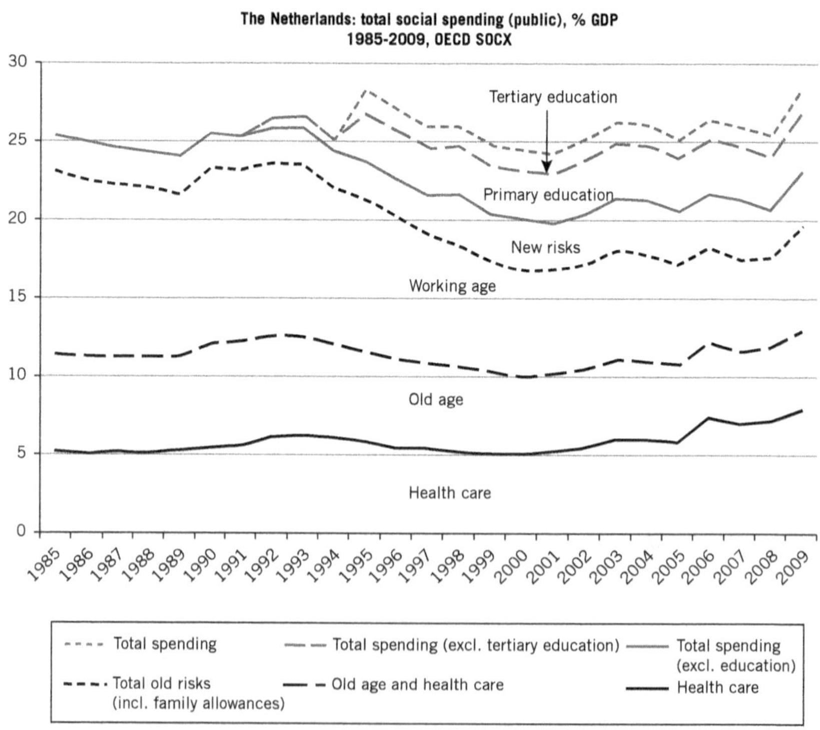

Figure 12.14. The Netherlands: total social spending (public), percentage of GDP, 1985–2009, OECD SOCX.

Table 12.13. Luxembourg: total social spending (public), percentage of GDP 1985–2009, OECD SOCX

LU		1985-1989	1990-1994	1995-1999	2000-2004	2005-2009	ppt change (05-09)–(85-89)
	PUBLIC SPENDING, AS A PERCENTAGE OF GDP						
(a)	“OLD1” HEALTH CARE	4.78	4.96	5.18	6.64	6.32	1.54
(b)	“OLD2” OLD AGE	5.24	8.46	8.56	7.22	6.96	1.72
(c)	“OLD3” OTHER BENEFITS + ALLOWANCES	5.80	4.80	5.32	6.30	6.14	0.34
	“OLD3” OTHER BENEFITS	4.62	3.40	3.56	4.26	4.02	–0.60
(d)	“NEW1” PARENTAL LEAVE	0.20	0.46	0.58	0.50	0.44	0.24
(e)	“NEW2” ELDERLY CARE	0.10	0.20	0.15			
(f)	“NEW3” CHILD CARE	0.22	0.52	0.80	1.30	1.50	1.28
	“NEW3” CHILD CARE + ALLOWANCES	1.40	1.92	2.56	3.34	3.62	2.22
(g)	“NEW4” ALMP	0.34	0.12	0.14	0.32	0.38	0.04
(h)	“NEW5” PRIMARY & SECONDARY EDUCATION			2.42	3.57	3.14	
(i)	“NEW6” TERTIARY EDUCATION						
(j)	TOTAL NEW 1-4 (a)	0.86	1.30	1.67	2.12	2.32	
	TOTAL NEW 1-4 (b)	2.04	2.70	3.43	4.16	4.44	
(k)	TOTAL OLD & NEW (education excluded)	16.68	19.52	20.73	22.28	21.74	

(continued)

Table 12.13. (Continued)

LU		1985-1989	1990-1994	1995-1999	2000-2004	2005-2009	ppt change (05-09)–(85-89)
	CASH, IN KIND, AND NOT CLASSIFIED SPENDING, AS A PERCENTAGE OF TOTAL SPENDING						
(l)	TOTAL CASH	66.54	70.28	69.66	62.05	60.90	–5.64
(m)	TOTAL IN KIND	31.43	29.10	29.67	36.52	37.35	5.93
(n)	TOTAL NOT CLASSIFIED	2.03	0.62	0.68	1.43	1.75	–0.28
	CONTEXTUAL FACTORS						
(o)	EMPLOYMENT RATE	59.24	60.51	59.88	62.79	63.99	4.74
(p)	UNEMPLOYMENT RATE	2.36	2.24	2.72	3.08	4.70	2.34
	BUDGETARY EFFORTS (INDICES)						
(q)	("OLD2" / 65+) / (GDP/cap)	100	158	153	131	126	
(r)	("NEW3a"/<5) / (GDP/CAP)	100	131	189	208	243	
	("NEW3b"/<5) / (GDP/CAP)	100	111	138	167	188	
(s)	("NEW4"/UN) / (GDP/cap)	100	35	20	44	34	
(t)	("NEW5"/5-19) / (GDP/cap)			100	112	123	

Table 12.14. The Netherlands: total social spending (public), percentage of GDP 1985–2009, OECD SOCX

NL		1985-1989	1990-1994	1995-1999	2000-2004	2005-2009	ppt change (05-09)–(85-89)
	PUBLIC SPENDING, AS A PERCENTAGE OF GDP						
(a)	"OLD1" HEALTH CARE	5.18	5.88	5.40	5.54	7.08	1.90
(b)	"OLD2" OLD AGE	6.10	6.42	5.50	5.02	4.80	–1.30
(c)	"OLD3" OTHER BENEFITS + ALLOWANCES	11.04	10.82	8.38	6.76	6.14	–4.90
	"OLD3" OTHER BENEFITS	9.66	9.74	7.54	6.06	5.48	–4.18
(d)	"NEW1" PARENTAL LEAVE	0.10					
(e)	"NEW2" ELDERLY CARE	0.54	0.50	0.58	0.72	0.90	0.36
(f)	"NEW3" CHILD CARE	0.42	0.38	0.50	0.90	1.08	0.66
	"NEW3" CHILD CARE + ALLOWANCES	1.80	1.46	1.34	1.60	1.74	–0.06
(g)	"NEW4" ALMP	1.28	1.38	1.64	1.66	1.48	0.20
(h)	"NEW5" PRIMARY & SECONDARY EDUCATION		0.72	3.02	3.33	3.44	
(i)	"NEW6" TERTIARY EDUCATION			1.37	1.31	1.36	
(j)	TOTAL NEW 1-4 (a)	2.34	2.26	2.72	3.28	3.46	
	TOTAL NEW 1-4 (b)	3.72	3.34	3.56	3.98	4.12	
(k)	TOTAL OLD & NEW (education excluded)	24.66	25.38	22.00	20.60	21.48	

(*continued*)

Table 12.14. (Continued)

NL		1985-1989	1990-1994	1995-1999	2000-2004	2005-2009	ppt change (05-09)–(85-89)
	CASH, IN KIND, AND NOT CLASSIFIED SPENDING, AS A PERCENTAGE OF TOTAL SPENDING						
(l)	TOTAL CASH	68.39	66.56	60.81	55.27	49.00	–19.38
(m)	TOTAL IN KIND	26.42	28.16	32.61	37.63	45.59	19.18
(n)	TOTAL NOT CLASSIFIED	5.20	5.28	6.59	7.10	5.40	0.21
	CONTEXTUAL FACTORS						
(o)	EMPLOYMENT RATE	55.90	63.25	67.87	72.07	73.96	18.06
(p)	UNEMPLOYMENT RATE	6.40	5.32	5.34	3.58	4.00	–2.40
	BUDGETARY EFFORTS (INDICES)						
(q)	("OLD2" / 65+) / (GDP/cap)	100	101	83	74	67	
(r)	("NEW3a"/<5) / (GDP/CAP)	100	87	116	208	267	
	("NEW3b"/<5) / (GDP/CAP)	100	78	72	86	100	
(s)	("NEW4"/UN) / (GDP/cap)	100	145	218	361	260	
(t)	("NEW5"/5-19) / (GDP/cap)		100	418	458	473	

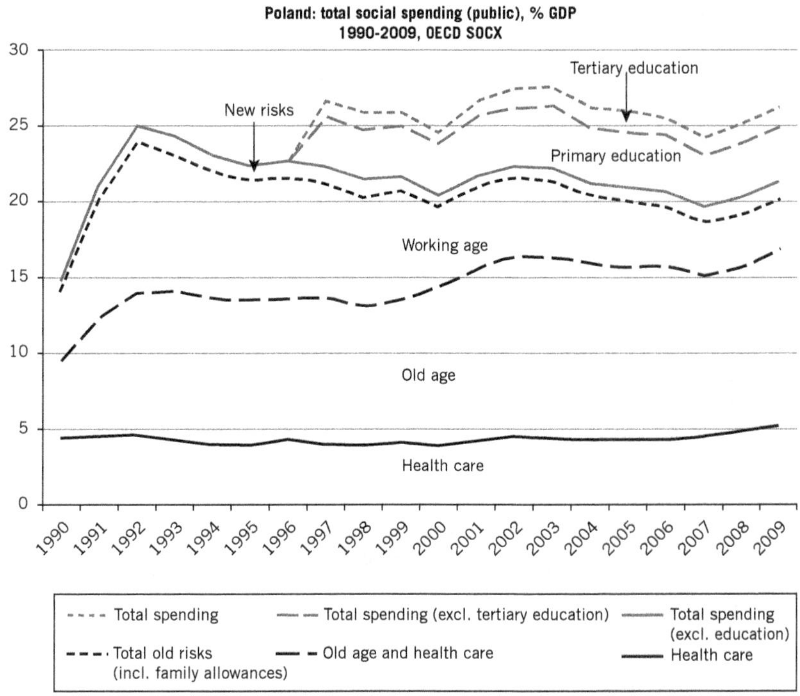

Figure 12.15. Poland: total social spending (public), percentage of GDP, 1990–2009, OECD SOCX.

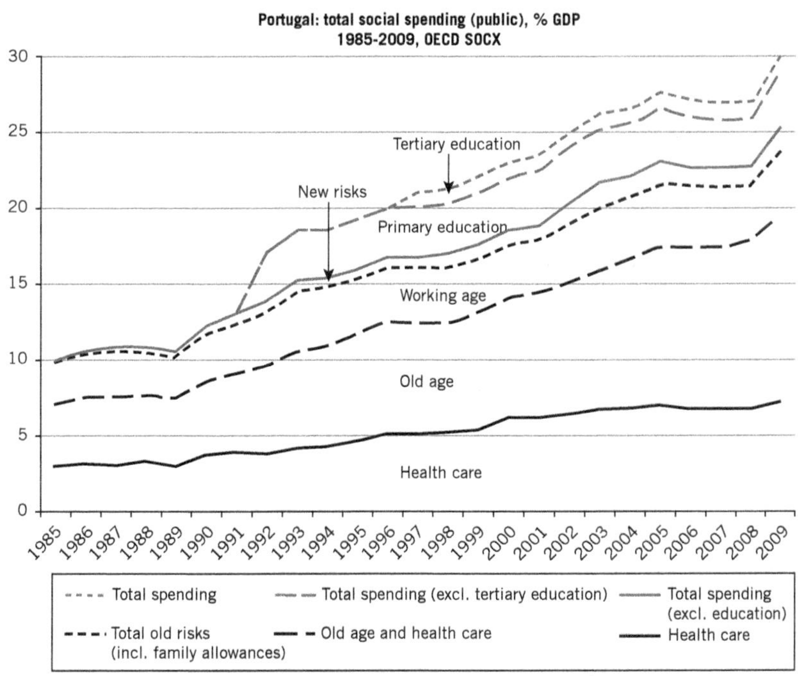

Figure 12.16. Portugal: total social spending (public), percentage of GDP, 1985–2009, OECD SOCX.

Table 12.15. Poland: total social spending (public), percentage of GDP 1985–2009, OECD SOCX

PL		1985-1989	1990-1994	1995-1999	2000-2004	2005-2009	ppt change (05-09)–(90-94)
	PUBLIC SPENDING, AS A PERCENTAGE OF GDP						
(a)	"OLD1" HEALTH CARE		4.36	4.06	4.26	4.64	0.28
(b)	"OLD2" OLD AGE		8.34	9.40	11.44	11.18	2.84
(c)	"OLD3" OTHER BENEFITS + ALLOWANCES		8.00	7.54	5.10	3.68	–4.32
	"OLD3" OTHER BENEFITS		6.58	7.00	4.62	3.30	–3.28
(d)	"NEW1" PARENTAL LEAVE		0.40	0.30	0.28	0.28	–0.12
(e)	"NEW2" ELDERLY CARE						
(f)	"NEW3" CHILD CARE		0.28	0.36	0.22	0.30	0.02
	"NEW3" CHILD CARE + ALLOWANCES		1.70	0.90	0.70	0.68	–1.02
(g)	"NEW4" ALMP		0.30	0.44	0.26	0.50	0.20
(h)	"NEW5" PRIMARY & SECONDARY EDUCATION			3.27	3.81	3.57	
(i)	"NEW6" TERTIARY EDUCATION			1.04	1.10	1.26	
(j)	TOTAL NEW 1-4 (a)		0.98	1.10	0.76	1.08	0.10
	TOTAL NEW 1-4 (b)		2.40	1.64	1.24	1.46	–0.94
(k)	TOTAL OLD & NEW (education excluded)		21.68	22.10	21.56	20.58	–1.10

	CASH, IN KIND, AND NOT CLASSIFIED SPENDING, AS A PERCENTAGE OF TOTAL SPENDING					
(l)	TOTAL CASH	74.71	76.01	76.72	72.59	–2.12
(m)	TOTAL IN KIND	23.97	22.00	22.07	24.98	1.01
(n)	TOTAL NOT CLASSIFIED	1.32	1.99	1.20	2.43	1.11
	CONTEXTUAL FACTORS					
(o)	EMPLOYMENT RATE	59.03	58.35	52.67	56.60	–2.43
(p)	UNEMPLOYMENT RATE	14.20	12.04	18.64	11.36	–2.84
	BUDGETARY EFFORTS (INDICES)					
(q)	("OLD2" / 65+) / (GDP/cap)	100	103	115	106	
(r)	("NEW3a"/<5) / (GDP/CAP)		100	124	174	
	("NEW3b"/<5) / (GDP/CAP)	100	54	73	73	
(s)	("NEW4"/UN) / (GDP/cap)	100	159	60	226	
(t)	("NEW5"/5-19) / (GDP/cap)		100	125	139	

Table 12.16. Portugal: total social spending (public), percentage of GDP 1985–2009, OECD SOCX

PT		1985-1989	1990-1994	1995-1999	2000-2004	2005-2009	ppt change (05-09)–(85-89)
	PUBLIC SPENDING, AS A PERCENTAGE OF GDP						
(a)	"OLD1" HEALTH CARE	3.12	3.98	5.10	6.46	6.86	3.74
(b)	"OLD2" OLD AGE	4.34	5.76	7.34	8.76	11.08	6.74
(c)	"OLD3" OTHER BENEFITS + ALLOWANCES	2.86	3.58	3.62	3.80	4.02	1.16
	"OLD3" OTHER BENEFITS	2.32	3.18	3.22	3.36	3.56	1.24
(d)	"NEW1" PARENTAL LEAVE	0.10	0.10	0.10	0.12	0.26	0.16
(e)	"NEW2" ELDERLY CARE				0.17	0.10	
(f)	"NEW3" CHILD CARE		0.10	0.20	0.56	0.50	
	"NEW3" CHILD CARE + ALLOWANCES	0.54	0.50	0.60	1.00	0.96	0.42
(g)	"NEW4" ALMP	0.20	0.46	0.44	0.54	0.50	0.30
(h)	"NEW5" PRIMARY & SECONDARY EDUCATION		3.25	3.34	3.54	3.32	
(i)	"NEW6" TERTIARY EDUCATION			0.94	0.99	1.14	
(j)	TOTAL NEW 1-4 (a)	0.30	0.66	0.74	1.39	1.36	
	TOTAL NEW 1-4 (b)	0.84	1.06	1.14	1.83	1.82	
(k)	TOTAL OLD & NEW (education excluded)	10.62	13.98	16.80	20.41	23.32	

	CASH, IN KIND, AND NOT CLASSIFIED SPENDING, AS A PERCENTAGE OF TOTAL SPENDING						
(l)	TOTAL CASH	69.01	67.42	65.87	62.13	65.85	−3.16
(m)	TOTAL IN KIND	29.50	29.27	31.52	35.22	32.01	2.52
(n)	TOTAL NOT CLASSIFIED	1.49	3.31	2.61	2.65	2.14	0.64
	CONTEXTUAL FACTORS						
(o)	EMPLOYMENT RATE	64.73	66.27	65.10	68.34	67.52	2.79
(p)	UNEMPLOYMENT RATE	7.26	5.08	6.34	5.88	9.04	1.78
	BUDGETARY EFFORTS (INDICES)						
(q)	("OLD2" / 65+) / (GDP/cap)	100	116	135	150	181	
(r)	("NEW3a"/<5) / (GDP/CAP)		100	209	588	543	
	("NEW3b"/<5) / (GDP/CAP)		100	125	210	209	
(s)	("NEW4"/UN) / (GDP/cap)	100	270	213	281	159	
(t)	("NEW5"/5-19) / (GDP/cap)		100	115	138	139	

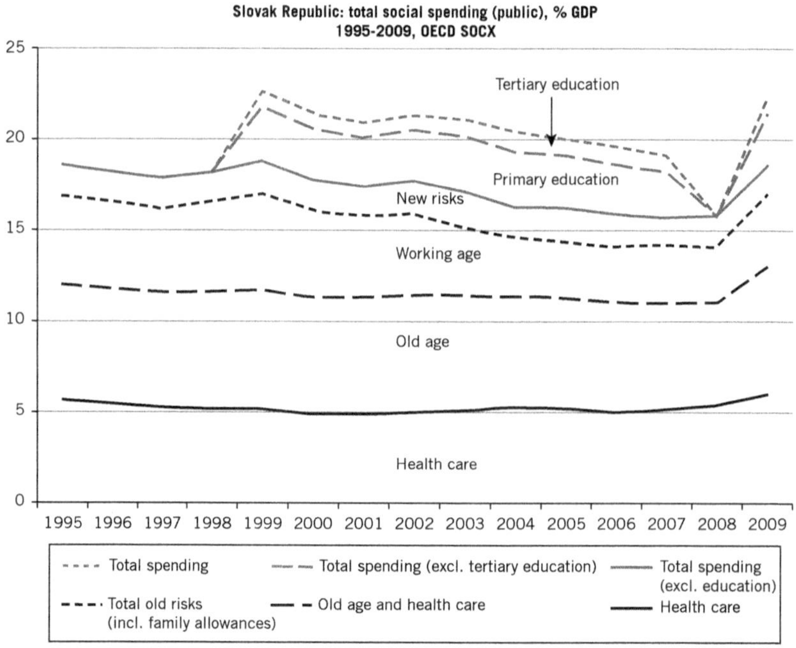

Figure 12.17. Slovak Republic: total social spending (public), percentage of GDP, 1995–2009, OECD SOCX.

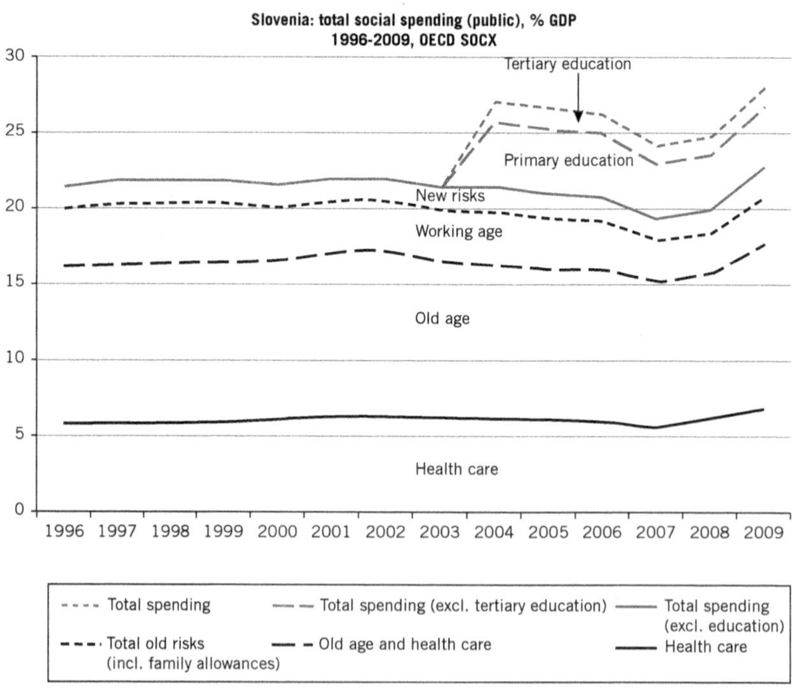

Figure 12.18. Slovenia: total social spending (public), percentage of GDP, 1996–2009, OECD SOCX.

Table 12.17. Slovak Republic: total social spending (public), percentage of GDP 1985–2009, OECD SOCX

SK		1985-1989	1990-1994	1995-1999	2000-2004	2005-2009	ppt change (05-09)–(95-99)
	PUBLIC SPENDING, AS A PERCENTAGE OF GDP						
(a)	"OLD1" HEALTH CARE			5.38	5.04	5.36	–0.02
(b)	"OLD2" OLD AGE			6.36	6.34	6.12	–0.24
(c)	"OLD3" OTHER BENEFITS + ALLOWANCES			4.92	4.14	3.28	–1.64
	"OLD3" OTHER BENEFITS			3.52	3.26	2.34	–1.18
(d)	"NEW1" PARENTAL LEAVE			0.66	0.54	0.50	–0.16
(e)	"NEW2" ELDERLY CARE			0.26	0.30	0.34	0.08
(f)	"NEW3" CHILD CARE			0.30	0.64	0.60	0.30
	"NEW3" CHILD CARE + ALLOWANCES			1.70	1.52	1.54	–0.16
(g)	"NEW4" ALMP			0.46	0.26	0.24	–0.22
(h)	"NEW5" PRIMARY & SECONDARY EDUCATION			3.02	2.86	2.73	
(i)	"NEW6" TERTIARY EDUCATION			0.83	0.92	0.92	0.09
(j)	TOTAL NEW 1-4 (a)			1.68	1.74	1.68	0.00
	TOTAL NEW 1-4 (b)			3.08	2.62	2.62	–0.46
(k)	TOTAL OLD & NEW (education excluded)			18.34	17.26	16.44	–1.90

(continued)

Table 12.17. (Continued)

SK		1985-1989	1990-1994	1995-1999	2000-2004	2005-2009	ppt change (05-09)–(95-99)
	CASH, IN KIND, AND NOT CLASSIFIED SPENDING, AS A PERCENTAGE OF TOTAL SPENDING						
(l)	TOTAL CASH			65.10	63.33	59.95	–5.15
(m)	TOTAL IN KIND			32.39	35.17	38.58	6.19
(n)	TOTAL NOT CLASSIFIED			2.51	1.50	1.47	–1.04
	CONTEXTUAL FACTORS						
(o)	EMPLOYMENT RATE			60.36	57.04	60.05	–0.32
(p)	UNEMPLOYMENT RATE			13.02	18.50	12.44	–0.58
	BUDGETARY EFFORTS (INDICES)						
(q)	(“OLD2” / 65+) / (GDP/cap)			100	97	90	
(r)	(“NEW3a”/<5) / (GDP/CAP)			100	280	260	
	(“NEW3b”/<5) / (GDP/CAP)			100	100	104	
(s)	(“NEW4”/UN) / (GDP/cap)			100	37	50	
(t)	(“NEW5”/5-19) / (GDP/cap)			100	102	90	

Table 12.18. Slovenia: total social spending (public), percentage of GDP 1985–2009, OECD SOCX

SI		1985-1989	1990-1994	1995-1999	2000-2004	2005-2009	ppt change (05-09)–(95-99)
	PUBLIC SPENDING, AS A PERCENTAGE OF GDP						
(a)	"OLD1" HEALTH CARE			5.85	6.20	6.12	0.27
(b)	"OLD2" OLD AGE			10.48	10.56	10.00	–0.48
(c)	"OLD3" OTHER BENEFITS + ALLOWANCES			3.95	3.42	3.02	–0.93
	"OLD3" OTHER BENEFITS			3.95	3.42	3.02	–0.93
(d)	"NEW1" PARENTAL LEAVE			0.50	0.48	0.54	0.04
(e)	"NEW2" ELDERLY CARE			0.10	0.10	0.10	0.00
(f)	"NEW3" CHILD CARE			0.83	0.80	0.72	–0.11
	"NEW3" CHILD CARE + ALLOWANCES			0.83	0.80	0.72	–0.11
(g)	"NEW4" ALMP				0.18	0.34	
(h)	"NEW5" PRIMARY & SECONDARY EDUCATION				4.33	4.01	
(i)	"NEW6" TERTIARY EDUCATION				1.34	1.29	
(j)	TOTAL NEW 1-4 (a)			1.43	1.56	1.70	
	TOTAL NEW 1-4 (b)			1.43	1.56	1.70	
(k)	TOTAL OLD & NEW (education excluded)			21.70	21.74	20.84	

(continued)

Table 12.18. (Continued)

SI		1985-1989	1990-1994	1995-1999	2000-2004	2005-2009	ppt change (05-09)–(95-99)
	CASH, IN KIND, AND NOT CLASSIFIED SPENDING, AS A PERCENTAGE OF TOTAL SPENDING						
(l)	TOTAL CASH			68.32	66.23	64.79	−3.53
(m)	TOTAL IN KIND			31.68	33.39	34.08	2.39
(n)	TOTAL NOT CLASSIFIED			0.00	0.37	1.14	1.14
	CONTEXTUAL FACTORS						
(o)	EMPLOYMENT RATE				63.76	67.28	
(p)	UNEMPLOYMENT RATE			7.15	6.44	5.54	−1.61
	BUDGETARY EFFORTS (INDICES)						
(q)	("OLD2" / 65+) / (GDP/cap)			100	91	79	
(r)	("NEW3a"/<5) / (GDP/CAP)			100	102	87	
	("NEW3b"/<5) / (GDP/CAP)			100	102	87	
(s)	("NEW4"/UN) / (GDP/cap)				100	203	
(t)	("NEW5"/5-19) / (GDP/cap)				100	98	

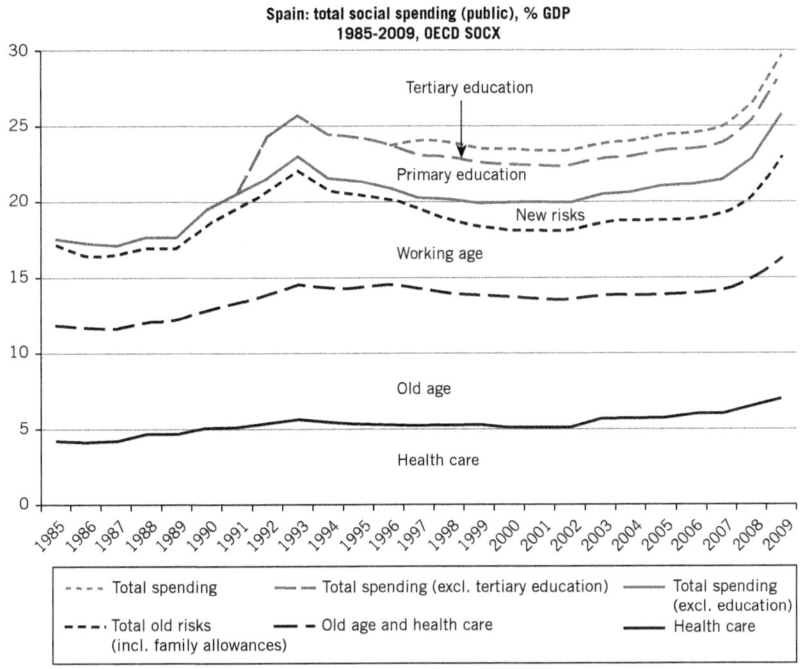

Figure 12.19. Spain: total social spending (public), percentage of GDP, 1985–2009, OECD SOCX.

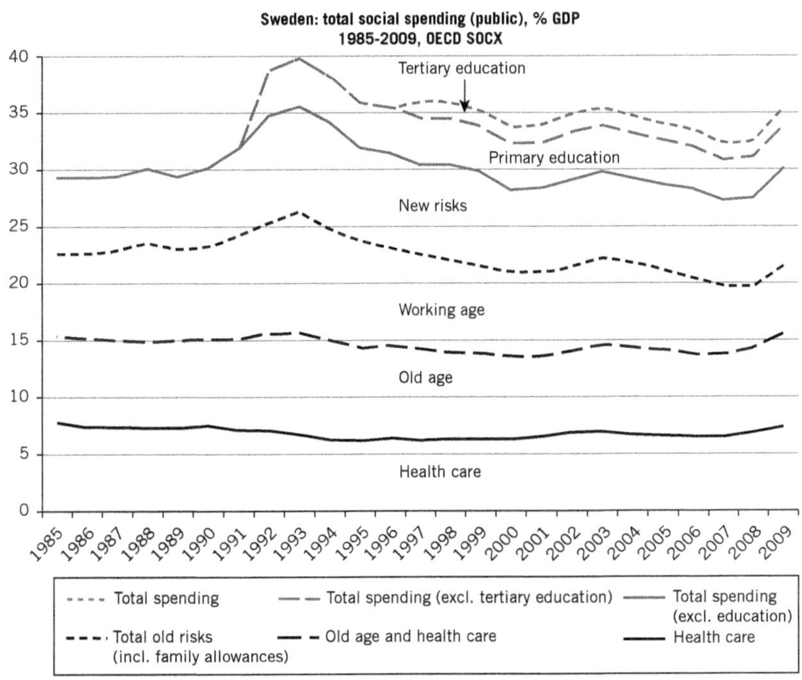

Figure 12.20. Sweden: total social spending (public), percentage of GDP, 1985–2009, OECD SOCX.

Table 12.19. Spain: total social spending (public), percentage of GDP 1985–2009, OECD SOCX

ES		1985-1989	1990-1994	1995-1999	2000-2004	2005-2009	ppt change (05-09)–(85-89)
	PUBLIC SPENDING, AS A PERCENTAGE OF GDP						
(a)	"OLD1" HEALTH CARE	4.46	5.40	5.34	5.42	6.28	1.82
(b)	"OLD2" OLD AGE	7.46	8.38	8.92	8.34	8.38	0.92
(c)	"OLD3" OTHER BENEFITS + ALLOWANCES	4.94	6.56	5.22	4.62	5.40	0.46
	"OLD3" OTHER BENEFITS	4.82	6.42	5.12	4.48	5.20	0.38
(d)	"NEW1" PARENTAL LEAVE	0.10	0.10	0.10	0.12	0.24	0.14
(e)	"NEW2" ELDERLY CARE		0.16	0.14	0.24	0.48	
(f)	"NEW3" CHILD CARE		0.10	0.28	0.70	0.80	
	"NEW3" CHILD CARE + ALLOWANCES	0.12	0.24	0.38	0.84	1.00	0.88
(g)	"NEW4" ALMP	0.60	0.58	0.56	0.80	0.92	0.32
(h)	"NEW5" PRIMARY & SECONDARY EDUCATION		2.79	2.83	2.43	2.44	
(i)	"NEW6" TERTIARY EDUCATION			0.98	1.04	1.07	
(j)	TOTAL NEW 1-4 (a)	0.70	0.94	1.08	1.86	2.44	
	TOTAL NEW 1-4 (b)	0.82	1.08	1.18	2.00	2.64	
(k)	TOTAL OLD & NEW (education excluded)	17.56	21.28	20.56	20.24	22.50	

	CASH, IN KIND, AND NOT CLASSIFIED SPENDING, AS A PERCENTAGE OF TOTAL SPENDING						
(l)	TOTAL CASH	70.75	70.16	67.66	62.86	60.50	–10.25
(m)	TOTAL IN KIND	25.82	27.26	29.99	33.68	35.85	10.03
(n)	TOTAL NOT CLASSIFIED	3.43	2.58	2.35	3.47	3.65	0.22
	CONTEXTUAL FACTORS						
(o)	EMPLOYMENT RATE	48.28	49.89	51.14	59.69	64.50	16.21
(p)	UNEMPLOYMENT RATE	17.70	17.32	17.24	11.18	11.08	–6.62
	BUDGETARY EFFORTS (INDICES)						
(q)	("OLD2" / 65+) / (GDP/cap)	100	99	94	83	84	
(r)	("NEW3a"/<5) / (GDP/CAP)		100	306	744	745	
	("NEW3b"/<5) / (GDP/CAP)		100	172	371	391	
(s)	("NEW4"/UN) / (GDP/cap)	100	97	85	187	225	
(t)	("NEW5"/5-19) / (GDP/cap)		100	116	116	127	

Table 12.20. Sweden: total social spending (public), percentage of GDP 1985–2009, OECD SOCX

SE		1985-1989	1990-1994	1995-1999	2000-2004	2005-2009	ppt change (05-09)–(85-89)
	PUBLIC SPENDING, AS A PERCENTAGE OF GDP						
(a)	"OLD1" HEALTH CARE	7.42	6.92	6.28	6.64	6.74	–0.68
(b)	"OLD2" OLD AGE	7.64	8.32	7.86	7.36	7.50	–0.14
(c)	"OLD3" OTHER BENEFITS + ALLOWANCES	7.86	9.54	8.40	7.44	6.26	–1.60
	"OLD3" OTHER BENEFITS	7.00	8.50	7.60	6.60	5.48	–1.52
(d)	"NEW1" PARENTAL LEAVE	0.78	1.10	0.62	0.60	0.72	–0.06
(e)	"NEW2" ELDERLY CARE	1.34	2.16	2.50	2.52	2.44	1.10
(f)	"NEW3" CHILD CARE	2.26	2.52	2.66	2.80	3.42	1.16
	"NEW3" CHILD CARE + ALLOWANCES	3.12	3.56	3.46	3.64	4.20	1.08
(g)	"NEW4" ALMP	2.22	2.74	2.46	1.58	1.30	–0.92
(h)	"NEW5" PRIMARY & SECONDARY EDUCATION		4.09	4.05	4.04	3.68	
(i)	"NEW6" TERTIARY EDUCATION			1.45	1.54	1.48	
(j)	TOTAL NEW 1-4 (a)	6.60	8.52	8.24	7.50	7.88	1.28
	TOTAL NEW 1-4 (b)	7.46	9.56	9.04	8.34	8.66	1.20
(k)	TOTAL OLD & NEW (education excluded)	29.52	33.30	30.78	28.94	28.38	–1.14

	CASH, IN KIND, AND NOT CLASSIFIED SPENDING, AS A PERCENTAGE OF TOTAL SPENDING						
(l)	TOTAL CASH	52.23	53.01	50.01	49.27	47.22	–5.01
(m)	TOTAL IN KIND	41.60	39.72	42.44	45.95	48.76	7.16
(n)	TOTAL NOT CLASSIFIED	6.17	7.27	7.55	4.78	4.02	–2.15
	CONTEXTUAL FACTORS						
(o)	EMPLOYMENT RATE	81.51	77.08	71.78	74.59	74.49	–7.01
(p)	UNEMPLOYMENT RATE	2.22	5.74	8.62	6.30	7.08	4.86
	BUDGETARY EFFORTS (INDICES)						
(q)	("OLD2" / 65+) / (GDP/cap)	100	108	104	99	99	
(r)	("NEW3a"/<5) / (GDP/CAP)	100	85	76	80	88	
	("NEW3b"/<5) / (GDP/CAP)	100	91	80	88	90	
(s)	("NEW4"/UN) / (GDP/cap)	100	63	30	30	19	
(t)	("NEW5"/5-19) / (GDP/cap)		100	95	93	88	

Table 12.21. United Kingdom: total social spending (public), percentage of GDP 1985–2009, OECD SOCX

UK		1985-1989	1990-1994	1995-1999	2000-2004	2005-2009	ppt change (05-09)–(85-89)
	PUBLIC SPENDING, AS A PERCENTAGE OF GDP						
(a)	"OLD1" HEALTH CARE	4.78	5.44	5.44	5.92	7.14	2.36
(b)	"OLD2" OLD AGE	5.12	5.28	5.28	5.46	5.62	0.50
(c)	"OLD3" OTHER BENEFITS + ALLOWANCES	6.86	6.84	6.80	5.98	6.12	–0.74
	"OLD3" OTHER BENEFITS	5.74	5.96	5.92	5.14	5.32	–0.42
(d)	"NEW1" PARENTAL LEAVE	0.10	0.10	0.10	0.10	0.34	0.24
(e)	"NEW2" ELDERLY CARE	0.38	0.38	0.48	0.48	0.54	0.16
(f)	"NEW3" CHILD CARE	0.40	0.42	0.72	1.10	1.36	0.96
	"NEW3" CHILD CARE + ALLOWANCES	1.52	1.30	1.60	1.94	2.16	0.64
(g)	"NEW4" ALMP	0.68	0.48	0.28	0.26	0.30	–0.38
(h)	"NEW5" PRIMARY & SECONDARY EDUCATION		3.44	2.67	2.67	3.02	
(i)	"NEW6" TERTIARY EDUCATION						
(j)	TOTAL NEW 1-4 (a)	1.56	1.38	1.58	1.94	2.54	0.98
	TOTAL NEW 1-4 (b)	2.68	2.26	2.46	2.78	3.34	0.66
(k)	TOTAL OLD & NEW (education excluded)	18.32	18.94	19.10	19.30	21.42	3.10

	CASH, IN KIND, AND NOT CLASSIFIED SPENDING, AS A PERCENTAGE OF TOTAL SPENDING						
(l)	TOTAL CASH	58.67	54.36	52.54	51.23	49.29	–9.38
(m)	TOTAL IN KIND	37.62	43.08	46.01	47.44	49.30	11.67
(n)	TOTAL NOT CLASSIFIED	3.70	2.55	1.45	1.33	1.41	–2.29
	CONTEXTUAL FACTORS						
(o)	EMPLOYMENT RATE	68.70	69.85	70.43	72.44	72.19	3.49
(p)	UNEMPLOYMENT RATE	9.66	8.96	7.04	5.04	5.74	–3.92
	BUDGETARY EFFORTS (INDICES)						
(q)	("OLD2" / 65+) / (GDP/cap)	100	101	101	105	111	
(r)	("NEW3a"/<5) / (GDP/CAP)	100	102	181	269	320	
	("NEW3b"/<5) / (GDP/CAP)	100	83	107	132	142	
(s)	("NEW4"/UN) / (GDP/cap)	100	78	54	76	76	
(t)	("NEW5"/5-19) / (GDP/cap)		100	76	76	91	

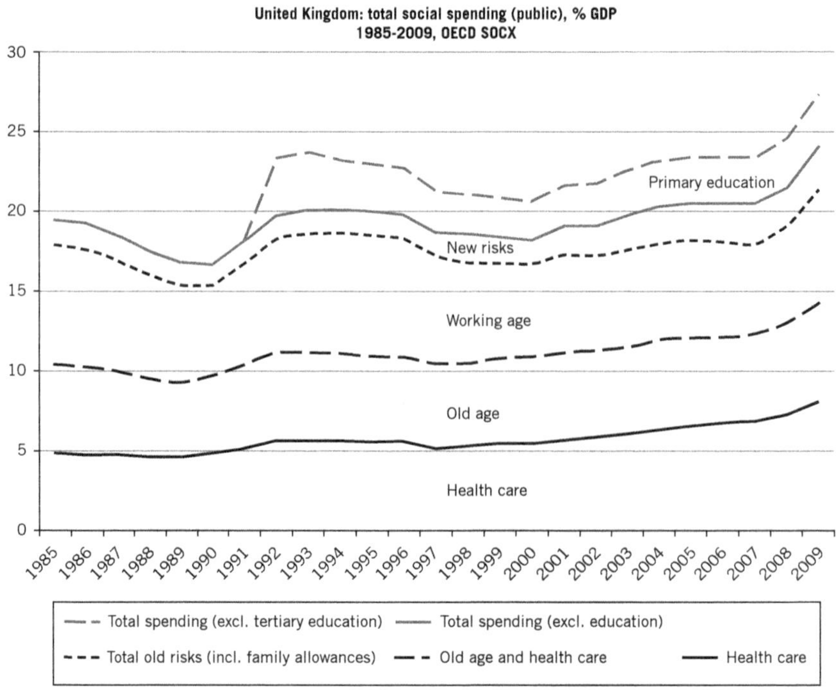

Figure 12.21. United Kingdom: total social spending (public), percentage of GDP, 1985–2009, OECD SOCX.

ACKNOWLEDGMENTS

We are grateful to Willem Adema, Bea Cantillon, Johan De Deken, Jeroen Horemans, Hendrik Larmuseau, Kim Lievens, Wim Van Lancker, Tim Van Rie, Frank Vandenbroucke, Gerlinde Verbist and Koen Vleminckx for helpful comments and discussion.

Sources:

Education data: OECD Education Statistics Database (expenditure by nature and resource).

Employment rate: OECD Country Statistical Profiles.

GDP: OECD Social Expenditure: Reference Series (for SK and SL data was used from the Education At A Glance publications).

OECD, Social Expenditure Statistics Detailed Data (Database).

Population Data: OECD Population Statistics (population).

Unemployment (1000s): OECD Annual Labour Force Survey (ALFS) Summary tables.

Unemployment rate: OECD Country Statistical Profiles.

NOTE

1 The OECD SOCX does not make the distinction between cash and in-kind benefits for ALMP spending and are, therefore, presented as "not classified" spending.

REFERENCES

Aaberge, R., & Langørgen, A. (2006). Measuring the benefits from public services: The effects of local government spending on the distribution of income in Norway. *Review of Income and Wealth, 52*(1), 61–83.

Aaberge, R., Bhuller, M., Langørgen, M., & Mogstad, M. (2010). The distributional impact of public services when needs differ. *Journal of Public Economics, 94*, 549–562.

Adelantado, J., & Calderón Cuevas, E. (2006). Globalization and the welfare state: The same strategies for similar problems? *Journal of European Social Policy, 16*(4), 374–386.

Adema, W., Einerh, M., Eklind, B., Lotz, J., & Pearson, M. (1996). *Net public social expenditure.* [Labour Market and Social Policy Occasional Paper No. 19]. Paris, France: OECD.

Adema, W. (1999). *Net social expenditure.* [Labour Market and Social Policy Occasional Paper No.3]. Paris, France: OECD.

Adema, W., & Ladaique, M. (2005). *Net social expenditure.* (2005 ed.). More comprehensive measures of social support [Social, Employment and Migration Working Paper, No.29]. Paris, France: OECD.

Adema, W., Fron, P. & Ladaique, M. (2011). Is the European welfare state really more expensive?: Indicators on social spending, 1980–2012; and a Manual to the OECD Social Expenditure Database (SOCX). OECD Social, Employment and Migration Working Papers, No. 124, OECD Publishing.

Afshartous, D., & Preston, R.A. (2010). Confidence intervals for dependent data: Equating non-overlap with statistical significance. *Computational Statistics & Data Analysis, 54*(10), 2296–305.

Airio, I. (2008). Change of Norm? In-work poverty in a comparative perspective. *Studies in Social Security and Health*, 92. Helsinki, Finland: The Social Insurance Institution, 134p.

Alber, J. (1988). Is there a crisis of the welfare state? Cross-national evidence from Europe, North-America and Japan. *European Sociological Review, 4*(3), 181–205.

Alkire, S., & Foster, J. (2011). Counting and multidimensional poverty measurement. *Journal of Public Economics, 95*(7-8),476–487.

Anderson, G. F., Reinhardt, U. E., Hussey, P. S., & Petrosyan, V. (2003). It's the prices, stupid: Why the United States is so different from other countries. *Health Affairs, 22*(3), 89–105.

Anderson, K. M. (2011). The Netherlands: Reconciling labour market flexicurity with security in old age. In K. Hinrichs & M. Jessoula (Eds.) *Labour market flexibility and pension reforms: flexible today, secure tomorrow?*, Houndmills, Basingstoke, United Kingdom: Palgrave Macmillan.

Andersson, J. (2004). A productive social citizenship? Reflections on the concept of productive social policies in the European tradition. In L. Magnusson & B. Strath (Eds.), *A European social citizenship: Preconditions for future social policies from a historical perspective* (pp. 69–88). Brussels, Belgium: P.I.E.-Peter Lange.

Andreβ, H.-J., & Lohmann, H. (2008). *The working poor in Europe*. London, England: Edward Elgar.

Antoninis, M., & Tsakloglou, P. (2001). Who benefits from public education in Greece? Evidence and policy implications. *Education Economics, 9*(2),197–222.

Araar, A., & Duclos, J-Y. (2007). DASP: Distributive Analysis Stata Package: PEP, CIRPÉE and World Bank, Université Laval.

Arneson, R. J. (1989). Equality and equal opportunity for welfare. *Philosophical Studies, 56*, 77–93.

Atkinson, A. B., & Micklewright, J. (1991). Unemployment compensation and labor market transitions: A critical review. *Journal of Economic Literature XXIX*, 1679–1727.

Atkinson, A.B. & Mogensen, G.V. (1993). *Welfare and work/incentives. A North European perspective*. Oxford, England: Clarendon Press.

Atkinson, A.B. (1998). *Poverty in Europe*. Oxford, England: Blackwell.

Atkinson, A. B., & Bourguignon, F. (2001). Poverty and inclusion from a world perspective. In J. E. Stiglitz & P.-A. Muet (Eds.), *Governance, equity and global markets*. New York, NY: Oxford University Press.

Atkinson, A. B., Cantillon, B., Marlier, E., & Nolan, B. (2002). *Social indicators: The EU and social exclusion*. Oxford, England: Oxford University Press.

Atkinson, A. B. (2003). Multidimensional deprivation: Contrasting social welfare and counting approaches. *Journal of Economic Inequality, 1*(1), 51–65.

Atkinson, A. B., & Piketty, T. (2006). *Top incomes over the twentieth century.* Oxford, England: Oxford University Press.

Atkinson, A. B. (2010). *Poverty and the EU: The new decade.* [DiSSE Working Paper Series]. Macerata, Italy: University of Macerata.

Atkinson, A. B., & Marlier, E. (2010). *Income and living conditions in Europe* [Eurostat Statistical Books]. Luxembourg: Publications Office of the European Union, 424p. ISBN 978-92-79-16351-7. Retrieved from doi: 10.2785/53320.

Atkinson, A. B., Marlier, E., Montaigne, F., & Reinstalder, A. (2010). Income poverty and income inequality. In A. B. Atkinson & E. Marlier (Eds.), *Income and living conditions in Europe* (pp. 101–132). Luxembourg: Publications Office of the European Union.

Aurich, P. (2009, July). *Levels, directions and divisions of change towards activation in Europe.* ISA World Congress 2010, RC 19.13, 'Comparing Activation Models and Policy', July 11–17, Gothenburg, Sweden.

Autor, D. H., Levy, F., & Murnane, R. J. (2003). The skill content of recent technological change: An empirical exploration. *The Quarterly Journal of Economics, 118*(4), 1279–1333.

Avdagic, S., Rhodes, M., & Visser, J. (2011). *Social pacts in Europe: Emergence, evolution and institutionalization.* Oxford, England: Oxford University Press.

Baccaro, L., & Simoni, M. (2008). Policy concertation in Europe: Understanding government choice. *Comparative Political Studies, 41*(10), 1323–1348.

Barbier, J.-C., & Ludwig-Mayerhofer, W. (2004). Introduction: The many worlds of activation. *European Societies, 6*(4), 423–436.

Barbier, J.-C. (2005). The European employment strategy, a channel for activating social protection? In J. Zeitlin & P. Pochet (Eds.), *The OMC in action: the European employment and social inclusion strategies* (pp. 417–446). Brussels, Belgium: P.I.E.-Peter Lang.

Bargain, O., & Orsini, K. (2007). Beans for breakfast? How exportable is the British Workfare Model? In O. Bargain (Ed.), *Microsimulation in action. Policy analysis in Europe using EUROMOD* [Research in Labour Economics 25], (pp. 165–198). Oxford, England: Elsevier.

Barr, N. (1992). Economic theory and the welfare state: A survey and interpretation. *Journal of Economic Literature, XXX* (June),741–803.

Barr, N. (2001). *The welfare state as piggy bank: Information, risk, uncertainty and the role of the State.* Oxford, England: Oxford University Press.

Barr, N. (2004). *The economics of the welfare state* (4th rev. ed.). Oxford, England: Oxford University Press.

Barr, N. (2012). *Economics of the welfare state* (5th ed.). Oxford, England: Oxford University Press.

Beblavý, M., & Mizsei, K. (2006). Make spurious poverty statistics history. *Development and Transition,* 4, June.

Beck, U. (1992). *Risk society: Towards a new modernity.* London, England: Sage.

Begg, I., Draxler, J., & Mortensen, J. (2008). *Is social Europe fit for globalisation? A study of the social impact of globalization in the European Union*. Brussels, Belgium: European Commission, Centre for European Policy Studies.

Bennet, K. S., & Hay, D.A. (2007). The role of family in the development of social skills in children with physical disabilities. *International Journal of Disability, Development and Education, 54*(4), 381–397.

Bernard, P., & Boucher, G. (2007). Institutional competitiveness, social investment, and welfare regimes. *Regulation & Governance, 1*(3), 213–229.

Berthoud, R., & Bryan, M. (2011). Income, deprivation and poverty: A longitudinal analysis. *Journal of Social Policy, 40*(01), 135–156.

Bertola, G., Boeri, T., & Nicoletti, G. (2011). *Welfare and employment in a United Europe*. Cambridge, MA: MIT Press.

Besharov, D. J., & Couch, K.A. (2012). *Counting the poor. New thinking about European poverty measures and lessons for the United States, international policy exchange*. New York, NY: Oxford University Press.

Betzelt, S., & Bothfeld, S. (2011). *Activation and labour market reforms in Europe: Challenges to social citizenship*. London, England: Palgrave Macmillan.

Beveridge, J. (1954). *Beveridge and his plan*. London, England: Hodder and Stoughton.

Biewen, M. (2009). Measuring state dependence in individual poverty histories when there is feedback to employment status and household composition? *Journal of Applied Econometrics, 24*, 1095–1116.

Blank, R. M. (2008). Presidential address: How to improve poverty measurement in the United States. *Journal of Policy Analysis and Management, 27*(2),233–254.

Boeri, T., & Garibaldi, P. (2009). Beyond eurosclerosis. *Economic Policy, 24*(59), 409–461.

Bonoli, G. (2005). The politics of the new social policies: Providing coverage against new social risks in mature welfare states. *Policy and Politics, 33*(3),431–449.

Bonoli, G. (2006). New social risks and the politics of post-industrial social policies. In K. Armingeon, & G. Boloni (Eds.), *The politics of post-industrial welfare states: Adapting post-war social policies to new social risks* (pp. 3–26). London, England and New York, NY: Routledge.

Bonoli, G. (2007). Time matters: Postindustrialization, new social risks and welfare state adaptation in advanced industrial democraties. *Comparative Political Studies, 40*(5),495–520.

Bonoli, G., & Palier, B. (2008). When past reforms open new opportunities: Comparing old-age insurance reforms in Bismarckian welfare systems. In B. Palier, & C. Martin (Eds.), *Reforming the Bismarkian welfare systems*. (pp. 21–39). Malden, MA: Blackwell.

Bonoli, G. (2011). Active labour market policy in a changing economic context. In J. Clasen, & D. Clegg (Eds.), *Regulating the risk of unemployment* (pp. 318–332). Oxford, England: Oxford University Press.

Bonoli, G. (2011). Transformations of the welfare state. Small states, big lessons. *Swiss Political Science Review, 17*,497–499.

Bonoli, G. (2012). Active labour market policy and social investment: A changing relationship. In N. Morel, B. Palier, & J. Palme (Eds.), *Towards a social investment welfare state? Ideas, policies and challenges* (pp. 181–204). Bristol, England: Policy Press.

Bosch, G., & Weinkopf, C. (2008). *Low-wage work in Germany*. New York, NY: Russell Sage Foundation.

Bosmans, K. (2011). *Distribution-sensitivity of rank-dependent poverty measures*. Mimeo.

Bourguignon, F., & Fields, G. S. (1990). Poverty measures and anti-poverty policy. *Recherches économiques de Louvain, 56*,409–427.

Bourguignon, F., & Chakravarty, S. R. (2003). The measurement of multidimensional poverty. *Journal of Economic Inequality, 1*(1), 25–49.

Bradshaw, J. (1993). *Budget standards for the United Kingdom*. Aldershot, England: Avebury.

Bradshaw, J., & Finch, N. (2010). Family benefits and services. In F. G. Castles, S. Leibfried, J. Lewis, H. Obinger, & C. Pierson (Eds.), *The Oxford handbook of the welfare state* (pp. 462–478). Oxford, England: Oxford University Press.

Brandolini, A. (2007). Measurement of income distribution in supranational entities: The case of the European Union. In S. Jenkins, & J. Micklewright (Eds.), *Inequality and poverty re-examined*, (pp. 62–83). Oxford, England: Oxford University Press.

Brandolini, A., & Smeeding, T. M. (2009). Income inequality in richer and OECD countries. In W. Salverda, B. Nolan, & T. M. Smeeding (Eds.) *The Oxford handbook of economic inequality* (pp. 71–100). Oxford, England: Oxford University Press.

Brandolini, A., Magri, S., & Smeeding, T. M. 2010). Asset-based measurement of poverty. *Journal of Policy Analysis and Management, 29*(2),267–284.

Breen, R., Luikx, R., Müller, W., & Pollak, R. (2009). Non-persistent inequality in educational attainment: Evidence from eight European countries. *American Journal of Sociology, 114*(5),1475–1521.

Breen, R., Luikx, R., Müller, W. & Pollak, R. (2010). Long-term trends in educational inequality in Europe: Class inequalities and gender differences. *European Sociological Review, 26*(1),31–48.

Brett, J. (2002). The experience of disability from the perspective of parents of children with profound impairment: Is it time for an alternative model of disability. *Disability & Society, 17*(7),825–843.

Brewer, M., Duncan, A., Shephard, A. & José Suarez, M. (2006). Did working families tax credit work? The impact of in-work support on labour supply in Great Britain. *Labour Economics, 13*,699–720.

Brink, A., Nordblom, K., & Wahlberg, R. (2007). Maximum fee versus child benefit: A welfare analysis of Swedish child-care fee reform. *International Tax and Public Finance 14*,(4),457–480.

Buchanan, J. M. (1975). The Samaritan's dilemma. In E. Phelps (Ed.), *Morality and economic theory* (pp. 71–85). New York, NY: Russell Sage.

Buhmann, B., Rainwater, L., Schmaus, G., & Smeeding, T. M. (1988). Equivalence scales, well-being, inequality, and poverty: sensitivity estimates across ten countries using the Luxembourg income study (LIS) database. *Review of Income and Wealth, 34*(2),115–142.

Burton, P., Phipps, S., & Woolley, F. (2007). Inequality within the household reconsidered. In S. Jenkins & J. Micklewright (Eds.), *Inequality and poverty Re-examined* (pp. 103–125). Oxford, England: Oxford University Press.

Callan, T., & Nolan, B. (1991). Concepts of poverty and the poverty line. *Journal of Economic Surveys, 5*(3), 243–261.

Callan, T., Smeeding, T. M., & Tsakloglou, P. (2008). Short-run distributional effects of public education transfers to tertiary education in seven European countries. *Education Economics, 16*(3), 275–288.

Callan, T., & Keane, C. (2009). Non-cash benefits and the distribution of economic welfare. *The Economic and Social Review, 40*(1), 49–71.

Caminada, K., Goudswaard, K. P., & Van Vliet, O. (2010). Patterns of welfare state indicators in the EU: Is there convergence? *Journal of Common Market Studies, 48*(3), 529–556.

Campbell, J. L., & Hall, J.A. (2006). Introduction. The State of Denmark. In J. L. Campbell, J. A. Hall, & O. K. Pedersen (Eds.), *National identity and the varieties of capitalism: The Danish experience*(pp. 1–50). Montreal; Canada and Ithaca, NY: McGill-Queen's University Press.

Cantillon, B. (1989). Socio-demografische veranderingen, inkomensverdeling en sociale zekerheid, 1976–1985. doctoraal proefschrift, Antwerp, Belgium: U.I.A.

Cantillon, B. (1997). The "zero-sum-crisis": stability in the distribution of income and welfare in a period of economic crisis. In N. Keilman (Ed.), *Poverty and economic inequality in industrialized Western societies* (pp. 183–203). Oslo, Norway: Scandinavian University Press.

Cantillon, B., Marx, I., & Van den Bosch, K. (1997). The challenge of poverty and social exclusion. In OECD (Ed.), *The new social policy agenda.* Paris, France: OECD.

Cantillon, B., Ghysels, J., Mussche, N., & Van Dam, R. (2001). Female employment differences, poverty and care provisions. *European Societies, 3*, 447–469.

Cantillon, B., Elchardus, M., Pestieau, P., & Van Parijs, P. (2003). *De nieuwe sociale kwesties.* Antwerpen/Apeldoorn: Garant.

Cantillon, B., Van Mechelen, N., Marx, I., & Van den Bosch, K. (2004). *The evolution of minimum income protection in 15 European countries, 1992–2001.* Antwerp, Belgium: UA/Berichten, Herman Deleeck Centre for Social Policy, University of Antwerp.

Cantillon, B., & Goedemé, T. (2006). Kinderbijslag in het werknemersstelsel: een terugblik op de toekomst. *Belgisch Tijdschrift voor Sociale Zekerheid. 48*(1), 7–34.

Cantillon, B. (2011). The paradox of the social investment state: growth, employment and poverty in the Lisbon era. *Journal of European Social Policy, 21*(5), 432–449.

Cantillon, B., & Van Mechelen, N. (2012). Between dream and reality...On anti-poverty policy, minimum income protection and the European social model. In B. Cantillon, H. Verschueren, & P. Ploscar (Eds.), *Social inclusion and social protection in the EU: Interactions between law and politics*. Antwerp, Belgium: Intersentia.

Cantillon, B., & Van Lancker, W. (2012). Solidarity and reciprocity in the social investment state: What can be learned from the case of Flemish school allowances and truancy? *Journal of Social Policy, 41*(4), 657–675.

Cantillon, B., Van Mechelen, N., Pintelon, O., & Van den Heede, A. (2012). *Household work-intensity and the adequacy of social protection in the EU* [CSB Working Paper No. 12/04]. Antwerp, Belgium: Herman Deleeck Centre for Social Policy, University of Antwerp.

Cappellari, L., & Jenkins, S. P. (2002). *Modelling low income transitions* [ISER Working Paper 2002-8]. Institute for Social and Economic Research, Colchester: University of Essex.Castles, F. G. (2004). *The future of the welfare state: Crisis myths and crisis realities*. Oxford, England: Oxford University Press.

Castles, F. G. (2005). Social expenditures in the 1990s: Data and determinants. *Policy & Politics, 33*(3), 411–430.

Castles, F. G. (2008). What welfare states do: A disaggregated expenditure approach. *Journal of Social Policy, 38*(1), 45–62.

Chaudhuri, S., & Ravallion, M. (1994). How well do static indicators identify the chronically poor? *Journal of Public Economics, 53*(3), 367–394.

Clark, G. L., & Whiteside, N. (2003). *Pension security in the 21st century*. Oxford, England: Oxford University Press.

Clark, T. N., & Lipset, S. M. (1991). Are social classes dying? *International Sociology, 6*(4), 397–410. doi: 10.1177/026858091006004002.

Clasen, J. (2005). *Reforming European welfare states: Germany and the United Kingdom compared*. Oxford, England: Oxford University Press.

Clasen, J., & Clegg, D. (2006). Beyond activation: Reforming European unemployment protection systems in post-industrial labour markets. *European Societies, 8*(4), 527–553.

Clasen, J. (2007). *Investigating welfare state change: The dependent variable problem in comparative analysis*. Cheltenham, England: Edward Elgar Publishing.

Clasen, J., & Clegg, D. (2011). Unemployment protection and labour market change in Europe. In J. Clasen, & D. Clegg (Eds.), *Regulating the risk of unemployment* (pp. 1–12). Oxford, England: Oxford University Press.

Clasen, J., & Clegg, D. (2011). *Regulating the risk of unemployment. National adaptations to post-industrial labour markets in Europe*. Oxford, England: Oxford University Press.

Clauwaert, S., & Harger, S. (2000). *Analysis of the implementation of the parental leave directive in the EU Member States*. Brussels, Belgium: European Trade Union Institute.

Clemenceau, A., & Museux, J. M. (2007). EU-SILC (Community Statistics on Income and Living Conditions: General presentation of the instrument). In *Comparative EU Statistics on Income and Living Conditions: Issues and Challenges*. Luxembourg: Office for Official Publications of the European Communities.

Coder, J., Fritzell, A., Hagenaars, M., Hauser, R., Jenkins, S., Saunders, P., Smeeding, T. M., & Wolfson, M. (1993). Poverty, inequality, and family living standards impacts across seven nations: The effect of noncash subsidies for health, education, and housing. *Review of Income and Wealth, 39*(3), 229–256.

Cohen, G. (1989). On the currency of egalitarian justice. *Ethics, 99*, 906–944.

Corazzini, L., Esposito, L., & Majorano, F. (2011). Exploring the absolutist vs. relativist perception of poverty using a cross-country questionnaire survey. *Journal of Economic Psychology, 32*(2), 273–283.

Corluy, V., & Verbist, G. (2010). Inkomen en diversiteit: onderzoek naar de inkomenspositie van migranten in België. Antwerp, Belgium: UA/Berichten, Herman Deleeck Centre for Social Policy, University of Antwerp.

Corluy, V., Marx, I., & Verbist, G. (2011). Employment chances and changes of immigrants in Belgium: The impact of citizenship. *International Journal of Comparative Sociology, 52*(4), 350–368.

Corluy, V., & Vandenbroucke, F. (2013). *Individual employment, household employment and risk of poverty in the EU. A decomposition analysis* [Eurostat Methodologies and Working Papers, 2013 edition]. Brussels: European Union; doi: 10.2785/41846

Coulter, F. A., Cowell, F. A., & Jenkins, S. (1992). Differences in needs and assessment of income distributions. *Bulletin of Economic Research, 44*(2), 77–124.

Coulter, F. A., Cowell, F.A., & Jenkins, S. (1992). Equivalence scale relativities and the extent of inequality and poverty. *Economic Journal, 102*(414),1067–1082.

Council of the European Communities. (1975). Council Decision of 22 July 1975 Concerning a Programme of Pilot Schemes and Studies to Combat Poverty. (In 75/458/EEC, pp. 34–35). Brussels, Belgium.

Council of the European Union. (1992). Council recommendation of 31 March 1992 on childcare.

Crettaz, E. (2011). *Fighting working poverty in post-industrial economies. Causes, trade-offs and policy solutions*. Cheltenham, England and Northampton, MA: Edward Elgar.

Crettaz, E., & Bonoli, G. (2011). Worlds of working poverty: National variations in mechanisms. In N. Fraser, R. Gutiérrez, & R. Peña-Casas (Eds.), *Working poverty in Europe: A comparative approach*. Houndmills, England: Palgrave Macmillan.

Cullen, J. B., & Gruber, J. (2000). Does unemployment insurance crowd out spousal labor supply? *Journal of Labor Economics, 18*(3), 546–572.

Cumming, G. (2009). Inference by eye: Reading the overlap of independent confidence intervals. *Statistics in Medicine, 28*(2), 205–220.

Daly, M. (2010). Assessing the EU approach to combating poverty and social exclusion in the last decade. In E. Marlier, D. Natali, & R. Van Dam (Eds.), *Europe 2020. Towards a more social EU?* (pp. 143–161). Brussels, Belgium: P.I.E. Peter Lang.

Daly, M. (2010b). Shifts in family policy in the UK under New Labour. *Journal of European Social Policy, 20*(5), 433–443.

Dawson, M., & de Witte, B. (2012). The EU legal framework of social inclusion and social protection: Between the Lisbon Strategy and the Lisbon Treaty. In B. Cantillon, H. Verschueren, & P. Ploscar (Eds.), *Social inclusion and social protection in the EU: Interaction between law and policy* (pp. 41–70). Antwerp, Belgium: Intersentia.

Deacon, A. & Bradshaw, J. (1983). *Reserved for the poor. The means test in British social policy*. Oxford, England: Martin Robertson & Company Ltd.

Deaton, A. (1992). *Understanding consumption*. Oxford, England: Clarendon Press.

Deaton, A. (1997). *The analysis of household surveys: A Microeconometric approach to development policy*. Baltimore, MD: John Hopkins University Press for the World Bank.

de Beer, P. (2007). Why work is not a panacea: A decomposition analysis of EU15 countries. *Journal of European Social Policy, 17*(4), 375–388.

Decancq, K. (2009). *Copula-based Measurement of Dependence between Dimensions of Well-being* [Health, Econometrics and Data Group (HEDG Working Papers 09/32]. HEDG, c/o Department of Economics, York, United Kingdom: University of York.

Decancq, K., Decoster, A., & Schokkaert, E. (2009). The evolution of world inequality in well-being. *World Development, 30*(1), 11–25.

Decancq, K., Van Ootegem, L., & Verhofstadt, E. (2013). What if we voted on the weights of a multidimensional well-being index? An illustration with Flemish data. *Fiscal Studies*.

Decancq, K., & Lugo, M. A. (2013). Weights in multidimensional indices of well-being: An overview. *Econometric Reviews, 32*(1), 7–34.

De Deken, J., & Kittel, B. (2007). Social expenditure under scrutiny: The problems of using aggregate spending data for assessing welfare state dynamics. In J. Clasen, & N. A. Siegel (Eds.), *Investigating welfare state change. The dependent variable problem in comparative analysis* (pp. 72–105). Cheltenham, England: Edward Elgar.

De Deken, J., & Clasen, J. (2011). Tracking caseloads: the changing composition of working-age benefit receipt in Europe. In J. Clasen, & D. Clegg (Eds.), *Regulating the risk of unemployment: national adaptations to post-industrial labour markets in Europe*. Oxford, England: Oxford University Press.

de Graaf-Zijl, M., & Nolan, B. (2011). Household joblessness and its impact on poverty and deprivation in Europe. *Journal of European Social Policy, 21*, 413–431.

De Henau, J., Meulders, D., & O'Dorchai, S. (2007). Parents' care and career. Comparing parental leave policies across EU15. In D. Del Boca, & C. Wetzels (Eds.), *Social policies, labour markets and motherhood* (pp. 63–106). Cambridge, England: Cambridge University Press.

Del Boca, D., Pasqua, S., Pronzato, C., & Wetzels, C. (2007). An empirical analysis of the effects of social policies on fertility, labour market participation and hourly wages of European women. In D. Del Boca, & C. Wetzels (Eds.), *Social policies, labour markets and motherhood* (pp. 271–303). Cambridge, England: Cambridge University Press.

Deleeck, H. (1966). *Maatschappelijke Zekerheid en inkomensverdeling in België. Proefschrift.* Antwerp, Belgium: SWU.

Deleeck, H., Huybrechs, J., & Cantillon, B. (1983). *Het Matteüseffect. De ongelijke verdeling van de sociale overheidsuitgaven in België.* Antwerp, Belgium: Kluwer.

Deleeck, H., Van den Bosch, K. & De Lathouwer, L. (1992).*Poverty and the adequacy of social security in the EC. A comparative analysis.* Aldershot, England: Avebury.

Delhey, J., & Kohler, U. (2006). From nationally bounded to pan-European inequalities? On the importance of foreign countries as reference groups. *European Sociological Review, 22*(2), 125–140.

Deneulin, S. (2002). Perfectionism, liberalism and paternalism in Sen and Nussbaum's capability approach. *Review of Political Economy, 14* (4), 497–518.

Deveci, N., Heurlen, K., & Sorensen, H. (2008, August). Non-market health care service in Denmark—Empirical studies of A, B and C methods. Paper presented at the International Association for Research in Income and Wealth (IARIW) conference, Portoroz, Slovenia.

de Vos, K., & Zaidi, A. (1997). Equivalence scale sensitivity of poverty statistics for the member states of the European community. *Review of Income and Wealth, 43*(3), 319–333.

de Vos, K., & Zaidi, A. (1998). Poverty measurement in the European Union: Country-specific or union-wide poverty lines? *Journal of Income Distribution, 8*(1), 77–92.

Dewilde, C. (2008). Armoede op oudere leeftijd: de impact van gezins- en loopbaantrajecten. In J. Vranken, G. Campaert, K. De Boyser, C. Dewilde, & D. Dierckx (Eds.), *Armoede en sociale uitsluiting, jaarboek 2008* (pp. 279–299). Leuven: Acco.

Dickens, R., & Ellwood, D. (2002). Whither poverty in Britain and the US?: The determinants of changing poverty and whether work will work. In R. Blundell, D. Card, & R. Freeman (Eds.), *Seeking a premier league economy.* Chicago, IL: University of Chicago Press.

Dingeldey, I. (2006). Between workfare and enabling—Different paths to transformation of the welfare state: A comparative analysis of activating labour market policies. *European Journal of Political Research, 46*(6), 823–851.

Dolado, J., Felgueroso, F., & Jimeno, J. (2000). *The role of the minimum wage in the welfare state: An appraisal* [IZA Discussion Paper No. 152]. Germany: Institute for the Study of Labor.

Dølvik, J. E. (2004). Industrial relations under EMU: Are renationalization and Europeanization two sides of the same coin? In A. Martin, & G. Ross (Eds.), *Euros and European. monetary integration and the European model of society* (pp. 278–308). Cambridge, England: Cambridge University Press.

Dowling, M., & Dolan, L. (2001). Families with children with disabilities—Inequalities and the social model. *Disability and Society, 16*(1), 21–35.

Duclos, J.-Y., Sahn, D. E., & Younger, S. D. (2006). Robust multidimensional poverty comparisons. *Economic Journal, 116*(514), 943–968.

Dunbar, G., Lewbel, A., & Pendakur, K. (2013). Children's resources in collective households: Identification, estimation and application to child poverty in Malawi. *American Economic Review, 103*(1), 438–471.

Duval, R., & Elmeskov, J. (2006). *The effects of EMU on structural reforms in labour and product markets* [Working Paper Series, 596] Frankfurt am Main, Germany: European Central Bank.

Duvander, A.-Z., Ferrarini, T., & Thalberg, S. (2006). Swedish parental leave and gender equality. In G. Rossi, & F. Angeli (Eds.), *Family and work: welfare policies in Europe* (pp. 217–238). Milan, Italy: Franco Angeli.

Dworkin, R. (1981a). What is equality? Part 1: Equality of welfare. *Philosophy and Public Affairs, 10*, 185–246.

Dworkin, R. (1981b). What is equality? Part 2: Equality of resources. *Philosophy and Public Affairs, 10*, 283–345.

Dyson, K., & Featherstone, K. (1999). *The road to Maastricht: Negotiating Economic Monetary Union*. Oxford, England: Oxford University Press.

Ebbinghaus, B. (2011). *The varieties of pension governance. Pension privatization in Europe*. Oxford, England: Oxford University Press.

Education data: OECD Education Statistics Database (expenditure by nature and resource).

Eichengreen, B. J. (2007). *The European economy since 1945: Coordinated capitalism and beyond*. Princeton, NJ: Princeton University Press.

Eichhorst, W., & Kaiser, L. C. (2006). *The German labor market: Still adjusting badly?* [IZA Discussion Paper No. 2215]. Germany: Institute for the Study of Labor.

Eichhorst, W., Feil, M., & Braun, C. (2008). *What have we learned? Assessing labor market institutions and indicators*. [IZA Discussion Paper No. 3470]. Germany: Institute for the Study of Labor.

Eichhorst, W., & Konle-Seidl, R. (2008). *Contingent convergence: A comparative analysis of activation policies* [IZA Discussion Paper No. 3905]. Germany: Institute for the Study of Labor.

Eichhorst, W., Kaufmann, O., & Konle-Seidl, R. (2008b). *Bringing the jobless into work?: Experiences with activation schemes in Europe and the US*. Berlin/Heidelberg, Germany: Springer.

Eichhorst, W., & Hemerijck, A. (2010). Welfare and employment: A European dilemma? In J. Alber & N. Gilbert (Eds.), *United in diversity? Comparing social models in Europe and America* (pp. 201–236). Oxford, England: Oxford University Press.

Eissa, N., & Hoynes, H. (2004). Taxes and the labor market participation of married couples: The earned income tax credit. *Journal of Public Economics, 88*,1931–1958.

Ellwood, D. T. (2000). The impact of earned income tax, credit and social policy reforms on work, marriage, and living arrangements. *National Tax Journal, 53*(4), 1063–1106.

Employment rate: OECD Country Statistical Profiles.

Erikson, R., & Goldthorpe, J. H. (1992). *The constant flux. A study of class mobility in industrial societies*. Oxford, England: Clarendon Press Oxford.

Esping-Andersen, G. (1990). *The three worlds of welfare capitalism*. Cambridge, England: Polity Press.

Esping-Andersen, G. (1993). *Changing classes: Stratification and mobility in post-industrial societies*. London, England: Sage.

Esping-Andersen, G. (1994). Welfare states and the economy. In N.J. Smelser, & R. Swedberg (Eds.), *The handbook of economic sociology* (pp. 711–732). Princeton, NJ/New York, NY: Princeton University Press/Russell Sage Foundation.

Esping-Andersen, G. (1996). *Welfare states in transition: National adaptations in global economies*. London, England: Sage.

Esping-Andersen, G. (1999). *Social foundations of postindustrial economies*. Oxford, England: Oxford University Press.

Esping-Andersen, G., Gallie, D. Hemerijck, A., & Myles, J. (2002). *Why we need a new welfare state*. Oxford, England: Oxford University Press.

Esping-Andersen, G. (2006). *Putting the horse in front of the cart: Towards a social model for mid-century Europe*[wrr-Lecture 2005]. Amsterdam, the Netherlands: Amsterdam University Press.

Esping-Andersen, G. (2008). Childhood investments and skill formation. *International Tax and Public Finance, 15*, 19–44.

Esping-Andersen, G. (2009). *The incomplete revolution. Adapting welfare states to women's new roles*. Cambridge, England: Polity Press.

Esping-Andersen, G., & Myles, J. (2009). Economic inequality and the "welfare state." In W. Salverda, B. Nolan, & T. Smeeding (Eds.), *Oxford handbook of economic inequality* (pp. 639–664). New York: Oxford University Press.

Estevez-Abe, M., Soskice, D., & Iversen, T (2001). Social protection and the formation of skills: A reinterpretation of the welfare state. In P.A. Hall, & D. Soskice (Eds.), *Varieties of capitalism. The institutional foundations of comparative advantage* (pp. 145–183). Oxford, England: Oxford University Press.

European Commission, and Economic Policy Committee. (2009). *Ageing Report: Economic and budgetary projections for the EU27 Member States (2008–2060).* [European Economy, No. 2/2009]. Luxembourg: Office for Official Publications of the European Communities.

European Commission, and OECD. (2006). *Eurostat-OECD methodological manual on purchasing power parities.* Paris, France: OECD. Retrieved from www.oecd.org/std/ppp/manual.

European Commission. (2000). *Social policy agenda* [Communication from the Commission]. Brussels, Belgium: Author.

European Commission. (2002). *Joint report on social inclusion.* Luxembourg: Office for Official Publications of the European Communities.

European Commission. (2004). *Joint report on social inclusion.* Luxembourg: Office for Official Publications of the European Communities.

European Commission. (2006). *Portfolio of overarching indicators and streamlined social inclusion, pensions, and health portfolios.* Brussels, Belgium: Author.

European Commission. (2007). *Joint report on social protection and social inclusion 2007. Social inclusion, pensions, healthcare and long term care.* Luxembourg: Office for Official Publications of the European Communities.

European Commission. (2009). *Portfolio of indicators for the monitoring of the European strategy for social protection and social inclusion* [2009 update]. Luxembourg: Office for Official Publications of the European Communities.

European Commission. (2009). *Joint report on social protection and social inclusion.* Brussels, Belgium: Author.

European Commission. (2010). *Seventeen percent of EU citizens were at-risk-of-poverty in 2008* [Statistics in Focus 9/2010]. Brussels, Belgium: Eurostat.

European Commission. (2010a). *Europe 2020. A strategy for smart, sustainable and inclusive growth* [Communication COM (2010) 2020]. Brussels, Belgium: Author.

European Commission. (2010b). *The European platform against poverty and social exclusion: A European framework for social and territorial cohesion* [COM(2010)]. Brussels, Belgium: Author.

European Commission. (2011a). *Employment and social developments in Europe.* Luxembourg: Publications Office of the European Communities.

European Commission. (2011b). *Joint employment report 2011.* Brussels, Belgium: Author.

European Commission. (2011c). *Early childhood education and care: Providing all our children with the best start for the world of tomorrow* [COM(2011) 66 final]. Brussels, Belgium: Author.

European Council. (2010). *European Council 17 June 2010 Conclusions*. Brussels, Belgium: Author.

European Foundation. (2004). *Working poor in the European Union*. Dublin, Ireland: European Foundation for the Improvement of Living and Working Conditions.

European Foundation. (2010). *Working poor in Europe*. Dublin, Ireland: European Foundation for the Improvement of Living and Working Conditions.

European Union. (2010). Regulation (EU) No 539/210 of the European Parliament and of the Council of 16 June 2010, p. 158. Retrieved from http://eur-lex.europa.eu/LexUriServ/LexUriServ.do?uri=OJ:L:2010:158:0001:0006:EN:PDF

European Union. (2012). *Employment and social developments in Europe 2011*. Luxembourg: Publications Office of the European Union. doi: 10.2767/44905.

Eurostat. (2008). *Comparative EU intermediate quality report*. Version 2—June 2010. Luxembourg: Author.

Eurostat. (2009). *Description of target variables: Cross-sectional and longitudinal, 2009 operation*. Luxembourg: Author.

Eurostat. (2010). *In-work poverty in the EU, methodologies and working papers* (2010 ed.). Luxembourg: Publications Office of the European Union.

Eurostat. (2010). *Social protection expenditure: Tables by functions, aggregated benefits and grouped schemes—in per cent of the GDP (spr_exp_gdp)* [last update: 06-12-2010]. Retrieved from(http://epp.eurostat.ec.europa.eu/portal/page/portal/social_protection/data/database).

Evandrou, M., Falkingham, J., Hills, J., & Le Grand, J. (1993). Welfare benefits in kind and income distribution. *Fiscal Studies, 14*(1), 57–76.

Evertsson, M., England, P., Mooi-Reci, I., Hermsen, J., De Bruijn, J., & Cotter, D. (2009). Is gender inequality greater at lower or higher educational levels? Common patterns in the Netherlands, Sweden, and the United States. *Social Politics 16,*(2), 210–241.

Expert Group on Household Income Statistics (The Canberra Group). (2001). *Final report and recommendations*. Ottawa, Canada: Canberra Group.

Fagan, C., & Walthery, P. (2007). The role and effectiveness of time policies for reconciliation. In OECD (Ed.), *Modernising social policy for the new life course*. Paris, France: OECD.

Fahey, T. (2007). The case for an EU-wide measure of poverty. *European Sociological Review, 23*(1), 35–47.

Fajertag, G., & Pochet, P. (2000). *Social pacts in Europe—New dynamics*. Brussels, Belgium: European Trade Union Institute/Observatoire Social Européen.

Falkingham, J., & Hills, J. (1995). *The dynamics of welfare: The welfare state and the life cycle*. Hemel Hempstead, England: Harvester Wheatsheaf.

Feinstein, J.S. (1993). The relationship between socioeconomic status and health: A review of literature. *Milbank Quarterly, 71*(2), 279–322.

Ferrarini, T. (2006). *Families, states and labour markets.* Cheltenham, England: Edward Elgar.

Ferreira, Francisco H. G., & Lugo, M. A. (2012). *Multidimensional poverty analysis. Looking for a middle ground* [Policy Research Working Paper Series]. Washington, DC: The World Bank. doi: 10.1093/wbro/lks013

Ferrera, M. (1996). The "Southern Model" of welfare in social Europe. *Journal of European Social Policy, 6*(1), 17–37.

Ferrera, M., Hemerijck, A., & Rhodes, M. (2000). *The future of social Europe: Recasting work and welfare in the new economy* [Report prepared for the Portuguese Presidency of the EU]. Oeiras, Portugal: Celta Editora.

Figari, F. (2011). Can in-work benefits improve social inclusion in the southern European countries? *Journal of European Social Policy, 20*, 301–315.

Finseraas, H. (2012). Anti-immigration attitudes, support for redistribution and party choice in Europe. In J. Kvist, J. Fritzell, B. Hvinden, & O. Kangas (Eds.), *Changing social equality: The Nordic welfare model in the 21st century* (pp. 23–44). Bristol, England: Policy Press.

Fischer, J. M., & Ravizza, M. (1993). *Perspectives on moral responsibility.* Ithaca, NY and London, England: Cornell University Press.

Fleckenstein, T. (2008). Restructuring welfare for the unemployed: The Hartz Legislation in Germany. *Journal of European Social Policy, 18*(2), 177–188.

Förster, M. (1993). *Comparing poverty in 13 OECD countries: Traditional and synthetic approaches* [Luxembourg Income Study Working Paper No. 100]. Luxembourg: Luxembourg Income Study.

Förster, M. F., Tarcali, G., & Till, M. (20024). *Income and non-income poverty in Europe: What is the minimum acceptable standard in an enlarged European Union?* Paper presented at 27th General Conference of the International Association for Research and Wealth (IARIW). Djurhamn, Sweden, 18–24th August 2002.

Förster, M. F. (2005). The European social space revisited: Comparing poverty in the enlarged European Union. *Journal of Comparative Policy Analysis, 7*(1), 29–48.

Foster, J., Greer, J., & Thorbecke, E. (1984). A class of decomposable poverty measures. *Econometrica, 52*(3), 761–766.

Foster, J. E., & Shorrocks, A. F. (1988). Poverty ordering. *Econometrica, 56*(1), 173–177.

Foster, J. E., & Shorrocks, A. F. (1991). Subgroup consistent poverty indices. *Econometrica, 59*(3), 687–709.

Foster, J. (2009). A class of chronic poverty measures. In T. Addison, D. Hulme, & R. Kanbur (Eds.) *Poverty dynamics: Interdisciplinary perspectives* (pp. 59–76). Oxford, England: Oxford University Press.

Foster, J., Greer, J., & Thorbecke, E. (2010). The Foster–Greer–Thorbecke (FGT) Poverty measures: 25 years later. *Journal of Economic Inequality, 8*, 491–524.

Fouarge, D. (2003). *Costs of non-social policy: Towards an economic framework of quality social policies—and the costs of not having them.* [Report for the Directorate-General for Employment, Social Affairs and Inclusion]. Brussels, Belgium: EU Network of Independent Experts on Social Inclusion, Directorate-General for Employment, Social Affairs and Inclusion.

Fraser, N., Gutiérrez, R., & Peña-Casas, R. (2011). *Working poverty in Europe: A comparative approach*. Bakingstoke, England: Palgrave Macmillan.

Frazer, H., & Marlier, E. (2010). *In-work poverty and labour market segmentation in the EU: Key lessons.* [Synthesis Report] Brussels, Belgium: EU Network of Independent Experts on Social Inclusion, Directorate-General for Employment, Social Affairs and Inclusion.

Frazer, H., Marlier, E., Natali, D., Van Dam, R., & Vanhercke, B. (2010). Europe 2020: Towards a more social EU? In E. Marlier, D. Natali, & R. Van Dam (Eds.), *Europe 2020. Towards a more social EU?* (pp. 15–44). Brussels, Belgium: P.I.E. Peter Lang.

Freeman, R., Topel, R., & Swedenborg, B. (1997). *The welfare state in transition: Reforming the Swedish model.* Chicago, IL: University of Chicago Press.

Freeman, R. (2007). *Labor market institutions around the world* [Working Paper 13242]. Cambridge, MA: National Bureau of Economic Research.

Frick, J. R., & Grabka, M. M. (2003). Imputed rent and income inequality: A decomposition analysis for Great Britain, West Germany and the U.S. *Review of Income and Wealth, 49*(4), 13–37.

Frick, J. R., & Krell, K. (2010). *Measuring income in household panel surveys for Germany: A comparison of EU-SILC and SOEP* [SOEP Papers on Multidisciplinary Panel Data Research, n° 265]. Berlin, Germany: Deutsches Institut für Wirtschaftsforschung (DIW).

Frick, J. R., & Krell, K. (2011). Einkommensmessungen in Haushaltspanelstudien für Deutschland: Ein Vergleich von EU-SILC und SOEP. *AStA Wirtschafts- und Sozialstatistisches Archiv, 5*(3), 221–248.

Fritzell, J., & Ritakallio, V.-M. (2010). Societal shifts and changed patterns of poverty. *International Journal of Social Welfare, 19*, S25–S41.

Fritzell, J., Bäckman, O., & Ritakallio, V.-M. (2012). Income inequality and poverty: Do the Nordic countries still constitute a family of their own? In J. Kvist, J. Fritzell, B. Hvinden, & O. Kangas (Eds.), *Changing social equality. The Nordic welfare model in the 21st century* (pp. 165–185). Bristol, England: Policy Press.

Gardiner, K., & Millar, J. (2006). How low-paid employees avoid poverty: An analysis by family type and household structure. *Journal of Social Policy, 35*, 351–369.

Garfinkel, I., Rainwater, L., & Smeeding, T.M. (2006). A re-examination of welfare states and inequality in rich nations: How in-kind transfers and indirect taxes change the story. *Journal of Policy Analysis and Management, 25*(4), 897–919.

Gauthier, A. H. (1996). *The state and the family: A comparative analysis of family policies in industrialized countries*. Oxford, England: The Clarendon Press at Oxford University Press.

Gauthier, A. H. (1999). Historical trends in state support for families in Europe (post-1945). *Children and Youth Servicer Review, 21*(11/12), 937–965.

Gazier, B. (2009). The European employment strategy in the tempest: Restoring a long-term perspective. In N. Morel, B. Palier, & J. Palme (Eds.), *What future for social investment?* (pp. 153–163). Stockholm, Sweden: Institute for Future Studies. Retrieved from http://hal-paris1.archives-ouvertes.fr/hal-00635239

Genschel, P., & Schwartz, P. (2011). Tax competition: A literature review. *Socio-Economic Review, 9*(2), 339–370.

GDP: OECD Social Expenditure: Reference Series (for SK and SL, data was used from the Education At A Glance publications).

Ghysels, J., & Van Vlasselaer, E. (2008). Child well-being in Flanders: a multidimensional account. *Social Indicators Research: An International and Interdisciplinary Journal For Quality-Of-Life Measurement, 89*(2),283–304.

Ghysels, J., & Van Lancker, W. (2010). De terugkeer van het mattheuseffect? De casus van de kinderopvang in Vlaanderen. *Tijdschrift voor Sociologie, 31*(2),151–163.

Ghysels, J., & Van Lancker, W. (2011). The unequal benefits of activation: An analysis of the social distribution of family policy among families with young children. *Journal of European Social Policy, 21*(5), 472–485.

Giddens, A. (1998). The social investment state. In A. Giddens (Ed.), *The Third Way: Renewal of Social Democracy* (pp. 99–128). Cambridge, England: Polity Press.

Giddens, A. (1998). *The Third Way: The Renewal of Social Democracy*. Cambridge: Polity Press.

Giddens, A. (2001). *The global Third Way debate*. Cambridge, England: Polity Press.

Gilbert, N. (2002). *Transformation of the welfare state: The silent surrender of public responsibility*. New York, NY: Oxford University Press.

Goedemé, T. (2010). *The standard error of estimates based on EU-SILC. An exploration through the Europe 2020 poverty indicators* [CSB Working Paper 10/09]. Antwerp, Belgium: Herman Deleeck Centre for Social Policy, University of Antwerp.

Goedemé, T. (2012). *The EU-SILC sample design variables: review and recommendations*. Paper presented at the Net-SILC2 workshop on standard error estimation and related sampling issues, Eurostat, Luxembourg, 29–30 March 2012.

Goedemé, T. (2013). How much confidence can we have in EU-SILC? Complex sample designs and the standard error of the Europe 2020 poverty indicators. *Social Indicators Research 110*(1), 89–110.

Goedemé, T., & Rottiers, S. (2011). Poverty in the enlarged European Union. A discussion about definitions and reference groups. *Sociology Compass, 5*(1), 77–91.

Goedhart, T., Halberstadt, V., Kapteyn, A., & van Praag, B. (1977). The poverty line: Concept and measurement. *Journal of Human Resources, 12*(4), 503–520.

Goodin, R. (1988). *Protecting the vulnerable. A re-analysis of our social responsibilities.* Chicago, IL: University of Chicago Press.

Goodin, R. E., & Grand, J. L. (1987). *Not only the poor. The middle classes and the welfare state.* London, England: Allen & Unwin.

Goos, M., Manning, A., & Salomons, A. (2009). The polarization of the European labor market. *American Economic Review Papers and Proceedings, 99*(2), 58–63.

Gorden, M., Rosenman, L., & Cuskelly, M. (2007). Constrained labour: maternal employment when children have disabilities. *Journal of Applied Research in Intellectual Disabilities, 20*, 236–246.

Gornick, J. C., Meyers, M. K., & Ross, K. E. (1997). Supporting the employment of mothers: Policy variation across fourteen welfare states. *Journal of European Social Policy, 7*(1), 45–70.

Gornick, J. C. (1999). *Gender equality in the labour market: Women's employment and earnings* [Luxemburg Income Study Working Paper No. 206]. Luxembourg: Luxemburg Income Study.

Gornick, J. C., & Meyers, M. K. (2003). *Families that work: Policies for reconciling parenthood and employment.* New York, NY: Russell Sage Foundation.

Gornick, J. C., & Hegewisch, A. (2010). *The impact of 'family-friendly policies' on women's employment outcomes and on the costs and benefits of doing business.* [commissioned report].Washington, DC: World Bank

Goul Andersen, J. (2011). Denmark: Ambiguous modernization of an inclusive unemployment protection system. In J. Clasen, & D. Clegg (Eds.), *Regulating the risk of unemployment* (pp. 187–207). Oxford, England: Oxford University Press.

Graziano, P. (2007). Adapting to the European employment strategy? Recent development in Italian employment policy. *The International Journal of Comparative Labour Law and Industrial Relations, 23*(4), 543–565.

Graziano, P. (2011). Chances and pitfalls of flexible labour markets: The case of the Spanish strategy of labour market flexibility. In *Activation and labour market reforms in Europe: Challenges to social citizenship.* Basingstoke, England: Palgrave Macmillan.

Gregg, P., & Wadsworth, J. (2008). Two sides to every story: measuring polarisation and inequality in the distribution of work. *Journal of the Royal Statistical Society: Series A (Statistics in Society), 171*, 857–875.

Gregg, P., Scutella, R., & Wadsworth, J. (2010). Reconciling workless measures at the individual and household level. Theory and evidence from the United States, Britain, Germany, Spain and Australia. *Journal of Population Economics, 23*(1), 139–167.

Grogger, J. (2003). The effects of time limits, the EITC, and other policy changes on welfare use, work, and income among female-headed families, *The Review of Economics and Statistics, 85*(2), 394–408.

Grosh, M. (1992). *From platitudes to practice: Targeting social programs in Latin America*. Washington, DC: World Bank.

Grover, C., & Stewart, J. (1999). 'Market Workfare': Social security and competitiveness in the 1990s. *Journal of Social Policy, 24*(1), 73–96.

Guio, A.-C. (2005a), *Income Poverty and Social Exclusion in the EU25,* Statistics in Focus, Luxembourg: Eurostat.

Guio, A.-C. (2005b), *Material Deprivation in the EU,* Statistics in Focus, Luxembourg: Eurostat.

Guio, A.-C. (2009). *What can be learned from deprivation indicators in Europe?* [Eurostat methodologies and working papers]. Luxembourg: Office for Official Publications of the European Communities.

Guio, A.-C., Gordon, D., & Marlier, E. (2012). *Measuring material deprivation in the EU* [Eurostat methodological and working Paper]. Luxembourg: Publications Office of the European Union.

Gustafsson, B., & Uusitalo, H. (1990). The welfare state and poverty in Finland and Sweden from the mid-1960s to the mid-1980s. *Review of Income and Wealth, 36*(3),249–266.

Gustafsson, B., & Lindblom, M. (1993). Poverty lines and poverty in seven European Countries, Australia, Canada and the USA. *Journal of European Social Policy, 3*(1),21–38.

Haas, L., & Rostgaard, T. (2011). Fathers' right to paid parental leave in the Nordic countries: Consequences for the gendered division of leave. *Community, Work & Family, 14*(2), 177–195.

Hacker, J., & Pierson, P. (2010). *Winner-take-all politics: How Washington made the rich richer—and abandoned the middle class.* New York, NY: Simon and Schuster.

Hagenaars, A. (1985). *The perception of poverty.* Amsterdam, the Netherlands: North Holland Publishers.

Hakim, C. (2000). *Work-lifestyle choices in the 21st century: Preference theory.* Oxford, England: Oxford University Press.

Hall, P. A., & Soskice, D. (2001). *Varieties of capitalism. The institutional foundations of comparative advantage.* Oxford, England: Oxford University Press.

Halleröd, B., & Heikkilä, M. (1999). Poverty and social exclusion in the Nordic countries. In M. Kautto, M. Heikkilä, B. Hvinden, S. Marklund, & N. Ploug (Eds.), *Nordic social policy. Changing welfare states* (pp. 185–234). London, England: Routledge.

Hanratty, M., & Blank, R. (1992). Down and out in North America: Recent trends in poverty rates in the United States and Canada. *Quarterly Journal of Economics, 107*(1), 233–254.

Harding, A., Warren, N., & Lloyd, B. (2006). *Moving beyond the traditional cash measures of economic well-being* [Working Paper 61]. Canberra, Australia: National Center for Economic and Social Modelling.

Hardy, S., & Adnett, N. (2002). The parental-leave directive: Towards a "family-friendly" social Europe? *European Journal of Industrial Relations, 8* (2), 157–172.

Hartman, H., Kartopawiro, J., & Jansen, F. (2010). Ziekteverzuim en arbeidsongeschiktheid. *De Nederlandse economie 2009* (173-187). Den Haag: Centraal Bureau voor de Statistiek.

Hauser, R. (2008). *Problems of the German contribution to EU-SILC: A research perspective, comparing EU-SILC, microcensus and SOEP* [DIW]. Berlin, Germany: The German Socio-Economic Panel (SOEP).

Heady, C., Mitrakos, T., & Tsakloglou, P. (2001). *The distributional impact of social transfers in the European Union: Evidence from the ECHP* [IZA Discussion paper series, No. 356]. Germany: Institute for the Study of Labor. Retrieved from http://www.econstor.eu/dspace/bitstream/10419/21216/1/dp356.pdf

Hemerijck, A., & Bakker, W. (1994). De pendule van perspectief, Convergentie en divergentie in het denken over de verzorgingsstaat. In G. Engbersen, A. Hemerijck, & W. Bakker (Eds.), *Zorgen in het Europese huis. Verkenningen over de grenzen van nationale verzorgingsstaten*. Amsterdam, the Netherlands: Boom.

Hemerijck, A., & Schludi, M. (2000). Sequences of policy failures and effective policy responses. In F. W. Scharpf, & V. A. Schmidt (Eds.), *Welfare and work in the open economy: From vulnerability to competitiveness* (Vol. I, pp. 125–228). Oxford, England: Oxford University Press.

Hemerijck, A. (2002). The self- transformation of the European social model(s). In G. Esping-Andersen with D. Gallie, A. Hemerijck, & J. Myles (Eds.), *Why we need a new welfare state* (pp. 173–214). Oxford, England: Oxford University Press.

Hemerijck, A. (2012). Two or three waves of welfare state transformation? In N. Morel, B. Palier, & J. Palme (Eds.) *Towards a social investment welfare state? Ideas, policies and challenges* (pp. 33–60). Bristol, England: Policy Press.

Hemerijck, A. (2013). *Changing welfare states*. Oxford, England: Oxford University Press.

Hemerijck, A. (2003). A paradoxical miracle: The politics of coalition government and social concertation in Dutch welfare reforms. In S. Jochem, & N. A. Siegel (Eds.), *Konzertierung, Verhandlungsdemokratie und Reformpolitik im Wohlfahrtsstaat* (pp. 232–270). Opladen: Leske + Budrich.

Hemerijck, A., & Eichhorst, W. (2009). *Whatever happened to the Bismarckian welfare state? From labor shedding to employment-friendly reforms* [IZA Discussion Paper No. 4085]. Bonn, Germany: Forschungsinstitut zur Zukunft der Arbeit / Institute for the Study of Labor.

Hernández-Quevado C., Jones A. M., López-Nicolás A., & Rice N. (2006). Socio-economic inequalities in health: A comparative longitudinal analysis using the European Community Household Panel. *Social Science & Medecine, 63*(5), 1246–1261.

Hills, J. (2004). *Inequality and the state.* Oxford, England: Oxford University Press.

Hoogenboom, M. (2011). The Netherlands: Two tiers for all. In J. Clasen, & D. Clegg (Eds.), *Regulating the risk of unemployment* (pp. 75–99). Oxford, England: Oxford University Press.

Hooghe, M., Reeskens, T., Stolle, D., & Trappers, A. (2009). Ethnic diversity and generalized trust in Europe. A cross-national multi-level study. *Comparative Political Studies,* 42(2), 198–223.

Horemans, J., & Marx, I. (2013). Should We Care about Part-Time Work from a Poverty Perspective? An Analysis of the EU15 Countries. In M. Koch, & M. Fritz (Eds.), *Destandardisation of employment in Europe* (pp. 169–189). Houndmills, England: Palgrave Macmillan.

Hotz, V. J., & Scholz, J. K. (2003). The earned income tax credit. In R. Moffit (Ed.), *Means-tested transfer programs in the U.S* (pp. 141–198). Chicago, IL: University of Chicago Press.

Hvinden, B., & Johansson, H. (2007). *Citizenship in Nordic welfare states. Dynamics of choice, duties and participation in a changing Europe.* London, England: Routledge.

Hvinden, B. (2009). Redistributive and regulatory disability provisions: Incompatibility or synergy? In G. Quinn, & L. Waddington (Eds.), *European yearbook of disability law* (pp. 5–27). Antwerp, Belgium: Intersentia.

Immergut, E., Anderson, K., & Schulze, I. (2007). *The handbook of pension politics in western Europe.* Oxford, England: Oxford University Press.

Immervoll, H., Sutherland, H., & de Vos, K. (2001). Reducing child poverty in the European Union: The role of child benefits. In K. Vleminckx, & T. M. Smeeding (Eds.), *Child well-being, child poverty, and child policy in modern nations: What do we know?* Bristol, England: The Policy Press.

Immervoll, H., & Barber, D. (2006). *Can parents afford to work? Childcare costs, tax-benefit policies and work incentives* [IZA Discussion Paper 1932]. Germany: Institute for the Study of Labor.

Iversen, T., & Wren, A. (1998). Equality, employment, and budgetary restraint: The trilemma of the service economy. *World Politics, 50*(4), 507–546.

Jaumotte, F. (2003). *Female labour market participation: Past trends and main determinants in OECD countries* [Economics Department Working Paper]. Paris, France: OECD.

Jenkins, S. P., & Lambert, P. (1997). Three "I"s of poverty curves, with an analysis of UK poverty trends." *Oxford Economic Papers, 49*, 317–27.

Jenkins, S. P., Brandolini, A., Micklewright, J., & Nolan, B. (2013). *The Great Recession and the distribution of household income.* Oxford, England: Oxford University.

Jenson, J. (2008). Writing women out, folding gender in: The European Union "modernises" social policy. *Social Politics, 15*(2),131–153.

Jenson, J. (2009). Lost in translation: the social investment perspective and gender equality. *Social Politics, 16*(4), 446–483.

Jenson, J. (2009). Redesigning citizenship regimes after neoliberalism. Moving towards social investment. In N. Morel, B. Palier, & J. Palme (Eds.), *What future for social investment?* (pp. 27–44). Stockholm, Sweden: Institute for Futures Studies Research.

Jenson, J. (2010). Diffusing ideas for after neoliberalism the social investment perspective in Europe and Latin America. *Global Social Policy, 10*(1), 59–84.

Jenson, J. (2012). Redesigning citizenship regimes after neoliberalism: moving towards social investment. In N. Morel, B. Palier, & J. Palme (Eds.), *Towards a social investment welfare state? Ideas, policies and challenges* (pp. 61–90). Bristol, England: Policy Press.

Jenson, J., & Saint-Martin, D. (2003). New routes to social cohesion? Citizenship and the social investment state. *Canadian Journal of Sociology, 28*(1), 77–99.

Jessoula, M., & Alti, T. (2010). Italy: An uncompleted departure from Bismark. In B. Palier (Ed.), *A long goodbye to Bismarck?* (pp. 157–182). Amsterdam, the Netherlands: Amsterdam University Press.

Juhász, G. (2006). Exporting or pulling down? The European social model and eastern enlargement in the EU. *European Journal of Social Quality, 6*(1), 82–108.

Kakwani, N. (1977). Measurement of tax progressivity: An international comparison. *Economic Journal, 87*, 71–80.

Kamerman, S. B. (1980). Childcare and family benefits: Policies of six industrialized countries. *Monthly Labour Review* (November): 23–28.

Kamerman, S. B. & Kahn, A. J. (2001). Child and family policies in an era of social policy retrenchment and restructuring. In K. Vleminckx, & T. M. Smeeding (Eds.), *Child well-being, child poverty and child policy in modern nations: What do we know?* (pp. 501–526). Bristol, England: Policy Press.

Kangas, O., & Ritakallio, V.-M. (2007). Relative to what? Cross national pictures of European poverty measured by regional, national and European standards. *European Societies, 9*(2), 119–145.

Kazepov, Y. (2010). Rescaling social policies towards multi-level governance in Europe: Some reflections on processes at state and actors involved. In Y. Kazepov (Ed.), *Rescaling social policies: Towards multi-level governance in Europe.* Vienna, Austria: Ashgate.

Kenworthy, L. (2004). *Egalitarian capitalism: Jobs, incomes and growth in affluent countries.* New York, NY: Russell Sage Foundation.

Kenworthy, L. (2008). *Jobs with equality.* Oxford, England: Oxford University Press.

Kenworthy, L. (2010). Labour market activation. In F.G. Castles, S. Leibfried, J. Lewis, H. Obinger, & C. Pierson (Eds.), *The Oxford handbook of the welfare state* (pp. 435–447). Oxford, England: Oxford University Press.

Kenworthy, L. (2011). *Progress for the poor.* Oxford, England: Oxford University Press.

Kersh, J., Hedvat, T. T., Hauser-Cram, P., & Warfield, M. E. (2006). The contribution of marital quality to the well-being of parents of children with developmental disabilities. *Journal of Intellectual Disability Research, 50*(12), 883–893.

Kind en Gezin. (2009). *Het Kind in Vlaanderen.* Brussels, Belgium: Kind en Gezin.

Knijn, T. (2012). *Work, family policies, and transitions to adulthood in Europe.* London, England: Palgrave Macmillan.

Korpi, W., & Palme, J. (1998). The paradox of redistribution and strategies of equality: Welfare state institutions, inequality, and poverty in the western countries. *American Sociological Review, 63*(5), 661–687.

Korthouwer, G. H. P. (2010). *Party politics as we knew it? Failure to dominate government, intraparty dynamics and welfare reforms in continental Europe.* Oisterwijk, the Netherlands: Uitgeverij BOXPress.

Kvist, J., Pedersen, L., & Köhler, P. (2008). Making all persons work: Modern Danish labour market policies. In W. Eichhorst, O. Kaufmann, & R. Konle-Seidl (Eds.), *Bringing the jobless into work? Experiences with activation schemes in Europe and the US* (pp. 221–256). Berlin and Heidelberg, Germany: Springer.

Kvist, J., Fritzell, J. Hvinden, B., & Kangas, O. (2012). *Changing social equality. The Nordic welfare model in the 21st century.* Bristol: Policy Press.

Lambert, P. (2002). *The distribution and redistribution of income* (Third edition) Manchester, England: Manchester University Press.

Lampedusa, G. T. di (2007) [1958] *The leopard* [Il Gattopardo]. New York, NY: William Collins PLC & Random House.

Lefebvre, M., & Pestieau, P. (2012). *L'Etat-providence en Europe. Performance et dumping social.* Paris, France: Éditions Rue d'Ulm/Presses de l'École normale supérieure.

Le Grand, J. (1982). *The strategy for equality: Redistribution and the social services.* London, England: Allen & Unwin.

Le Grand, J. (2007). *The other invisible hand.* Princeton, NJ: Princeton University Press.

Le Grand, J., Propper, C., & Smith, S. (2008). *The economics of social problems* (4th ed.). Hamphire, England: Palgrave Macmillan.

Lelkes, O., Medgyesi, M., Tóth, I. G., & Ward, T. (2009). Income distribution and the risk of poverty. In T. Ward, O. Lelkes, H. Sutherland, & I. G. Tóth (Eds.), *European inequalities. Social inclusion and income distribution in the European Union* (pp. 17–44). Budapest, Hungary: Tárki.

Lelkes, O., & Zolyomi, E. (2011). *Poverty and social exclusion of migrants in the European Union* [Policy Brief]. Vienna, Austria: European Centre. Retrieved from http://www.euro.centre.org/data/1298540538_34816.pdf

Lessenich, S. (1995). *Wohlfahrstaat. Arbeitsmarkt und Sozialpolitik in Spanien. Eine exemplarische Analyse postautoritären Wandels.* Oplade: Leske & Budrich, 77–84.

Levy, F. (2010). *How technology changes demands for human skills* [OECD Education Working Paper No. 45]. Paris, France: OECD.

Lewis, J. (2006). Work/family reconciliation, equal opportunities, and social policies: The interpretation of policy trajectories at the EU level and the meaning of gender equality. *Journal of European Public Policy, 13*(3), 420–437.

Lewis, J. (2006). *Children, changing families and welfare states.* Cheltenham, England: Edward Elgar.

Lewis, J., Campbell, M., & Huerta, C. (2008). Patterns of paid and unpaid work in Western Europe: Gender, commodification, preferences and the implications for policy. *Journal of European Social Policy, 18*(1), 21–37.

Lewis, J. (2009). *Work-family balance, gender and policy.* Cheltenham, England: Edward Elgar.

Ligon, E., & Schechter, L. (2003). Measuring vulnerability. *The Economic Journal, 113*(486), C95–C102.

Lindsay, C., McQuaid, R. W, & Dutton, M. (2007). New approaches to employability in the UK: Combining "human capital development" and "work first" strategies? *Journal of Social Policy, 36*(4), 539–560.

Lindvall, J. (2010). *Mass unemployment and the state.* Oxford, England: Oxford University Press.

Lohmann, H., & Andreβ, H. J. (2008). Explaining in-work poverty within and across countries. In H. J. Andreβ, & H. Lohmann (Eds.), *The working poor in Europe; Employment, poverty and globalization* (pp. 293-314). London, England: Edward Elgar.

Lohmann, H., & Marx, I. (2008). The different faces of in-work poverty across welfare state regimes. In H. J. Andreβ, & H. Lohmann (Eds.), *The working poor in Europe; Employment, poverty and globalization* (pp. 17–46). London, England: Edward Elgar.

Lohmann, H. (2009). Welfare states, labour market institutions and the working poor: A comparative analysis of 20 European countries. *European Sociological Review, 25*(4),489–504

Lohmann, H. (2011). Comparability of EU-SILC survey and register data: The relationship among employment, earnings and poverty. *Journal of European Social Policy, 21*(1), 37–54.

Lucifora, C., & Salverda, W. (2008). Low pay. In W. Salverda, B. Nolan, & T. M. Smeeding (Eds.), *Oxford handbook of economic inequality* (pp. 256–283). Oxford, England: Oxford University Press.

Maasoumi, E., & Lugo, M. A. (2008). The information basis of multivariate poverty assessments. In N. Kakwani, & J. Silber (Eds.), *Quantitative approaches to multidimensional poverty measurement* (pp. 1–29). New York: Palgrave MacMillan.

Mack, J., & Lansley, S. (1985). *Poor Britain*. London, England: George Allen & Unwin.

Mahon, R. (2002). Childcare: Toward what kind of social Europe. *Social Politics, 9*(3), 343–379.

Mahon, R. (2006). The OECD and the work/family reconciliation agenda: Competing frames. In J. E. Lewi (Ed.), *Children, changing families and welfare states* (pp. 173–197). Cheltenham, England: Edward Elgar Publishing.

Maitre, B., Nolan, B., & Whelan, C. T. (2011). *Low pay, in-work poverty and economic vulnerability: A comparative analysis using EU-SILC*. Manchester, England: The Manchester School.

Marical, F., Mira d'Ercole, M., Vaalavuo, M., & Verbist, G. (2008). Publicly-provided services and the distribution of households' economics resources. *OECD Economic Studies, 44*(1), 9–47.

Marlier, E., Atkinson, A. B., Cantillon, B., & Nolan, B. (2007). *The EU and social inclusion. Facing the challenges*. Bristol: The Policy Press.

Marx, I., & Verbist, G. (1998). Low-paid work and poverty: A cross-country perspective. In S. Bazen, M. Gregory, & W. Salverda (Eds.), *Low-wage employment in Europe*. Cheltenham, England: Edward Elgar.

Marx, I., & G. Verbist. (2008). Combating in-work poverty in Continental Europe: The policy options assessed. In H. J. Andreβ, & H. Lohmann (Eds.), *The working poor in Europe* (pp. 273–292). London, England: Edward Elgar.

Marx, I., Vanhille, J., & Verbist, G. (2012a.) Combating in-work poverty in Continental Europe: An investigation using the Belgian case. *Journal of Social Policy, 41*(1), 19–41.

Marx, I., Vandenbroucke, P., & Verbist, G. (2012b). Can higher employment levels bring down poverty in the EU? Regression based simulations of the Europe 2020 target. *Journal of European Social Policy, 22*(5), 472–486.

Marx, I., Marchal, S., & Nolan, B. (2013). Mind the gap: Net incomes of minimum wage workers in the EU & the US. In I. Marx, & K. Nelson (Eds.), *Minimum income protection in flux* (pp. 54–80). Houndmills and Basingstoke, Hampshire, England: Palgrave MacMillan.

Matsaganis, M., & Verbist, G. (2009). Distributional effects of publicly funded childcare. In T. Ward, O. Lelkes, H. Sutherland, & I. Toth (Eds.), *European inequalities. Social inclusion and income distribution in the European Union* (pp. 177–185). Budapest, Hungary: Tarki.

Mätzke, M., & Ostner, I. (2010). Introduction: change and continuity in recent family policies. *Journal of European Social Policy, 20*, 387–398.

Mau, S., & Burkhardt, C. (2009). Migration and welfare state solidarity in Western Europe. *Journal of European Social Policy, 9*(3), 213–229.

Meeusen, L., & Nys, A. (2012). *Social spending in Europe* [CSB Working Paper No. 12/07]. Antwerp, Belgium: Herman Deleeck Centre for Social Policy, University of Antwerp.

Merton, R. K. (1968). The Matthew effect in science: The reward and communication systems of science are considered. *Science, 159*(3810), 56–63.

Meyer, B. D., & Rosenbaum, B. T. (2001). Welfare, the earned income tax credit, and the labor supply of single mothers. *The Quarterly Journal of Economics, 116*(3), 1063–1115.

Ministry of Social Affairs and Health. (1999). *Poverty and social exclusion in Finland in the 1990s*. Helsinki, Finland: Author.

Mishra, R. (1990). *The welfare state in capitalist society. Policies of retrenchment and maintenance in Europe, North America and Australia*. New York, NY: Harvester Wheatsheaf.

MISSOC. (2011). Mutual Information System on Social Protection on-line tables at Eurostat website http://ec.europa.eu/employment_social/missoc/db/public/compareTables.do?lang=en accessed 26.12.2011.

Montanari, I. (2000). From family wage to marriage subsidy and child benefits: Controversy and consensus in the development of family support. *Journal of European Social Policy, 10*(4), 307–333.

Morel, N., Palier, B., & Palme, J. (2009). *What future for social investment?* [Research Report, 2009/1]. Stockholm, Sweden: Institute for Future.

Morel, N., Palier, B., & Palme, J. (2012). *Towards a social investment welfare state? Ideas, policies and challenges*. Bristol, England: The Policy Press.

Morgan, K. J., & Zippel, K. (2003). Paid to care: The origins and effects of care leave policies in Western Europe. *Social Politics, 10*(1), 49–85.

Morgan, K. J. (2008). Working mothers and the welfare state: Religion and the politics of work-family policies in Western Europe and the United States. Stanford, CA: Stanford University Press.

Morgan, K. J. (2012). Promoting social investment through work-family policies: Which nations do it and why? In N. Morel, B. Palier, & J. Palme (Eds.), *Towards a social investment welfare state? Ideas, policies and challenges* (pp. 153–179). Bristol, England: Policy Press.

Morris, N., & Preston, I. (1986). Inequality, poverty and the redistribution of income. *Bulletin of Economic Research, 38*(4),275–344.

Morrison, Chr., & Murtin, F. (2010). *The Kuznets Curve of education: A global perspective of education inequalities*. Centre for the Economics of Education (LSE) DP116. Retrieved from http://cee.lse.ac.uk/ceedps/ceedp116.pdf.

Moss, P. (1990). *Kinderopvang en -verzorging in de Europese Gemeenschap 1985–1990*. Brussel: Europese Commissie—Netwerk Kinderopvang.

Moss, P. (2011). *International review of leave policies and related research 2011*. London, England: International Network on Leave Policies and Research.

Myrdal, A., & Myrdal, G. (1934). Kris i befolkningsfrågan (Crisis in the Population Question).

Narayan, D., Patel, R., Schafft, K., Rademacher, A., & Koch-Schulte, S. (2000). *Voices of the poor. Can Anyone Hear Us?*. New York: Published for the World Bank, Oxford University Press.

Nelson, K. (2011). Social assistance and EU poverty thresholds 1990–2008. Are European welfare systems providing just and fair protection against low income? *European Sociological Review* 0, 1-16. doi: 10.1093/esr/jcr080

Nickell, S. (2004). Poverty and worklessness in Britain. *The Economique Journal, 114*(494), C1–C25.

Nikolai, R. (2009). Towards social investment? Patterns of public policy in the OECD world. In N. Morel, B. Palier, & J. Palme (Eds.) *What future for social investment* (pp. 99–118). Stockholm, Sweden: Institute for Futures Studies.

Nolan, B., & Marx, I. (2000). Low pay and household poverty. In M. Gregory, W. Salverda, & S. Bazen (Eds.), *Labour market inequalities: Problems and policies of low-wage employment in international perspective* (pp. 100–199). Oxford, England: Oxford University Press.

Nolan, B., & Russell, H. (2001). *Non-cash Benefits and Poverty in Ireland.* [Policy Research Series Paper No. 39].Dublin: The Economic and Social Research Institute.

Nolan, B., & Marx, I. (2008). Poverty and social exclusion. In W. Salverda, B. Nolan, & T. M. Smeeding (Eds.), *Oxford handbook of economic inequality.* Oxford, England: Oxford University Press.

Nolan, B., & Whelan, C. T. (2011a). *The EU 2020 poverty target* [GINI Discussion Paper Series]. Amsterdam, the Netherlands: Amsterdams Instituut voor Arbeidsstudies (AIAS).

Nolan, B., & Whelan, C. T. (2011b). *Poverty and deprivation in Europe.* Oxford, England: Oxford University Press.

Notten, G., & de Neubourg, C. (2011). Monitoring absolute and relative poverty: "Not enough" is not the same as "much less." *Review of Income and Wealth, 57*(2), 247–269.

Nussbaum, M. (2001). *Upheavals of thought: The intelligence of emotions.* Cambridge, England: Cambridge University Press.

Nussbaum, M. (2006). *Frontiers of justice: disability, nationality, species membership.* Cambridge, MA: Belknap Press of Harvard University Press.

Nussbaum, M. (2011). *Creating capabilities. The human development approach.* Cambridge, MA: The Belknap Press of Harvard University Press.

O'Neill, D., & Sweetman, O. (1998). Intergenerational mobility in Britain: Evidence from unemployment patterns. *Oxford Bulletin of Economics and Statistics, 60*(4),431–447. doi: 10.1111/1468-0084.00108

OECD. Social Expenditure Statistics Detailed Data (Database).

OECD. (1994). *The OECD jobs study. Facts, analysis, strategies.* Paris, France: OECD.

OECD. (2001). *Employment outlook 2001*. Paris, France: OECD.

OECD. (2006). *Projecting OECD health and long-term care expenditures: What are the main drivers?* [OECD Economic Department Working Papers. No. 477]. Paris, France: OECD.

OECD. (2006a). *OECD employment outlook*. Paris, France: OECD.

OECD. (2006b). *Education at a glance*. [OECD Indicators]. Paris, France: OECD.

OECD. (2007). *Babies and bosses*. Paris, France: OECD.

OECD. (2007). *Employment outlook*. Paris, France: OECD.

OECD. (2008). *Growing unequal? Income distribution and poverty in OECD countries*. Paris, France: OECD.

OECD. (2009). *Is work the best antidote to poverty?* [Employment outlook]. Paris, France: OECD.

OECD. (2009). *Employment outlook*. Paris, France: OECD.

OECD. (2010). *Education at a glance 2010*. Paris, France: OECD.

OECD. (2010). *Sickness, disability and work: Breaking the barriers. A synthesis of findings across OECD countries*. Paris, France: OECD.

OECD. (2011). *Divided we stand: Why inequality keeps rising*. E-book available online at: www.oecd-ilibrary.org.

OECD. (2011). *Doing better for families*. Paris, France: OECD.

OECD. (2011). *Help Wanted? Providing and paying for long-term care*. Paris, France: OECD.

O'Neill, D., & Sweetman, O. (1998). Intergenerational mobility in Britain: Evidence from unemployment patterns. *Oxford Bulletin of Economics and Statistics, 60*(4), 431–447.

Oosterlynck, S., Kazepov, Y., Novy, A., Cools, P., Barberis, E., Wukovitsch, F., Sarius, T., & Leubolt, B. *The butterfly and the elephant: Local social innovation, the welfare state and new poverty dynamics*. Mimeo.

Orloff, A. S. (1993). Gender and the social rights of citizenship: The comparative analysis of gender relations and welfare states. *American Sociological Review, 58*, 301–328.

Orloff, A. S. (2006). From maternalism to "employment for all": State policies to promote women's employment across the affluent democracies. In J. Levy (Ed.), *The state after statism* (pp. 230–270). Cambridge, MA: Harvard University Press. Orloff, A. S. (2009). Gendering the comparative analysis of welfare states: an unfinished agenda. *Sociological Theory, 27*(3), 317–343.

Orloff, A. S. (2010). Gender. In F. G. Castles, S. Leibfried, J. Lewis, H. Obinger, & C. Pierson (Eds.), *The Oxford handbook of the welfare state* (pp. 252–264). Oxford, England: Oxford University Press.

Orshansky, M. (1965). Counting the poor: Another look at the poverty profile. *Social Security Bulletin, 28*(1), 3–29.

Orshansky, M. (1969). How poverty is measured. *Monthly Labor Review, 92*(2), 37–41.

Paats, M., & Tiit, E. -M. (2010). Income from own-consumption. InA. B. Atkinson, & E. Marlier (Eds.), *Income and living conditions in Europe* (pp. 179–194). Luxembourg: Publications Office of the European Union.

Pakulski, J., & Waters, M. (1996). *The death of class*. London, England: Sage.

Palier, B., & Martin, C. (2007). Editorial introduction. From a 'frozen landscape" to structural reforms: The sequential transformation of Bismarckian welfare systems. *Social Policy and Administration, 41*(6), 535–554.

Palier, B. (2010). *The politics of reform in Bismarckian welfare states*. Amsterdam, the Netherlands: Amsterdam University.

Palier, B. (2010a). *A long goodbye to Bismarck? The politics of welfare reforms in Continental Europe*. Amsterdam, the Netherlands: Amsterdam University Press.

Palier, B. (2010b). Continental Western Europe. In F. G. Castles, S. Leibfried, J. Lewis, H. Obinger, & C. Pierson (Eds.), *The Oxford handbook of the welfare state* (pp. 601–615). Oxford, England: Oxford University Press.

Palier, B. (2010c). The dualization of the French welfare system. In B. Palier (Ed.), A long goodbye to Bismarck? (pp. 73–100). Amsterdam, the Netherlands: Amsterdam University Press.

Palier, B., & Thelen, K. (2010). Institutionalizing dualism: Complementarities and change in France and Germany. *Politics and Society, 38*(1), 119–148.

Palme, J. (2005). Features of the Swedish pension reform. *The Japanese Journal of Social Security Policy, 4*(1),42–53.

Paulus, A., Sutherland, H., & Tsakloglou, P. (2010). The distributional impact of in-kind public benefits in European countries. *Journal of Policy Analysis and Management, 29*(2), 243–266.

Payne, G., Laporte, A., Deber, R., & Coyte, P. C. (2007). Counting backward to health care's future: Using time-to-death modeling to identify changes in end-of-life morbidity and the impact of aging on health care expenditures. *The Milbank Quarterly, 85*(2), 213–257.

Pearson, M. (2009). *Disparities in health expenditure across OECD countries: Why does the United States spend so much more than other countries?* [Written Statement to Senate Special Committee on Aging].

Peeters, H., Debels, A., & Verpoorten, R. (2013). Excluding institutionalized elderly from surveys: Consequences for income and poverty statistics. *Social Indicators Research, 110*, 751–769.

Pfau-Effinger, B., & Rostgaard, T. (2011). *Care between work and welfare in European societies*. London, England: Palgrave Macmillan.

Pierson, P. (1994). *Dismantling the welfare state? Reagan, Thatcher, and the politics of retrenchment*. Cambridge, England: Cambridge University Press.

Pierson, P. (1995). *The new politics of the welfare state*. Bremen: Zentrum für Sozialpolitik, (ZeS-Arbeitspapier nr. 3/95).

Pierson, P. (1998). Irresistible forces, immovable objects: Post-industrial welfare states confront permanent austerity. *Journal of European Public Policy, 5*(4), 539–560.

Pierson, P. (2001). Coping with permanent austerity: Welfare state restructuring in affluent democracies. In P. Pierson (Ed.), *The new politics of the welfare state* (pp. 410–456). Oxford, England: Oxford University Press.

Pierson, P. (2001). *The new politics of the welfare state*. Oxford, England: Oxford University Press.

Pierson, P. (2004). *Politics in time: History, institutions, and social analysis*. Princeton, NJ/Oxford, England: Princeton University Press.

Pierson, P. (2011). *The welfare state over the very long run* [ZeS-Working Paper No. 02/2011]. Retrieved from http://econstor.eu/bitstream/10419/46215/1/65484416X.pdf

Pintelon, O., Cantillon, B., Van den Bosch, K., & Whelan, C. (2013). The social stratification of social risks: The relevance of class for social investment strategies. *Journal of European Social Policy, 23*(1), 52–67. http://dx.doi.org/doi:10.1177/0958928712463156.

Pogge, T. (2002) Can the capability approach be justified? *Philosophical Topics, 30*(2), 167–228.

Pollitt, C. (2003). Joined-up government: A survey. *Political Studies Review, 1*(1),34–39.

Pollitt, C., & Bouckaert, G. (2004). *Public management: A comparative analysis* (2nd ed.). Oxford, England: Oxford University Press. Population Data: OECD Population Statistics (population).

Public Policy and Management Institute. (2011). *Evaluation of the effectiveness and impact of the social OMC since 2006. Recommendations for improving and strengthening effectiveness and impact of the social OMC*. Report Commissioned by the European Commission, Directorate-General for Employment, Social Affairs and Inclusion, Vilnius, Lithuania.

Radner, D. (1997). Non-cash income, equivalence scales and the measurement of economic well-being. *Review of Income and Wealth, 43*(1), 71–88.

Rainwater, L. (1982) Stigma in income-tested programs. In I. Garfinkel (Ed.), *Income tested transfer programs: The case for and against* (pp. 19–46). New York, NY: New York Academic Press.

Ravallion, M. (1994). *Poverty comparisons*. Chur, Switzerland: Harwood Academic Press.

Ravallion, M., & Bidani, B. (1994). How robust is a poverty profile? *The World Bank Economic Review, 8*(1), 75–102.

Ravallion, M. (2008). On the welfarist rationale for relative poverty lines. In K. Basu, & R. Kanbur (Eds.), *Arguments for a better world: Essays in honor of Amartya Sen*. Oxford, England: Oxford University Press.

Ravallion, M. (2010). *Poverty lines across the world*. [Policy Research Working Paper Series]. Washington, DC: The World Bank.

Ravallion, M. (2011). On multidimensional indices of poverty. *Journal of Economic Inequality, 9*(2), 235–248.

Ravallion, M, & Chen, S. (2011). Weakly relative poverty. *Review of Economics and Statistics, 93*(4), 1251–1261.

Rawls, J. (1971). *A theory of justice.* Cambridge, MA: Belknap Press of Harvard University Press.

Ray, R., Gornick, J. C., & Schmitt, J. (2010). Who cares? Assessing generosity and gender equality in parental leave policy designs in 21 countries. *Journal of European Social Policy, 20*(3), 196–216.

Rigney, D. (2010). *The Matthew effect: How advantage begets further advantage.* New York: Columbia University Press.

Ringen, S. (1987). *The possibility of politics: A study in the political economy of the welfare state.* Oxford, England: Clarendon Press.

Ritzen, J. (2011). *A renaissance for social mobility and its significance for the bridge towards postsecondary education* [UNU-MERIT Working Paper Series 2011-057]. Retrieved from http://www.merit.unu.edu/publications/wppdf/2011/wp2011-057.pdf.

Rodrik, D. (1997). *Has globalization gone too far?* Washington, DC: Institute for International Economics.

Roemer, J. (1993). A pragmatic theory of responsibility for the egalitarian planner. *Philosophy and Public Affairs, 22*, 146–166.

Roemer, J. (1998). *Equality of opportunity.* Cambridge, MA: Harvard University Press.

Room, G. (1995). *Beyond the threshold: The measurement and analysis of social exclusion.* Oxford, England: Blackwell.

Rosanvallon, P. (1995). *La nouvelle question sociale.* Paris, France: Repenser L'Etat-providence.

Rosanvallon, P. (2011). The metamorphoses of democratic legitimacy: Impartiality, reflexivity, proximity. *Constellations, 18*(2), 114–123. Article first published online: 22 May 2011 doi/10.1111/j.1467-8675.2011.00631.x

Rosenberg, N. (1982) *Inside the black box: Technology and economics.* Cambridge, MA: University Press.

Rowntree, B. (2000) [1901]. Seebohm. *Poverty: A Study of Town Life.* Bristol, England: The Policy Press.

Rubery, J., Grimshaw, D., Fagan, C., Figueiredo, H., & Smith, M. (2003). Gender equality still on the agenda—but for how long? *Industrial Relations Journal, 34*(5), 477–497.

Ruggeri Laderchi, C., Saith, R., & Stewart, F. (2003). Does it matter that we don't agree on the definition of poverty? A comparison of four approaches. [QEH Working Paper Series 107]. Oxford, England: University of Oxford.

Sabel, C. F., Saxenian, A. L., & Miettinen, R., Kristensen, P. H., & Hautamäki, J. (2010). *Individualized service provision in the new welfare state: Lessons from special education in Finland.* Helsinki, Finland: SITRA.

Sainsbury, D. (1991). Analysing welfare state variations: The merits and limitations of models based on the residual-institutional distinction. *Scandinavian Political Studies, 14*(1), 1–30.

Sainsbury, D. (1994). *Gendering welfare states.* London, England: Sage.

Sala-i-Martin. (1996). Regional cohesion: Evidence and theories of regional growth and convergence. *European Economic Review 40*,1325–1352.

Salverda, W., Van Klaveren, M., & van der Meer, M. (2008). *Low wage work in the Netherlands.* New York, NY: Russell Sage Foundation.

Sauli, H., & Törmälehto. V.-M. (2010). The distributional impact of imputed rent. In A.B. Atkinson, & E. Marlier (Eds.), *Income and living conditions in Europe* (pp. 155–178). Luxembourg: Publications Office of the European Union.

Scharpf, F. W. (1991). *Crisis and choice in European social democracy.* Ithaca, NY: Cornell University Press.

Scharpf, F. W. (2000). The viability of advanced welfare states in the international economy: Vulnerabilities and options. *Journal of European Public Policy, 7*(2), 190–228.

Schenker, N., & Gentleman, J. F. (2001). On judging the significance of differences by examining the overlap between confidence intervals. *The American Statistician, 55*(3), 182–186.

Schleicher, A. (2009). Securing quality and equity in education: Lessons from PISA. *Prospects, 39*, 251–263.

Schmid, G. (2006). Social risk management through transitional labour markets. *Socioeconomic Review, 4*(1), 1–33.

Schmid, G. (2008). *Full employment in Europe: Managing labour market transition and risks.* Cheltenham, England: Edward Elgar.

Schmidt, M. (1983). The welfare state and the economy in periods of economic crisis: A comparative study of twenty-three OECD nations. *European Journal of Political Research,* (1), 1–26.

Schmitt, C., & Starke, P. (2011). Explaining convergence of OECD welfare states: A conditional approach. *Journal of European Social Policy, 21*(2), 120–135.

Schoon, I. (2010). Childhood cognitive ability and adult academic attainment: Evidence from three British cohort studies. *Longitudinal and Life Course Studies, 1*(3), 241–258.

Schuetz, G., Ursprung, H. W., & Woessmann, L. (2008). Education policy and equality of opportunity. *Kyklos, 61*(2), 279–308.

Scott, J. (1996). *Stratification and power: Structures of class, status and command.* Cambridge, England: Polity Press.

Scruggs, L. (2008). Social rights, welfare generosity, and inequality. In P. Baramendi, & C. Anderson (Eds.) *Democracy, inequality and* representation (pp. 62–90). New York, NY: Russell Sage Foundation.

Sefton, T. (2002). *Recent changes in the distribution of the social wage* [CASE paper 62]. London, England: London School of Economics.

Seidl, C. (1998). Poverty measurement: A survey. In D. Bös, M. Ros, & C. Seidl (Eds.), *Welfare and efficiency in public economics.* Heidelberg, Germany: Springer-Verlag.

Sen, A. (1976. Poverty: An ordinal approach to measurement. *Econometrica, 44*(2), 219–231.

Sen, A. (1980). Equality of what? In A. Sen (Ed.), *Choice, welfare and measurement* (pp. 353–372). Oxford, England: Blackwell.

Sen, A. (1983). Poor, relatively speaking. *Oxford Economic Papers, 35*(2), 153–169.

Sen, A. (1985). A sociological approach to the measurement of poverty: A reply to Professor Peter Townsend. *Oxford Economic Papers, 37*(4), 669–676.

Sen, A. (1985). *Commodities and capabilities.* Amsterdam, the Netherlands: Elsevier.

Sen, A. (1992). *Inequality re-examined.* Oxford, England: Clarendon Press.

Sen, A. (1993). Capability and well-being. In M. Nussbaum, & A. Sen (Eds), *The quality of life.* Oxford. England: Clarendon Press.

Sen, A. (1999). *Development as freedom.* Oxford, England: Oxford University Press.

Sen, A. (2001). Economic development and capability expansion in historical perspective. *Pacific Economic Review, 6*(2),179–191.

Sen, A. (2009). *The idea of justice.* London, England: Allen-Lane/Penguin Books.

Serrano Pascual, A. (2004). *Are activation policies converging in Europe?* Brussels, Belgium: ETUI.

Seshamani, M., & Gray, A. M. (2004). A longitudinal study of the effects of age and time to death on hospital costs. *Journal of Health Economics, 23*(2), 217–235.

Shavit, Y., & Blossfeld, H.P. (1993). *Persistent inequality. Changing educational attainment in thirteen countries.* Boulder, CO: Westview Press.

Siegel, N. (2007). When (only) money matters: The pros and cons of expenditure analysis. In J. Clasen, & N. Siegel (Eds.), *Investigating welfare state change. The dependent variable problem in comparative analysis* (pp. 43–71). Cheltenham, England: Edward Elgar.

Sinn, H.-W. (1990). Tax harmonization and tax competition in Europe. *European Economic Review, 34*, 489–504.

Sjöberg, O. (2011). Sweden: Ambivalent adjustment. In J. Clasen, & D. Clegg (Eds.), *Regulating the risk of unemployment* (pp. 208–231). Oxford, England: Oxford University Press.

Skocpol, T. (1991). Targeting within universalism: Politically viable policies to combat poverty in the United States. In C. Jencks, & P. E. Peterson (Eds.), *The urban underclass.* Washington, DC: The Brookings Institution.

Skocpol, T., & Ritter, G. (1991). Gender and the origins of modern social policies in Britain and the United States. *Studies in American Political Development, 5*, 36–93.

Skolverket. (2000). *Childcare in Sweden.* Stockholm: Author.

Skolverket. (2007). *Five year with the maximum fee.* Stockholm: Author.

Slesnick, D.T. (1993). Gaining ground: Poverty in the postwar United States. *Journal of Political Economy, 101*(1), 1–38.

Smeeding, T. M. (1977). The antipoverty effectiveness of in-kind transfers. *Journal of Human Resources, 12*, 360–378.

Smeeding, T. M. (1982). *Alternative methods for valuing selected in-kind transfer benefits and measuring their effect on poverty* [U.S. Bureau of Census Technical Paper No. 50]. Washington, DC: U.S. Government Printing Office.

Smeeding, T. M., Saunders, P., Coder, J., Jenkins, S., Fritzell, J., Hagenaars, A. J. M., . . . Wolfson, M. (1993). Poverty, inequality, and family living standards impact across seven nations: The effect of noncash subsidies for health, education and housing. *Review of Income and Wealth, 39*(3), 229–256.

Smeeding, T. M. (2005). Public policy and economic inequality: The United States in comparative perspective. *Social Science Quarterly, 86*(5), 1–50.

Social Protection Committee. (2009). *Growth, jobs and social progress in the EU. A contribution to the evaluation of the social dimension of the Lisbon Strategy.* Brussels, Belgium: European Commission, Directorate-General for Employment, Social Affairs and Equal Opportunities,

Starke, P. (2006). The politics of welfare state retrenchment: A literature review. *Social Policy and Administration, 40*(1), 104–120.

Starke, P. (2008). *Radical welfare state retrenchment: A comparative analysis.* Houndmills, England/New York, NY: Palgrave Macmillan.

Steinmo, S. (1993). *Taxation and democracy.* New Haven, CT: Yale University Press.

Stiglitz, J. E., Sen, A., & Fitoussi, J.-P. (2009). *Report by the Commission on the measurement of economic performance and social progress* [Commission on the Measurement of Economic Performance and Social Progress]. Mimeo. Retrieved from http://www.stiglitz-sen-fitoussi.fr

Storms, B., & Van den Bosch, K. (2009). *Wat Heeft Een Gezin Minimaal Nodig? Een Budgetstandaard Voor Vlaanderen.* Leuven: Acco.

Storms, B., Goedemé, T., & Van den Bosch, K. (2011). *Reference budgets: Are they an alternative to the current European poverty line?* Paper presented at the FISS Conference, Sigtuna, Sweden.

Storms, B., Goedemé, T., Van den Bosch, K., & Devuyst, K. (2013). *Towards a common framework for developing cross-nationally comparable reference budgets in Europe.* ImPRovE Working Papers, Methodological paper 13/02, Antwerp: Herman Deleeck Centre for Social Policy; University of Antwerp.

Streeck, W. (1992). Productive constraints: On the institutional conditions of diversified quality production. In W. Streeck (Ed.), *Institutions and economic performance* (pp. 1–40). London, England: Sage.

Streeck, W. (2000). Competitive solidarity: Rethinking the "European social model." In K. Hinrichs, H. Kitschelt, & H. Wiesenthal (Eds.), *Kontingenz*

und Krise: Institutionenpolitik in kapitalistischen und postsozialistischen Gesellschaften (pp. 245–261). Frankfurt am Main, Germany: Campus.
Subramanian, S. (2002). Counting the poor: An elementary difficulty in the measurement of poverty. *Economics and Philosophy, 18*(02), 277–85.
Swank, D. (2002). *Global capital, political institutions, and policy change in developed welfare states.* Cambridge, England: Cambridge University Press.
Swank, D., & Steinmo, S (2002). The new political economy of taxation in advanced capitalist economies. *American Journal of Political Science, 46*, 642–655.
Swank, D. (2006). Tax policy in the era of internationalization: Explaining the spread of neoliberalism. *International Organization, 60*(4), 847–882.
Tanzi, V. (1995). *Taxation in an integrating world.* Washington, DC: Brooking Institution.
Taylor-Gooby, P. (2004). *New risks, new welfare: The transformation of the European welfare state.* Oxford, England: Oxford University Press.
Taylor-Gooby, P. (2008). The new welfare settlement in Europe. *European Societies, 10*(1), 3–24.
Taylor-Gooby, P. (2012). *New paradigms in public policy*. Oxford, England: Oxford University Press.
The Social Protection Committee. (2009). *Growth, jobs and social progress in the EU. A contribution to the evaluation of the social dimension of the Lisbon Strategy*. Brussels, Belgium: European Commission Directorate-General for Employment, Social Affairs and Equal Opportunities.
Thorbecke, E. (2008). Multidimensional poverty: Conceptual and measurement Issues. In N. Kakwani, & J. Silber (Eds.) *The many dimensions of* poverty (pp. 3–19). New York, NY: Palgrave MacMillan.
Titmuss, R. (1969). *The gift relationship: From human blood to social policy.* London, England: Routledge.
Tobin, J. (1970). On limiting the domain of inequality. *Journal of Law and Economics, 13*(2), 263–277.
Touraine, A. (1969). *La Société post-industrielle. Naissance d'une société.* Paris, France: Editions Denoel.
Townsend, P. (1979). *Poverty in the United Kingdom. A survey of household resources and standards of living.* Middlesex [England]: Penguin Books.
Townsend, P. (1985). A sociological approach to the measurement of poverty—a rejoinder to Professor Amartya Sen. *Oxford Economic Papers, 37*(4), 659–68.
Tsui, K.Y. (2002). Multidimensional poverty indices. *Social Choice and Welfare, 19*, 69–93.
Ungerson, C. (2004). Whose empowerment and independence? A cross-national perspective on "cash for care" schemes? *Ageing and Society, 24*, 189–212.
Unemployment (1000s): OECD Annual Labour Force Survey (ALFS) Summary tables.
Unemployment rate: OECD Country Statistical Profiles.

Uunk, W., Kalmijn, M., & Muffels, R. T. (2005). The impact of young children on women's labour supply. *Acta Sociologica, 48*(1), 41–62.

Vaalavuo, M. (2011). *Towards an improved measure of income inequality. The impact of public services in income distribution. An international comparison* (Unpublished doctoral dissertation). European University Institute, Florence, Italy.

Vail, M. I. (2010). *Recasting welfare capitalism: Economic adjustment in contemporary France and Germany*. Philadelphia, PA: Temple University Press.

Van Berkel, R., & Borghi, V. (2008). Introduction: The governance of activation. *Social Policy and Society, 7*(3), 331–340.

Van Berkel, R., de Graaf, W., & Sirovátka, T. (2011). *The governance of active welfare states in Europe*. London, England: Palgrave Macmillan.

Vandecasteele, L. (2010). Life course risks or cumulative disadvantage? The structuring effect of social stratification determinants and life course events on poverty transitions in Europe. *European Sociological Review*, 2010, 1–18. doi: 10.1093/esr/jcq005

Vandecasteele, L. (2010). Poverty trajectories after risky life events in different European welfare regimes. *European Societies, 12*(2), 257–278.

Van den Bosch, K. (2001). *Identifying the poor. Using subjective and consensual measures*. Aldershot, England: Ashgate.

Vandenbroeck, M. (2006). *Globalisation and privatisation: The impact on childcare policy and practice.* [Working Papers in Early Childhood Development No. 38]. The Hague, the Netherlands: Bernard Van Leer Foundation.

Vandenbroucke, F. (2001). *Social justice and individual ethics in an open society: Equality, responsibility, and incentives*. Berlin, Germany and New York, NY: Springer.

Vandenbroucke, F. (2002a). Foreword.In G. Esping-Andersen with D. Gallie, A. Hemerijck, & J. Myles (Eds.), *Why we need a new welfare state* (pp. viii–xxiv). Oxford, England: Oxford University Press.

Vandenbroucke, F. (2002b, June). *The EU and social protection: What should the European Convention propose?* Paper presented at the Max Planck Institute for the Study of Societies. Köln, Germany.

Vandenbroucke, F, & Vleminckx, K. (2011). Disappointing poverty trends: Is the social investment state to blame? *Journal of European Social Policy, 21*(5), 450–471.

Vandenbroucke, F. (2012). *Europe: The social challenge. Defining the Union's social objective is a necessity rather than a luxury* [Observatoire social Européen (OSE) Opinion Paper No. 11]. Bruxelles, Belgium: OSE.

Vandenbroucke, F., Diris, R., & Verbist, G. (2013). *Excessive Social Imbalances and the Performance of Welfare States in the EU* [Euroforum Policy Paper]. Leuven, Belgium: KU Leuven.

Vandenbroucke, F., Cantillon, B., Van Mechelen, N., Goedemé, T., & Van Lancker, A. (2013). The EU and minimum income protection: Clarifying the policy conundrum. In I. Marx, & K. Nelson (Eds.), *Minimum income protection in* flux (pp. 271–317). Houndmills and Basingstoke, Hampshire, England: Palgrave MacMillan.

Van der Lippe, T., & van Dijck, L. (2002). Comparative research on women's employment. *Annual Review of Sociology, 28*, 221–241.

Van Gennep, A.T.G. (2000). *Emancipatie van de zwaksten in de samenleving: Over paradigma's van verstandelijke handicap*. Amsterdam, the Netherlands: Boom.

Van Gerven, M. (2008). *The broad tracks of path dependent benefit reforms: A longitudinal study of social benefit reforms in three European countries, 1980–2006.* [Studies in Social Security and Health] Helsinki, Finland: Social Insurance Institution Finland.

Vanhercke, B., & Lelie, P. (2012). Benchmarking social Europe a decade on: Demystifying the OMC's learning tools. In A. Fennan, & F. Knuepling (Eds.), *Benchmarking in federal systems: Australian and international experiences* (pp. 145–184). Melbourne, Australia: Productivity Commission.

Van Kerm, P. (2007). *Extreme incomes and the estimation of poverty and inequality indicators from EU-SILC* [IRISS Working Paper Series, 51]. Luxembourg: CEPS-Instead.

Van Lancker, W. (2012). The European world of temporary employment: Gendered and poor?, *European Societies, 14*(1), 125–142.

Van Lancker, W., & Ghysels, J. (2012). Who benefits? The social distribution of subsidized childcare in Sweden and Flanders. *Acta Sociologica, 55*(2), 125–142.

Van Lancker, W. (2013). Putting the child-centred investment strategy to the test: Evidence for the EU27, *European Journal of Social Security, 15*(1), 4–27.

Van Mechelen, N., Marx, I., Marchal, S., Goedemé, T., & Cantillon, B. (2010). *The evolution of social assistance and minimum wages in 25 European countries, 2001–2009*. Antwerp, Belgium: Herman Deleeck Centre for Social Policy.

Van Mechelen, N., Marchal, S., Goedemé, T., Marx, I., & Cantillon, B. (2011). *The CSB-Minimum Income Protection Indicators dataset (CSB-MIPI).* [CSB Working Paper No. 5/11]. Antwerp, Belgium: Herman Deleeck Centre for Social Policy, University of Antwerp.

Van Mechelen, N., & Bradshaw, J. (2013). Child poverty as a government priority: Child benefit packages for working families, 1992–2009. In I. Marx, & K. Nelson (Eds.), *Minimum income protection in flux* (pp. 81–107). Houndmills, Basingstoke, Hampshire, England: Palgrave Macmillan.

Van Mechelen, N., & Marchal, S. (2013). Struggle for life: Social assistance benefits, 1992–2009. In I. Marx, & K. Nelson (Eds.), *Minimum income protection in flux* (pp. 28–53). Houndmills, Basingstoke, Hampshire, England: Palgrave Macmillan.

Van Oorschot, W. (2000). Who should get what, and why? On deservingness criteria and the conditionality of solidarity among the public. *Policy and Politics, 28*(1), 33–48.

Van Vliet, O. (2011). *Convergence and Europeanisation. The political economy of social and labour market policies*. Leiden, the Netherlands: Leiden University Press.

Verbist, G., Förster, M., & Vaalavuo, M. (2012). *The impact of publicly provided services on the distribution of resources: A review of new results and methods* [Social, Employment and Migration Working Paper, No 130]. Paris, France: OECD Publishing.

Verma, V., & Betti, G. (2010). Data accuracy in EU-SILC. In A. B. Atkinson, & E. Marlier (Eds.), *Income and living conditions in Europe*. Luxembourg: Eurostat.

Verschueren, H. (2012). Union law and the fight against poverty: Which legal instruments? In B. Cantillon, H. Verschueren, & P. Ploscar (Eds.), *Social inclusion and social protection in the EU: Interaction between law and policy* (pp. 205–230). Antwerp, Belgium: Intersentia.

Vincent-Jones, P. (2009). *Individual responsibility and welfare contractualism. A relational evaluation*. Oxford, England: The Foundation for Law, Justice and Society in affiliation with The Centre for Socio-Legal Studies, University of Oxford. Retrieved from http://www.fljs.org/uploads/documents/Vincent-Jones.pdf

Von Rhein-Kress, G. (1993). Coping with economic crisis: Labour supply as a policy instrument. In F. Castles (Ed.), *Families of nations. Patterns of public policy in Western democracies* (pp. 131–178). Aldershot, England: Darthmouth.

Vranken, J. (2002, February). *Belgian reports on poverty*. Paper presented at the conference "Reporting on Income Distribution and Poverty—Perspectives from a German and an European Point of View," organized by Hans Böckler Stiftung, Berlin, Germany.

Vrooman, C. J. (2009). *Rules of relief: Institutions of social security, and their impact*. The Hague, the Netherlands: SCP.

Wagner, G., Frick, J., & Schupp, J. (2007). The German Socio-Economic Panel Study (SOEP)—Scope, evolution and enhancements. Schmollers Jahrbuch: *Journal of Applied Social Science Studies* / Zeitschrift für Wirtschafts- und Sozialwissenschaften, *127*(1), 139–69.

Ward, T., Lelkes, O., Sutherland, H., & Tóth, I. G. (2009). *European inequalities. Social inclusion and income distribution in the European Union*. Budapest, Hungary: Tárki.

Weishaupt, J. T. (2011). *From the manpower revolution to the activation paradigm. Explaining institutional continuity and change in an integrating Europe*. Amsterdam, the Netherlands: Amsterdam University Press.

Weishaupt, J. T. (2013). Origin and genesis of activation policies in "old" Europe: Toward a balanced approach?, In I. Marx, & K. Nelson (Eds.), *Minimum income protection in flux* (pp.190-216). Houndmills and Basingstoke, Hampshire, England: Palgrave Macmillan.

Wennemo, I. (1992). The development of family policy: A comparison of family benefits and tax reductions for families in 18 OECD countries. *Acta Sociologica, 35*, 201–217.

Whelan, C. T., Layte, R., Maitre, B., Gannon, B., Nolan, B., Watson, D., & Williams, J. (2003). *Monitoring poverty trends in Ireland: Results from the 2001 Living in Ireland Survey*. Dublin, Ireland: Economic and Social Research Institute.

Whelan, C. T., & Maître, B. (2009). The 'Europeanisation' of reference groups. A reconsideration using EU-SILC. *European Societies, 11*(2), 283–309.

White, S. (1999). Rights and responsibilities: A Social Democratic perspective. In A. Gamble, & T. Wright (Eds.), *The new social democracy* (pp. 166–179). Oxford, England: Blackwell.

Whiteford, P., & Adema, W. (2007). *What works best in reducing child poverty: A benefit or work strategy?* [Social Employment and Migration Working Papers, No. 51]. Paris, France: OECD.

Whiteford, P. (2008). How much redistribution do governments achieve? The role of cash transfers and household taxes. In *Growing unequal: Income distribution and poverty in OECD countries* (pp. 97–121). Paris, France: OECD.

Wilthagen, T. (1998). *Flexicurity: A new paradigm for labour market reform?* [WZB Discussion Paper, FS 1, pp. 98–202]. Berlin, Germany: Social Science Research Center Berlin (WZB).

Wilthagen, T., Tros, F., & van Lieshout, H. (2004). Towards flexicurity? Balancing flexibility and security in EU Member States. *European Journal of Social Security, 23*(4), 113–136.

Wolfe, R., & Hanley, J. (2002). If we're so different, why do we keep overlapping? When 1 plus 1 doesn't make 2. *CMAJ: Canadian Medical Association Journal, 166*(1), 65–66.

Wolff, P., Montaigne, F., & Rojas Gonzáles, G. (2010). Investing in statistics: EU-SILC. In A. B. Atkinson, & E. Marlier (Eds.), *Income and living conditions in Europe* (pp. 37–55). Luxembourg: Office for Official Publications of the European Communities.

World Bank. (1990). *World development report 1990: Poverty*. Oxford, England: Oxford University Press.

Wright, S. (2011). Steering with sticks, rowing for rewards: The new governance of activation in the UK. In *The governance of active welfare states in Europe*. London, England: Palgrave Macmillan.

Zaidi, A. M., & de Vos, K. (2001).Trends in consumption-based poverty and inequality in the European Union during the 1980s. *Journal of Population Economics, 14*(2), 367–390.

Zeitlin, J. (2010). Towards a stronger OMC in a more social Europe 2020: A new governance architecture for EU Policy coordination. In E. Marlier, & D. Natali with R. Van Dam (Eds.), *Europe 2020. Towards a more social EU?* (pp. 253–273). Brussels, Belgium: P.I.E. Peter Lang.

Zheng, B. (1997). Aggregate poverty measures. *Journal of Economic Surveys, 11*(2), 123–162.

Zheng, B. (2000). Poverty orderings. *Journal of Economic Surveys, 14*(4), 427–466.

INDEX

Boxes, tables, and figures are indicated by an italic "*b*", "*t*", or "*f*" following the page number.